THE WORLD'S MOST UNLIKABL

# THE IRREDEEMABLE
# ANT-MAN



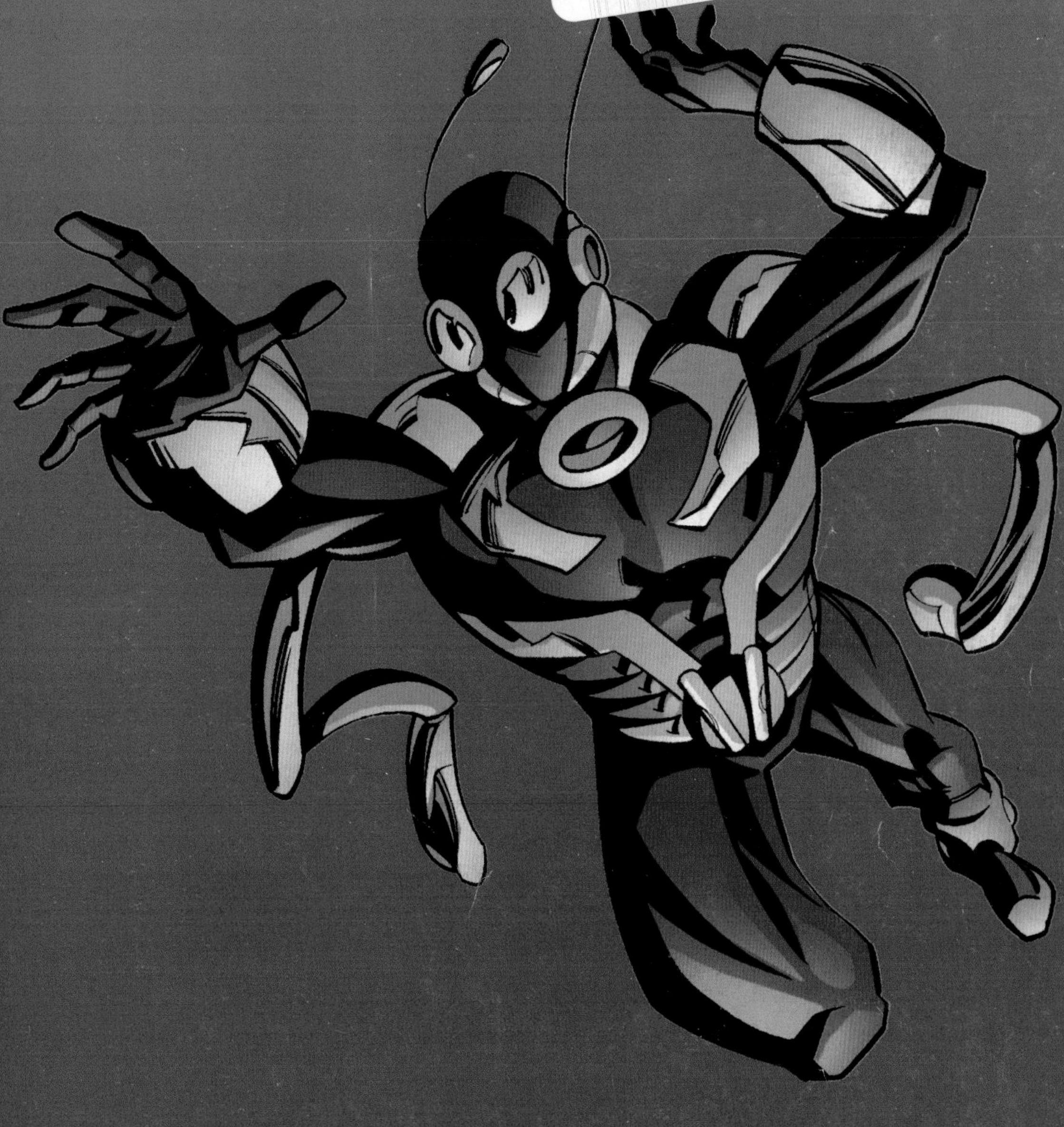

# THE WORLD'S MOST UNLIKABLE SUPER HERO
## THE IRREDEEMABLE
# ANT-MAN

WRITER: ROBERT KIRKMAN
PENCILER: PHIL HESTER
INKER: ANDE PARKS
COLORISTS: VAL STAPLES & BILL CRABTREE
LETTERER: VIRTUAL CALLIGRAPHY'S RUS WOOTON
COVER ART: PHIL HESTER, ANDE PARKS & BILL CRABTREE
MIGHTY AVENGERS #1 COVER ART: FRANK CHO
& JASON KEITH
EDITOR: AUBREY SITTERSON
EXECUTIVE EDITOR: TOM BREVOORT

COLLECTION EDITOR: CORY LEVINE
EDITORIAL ASSISTANT: ALEX STARBUCK
ASSISTANT EDITOR: JOHN DENNING
EDITORS, SPECIAL PROJECTS: JENNIFER GRÜNWALD
& MARK D. BEAZLEY
SENIOR EDITOR, SPECIAL PROJECTS: JEFF YOUNGQUIST
SENIOR VICE PRESIDENT OF SALES: DAVID GABRIEL
PRODUCTION: JERRY KALINOWSKI
BOOK DESIGNER: DAYLE CHESLER
VICE PRESIDENT OF CREATIVE: TOM MARVELLI

EDITOR IN CHIEF: JOE QUESADA
PUBLISHER: DAN BUCKLEY
EXECUTIVE PRODUCER: ALAN FINE

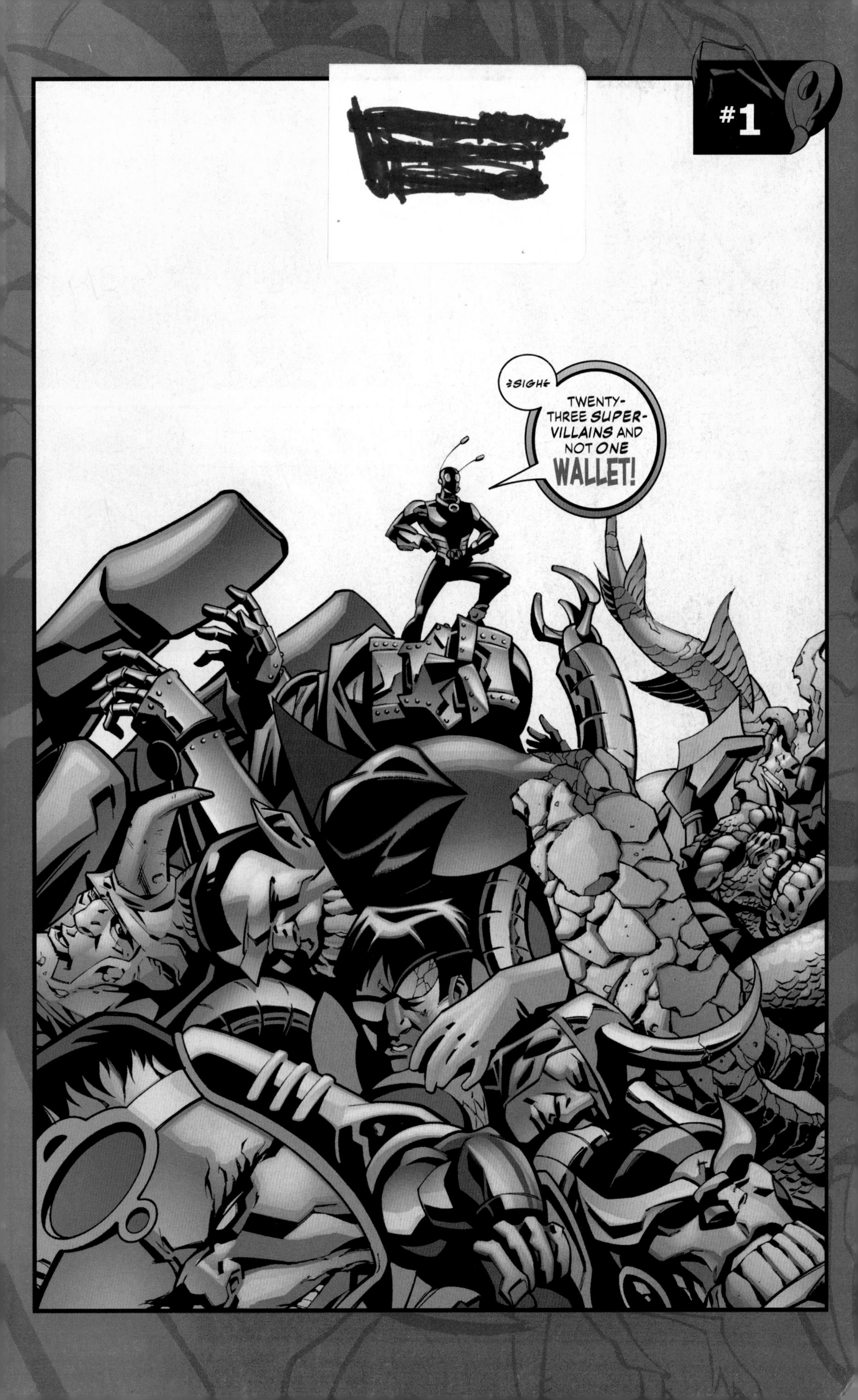
[redacted]
#1
SIGH
TWENTY-THREE SUPER-VILLAINS AND NOT ONE WALLET!

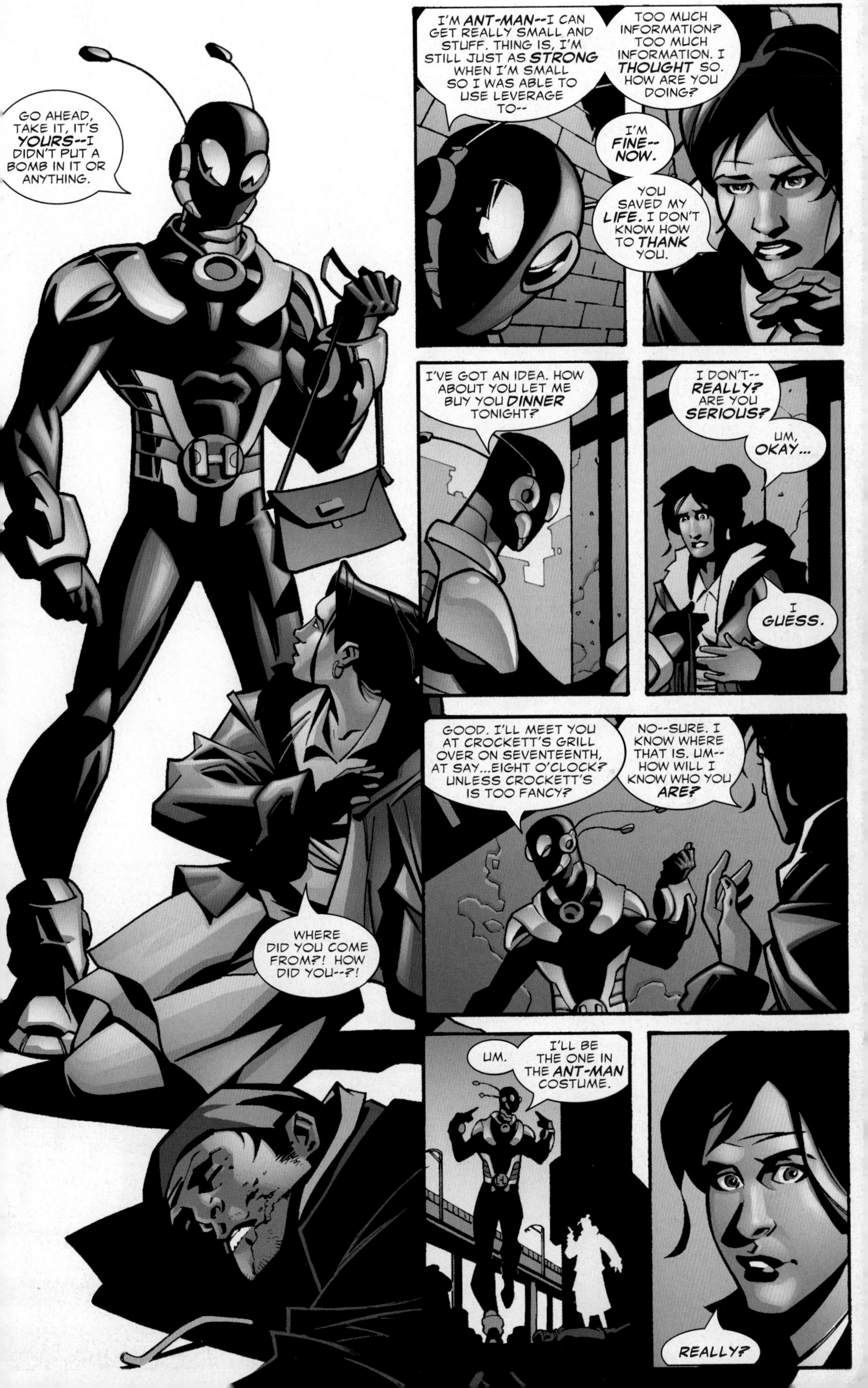
GO AHEAD, TAKE IT, IT'S YOURS--I DIDN'T PUT A BOMB IN IT OR ANYTHING.
WHERE DID YOU COME FROM?! HOW DID YOU--?!
I'M ANT-MAN--I CAN GET REALLY SMALL AND STUFF. THING IS, I'M STILL JUST AS STRONG WHEN I'M SMALL SO I WAS ABLE TO USE LEVERAGE TO--
TOO MUCH INFORMATION? TOO MUCH INFORMATION. I THOUGHT SO. HOW ARE YOU DOING?
I'M FINE-- NOW.
YOU SAVED MY LIFE. I DON'T KNOW HOW TO THANK YOU.
I'VE GOT AN IDEA. HOW ABOUT YOU LET ME BUY YOU DINNER TONIGHT?
I DON'T-- REALLY? ARE YOU SERIOUS?
UM, OKAY...
I GUESS.
GOOD. I'LL MEET YOU AT CROCKETT'S GRILL OVER ON SEVENTEENTH, AT SAY...EIGHT O'CLOCK? UNLESS CROCKETT'S IS TOO FANCY?
NO--SURE. I KNOW WHERE THAT IS. UM-- HOW WILL I KNOW WHO YOU ARE?
UM.
I'LL BE THE ONE IN THE ANT-MAN COSTUME.
REALLY?

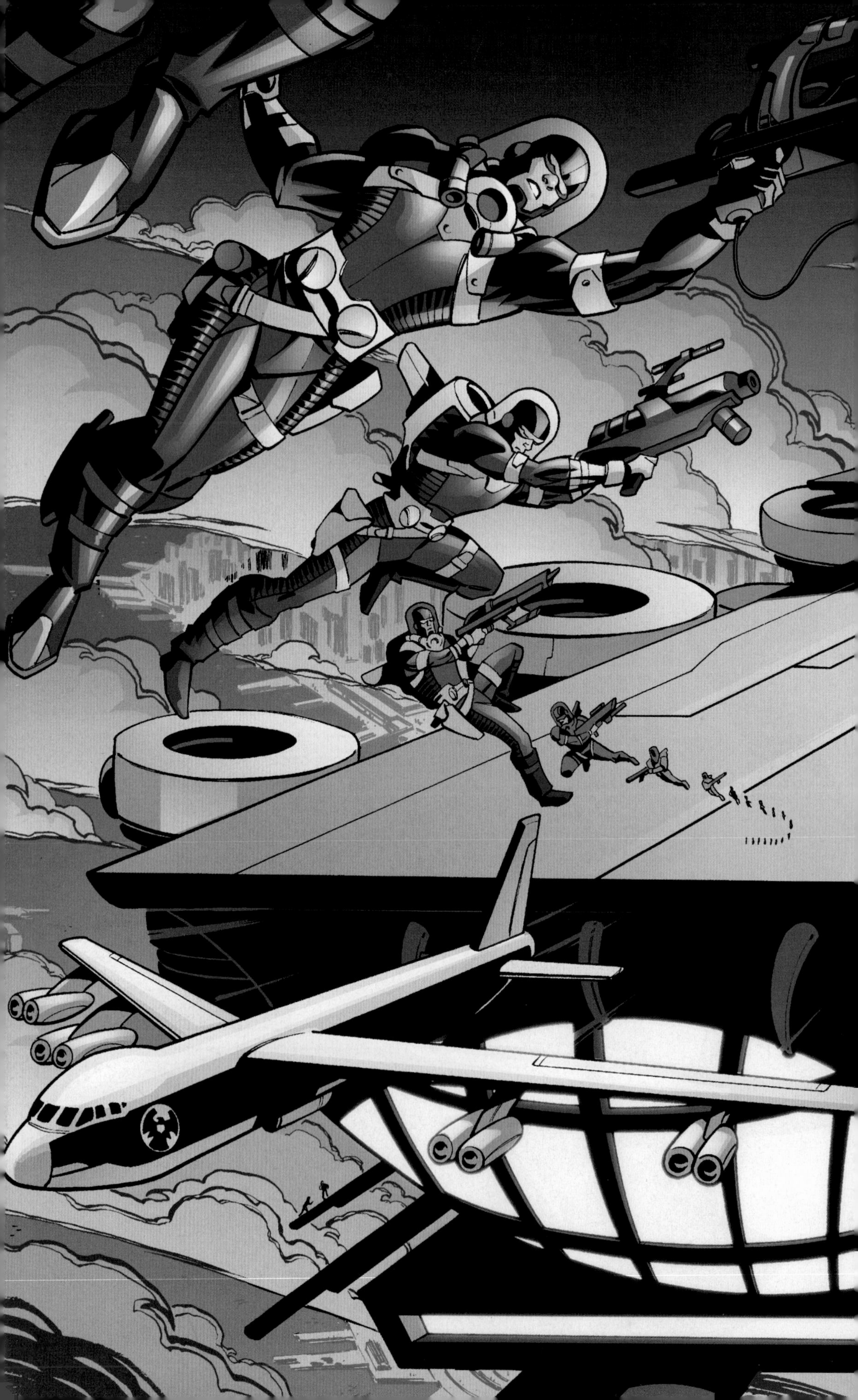

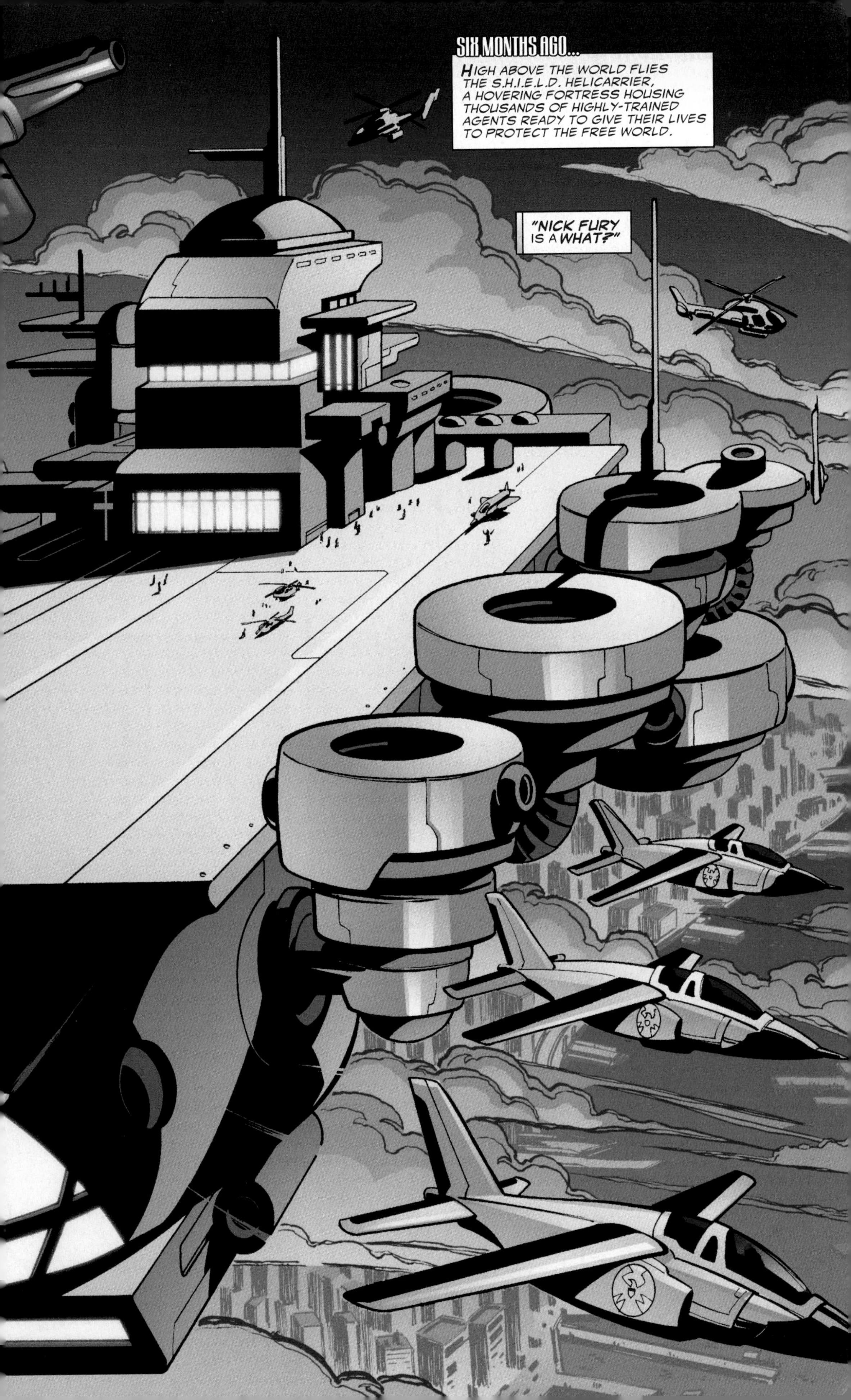
SIX MONTHS AGO...
HIGH ABOVE THE WORLD FLIES THE S.H.I.E.L.D. HELICARRIER, A HOVERING FORTRESS HOUSING THOUSANDS OF HIGHLY-TRAINED AGENTS READY TO GIVE THEIR LIVES TO PROTECT THE FREE WORLD.
"NICK FURY IS A WHAT?"

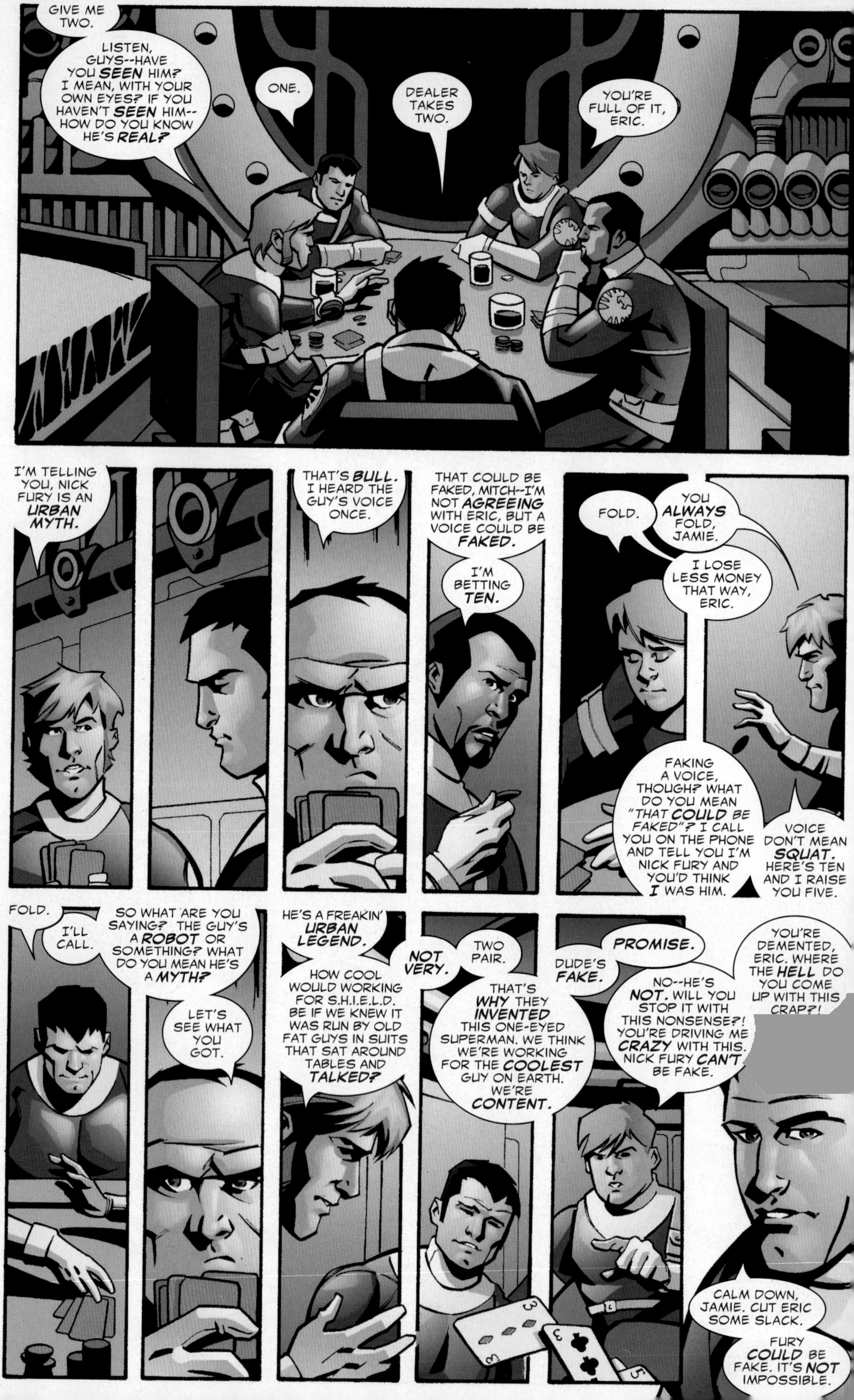
GIVE ME TWO.
LISTEN, GUYS--HAVE YOU SEEN HIM? I MEAN, WITH YOUR OWN EYES? IF YOU HAVEN'T SEEN HIM-- HOW DO YOU KNOW HE'S REAL?
ONE.
DEALER TAKES TWO.
YOU'RE FULL OF IT, ERIC.
I'M TELLING YOU, NICK FURY IS AN URBAN MYTH.
THAT'S BULL. I HEARD THE GUY'S VOICE ONCE.
THAT COULD BE FAKED, MITCH--I'M NOT AGREEING WITH ERIC, BUT A VOICE COULD BE FAKED.
I'M BETTING TEN.
FOLD.
YOU ALWAYS FOLD, JAMIE.
I LOSE LESS MONEY THAT WAY, ERIC.
FAKING A VOICE, THOUGH? WHAT DO YOU MEAN "THAT COULD BE FAKED"? I CALL YOU ON THE PHONE AND TELL YOU I'M NICK FURY AND YOU'D THINK I WAS HIM.
VOICE DON'T MEAN SQUAT. HERE'S TEN AND I RAISE YOU FIVE.
FOLD.
I'LL CALL.
SO WHAT ARE YOU SAYING? THE GUY'S A ROBOT OR SOMETHING? WHAT DO YOU MEAN HE'S A MYTH?
LET'S SEE WHAT YOU GOT.
HE'S A FREAKIN' URBAN LEGEND.
HOW COOL WOULD WORKING FOR S.H.I.E.L.D. BE IF WE KNEW IT WAS RUN BY OLD FAT GUYS IN SUITS THAT SAT AROUND TABLES AND TALKED?
NOT VERY.
TWO PAIR.
THAT'S WHY THEY INVENTED THIS ONE-EYED SUPERMAN. WE THINK WE'RE WORKING FOR THE COOLEST GUY ON EARTH. WE'RE CONTENT.
DUDE'S FAKE.
PROMISE.
NO--HE'S NOT. WILL YOU STOP IT WITH THIS NONSENSE?! YOU'RE DRIVING ME CRAZY WITH THIS. NICK FURY CAN'T BE FAKE.
YOU'RE DEMENTED, ERIC. WHERE THE HELL DO YOU COME UP WITH THIS CRAP?!
CALM DOWN, JAMIE. CUT ERIC SOME SLACK.
FURY COULD BE FAKE. IT'S NOT IMPOSSIBLE.

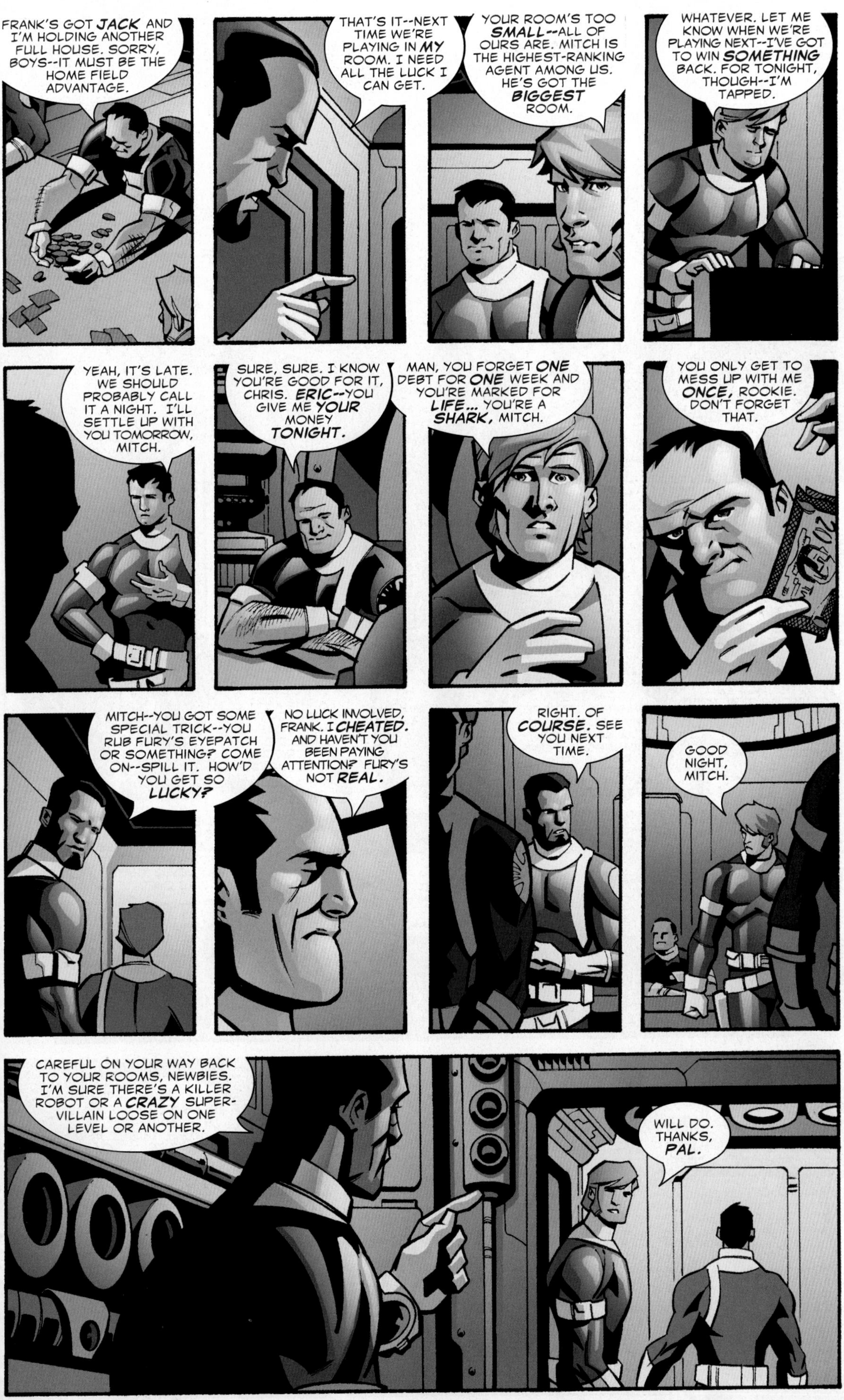
FRANK'S GOT JACK AND I'M HOLDING ANOTHER FULL HOUSE. SORRY, BOYS--IT MUST BE THE HOME FIELD ADVANTAGE.
THAT'S IT--NEXT TIME WE'RE PLAYING IN MY ROOM. I NEED ALL THE LUCK I CAN GET.
YOUR ROOM'S TOO SMALL--ALL OF OURS ARE. MITCH IS THE HIGHEST-RANKING AGENT AMONG US. HE'S GOT THE BIGGEST ROOM.
WHATEVER. LET ME KNOW WHEN WE'RE PLAYING NEXT--I'VE GOT TO WIN SOMETHING BACK. FOR TONIGHT, THOUGH--I'M TAPPED.
YEAH, IT'S LATE. WE SHOULD PROBABLY CALL IT A NIGHT. I'LL SETTLE UP WITH YOU TOMORROW, MITCH.
SURE, SURE. I KNOW YOU'RE GOOD FOR IT, CHRIS. ERIC--YOU GIVE ME YOUR MONEY TONIGHT.
MAN, YOU FORGET ONE DEBT FOR ONE WEEK AND YOU'RE MARKED FOR LIFE... YOU'RE A SHARK, MITCH.
YOU ONLY GET TO MESS UP WITH ME ONCE, ROOKIE. DON'T FORGET THAT.
MITCH--YOU GOT SOME SPECIAL TRICK--YOU RUB FURY'S EYEPATCH OR SOMETHING? COME ON--SPILL IT. HOW'D YOU GET SO LUCKY?
NO LUCK INVOLVED, FRANK. I CHEATED. AND HAVEN'T YOU BEEN PAYING ATTENTION? FURY'S NOT REAL.
RIGHT. OF COURSE. SEE YOU NEXT TIME.
GOOD NIGHT, MITCH.
CAREFUL ON YOUR WAY BACK TO YOUR ROOMS, NEWBIES. I'M SURE THERE'S A KILLER ROBOT OR A CRAZY SUPER-VILLAIN LOOSE ON ONE LEVEL OR ANOTHER.
WILL DO. THANKS, PAL.

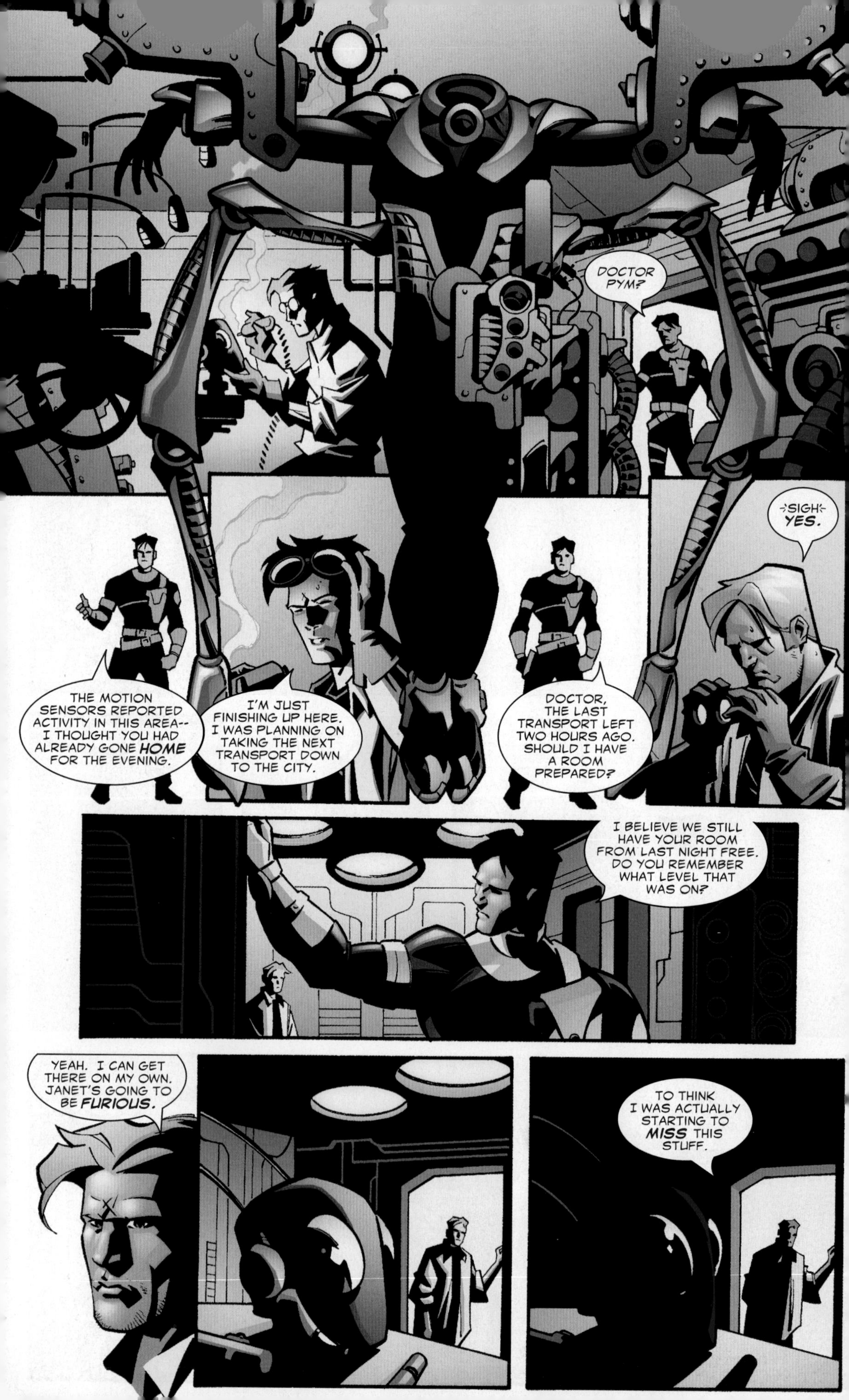
DOCTOR PYM?
THE MOTION SENSORS REPORTED ACTIVITY IN THIS AREA-- I THOUGHT YOU HAD ALREADY GONE HOME FOR THE EVENING.
I'M JUST FINISHING UP HERE. I WAS PLANNING ON TAKING THE NEXT TRANSPORT DOWN TO THE CITY.
DOCTOR, THE LAST TRANSPORT LEFT TWO HOURS AGO. SHOULD I HAVE A ROOM PREPARED?
-SIGH- YES.
I BELIEVE WE STILL HAVE YOUR ROOM FROM LAST NIGHT FREE. DO YOU REMEMBER WHAT LEVEL THAT WAS ON?
YEAH. I CAN GET THERE ON MY OWN. JANET'S GOING TO BE FURIOUS.
TO THINK I WAS ACTUALLY STARTING TO MISS THIS STUFF.

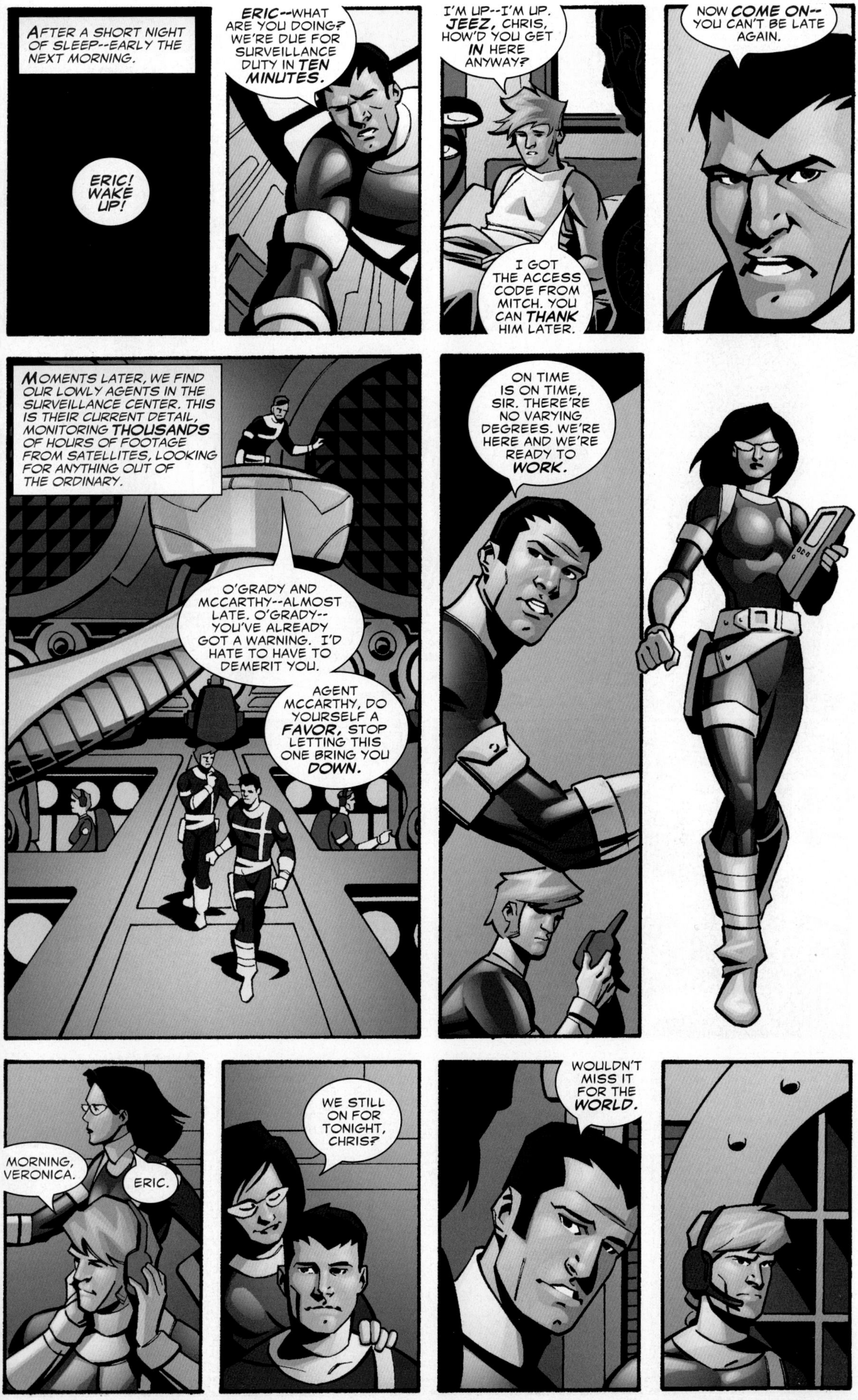
AFTER A SHORT NIGHT OF SLEEP--EARLY THE NEXT MORNING.
ERIC! WAKE UP!
ERIC--WHAT ARE YOU DOING? WE'RE DUE FOR SURVEILLANCE DUTY IN TEN MINUTES.
I'M UP--I'M UP. JEEZ, CHRIS, HOW'D YOU GET IN HERE ANYWAY?
I GOT THE ACCESS CODE FROM MITCH. YOU CAN THANK HIM LATER.
NOW COME ON--YOU CAN'T BE LATE AGAIN.
MOMENTS LATER, WE FIND OUR LOWLY AGENTS IN THE SURVEILLANCE CENTER. THIS IS THEIR CURRENT DETAIL, MONITORING THOUSANDS OF HOURS OF FOOTAGE FROM SATELLITES, LOOKING FOR ANYTHING OUT OF THE ORDINARY.
O'GRADY AND MCCARTHY--ALMOST LATE. O'GRADY--YOU'VE ALREADY GOT A WARNING. I'D HATE TO HAVE TO DEMERIT YOU.
AGENT MCCARTHY, DO YOURSELF A FAVOR, STOP LETTING THIS ONE BRING YOU DOWN.
ON TIME IS ON TIME, SIR. THERE'RE NO VARYING DEGREES. WE'RE HERE AND WE'RE READY TO WORK.
MORNING, VERONICA.
ERIC.
WE STILL ON FOR TONIGHT, CHRIS?
WOULDN'T MISS IT FOR THE WORLD.

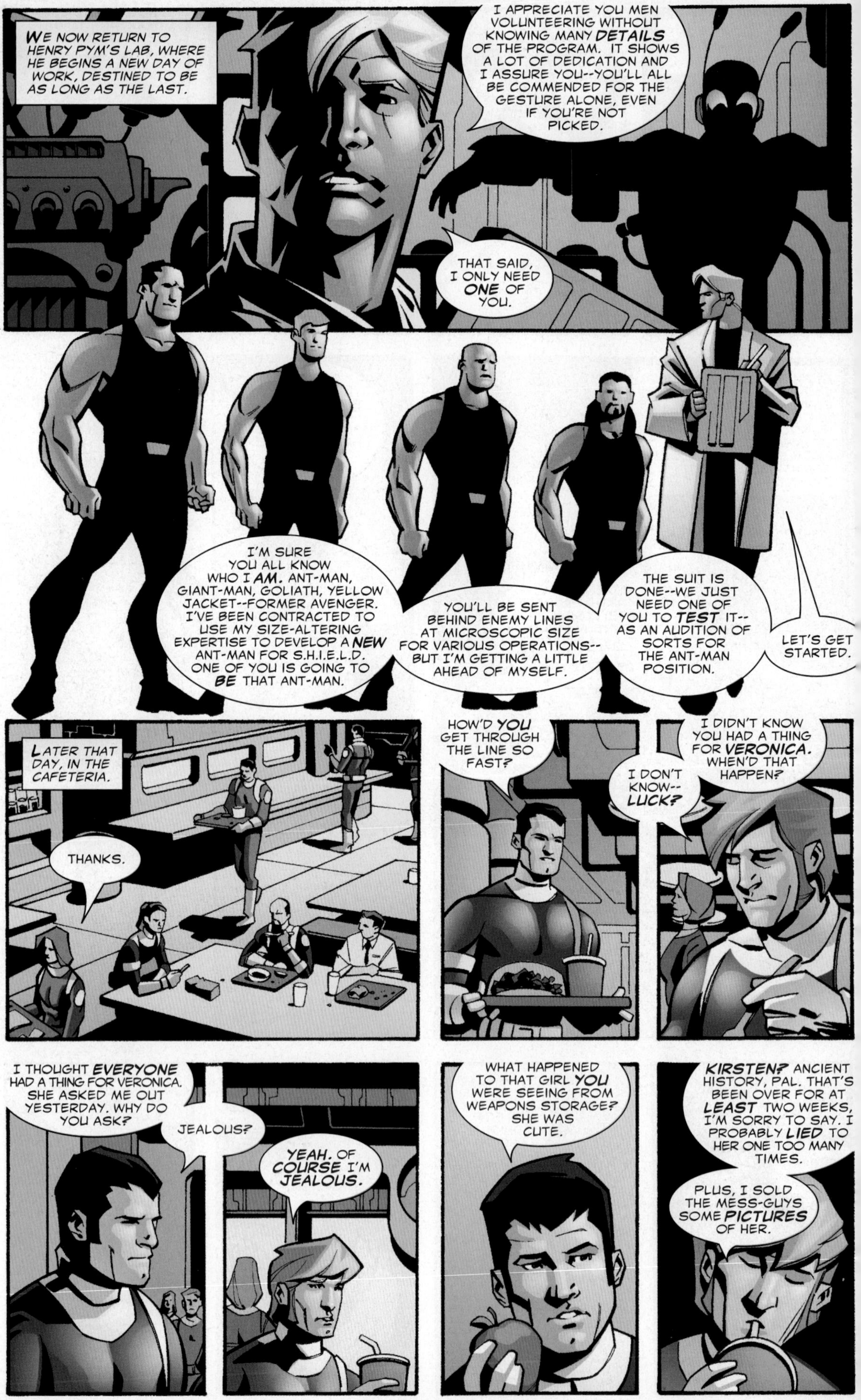

WE NOW RETURN TO HENRY PYM'S LAB, WHERE HE BEGINS A NEW DAY OF WORK, DESTINED TO BE AS LONG AS THE LAST.
I APPRECIATE YOU MEN VOLUNTEERING WITHOUT KNOWING MANY DETAILS OF THE PROGRAM. IT SHOWS A LOT OF DEDICATION AND I ASSURE YOU--YOU'LL ALL BE COMMENDED FOR THE GESTURE ALONE, EVEN IF YOU'RE NOT PICKED.
THAT SAID, I ONLY NEED ONE OF YOU.
I'M SURE YOU ALL KNOW WHO I AM. ANT-MAN, GIANT-MAN, GOLIATH, YELLOW JACKET--FORMER AVENGER. I'VE BEEN CONTRACTED TO USE MY SIZE-ALTERING EXPERTISE TO DEVELOP A NEW ANT-MAN FOR S.H.I.E.L.D. ONE OF YOU IS GOING TO BE THAT ANT-MAN.
YOU'LL BE SENT BEHIND ENEMY LINES AT MICROSCOPIC SIZE FOR VARIOUS OPERATIONS--BUT I'M GETTING A LITTLE AHEAD OF MYSELF.
THE SUIT IS DONE--WE JUST NEED ONE OF YOU TO TEST IT--AS AN AUDITION OF SORTS FOR THE ANT-MAN POSITION.
LET'S GET STARTED.
LATER THAT DAY, IN THE CAFETERIA.
THANKS.
HOW'D YOU GET THROUGH THE LINE SO FAST?
I DON'T KNOW--LUCK?
I DIDN'T KNOW YOU HAD A THING FOR VERONICA. WHEN'D THAT HAPPEN?
I THOUGHT EVERYONE HAD A THING FOR VERONICA. SHE ASKED ME OUT YESTERDAY. WHY DO YOU ASK?
JEALOUS?
YEAH. OF COURSE I'M JEALOUS.
WHAT HAPPENED TO THAT GIRL YOU WERE SEEING FROM WEAPONS STORAGE? SHE WAS CUTE.
KIRSTEN? ANCIENT HISTORY, PAL. THAT'S BEEN OVER FOR AT LEAST TWO WEEKS, I'M SORRY TO SAY. I PROBABLY LIED TO HER ONE TOO MANY TIMES.
PLUS, I SOLD THE MESS-GUYS SOME PICTURES OF HER.

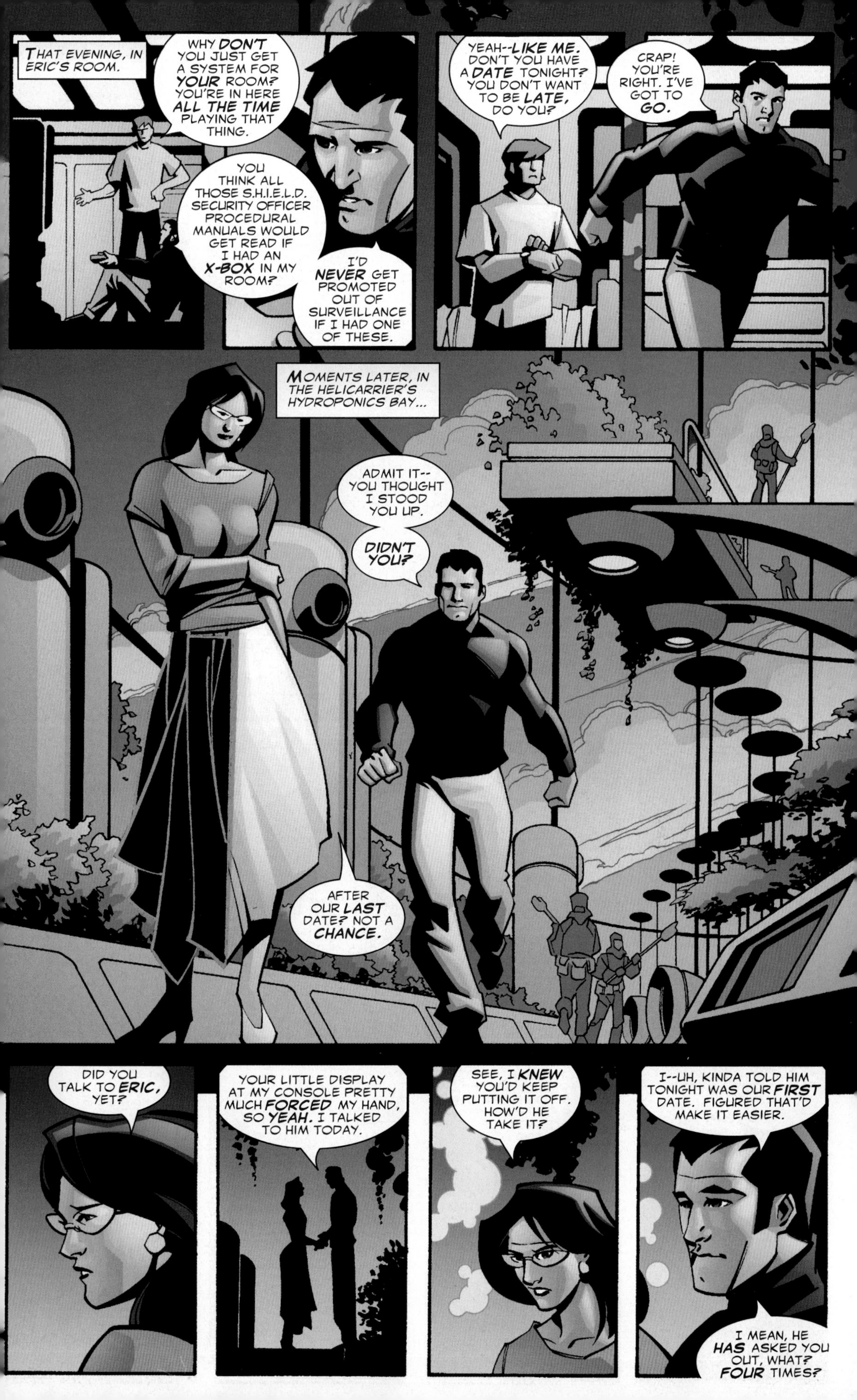
THAT EVENING, IN ERIC'S ROOM.
WHY DON'T YOU JUST GET A SYSTEM FOR YOUR ROOM? YOU'RE IN HERE ALL THE TIME PLAYING THAT THING.
YOU THINK ALL THOSE S.H.I.E.L.D. SECURITY OFFICER PROCEDURAL MANUALS WOULD GET READ IF I HAD AN X-BOX IN MY ROOM?
I'D NEVER GET PROMOTED OUT OF SURVEILLANCE IF I HAD ONE OF THESE.
YEAH--LIKE ME. DON'T YOU HAVE A DATE TONIGHT? YOU DON'T WANT TO BE LATE, DO YOU?
CRAP! YOU'RE RIGHT. I'VE GOT TO GO.
MOMENTS LATER, IN THE HELICARRIER'S HYDROPONICS BAY...
ADMIT IT-- YOU THOUGHT I STOOD YOU UP.
DIDN'T YOU?
AFTER OUR LAST DATE? NOT A CHANCE.
DID YOU TALK TO ERIC, YET?
YOUR LITTLE DISPLAY AT MY CONSOLE PRETTY MUCH FORCED MY HAND, SO YEAH. I TALKED TO HIM TODAY.
SEE, I KNEW YOU'D KEEP PUTTING IT OFF. HOW'D HE TAKE IT?
I--UH, KINDA TOLD HIM TONIGHT WAS OUR FIRST DATE. FIGURED THAT'D MAKE IT EASIER.
I MEAN, HE HAS ASKED YOU OUT, WHAT? FOUR TIMES?

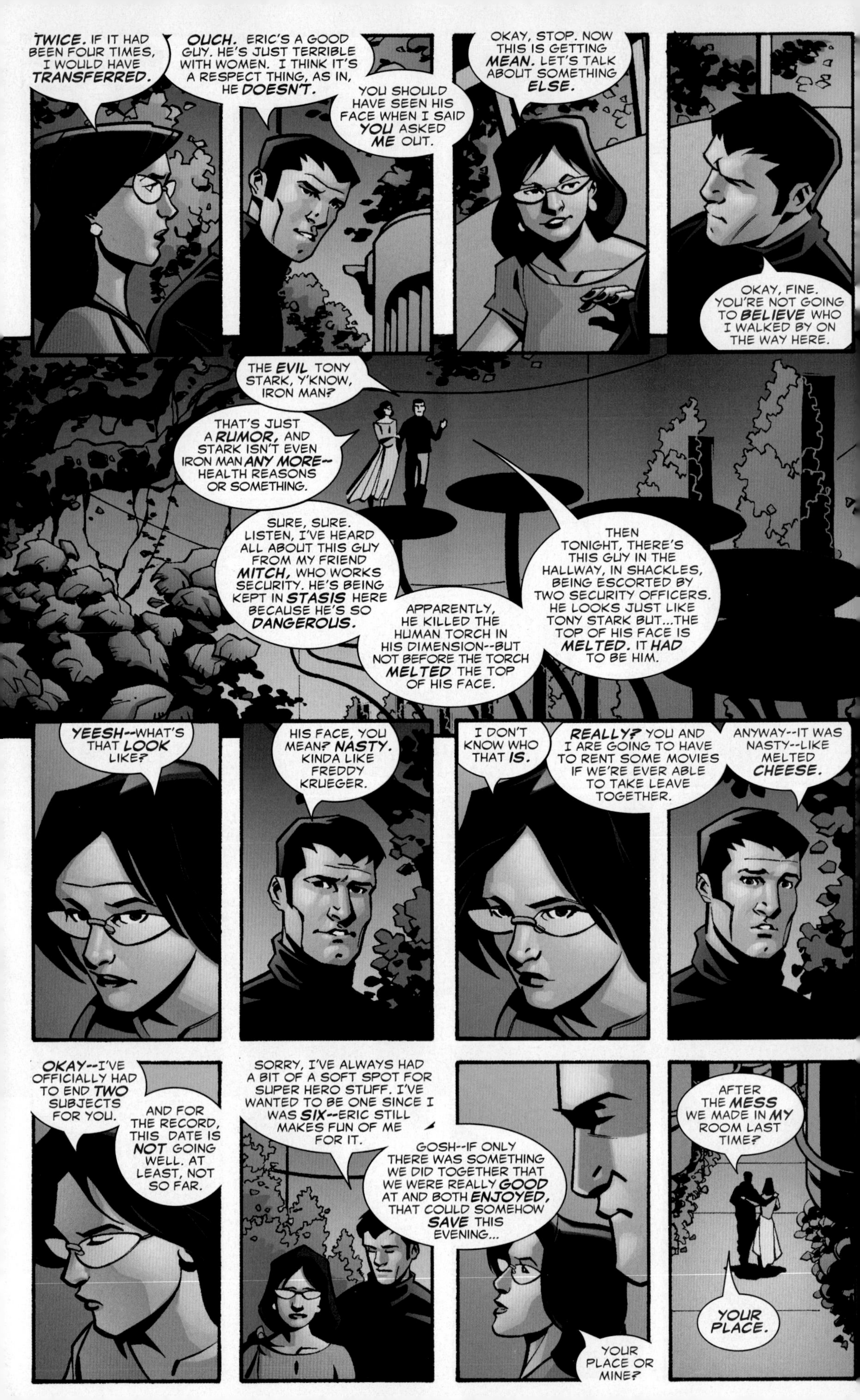
TWICE. IF IT HAD BEEN FOUR TIMES, I WOULD HAVE TRANSFERRED.
OUCH. ERIC'S A GOOD GUY. HE'S JUST TERRIBLE WITH WOMEN. I THINK IT'S A RESPECT THING, AS IN, HE DOESN'T.
YOU SHOULD HAVE SEEN HIS FACE WHEN I SAID YOU ASKED ME OUT.
OKAY, STOP. NOW THIS IS GETTING MEAN. LET'S TALK ABOUT SOMETHING ELSE.
OKAY, FINE. YOU'RE NOT GOING TO BELIEVE WHO I WALKED BY ON THE WAY HERE.
THE EVIL TONY STARK, Y'KNOW, IRON MAN?
THAT'S JUST A RUMOR, AND STARK ISN'T EVEN IRON MAN ANY MORE--HEALTH REASONS OR SOMETHING.
SURE, SURE. LISTEN, I'VE HEARD ALL ABOUT THIS GUY FROM MY FRIEND MITCH, WHO WORKS SECURITY. HE'S BEING KEPT IN STASIS HERE BECAUSE HE'S SO DANGEROUS.
APPARENTLY, HE KILLED THE HUMAN TORCH IN HIS DIMENSION--BUT NOT BEFORE THE TORCH MELTED THE TOP OF HIS FACE.
THEN TONIGHT, THERE'S THIS GUY IN THE HALLWAY, IN SHACKLES, BEING ESCORTED BY TWO SECURITY OFFICERS. HE LOOKS JUST LIKE TONY STARK BUT...THE TOP OF HIS FACE IS MELTED. IT HAD TO BE HIM.
YEESH--WHAT'S THAT LOOK LIKE?
HIS FACE, YOU MEAN? NASTY. KINDA LIKE FREDDY KRUEGER.
I DON'T KNOW WHO THAT IS.
REALLY? YOU AND I ARE GOING TO HAVE TO RENT SOME MOVIES IF WE'RE EVER ABLE TO TAKE LEAVE TOGETHER.
ANYWAY--IT WAS NASTY--LIKE MELTED CHEESE.
OKAY--I'VE OFFICIALLY HAD TO END TWO SUBJECTS FOR YOU.
AND FOR THE RECORD, THIS DATE IS NOT GOING WELL. AT LEAST, NOT SO FAR.
SORRY, I'VE ALWAYS HAD A BIT OF A SOFT SPOT FOR SUPER HERO STUFF. I'VE WANTED TO BE ONE SINCE I WAS SIX--ERIC STILL MAKES FUN OF ME FOR IT.
GOSH--IF ONLY THERE WAS SOMETHING WE DID TOGETHER THAT WE WERE REALLY GOOD AT AND BOTH ENJOYED, THAT COULD SOMEHOW SAVE THIS EVENING...
YOUR PLACE OR MINE?
AFTER THE MESS WE MADE IN MY ROOM LAST TIME?
YOUR PLACE.

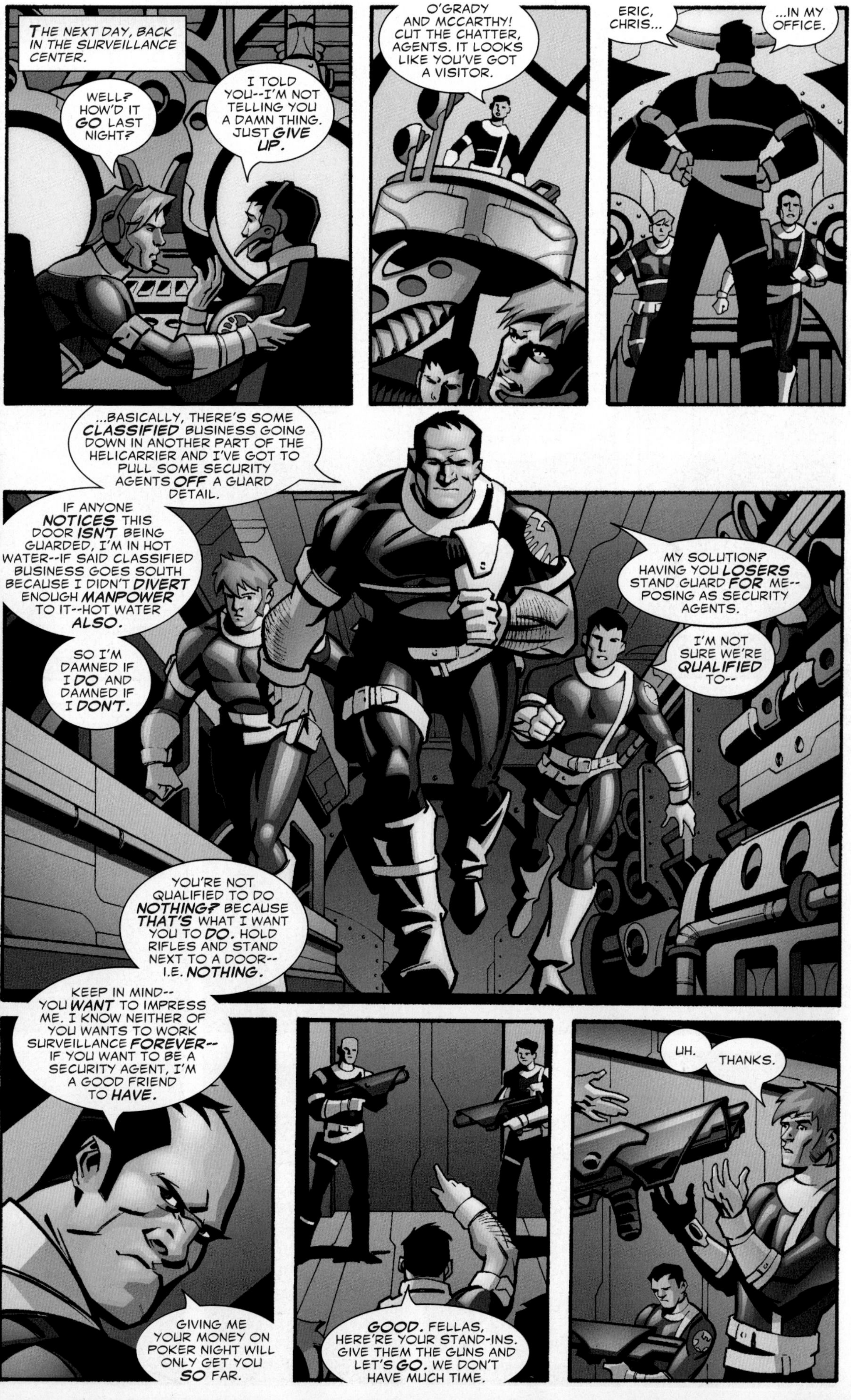
THE NEXT DAY, BACK IN THE SURVEILLANCE CENTER.
WELL? HOW'D IT GO LAST NIGHT?
I TOLD YOU--I'M NOT TELLING YOU A DAMN THING. JUST GIVE UP.
O'GRADY AND MCCARTHY! CUT THE CHATTER, AGENTS. IT LOOKS LIKE YOU'VE GOT A VISITOR.
ERIC, CHRIS...
...IN MY OFFICE.
...BASICALLY, THERE'S SOME CLASSIFIED BUSINESS GOING DOWN IN ANOTHER PART OF THE HELICARRIER AND I'VE GOT TO PULL SOME SECURITY AGENTS OFF A GUARD DETAIL.
IF ANYONE NOTICES THIS DOOR ISN'T BEING GUARDED, I'M IN HOT WATER--IF SAID CLASSIFIED BUSINESS GOES SOUTH BECAUSE I DIDN'T DIVERT ENOUGH MANPOWER TO IT--HOT WATER ALSO.
SO I'M DAMNED IF I DO AND DAMNED IF I DON'T.
MY SOLUTION? HAVING YOU LOSERS STAND GUARD FOR ME--POSING AS SECURITY AGENTS.
I'M NOT SURE WE'RE QUALIFIED TO--
YOU'RE NOT QUALIFIED TO DO NOTHING? BECAUSE THAT'S WHAT I WANT YOU TO DO. HOLD RIFLES AND STAND NEXT TO A DOOR--I.E. NOTHING.
KEEP IN MIND--YOU WANT TO IMPRESS ME. I KNOW NEITHER OF YOU WANTS TO WORK SURVEILLANCE FOREVER--IF YOU WANT TO BE A SECURITY AGENT, I'M A GOOD FRIEND TO HAVE.
GIVING ME YOUR MONEY ON POKER NIGHT WILL ONLY GET YOU SO FAR.
GOOD. FELLAS, HERE'RE YOUR STAND-INS. GIVE THEM THE GUNS AND LET'S GO. WE DON'T HAVE MUCH TIME.
UH.
THANKS.

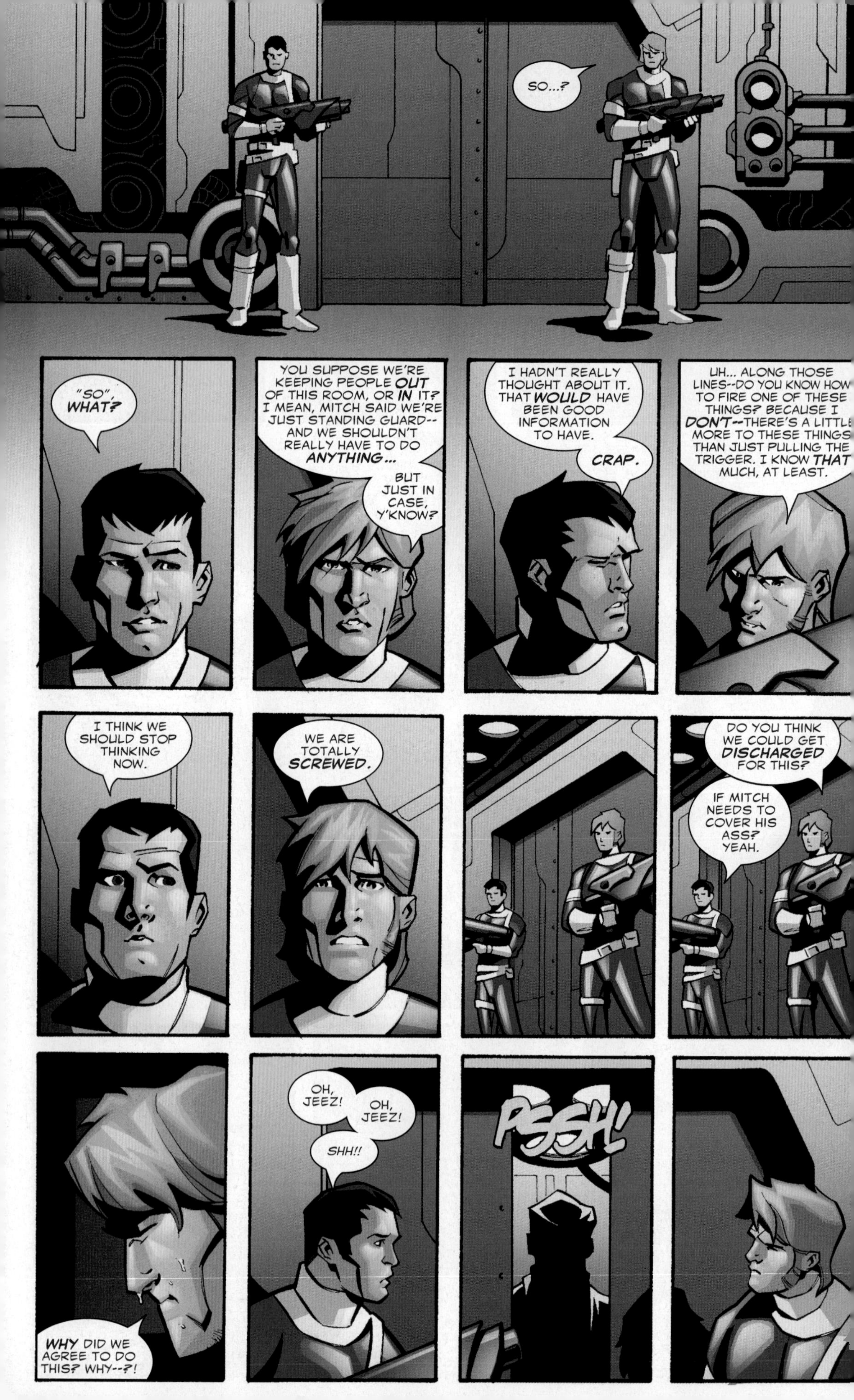
SO...?
"SO", WHAT?
YOU SUPPOSE WE'RE KEEPING PEOPLE OUT OF THIS ROOM, OR IN IT? I MEAN, MITCH SAID WE'RE JUST STANDING GUARD-- AND WE SHOULDN'T REALLY HAVE TO DO ANYTHING...
BUT JUST IN CASE, Y'KNOW?
I HADN'T REALLY THOUGHT ABOUT IT. THAT WOULD HAVE BEEN GOOD INFORMATION TO HAVE.
CRAP.
UH... ALONG THOSE LINES--DO YOU KNOW HOW TO FIRE ONE OF THESE THINGS? BECAUSE I DON'T--THERE'S A LITTLE MORE TO THESE THINGS THAN JUST PULLING THE TRIGGER. I KNOW THAT MUCH, AT LEAST.
I THINK WE SHOULD STOP THINKING NOW.
WE ARE TOTALLY SCREWED.
DO YOU THINK WE COULD GET DISCHARGED FOR THIS?
IF MITCH NEEDS TO COVER HIS ASS? YEAH.
WHY DID WE AGREE TO DO THIS? WHY--?!
OH, JEEZ!
OH, JEEZ!
SHH!!
PSSSH!

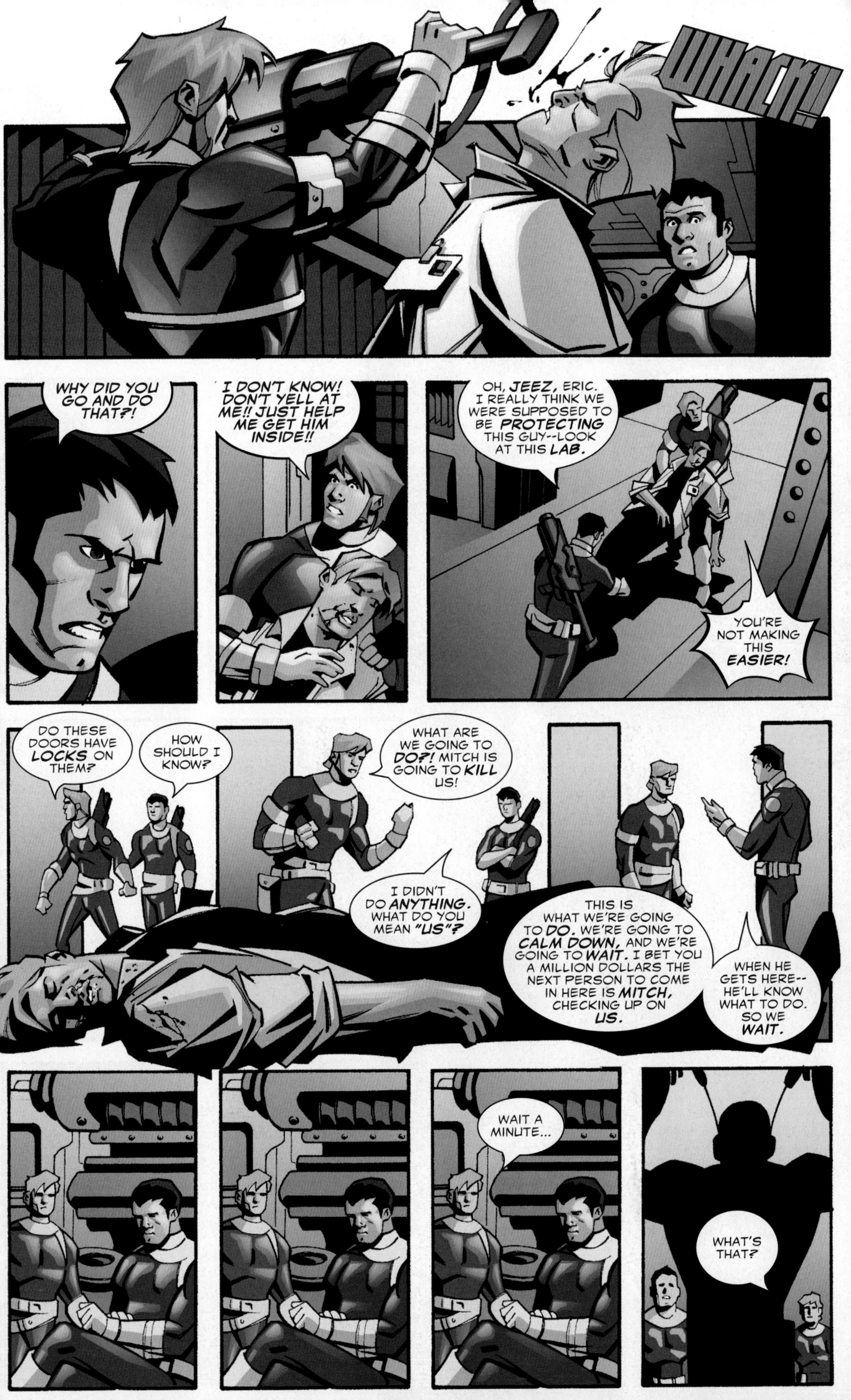
WHACK!!
WHY DID YOU GO AND DO THAT?!
I DON'T KNOW! DON'T YELL AT ME!! JUST HELP ME GET HIM INSIDE!!
OH, JEEZ, ERIC. I REALLY THINK WE WERE SUPPOSED TO BE PROTECTING THIS GUY--LOOK AT THIS LAB.
YOU'RE NOT MAKING THIS EASIER!
DO THESE DOORS HAVE LOCKS ON THEM?
HOW SHOULD I KNOW?
WHAT ARE WE GOING TO DO?! MITCH IS GOING TO KILL US!
I DIDN'T DO ANYTHING. WHAT DO YOU MEAN "US"?
THIS IS WHAT WE'RE GOING TO DO. WE'RE GOING TO CALM DOWN, AND WE'RE GOING TO WAIT. I BET YOU A MILLION DOLLARS THE NEXT PERSON TO COME IN HERE IS MITCH, CHECKING UP ON US.
WHEN HE GETS HERE-- HE'LL KNOW WHAT TO DO. SO WE WAIT.
WAIT A MINUTE...
WHAT'S THAT?

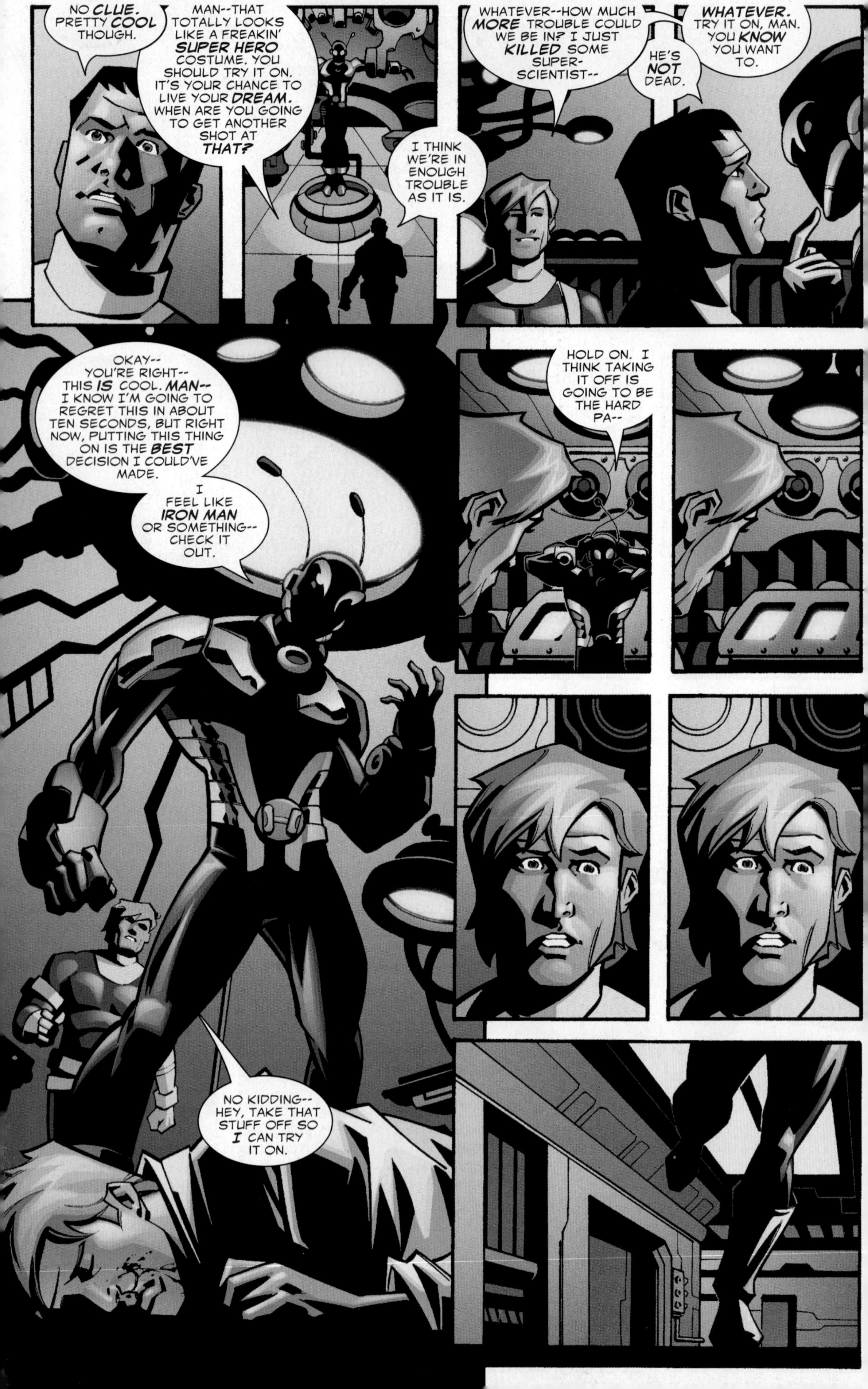
NO CLUE. PRETTY COOL THOUGH.
MAN--THAT TOTALLY LOOKS LIKE A FREAKIN' SUPER HERO COSTUME. YOU SHOULD TRY IT ON. IT'S YOUR CHANCE TO LIVE YOUR DREAM. WHEN ARE YOU GOING TO GET ANOTHER SHOT AT THAT?
I THINK WE'RE IN ENOUGH TROUBLE AS IT IS.
WHATEVER--HOW MUCH MORE TROUBLE COULD WE BE IN? I JUST KILLED SOME SUPER-SCIENTIST--
HE'S NOT DEAD.
WHATEVER. TRY IT ON, MAN. YOU KNOW YOU WANT TO.
OKAY-- YOU'RE RIGHT-- THIS IS COOL. MAN-- I KNOW I'M GOING TO REGRET THIS IN ABOUT TEN SECONDS, BUT RIGHT NOW, PUTTING THIS THING ON IS THE BEST DECISION I COULD'VE MADE.
I FEEL LIKE IRON MAN OR SOMETHING-- CHECK IT OUT.
NO KIDDING-- HEY, TAKE THAT STUFF OFF SO I CAN TRY IT ON.
HOLD ON. I THINK TAKING IT OFF IS GOING TO BE THE HARD PA--

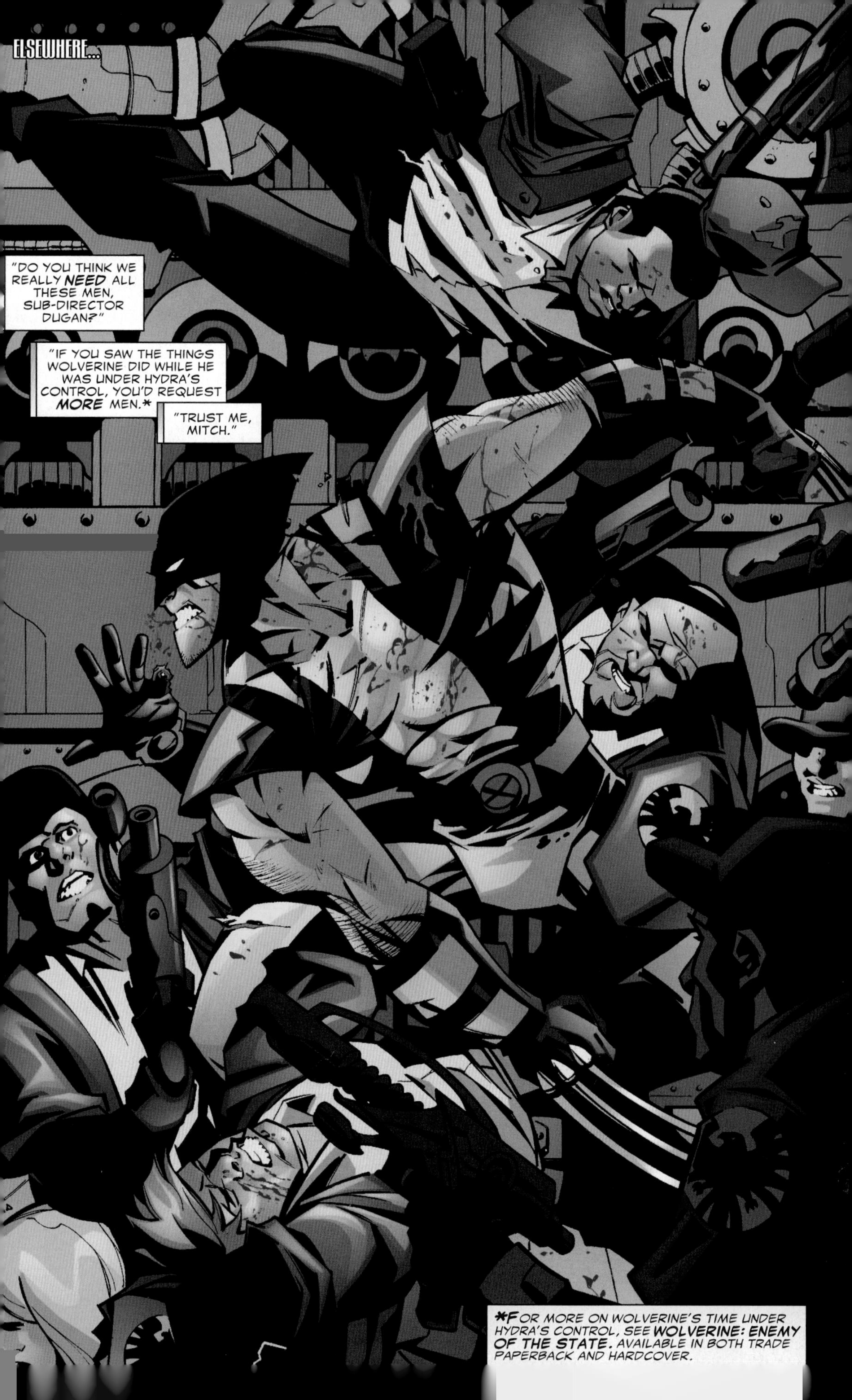
ELSEWHERE...
"DO YOU THINK WE REALLY NEED ALL THESE MEN, SUB-DIRECTOR DUGAN?"
"IF YOU SAW THE THINGS WOLVERINE DID WHILE HE WAS UNDER HYDRA'S CONTROL, YOU'D REQUEST MORE MEN.*
"TRUST ME, MITCH."
*FOR MORE ON WOLVERINE'S TIME UNDER HYDRA'S CONTROL, SEE WOLVERINE: ENEMY OF THE STATE. AVAILABLE IN BOTH TRADE PAPERBACK AND HARDCOVER.

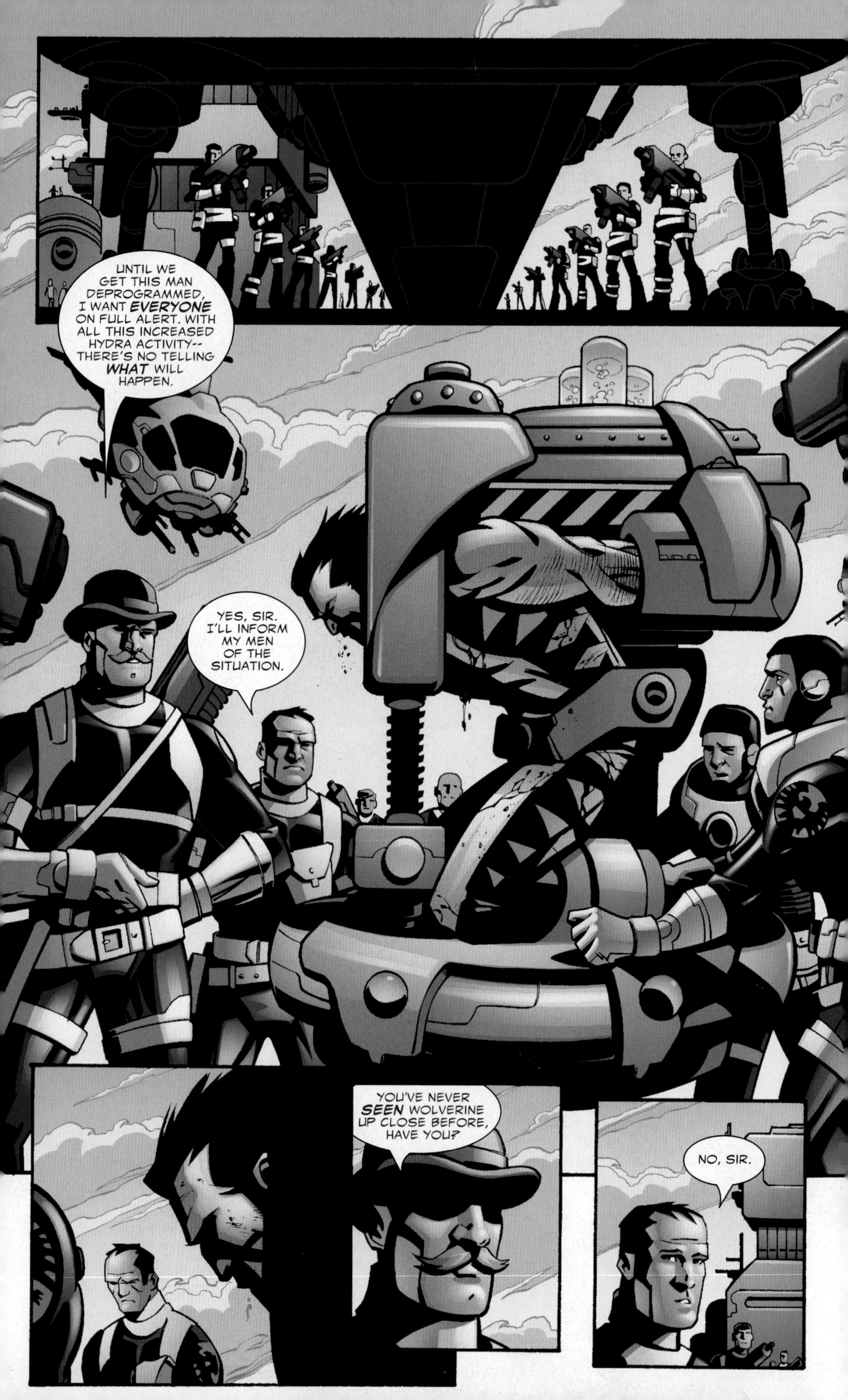
UNTIL WE GET THIS MAN DEPROGRAMMED, I WANT EVERYONE ON FULL ALERT. WITH ALL THIS INCREASED HYDRA ACTIVITY-- THERE'S NO TELLING WHAT WILL HAPPEN.
YES, SIR. I'LL INFORM MY MEN OF THE SITUATION.
YOU'VE NEVER SEEN WOLVERINE UP CLOSE BEFORE, HAVE YOU?
NO, SIR.

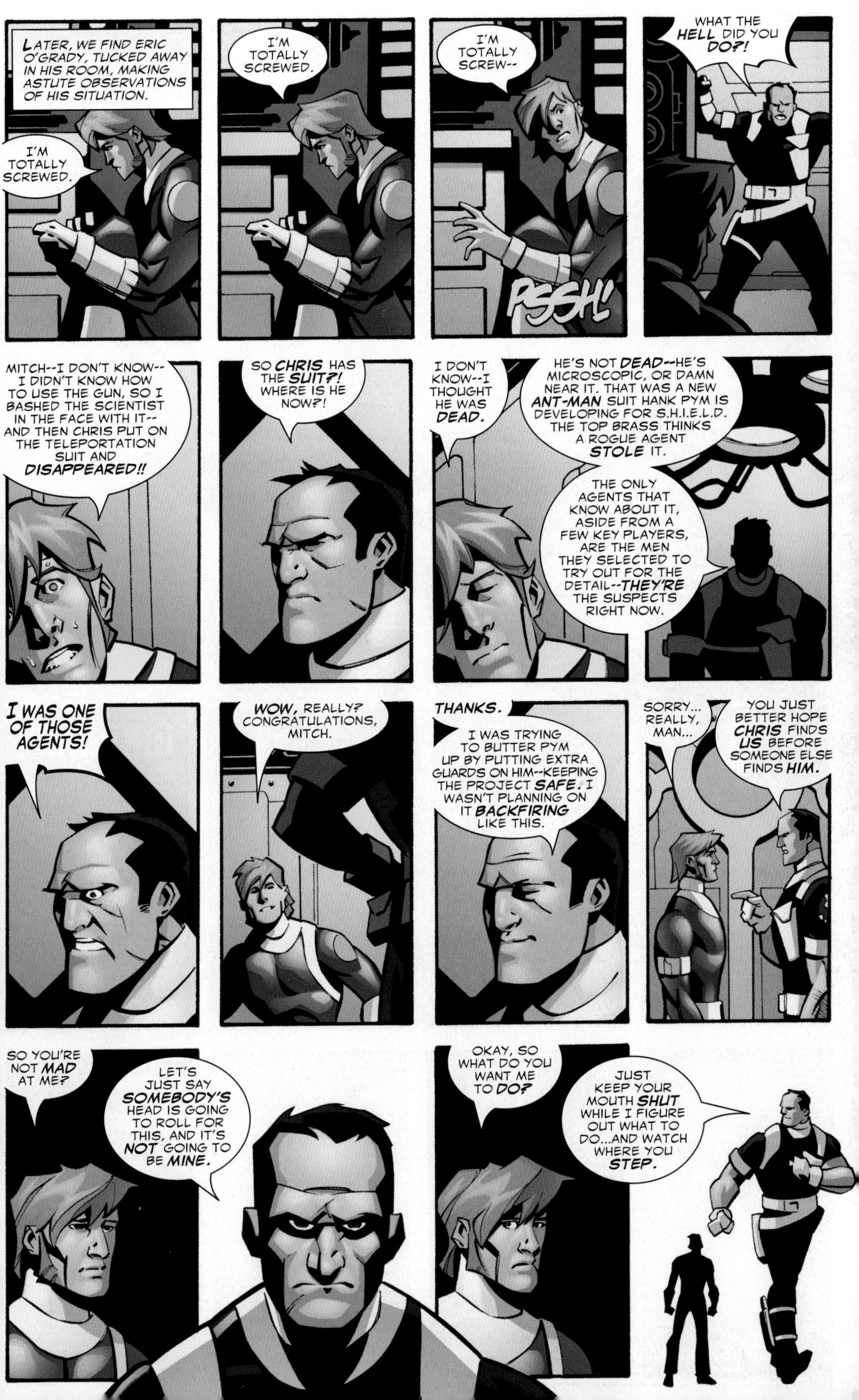
LATER, WE FIND ERIC O'GRADY, TUCKED AWAY IN HIS ROOM, MAKING ASTUTE OBSERVATIONS OF HIS SITUATION.
I'M TOTALLY SCREWED.
I'M TOTALLY SCREWED.
I'M TOTALLY SCREW--
PSSH!
WHAT THE HELL DID YOU DO?!
MITCH--I DON'T KNOW--I DIDN'T KNOW HOW TO USE THE GUN, SO I BASHED THE SCIENTIST IN THE FACE WITH IT--AND THEN CHRIS PUT ON THE TELEPORTATION SUIT AND DISAPPEARED!!
SO CHRIS HAS THE SUIT?! WHERE IS HE NOW?!
I DON'T KNOW--I THOUGHT HE WAS DEAD.
HE'S NOT DEAD--HE'S MICROSCOPIC, OR DAMN NEAR IT. THAT WAS A NEW ANT-MAN SUIT HANK PYM IS DEVELOPING FOR S.H.I.E.L.D. THE TOP BRASS THINKS A ROGUE AGENT STOLE IT.
THE ONLY AGENTS THAT KNOW ABOUT IT, ASIDE FROM A FEW KEY PLAYERS, ARE THE MEN THEY SELECTED TO TRY OUT FOR THE DETAIL--THEY'RE THE SUSPECTS RIGHT NOW.
I WAS ONE OF THOSE AGENTS!
WOW, REALLY? CONGRATULATIONS, MITCH.
THANKS.
I WAS TRYING TO BUTTER PYM UP BY PUTTING EXTRA GUARDS ON HIM--KEEPING THE PROJECT SAFE. I WASN'T PLANNING ON IT BACKFIRING LIKE THIS.
SORRY... REALLY, MAN...
YOU JUST BETTER HOPE CHRIS FINDS US BEFORE SOMEONE ELSE FINDS HIM.
SO YOU'RE NOT MAD AT ME?
LET'S JUST SAY SOMEBODY'S HEAD IS GOING TO ROLL FOR THIS, AND IT'S NOT GOING TO BE MINE.
OKAY, SO WHAT DO YOU WANT ME TO DO?
JUST KEEP YOUR MOUTH SHUT WHILE I FIGURE OUT WHAT TO DO...AND WATCH WHERE YOU STEP.

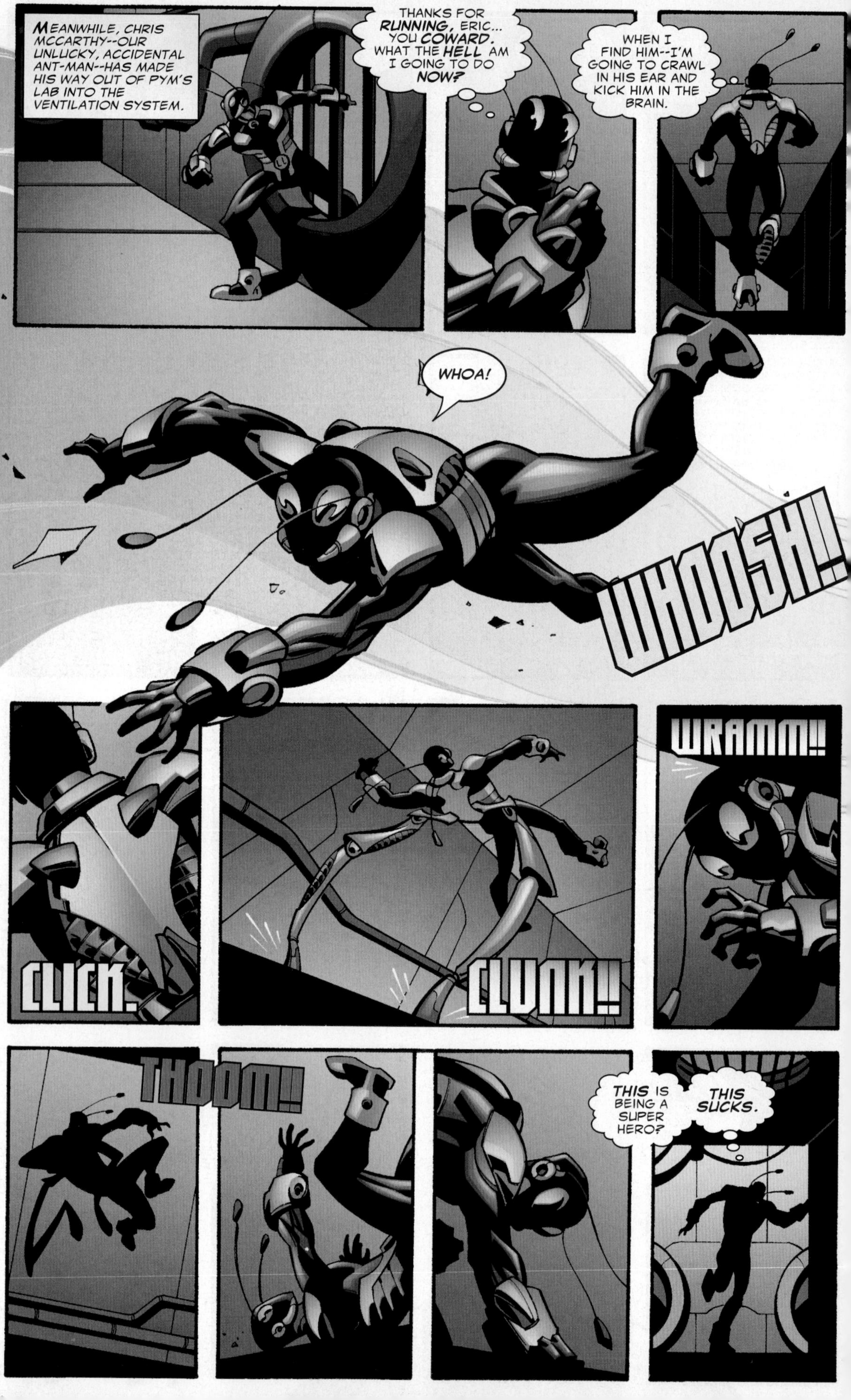
MEANWHILE, CHRIS McCARTHY--OUR UNLUCKY, ACCIDENTAL ANT-MAN--HAS MADE HIS WAY OUT OF PYM'S LAB INTO THE VENTILATION SYSTEM.
THANKS FOR RUNNING, ERIC... YOU COWARD. WHAT THE HELL AM I GOING TO DO NOW?
WHEN I FIND HIM--I'M GOING TO CRAWL IN HIS EAR AND KICK HIM IN THE BRAIN.
WHOA!
WHOOSH!!
CLICK.
CLUNK!!
WRAMM!!
THOOM!!
THIS IS BEING A SUPER HERO?
THIS SUCKS.

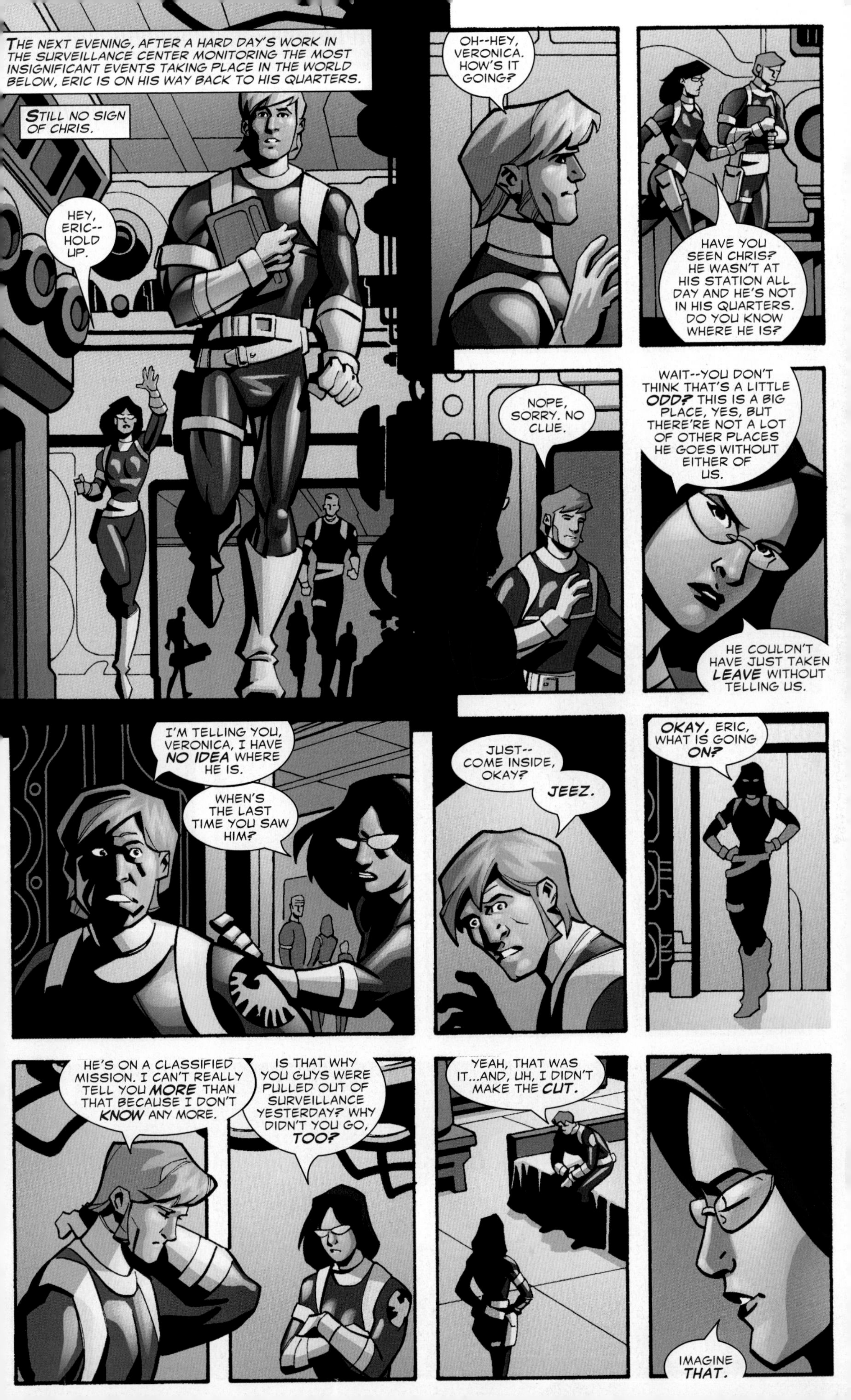
THE NEXT EVENING, AFTER A HARD DAY'S WORK IN THE SURVEILLANCE CENTER MONITORING THE MOST INSIGNIFICANT EVENTS TAKING PLACE IN THE WORLD BELOW, ERIC IS ON HIS WAY BACK TO HIS QUARTERS.
STILL NO SIGN OF CHRIS.
HEY, ERIC-- HOLD UP.
OH--HEY, VERONICA. HOW'S IT GOING?
HAVE YOU SEEN CHRIS? HE WASN'T AT HIS STATION ALL DAY AND HE'S NOT IN HIS QUARTERS. DO YOU KNOW WHERE HE IS?
NOPE, SORRY. NO CLUE.
WAIT--YOU DON'T THINK THAT'S A LITTLE ODD? THIS IS A BIG PLACE, YES, BUT THERE'RE NOT A LOT OF OTHER PLACES HE GOES WITHOUT EITHER OF US.
HE COULDN'T HAVE JUST TAKEN LEAVE WITHOUT TELLING US.
I'M TELLING YOU, VERONICA, I HAVE NO IDEA WHERE HE IS.
WHEN'S THE LAST TIME YOU SAW HIM?
JUST-- COME INSIDE, OKAY?
JEEZ.
OKAY, ERIC, WHAT IS GOING ON?
HE'S ON A CLASSIFIED MISSION. I CAN'T REALLY TELL YOU MORE THAN THAT BECAUSE I DON'T KNOW ANY MORE.
IS THAT WHY YOU GUYS WERE PULLED OUT OF SURVEILLANCE YESTERDAY? WHY DIDN'T YOU GO, TOO?
YEAH, THAT WAS IT...AND, UH, I DIDN'T MAKE THE CUT.
IMAGINE THAT.

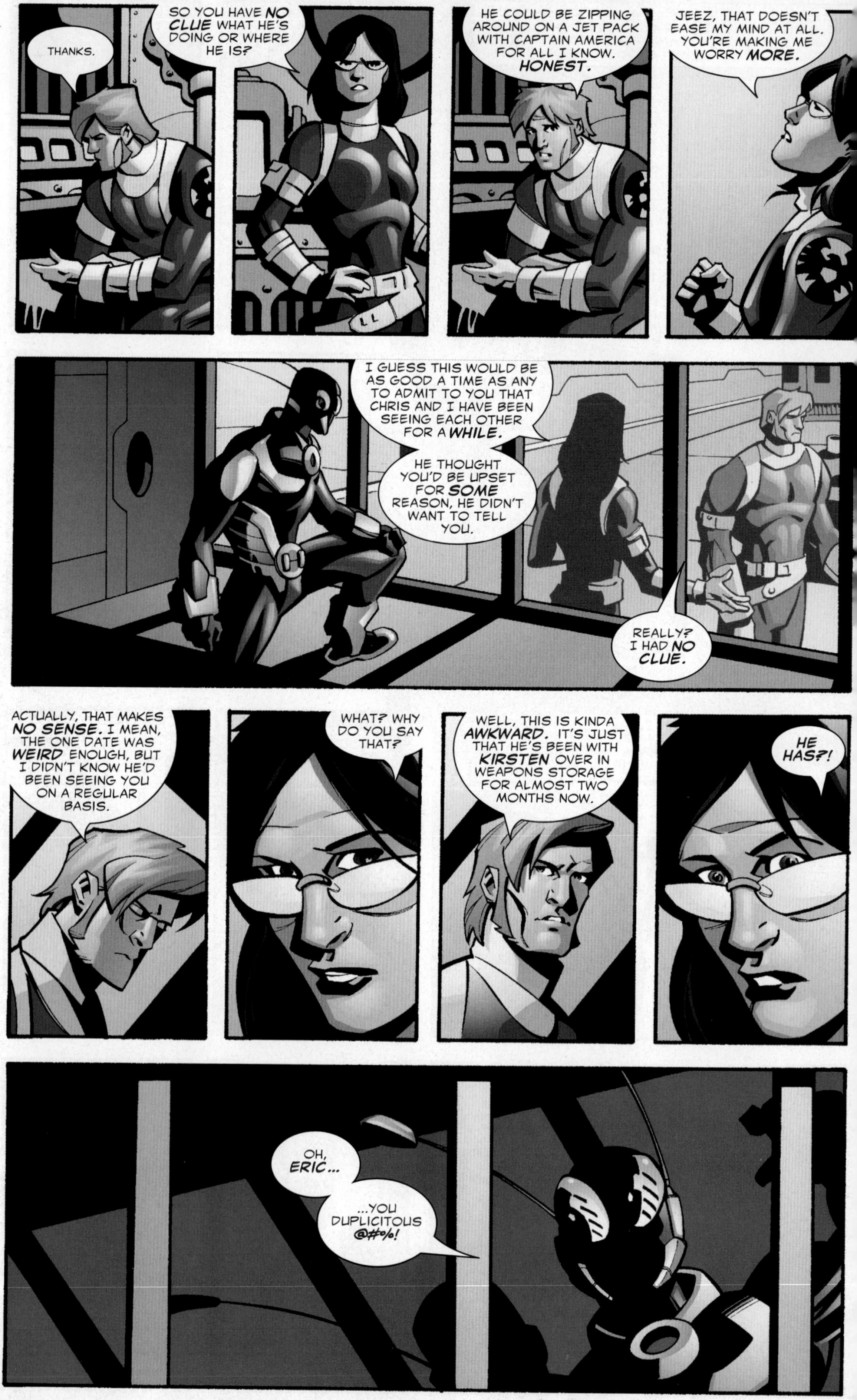
THANKS.
SO YOU HAVE NO CLUE WHAT HE'S DOING OR WHERE HE IS?
HE COULD BE ZIPPING AROUND ON A JET PACK WITH CAPTAIN AMERICA FOR ALL I KNOW. HONEST.
JEEZ, THAT DOESN'T EASE MY MIND AT ALL. YOU'RE MAKING ME WORRY MORE.
I GUESS THIS WOULD BE AS GOOD A TIME AS ANY TO ADMIT TO YOU THAT CHRIS AND I HAVE BEEN SEEING EACH OTHER FOR A WHILE.
HE THOUGHT YOU'D BE UPSET FOR SOME REASON, HE DIDN'T WANT TO TELL YOU.
REALLY? I HAD NO CLUE.
ACTUALLY, THAT MAKES NO SENSE. I MEAN, THE ONE DATE WAS WEIRD ENOUGH, BUT I DIDN'T KNOW HE'D BEEN SEEING YOU ON A REGULAR BASIS.
WHAT? WHY DO YOU SAY THAT?
WELL, THIS IS KINDA AWKWARD. IT'S JUST THAT HE'S BEEN WITH KIRSTEN OVER IN WEAPONS STORAGE FOR ALMOST TWO MONTHS NOW.
HE HAS?!
OH, ERIC...
...YOU DUPLICITOUS @#%!

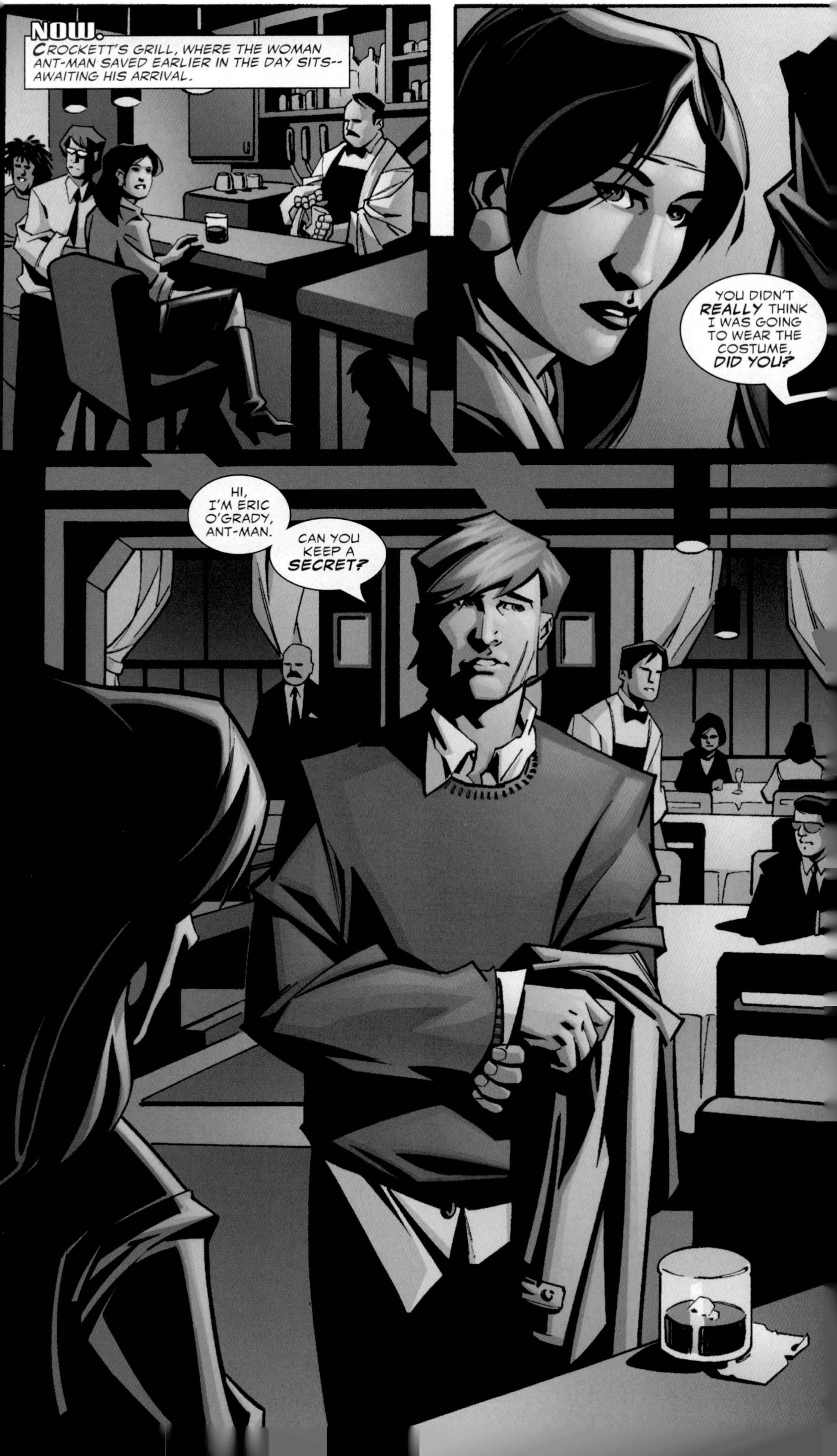
NOW.
CROCKETT'S GRILL, WHERE THE WOMAN ANT-MAN SAVED EARLIER IN THE DAY SITS-- AWAITING HIS ARRIVAL.
YOU DIDN'T REALLY THINK I WAS GOING TO WEAR THE COSTUME, DID YOU?
HI, I'M ERIC O'GRADY, ANT-MAN.
CAN YOU KEEP A SECRET?

#2

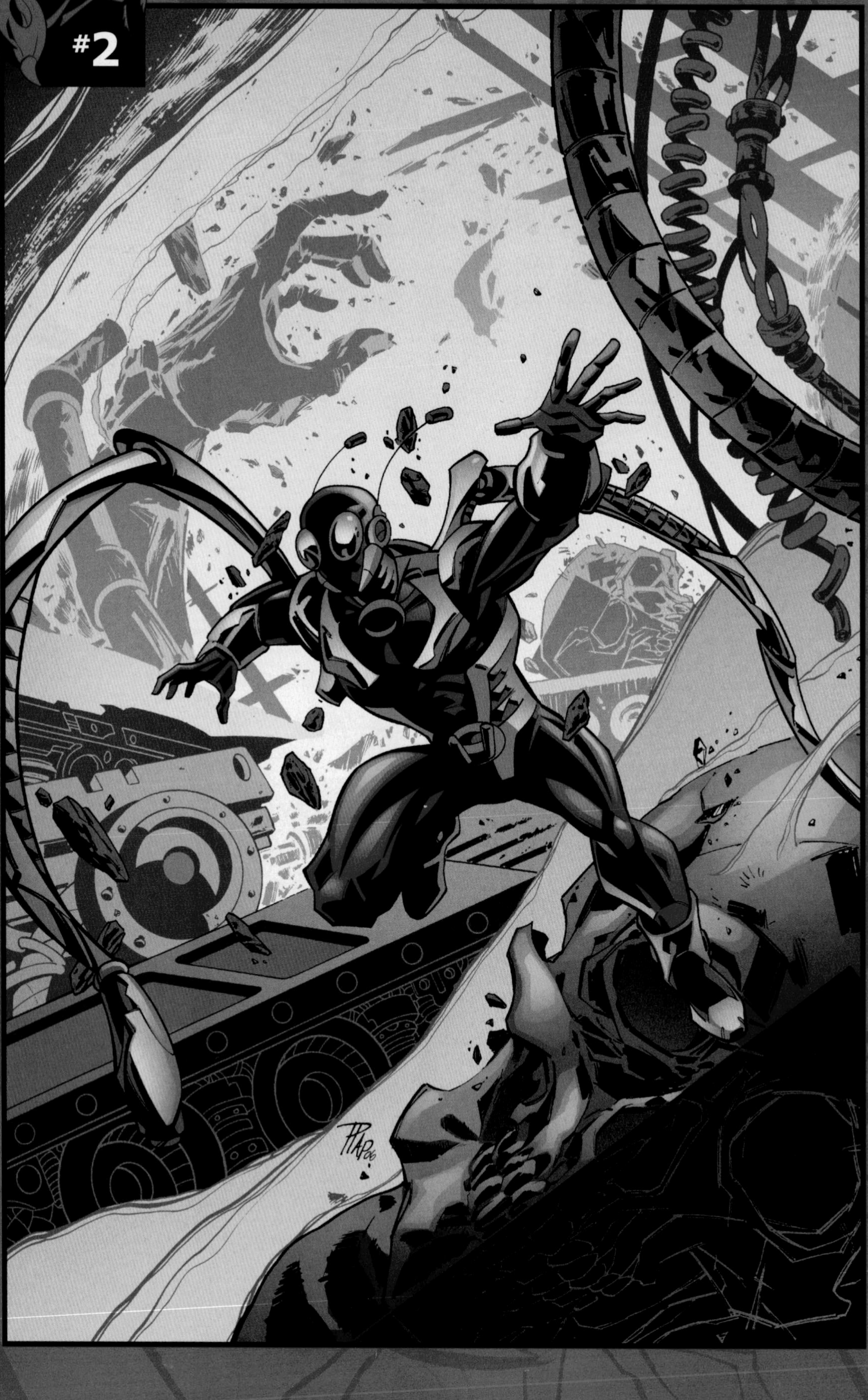

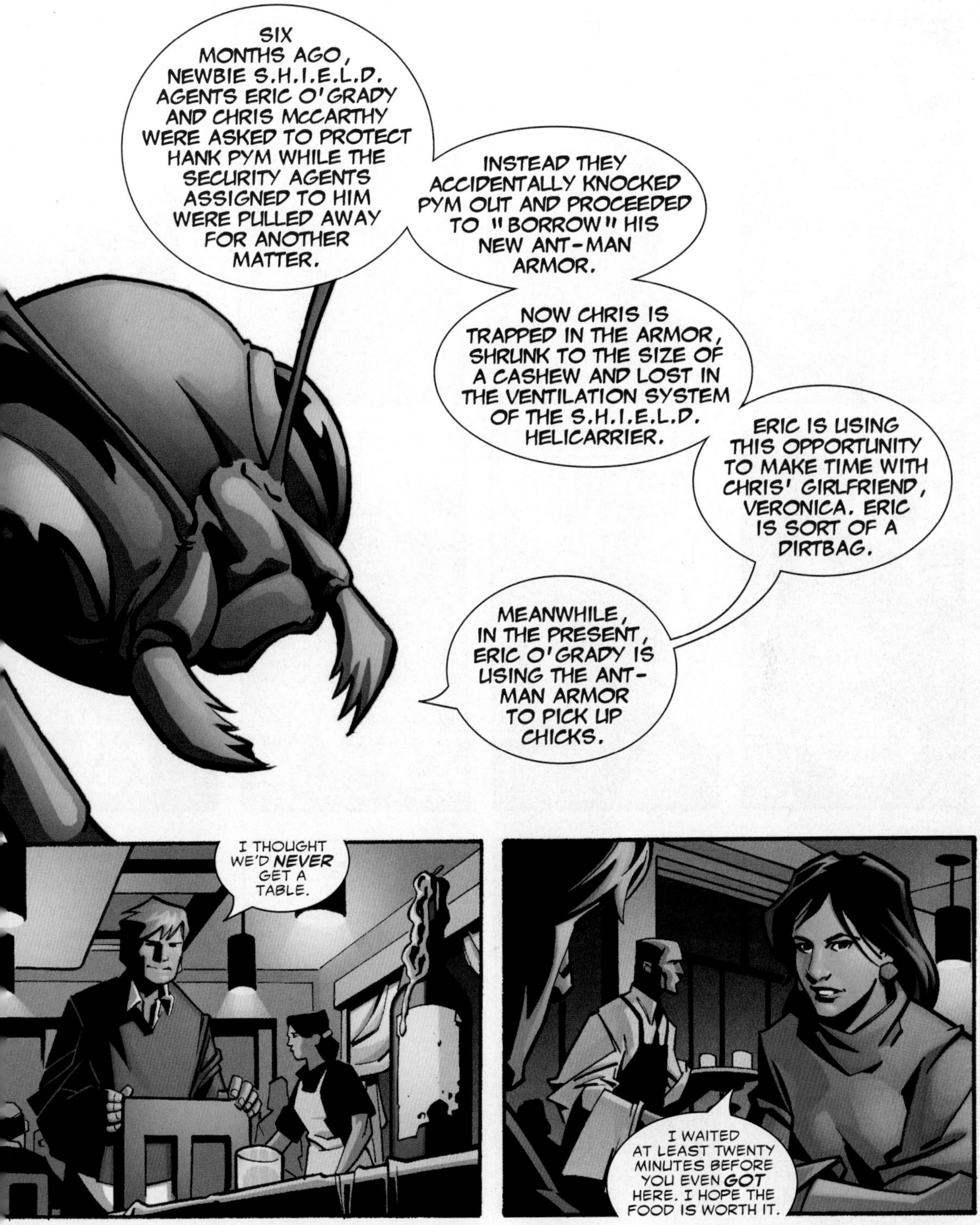
SIX MONTHS AGO, NEWBIE S.H.I.E.L.D. AGENTS ERIC O'GRADY AND CHRIS McCARTHY WERE ASKED TO PROTECT HANK PYM WHILE THE SECURITY AGENTS ASSIGNED TO HIM WERE PULLED AWAY FOR ANOTHER MATTER.
INSTEAD THEY ACCIDENTALLY KNOCKED PYM OUT AND PROCEEDED TO "BORROW" HIS NEW ANT-MAN ARMOR.
NOW CHRIS IS TRAPPED IN THE ARMOR, SHRUNK TO THE SIZE OF A CASHEW AND LOST IN THE VENTILATION SYSTEM OF THE S.H.I.E.L.D. HELICARRIER.
ERIC IS USING THIS OPPORTUNITY TO MAKE TIME WITH CHRIS' GIRLFRIEND, VERONICA. ERIC IS SORT OF A DIRTBAG.
MEANWHILE, IN THE PRESENT, ERIC O'GRADY IS USING THE ANT-MAN ARMOR TO PICK UP CHICKS.
I THOUGHT WE'D ***NEVER*** GET A TABLE.
I WAITED AT LEAST TWENTY MINUTES BEFORE YOU EVEN ***GOT*** HERE. I HOPE THE FOOD IS WORTH IT.

# SHOCK & AWE

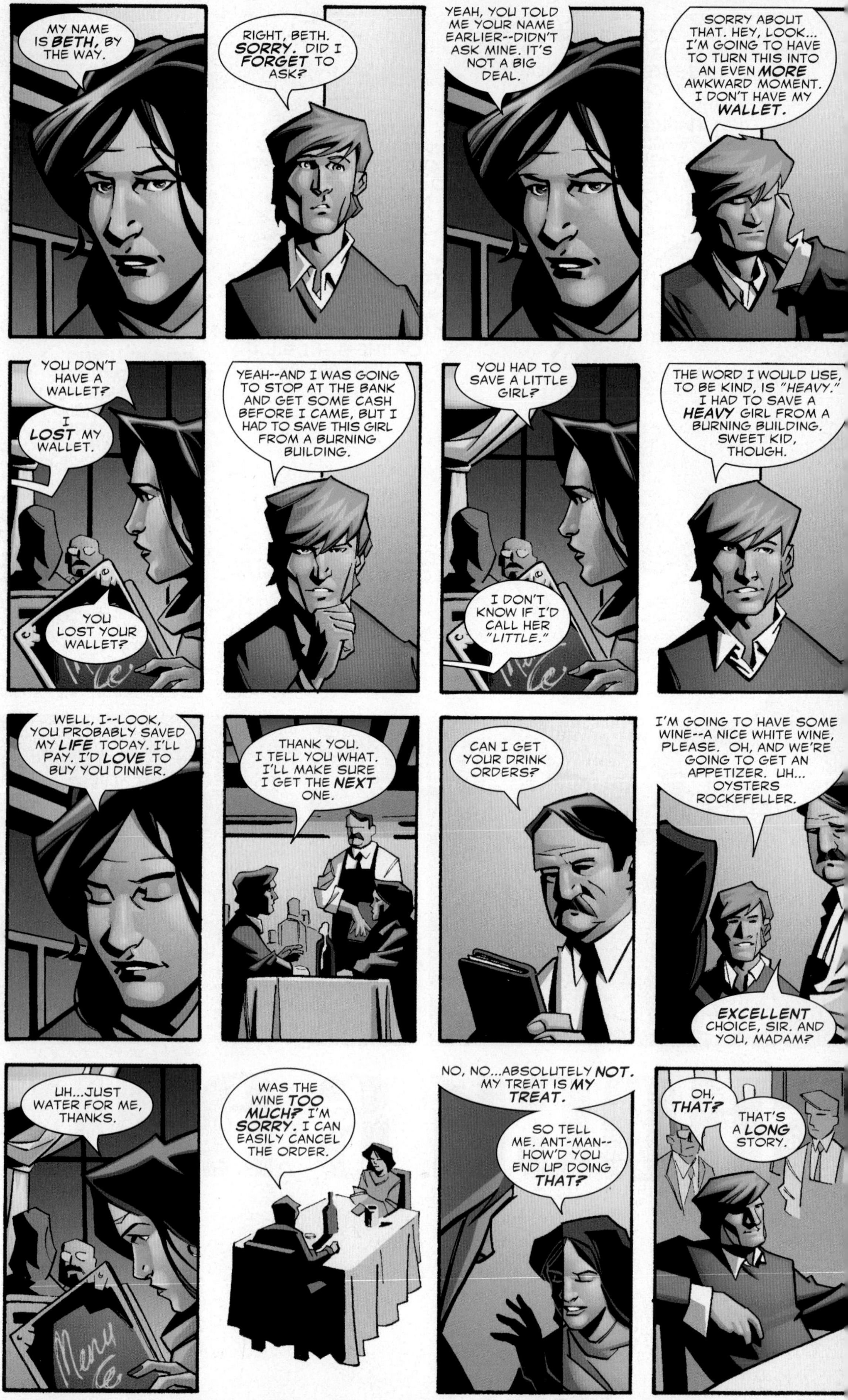
MY NAME IS BETH, BY THE WAY.
RIGHT, BETH. SORRY. DID I FORGET TO ASK?
YEAH, YOU TOLD ME YOUR NAME EARLIER--DIDN'T ASK MINE. IT'S NOT A BIG DEAL.
SORRY ABOUT THAT. HEY, LOOK... I'M GOING TO HAVE TO TURN THIS INTO AN EVEN MORE AWKWARD MOMENT. I DON'T HAVE MY WALLET.
YOU DON'T HAVE A WALLET?
I LOST MY WALLET.
YOU LOST YOUR WALLET?
YEAH--AND I WAS GOING TO STOP AT THE BANK AND GET SOME CASH BEFORE I CAME, BUT I HAD TO SAVE THIS GIRL FROM A BURNING BUILDING.
YOU HAD TO SAVE A LITTLE GIRL?
I DON'T KNOW IF I'D CALL HER "LITTLE."
THE WORD I WOULD USE, TO BE KIND, IS "HEAVY." I HAD TO SAVE A HEAVY GIRL FROM A BURNING BUILDING. SWEET KID, THOUGH.
WELL, I--LOOK, YOU PROBABLY SAVED MY LIFE TODAY. I'LL PAY. I'D LOVE TO BUY YOU DINNER.
THANK YOU. I TELL YOU WHAT. I'LL MAKE SURE I GET THE NEXT ONE.
CAN I GET YOUR DRINK ORDERS?
I'M GOING TO HAVE SOME WINE--A NICE WHITE WINE, PLEASE. OH, AND WE'RE GOING TO GET AN APPETIZER. UH... OYSTERS ROCKEFELLER.
EXCELLENT CHOICE, SIR. AND YOU, MADAM?
UH...JUST WATER FOR ME, THANKS.
WAS THE WINE TOO MUCH? I'M SORRY. I CAN EASILY CANCEL THE ORDER.
NO, NO...ABSOLUTELY NOT. MY TREAT IS MY TREAT.
SO TELL ME. ANT-MAN-- HOW'D YOU END UP DOING THAT?
OH, THAT?
THAT'S A LONG STORY.

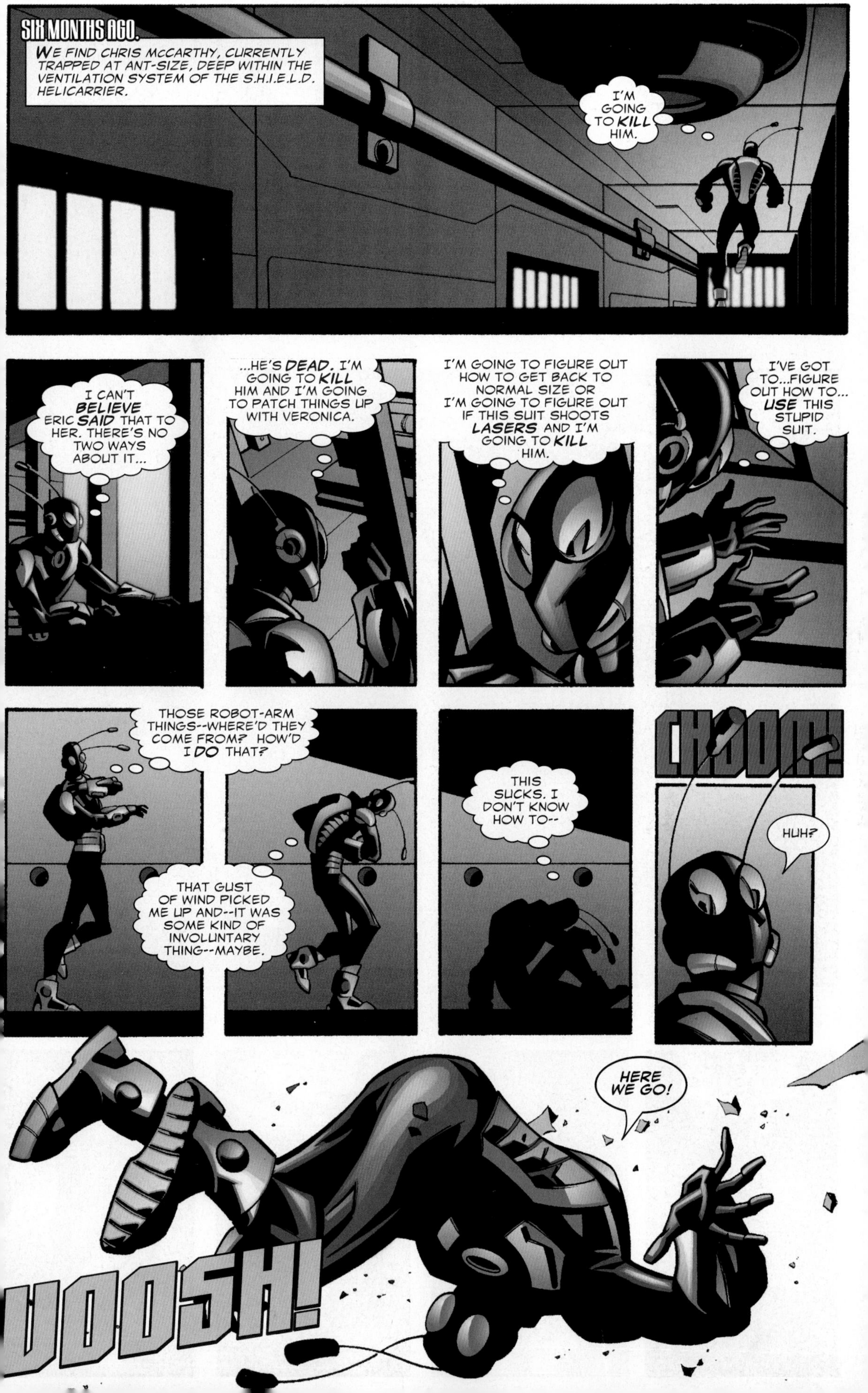
SIX MONTHS AGO.
WE FIND CHRIS McCARTHY, CURRENTLY TRAPPED AT ANT-SIZE, DEEP WITHIN THE VENTILATION SYSTEM OF THE S.H.I.E.L.D. HELICARRIER.
I'M GOING TO KILL HIM.
I CAN'T BELIEVE ERIC SAID THAT TO HER. THERE'S NO TWO WAYS ABOUT IT...
...HE'S DEAD. I'M GOING TO KILL HIM AND I'M GOING TO PATCH THINGS UP WITH VERONICA.
I'M GOING TO FIGURE OUT HOW TO GET BACK TO NORMAL SIZE OR I'M GOING TO FIGURE OUT IF THIS SUIT SHOOTS LASERS AND I'M GOING TO KILL HIM.
I'VE GOT TO...FIGURE OUT HOW TO... USE THIS STUPID SUIT.
THOSE ROBOT-ARM THINGS--WHERE'D THEY COME FROM? HOW'D I DO THAT?
THAT GUST OF WIND PICKED ME UP AND--IT WAS SOME KIND OF INVOLUNTARY THING--MAYBE.
THIS SUCKS. I DON'T KNOW HOW TO--
CHOOM!
HUH?
HERE WE GO!
VOOSH!

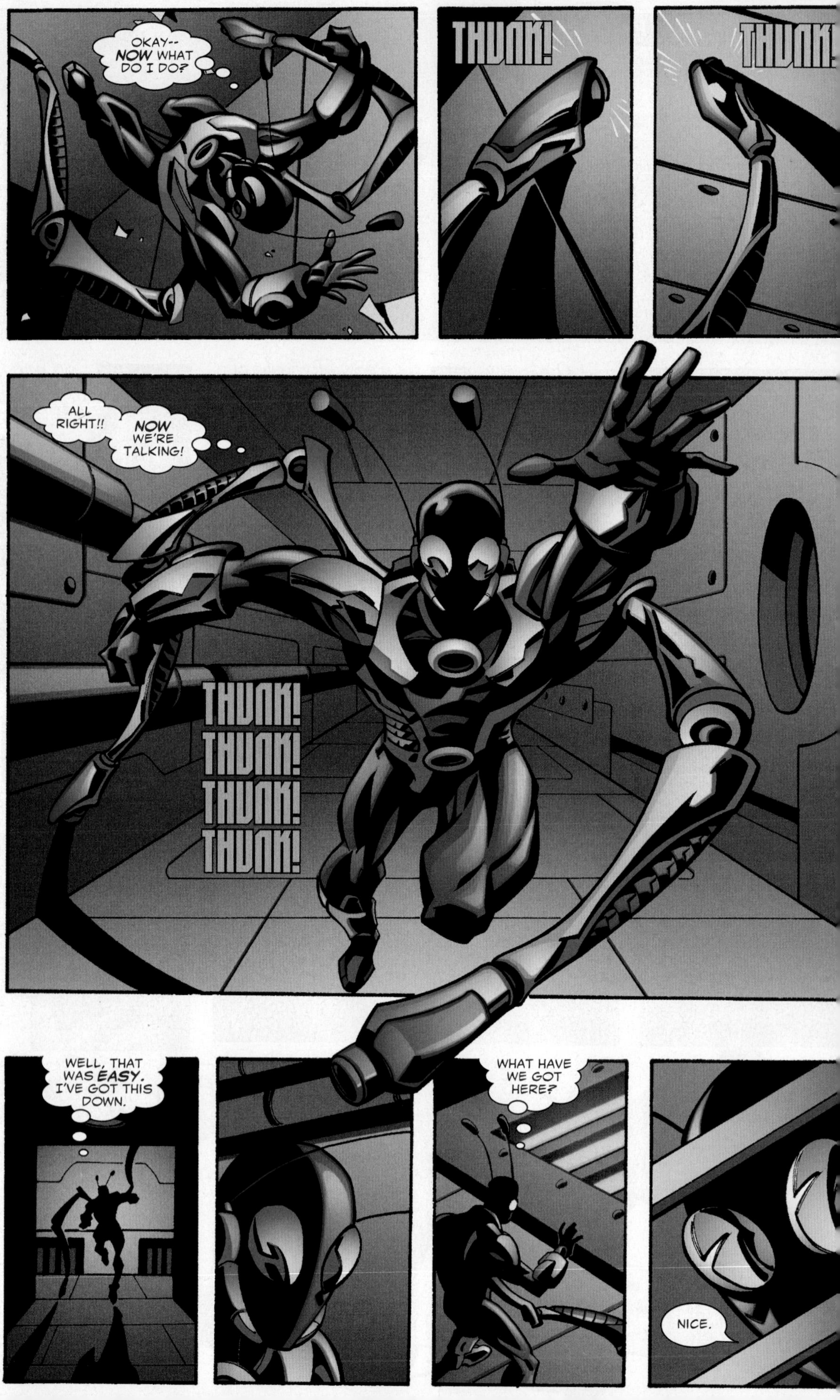
OKAY-- NOW WHAT DO I DO?
THUNK!
THUNK!
ALL RIGHT!!
NOW WE'RE TALKING!
THUNK! THUNK! THUNK! THUNK!
WELL, THAT WAS EASY. I'VE GOT THIS DOWN.
WHAT HAVE WE GOT HERE?
NICE.

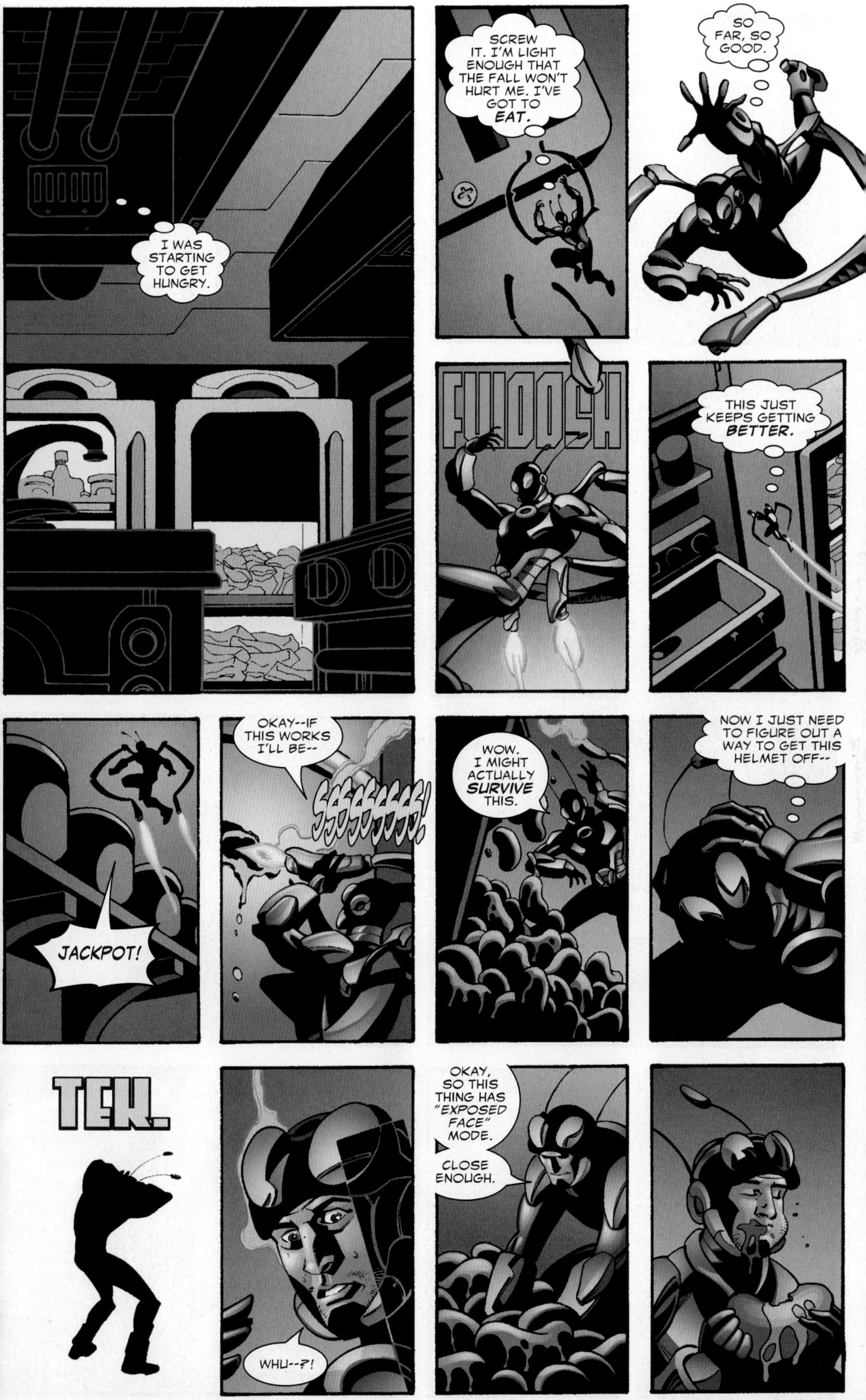
I WAS STARTING TO GET HUNGRY.
SCREW IT. I'M LIGHT ENOUGH THAT THE FALL WON'T HURT ME. I'VE GOT TO EAT.
SO FAR, SO GOOD.
FWOOSH
THIS JUST KEEPS GETTING BETTER.
JACKPOT!
OKAY--IF THIS WORKS I'LL BE--
SSSSSSSSS!
WOW. I MIGHT ACTUALLY SURVIVE THIS.
NOW I JUST NEED TO FIGURE OUT A WAY TO GET THIS HELMET OFF--
TEK.
WHU--?!
OKAY, SO THIS THING HAS "EXPOSED FACE" MODE.
CLOSE ENOUGH.

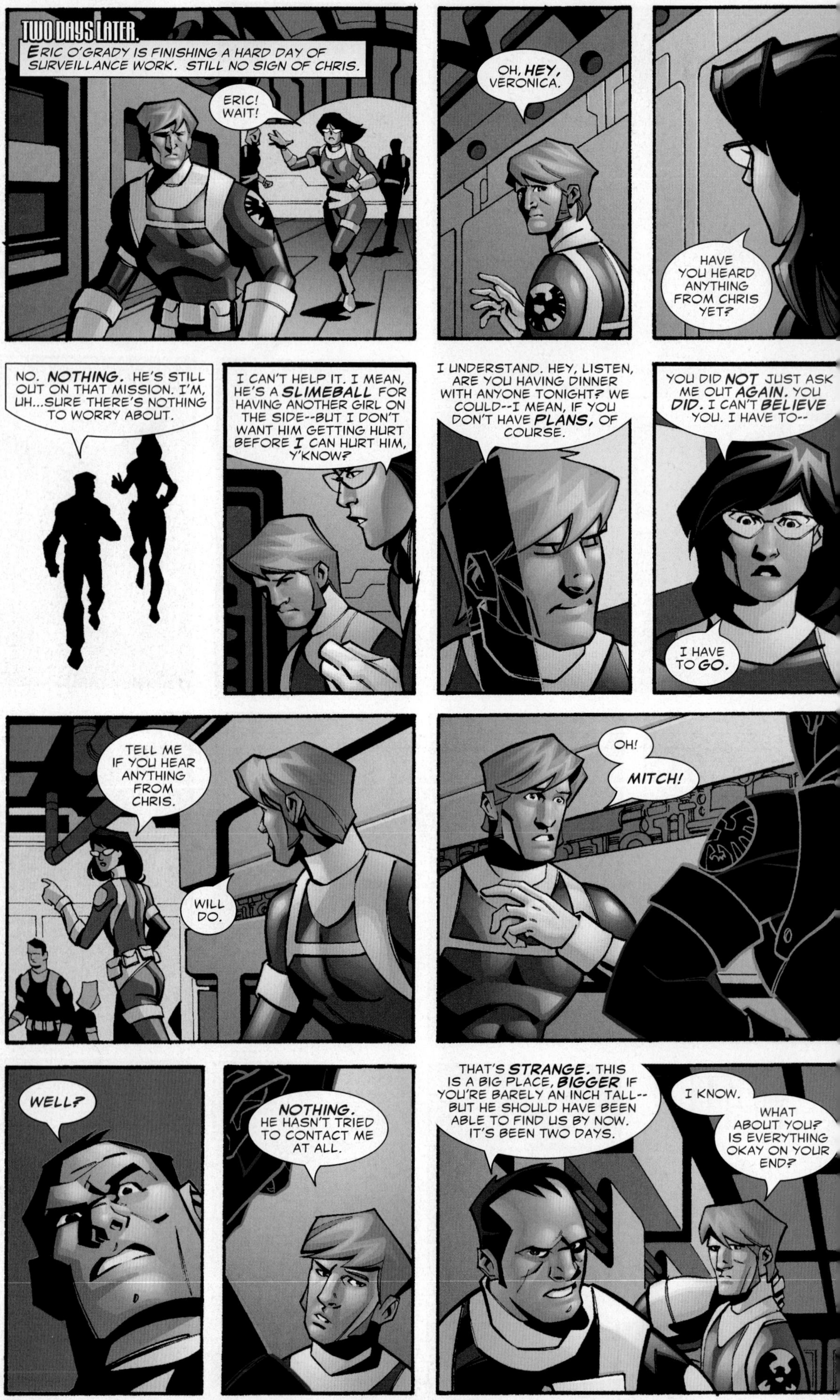
TWO DAYS LATER.
ERIC O'GRADY IS FINISHING A HARD DAY OF SURVEILLANCE WORK. STILL NO SIGN OF CHRIS.
ERIC! WAIT!
OH, HEY, VERONICA.
HAVE YOU HEARD ANYTHING FROM CHRIS YET?
NO. NOTHING. HE'S STILL OUT ON THAT MISSION. I'M, UH...SURE THERE'S NOTHING TO WORRY ABOUT.
I CAN'T HELP IT. I MEAN, HE'S A SLIMEBALL FOR HAVING ANOTHER GIRL ON THE SIDE--BUT I DON'T WANT HIM GETTING HURT BEFORE I CAN HURT HIM, Y'KNOW?
I UNDERSTAND. HEY, LISTEN, ARE YOU HAVING DINNER WITH ANYONE TONIGHT? WE COULD--I MEAN, IF YOU DON'T HAVE PLANS, OF COURSE.
YOU DID NOT JUST ASK ME OUT AGAIN. YOU DID. I CAN'T BELIEVE YOU. I HAVE TO--
I HAVE TO GO.
TELL ME IF YOU HEAR ANYTHING FROM CHRIS.
WILL DO.
OH!
MITCH!
WELL?
NOTHING. HE HASN'T TRIED TO CONTACT ME AT ALL.
THAT'S STRANGE. THIS IS A BIG PLACE, BIGGER IF YOU'RE BARELY AN INCH TALL--BUT HE SHOULD HAVE BEEN ABLE TO FIND US BY NOW. IT'S BEEN TWO DAYS.
I KNOW.
WHAT ABOUT YOU? IS EVERYTHING OKAY ON YOUR END?

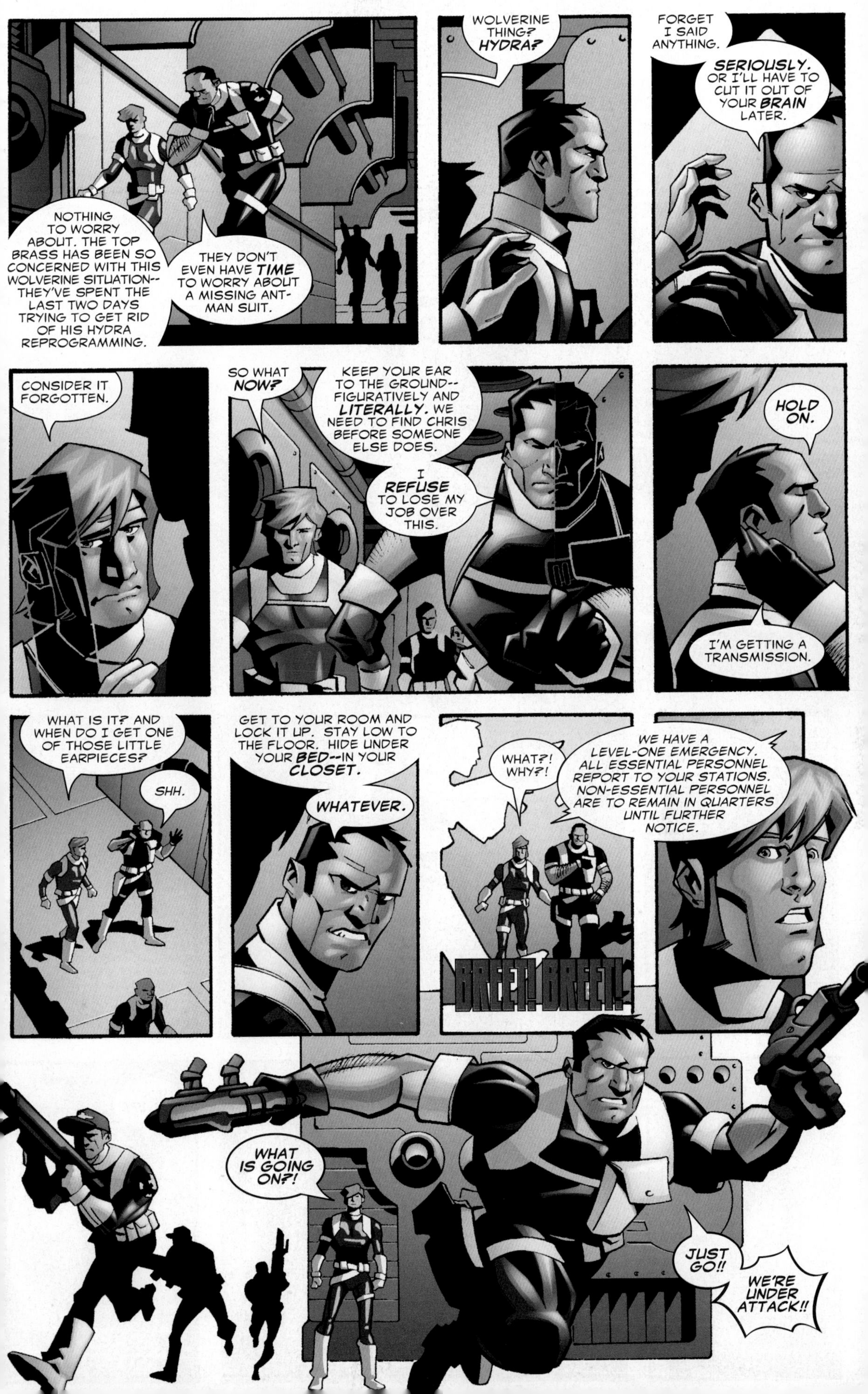
NOTHING TO WORRY ABOUT. THE TOP BRASS HAS BEEN SO CONCERNED WITH THIS WOLVERINE SITUATION-- THEY'VE SPENT THE LAST TWO DAYS TRYING TO GET RID OF HIS HYDRA REPROGRAMMING.
THEY DON'T EVEN HAVE TIME TO WORRY ABOUT A MISSING ANT-MAN SUIT.
WOLVERINE THING? HYDRA?
FORGET I SAID ANYTHING.
SERIOUSLY. OR I'LL HAVE TO CUT IT OUT OF YOUR BRAIN LATER.
CONSIDER IT FORGOTTEN.
SO WHAT NOW?
KEEP YOUR EAR TO THE GROUND-- FIGURATIVELY AND LITERALLY. WE NEED TO FIND CHRIS BEFORE SOMEONE ELSE DOES.
I REFUSE TO LOSE MY JOB OVER THIS.
HOLD ON.
I'M GETTING A TRANSMISSION.
WHAT IS IT? AND WHEN DO I GET ONE OF THOSE LITTLE EARPIECES?
SHH.
GET TO YOUR ROOM AND LOCK IT UP. STAY LOW TO THE FLOOR. HIDE UNDER YOUR BED--IN YOUR CLOSET.
WHATEVER.
WHAT?! WHY?!
WE HAVE A LEVEL-ONE EMERGENCY. ALL ESSENTIAL PERSONNEL REPORT TO YOUR STATIONS. NON-ESSENTIAL PERSONNEL ARE TO REMAIN IN QUARTERS UNTIL FURTHER NOTICE.
BREET! BREET!
WHAT IS GOING ON?!
JUST GO!!
WE'RE UNDER ATTACK!!

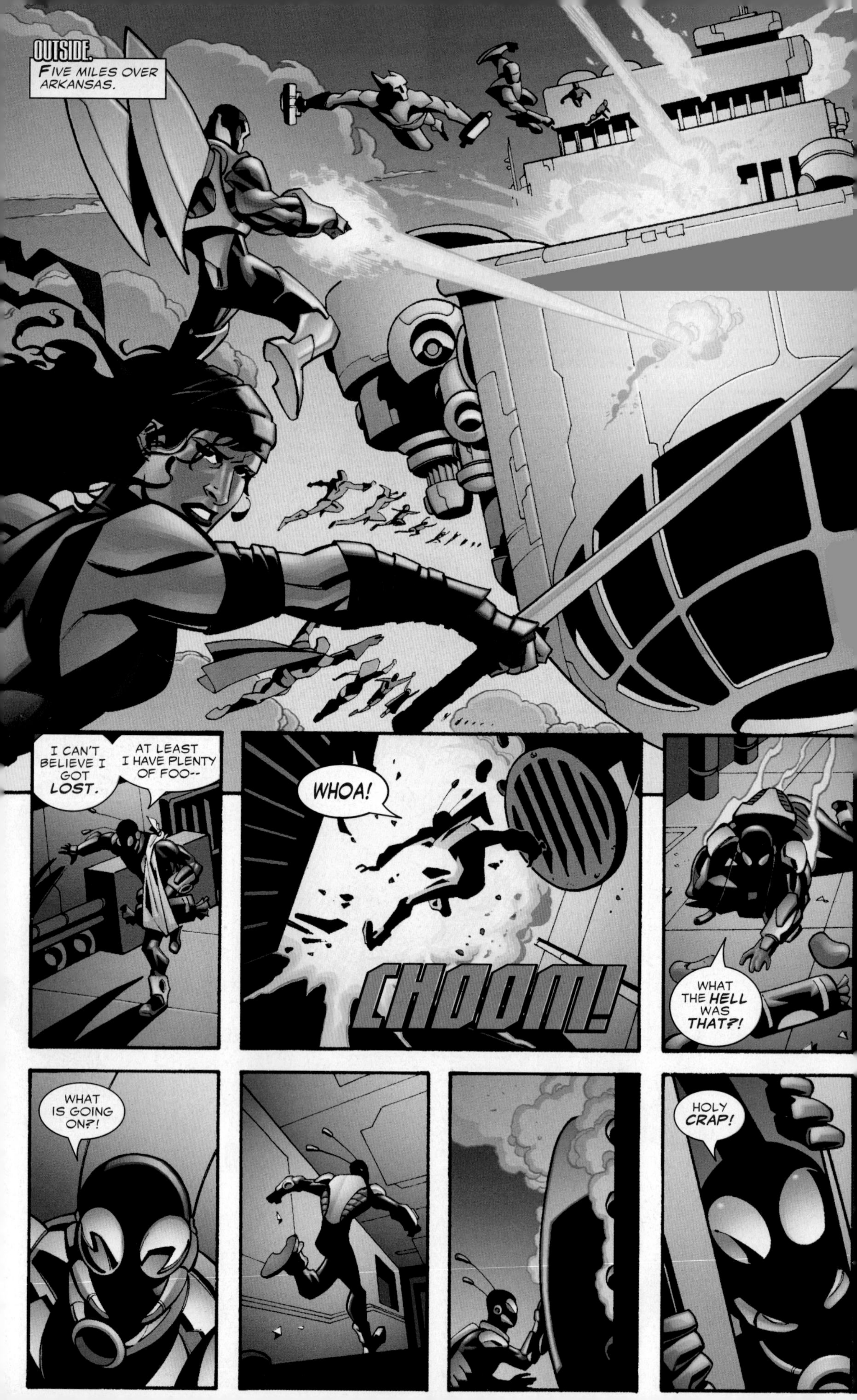
OUTSIDE.
FIVE MILES OVER ARKANSAS.
I CAN'T BELIEVE I GOT LOST.
AT LEAST I HAVE PLENTY OF FOO--
WHOA!
CHOOM!
WHAT THE HELL WAS THAT?!
WHAT IS GOING ON?!
HOLY CRAP!

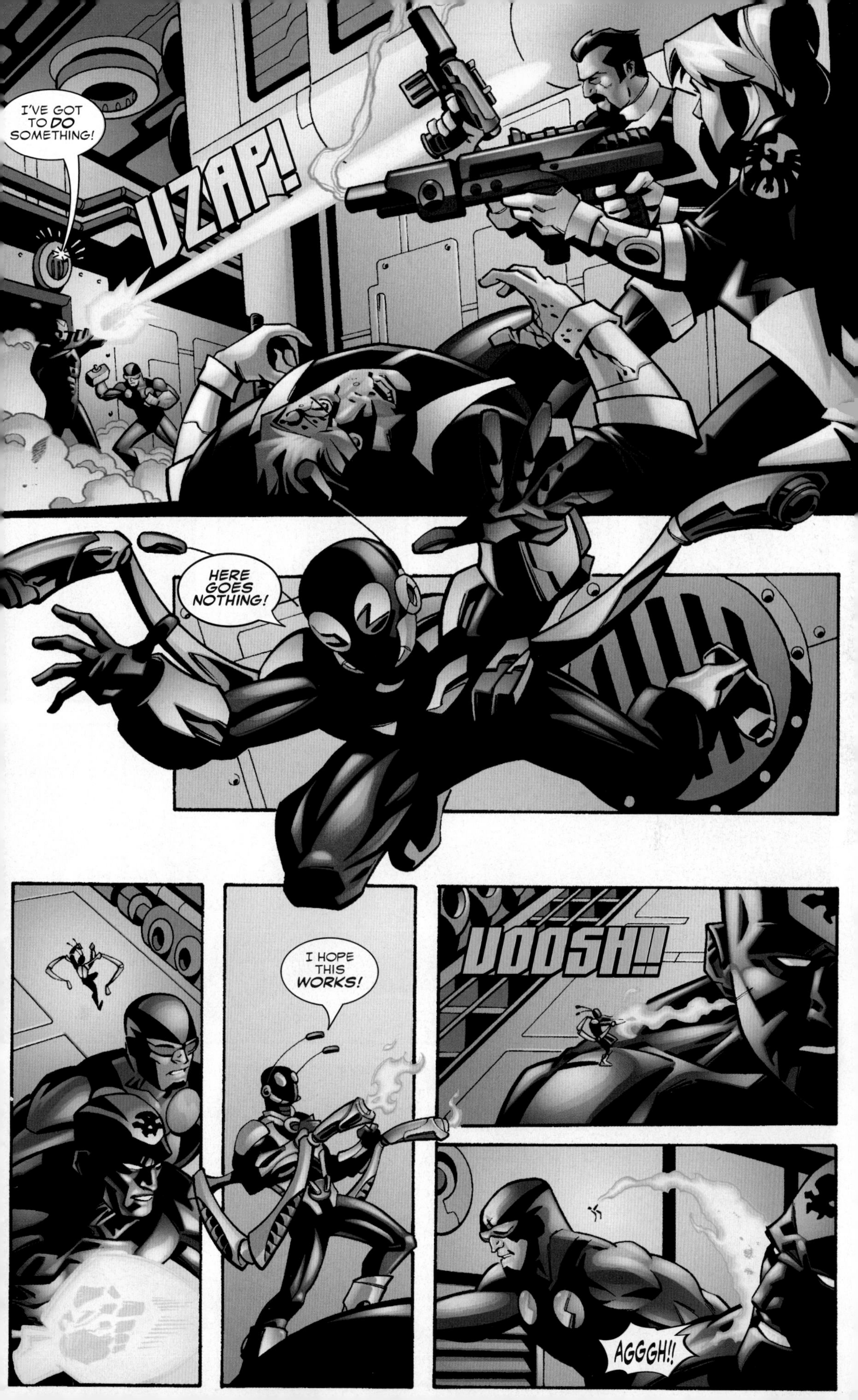
I'VE GOT TO DO SOMETHING!
VZAP!
HERE GOES NOTHING!
I HOPE THIS WORKS!
VOOSH!!
AGGGH!!

I CAN'T BELIEVE THIS IS ACTUALLY WORKING!

GAAAH!!

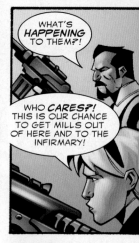

WHAT'S HAPPENING TO THEM?!

WHO CARES?! THIS IS OUR CHANCE TO GET MILLS OUT OF HERE AND TO THE INFIRMARY!

OUT--NOW! THE AGENTS ARE RUNNING! THEY MUST HAVE GASSED THIS CORRIDOR! IT'S MELTING YOUR BRAIN STEMS OR SOMETHING!

OOF!!

THOOM!

JEEZ.

TEK.

OH, MAN! OH, MAN!

KICK ASS!

I'M FULL-SIZE AGAIN!

SKROOM!!

NEVER MIND!

THIS SUCKS!

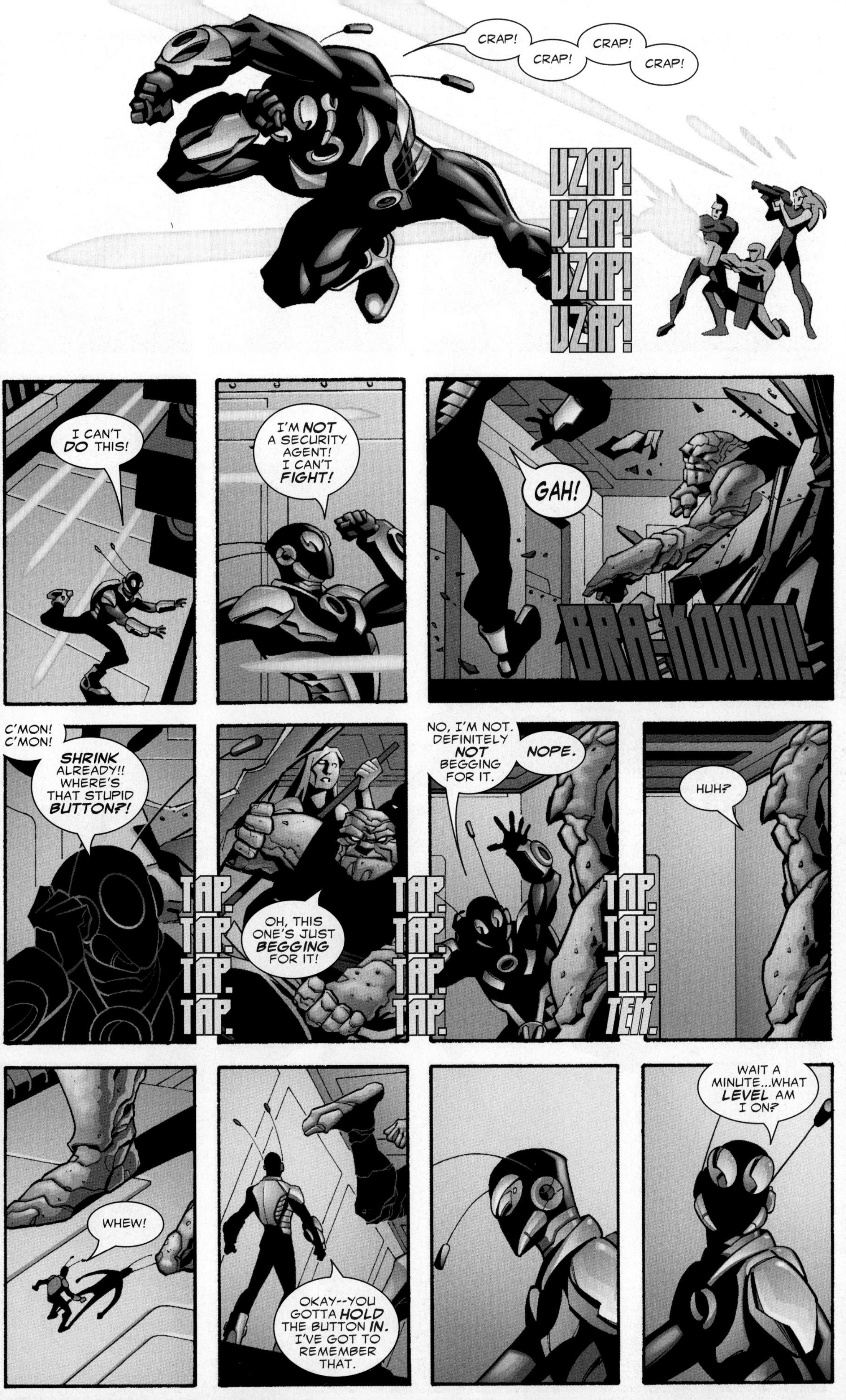
CRAP!
CRAP!
CRAP!
CRAP!
VZAP! VZAP! VZAP! VZAP!
I CAN'T DO THIS!
I'M NOT A SECURITY AGENT! I CAN'T FIGHT!
GAH!
BRA-KOOM!
C'MON! C'MON!
SHRINK ALREADY!! WHERE'S THAT STUPID BUTTON?!
TAP. TAP. TAP. TAP.
OH, THIS ONE'S JUST BEGGING FOR IT!
TAP. TAP. TAP. TAP.
NO, I'M NOT. DEFINITELY NOT BEGGING FOR IT.
NOPE.
TAP. TAP. TAP. TEK.
HUH?
WHEW!
OKAY--YOU GOTTA HOLD THE BUTTON IN. I'VE GOT TO REMEMBER THAT.
WAIT A MINUTE...WHAT LEVEL AM I ON?

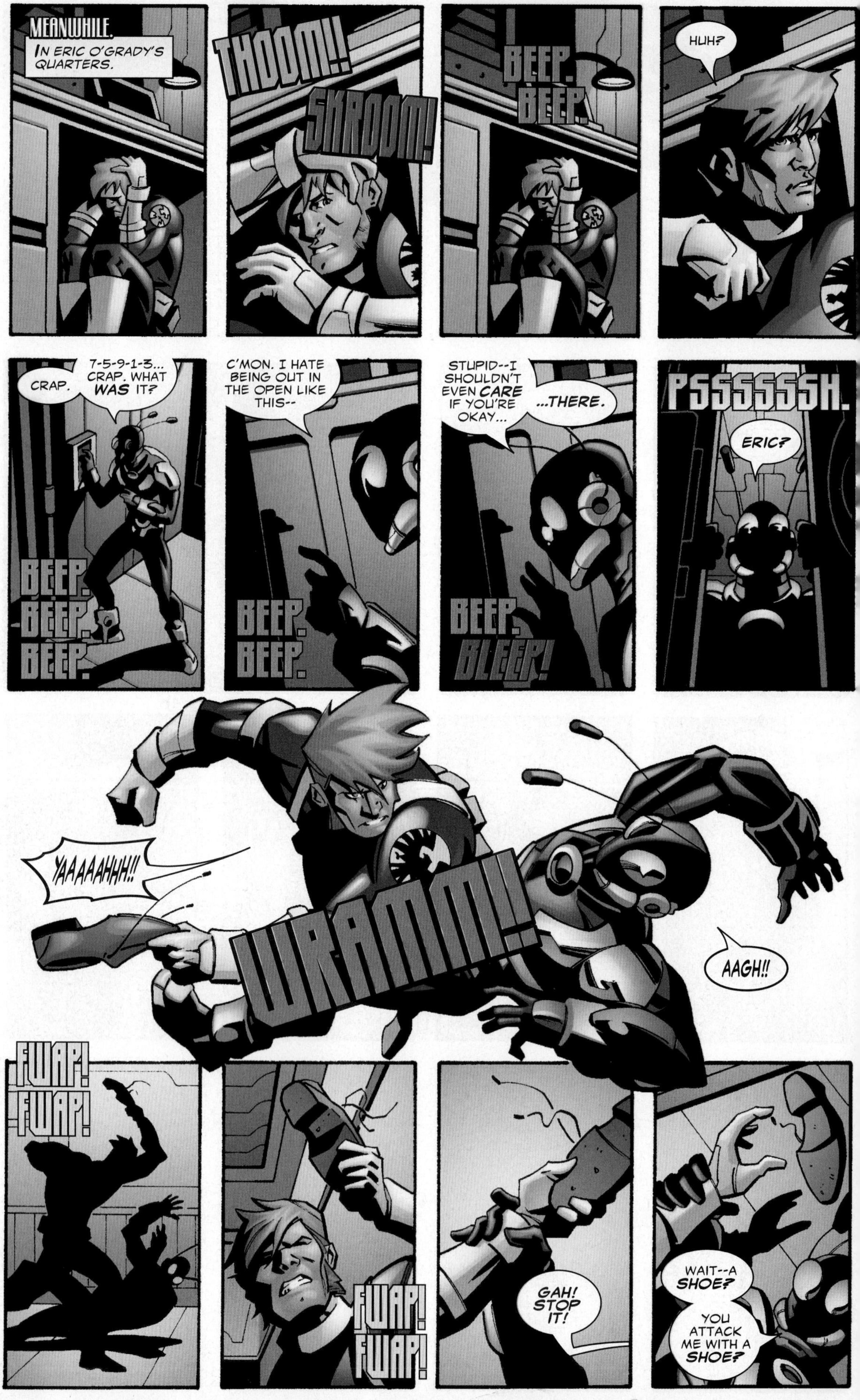
MEANWHILE.
IN ERIC O'GRADY'S QUARTERS.
THOOM!!
SKROOM!
BEEP. BEEP.
HUH?
CRAP.
7-5-9-1-3... CRAP. WHAT WAS IT?
BEEP. BEEP. BEEP.
C'MON. I HATE BEING OUT IN THE OPEN LIKE THIS--
BEEP. BEEP.
STUPID--I SHOULDN'T EVEN CARE IF YOU'RE OKAY...
...THERE.
BEEP. BLEEP!
PSSSSSSH.
ERIC?
YAAAAAHHH!!
WRAMM!!
AAGH!!
FWAP! FWAP!
FWAP! FWAP!
GAH! STOP IT!
WAIT--A SHOE?
YOU ATTACK ME WITH A SHOE?

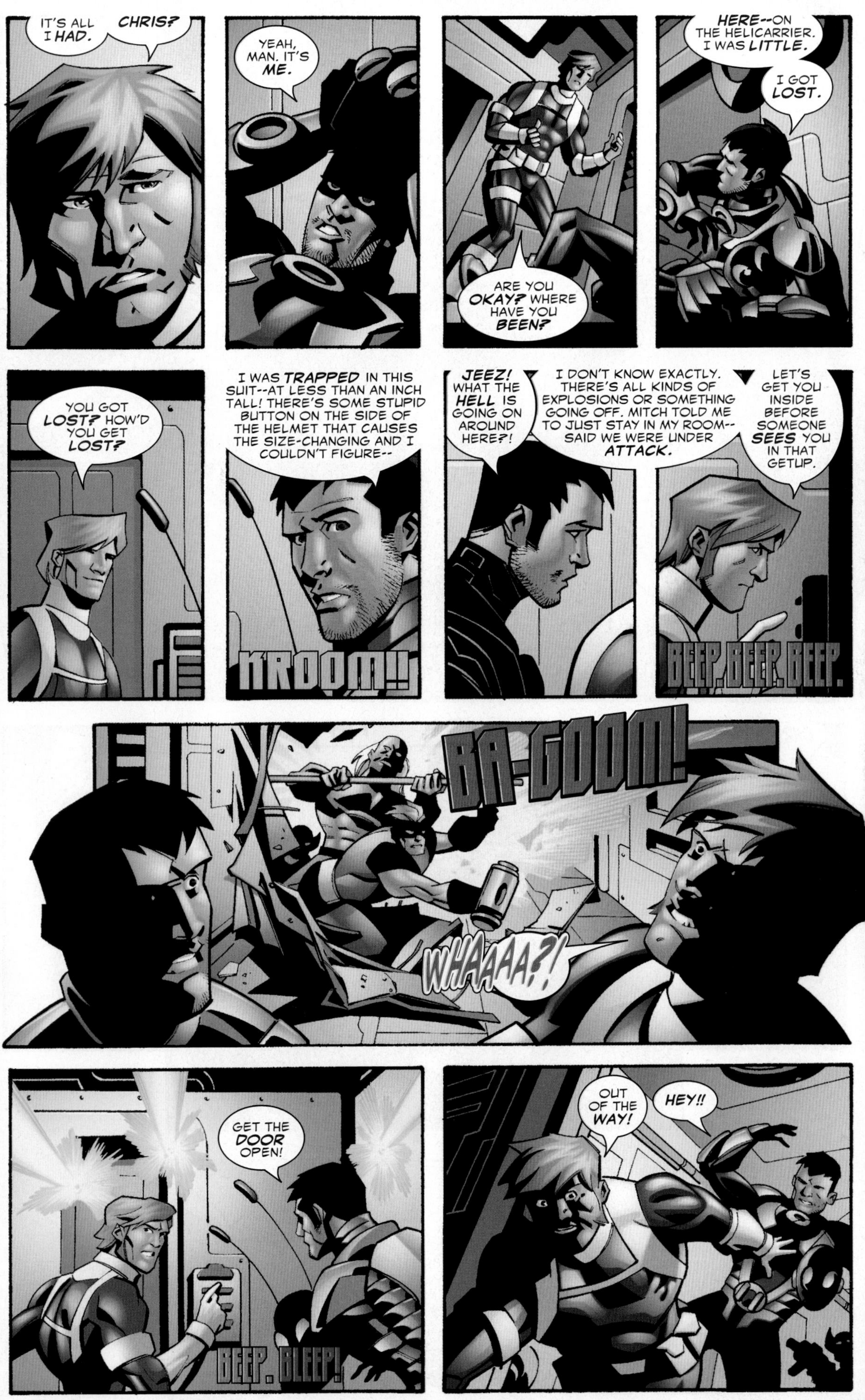
IT'S ALL I HAD.
CHRIS?
YEAH, MAN. IT'S ME.
ARE YOU OKAY? WHERE HAVE YOU BEEN?
HERE--ON THE HELICARRIER. I WAS LITTLE.
I GOT LOST.
YOU GOT LOST? HOW'D YOU GET LOST?
I WAS TRAPPED IN THIS SUIT--AT LESS THAN AN INCH TALL! THERE'S SOME STUPID BUTTON ON THE SIDE OF THE HELMET THAT CAUSES THE SIZE-CHANGING AND I COULDN'T FIGURE--
KROOM!!
JEEZ! WHAT THE HELL IS GOING ON AROUND HERE?!
I DON'T KNOW EXACTLY. THERE'S ALL KINDS OF EXPLOSIONS OR SOMETHING GOING OFF. MITCH TOLD ME TO JUST STAY IN MY ROOM--SAID WE WERE UNDER ATTACK.
LET'S GET YOU INSIDE BEFORE SOMEONE SEES YOU IN THAT GETUP.
BEEP. BEEP. BEEP.
BA-GOOM!
WHAAAA?!
GET THE DOOR OPEN!
BEEP. BLEEP!
OUT OF THE WAY!
HEY!!

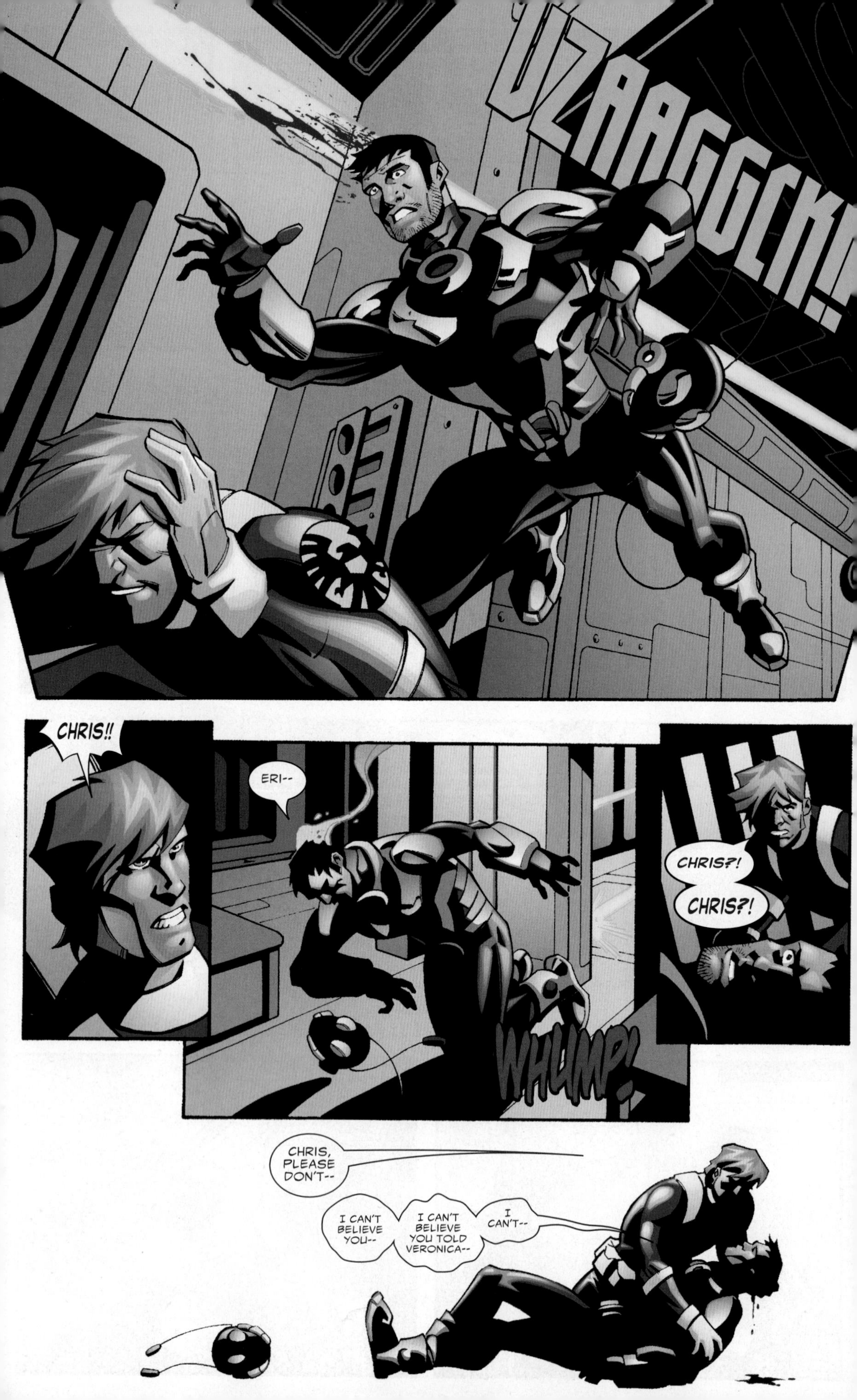
DZAAGGCK!!
CHRIS!!
ERI--
WHUMP!
CHRIS?!
CHRIS?!
CHRIS, PLEASE DON'T--
I CAN'T BELIEVE YOU--
I CAN'T BELIEVE YOU TOLD VERONICA--
I CAN'T--

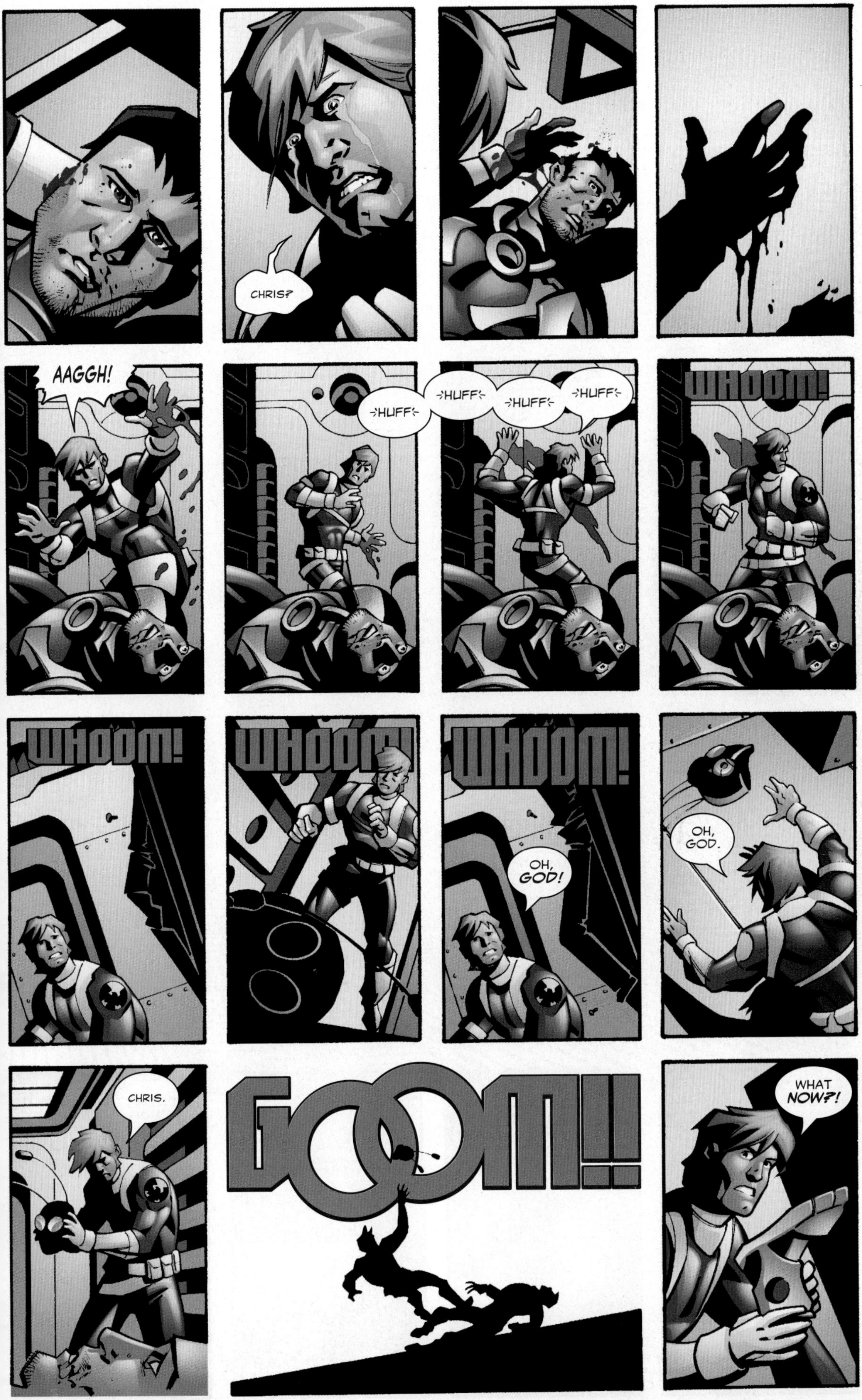
CHRIS?
AAGGH!
HUFF
HUFF
HUFF
HUFF
WHOOM!
WHOOM!
WHOOM!
WHOOM!
OH, GOD!
OH, GOD.
CHRIS.
GOOM!!
WHAT NOW?!

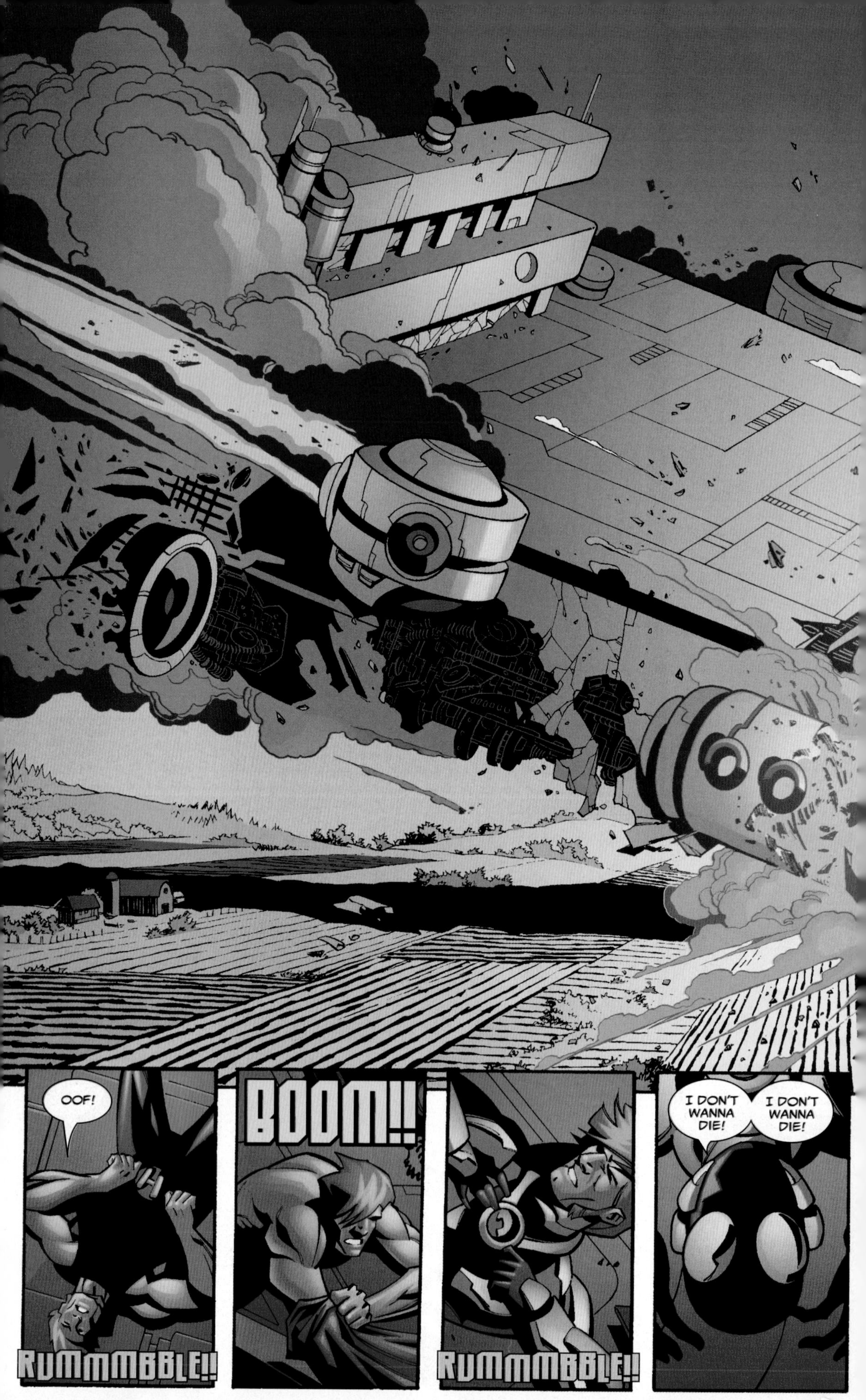
OOF!
RUMMMMBBLE!!
BOOM!!
RUMMMMBBLE!!
I DON'T WANNA DIE!
I DON'T WANNA DIE!

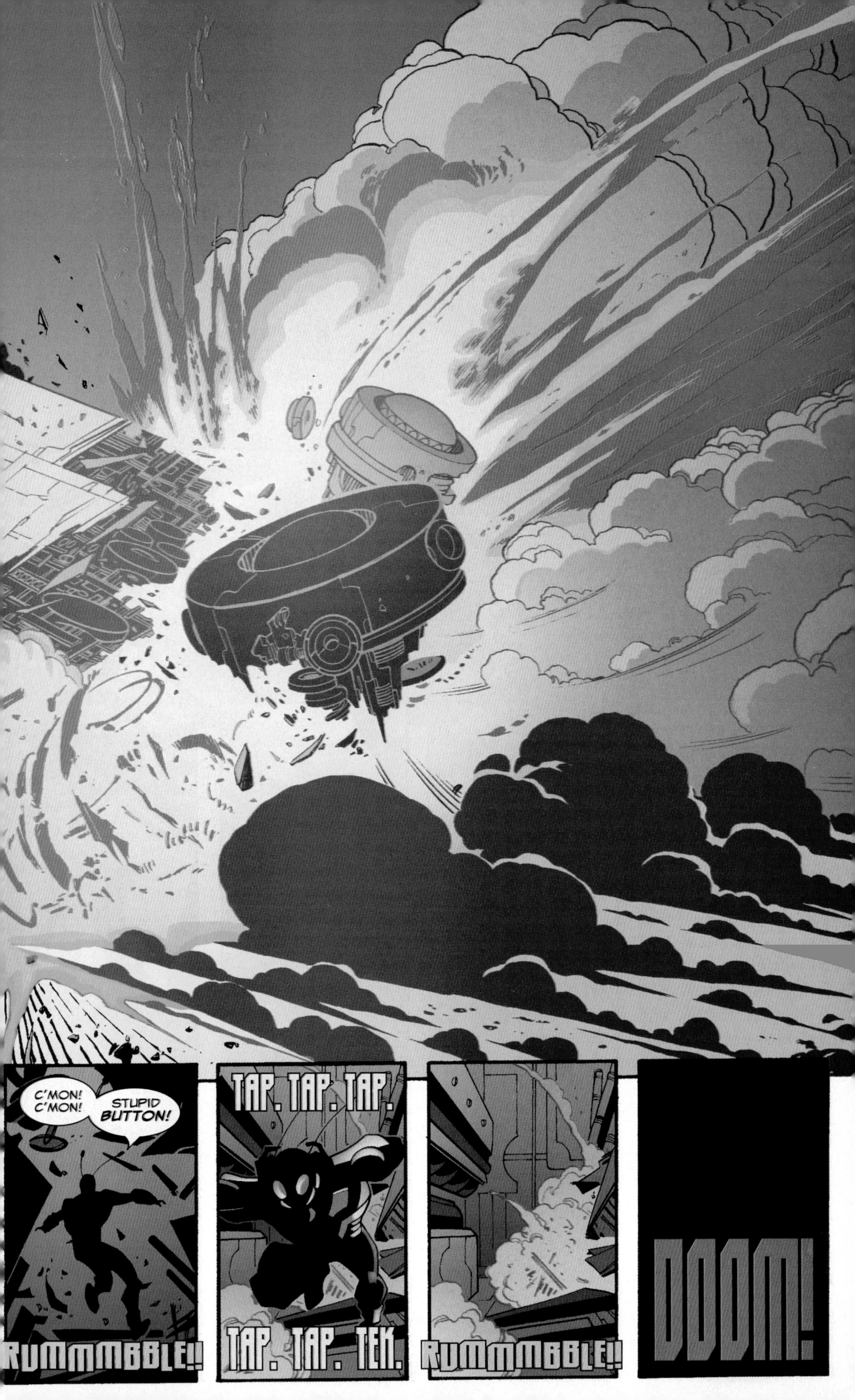
C'MON! C'MON!
STUPID BUTTON!
RUMMMMBBLE!!
TAP. TAP. TAP.
TAP. TAP. TEK.
RUMMMMBBLE!!
DOOM!

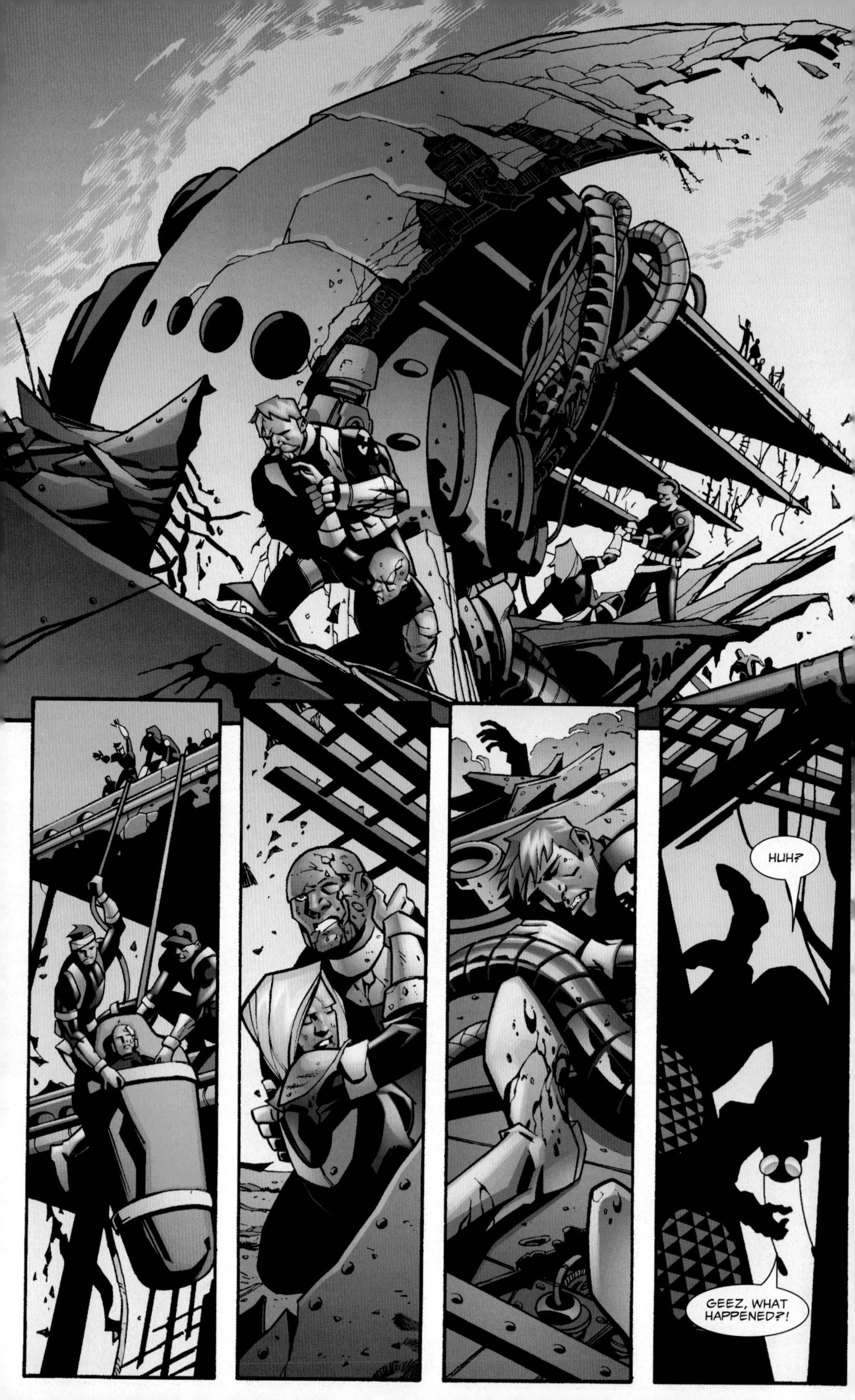
HUH?
GEEZ, WHAT HAPPENED?!

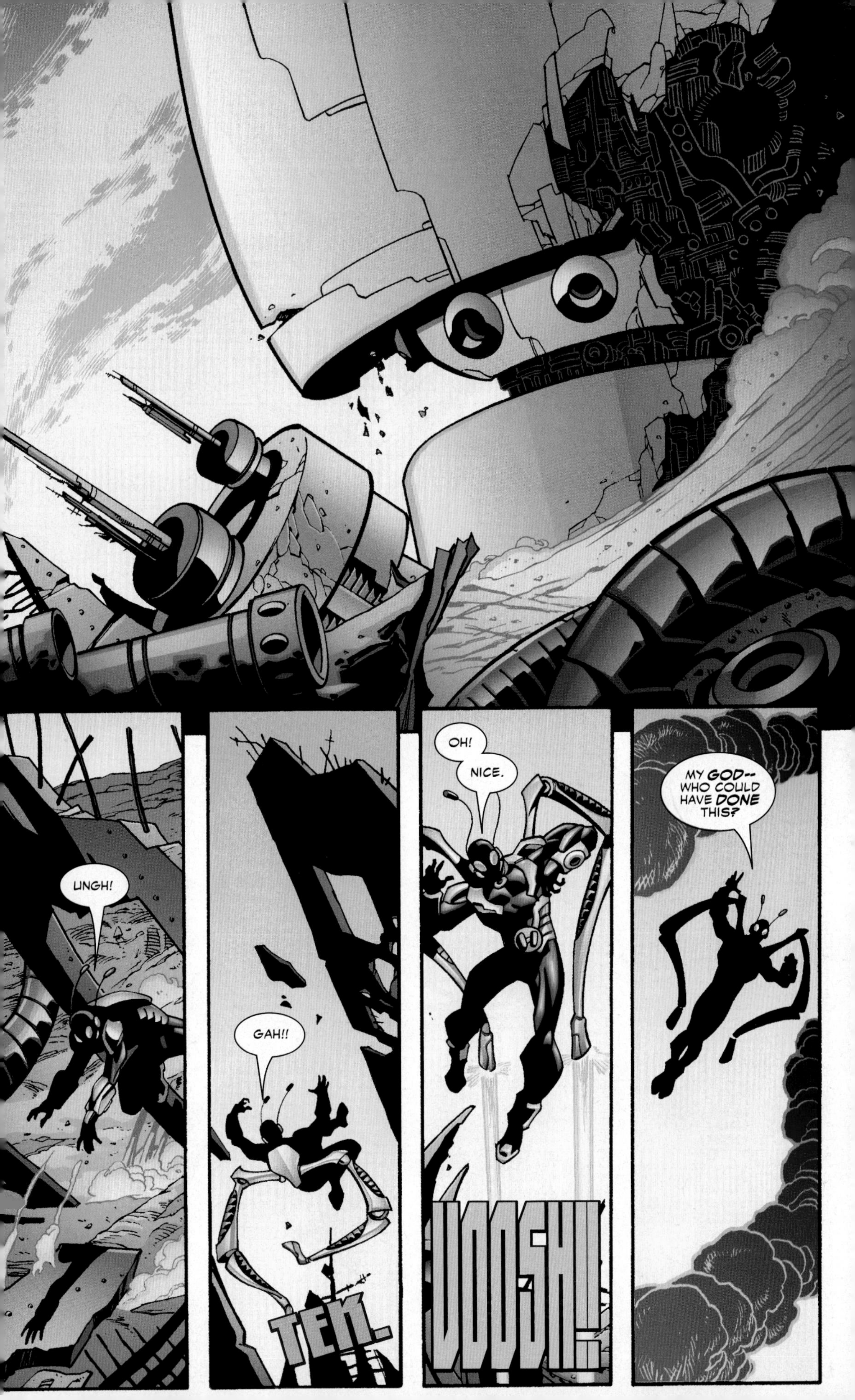
UNGH!
GAH!!
TEK.
OH!
NICE.
VOOSH!!
MY GOD--
WHO COULD
HAVE DONE
THIS?

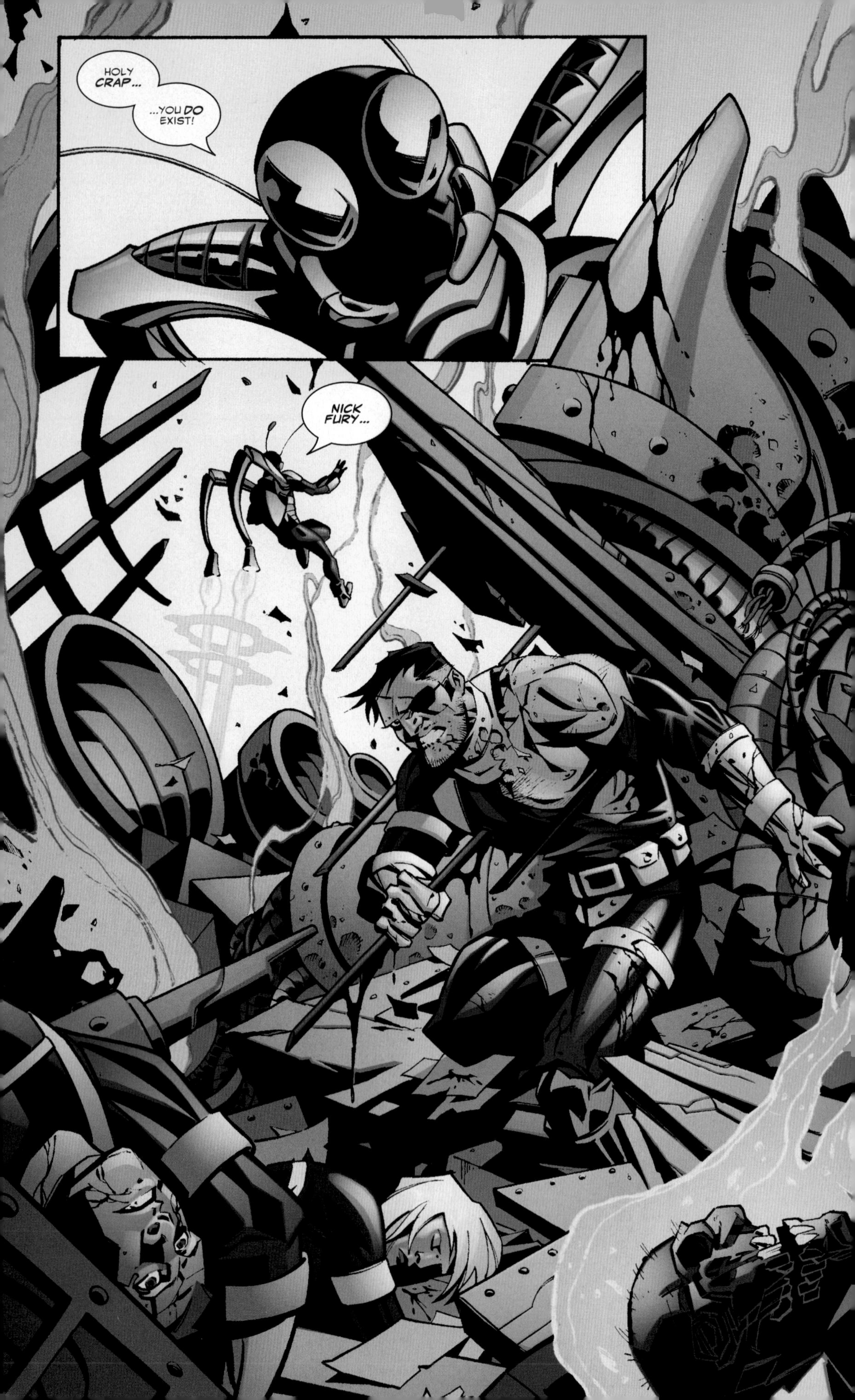
HOLY CRAP...
...YOU DO EXIST!
NICK FURY...

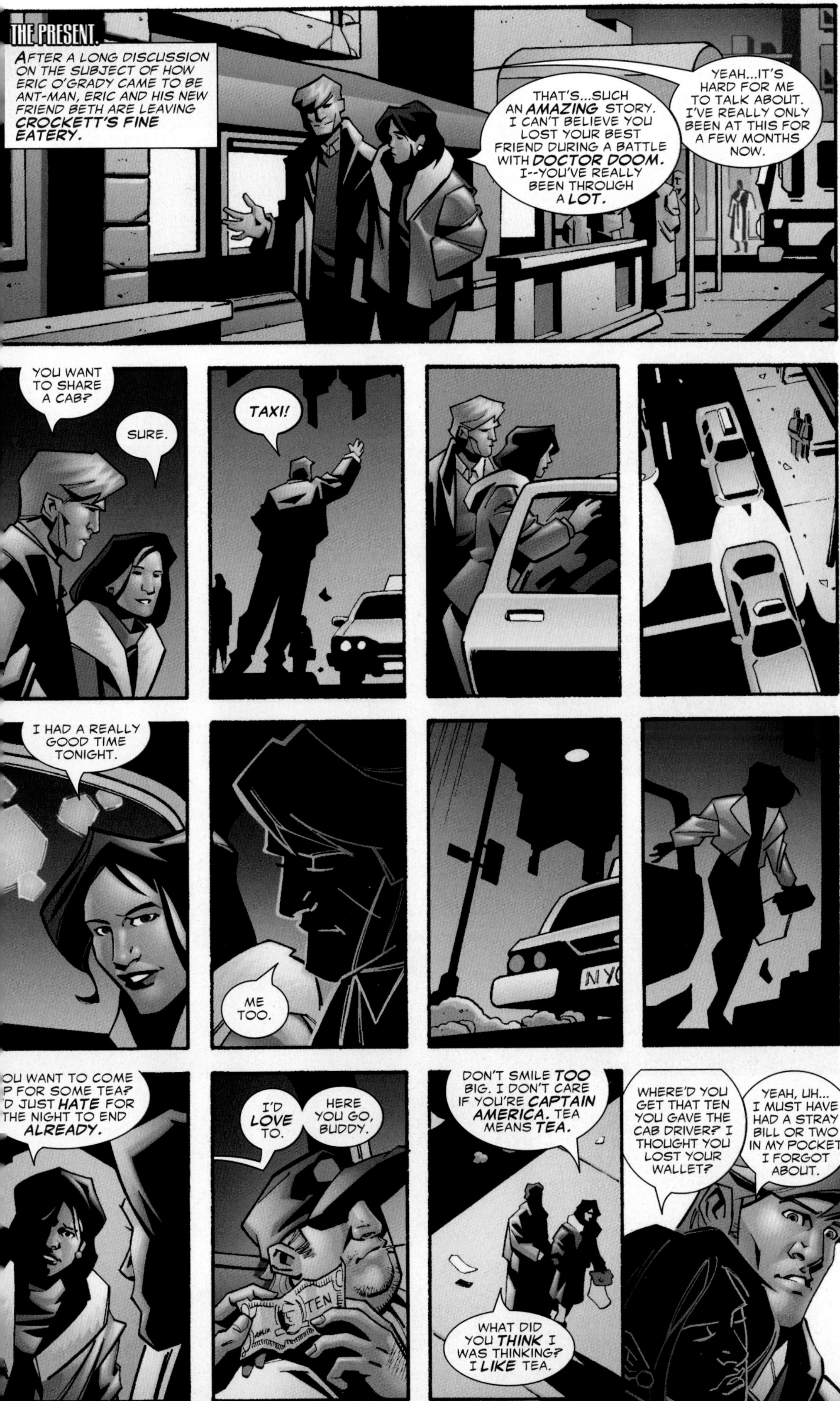
THE PRESENT.
AFTER A LONG DISCUSSION ON THE SUBJECT OF HOW ERIC O'GRADY CAME TO BE ANT-MAN, ERIC AND HIS NEW FRIEND BETH ARE LEAVING CROCKETT'S FINE EATERY.
THAT'S...SUCH AN AMAZING STORY. I CAN'T BELIEVE YOU LOST YOUR BEST FRIEND DURING A BATTLE WITH DOCTOR DOOM. I--YOU'VE REALLY BEEN THROUGH A LOT.
YEAH...IT'S HARD FOR ME TO TALK ABOUT. I'VE REALLY ONLY BEEN AT THIS FOR A FEW MONTHS NOW.
YOU WANT TO SHARE A CAB?
SURE.
TAXI!
I HAD A REALLY GOOD TIME TONIGHT.
ME TOO.
NYC
OU WANT TO COME P FOR SOME TEA? D JUST HATE FOR THE NIGHT TO END ALREADY.
I'D LOVE TO.
HERE YOU GO, BUDDY.
TEN
DON'T SMILE TOO BIG. I DON'T CARE IF YOU'RE CAPTAIN AMERICA. TEA MEANS TEA.
WHAT DID YOU THINK I WAS THINKING? I LIKE TEA.
WHERE'D YOU GET THAT TEN YOU GAVE THE CAB DRIVER? I THOUGHT YOU LOST YOUR WALLET?
YEAH, UH... I MUST HAVE HAD A STRAY BILL OR TWO IN MY POCKET I FORGOT ABOUT.

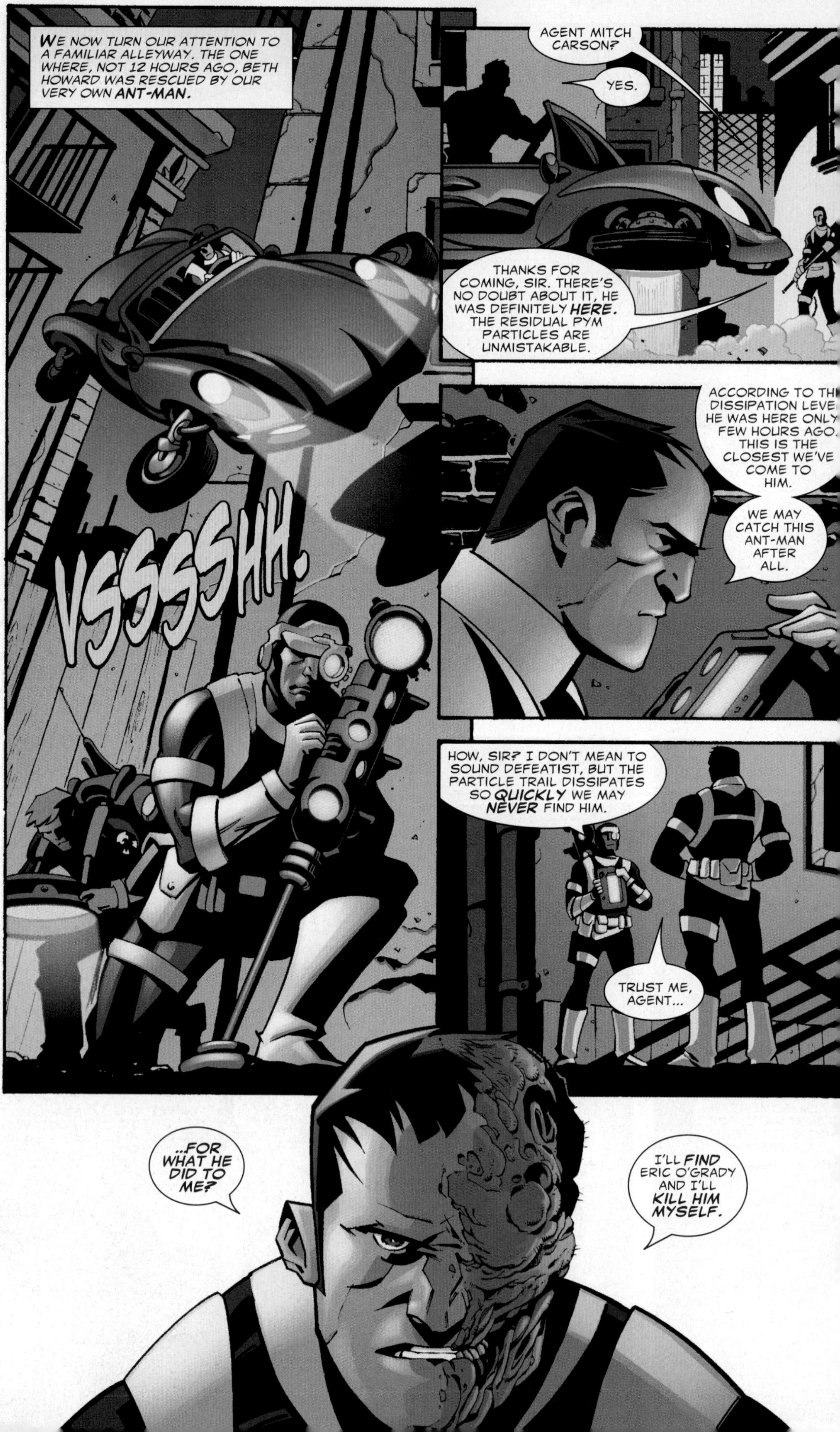
WE NOW TURN OUR ATTENTION TO A FAMILIAR ALLEYWAY. THE ONE WHERE, NOT 12 HOURS AGO, BETH HOWARD WAS RESCUED BY OUR VERY OWN ANT-MAN.
VSSSSHH.
AGENT MITCH CARSON?
YES.
THANKS FOR COMING, SIR. THERE'S NO DOUBT ABOUT IT, HE WAS DEFINITELY HERE. THE RESIDUAL PYM PARTICLES ARE UNMISTAKABLE.
ACCORDING TO TH DISSIPATION LEVE HE WAS HERE ONLY FEW HOURS AGO. THIS IS THE CLOSEST WE'VE COME TO HIM.
WE MAY CATCH THIS ANT-MAN AFTER ALL.
HOW, SIR? I DON'T MEAN TO SOUND DEFEATIST, BUT THE PARTICLE TRAIL DISSIPATES SO QUICKLY WE MAY NEVER FIND HIM.
TRUST ME, AGENT...
...FOR WHAT HE DID TO ME?
I'LL FIND ERIC O'GRADY AND I'LL KILL HIM MYSELF.

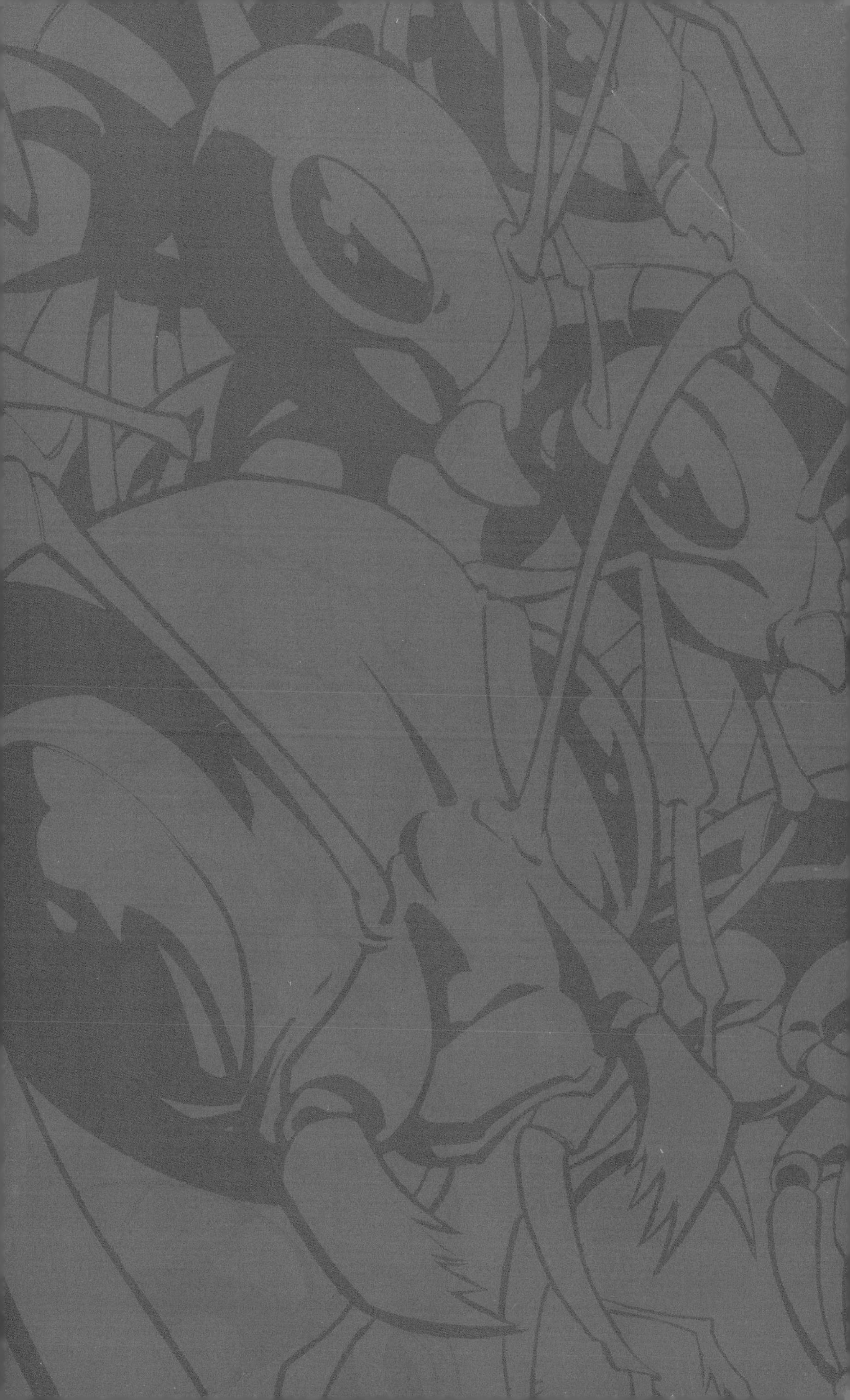

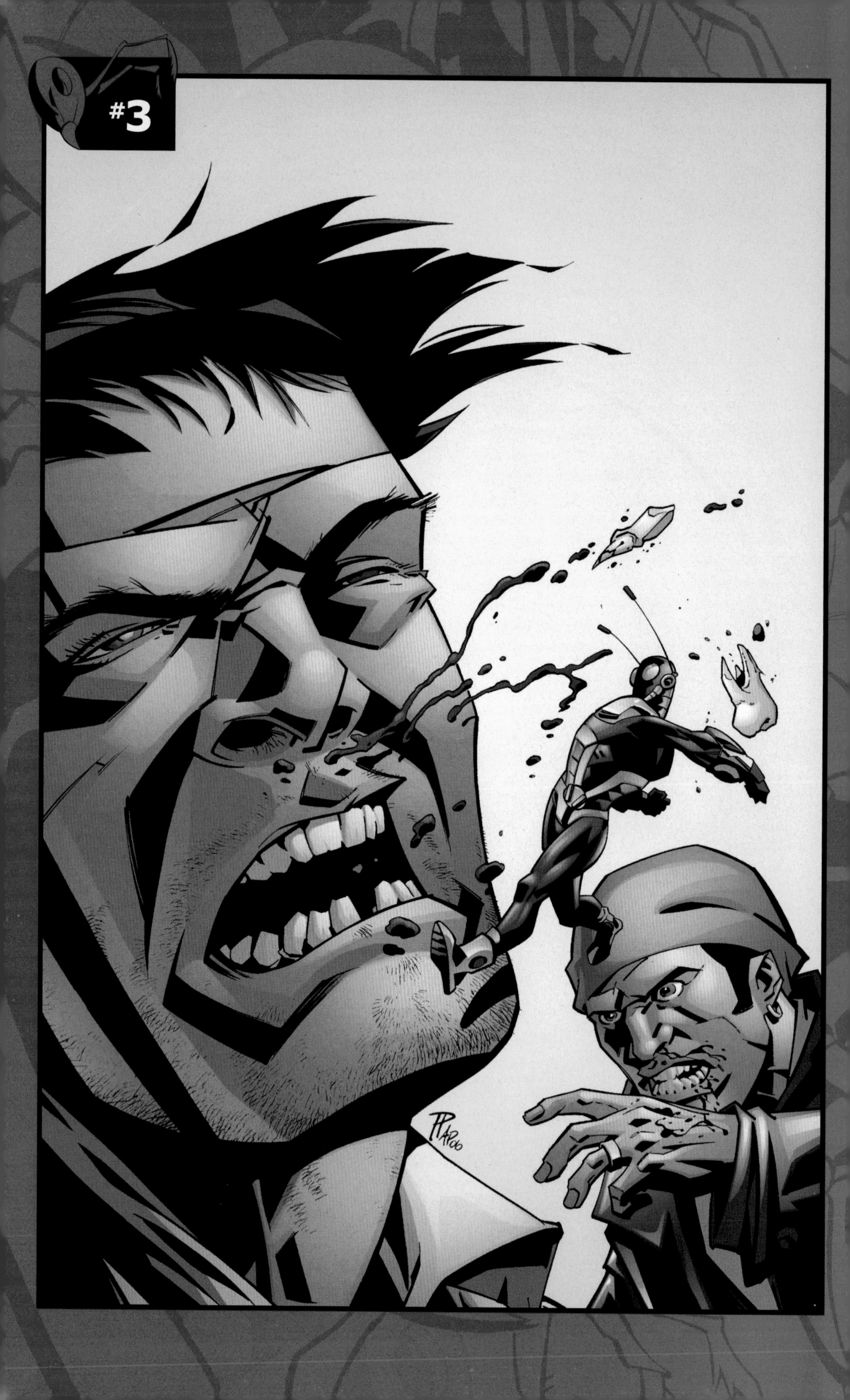

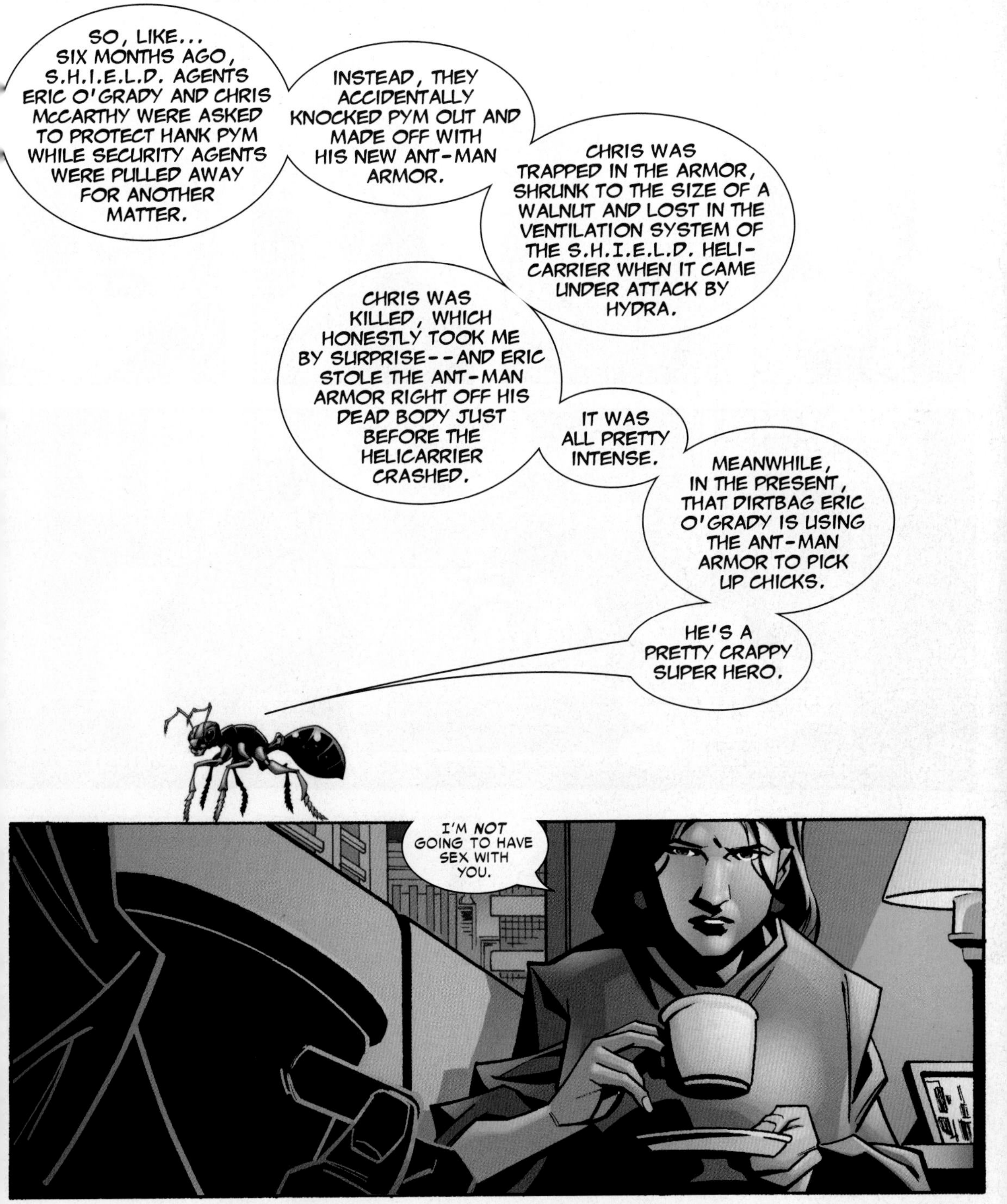
SO, LIKE... SIX MONTHS AGO, S.H.I.E.L.D. AGENTS ERIC O'GRADY AND CHRIS McCARTHY WERE ASKED TO PROTECT HANK PYM WHILE SECURITY AGENTS WERE PULLED AWAY FOR ANOTHER MATTER.
INSTEAD, THEY ACCIDENTALLY KNOCKED PYM OUT AND MADE OFF WITH HIS NEW ANT-MAN ARMOR.
CHRIS WAS TRAPPED IN THE ARMOR, SHRUNK TO THE SIZE OF A WALNUT AND LOST IN THE VENTILATION SYSTEM OF THE S.H.I.E.L.D. HELI-CARRIER WHEN IT CAME UNDER ATTACK BY HYDRA.
CHRIS WAS KILLED, WHICH HONESTLY TOOK ME BY SURPRISE--AND ERIC STOLE THE ANT-MAN ARMOR RIGHT OFF HIS DEAD BODY JUST BEFORE THE HELICARRIER CRASHED.
IT WAS ALL PRETTY INTENSE.
MEANWHILE, IN THE PRESENT, THAT DIRTBAG ERIC O'GRADY IS USING THE ANT-MAN ARMOR TO PICK UP CHICKS.
HE'S A PRETTY CRAPPY SUPER HERO.
I'M *NOT* GOING TO HAVE SEX WITH YOU.

# HOMECOMING

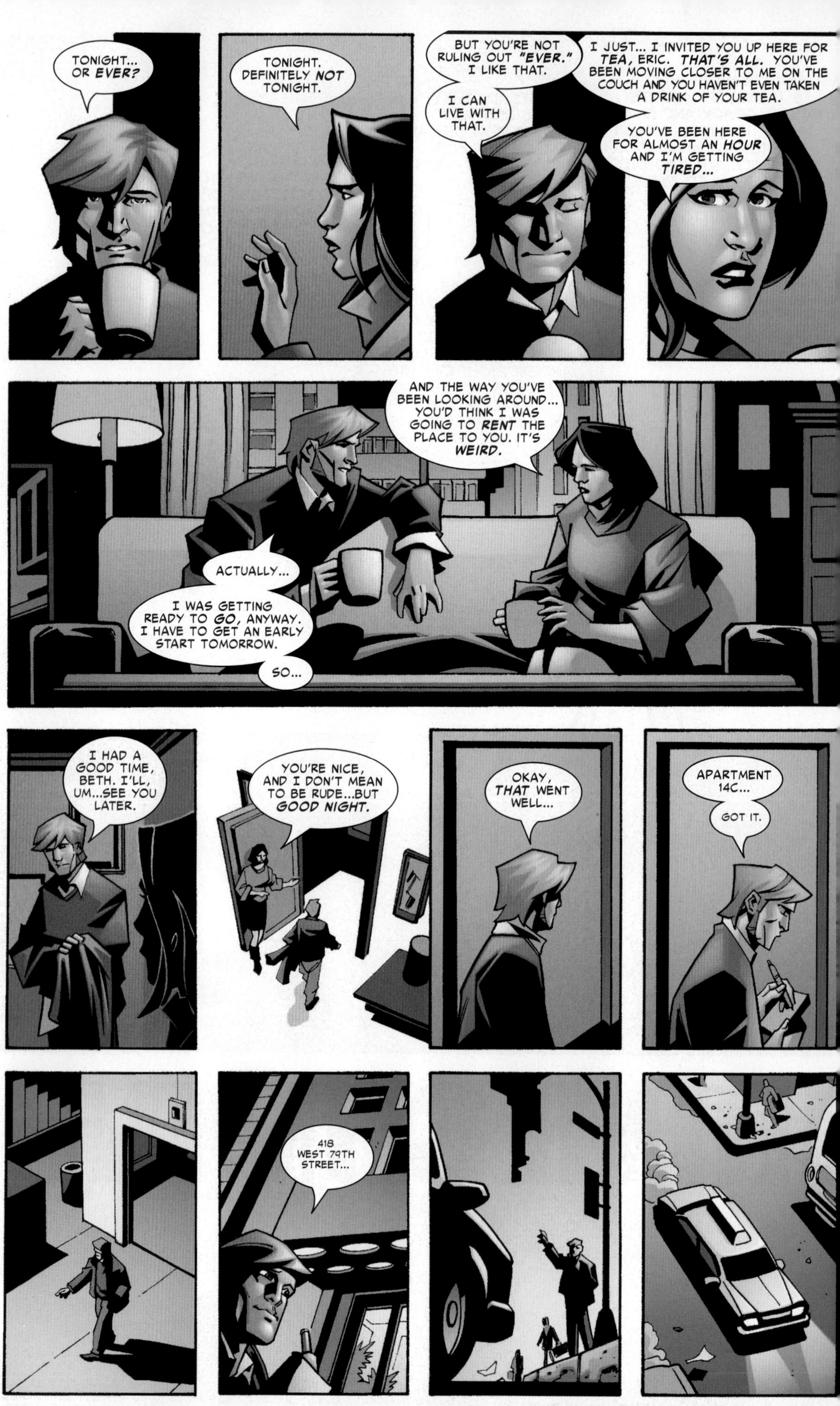
TONIGHT... OR EVER?
TONIGHT. DEFINITELY NOT TONIGHT.
BUT YOU'RE NOT RULING OUT "EVER." I LIKE THAT.
I CAN LIVE WITH THAT.
I JUST... I INVITED YOU UP HERE FOR TEA, ERIC. THAT'S ALL. YOU'VE BEEN MOVING CLOSER TO ME ON THE COUCH AND YOU HAVEN'T EVEN TAKEN A DRINK OF YOUR TEA.
YOU'VE BEEN HERE FOR ALMOST AN HOUR AND I'M GETTING TIRED...
AND THE WAY YOU'VE BEEN LOOKING AROUND... YOU'D THINK I WAS GOING TO RENT THE PLACE TO YOU. IT'S WEIRD.
ACTUALLY...
I WAS GETTING READY TO GO, ANYWAY. I HAVE TO GET AN EARLY START TOMORROW.
SO...
I HAD A GOOD TIME, BETH. I'LL, UM...SEE YOU LATER.
YOU'RE NICE, AND I DON'T MEAN TO BE RUDE...BUT GOOD NIGHT.
OKAY, THAT WENT WELL...
APARTMENT 14C...
GOT IT.
418 WEST 79TH STREET...

WAIT FOR ME. I'LL BE OUT IN *TWO* MINUTES.

TAKE ME BACK TO 418 WEST 79TH STREET, PLEASE.

HERE YOU GO.

THANKS.

DING.

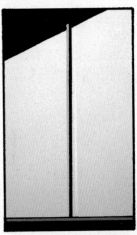

DING.

14C...

14C...

AH! HERE WE GO.

HOME *SWEET* HOME...

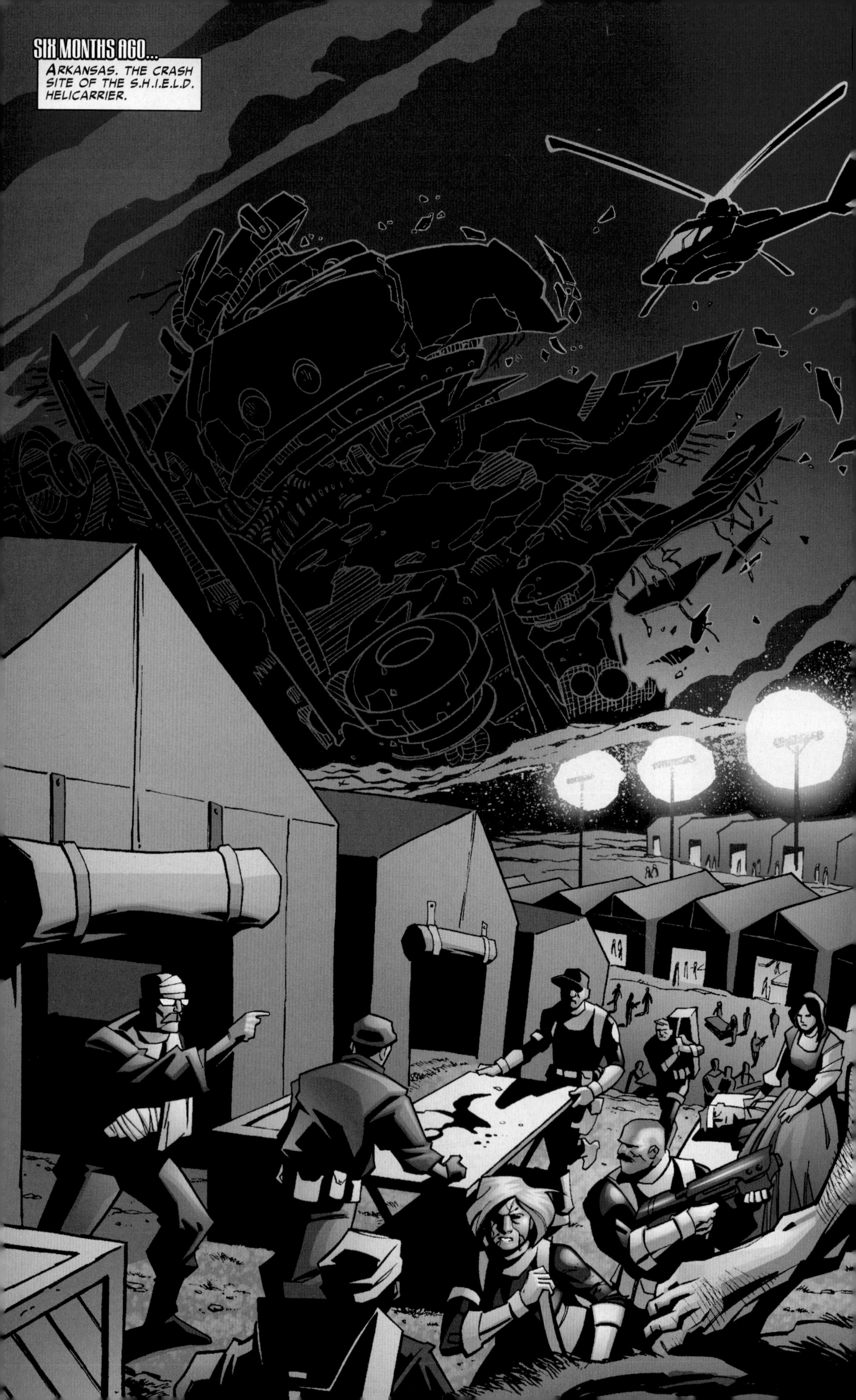
SIX MONTHS AGO...
ARKANSAS. THE CRASH SITE OF THE S.H.I.E.L.D. HELICARRIER.

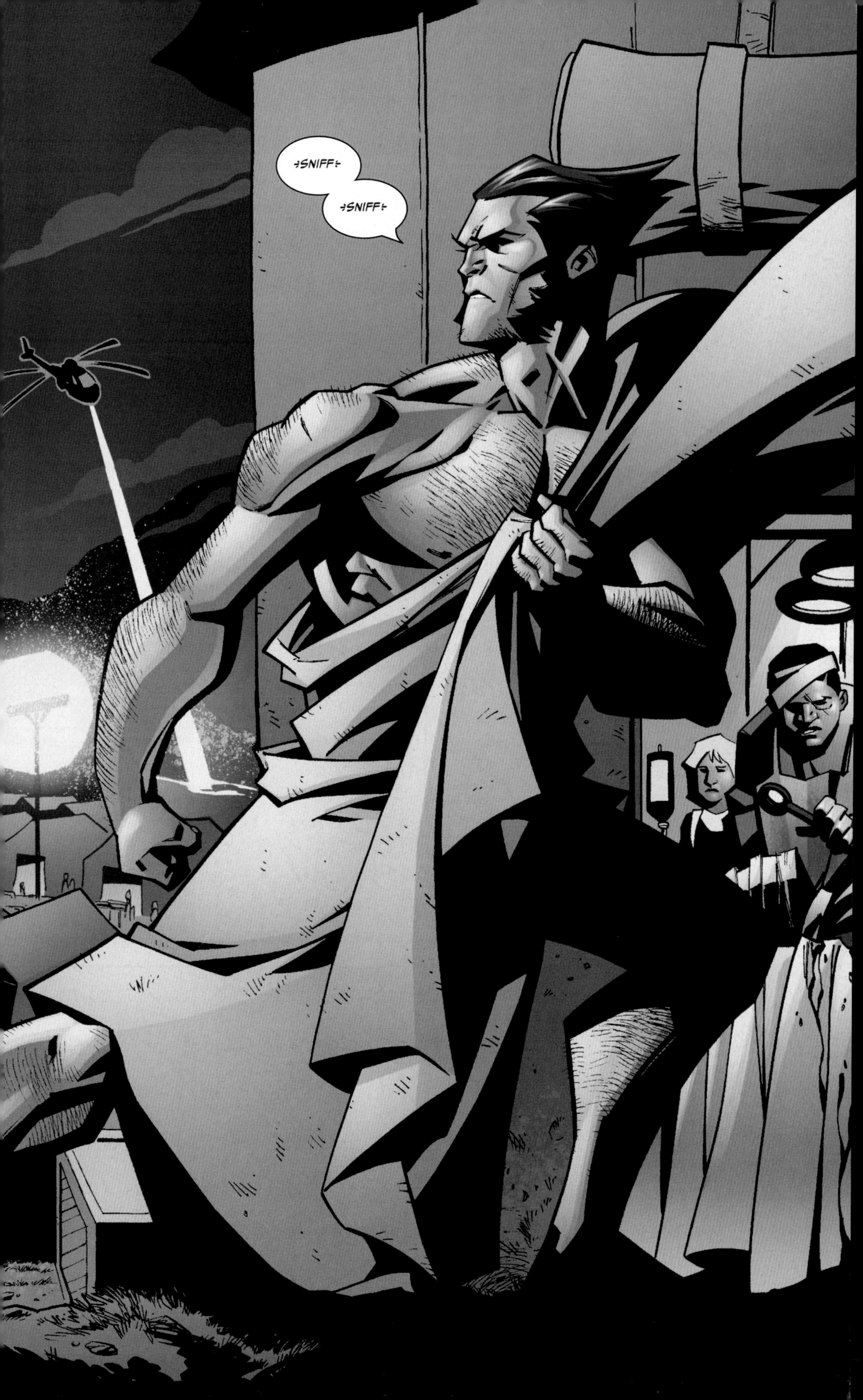
SNIFF
SNIFF

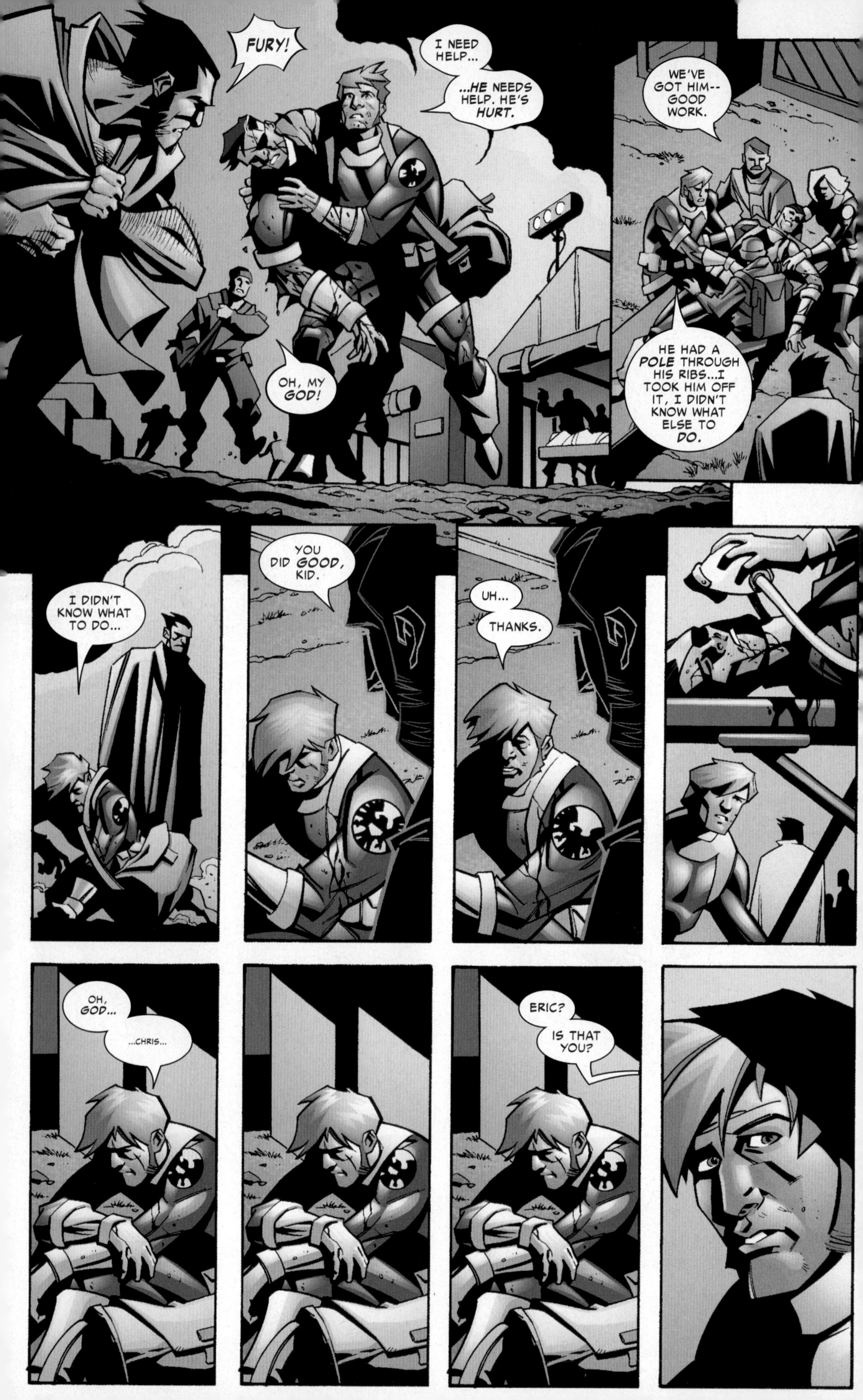
FURY!
I NEED HELP...
...HE NEEDS HELP. HE'S HURT.
OH, MY GOD!
WE'VE GOT HIM-- GOOD WORK.
HE HAD A POLE THROUGH HIS RIBS...I TOOK HIM OFF IT, I DIDN'T KNOW WHAT ELSE TO DO.
I DIDN'T KNOW WHAT TO DO...
YOU DID GOOD, KID.
UH...
THANKS.
OH, GOD...
...CHRIS...
ERIC?
IS THAT YOU?

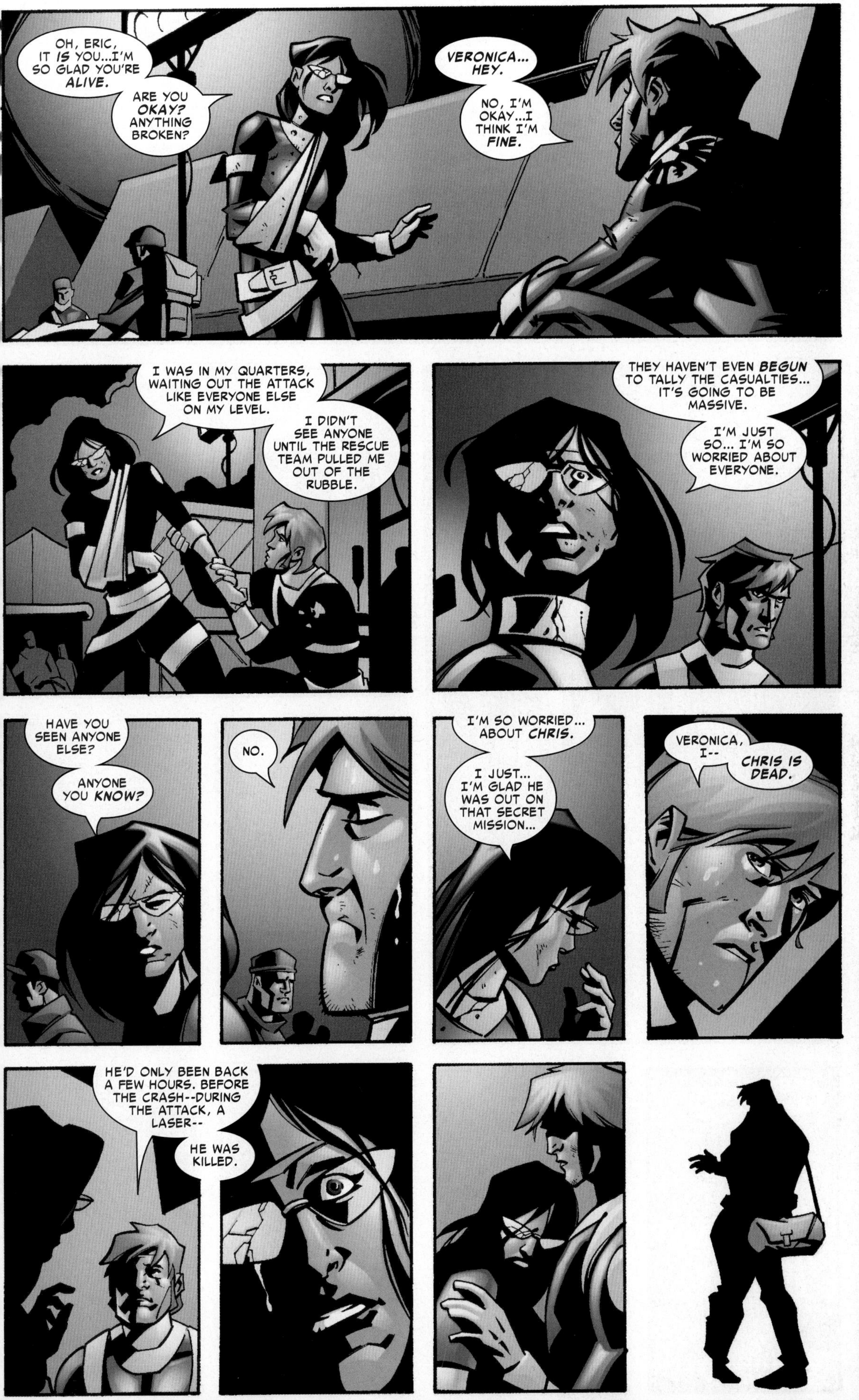
OH, ERIC, IT IS YOU...I'M SO GLAD YOU'RE ALIVE.
ARE YOU OKAY? ANYTHING BROKEN?
VERONICA... HEY.
NO, I'M OKAY...I THINK I'M FINE.
I WAS IN MY QUARTERS, WAITING OUT THE ATTACK LIKE EVERYONE ELSE ON MY LEVEL.
I DIDN'T SEE ANYONE UNTIL THE RESCUE TEAM PULLED ME OUT OF THE RUBBLE.
THEY HAVEN'T EVEN BEGUN TO TALLY THE CASUALTIES... IT'S GOING TO BE MASSIVE.
I'M JUST SO... I'M SO WORRIED ABOUT EVERYONE.
HAVE YOU SEEN ANYONE ELSE?
ANYONE YOU KNOW?
NO.
I'M SO WORRIED... ABOUT CHRIS.
I JUST... I'M GLAD HE WAS OUT ON THAT SECRET MISSION...
VERONICA, I--
CHRIS IS DEAD.
HE'D ONLY BEEN BACK A FEW HOURS. BEFORE THE CRASH--DURING THE ATTACK, A LASER--
HE WAS KILLED.

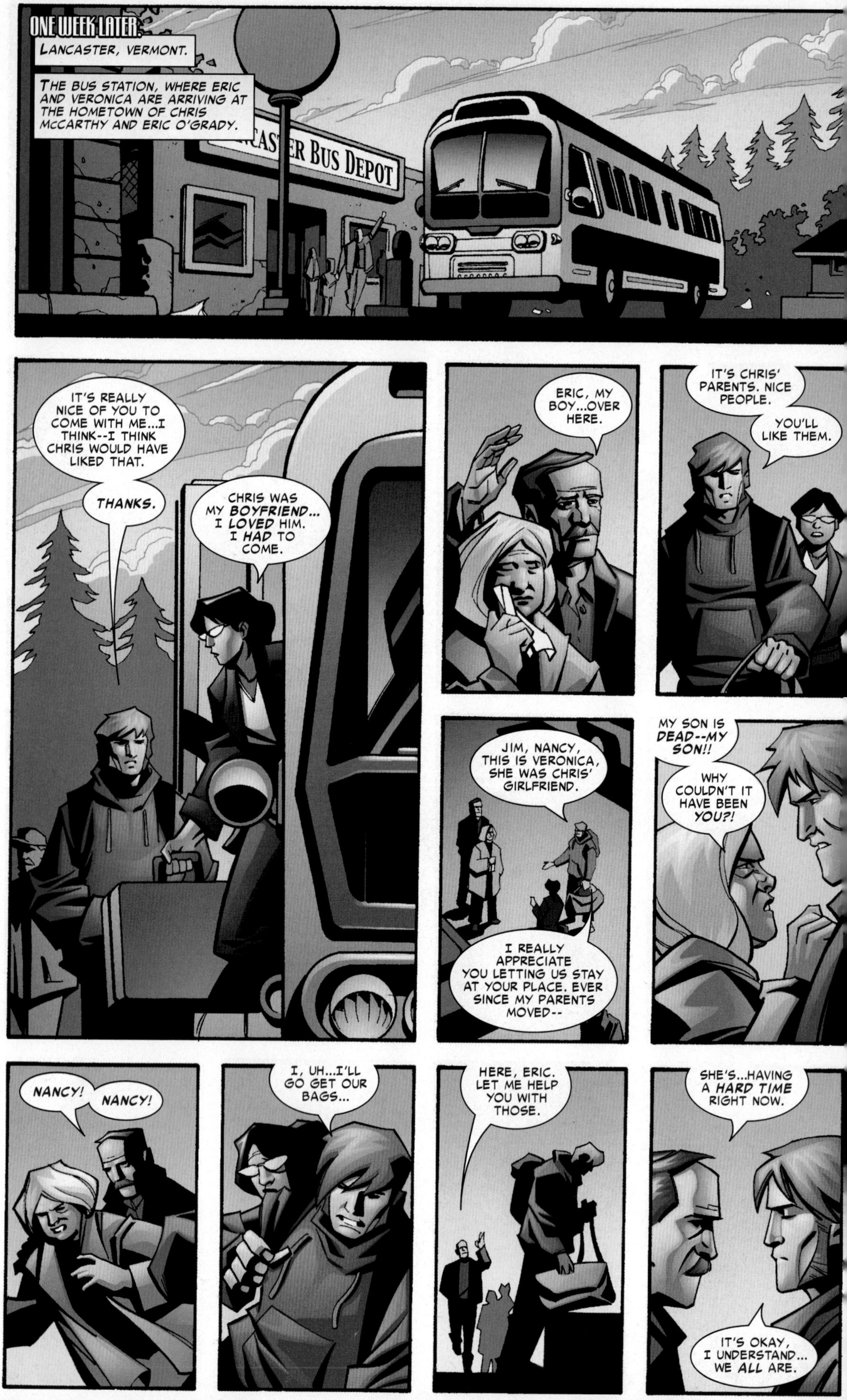
ONE WEEK LATER:
LANCASTER, VERMONT.
THE BUS STATION, WHERE ERIC AND VERONICA ARE ARRIVING AT THE HOMETOWN OF CHRIS McCARTHY AND ERIC O'GRADY.
ER BUS DEPOT
IT'S REALLY NICE OF YOU TO COME WITH ME...I THINK--I THINK CHRIS WOULD HAVE LIKED THAT.
THANKS.
CHRIS WAS MY BOYFRIEND... I LOVED HIM. I HAD TO COME.
ERIC, MY BOY...OVER HERE.
IT'S CHRIS' PARENTS. NICE PEOPLE.
YOU'LL LIKE THEM.
JIM, NANCY, THIS IS VERONICA, SHE WAS CHRIS' GIRLFRIEND.
I REALLY APPRECIATE YOU LETTING US STAY AT YOUR PLACE. EVER SINCE MY PARENTS MOVED--
MY SON IS DEAD--MY SON!!
WHY COULDN'T IT HAVE BEEN YOU?!
NANCY!
NANCY!
I, UH...I'LL GO GET OUR BAGS...
HERE, ERIC. LET ME HELP YOU WITH THOSE.
SHE'S...HAVING A HARD TIME RIGHT NOW.
IT'S OKAY, I UNDERSTAND... WE ALL ARE.

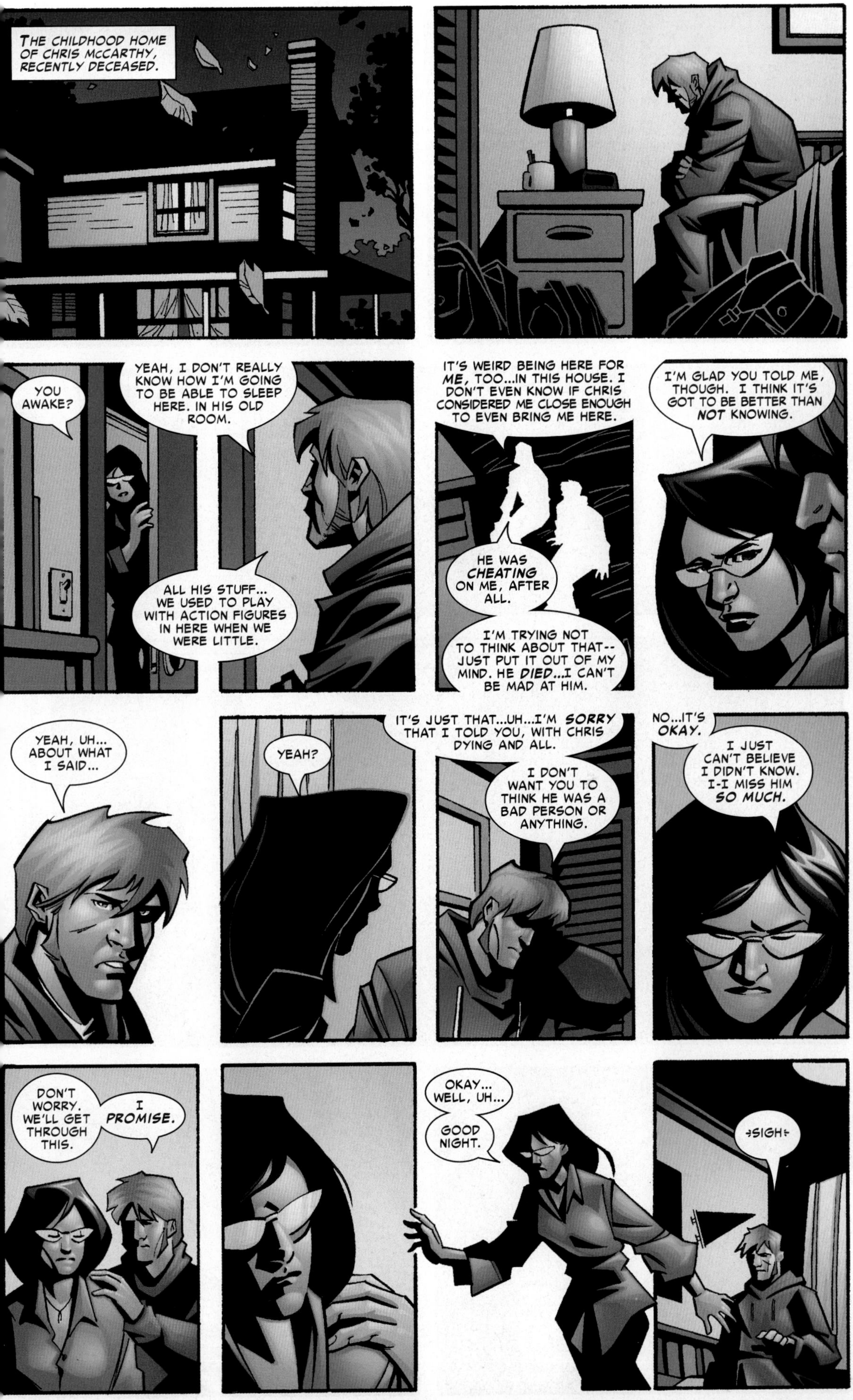
THE CHILDHOOD HOME OF CHRIS McCARTHY, RECENTLY DECEASED.
YOU AWAKE?
YEAH, I DON'T REALLY KNOW HOW I'M GOING TO BE ABLE TO SLEEP HERE. IN HIS OLD ROOM.
ALL HIS STUFF... WE USED TO PLAY WITH ACTION FIGURES IN HERE WHEN WE WERE LITTLE.
IT'S WEIRD BEING HERE FOR ME, TOO...IN THIS HOUSE. I DON'T EVEN KNOW IF CHRIS CONSIDERED ME CLOSE ENOUGH TO EVEN BRING ME HERE.
HE WAS CHEATING ON ME, AFTER ALL.
I'M TRYING NOT TO THINK ABOUT THAT-- JUST PUT IT OUT OF MY MIND. HE DIED...I CAN'T BE MAD AT HIM.
I'M GLAD YOU TOLD ME, THOUGH. I THINK IT'S GOT TO BE BETTER THAN NOT KNOWING.
YEAH, UH... ABOUT WHAT I SAID...
YEAH?
IT'S JUST THAT...UH...I'M SORRY THAT I TOLD YOU, WITH CHRIS DYING AND ALL.
I DON'T WANT YOU TO THINK HE WAS A BAD PERSON OR ANYTHING.
NO...IT'S OKAY.
I JUST CAN'T BELIEVE I DIDN'T KNOW. I-I MISS HIM SO MUCH.
DON'T WORRY. WE'LL GET THROUGH THIS.
I PROMISE.
OKAY... WELL, UH...
GOOD NIGHT.
SIGH

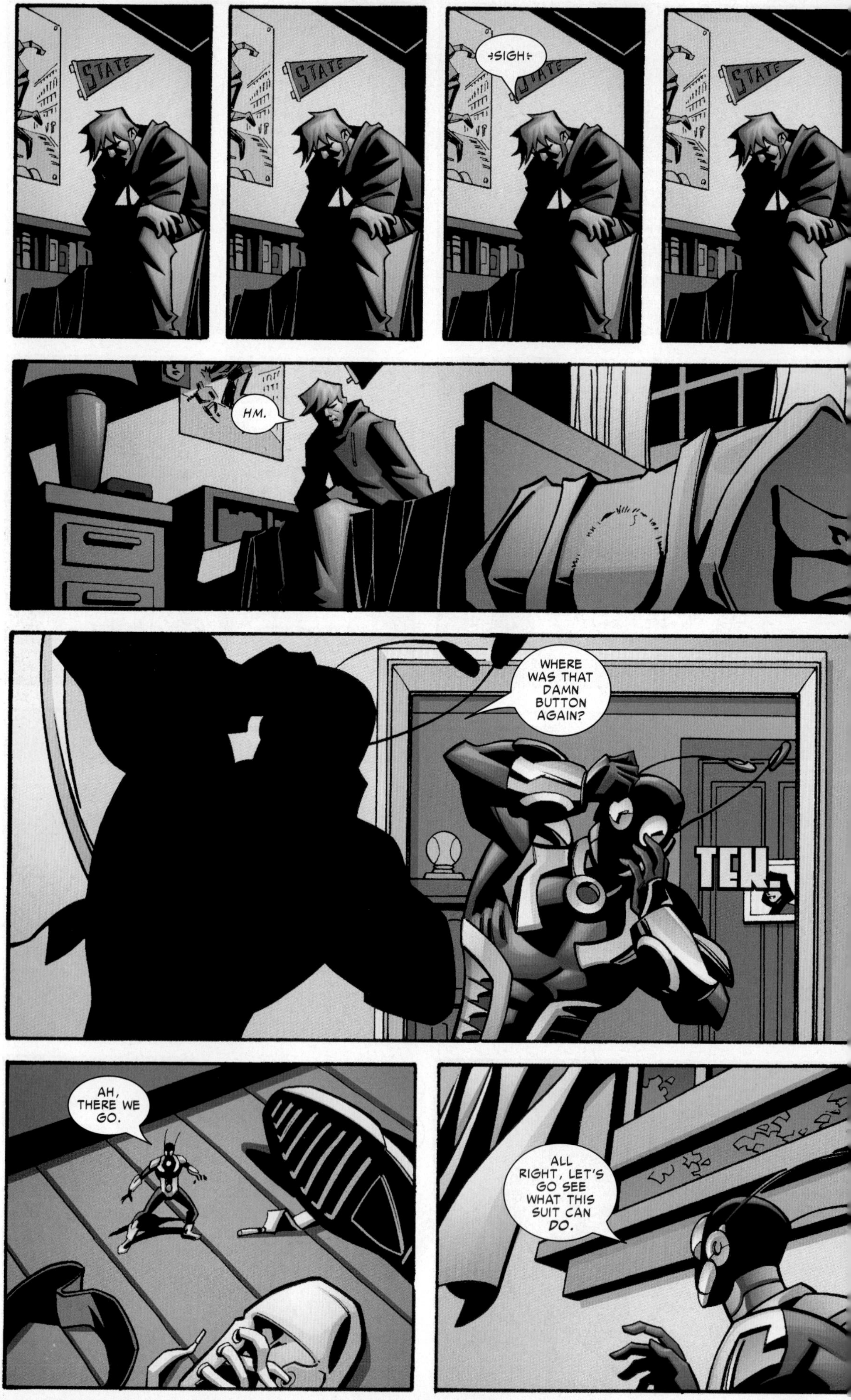
STATE
STATE
SIGH
STATE
STATE
HM.
WHERE WAS THAT DAMN BUTTON AGAIN?
TEK
AH, THERE WE GO.
ALL RIGHT, LET'S GO SEE WHAT THIS SUIT CAN DO.

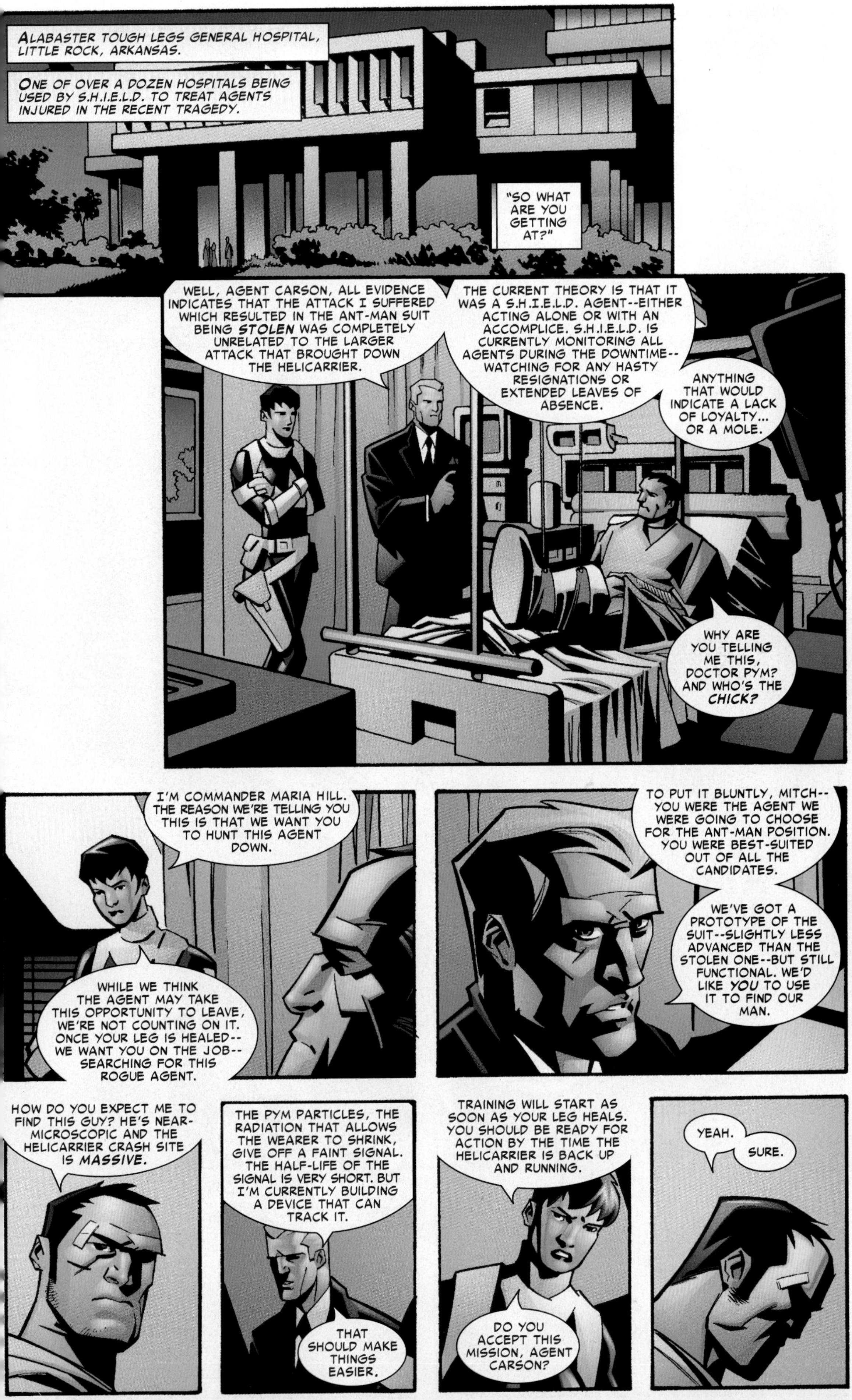
ALABASTER TOUGH LEGS GENERAL HOSPITAL, LITTLE ROCK, ARKANSAS.
ONE OF OVER A DOZEN HOSPITALS BEING USED BY S.H.I.E.L.D. TO TREAT AGENTS INJURED IN THE RECENT TRAGEDY.
"SO WHAT ARE YOU GETTING AT?"
WELL, AGENT CARSON, ALL EVIDENCE INDICATES THAT THE ATTACK I SUFFERED WHICH RESULTED IN THE ANT-MAN SUIT BEING STOLEN WAS COMPLETELY UNRELATED TO THE LARGER ATTACK THAT BROUGHT DOWN THE HELICARRIER.
THE CURRENT THEORY IS THAT IT WAS A S.H.I.E.L.D. AGENT--EITHER ACTING ALONE OR WITH AN ACCOMPLICE. S.H.I.E.L.D. IS CURRENTLY MONITORING ALL AGENTS DURING THE DOWNTIME--WATCHING FOR ANY HASTY RESIGNATIONS OR EXTENDED LEAVES OF ABSENCE.
ANYTHING THAT WOULD INDICATE A LACK OF LOYALTY... OR A MOLE.
WHY ARE YOU TELLING ME THIS, DOCTOR PYM? AND WHO'S THE CHICK?
I'M COMMANDER MARIA HILL. THE REASON WE'RE TELLING YOU THIS IS THAT WE WANT YOU TO HUNT THIS AGENT DOWN.
WHILE WE THINK THE AGENT MAY TAKE THIS OPPORTUNITY TO LEAVE, WE'RE NOT COUNTING ON IT. ONCE YOUR LEG IS HEALED--WE WANT YOU ON THE JOB--SEARCHING FOR THIS ROGUE AGENT.
TO PUT IT BLUNTLY, MITCH--YOU WERE THE AGENT WE WERE GOING TO CHOOSE FOR THE ANT-MAN POSITION. YOU WERE BEST-SUITED OUT OF ALL THE CANDIDATES.
WE'VE GOT A PROTOTYPE OF THE SUIT--SLIGHTLY LESS ADVANCED THAN THE STOLEN ONE--BUT STILL FUNCTIONAL. WE'D LIKE YOU TO USE IT TO FIND OUR MAN.
HOW DO YOU EXPECT ME TO FIND THIS GUY? HE'S NEAR-MICROSCOPIC AND THE HELICARRIER CRASH SITE IS MASSIVE.
THE PYM PARTICLES, THE RADIATION THAT ALLOWS THE WEARER TO SHRINK, GIVE OFF A FAINT SIGNAL. THE HALF-LIFE OF THE SIGNAL IS VERY SHORT. BUT I'M CURRENTLY BUILDING A DEVICE THAT CAN TRACK IT.
THAT SHOULD MAKE THINGS EASIER.
TRAINING WILL START AS SOON AS YOUR LEG HEALS. YOU SHOULD BE READY FOR ACTION BY THE TIME THE HELICARRIER IS BACK UP AND RUNNING.
DO YOU ACCEPT THIS MISSION, AGENT CARSON?
YEAH.
SURE.

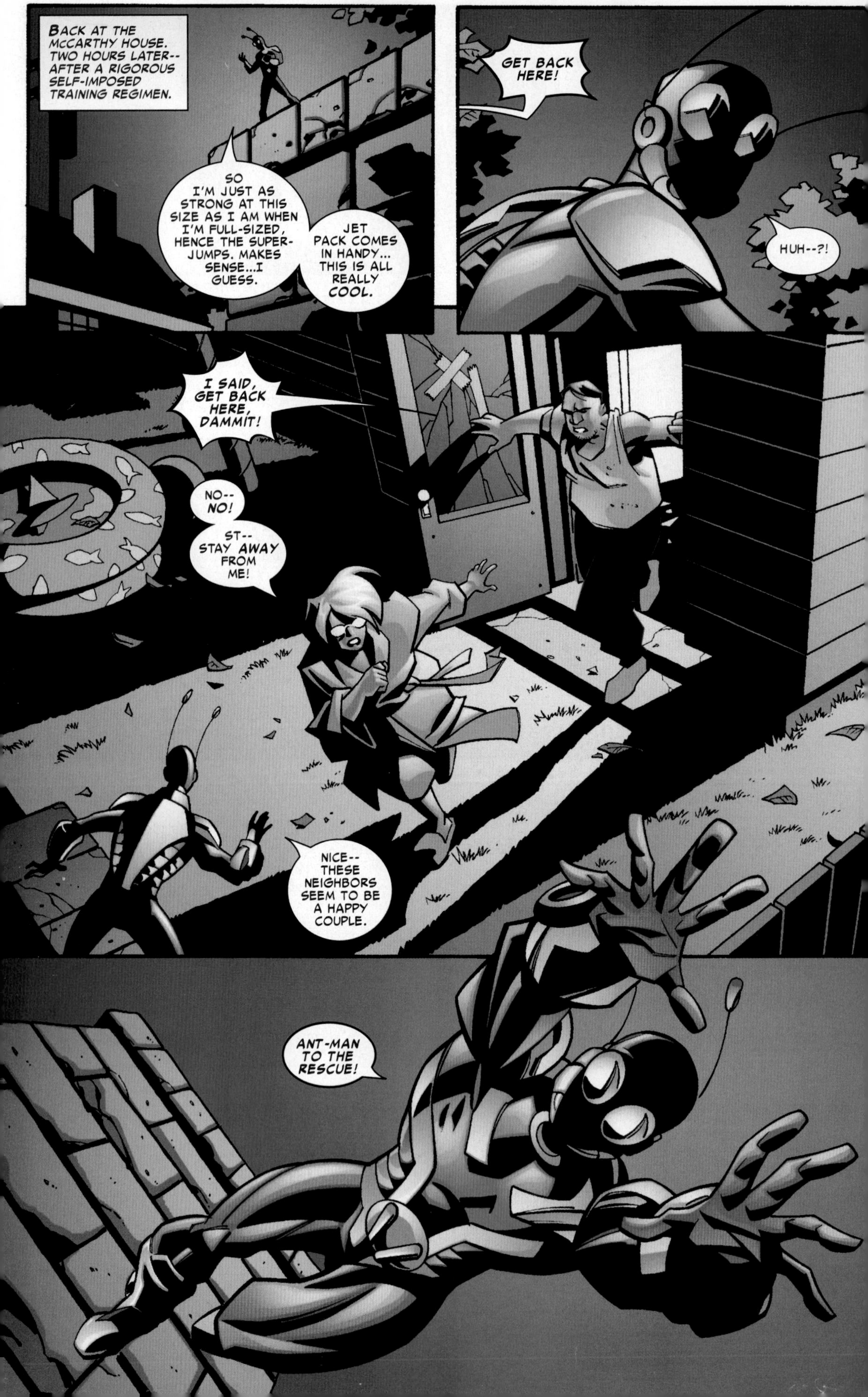
BACK AT THE McCARTHY HOUSE. TWO HOURS LATER-- AFTER A RIGOROUS SELF-IMPOSED TRAINING REGIMEN.
SO I'M JUST AS STRONG AT THIS SIZE AS I AM WHEN I'M FULL-SIZED, HENCE THE SUPER-JUMPS. MAKES SENSE...I GUESS.
JET PACK COMES IN HANDY... THIS IS ALL REALLY COOL.
GET BACK HERE!
HUH--?!
I SAID, GET BACK HERE, DAMMIT!
NO-- NO!
ST-- STAY AWAY FROM ME!
NICE-- THESE NEIGHBORS SEEM TO BE A HAPPY COUPLE.
ANT-MAN TO THE RESCUE!

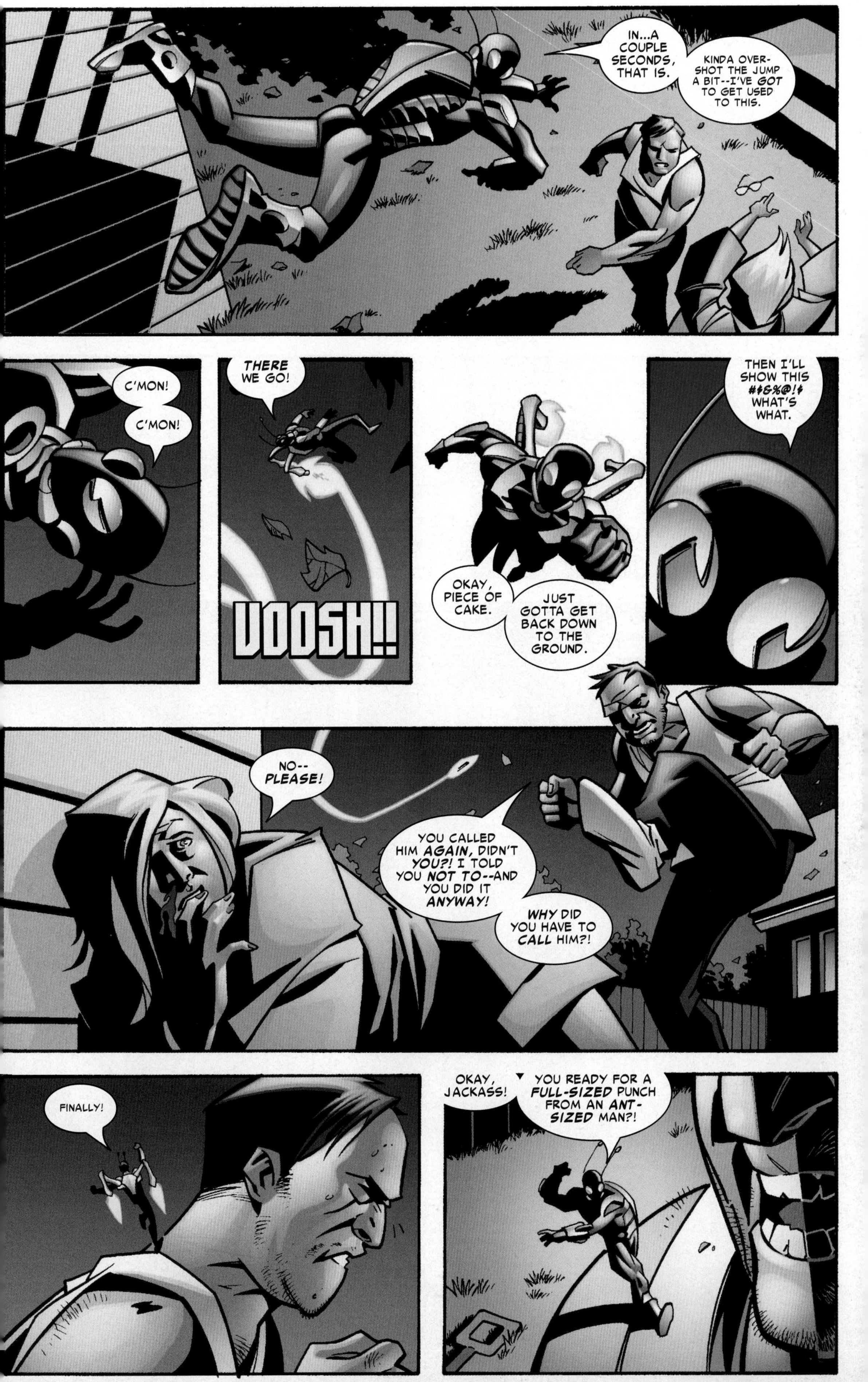
IN...A COUPLE SECONDS, THAT IS.
KINDA OVER-SHOT THE JUMP A BIT--I'VE GOT TO GET USED TO THIS.
C'MON!
C'MON!
THERE WE GO!
VOOSH!!
OKAY, PIECE OF CAKE.
JUST GOTTA GET BACK DOWN TO THE GROUND.
THEN I'LL SHOW THIS #$&%@!$ WHAT'S WHAT.
NO--PLEASE!
YOU CALLED HIM AGAIN, DIDN'T YOU?! I TOLD YOU NOT TO--AND YOU DID IT ANYWAY!
WHY DID YOU HAVE TO CALL HIM?!
FINALLY!
OKAY, JACKASS!
YOU READY FOR A FULL-SIZED PUNCH FROM AN ANT-SIZED MAN?!

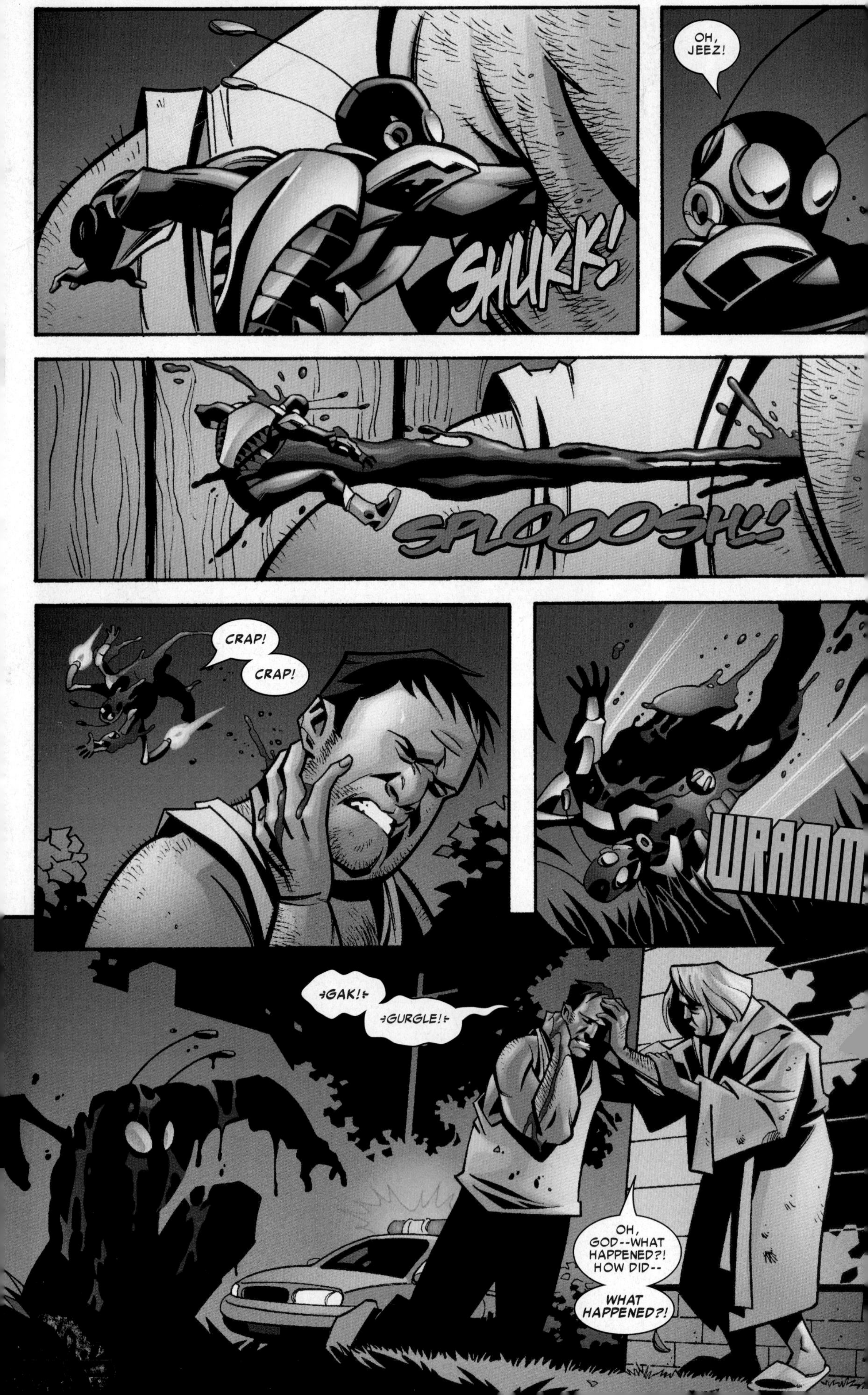
SHUKK!
OH, JEEZ!
SPLOOOSH!!
CRAP!
CRAP!
WRAMM
GAK!
GURGLE!
OH, GOD--WHAT HAPPENED?! HOW DID--
WHAT HAPPENED?!

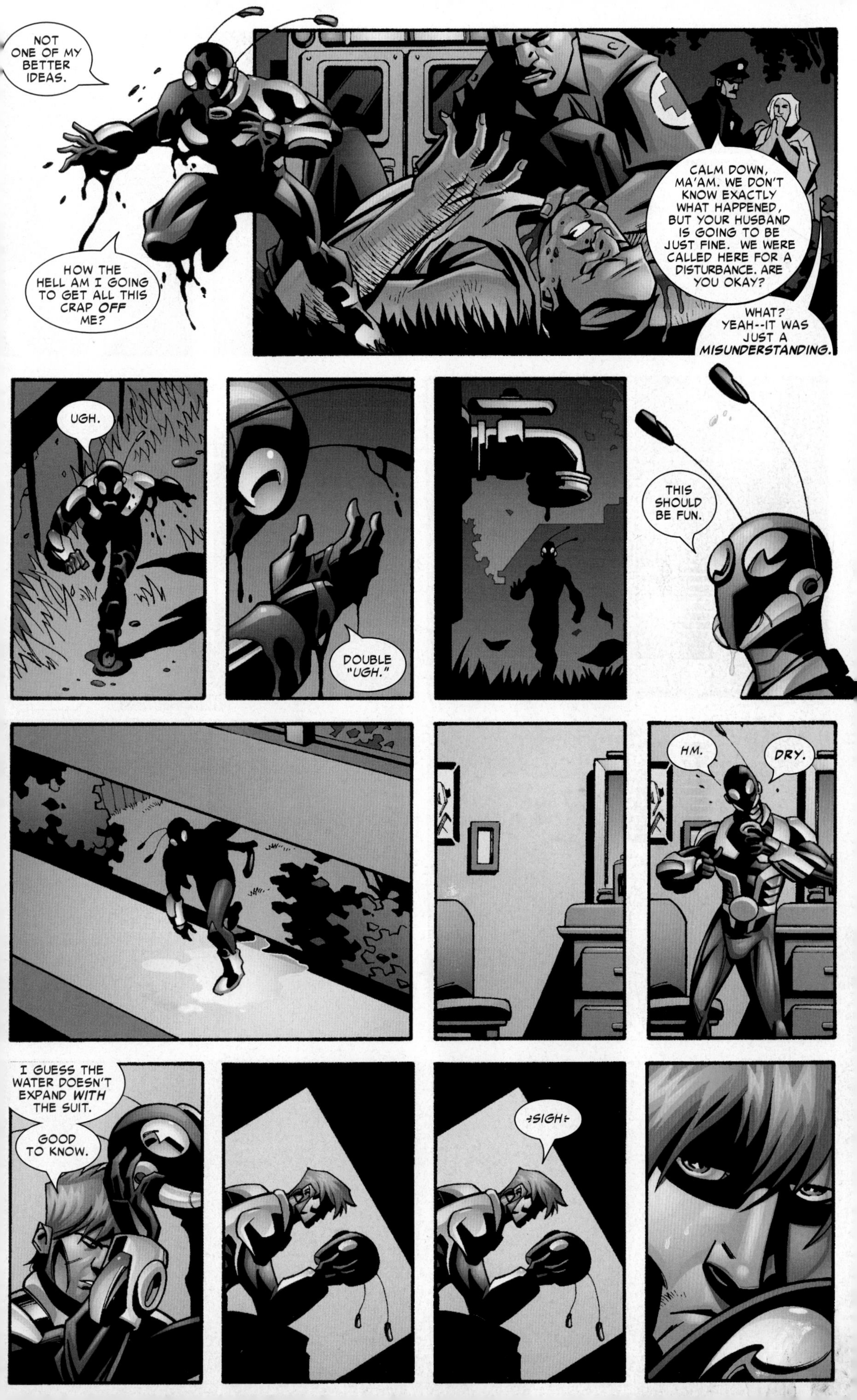
NOT ONE OF MY BETTER IDEAS.
HOW THE HELL AM I GOING TO GET ALL THIS CRAP OFF ME?
CALM DOWN, MA'AM. WE DON'T KNOW EXACTLY WHAT HAPPENED, BUT YOUR HUSBAND IS GOING TO BE JUST FINE. WE WERE CALLED HERE FOR A DISTURBANCE. ARE YOU OKAY?
WHAT? YEAH--IT WAS JUST A MISUNDERSTANDING.
UGH.
DOUBLE "UGH."
THIS SHOULD BE FUN.
HM.
DRY.
I GUESS THE WATER DOESN'T EXPAND WITH THE SUIT.
GOOD TO KNOW.
SIGH

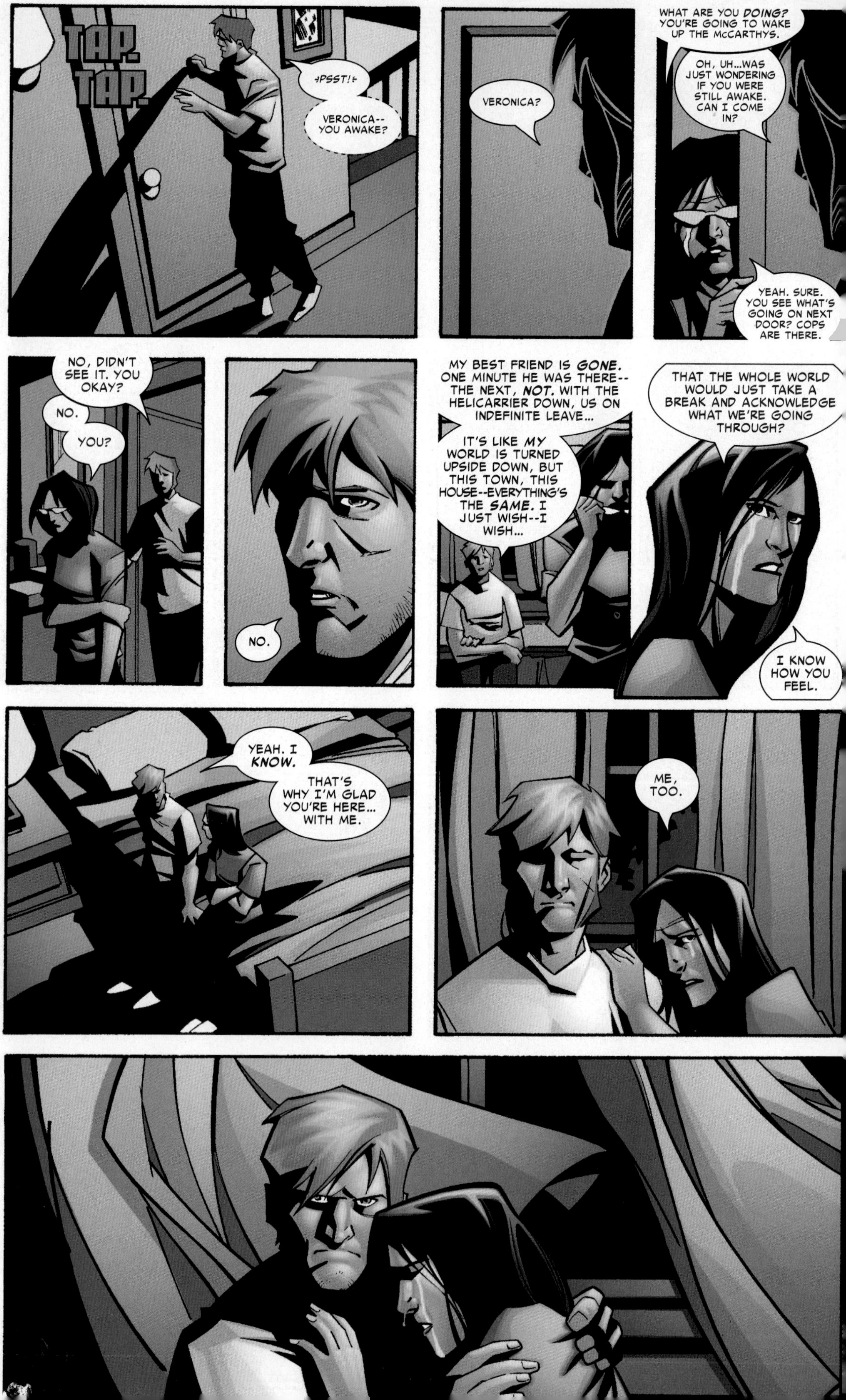
TAP. TAP.
PSST!
VERONICA-- YOU AWAKE?
VERONICA?
WHAT ARE YOU DOING? YOU'RE GOING TO WAKE UP THE McCARTHYS.
OH, UH...WAS JUST WONDERING IF YOU WERE STILL AWAKE. CAN I COME IN?
YEAH. SURE. YOU SEE WHAT'S GOING ON NEXT DOOR? COPS ARE THERE.
NO, DIDN'T SEE IT. YOU OKAY?
NO.
YOU?
NO.
MY BEST FRIEND IS GONE. ONE MINUTE HE WAS THERE-- THE NEXT, NOT. WITH THE HELICARRIER DOWN, US ON INDEFINITE LEAVE...
IT'S LIKE MY WORLD IS TURNED UPSIDE DOWN, BUT THIS TOWN, THIS HOUSE--EVERYTHING'S THE SAME. I JUST WISH--I WISH...
THAT THE WHOLE WORLD WOULD JUST TAKE A BREAK AND ACKNOWLEDGE WHAT WE'RE GOING THROUGH?
I KNOW HOW YOU FEEL.
YEAH. I KNOW.
THAT'S WHY I'M GLAD YOU'RE HERE... WITH ME.
ME, TOO.

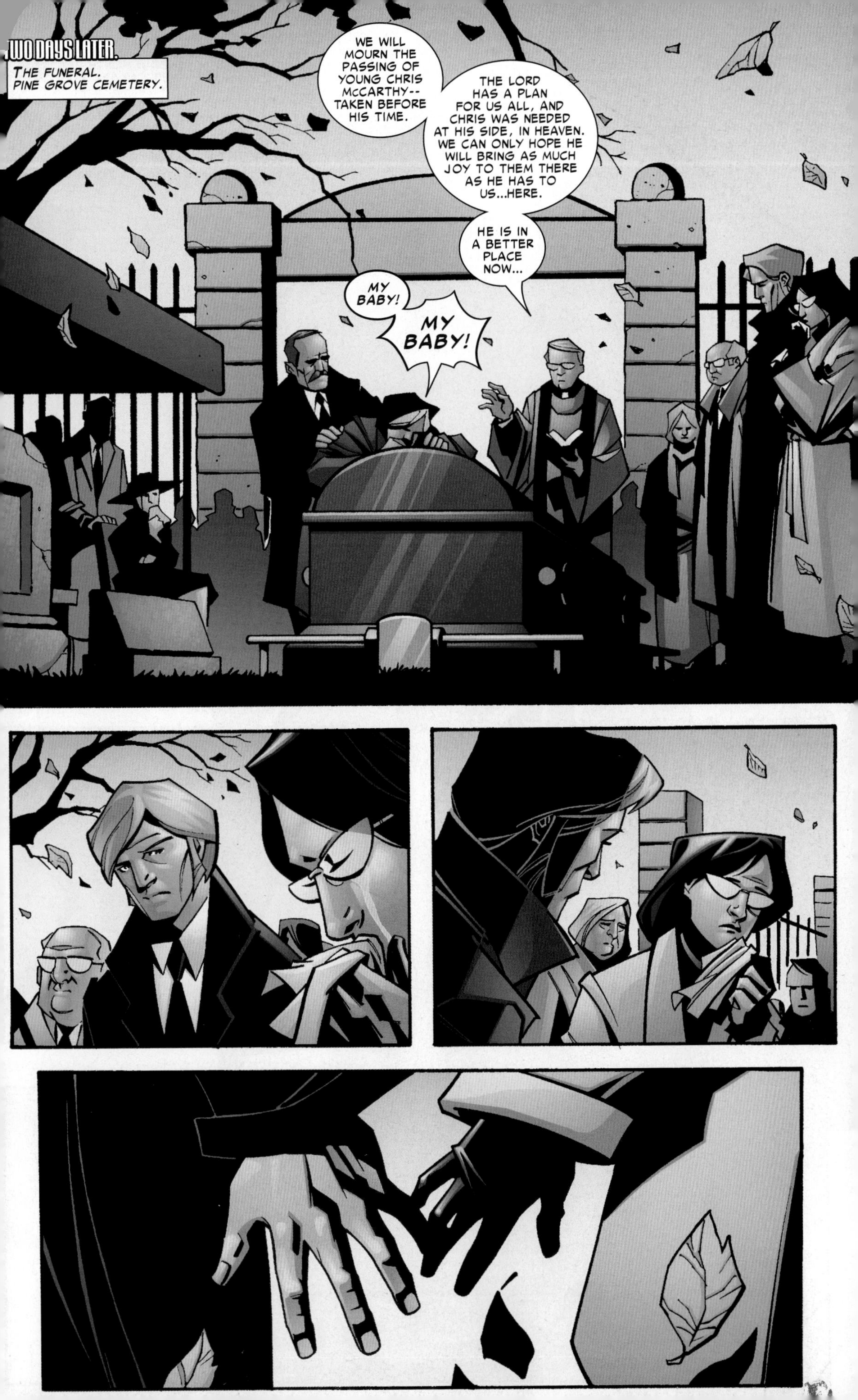
TWO DAYS LATER.
THE FUNERAL. PINE GROVE CEMETERY.
WE WILL MOURN THE PASSING OF YOUNG CHRIS McCARTHY-- TAKEN BEFORE HIS TIME.
THE LORD HAS A PLAN FOR US ALL, AND CHRIS WAS NEEDED AT HIS SIDE, IN HEAVEN. WE CAN ONLY HOPE HE WILL BRING AS MUCH JOY TO THEM THERE AS HE HAS TO US...HERE.
HE IS IN A BETTER PLACE NOW...
MY BABY!
MY BABY!

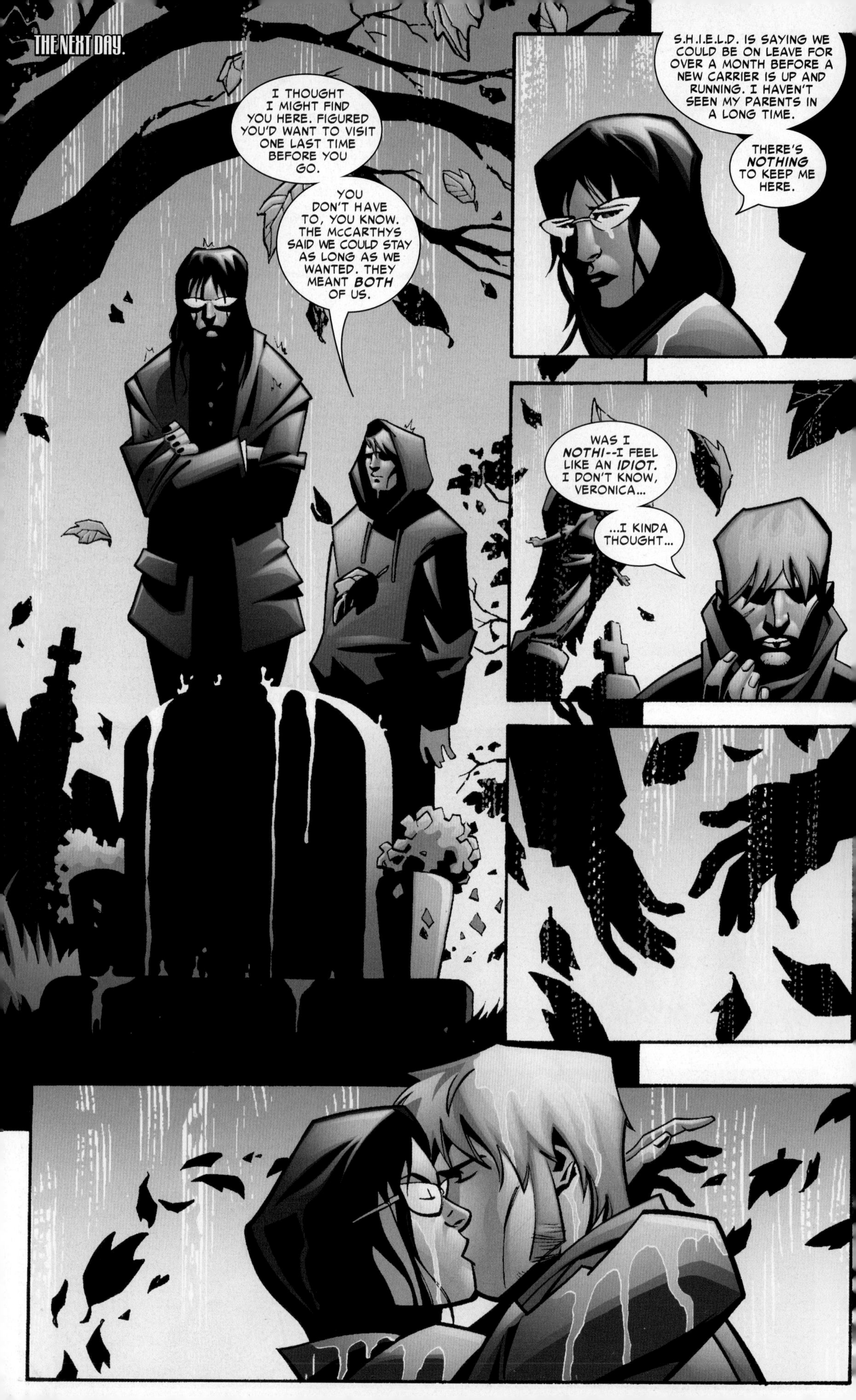
THE NEXT DAY.
I THOUGHT I MIGHT FIND YOU HERE. FIGURED YOU'D WANT TO VISIT ONE LAST TIME BEFORE YOU GO.
YOU DON'T HAVE TO, YOU KNOW. THE McCARTHYS SAID WE COULD STAY AS LONG AS WE WANTED. THEY MEANT BOTH OF US.
S.H.I.E.L.D. IS SAYING WE COULD BE ON LEAVE FOR OVER A MONTH BEFORE A NEW CARRIER IS UP AND RUNNING. I HAVEN'T SEEN MY PARENTS IN A LONG TIME.
THERE'S NOTHING TO KEEP ME HERE.
WAS I NOTHI--I FEEL LIKE AN IDIOT. I DON'T KNOW, VERONICA...
...I KINDA THOUGHT...

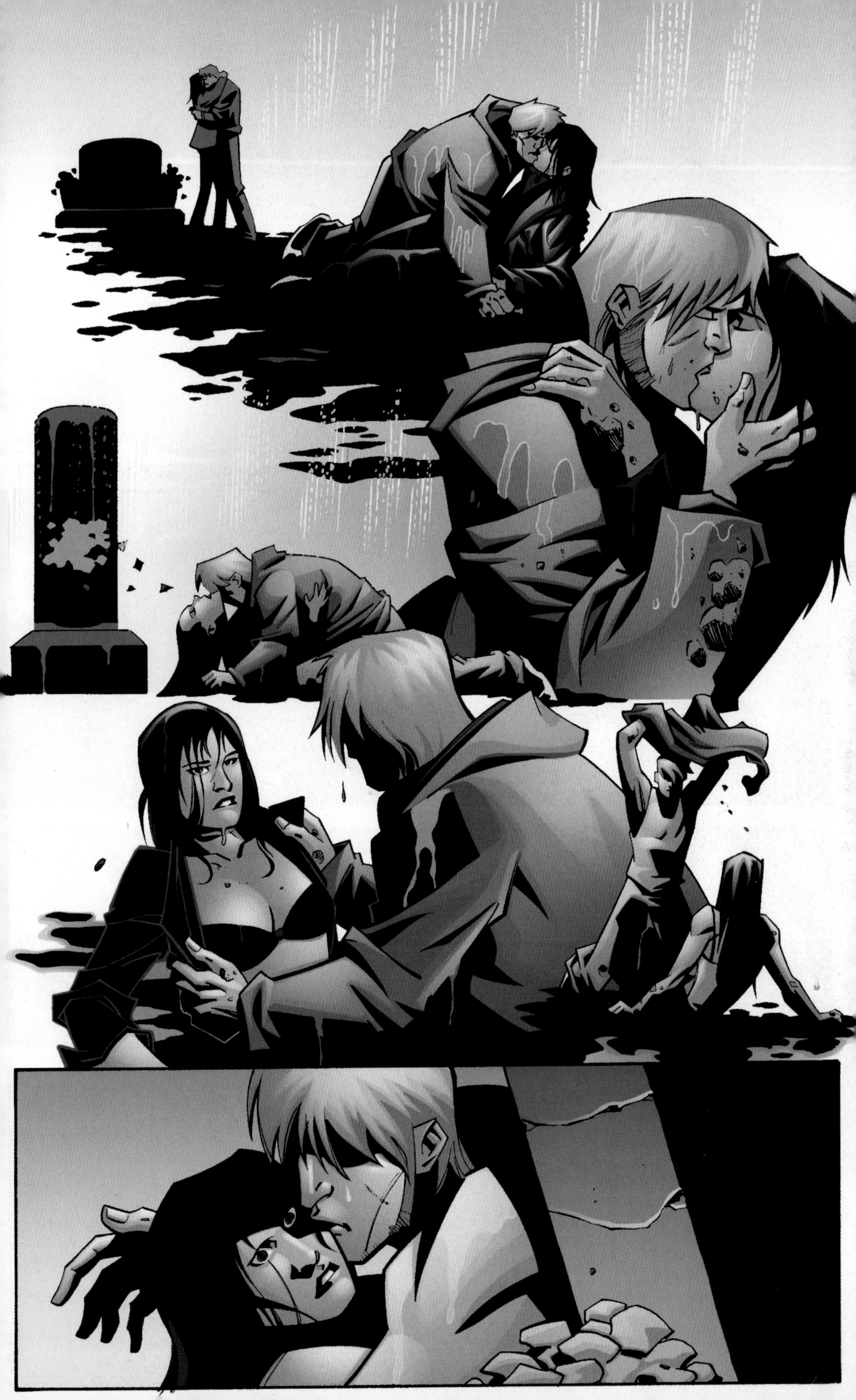

GET OFF ME!

WHAT IS IT? WHAT DID I DO?

NO. JUST... NO. THERE'S NO WAY I'M DOING THIS.

NO.

CHRIS MCCARTHY
TAKEN BEFORE HIS TIME

CHRIS MCCARTHY
TAKEN BEFORE HIS TIME

WHAT ARE YOU LOOKING AT?

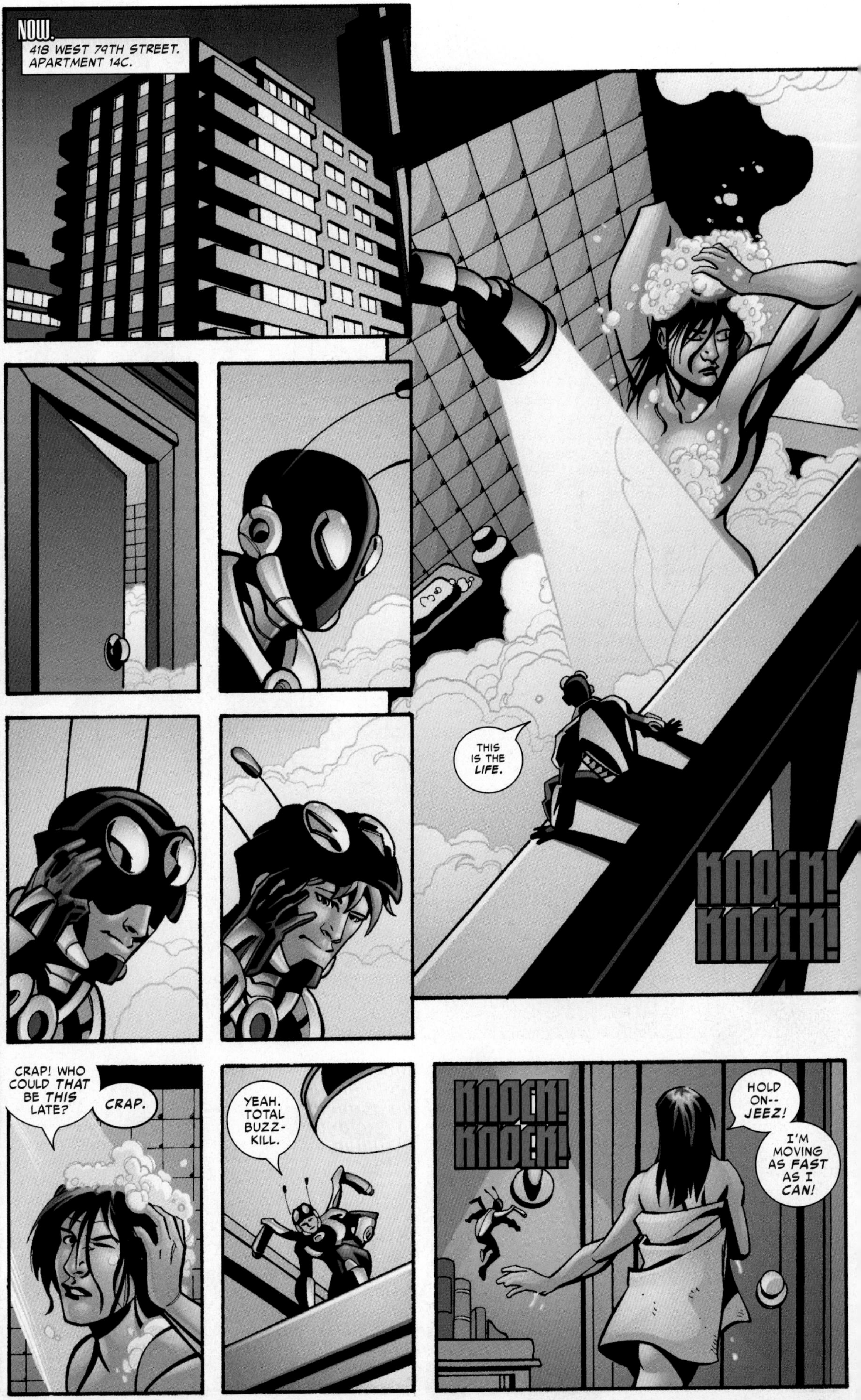
NOW.
418 WEST 79TH STREET. APARTMENT 14C.
THIS IS THE LIFE.
KNOCK! KNOCK!
CRAP! WHO COULD THAT BE THIS LATE?
CRAP.
YEAH. TOTAL BUZZ-KILL.
KNOCK! KNOCK!
HOLD ON-- JEEZ!
I'M MOVING AS FAST AS I CAN!

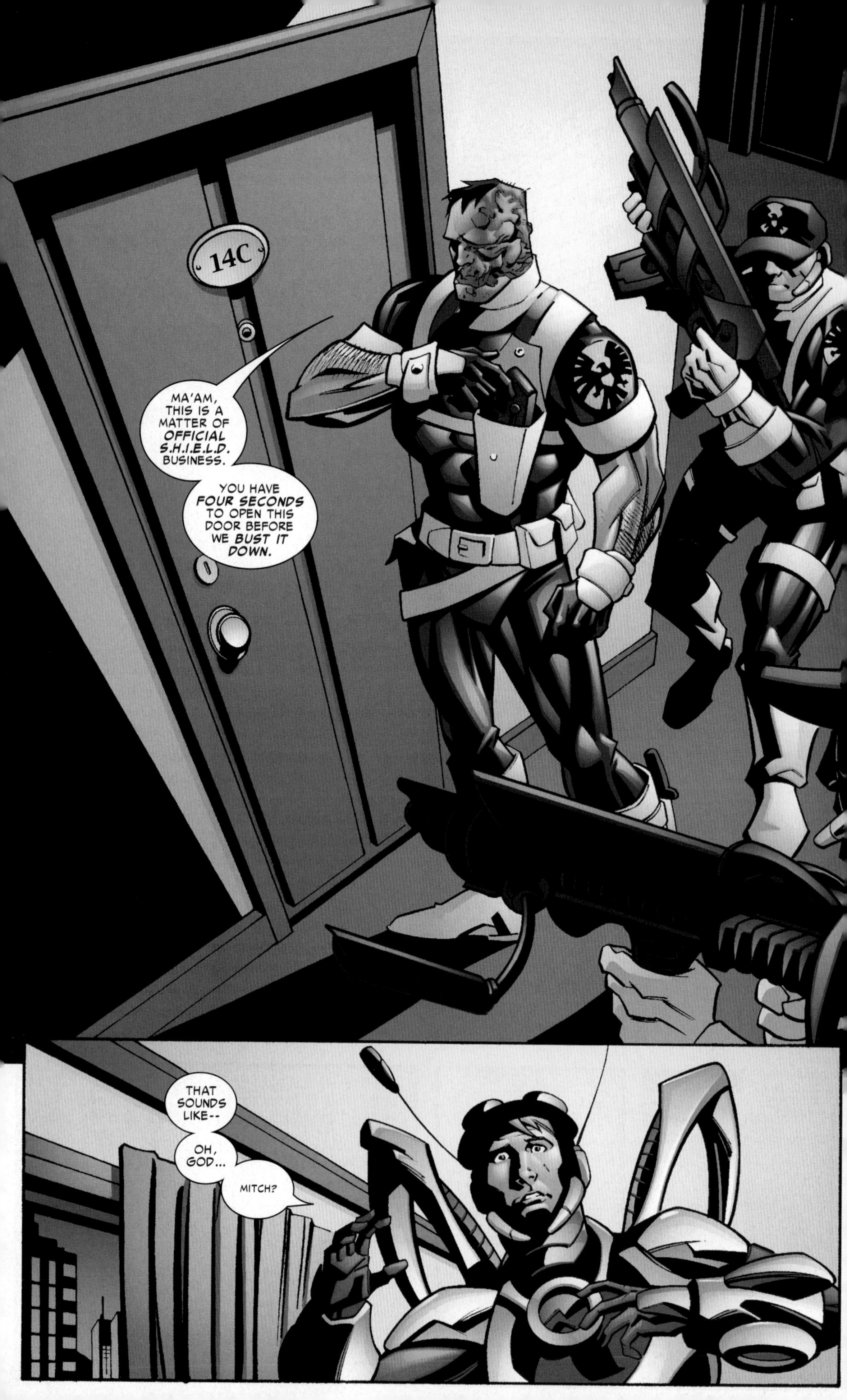
MA'AM, THIS IS A MATTER OF OFFICIAL S.H.I.E.L.D. BUSINESS.
YOU HAVE FOUR SECONDS TO OPEN THIS DOOR BEFORE WE BUST IT DOWN.
THAT SOUNDS LIKE--
OH, GOD...
MITCH?

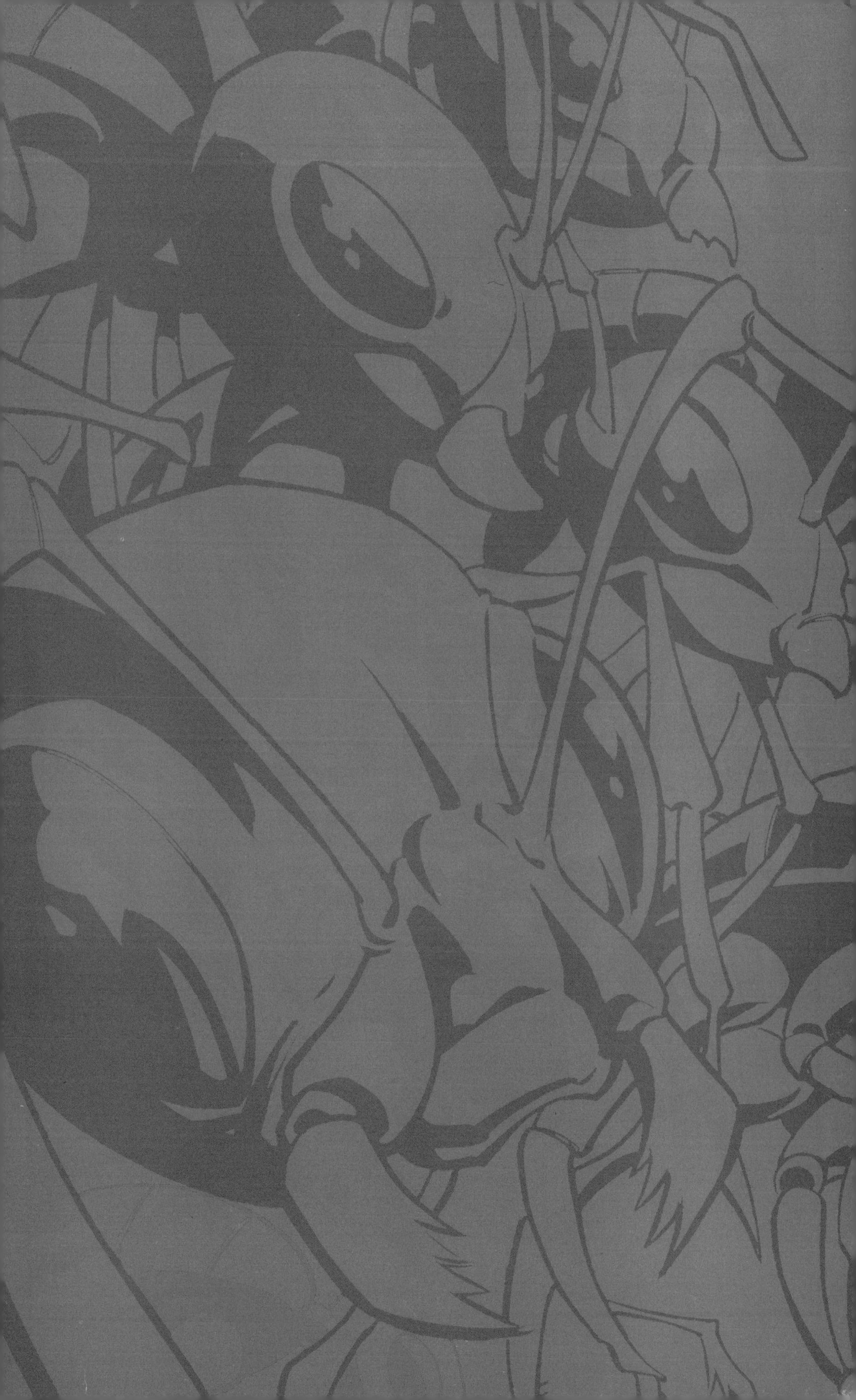

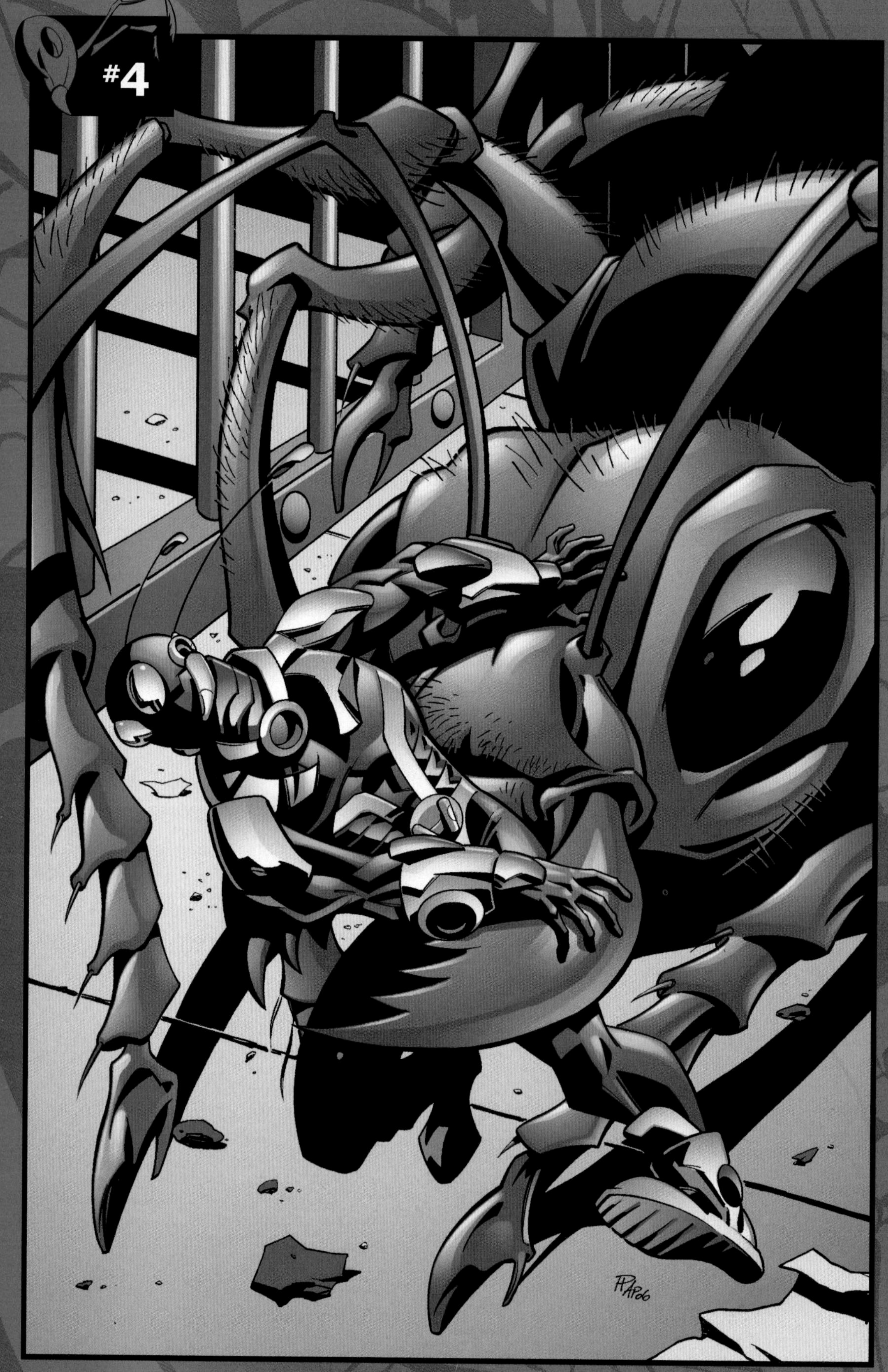
#4

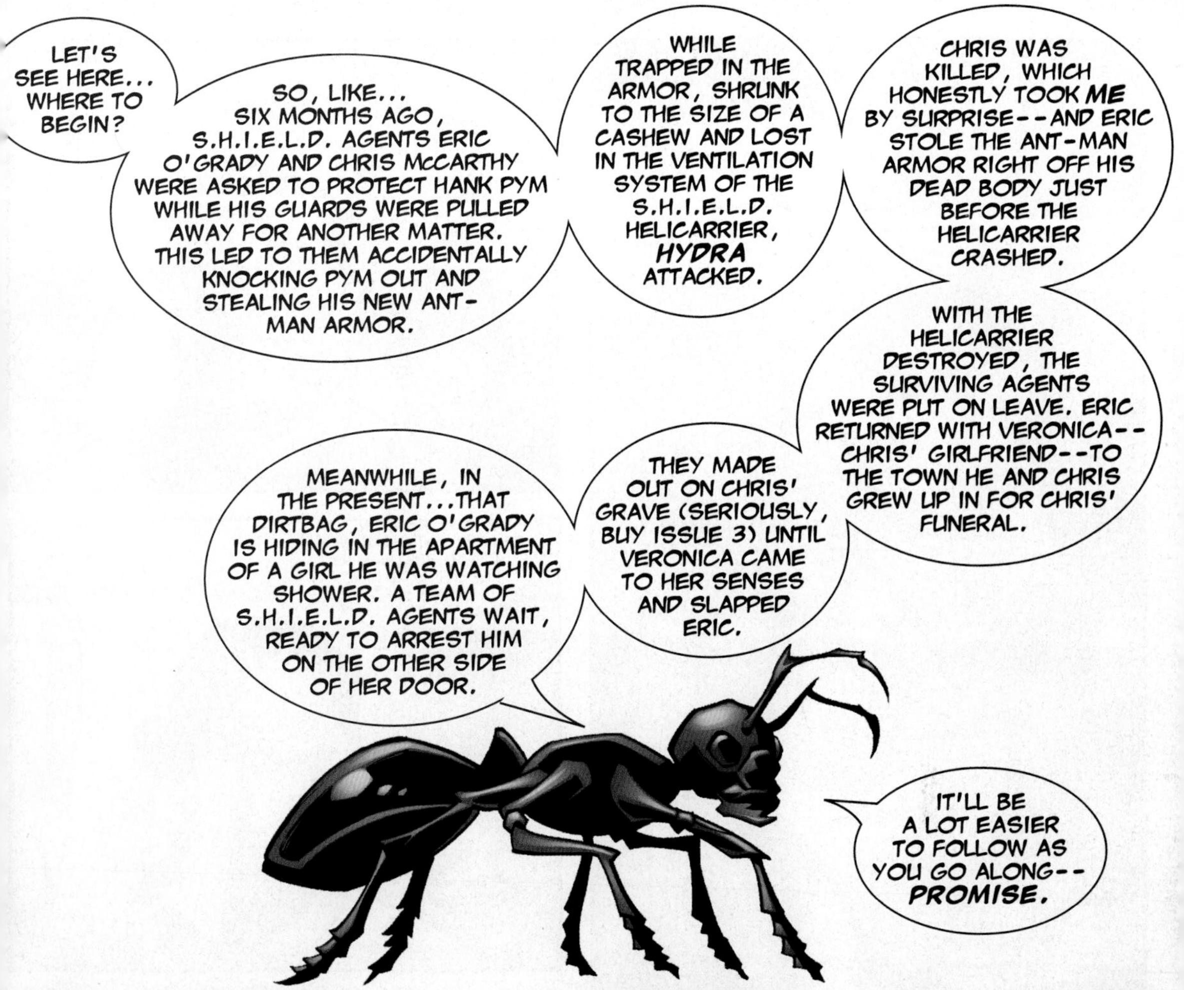
LET'S SEE HERE... WHERE TO BEGIN?
SO, LIKE... SIX MONTHS AGO, S.H.I.E.L.D. AGENTS ERIC O'GRADY AND CHRIS McCARTHY WERE ASKED TO PROTECT HANK PYM WHILE HIS GUARDS WERE PULLED AWAY FOR ANOTHER MATTER. THIS LED TO THEM ACCIDENTALLY KNOCKING PYM OUT AND STEALING HIS NEW ANT-MAN ARMOR.
WHILE TRAPPED IN THE ARMOR, SHRUNK TO THE SIZE OF A CASHEW AND LOST IN THE VENTILATION SYSTEM OF THE S.H.I.E.L.D. HELICARRIER, HYDRA ATTACKED.
CHRIS WAS KILLED, WHICH HONESTLY TOOK ME BY SURPRISE--AND ERIC STOLE THE ANT-MAN ARMOR RIGHT OFF HIS DEAD BODY JUST BEFORE THE HELICARRIER CRASHED.
WITH THE HELICARRIER DESTROYED, THE SURVIVING AGENTS WERE PUT ON LEAVE. ERIC RETURNED WITH VERONICA--CHRIS' GIRLFRIEND--TO THE TOWN HE AND CHRIS GREW UP IN FOR CHRIS' FUNERAL.
THEY MADE OUT ON CHRIS' GRAVE (SERIOUSLY, BUY ISSUE 3) UNTIL VERONICA CAME TO HER SENSES AND SLAPPED ERIC.
MEANWHILE, IN THE PRESENT...THAT DIRTBAG, ERIC O'GRADY IS HIDING IN THE APARTMENT OF A GIRL HE WAS WATCHING SHOWER. A TEAM OF S.H.I.E.L.D. AGENTS WAIT, READY TO ARREST HIM ON THE OTHER SIDE OF HER DOOR.
IT'LL BE A LOT EASIER TO FOLLOW AS YOU GO ALONG--PROMISE.

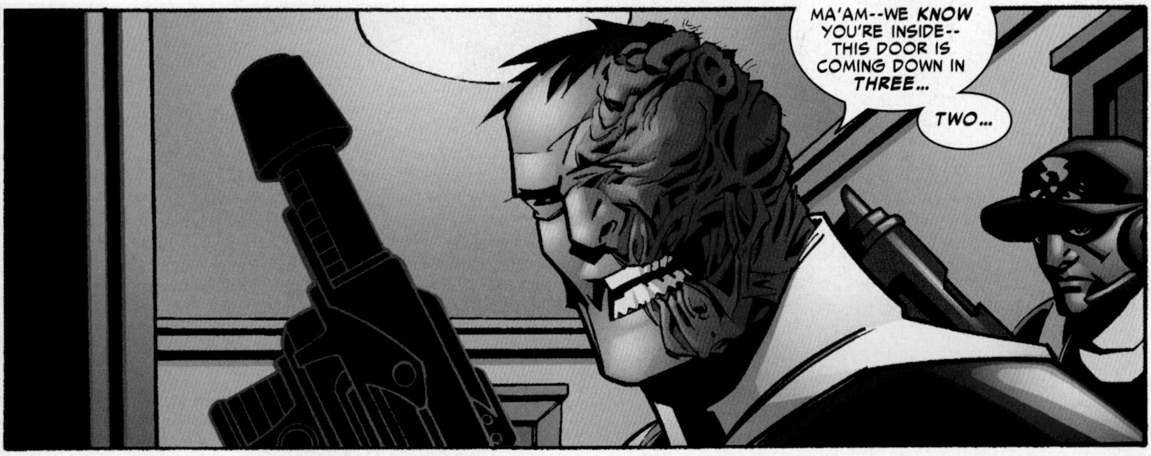
MA'AM--WE KNOW YOU'RE INSIDE--THIS DOOR IS COMING DOWN IN THREE...
TWO...

# THE DAILY GRIND

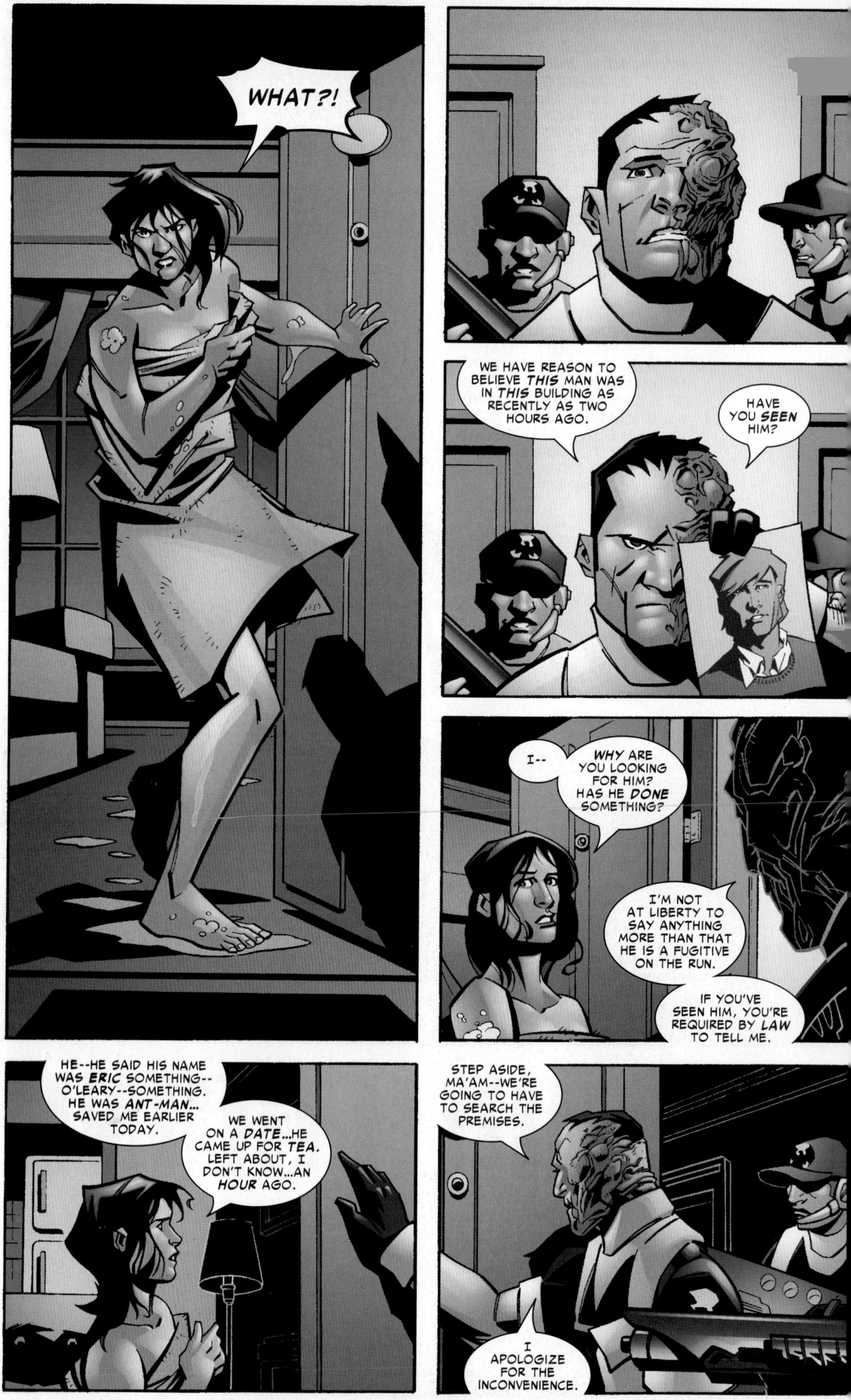
WHAT?!
WE HAVE REASON TO BELIEVE THIS MAN WAS IN THIS BUILDING AS RECENTLY AS TWO HOURS AGO.
HAVE YOU SEEN HIM?
I--
WHY ARE YOU LOOKING FOR HIM? HAS HE DONE SOMETHING?
I'M NOT AT LIBERTY TO SAY ANYTHING MORE THAN THAT HE IS A FUGITIVE ON THE RUN.
IF YOU'VE SEEN HIM, YOU'RE REQUIRED BY LAW TO TELL ME.
HE--HE SAID HIS NAME WAS ERIC SOMETHING--O'LEARY--SOMETHING. HE WAS ANT-MAN... SAVED ME EARLIER TODAY.
WE WENT ON A DATE...HE CAME UP FOR TEA. LEFT ABOUT, I DON'T KNOW...AN HOUR AGO.
STEP ASIDE, MA'AM--WE'RE GOING TO HAVE TO SEARCH THE PREMISES.
I APOLOGIZE FOR THE INCONVENIENCE.

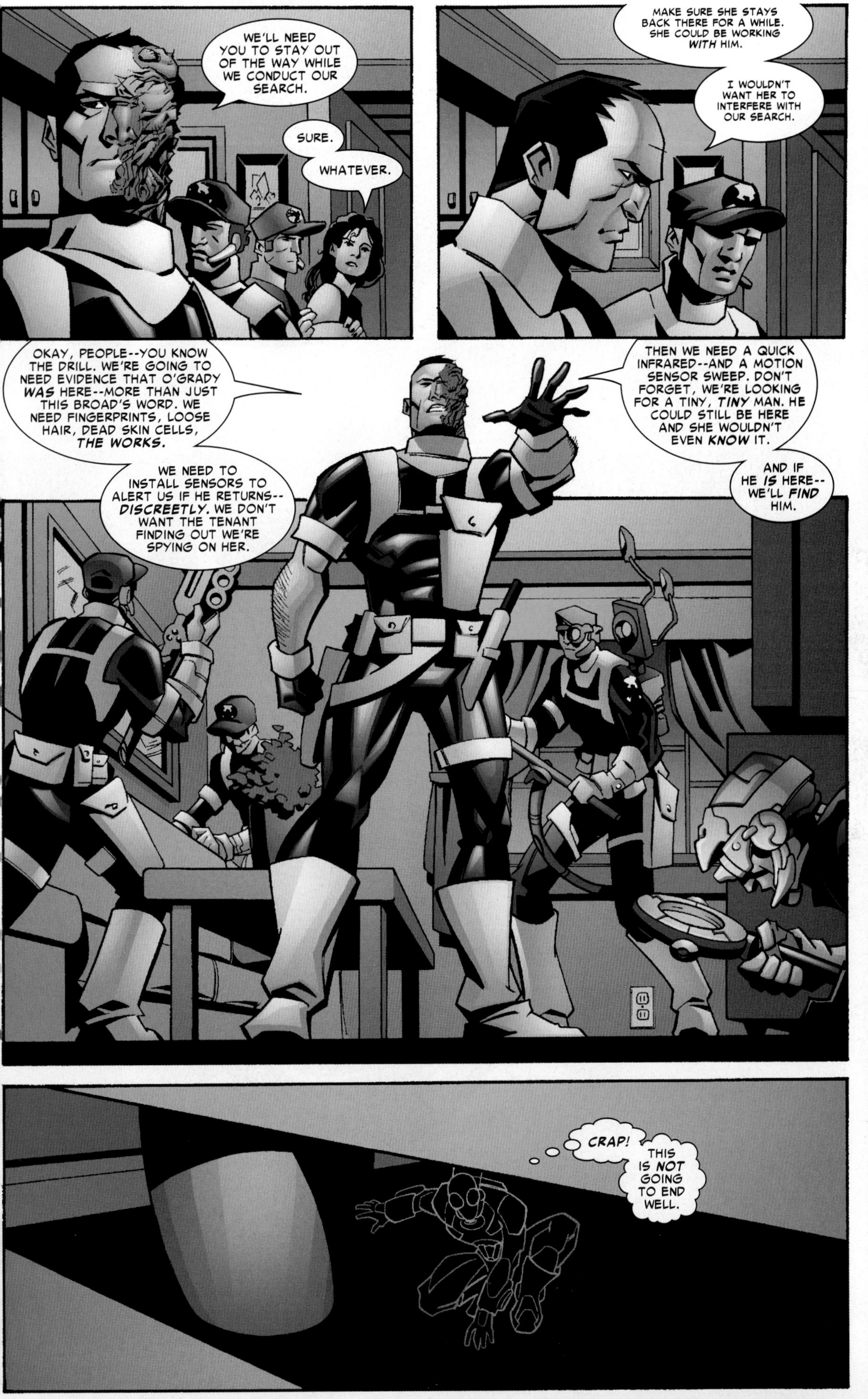
WE'LL NEED YOU TO STAY OUT OF THE WAY WHILE WE CONDUCT OUR SEARCH.
SURE.
WHATEVER.
MAKE SURE SHE STAYS BACK THERE FOR A WHILE. SHE COULD BE WORKING WITH HIM.
I WOULDN'T WANT HER TO INTERFERE WITH OUR SEARCH.
OKAY, PEOPLE--YOU KNOW THE DRILL. WE'RE GOING TO NEED EVIDENCE THAT O'GRADY WAS HERE--MORE THAN JUST THIS BROAD'S WORD. WE NEED FINGERPRINTS, LOOSE HAIR, DEAD SKIN CELLS, THE WORKS.
WE NEED TO INSTALL SENSORS TO ALERT US IF HE RETURNS--DISCREETLY. WE DON'T WANT THE TENANT FINDING OUT WE'RE SPYING ON HER.
THEN WE NEED A QUICK INFRARED--AND A MOTION SENSOR SWEEP. DON'T FORGET, WE'RE LOOKING FOR A TINY, TINY MAN. HE COULD STILL BE HERE AND SHE WOULDN'T EVEN KNOW IT.
AND IF HE IS HERE--WE'LL FIND HIM.
CRAP!
THIS IS NOT GOING TO END WELL.

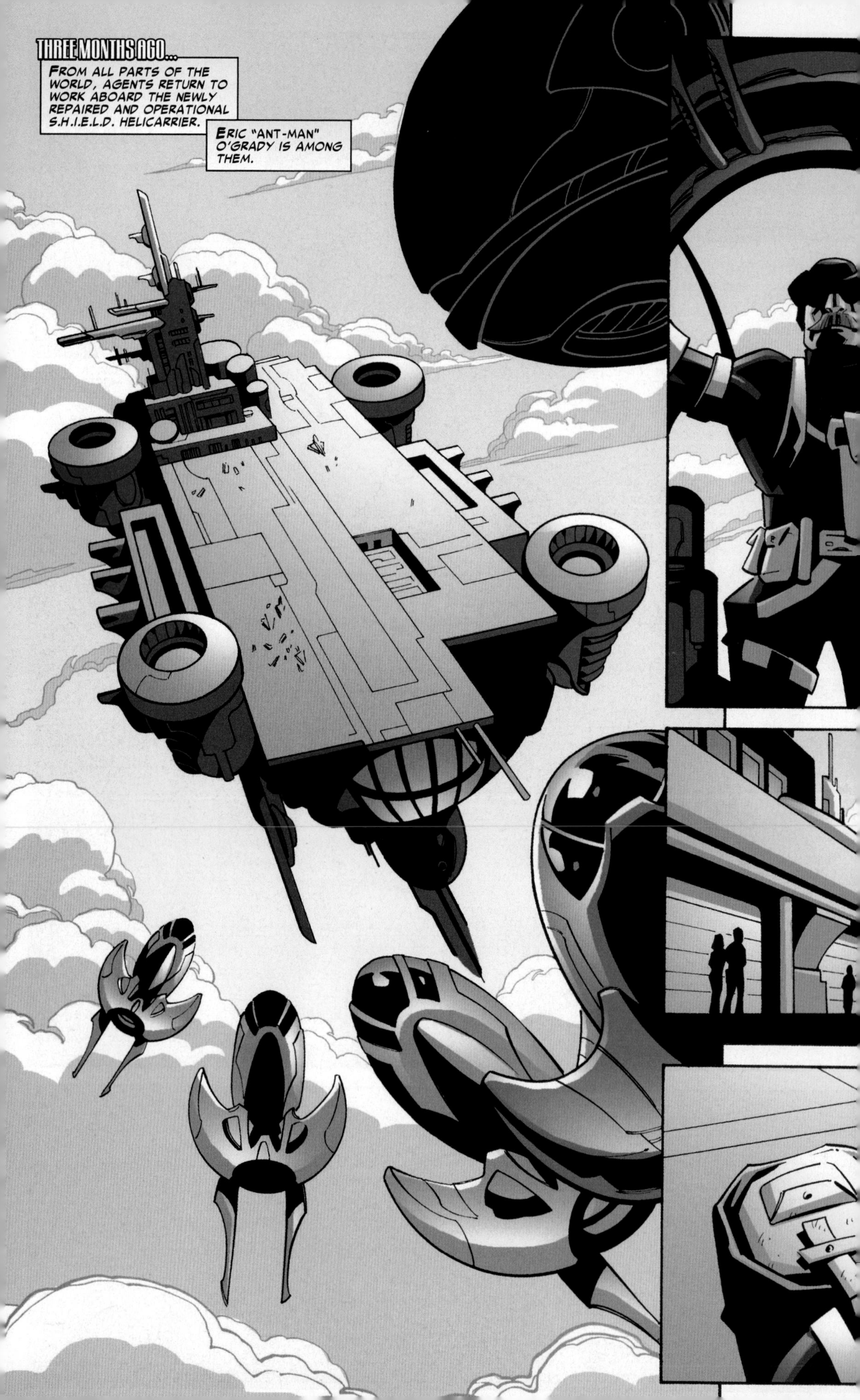
THREE MONTHS AGO...
FROM ALL PARTS OF THE WORLD, AGENTS RETURN TO WORK ABOARD THE NEWLY REPAIRED AND OPERATIONAL S.H.I.E.L.D. HELICARRIER.
ERIC "ANT-MAN" O'GRADY IS AMONG THEM.

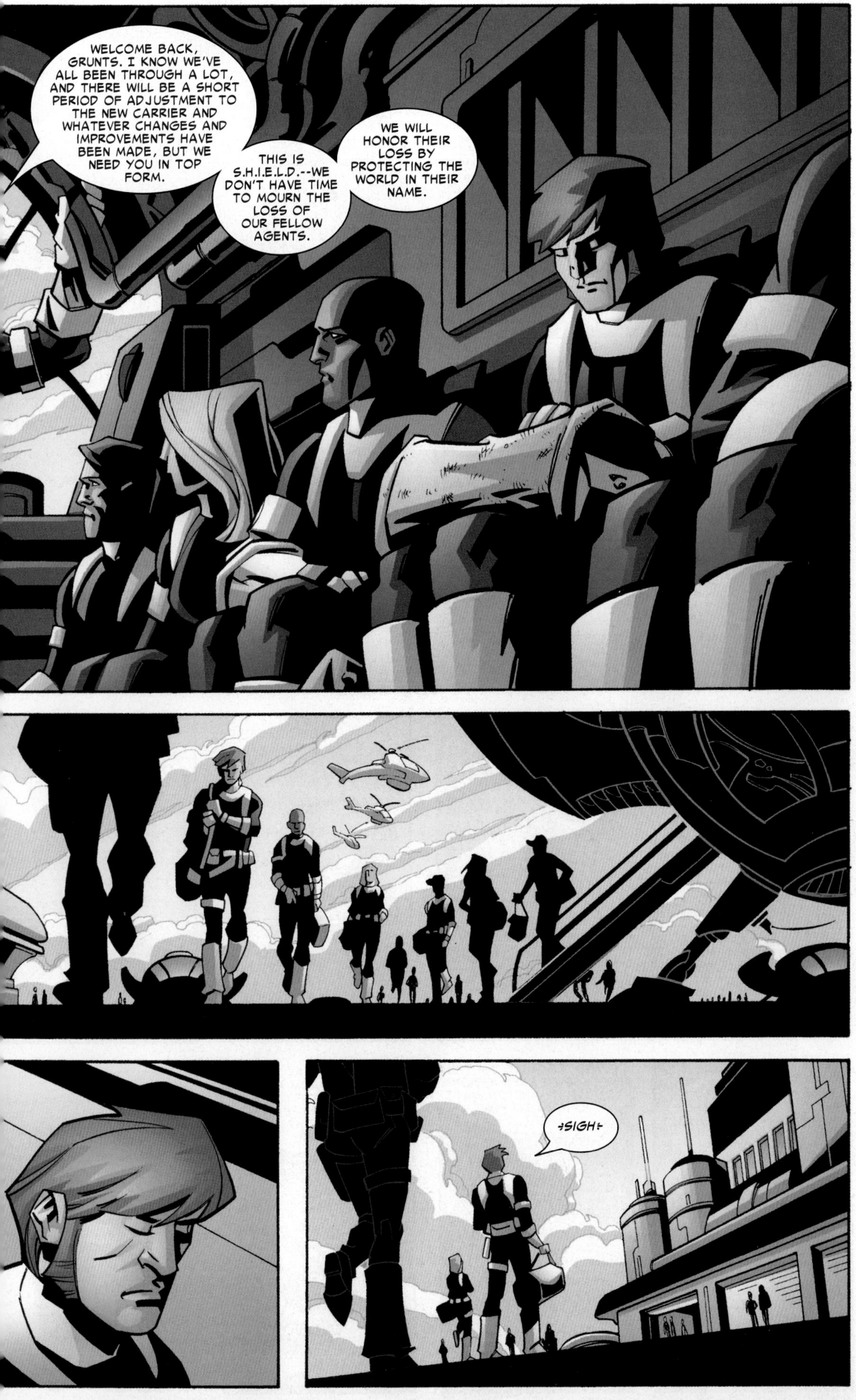
WELCOME BACK, GRUNTS. I KNOW WE'VE ALL BEEN THROUGH A LOT, AND THERE WILL BE A SHORT PERIOD OF ADJUSTMENT TO THE NEW CARRIER AND WHATEVER CHANGES AND IMPROVEMENTS HAVE BEEN MADE, BUT WE NEED YOU IN TOP FORM.
THIS IS S.H.I.E.L.D.--WE DON'T HAVE TIME TO MOURN THE LOSS OF OUR FELLOW AGENTS.
WE WILL HONOR THEIR LOSS BY PROTECTING THE WORLD IN THEIR NAME.
SIGH

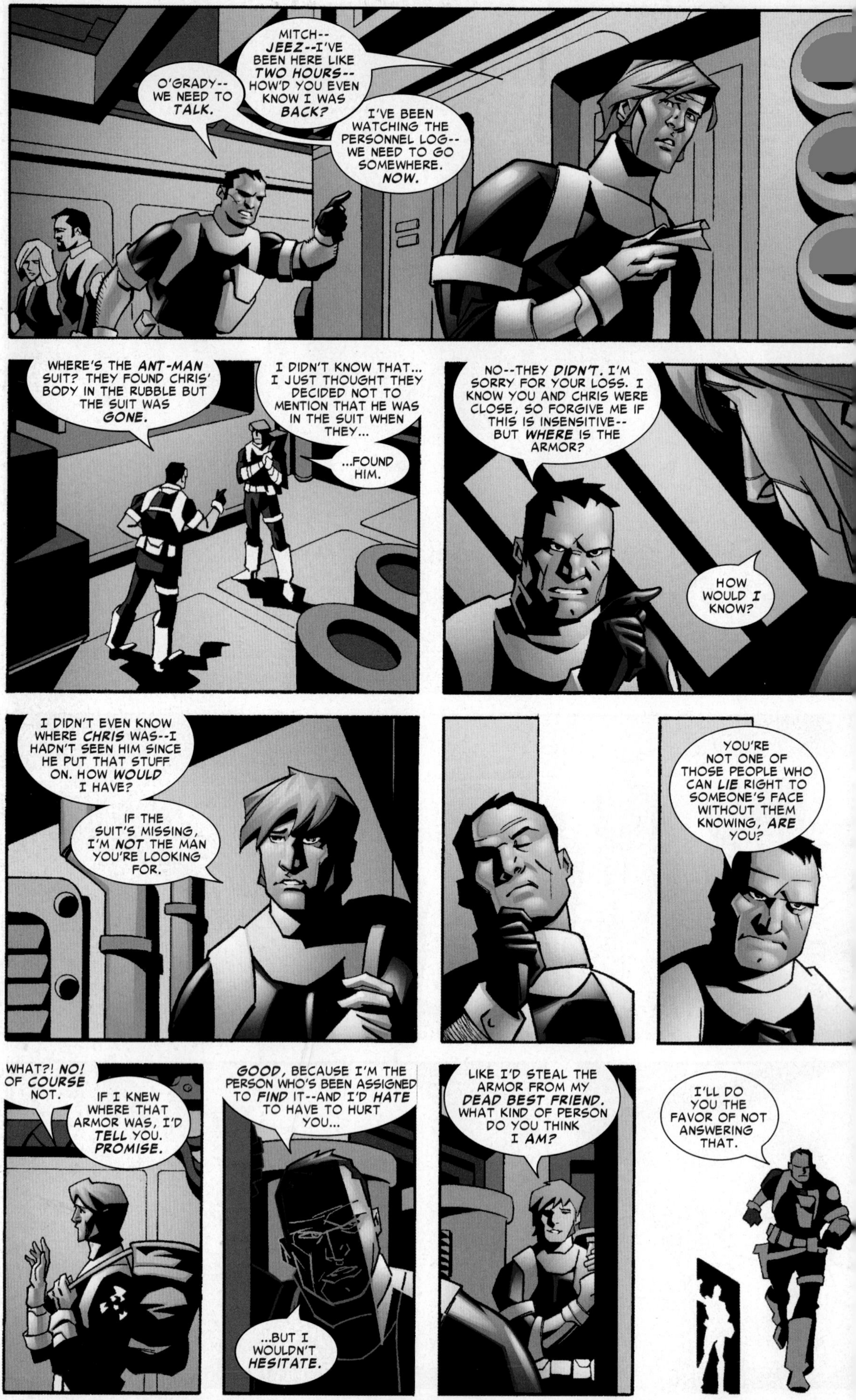
O'GRADY--
WE NEED TO TALK.
MITCH--
JEEZ--I'VE BEEN HERE LIKE TWO HOURS--HOW'D YOU EVEN KNOW I WAS BACK?
I'VE BEEN WATCHING THE PERSONNEL LOG--WE NEED TO GO SOMEWHERE. NOW.
WHERE'S THE ANT-MAN SUIT? THEY FOUND CHRIS' BODY IN THE RUBBLE BUT THE SUIT WAS GONE.
I DIDN'T KNOW THAT... I JUST THOUGHT THEY DECIDED NOT TO MENTION THAT HE WAS IN THE SUIT WHEN THEY...
...FOUND HIM.
NO--THEY DIDN'T. I'M SORRY FOR YOUR LOSS. I KNOW YOU AND CHRIS WERE CLOSE, SO FORGIVE ME IF THIS IS INSENSITIVE--BUT WHERE IS THE ARMOR?
HOW WOULD I KNOW?
I DIDN'T EVEN KNOW WHERE CHRIS WAS--I HADN'T SEEN HIM SINCE HE PUT THAT STUFF ON. HOW WOULD I HAVE?
IF THE SUIT'S MISSING, I'M NOT THE MAN YOU'RE LOOKING FOR.
YOU'RE NOT ONE OF THOSE PEOPLE WHO CAN LIE RIGHT TO SOMEONE'S FACE WITHOUT THEM KNOWING, ARE YOU?
WHAT?! NO! OF COURSE NOT.
IF I KNEW WHERE THAT ARMOR WAS, I'D TELL YOU. PROMISE.
GOOD, BECAUSE I'M THE PERSON WHO'S ASSIGNED TO FIND IT--AND I'D HATE TO HAVE TO HURT YOU...
...BUT I WOULDN'T HESITATE.
LIKE I'D STEAL THE ARMOR FROM MY DEAD BEST FRIEND. WHAT KIND OF PERSON DO YOU THINK I AM?
I'LL DO YOU THE FAVOR OF NOT ANSWERING THAT.

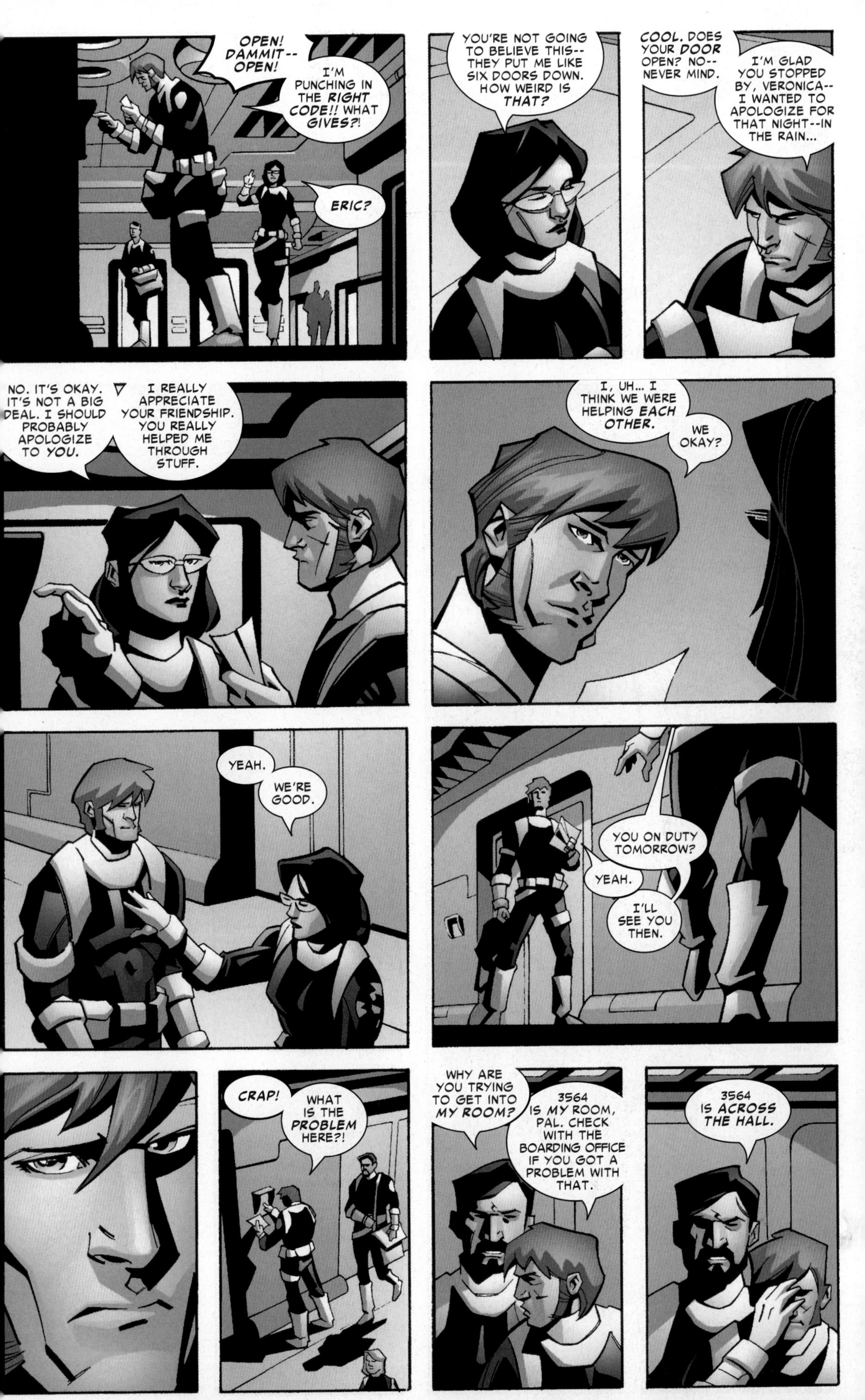
OPEN! DAMMIT-- OPEN!
I'M PUNCHING IN THE RIGHT CODE!! WHAT GIVES?!
ERIC?
YOU'RE NOT GOING TO BELIEVE THIS-- THEY PUT ME LIKE SIX DOORS DOWN. HOW WEIRD IS THAT?
COOL. DOES YOUR DOOR OPEN? NO-- NEVER MIND.
I'M GLAD YOU STOPPED BY, VERONICA-- I WANTED TO APOLOGIZE FOR THAT NIGHT--IN THE RAIN...
NO. IT'S OKAY. IT'S NOT A BIG DEAL. I SHOULD PROBABLY APOLOGIZE TO YOU.
I REALLY APPRECIATE YOUR FRIENDSHIP. YOU REALLY HELPED ME THROUGH STUFF.
I, UH... I THINK WE WERE HELPING EACH OTHER.
WE OKAY?
YEAH.
WE'RE GOOD.
YOU ON DUTY TOMORROW?
YEAH.
I'LL SEE YOU THEN.
CRAP!
WHAT IS THE PROBLEM HERE?!
WHY ARE YOU TRYING TO GET INTO MY ROOM?
3564 IS MY ROOM, PAL. CHECK WITH THE BOARDING OFFICE IF YOU GOT A PROBLEM WITH THAT.
3564 IS ACROSS THE HALL.

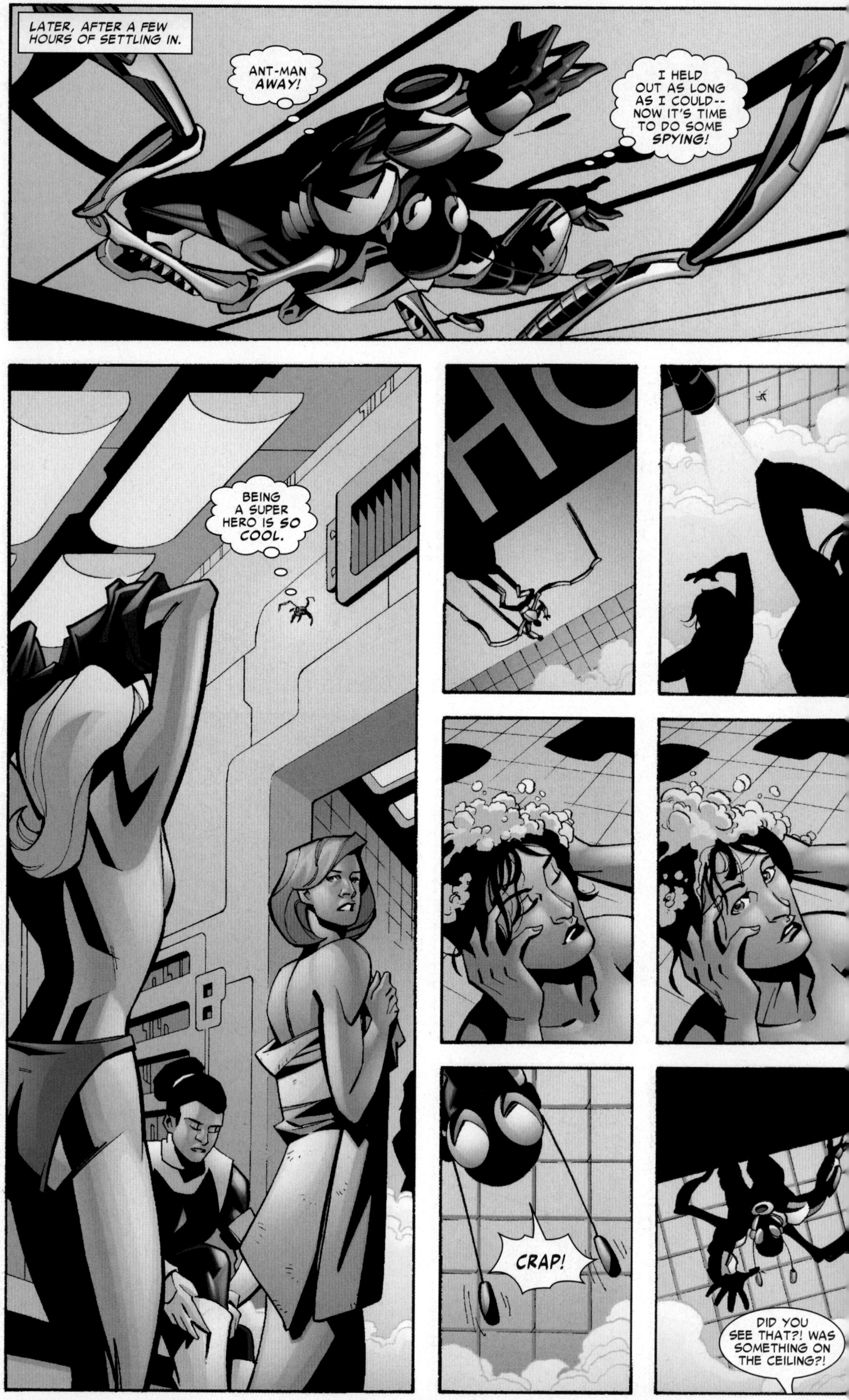
LATER, AFTER A FEW HOURS OF SETTLING IN.
ANT-MAN AWAY!
I HELD OUT AS LONG AS I COULD-- NOW IT'S TIME TO DO SOME SPYING!
BEING A SUPER HERO IS SO COOL.
CRAP!
DID YOU SEE THAT?! WAS SOMETHING ON THE CEILING?!

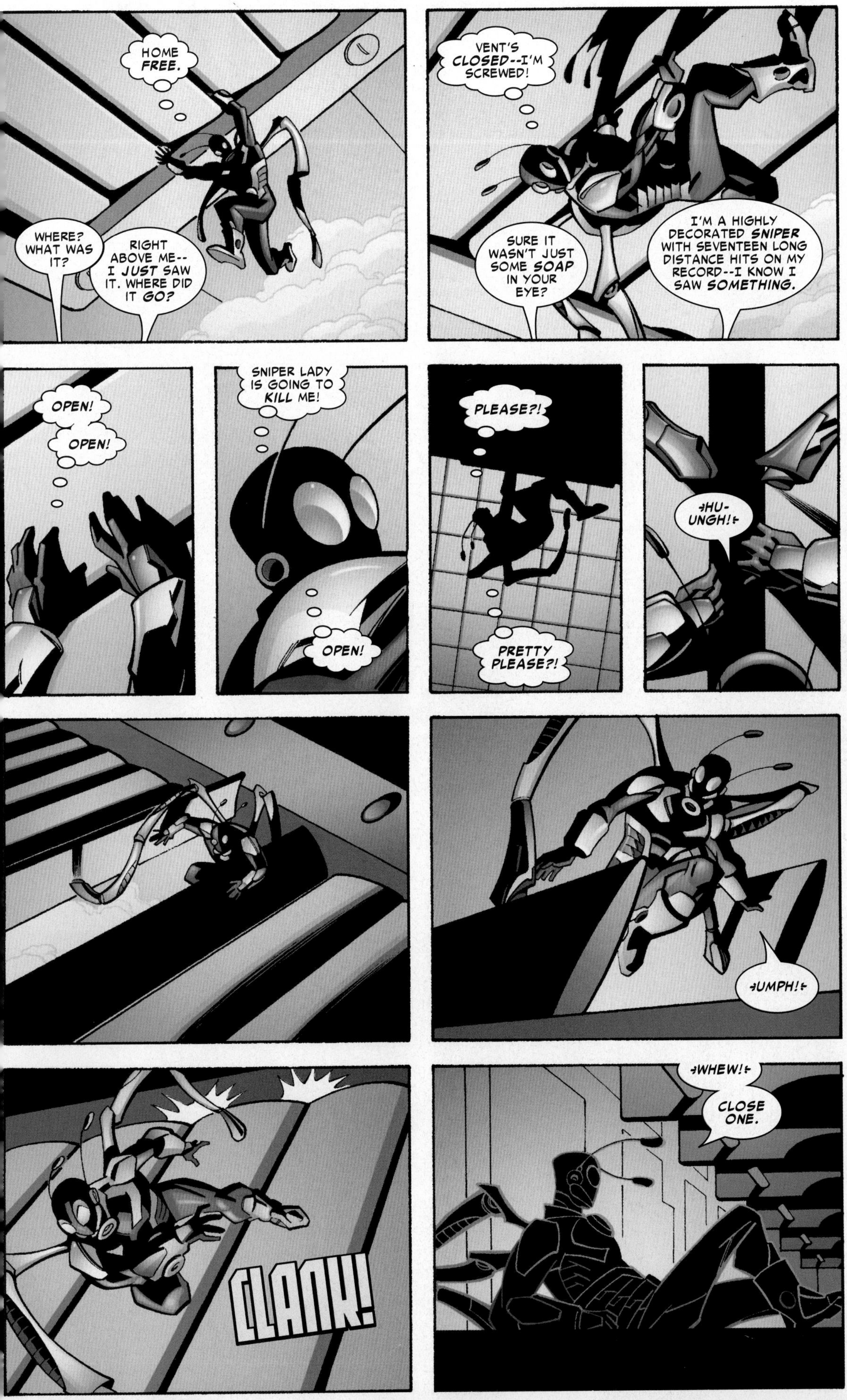
HOME FREE.
WHERE? WHAT WAS IT?
RIGHT ABOVE ME-- I JUST SAW IT. WHERE DID IT GO?
VENT'S CLOSED--I'M SCREWED!
SURE IT WASN'T JUST SOME SOAP IN YOUR EYE?
I'M A HIGHLY DECORATED SNIPER WITH SEVENTEEN LONG DISTANCE HITS ON MY RECORD--I KNOW I SAW SOMETHING.
OPEN!
OPEN!
SNIPER LADY IS GOING TO KILL ME!
OPEN!
PLEASE?!
PRETTY PLEASE?!
HU-UNGH!
UMPH!
CLANK!
WHEW!
CLOSE ONE.

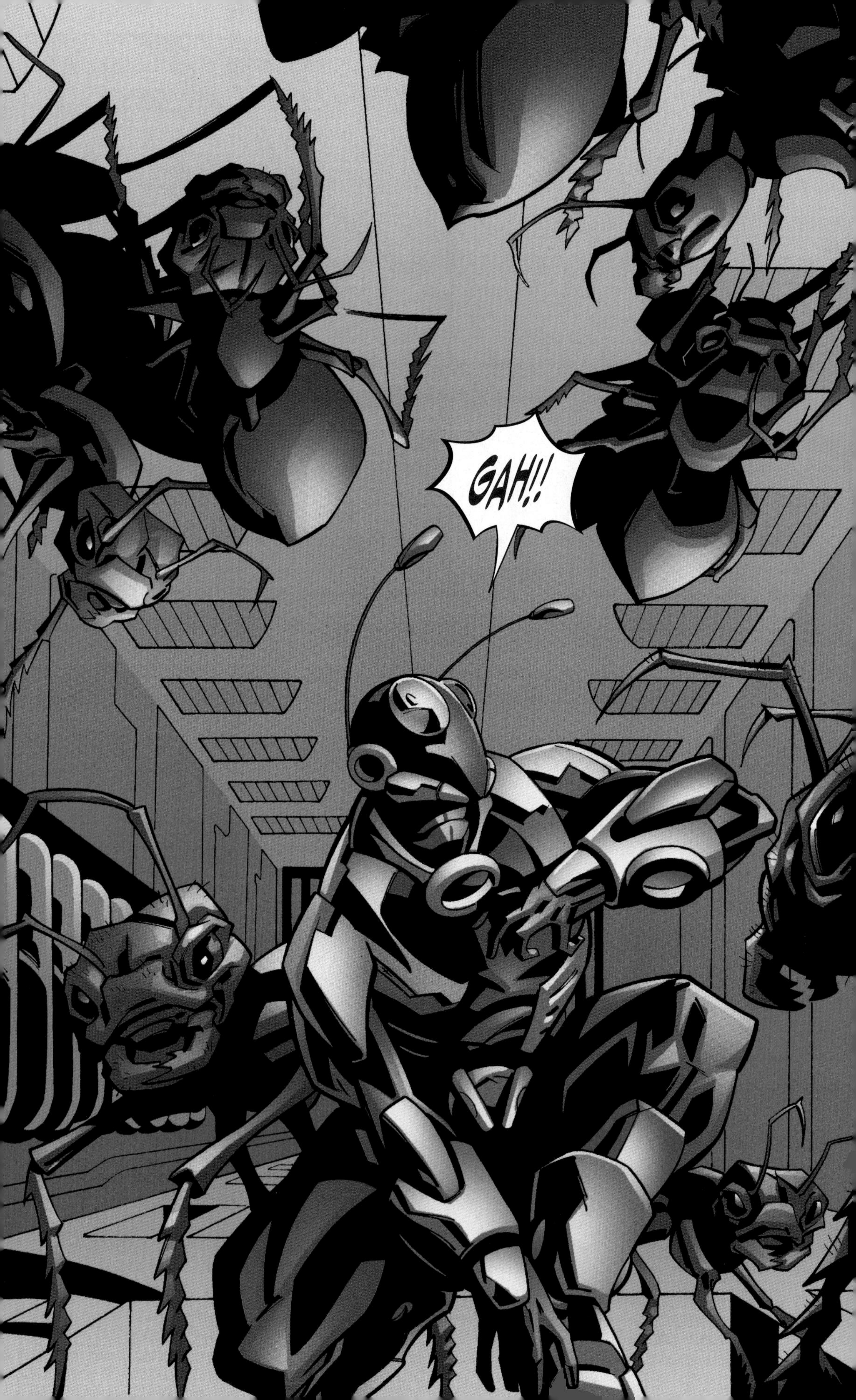
GAH!!

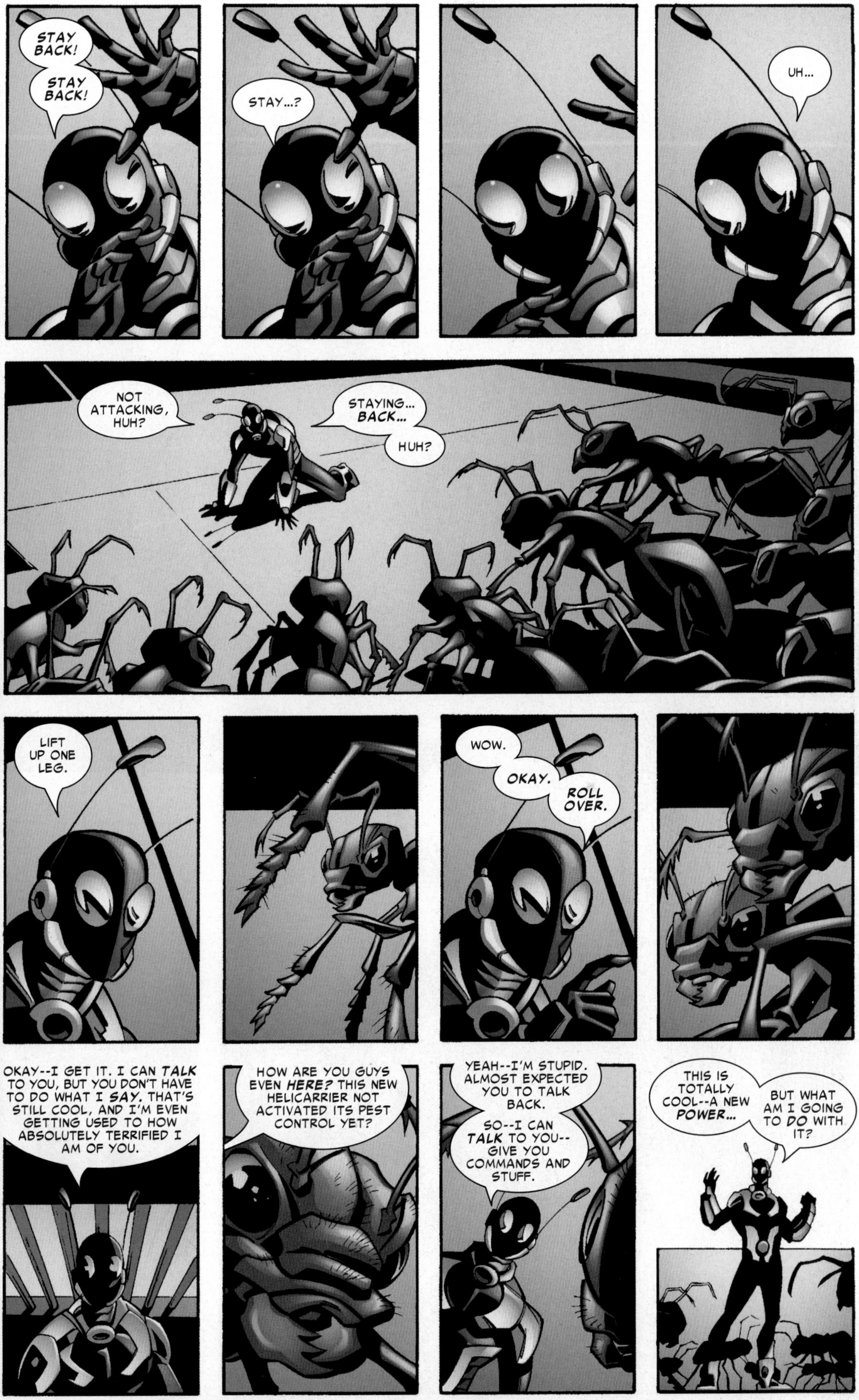
STAY BACK!
STAY BACK!
STAY...?
UH...
NOT ATTACKING, HUH?
STAYING... BACK...
HUH?
LIFT UP ONE LEG.
WOW.
OKAY.
ROLL OVER.
OKAY--I GET IT. I CAN TALK TO YOU, BUT YOU DON'T HAVE TO DO WHAT I SAY. THAT'S STILL COOL, AND I'M EVEN GETTING USED TO HOW ABSOLUTELY TERRIFIED I AM OF YOU.
HOW ARE YOU GUYS EVEN HERE? THIS NEW HELICARRIER NOT ACTIVATED ITS PEST CONTROL YET?
YEAH--I'M STUPID. ALMOST EXPECTED YOU TO TALK BACK.
SO--I CAN TALK TO YOU--GIVE YOU COMMANDS AND STUFF.
THIS IS TOTALLY COOL--A NEW POWER...
BUT WHAT AM I GOING TO DO WITH IT?

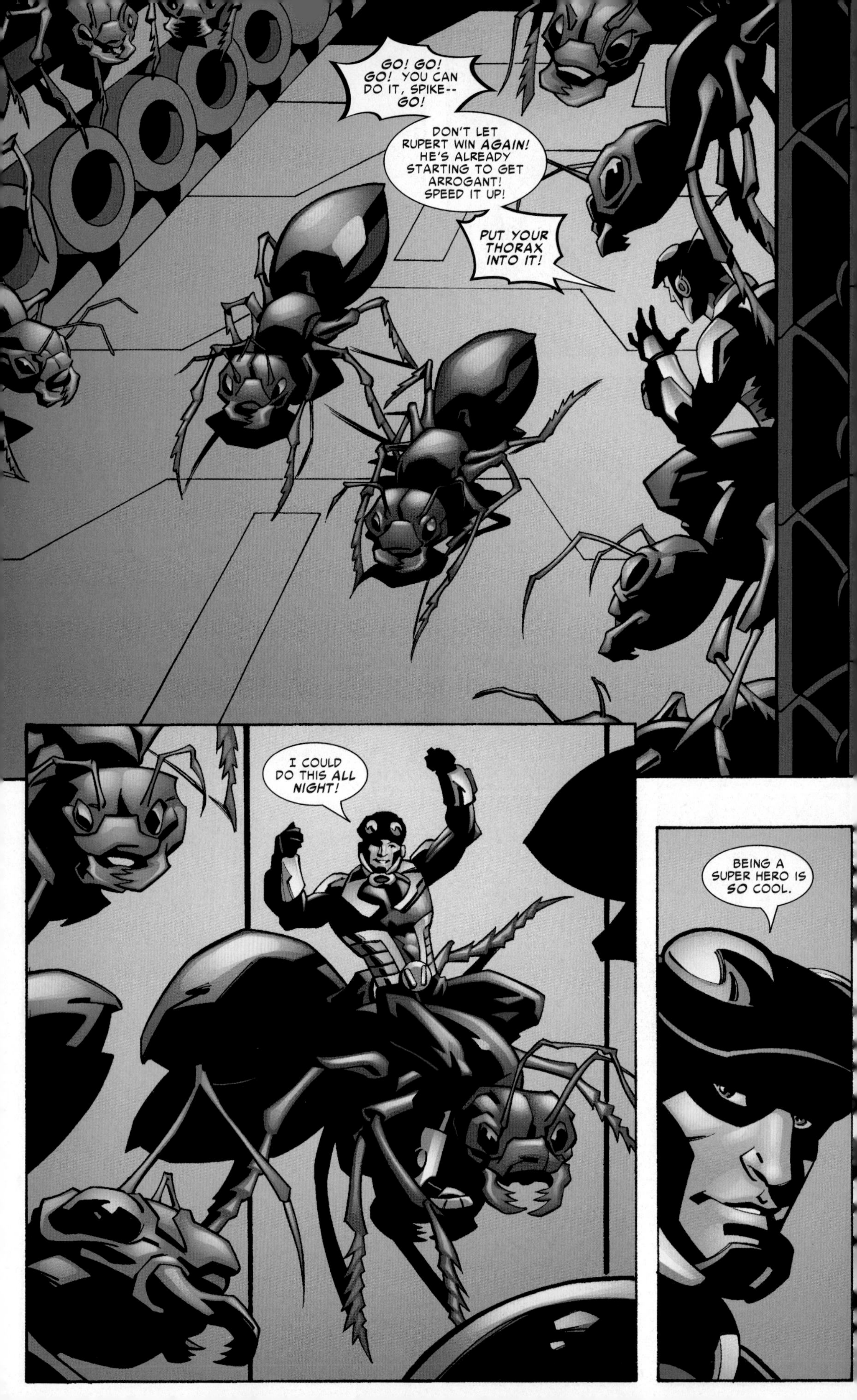
GO! GO! GO! YOU CAN DO IT, SPIKE-- GO!
DON'T LET RUPERT WIN AGAIN! HE'S ALREADY STARTING TO GET ARROGANT! SPEED IT UP!
PUT YOUR THORAX INTO IT!
I COULD DO THIS ALL NIGHT!
BEING A SUPER HERO IS SO COOL.

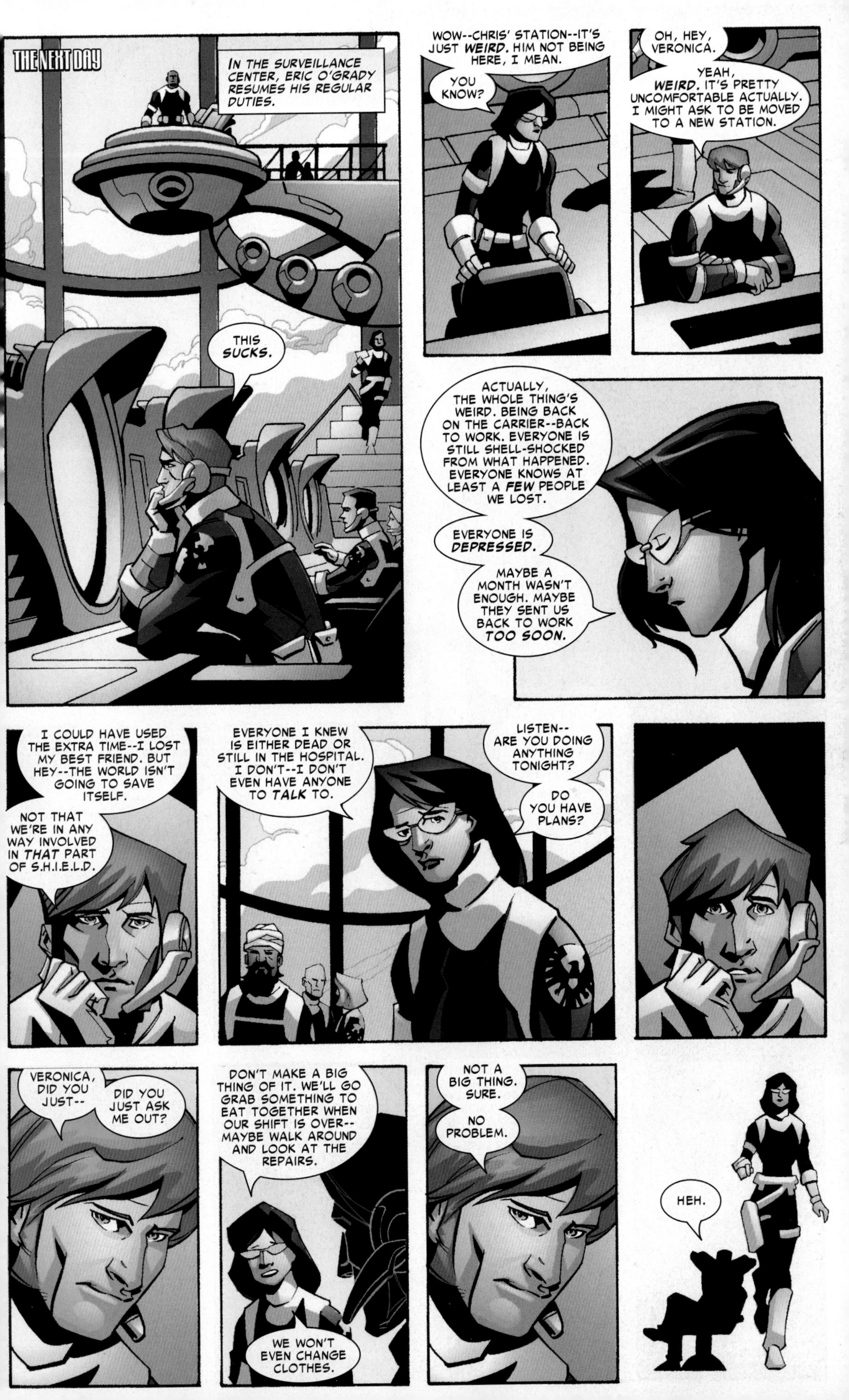
THE NEXT DAY
IN THE SURVEILLANCE CENTER, ERIC O'GRADY RESUMES HIS REGULAR DUTIES.
THIS SUCKS.
WOW--CHRIS' STATION--IT'S JUST WEIRD. HIM NOT BEING HERE, I MEAN.
YOU KNOW?
OH, HEY, VERONICA.
YEAH, WEIRD. IT'S PRETTY UNCOMFORTABLE ACTUALLY. I MIGHT ASK TO BE MOVED TO A NEW STATION.
ACTUALLY, THE WHOLE THING'S WEIRD. BEING BACK ON THE CARRIER--BACK TO WORK. EVERYONE IS STILL SHELL-SHOCKED FROM WHAT HAPPENED. EVERYONE KNOWS AT LEAST A FEW PEOPLE WE LOST.
EVERYONE IS DEPRESSED.
MAYBE A MONTH WASN'T ENOUGH. MAYBE THEY SENT US BACK TO WORK TOO SOON.
I COULD HAVE USED THE EXTRA TIME--I LOST MY BEST FRIEND. BUT HEY--THE WORLD ISN'T GOING TO SAVE ITSELF.
NOT THAT WE'RE IN ANY WAY INVOLVED IN THAT PART OF S.H.I.E.L.D.
EVERYONE I KNEW IS EITHER DEAD OR STILL IN THE HOSPITAL. I DON'T--I DON'T EVEN HAVE ANYONE TO TALK TO.
LISTEN--ARE YOU DOING ANYTHING TONIGHT?
DO YOU HAVE PLANS?
VERONICA, DID YOU JUST--
DID YOU JUST ASK ME OUT?
DON'T MAKE A BIG THING OF IT. WE'LL GO GRAB SOMETHING TO EAT TOGETHER WHEN OUR SHIFT IS OVER--MAYBE WALK AROUND AND LOOK AT THE REPAIRS.
WE WON'T EVEN CHANGE CLOTHES.
NOT A BIG THING. SURE.
NO PROBLEM.
HEH.

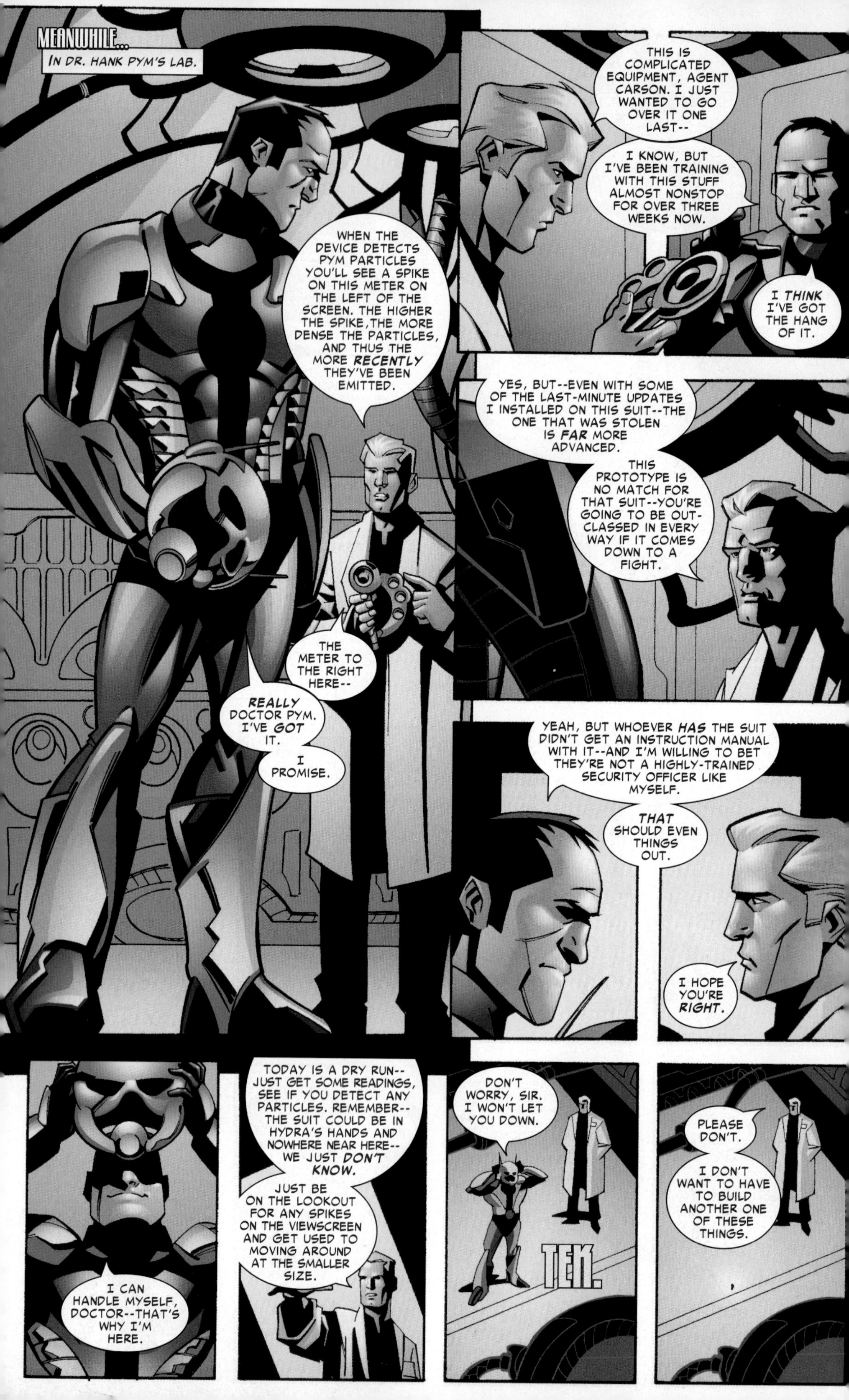
MEANWHILE...
IN DR. HANK PYM'S LAB.
WHEN THE DEVICE DETECTS PYM PARTICLES YOU'LL SEE A SPIKE ON THIS METER ON THE LEFT OF THE SCREEN. THE HIGHER THE SPIKE, THE MORE DENSE THE PARTICLES, AND THUS THE MORE RECENTLY THEY'VE BEEN EMITTED.
THE METER TO THE RIGHT HERE--
REALLY DOCTOR PYM. I'VE GOT IT.
I PROMISE.
THIS IS COMPLICATED EQUIPMENT, AGENT CARSON. I JUST WANTED TO GO OVER IT ONE LAST--
I KNOW, BUT I'VE BEEN TRAINING WITH THIS STUFF ALMOST NONSTOP FOR OVER THREE WEEKS NOW.
I THINK I'VE GOT THE HANG OF IT.
YES, BUT--EVEN WITH SOME OF THE LAST-MINUTE UPDATES I INSTALLED ON THIS SUIT--THE ONE THAT WAS STOLEN IS FAR MORE ADVANCED.
THIS PROTOTYPE IS NO MATCH FOR THAT SUIT--YOU'RE GOING TO BE OUT-CLASSED IN EVERY WAY IF IT COMES DOWN TO A FIGHT.
YEAH, BUT WHOEVER HAS THE SUIT DIDN'T GET AN INSTRUCTION MANUAL WITH IT--AND I'M WILLING TO BET THEY'RE NOT A HIGHLY-TRAINED SECURITY OFFICER LIKE MYSELF.
THAT SHOULD EVEN THINGS OUT.
I HOPE YOU'RE RIGHT.
I CAN HANDLE MYSELF, DOCTOR--THAT'S WHY I'M HERE.
TODAY IS A DRY RUN--JUST GET SOME READINGS, SEE IF YOU DETECT ANY PARTICLES. REMEMBER--THE SUIT COULD BE IN HYDRA'S HANDS AND NOWHERE NEAR HERE--WE JUST DON'T KNOW.
JUST BE ON THE LOOKOUT FOR ANY SPIKES ON THE VIEWSCREEN AND GET USED TO MOVING AROUND AT THE SMALLER SIZE.
DON'T WORRY, SIR. I WON'T LET YOU DOWN.
TEK.
PLEASE DON'T.
I DON'T WANT TO HAVE TO BUILD ANOTHER ONE OF THESE THINGS.

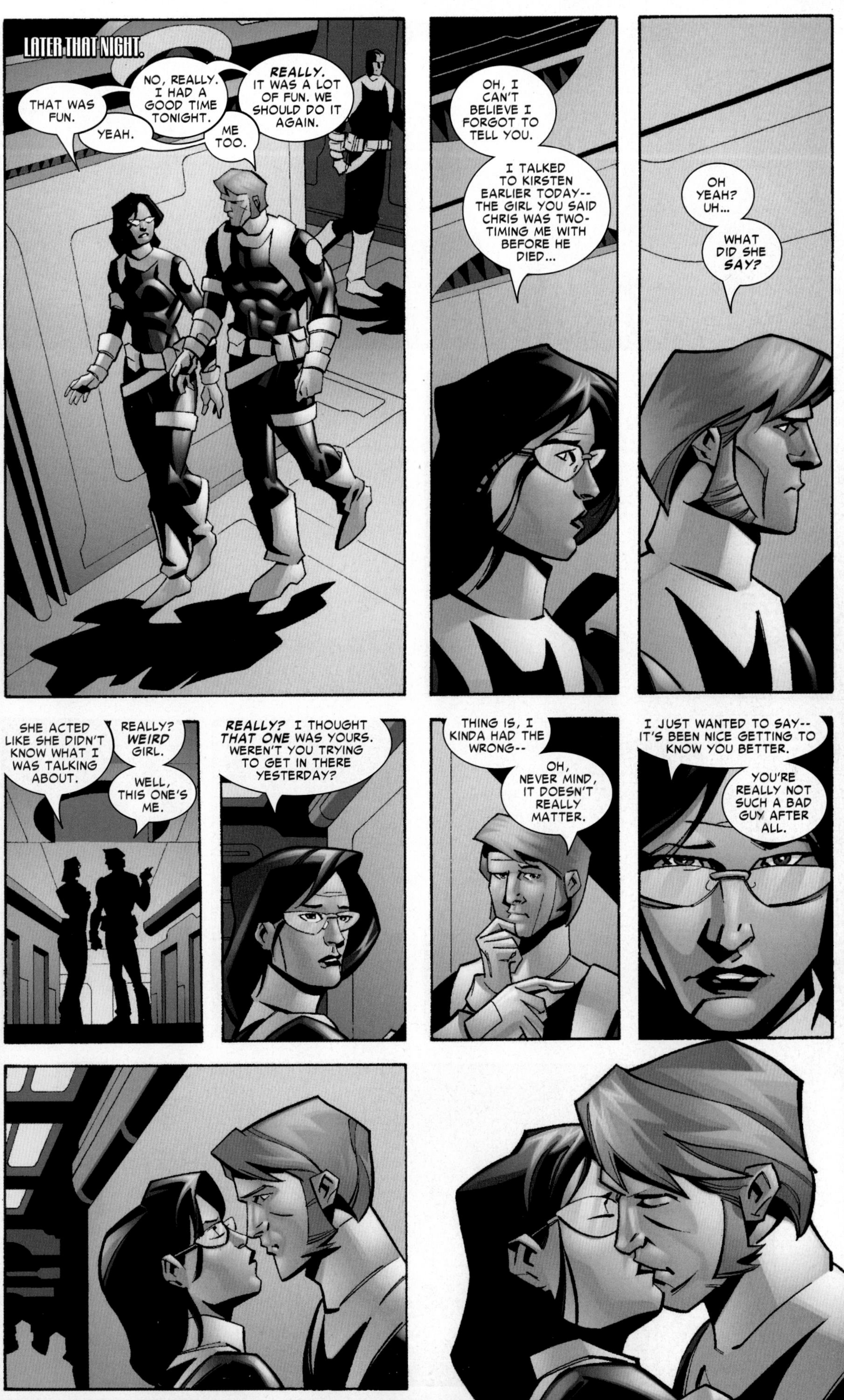
LATER THAT NIGHT.
THAT WAS FUN.
YEAH.
NO, REALLY. I HAD A GOOD TIME TONIGHT.
ME TOO.
REALLY. IT WAS A LOT OF FUN. WE SHOULD DO IT AGAIN.
OH, I CAN'T BELIEVE I FORGOT TO TELL YOU.
I TALKED TO KIRSTEN EARLIER TODAY-- THE GIRL YOU SAID CHRIS WAS TWO-TIMING ME WITH BEFORE HE DIED...
OH YEAH? UH...
WHAT DID SHE SAY?
SHE ACTED LIKE SHE DIDN'T KNOW WHAT I WAS TALKING ABOUT.
REALLY? WEIRD GIRL.
WELL, THIS ONE'S ME.
REALLY? I THOUGHT THAT ONE WAS YOURS. WEREN'T YOU TRYING TO GET IN THERE YESTERDAY?
THING IS, I KINDA HAD THE WRONG--
OH, NEVER MIND, IT DOESN'T REALLY MATTER.
I JUST WANTED TO SAY-- IT'S BEEN NICE GETTING TO KNOW YOU BETTER.
YOU'RE REALLY NOT SUCH A BAD GUY AFTER ALL.

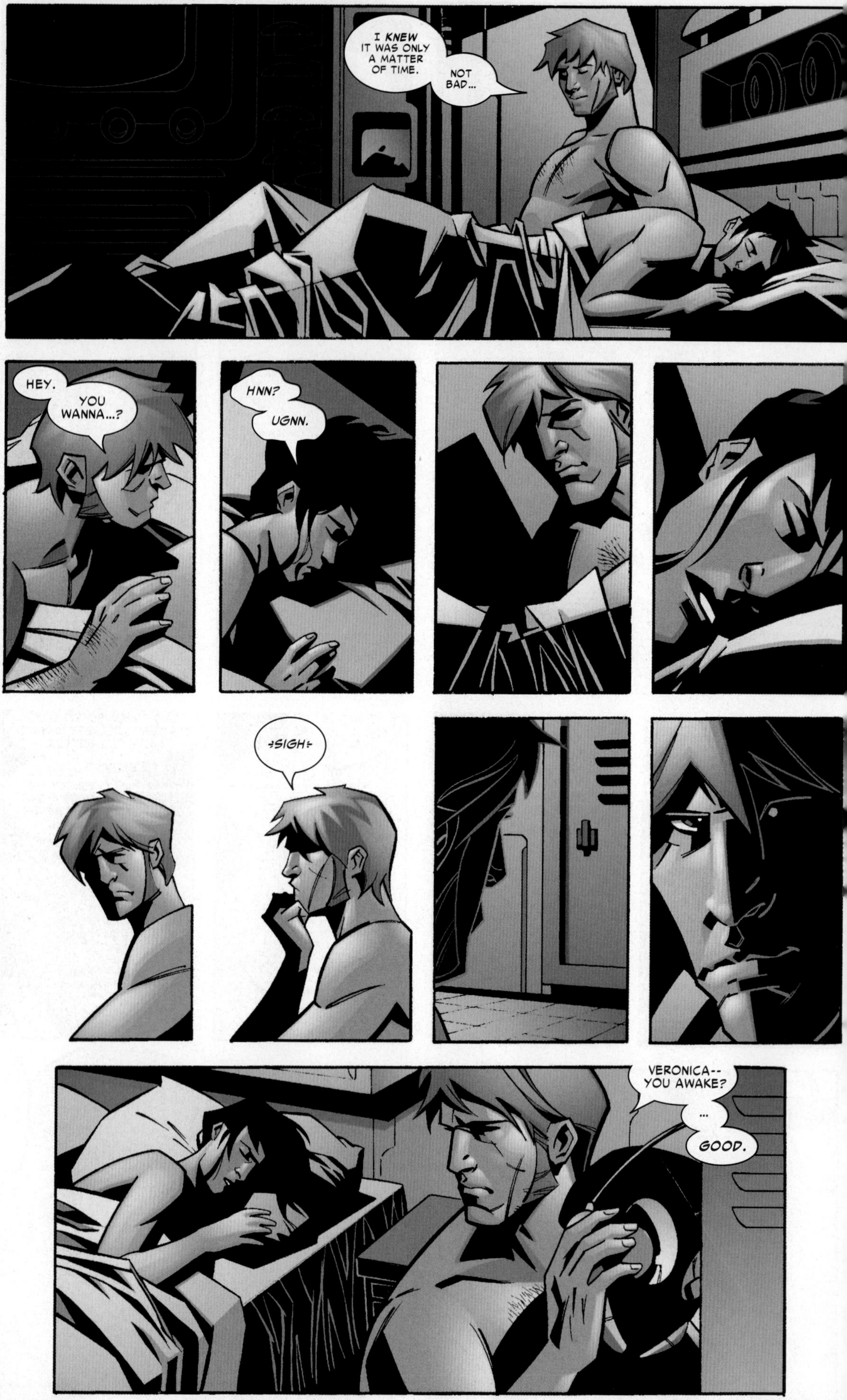
I KNEW IT WAS ONLY A MATTER OF TIME.
NOT BAD...
HEY.
YOU WANNA...?
HNN?
UGNN.
-SIGH-
VERONICA-- YOU AWAKE?
...
GOOD.

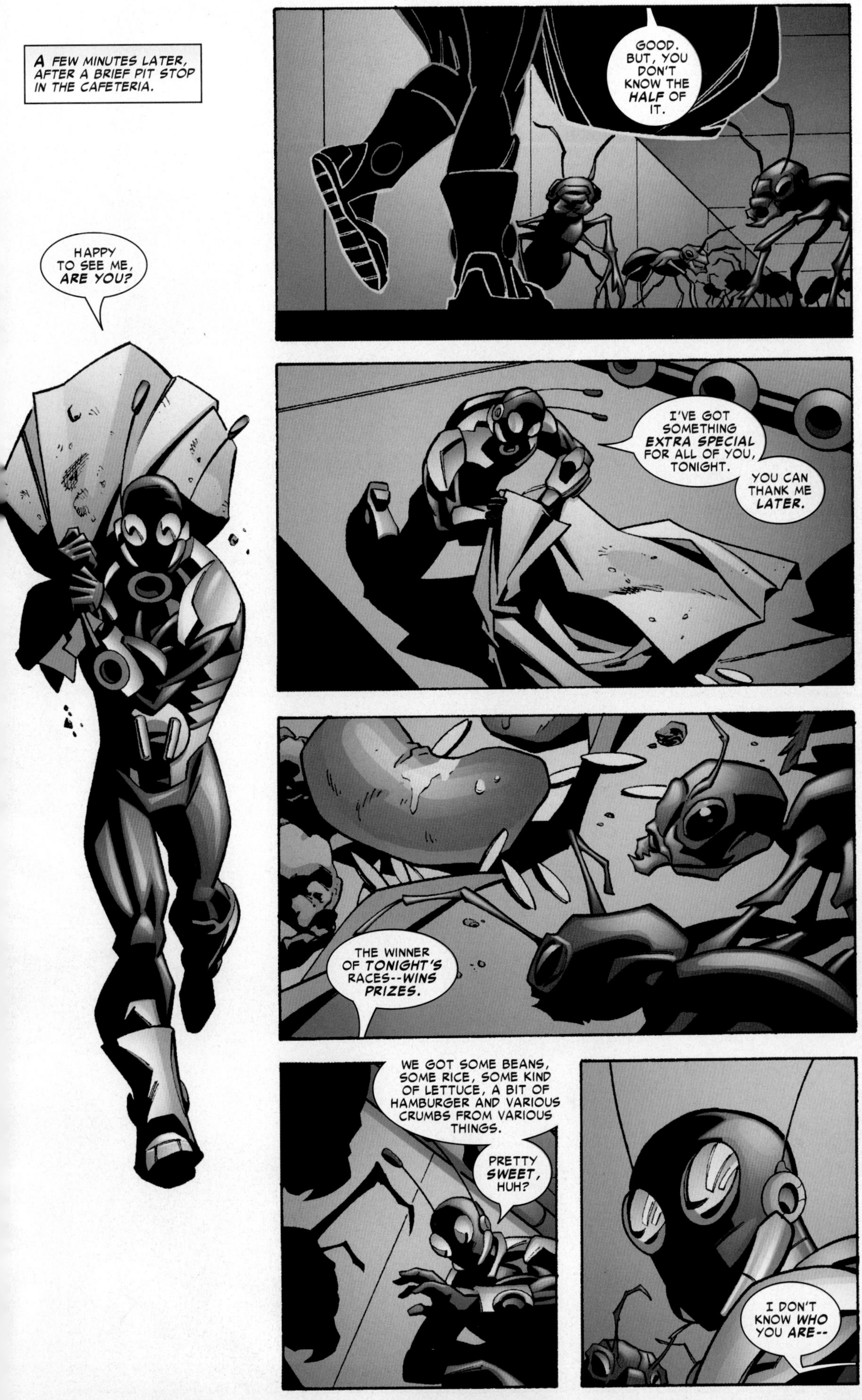
A FEW MINUTES LATER, AFTER A BRIEF PIT STOP IN THE CAFETERIA.
HAPPY TO SEE ME, ARE YOU?
GOOD. BUT, YOU DON'T KNOW THE HALF OF IT.
I'VE GOT SOMETHING EXTRA SPECIAL FOR ALL OF YOU, TONIGHT.
YOU CAN THANK ME LATER.
THE WINNER OF TONIGHT'S RACES--WINS PRIZES.
WE GOT SOME BEANS, SOME RICE, SOME KIND OF LETTUCE, A BIT OF HAMBURGER AND VARIOUS CRUMBS FROM VARIOUS THINGS.
PRETTY SWEET, HUH?
I DON'T KNOW WHO YOU ARE--

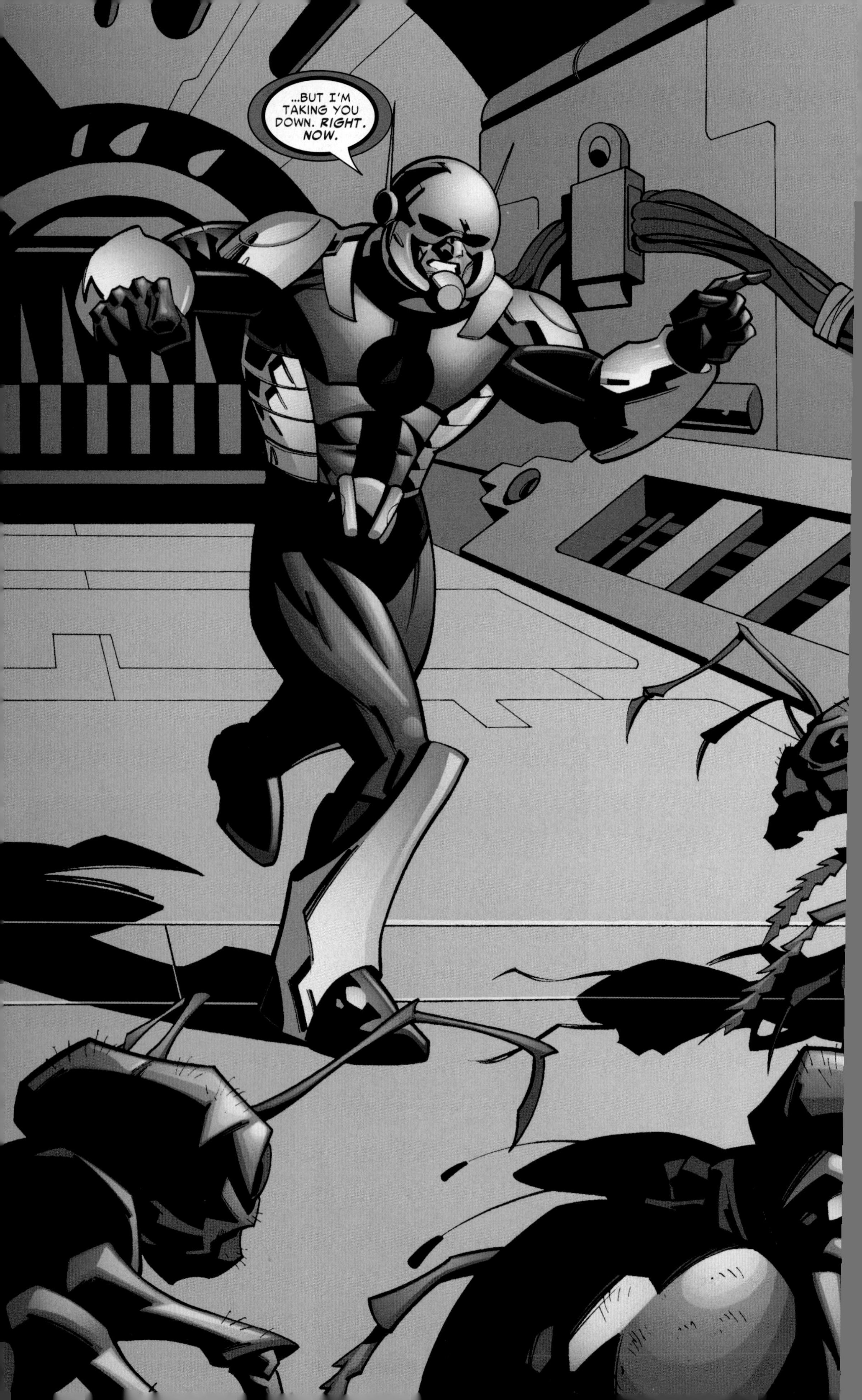
...BUT I'M TAKING YOU DOWN. RIGHT. NOW.

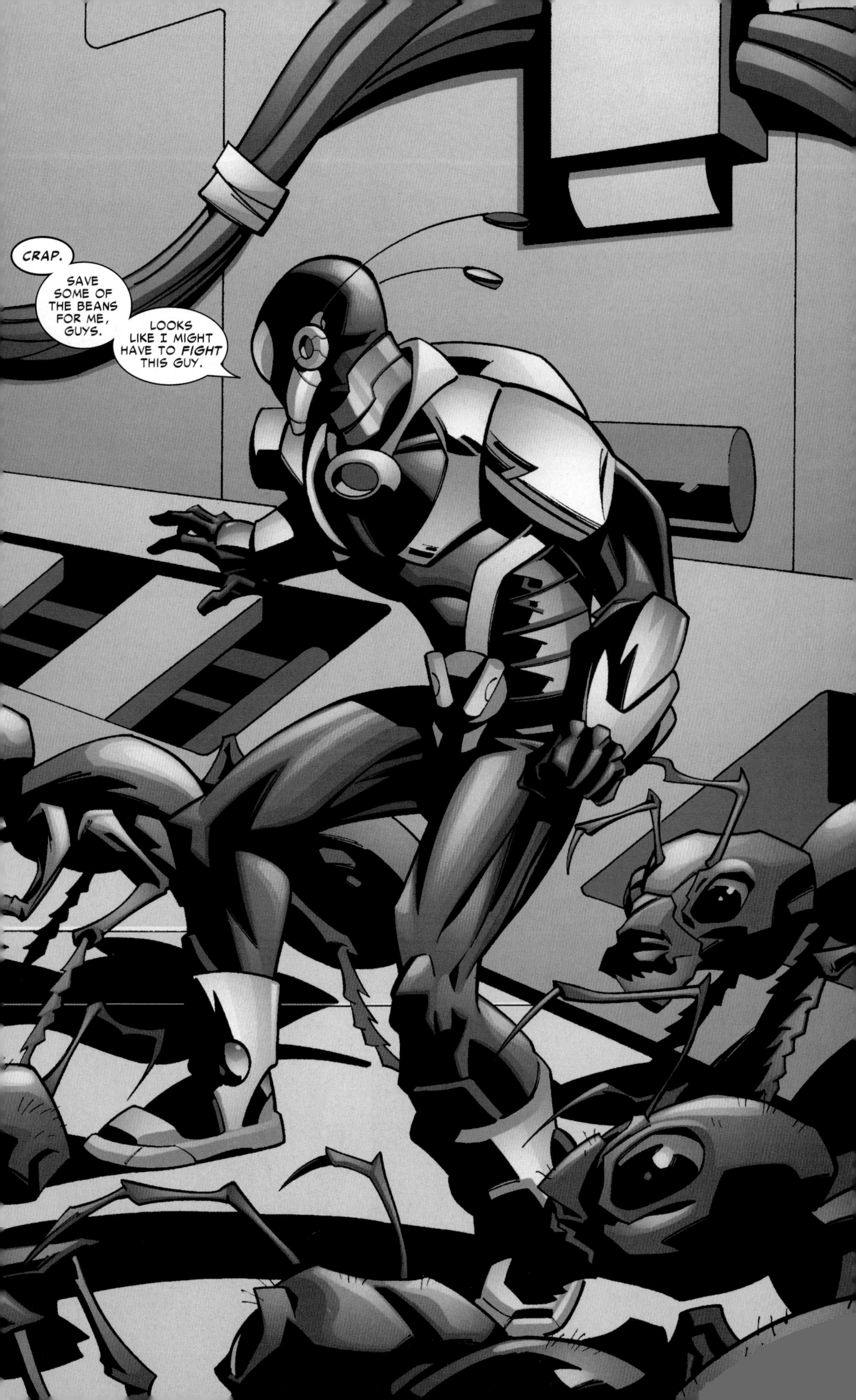
CRAP.
SAVE SOME OF THE BEANS FOR ME, GUYS.
LOOKS LIKE I MIGHT HAVE TO FIGHT THIS GUY.

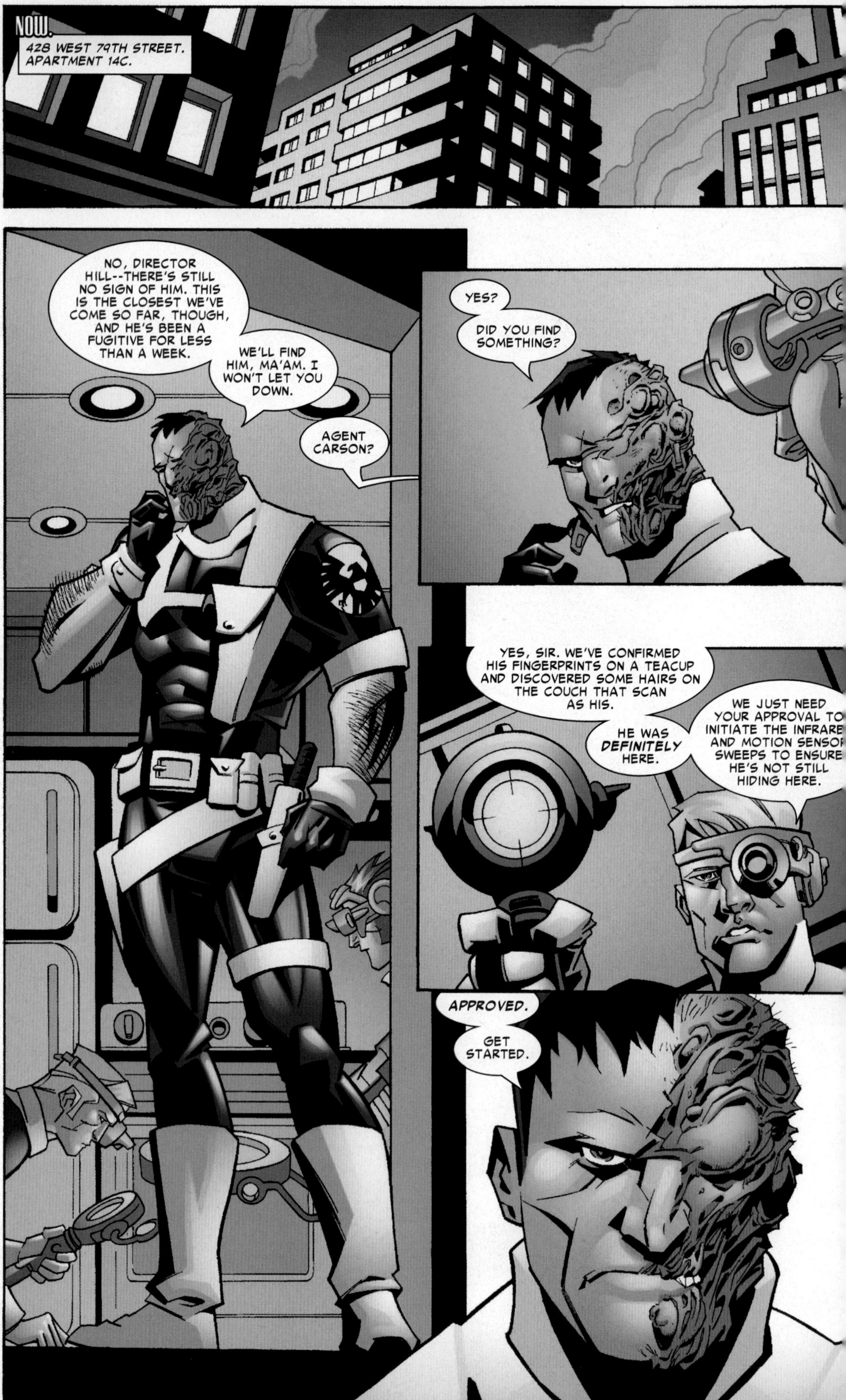
NOW.
428 WEST 79TH STREET. APARTMENT 14C.
NO, DIRECTOR HILL--THERE'S STILL NO SIGN OF HIM. THIS IS THE CLOSEST WE'VE COME SO FAR, THOUGH, AND HE'S BEEN A FUGITIVE FOR LESS THAN A WEEK.
WE'LL FIND HIM, MA'AM. I WON'T LET YOU DOWN.
AGENT CARSON?
YES?
DID YOU FIND SOMETHING?
YES, SIR. WE'VE CONFIRMED HIS FINGERPRINTS ON A TEACUP AND DISCOVERED SOME HAIRS ON THE COUCH THAT SCAN AS HIS.
HE WAS *DEFINITELY* HERE.
WE JUST NEED YOUR APPROVAL TO INITIATE THE INFRARE AND MOTION SENSO SWEEPS TO ENSURE HE'S NOT STILL HIDING HERE.
*APPROVED.*
GET STARTED.

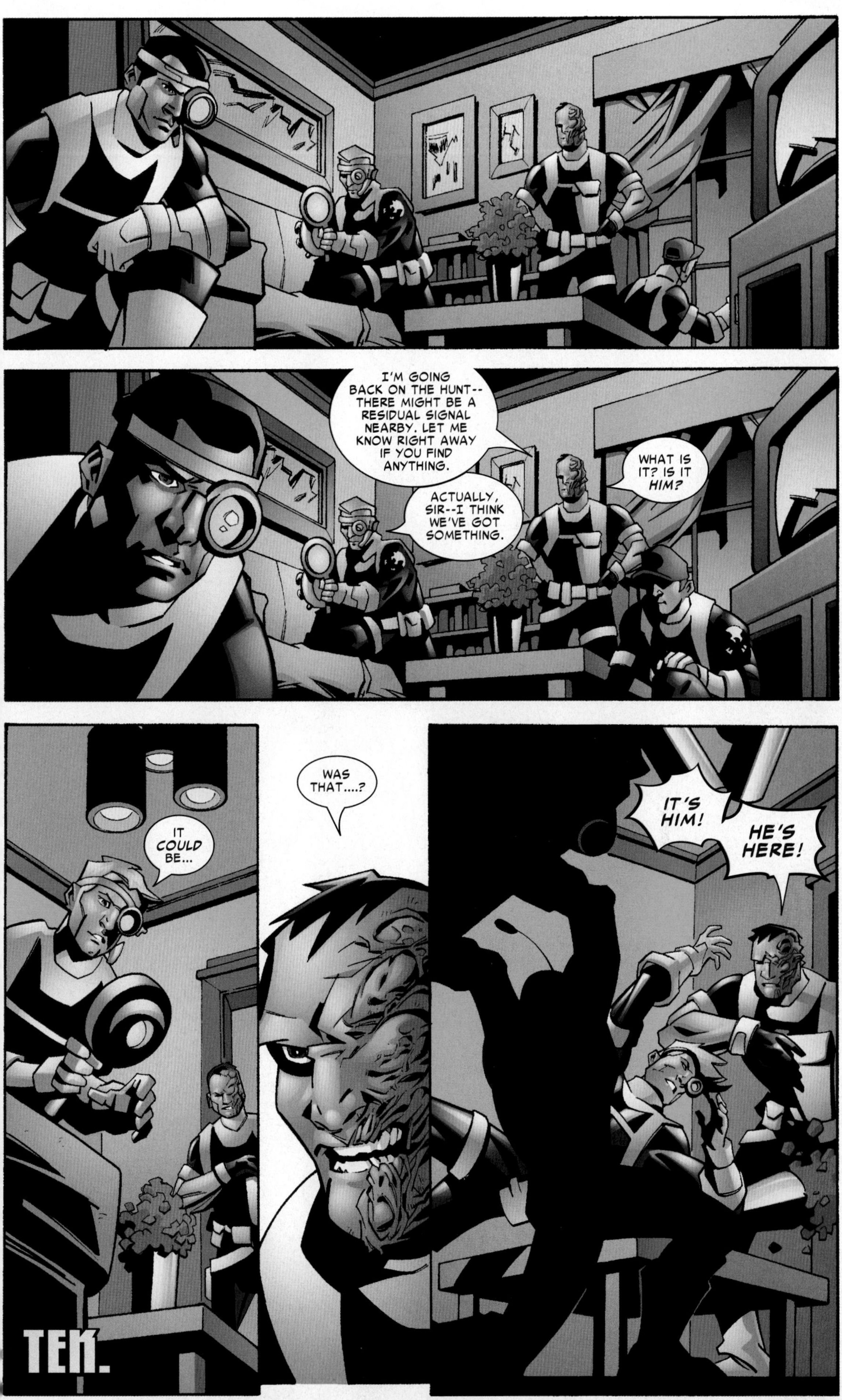
I'M GOING BACK ON THE HUNT-- THERE MIGHT BE A RESIDUAL SIGNAL NEARBY. LET ME KNOW RIGHT AWAY IF YOU FIND ANYTHING.
ACTUALLY, SIR--I THINK WE'VE GOT SOMETHING.
WHAT IS IT? IS IT HIM?
IT COULD BE...
WAS THAT....?
IT'S HIM!
HE'S HERE!
TEK.

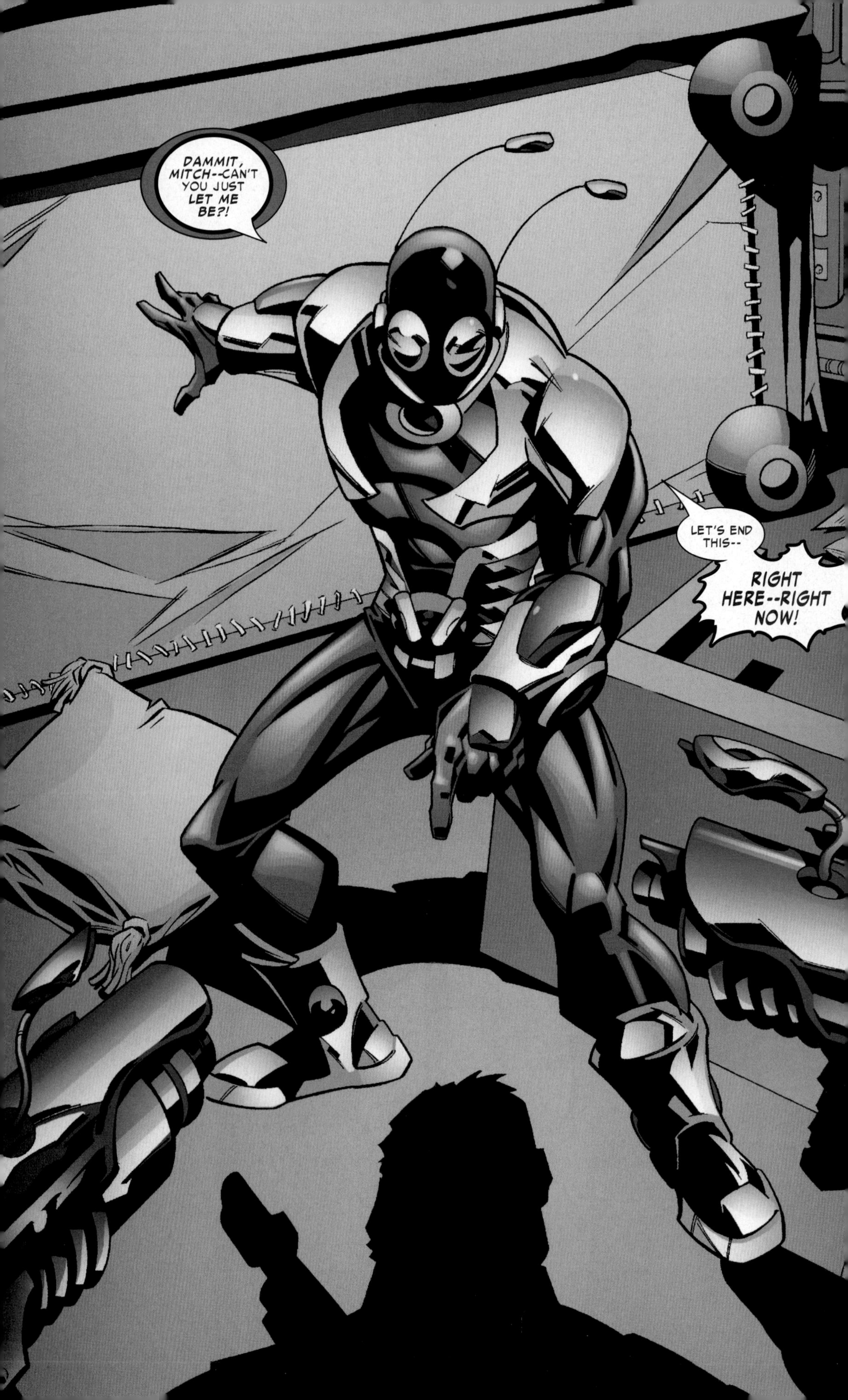
DAMMIT, MITCH--CAN'T YOU JUST LET ME BE?!
LET'S END THIS--
RIGHT HERE--RIGHT NOW!

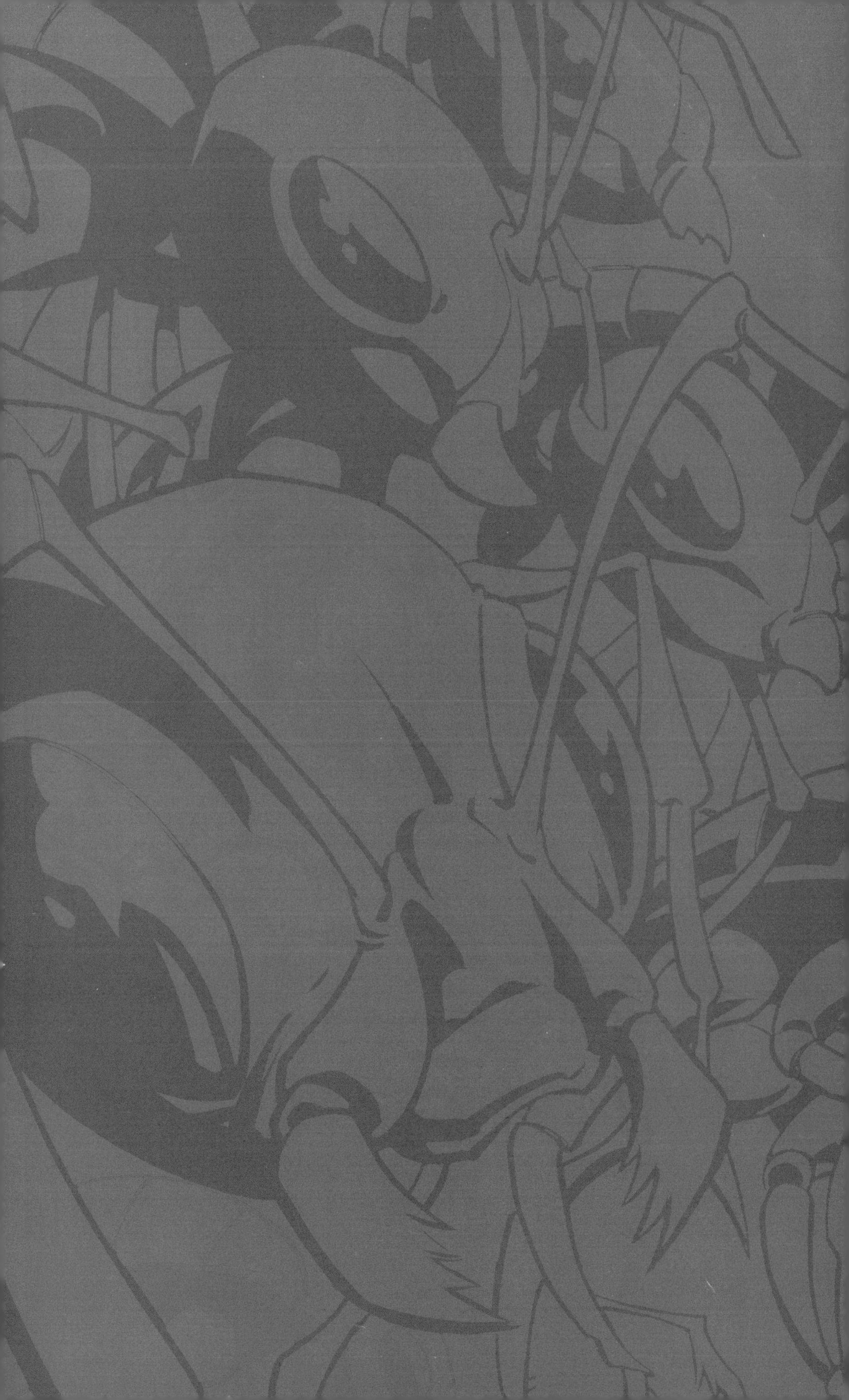

#5

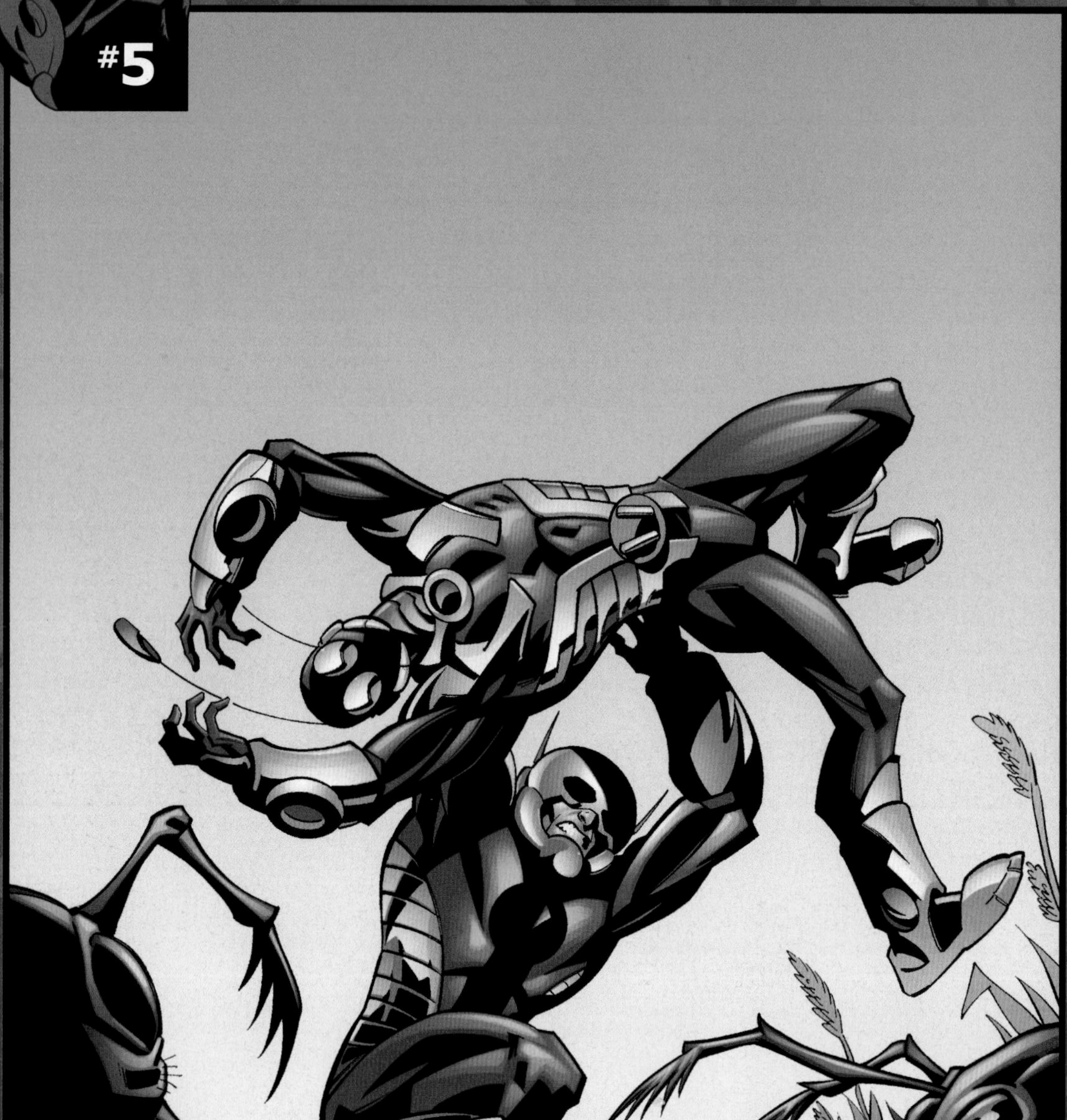

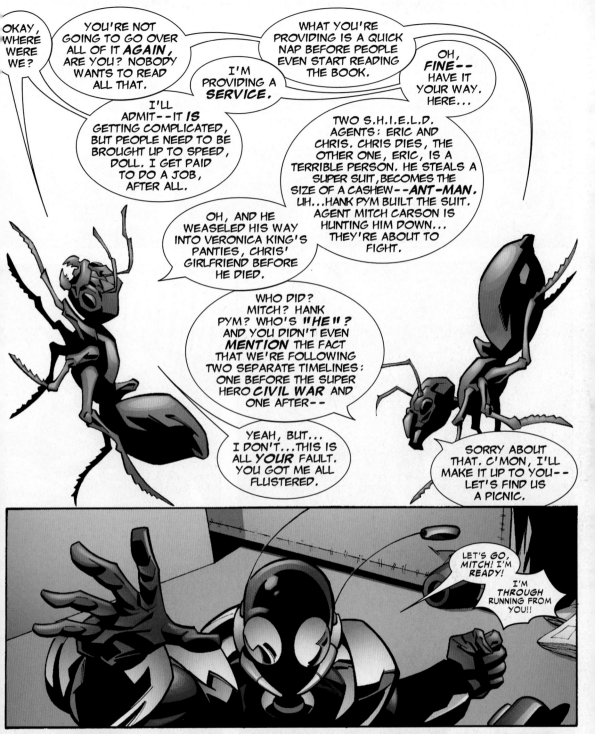

OKAY, WHERE WERE WE?

YOU'RE NOT GOING TO GO OVER ALL OF IT *AGAIN*, ARE YOU? NOBODY WANTS TO READ ALL THAT.

WHAT YOU'RE PROVIDING IS A QUICK NAP BEFORE PEOPLE EVEN START READING THE BOOK.

I'M PROVIDING A *SERVICE*.

OH, *FINE*-- HAVE IT YOUR WAY. HERE...

I'LL ADMIT--IT *IS* GETTING COMPLICATED, BUT PEOPLE NEED TO BE BROUGHT UP TO SPEED, DOLL. I GET PAID TO DO A JOB, AFTER ALL.

TWO S.H.I.E.L.D. AGENTS; ERIC AND CHRIS. CHRIS DIES, THE OTHER ONE, ERIC, IS A TERRIBLE PERSON. HE STEALS A SUPER SUIT, BECOMES THE SIZE OF A CASHEW--*ANT-MAN*. UH...HANK PYM BUILT THE SUIT. AGENT MITCH CARSON IS HUNTING HIM DOWN... THEY'RE ABOUT TO FIGHT.

OH, AND HE WEASELED HIS WAY INTO VERONICA KING'S PANTIES, CHRIS' GIRLFRIEND BEFORE HE DIED.

WHO DID? MITCH? HANK PYM? WHO'S *"HE"*? AND YOU DIDN'T EVEN *MENTION* THE FACT THAT WE'RE FOLLOWING TWO SEPARATE TIMELINES: ONE BEFORE THE SUPER HERO *CIVIL WAR* AND ONE AFTER--

YEAH, BUT... I DON'T...THIS IS ALL *YOUR* FAULT. YOU GOT ME ALL FLUSTERED.

SORRY ABOUT THAT. C'MON, I'LL MAKE IT UP TO YOU-- LET'S FIND US A PICNIC.

LET'S GO, MITCH! I'M READY!

I'M THROUGH RUNNING FROM YOU!!

# CONFRONTATION

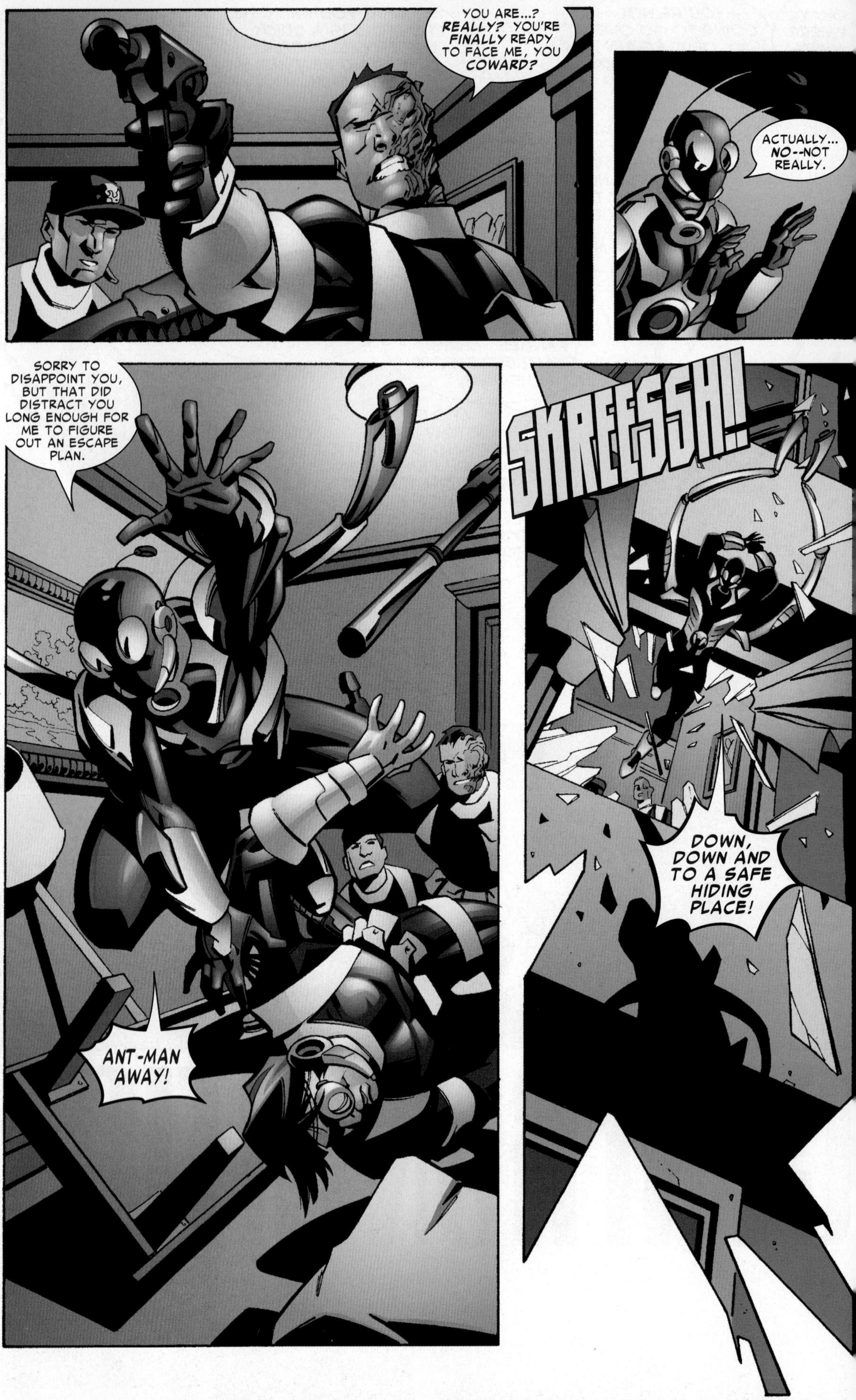
YOU ARE...? REALLY? YOU'RE FINALLY READY TO FACE ME, YOU COWARD?
ACTUALLY... NO--NOT REALLY.
SORRY TO DISAPPOINT YOU, BUT THAT DID DISTRACT YOU LONG ENOUGH FOR ME TO FIGURE OUT AN ESCAPE PLAN.
ANT-MAN AWAY!
SKREESSH!!
DOWN, DOWN AND TO A SAFE HIDING PLACE!

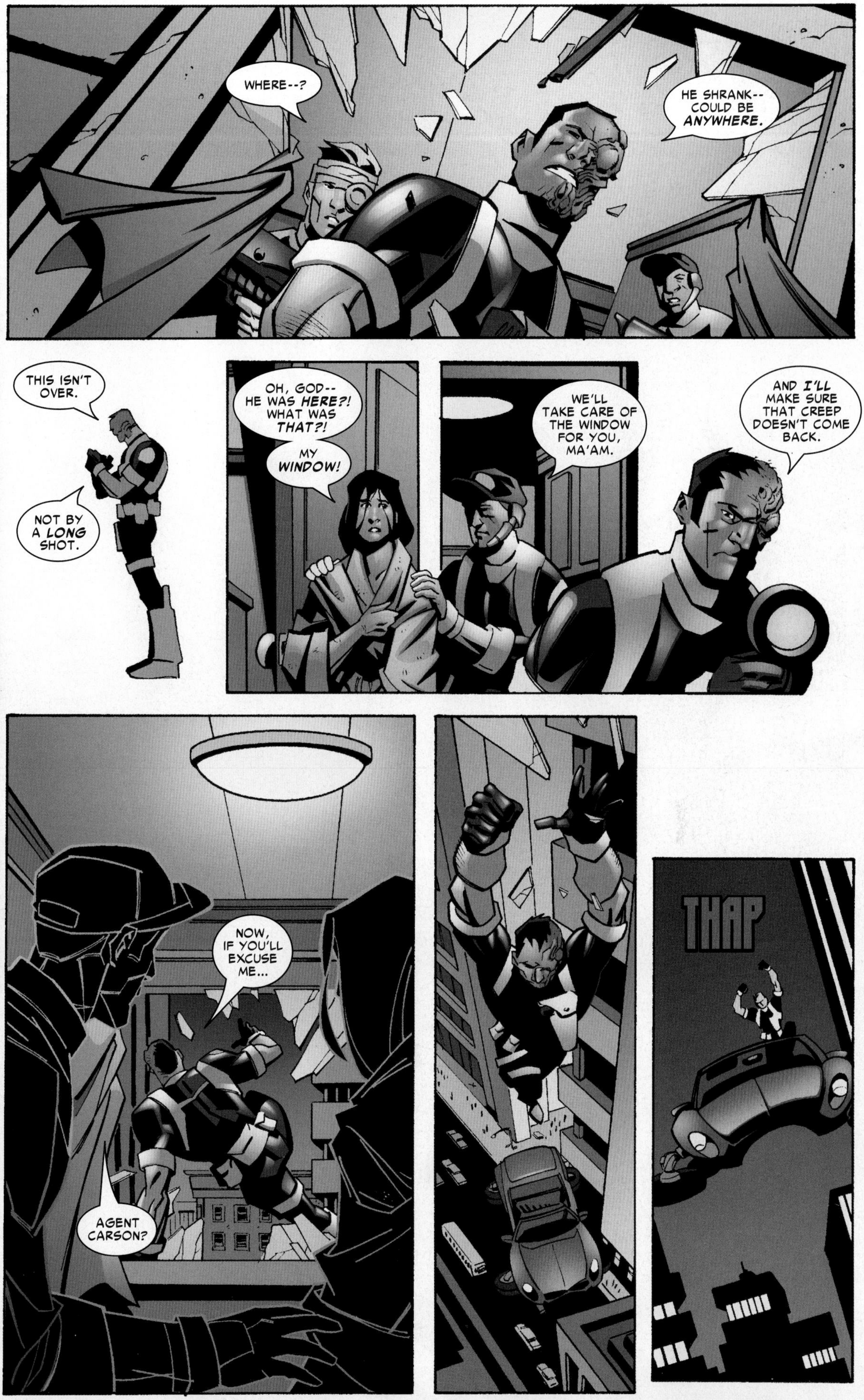
WHERE--?
HE SHRANK-- COULD BE ANYWHERE.
THIS ISN'T OVER.
NOT BY A LONG SHOT.
OH, GOD-- HE WAS HERE?! WHAT WAS THAT?!
MY WINDOW!
WE'LL TAKE CARE OF THE WINDOW FOR YOU, MA'AM.
AND I'LL MAKE SURE THAT CREEP DOESN'T COME BACK.
NOW, IF YOU'LL EXCUSE ME...
AGENT CARSON?
THAP

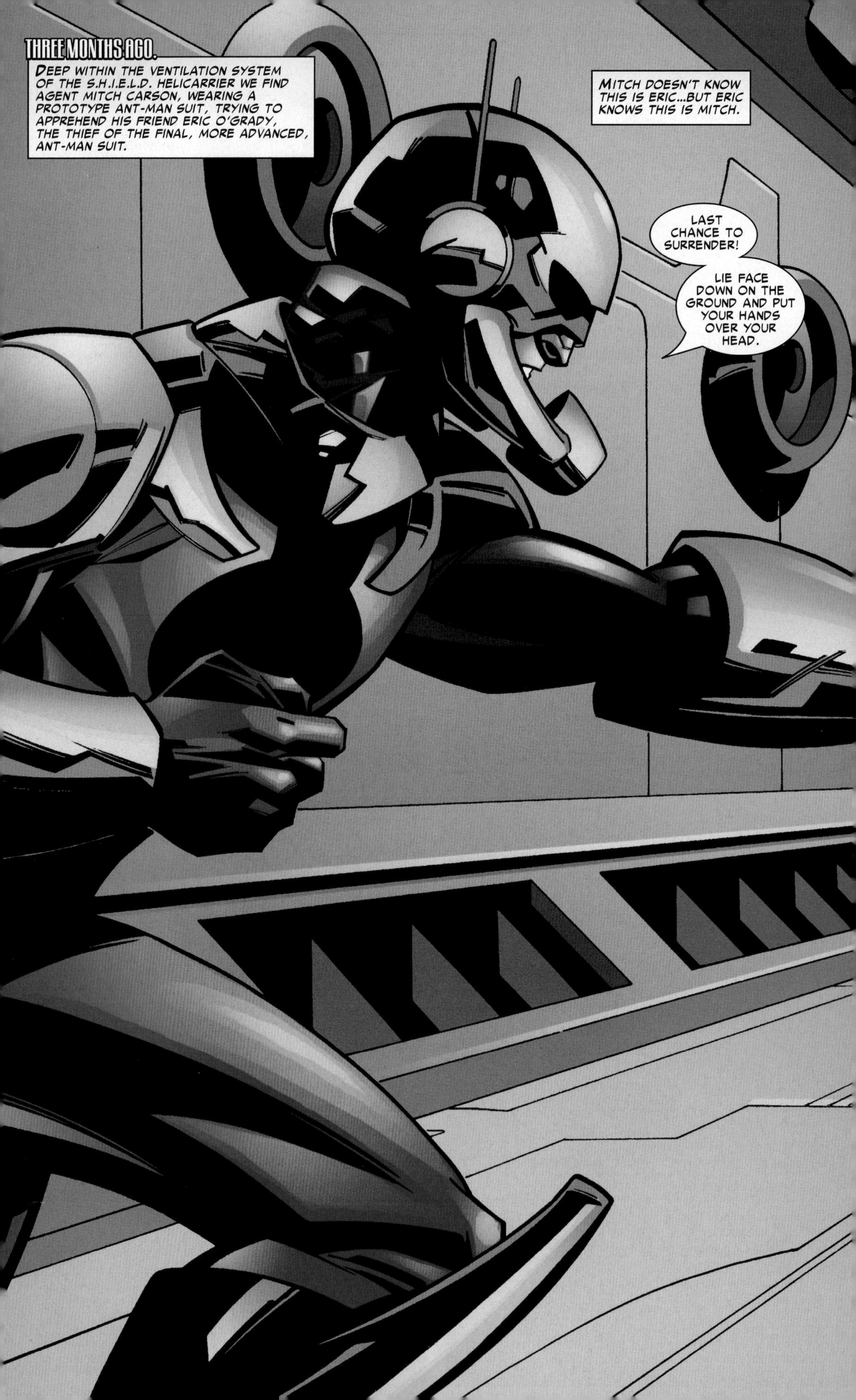
THREE MONTHS AGO.
DEEP WITHIN THE VENTILATION SYSTEM OF THE S.H.I.E.L.D. HELICARRIER WE FIND AGENT MITCH CARSON, WEARING A PROTOTYPE ANT-MAN SUIT, TRYING TO APPREHEND HIS FRIEND ERIC O'GRADY, THE THIEF OF THE FINAL, MORE ADVANCED, ANT-MAN SUIT.
MITCH DOESN'T KNOW THIS IS ERIC...BUT ERIC KNOWS THIS IS MITCH.
LAST CHANCE TO SURRENDER!
LIE FACE DOWN ON THE GROUND AND PUT YOUR HANDS OVER YOUR HEAD.

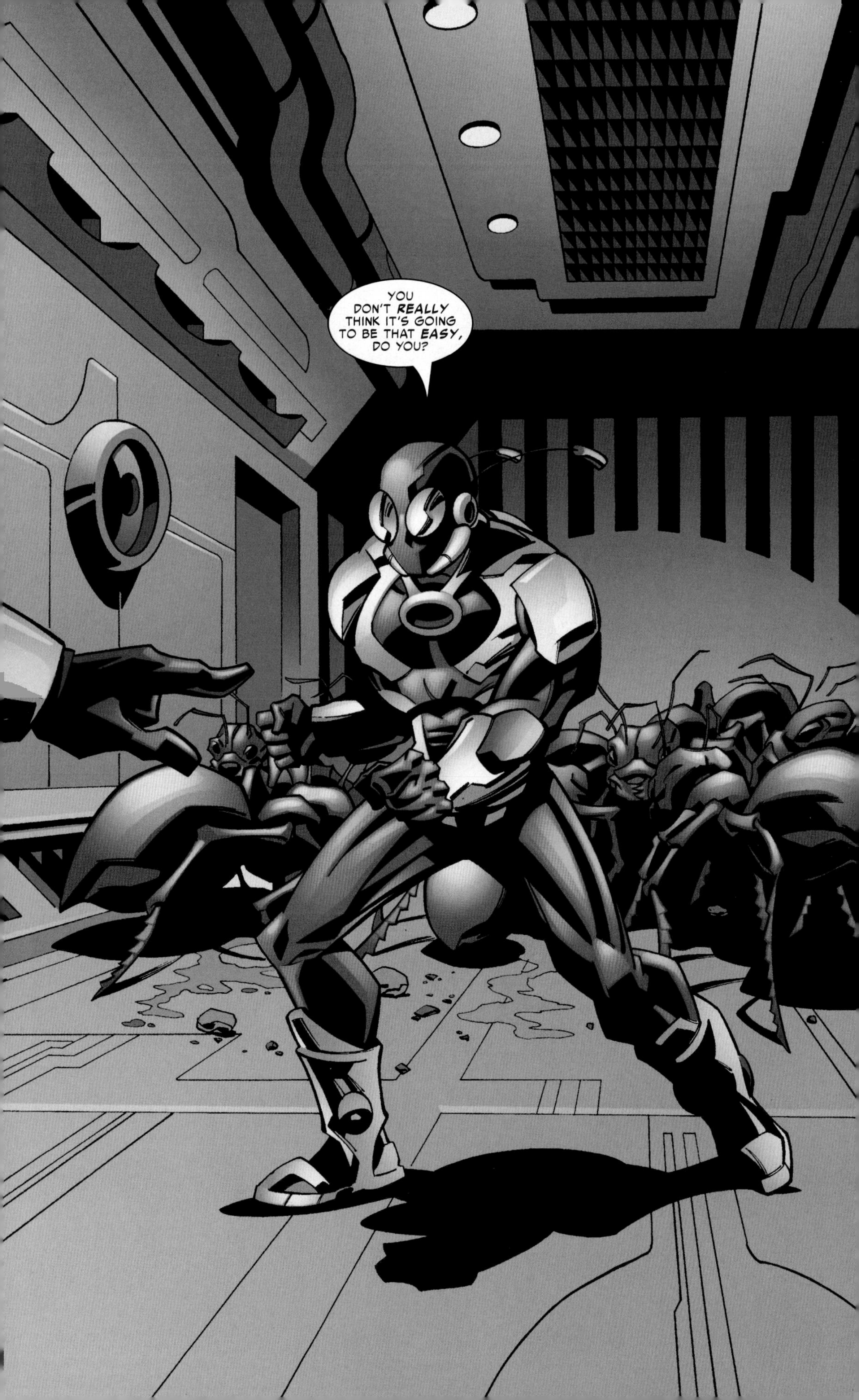
YOU DON'T REALLY THINK IT'S GOING TO BE THAT EASY, DO YOU?

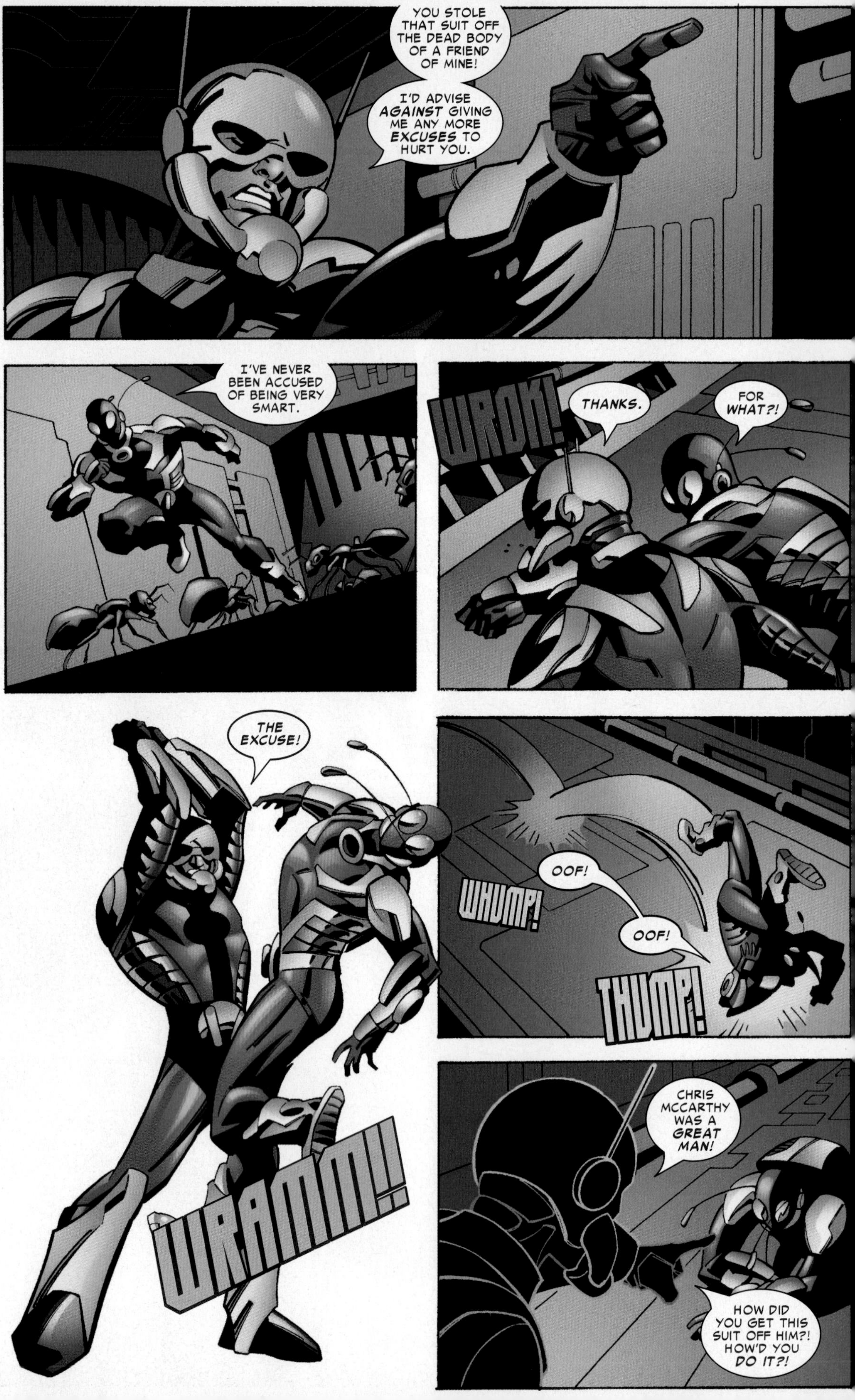
YOU STOLE THAT SUIT OFF THE DEAD BODY OF A FRIEND OF MINE!
I'D ADVISE AGAINST GIVING ME ANY MORE EXCUSES TO HURT YOU.
I'VE NEVER BEEN ACCUSED OF BEING VERY SMART.
WROK!
THANKS.
FOR WHAT?!
THE EXCUSE!
WRAMM!!
WHUMP!
OOF!
OOF!
THUMP!
CHRIS MCCARTHY WAS A GREAT MAN!
HOW DID YOU GET THIS SUIT OFF HIM?! HOW'D YOU DO IT?!

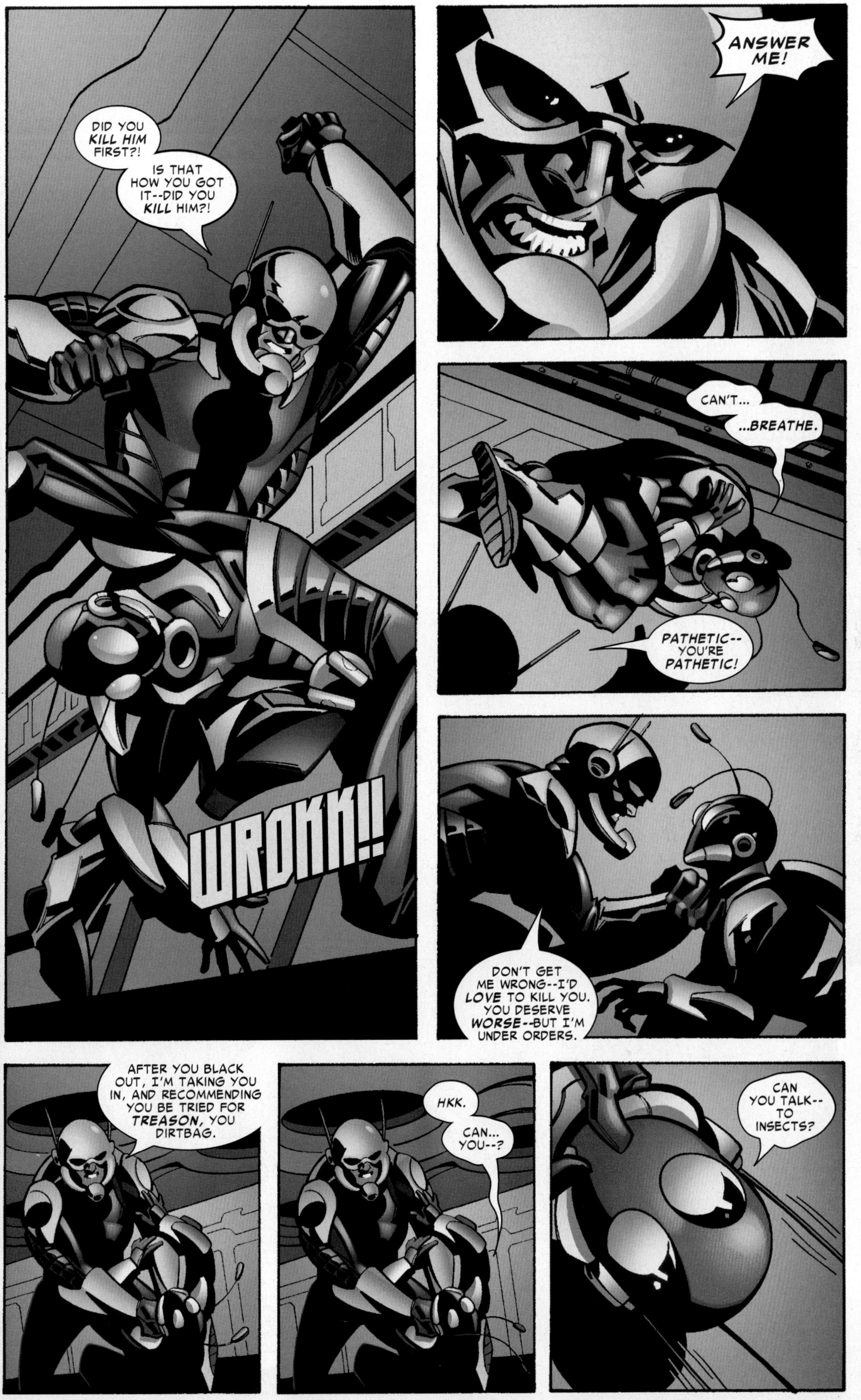
DID YOU KILL HIM FIRST?!
IS THAT HOW YOU GOT IT--DID YOU KILL HIM?!
WROKK!!
ANSWER ME!
CAN'T...
...BREATHE.
PATHETIC--YOU'RE PATHETIC!
DON'T GET ME WRONG--I'D LOVE TO KILL YOU. YOU DESERVE WORSE--BUT I'M UNDER ORDERS.
AFTER YOU BLACK OUT, I'M TAKING YOU IN, AND RECOMMENDING YOU BE TRIED FOR TREASON, YOU DIRTBAG.
HKK.
CAN... YOU--?
CAN YOU TALK--TO INSECTS?

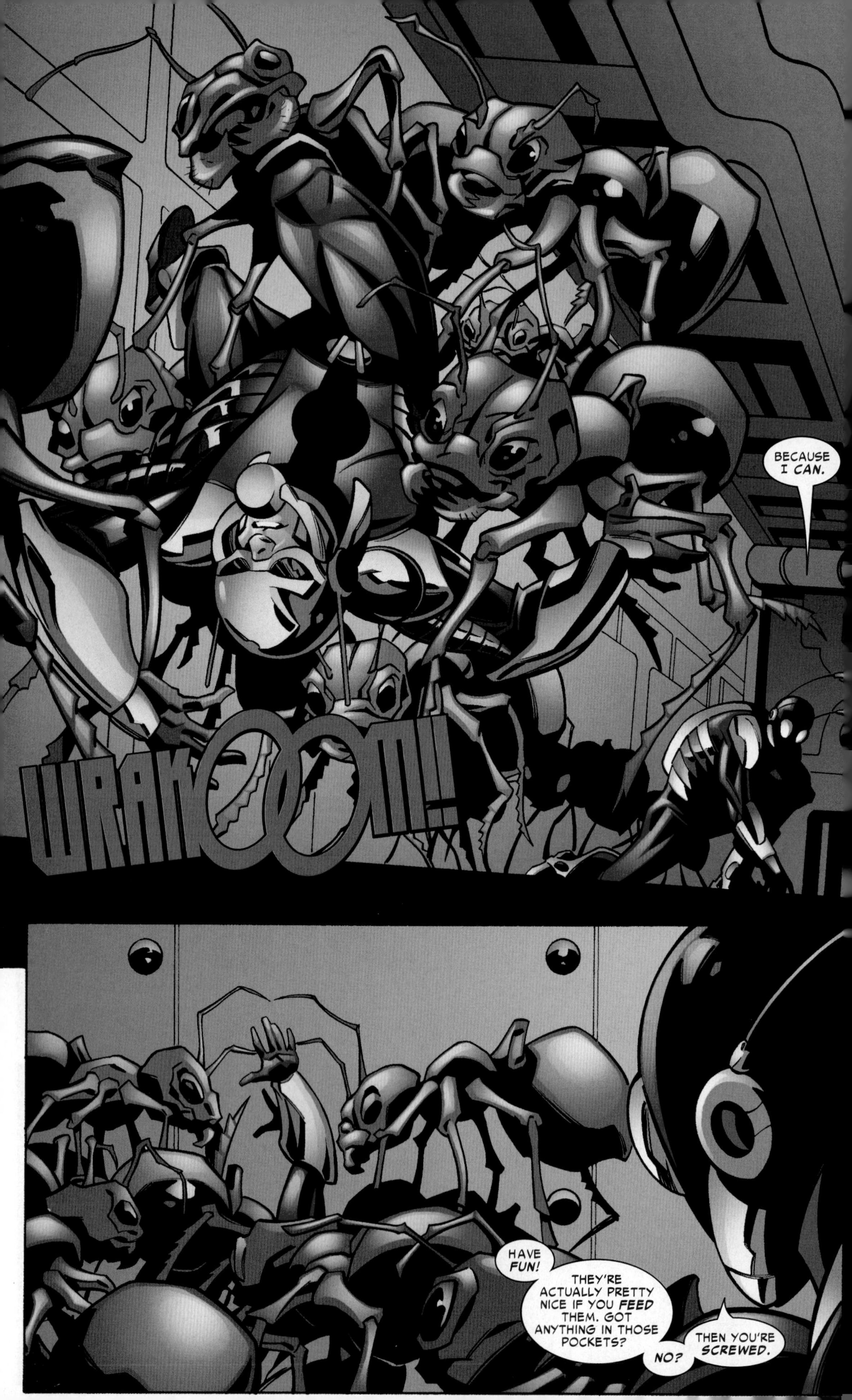

BECAUSE I CAN.
WRAKOOOM!!
HAVE FUN!
THEY'RE ACTUALLY PRETTY NICE IF YOU FEED THEM. GOT ANYTHING IN THOSE POCKETS?
NO?
THEN YOU'RE SCREWED.

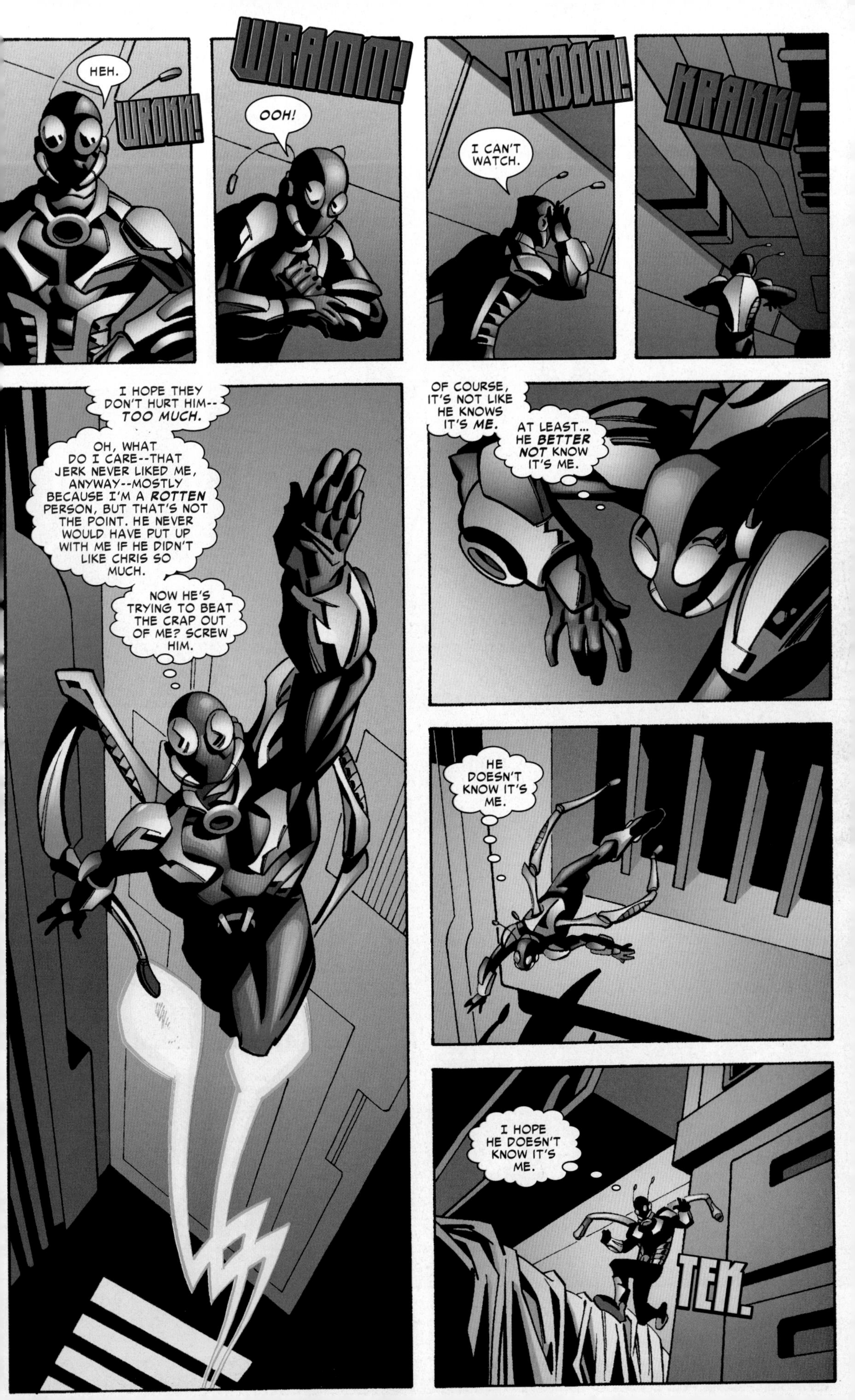
HEH.
WROKK!
WRAMM!
OOH!
KROOM!
I CAN'T WATCH.
KRAKK!
I HOPE THEY DON'T HURT HIM-- TOO MUCH.
OH, WHAT DO I CARE--THAT JERK NEVER LIKED ME, ANYWAY--MOSTLY BECAUSE I'M A ROTTEN PERSON, BUT THAT'S NOT THE POINT. HE NEVER WOULD HAVE PUT UP WITH ME IF HE DIDN'T LIKE CHRIS SO MUCH.
NOW HE'S TRYING TO BEAT THE CRAP OUT OF ME? SCREW HIM.
OF COURSE, IT'S NOT LIKE HE KNOWS IT'S ME.
AT LEAST... HE BETTER NOT KNOW IT'S ME.
HE DOESN'T KNOW IT'S ME.
I HOPE HE DOESN'T KNOW IT'S ME.
TEK.

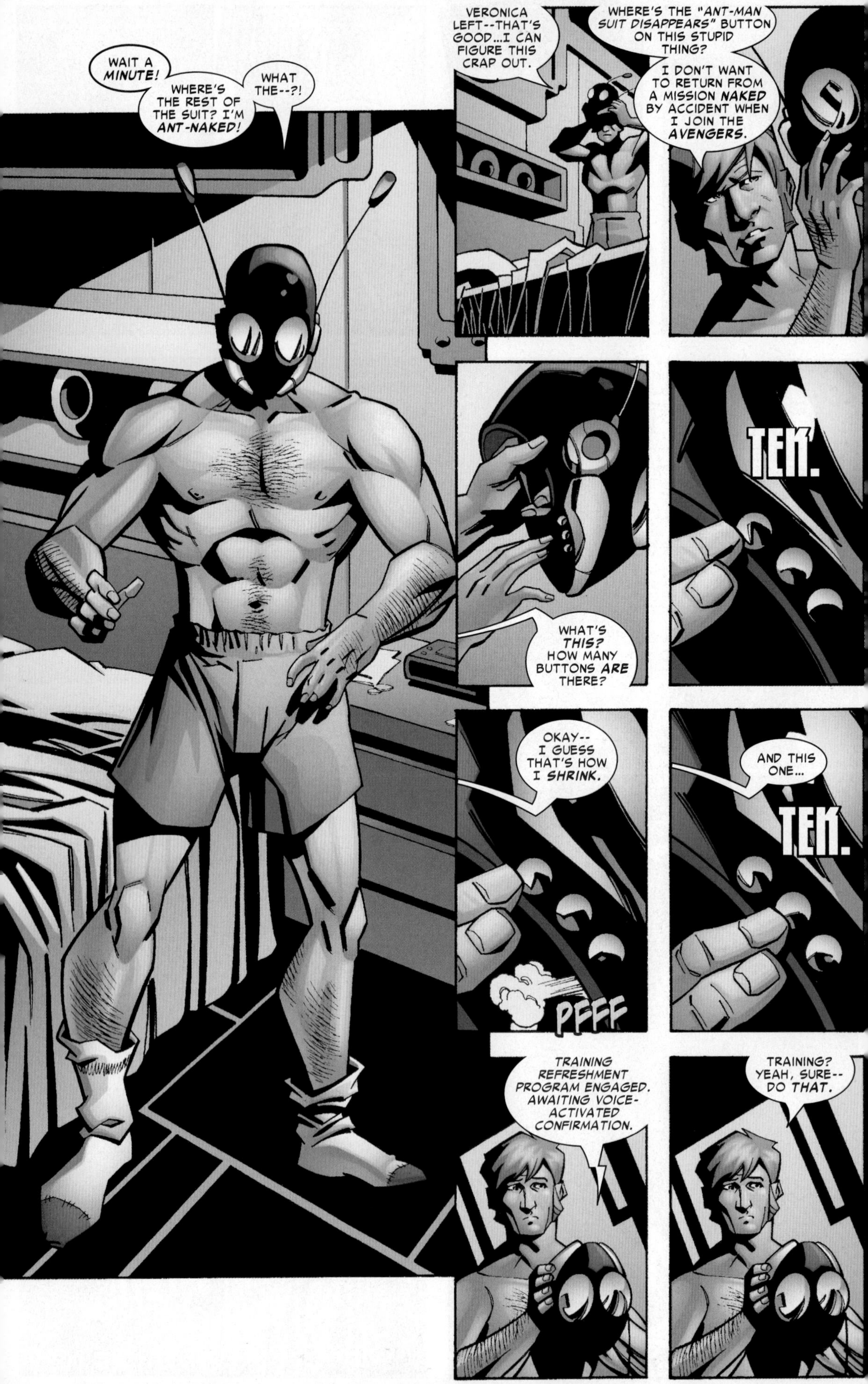

WAIT A MINUTE!
WHERE'S THE REST OF THE SUIT? I'M ANT-NAKED!
WHAT THE--?!
VERONICA LEFT--THAT'S GOOD...I CAN FIGURE THIS CRAP OUT.
WHERE'S THE "ANT-MAN SUIT DISAPPEARS" BUTTON ON THIS STUPID THING?
I DON'T WANT TO RETURN FROM A MISSION NAKED BY ACCIDENT WHEN I JOIN THE AVENGERS.
WHAT'S THIS? HOW MANY BUTTONS ARE THERE?
TEK.
OKAY-- I GUESS THAT'S HOW I SHRINK.
PFFF
AND THIS ONE...
TEK.
TRAINING REFRESHMENT PROGRAM ENGAGED. AWAITING VOICE-ACTIVATED CONFIRMATION.
TRAINING? YEAH, SURE-- DO THAT.

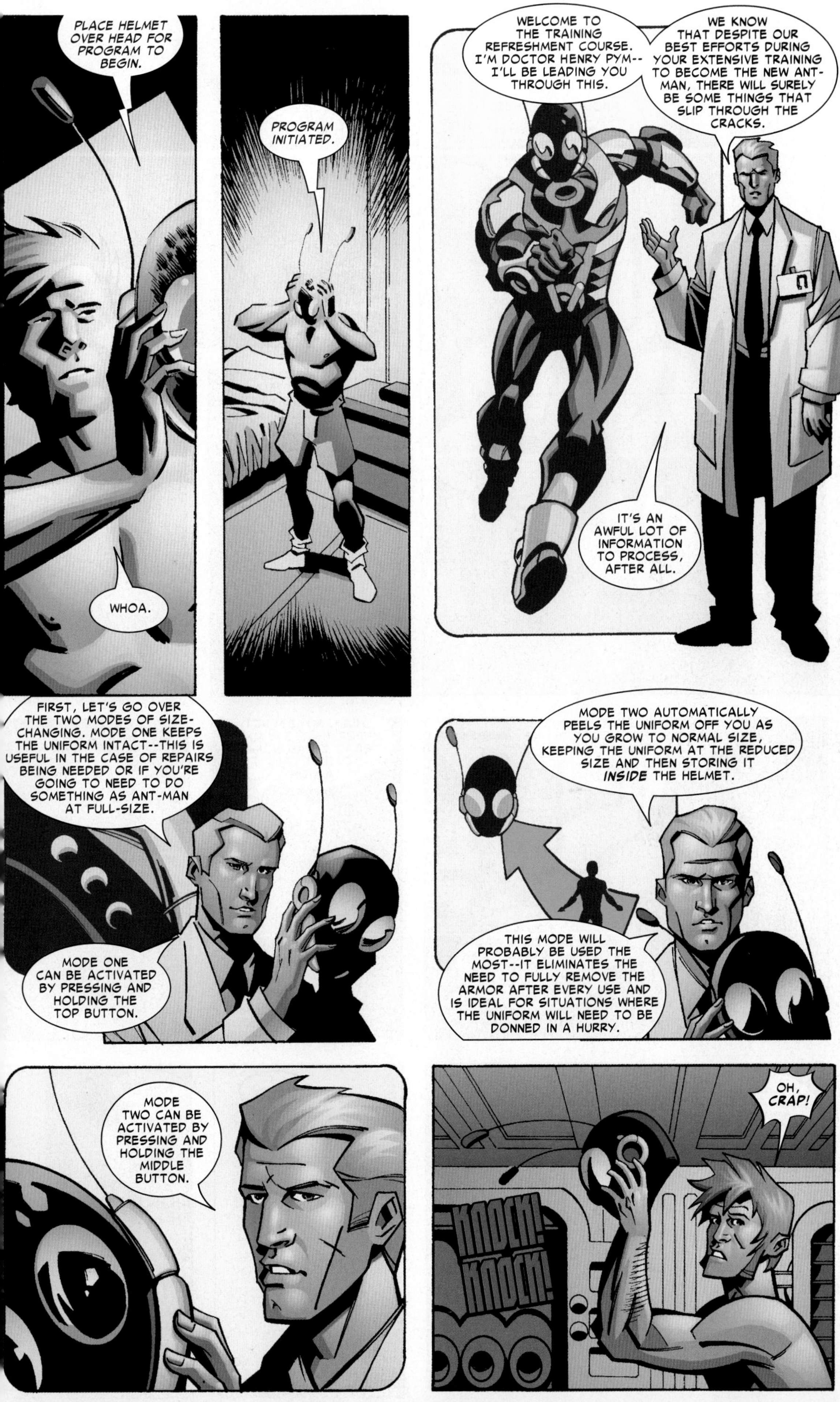
PLACE HELMET OVER HEAD FOR PROGRAM TO BEGIN.
WHOA.
PROGRAM INITIATED.
WELCOME TO THE TRAINING REFRESHMENT COURSE. I'M DOCTOR HENRY PYM--I'LL BE LEADING YOU THROUGH THIS.
WE KNOW THAT DESPITE OUR BEST EFFORTS DURING YOUR EXTENSIVE TRAINING TO BECOME THE NEW ANT-MAN, THERE WILL SURELY BE SOME THINGS THAT SLIP THROUGH THE CRACKS.
IT'S AN AWFUL LOT OF INFORMATION TO PROCESS, AFTER ALL.
FIRST, LET'S GO OVER THE TWO MODES OF SIZE-CHANGING. MODE ONE KEEPS THE UNIFORM INTACT--THIS IS USEFUL IN THE CASE OF REPAIRS BEING NEEDED OR IF YOU'RE GOING TO NEED TO DO SOMETHING AS ANT-MAN AT FULL-SIZE.
MODE ONE CAN BE ACTIVATED BY PRESSING AND HOLDING THE TOP BUTTON.
MODE TWO AUTOMATICALLY PEELS THE UNIFORM OFF YOU AS YOU GROW TO NORMAL SIZE, KEEPING THE UNIFORM AT THE REDUCED SIZE AND THEN STORING IT *INSIDE* THE HELMET.
THIS MODE WILL PROBABLY BE USED THE MOST--IT ELIMINATES THE NEED TO FULLY REMOVE THE ARMOR AFTER EVERY USE AND IS IDEAL FOR SITUATIONS WHERE THE UNIFORM WILL NEED TO BE DONNED IN A HURRY.
MODE TWO CAN BE ACTIVATED BY PRESSING AND HOLDING THE MIDDLE BUTTON.
KNOCK! KNOCK!
OH, *CRAP!*

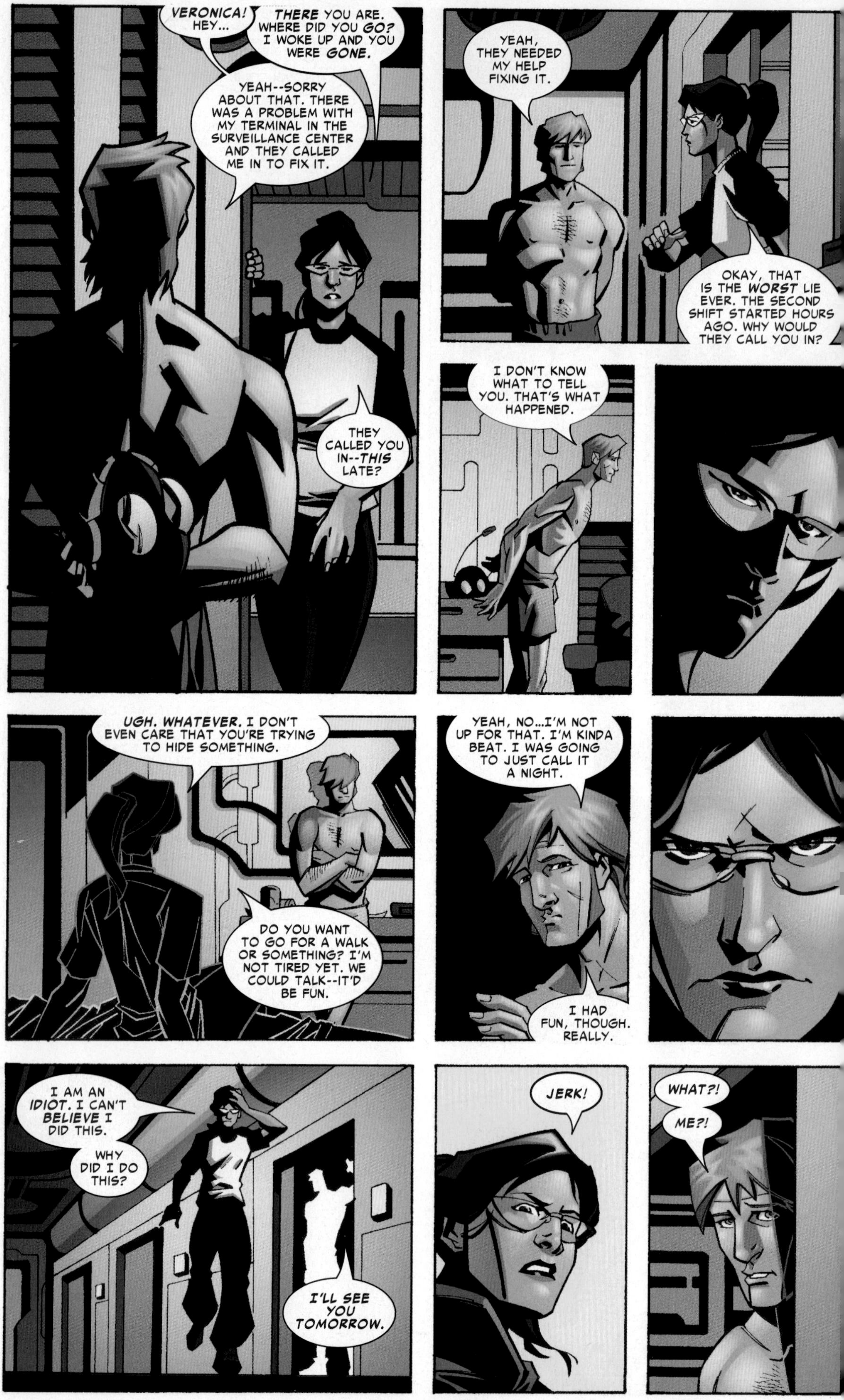

VERONICA! HEY...
THERE YOU ARE. WHERE DID YOU GO? I WOKE UP AND YOU WERE GONE.
YEAH--SORRY ABOUT THAT. THERE WAS A PROBLEM WITH MY TERMINAL IN THE SURVEILLANCE CENTER AND THEY CALLED ME IN TO FIX IT.
THEY CALLED YOU IN--THIS LATE?
YEAH, THEY NEEDED MY HELP FIXING IT.
OKAY, THAT IS THE WORST LIE EVER. THE SECOND SHIFT STARTED HOURS AGO. WHY WOULD THEY CALL YOU IN?
I DON'T KNOW WHAT TO TELL YOU. THAT'S WHAT HAPPENED.
UGH. WHATEVER. I DON'T EVEN CARE THAT YOU'RE TRYING TO HIDE SOMETHING.
DO YOU WANT TO GO FOR A WALK OR SOMETHING? I'M NOT TIRED YET. WE COULD TALK--IT'D BE FUN.
YEAH, NO...I'M NOT UP FOR THAT. I'M KINDA BEAT. I WAS GOING TO JUST CALL IT A NIGHT.
I HAD FUN, THOUGH. REALLY.
I AM AN IDIOT. I CAN'T BELIEVE I DID THIS.
WHY DID I DO THIS?
I'LL SEE YOU TOMORROW.
JERK!
WHAT?!
ME?!

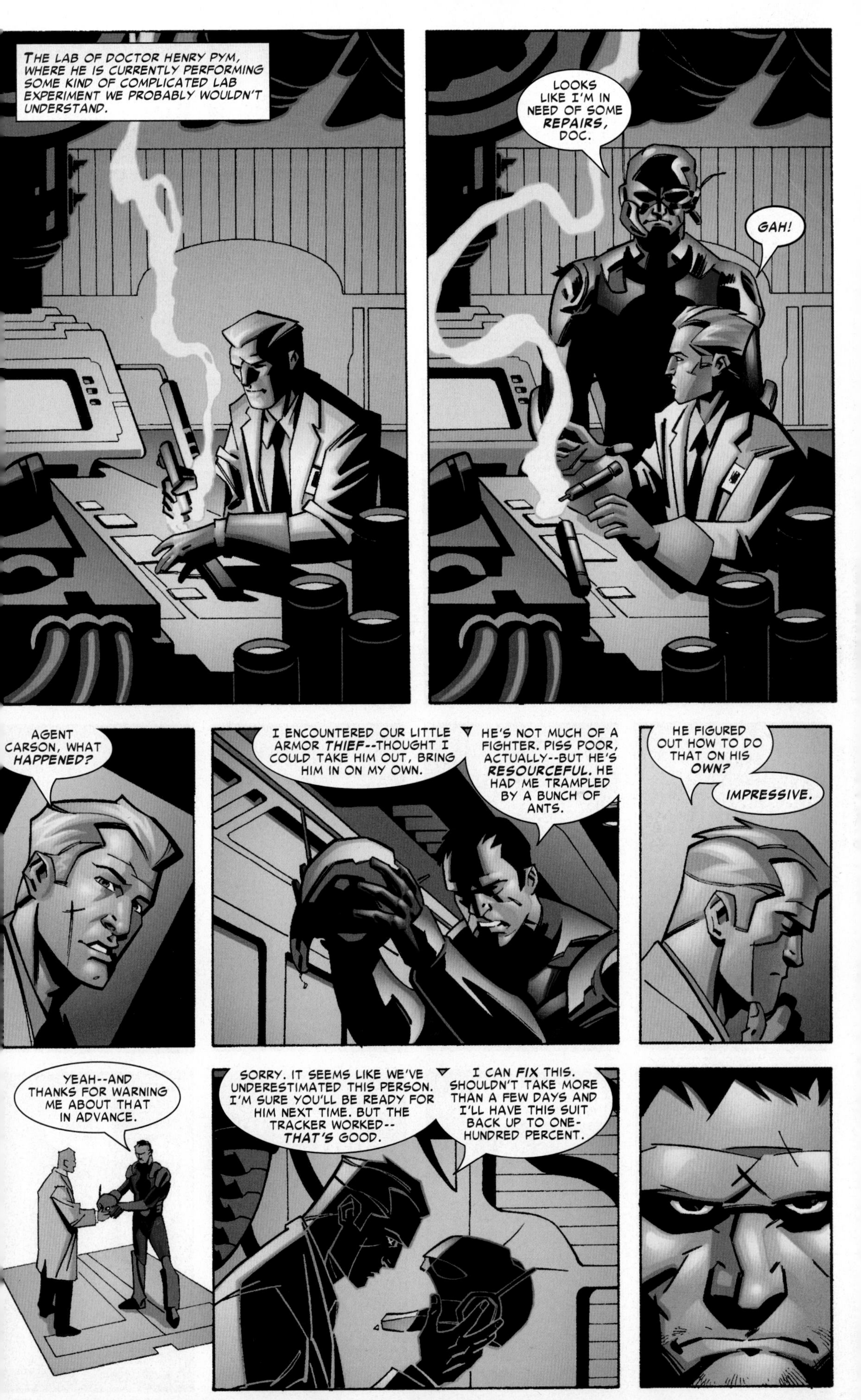
THE LAB OF DOCTOR HENRY PYM, WHERE HE IS CURRENTLY PERFORMING SOME KIND OF COMPLICATED LAB EXPERIMENT WE PROBABLY WOULDN'T UNDERSTAND.
LOOKS LIKE I'M IN NEED OF SOME REPAIRS, DOC.
GAH!
AGENT CARSON, WHAT HAPPENED?
I ENCOUNTERED OUR LITTLE ARMOR THIEF--THOUGHT I COULD TAKE HIM OUT, BRING HIM IN ON MY OWN.
HE'S NOT MUCH OF A FIGHTER. PISS POOR, ACTUALLY--BUT HE'S RESOURCEFUL. HE HAD ME TRAMPLED BY A BUNCH OF ANTS.
HE FIGURED OUT HOW TO DO THAT ON HIS OWN?
IMPRESSIVE.
YEAH--AND THANKS FOR WARNING ME ABOUT THAT IN ADVANCE.
SORRY. IT SEEMS LIKE WE'VE UNDERESTIMATED THIS PERSON. I'M SURE YOU'LL BE READY FOR HIM NEXT TIME. BUT THE TRACKER WORKED-- THAT'S GOOD.
I CAN FIX THIS. SHOULDN'T TAKE MORE THAN A FEW DAYS AND I'LL HAVE THIS SUIT BACK UP TO ONE-HUNDRED PERCENT.

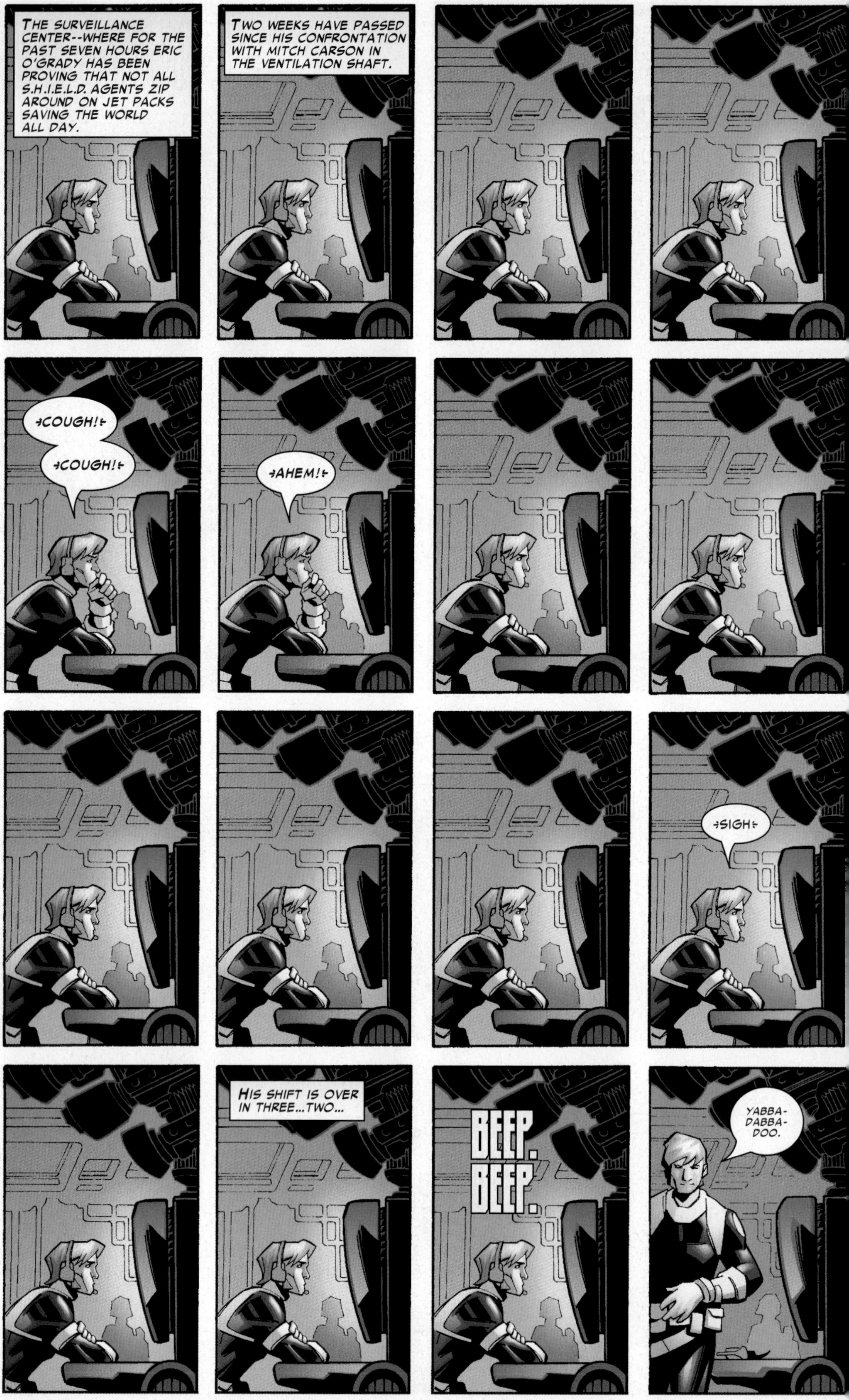
THE SURVEILLANCE CENTER--WHERE FOR THE PAST SEVEN HOURS ERIC O'GRADY HAS BEEN PROVING THAT NOT ALL S.H.I.E.L.D. AGENTS ZIP AROUND ON JET PACKS SAVING THE WORLD ALL DAY.
TWO WEEKS HAVE PASSED SINCE HIS CONFRONTATION WITH MITCH CARSON IN THE VENTILATION SHAFT.
COUGH!
COUGH!
AHEM!
SIGH
HIS SHIFT IS OVER IN THREE...TWO...
BEEP.
BEEP.
YABBA-DABBA-DOO.

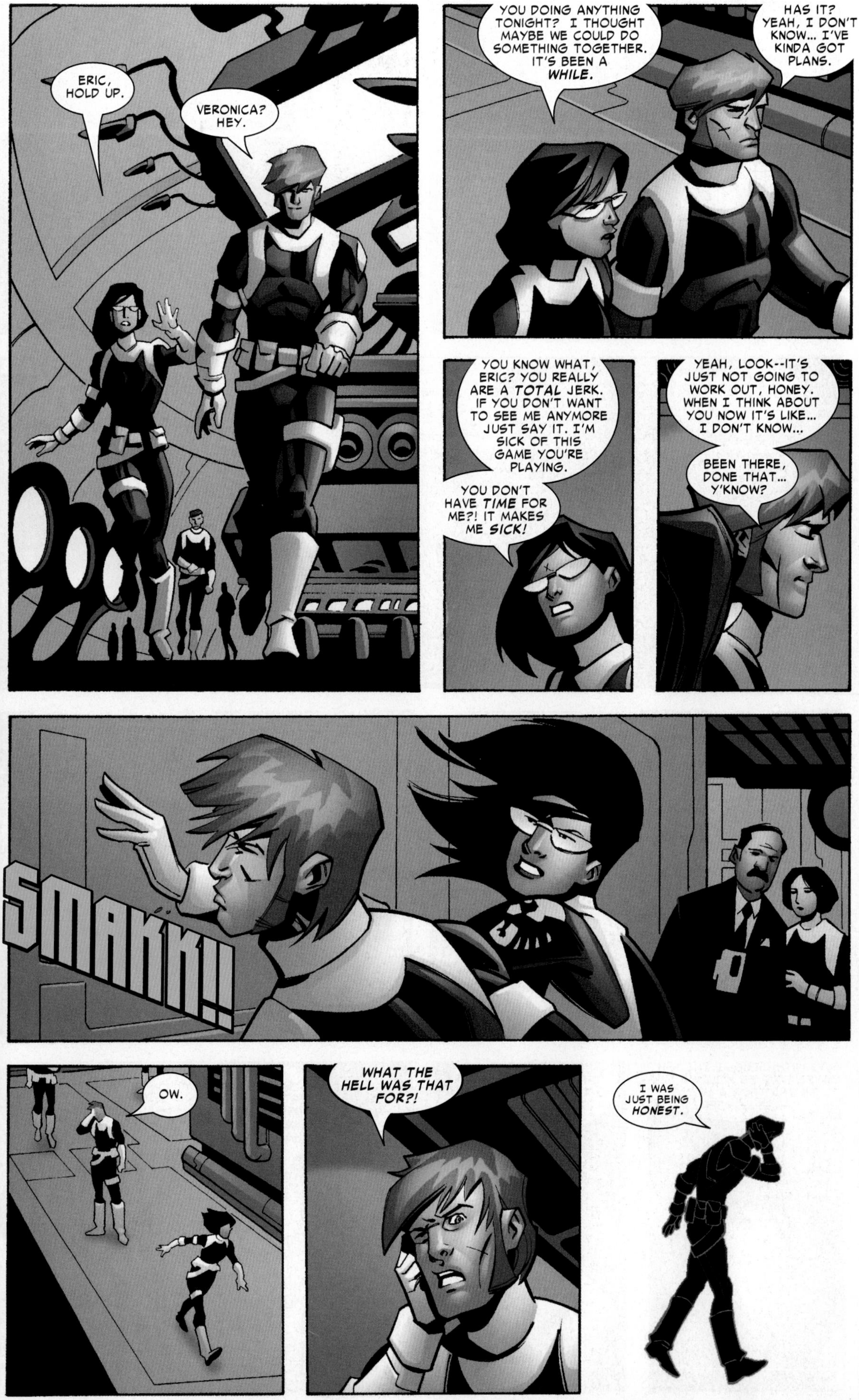

ERIC, HOLD UP.
VERONICA? HEY.
YOU DOING ANYTHING TONIGHT? I THOUGHT MAYBE WE COULD DO SOMETHING TOGETHER. IT'S BEEN A WHILE.
HAS IT? YEAH, I DON'T KNOW... I'VE KINDA GOT PLANS.
YOU KNOW WHAT, ERIC? YOU REALLY ARE A TOTAL JERK. IF YOU DON'T WANT TO SEE ME ANYMORE JUST SAY IT. I'M SICK OF THIS GAME YOU'RE PLAYING.
YOU DON'T HAVE TIME FOR ME?! IT MAKES ME SICK!
YEAH, LOOK--IT'S JUST NOT GOING TO WORK OUT, HONEY. WHEN I THINK ABOUT YOU NOW IT'S LIKE... I DON'T KNOW...
BEEN THERE, DONE THAT... Y'KNOW?
SMAKK!!
OW.
WHAT THE HELL WAS THAT FOR?!
I WAS JUST BEING HONEST.

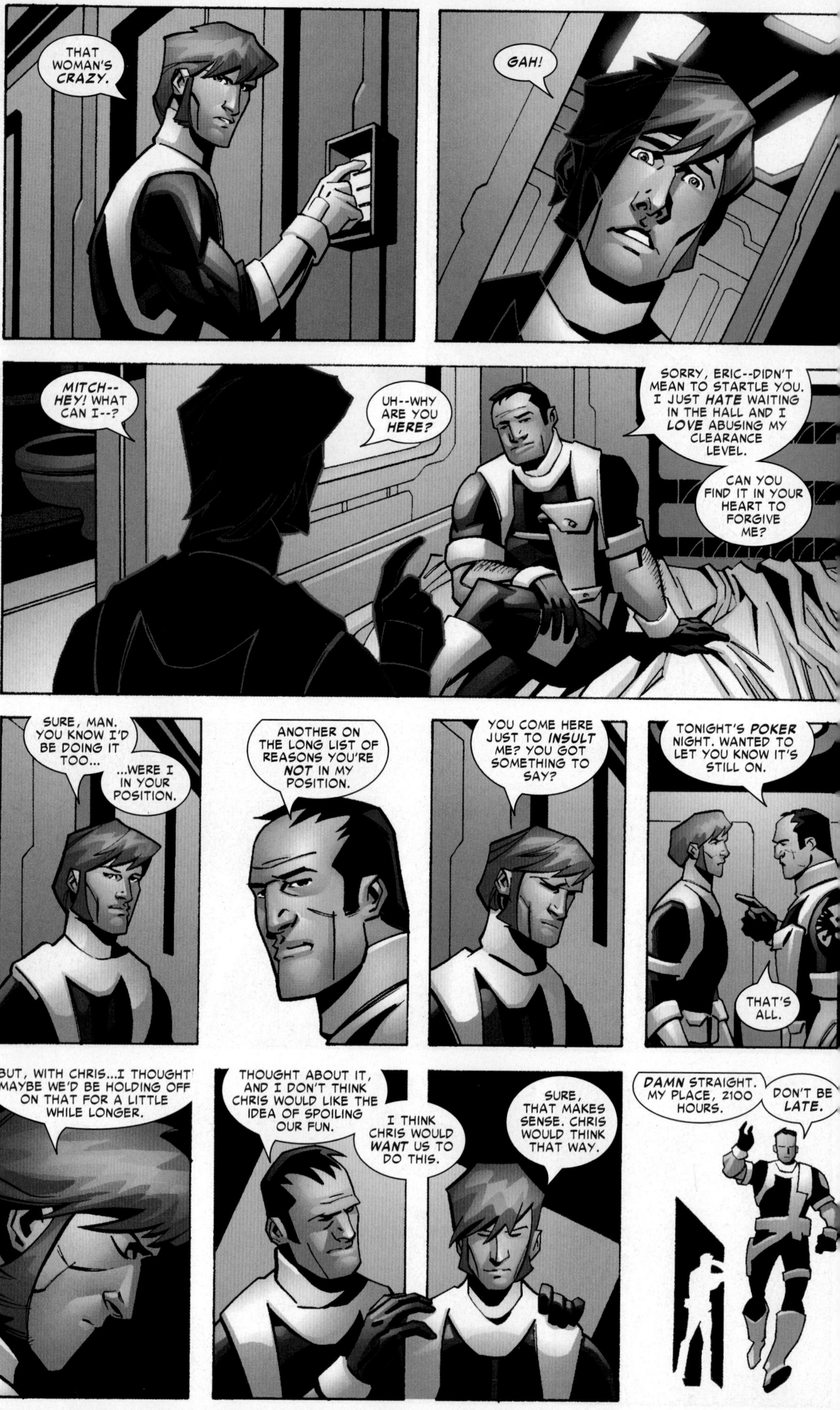
THAT WOMAN'S CRAZY.
GAH!
MITCH-- HEY! WHAT CAN I--?
UH--WHY ARE YOU HERE?
SORRY, ERIC--DIDN'T MEAN TO STARTLE YOU. I JUST HATE WAITING IN THE HALL AND I LOVE ABUSING MY CLEARANCE LEVEL.
CAN YOU FIND IT IN YOUR HEART TO FORGIVE ME?
SURE, MAN. YOU KNOW I'D BE DOING IT TOO...
...WERE I IN YOUR POSITION.
ANOTHER ON THE LONG LIST OF REASONS YOU'RE NOT IN MY POSITION.
YOU COME HERE JUST TO INSULT ME? YOU GOT SOMETHING TO SAY?
TONIGHT'S POKER NIGHT. WANTED TO LET YOU KNOW IT'S STILL ON.
THAT'S ALL.
BUT, WITH CHRIS...I THOUGHT MAYBE WE'D BE HOLDING OFF ON THAT FOR A LITTLE WHILE LONGER.
THOUGHT ABOUT IT, AND I DON'T THINK CHRIS WOULD LIKE THE IDEA OF SPOILING OUR FUN.
I THINK CHRIS WOULD WANT US TO DO THIS.
SURE, THAT MAKES SENSE. CHRIS WOULD THINK THAT WAY.
DAMN STRAIGHT. MY PLACE, 2100 HOURS.
DON'T BE LATE.

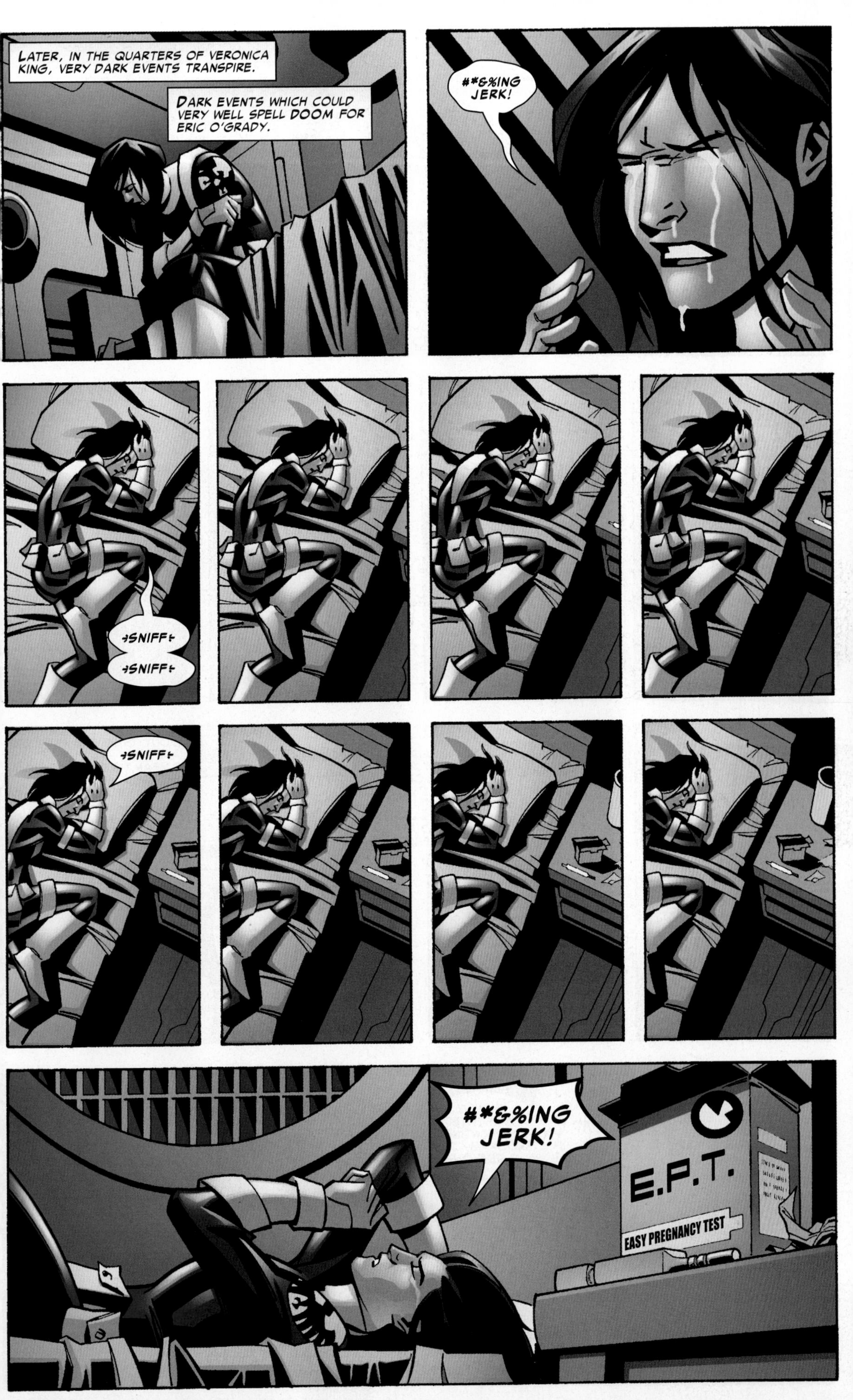
LATER, IN THE QUARTERS OF VERONICA KING, VERY DARK EVENTS TRANSPIRE.
DARK EVENTS WHICH COULD VERY WELL SPELL DOOM FOR ERIC O'GRADY.
#*&%ING JERK!
SNIFF
SNIFF
SNIFF
#*&%ING JERK!
E.P.T.
EASY PREGNANCY TEST

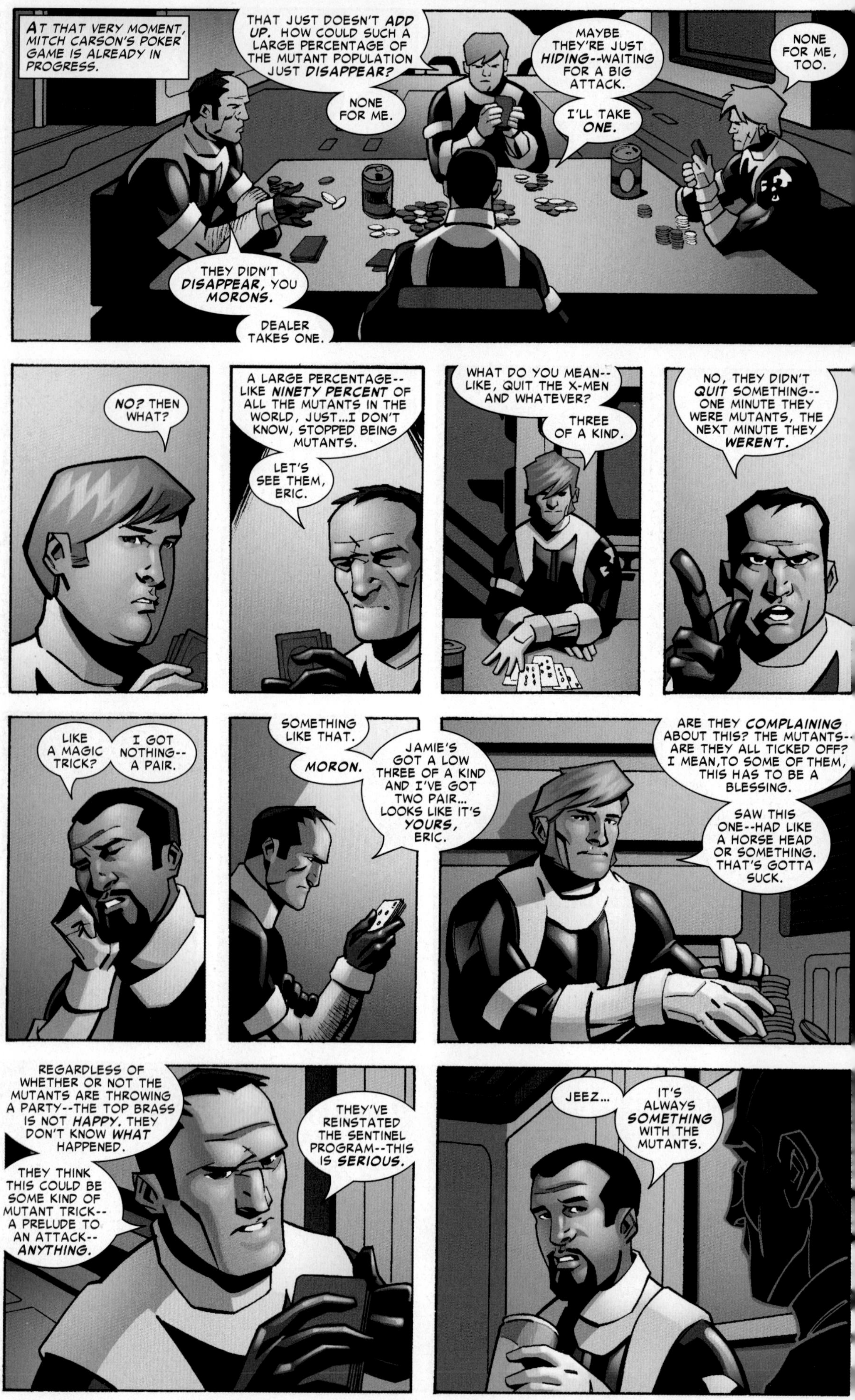

AT THAT VERY MOMENT, MITCH CARSON'S POKER GAME IS ALREADY IN PROGRESS.
THAT JUST DOESN'T ADD UP. HOW COULD SUCH A LARGE PERCENTAGE OF THE MUTANT POPULATION JUST DISAPPEAR?
NONE FOR ME.
MAYBE THEY'RE JUST HIDING--WAITING FOR A BIG ATTACK.
I'LL TAKE ONE.
NONE FOR ME, TOO.
THEY DIDN'T DISAPPEAR, YOU MORONS.
DEALER TAKES ONE.
NO? THEN WHAT?
A LARGE PERCENTAGE--LIKE NINETY PERCENT OF ALL THE MUTANTS IN THE WORLD, JUST...I DON'T KNOW, STOPPED BEING MUTANTS.
LET'S SEE THEM, ERIC.
WHAT DO YOU MEAN--LIKE, QUIT THE X-MEN AND WHATEVER?
THREE OF A KIND.
NO, THEY DIDN'T QUIT SOMETHING--ONE MINUTE THEY WERE MUTANTS, THE NEXT MINUTE THEY WEREN'T.
LIKE A MAGIC TRICK?
I GOT NOTHING--A PAIR.
SOMETHING LIKE THAT.
MORON.
JAMIE'S GOT A LOW THREE OF A KIND AND I'VE GOT TWO PAIR... LOOKS LIKE IT'S YOURS, ERIC.
ARE THEY COMPLAINING ABOUT THIS? THE MUTANTS--ARE THEY ALL TICKED OFF? I MEAN,TO SOME OF THEM, THIS HAS TO BE A BLESSING.
SAW THIS ONE--HAD LIKE A HORSE HEAD OR SOMETHING. THAT'S GOTTA SUCK.
REGARDLESS OF WHETHER OR NOT THE MUTANTS ARE THROWING A PARTY--THE TOP BRASS IS NOT HAPPY. THEY DON'T KNOW WHAT HAPPENED.
THEY THINK THIS COULD BE SOME KIND OF MUTANT TRICK--A PRELUDE TO AN ATTACK--ANYTHING.
THEY'VE REINSTATED THE SENTINEL PROGRAM--THIS IS SERIOUS.
JEEZ...
IT'S ALWAYS SOMETHING WITH THE MUTANTS.

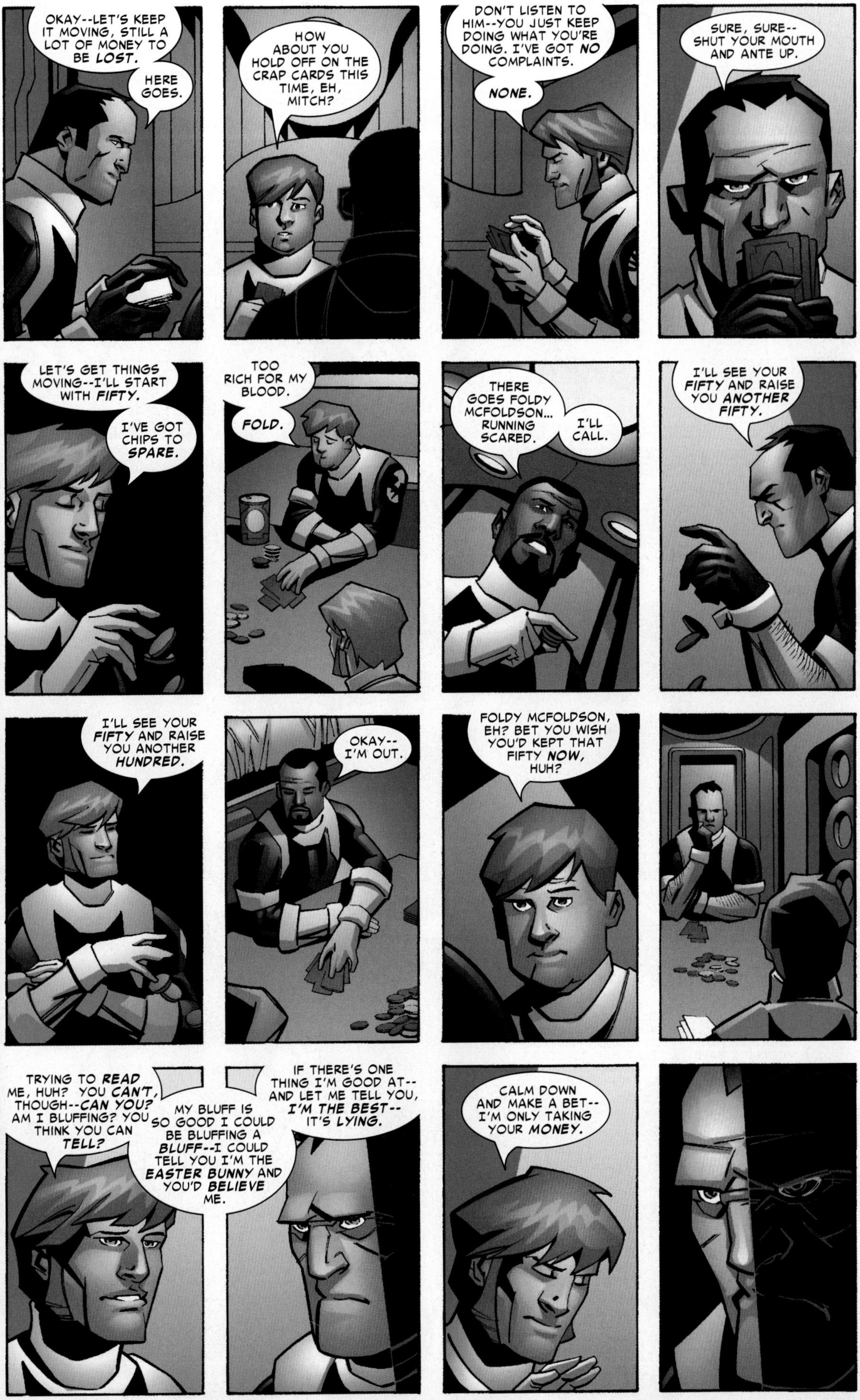
OKAY--LET'S KEEP IT MOVING, STILL A LOT OF MONEY TO BE LOST.
HERE GOES.
HOW ABOUT YOU HOLD OFF ON THE CRAP CARDS THIS TIME, EH, MITCH?
DON'T LISTEN TO HIM--YOU JUST KEEP DOING WHAT YOU'RE DOING. I'VE GOT NO COMPLAINTS.
NONE.
SURE, SURE--SHUT YOUR MOUTH AND ANTE UP.
LET'S GET THINGS MOVING--I'LL START WITH FIFTY.
I'VE GOT CHIPS TO SPARE.
TOO RICH FOR MY BLOOD.
FOLD.
THERE GOES FOLDY MCFOLDSON... RUNNING SCARED.
I'LL CALL.
I'LL SEE YOUR FIFTY AND RAISE YOU ANOTHER FIFTY.
I'LL SEE YOUR FIFTY AND RAISE YOU ANOTHER HUNDRED.
OKAY--I'M OUT.
FOLDY MCFOLDSON, EH? BET YOU WISH YOU'D KEPT THAT FIFTY NOW, HUH?
TRYING TO READ ME, HUH? YOU CAN'T, THOUGH--CAN YOU? AM I BLUFFING? YOU THINK YOU CAN TELL?
MY BLUFF IS SO GOOD I COULD BE BLUFFING A BLUFF--I COULD TELL YOU I'M THE EASTER BUNNY AND YOU'D BELIEVE ME.
IF THERE'S ONE THING I'M GOOD AT--AND LET ME TELL YOU, I'M THE BEST--IT'S LYING.
CALM DOWN AND MAKE A BET--I'M ONLY TAKING YOUR MONEY.

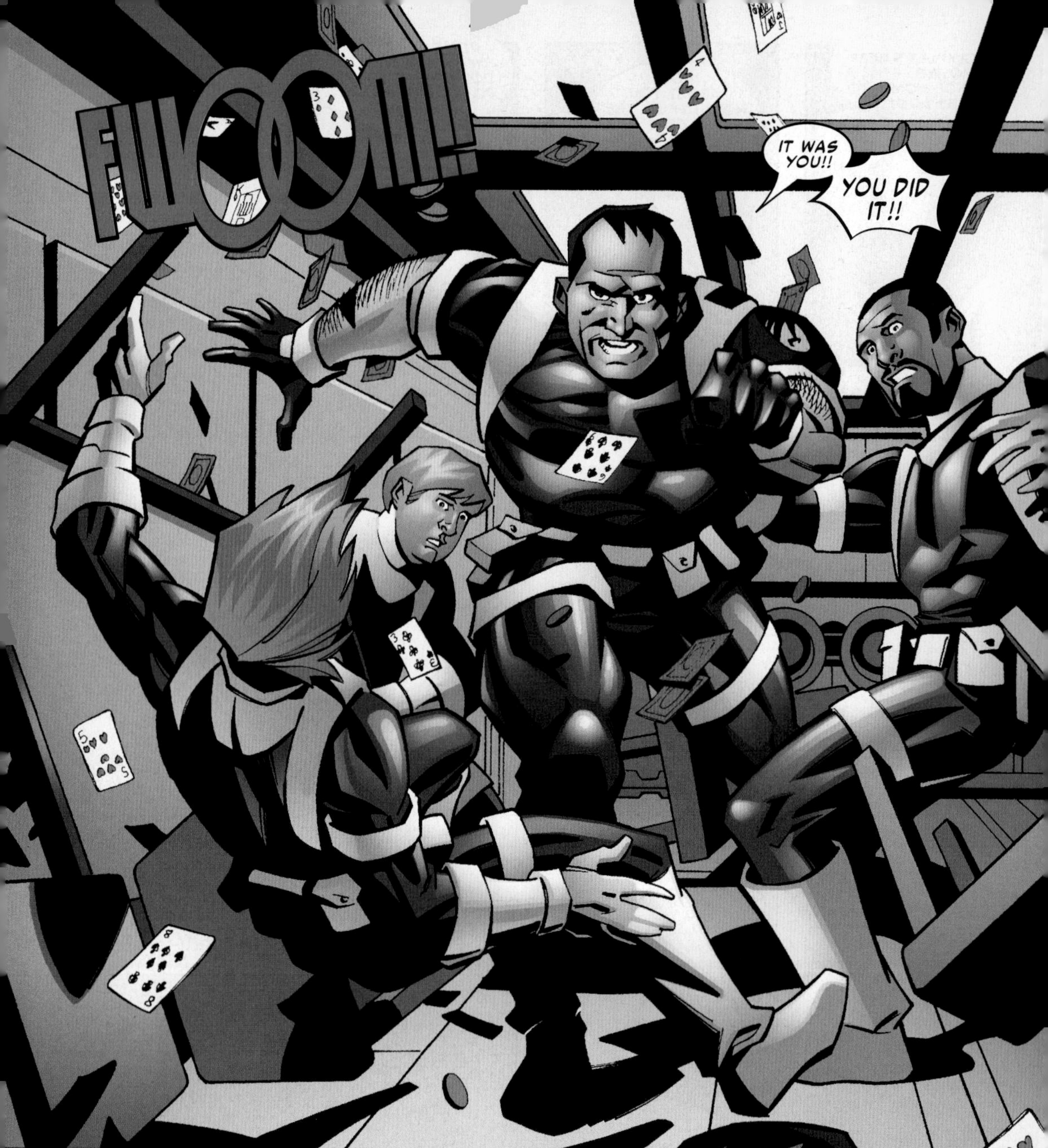
FWOOM!!
IT WAS YOU!!
YOU DID IT!!

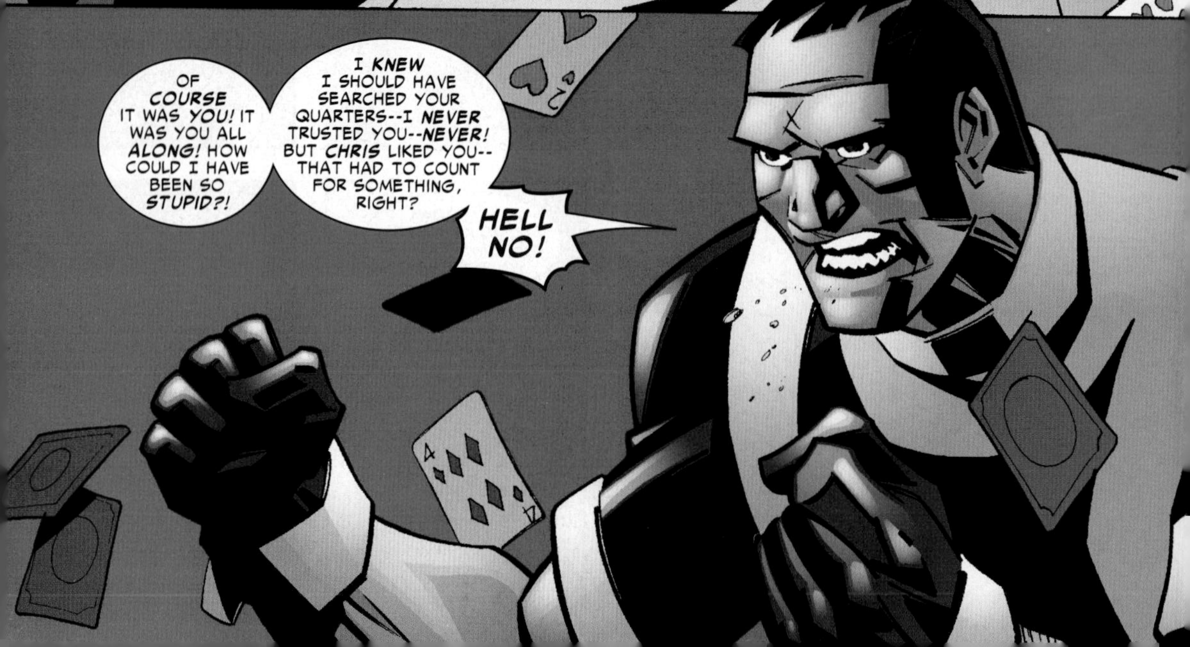
OF COURSE IT WAS YOU! IT WAS YOU ALL ALONG! HOW COULD I HAVE BEEN SO STUPID?!
I KNEW I SHOULD HAVE SEARCHED YOUR QUARTERS--I NEVER TRUSTED YOU--NEVER! BUT CHRIS LIKED YOU--THAT HAD TO COUNT FOR SOMETHING, RIGHT?
HELL NO!

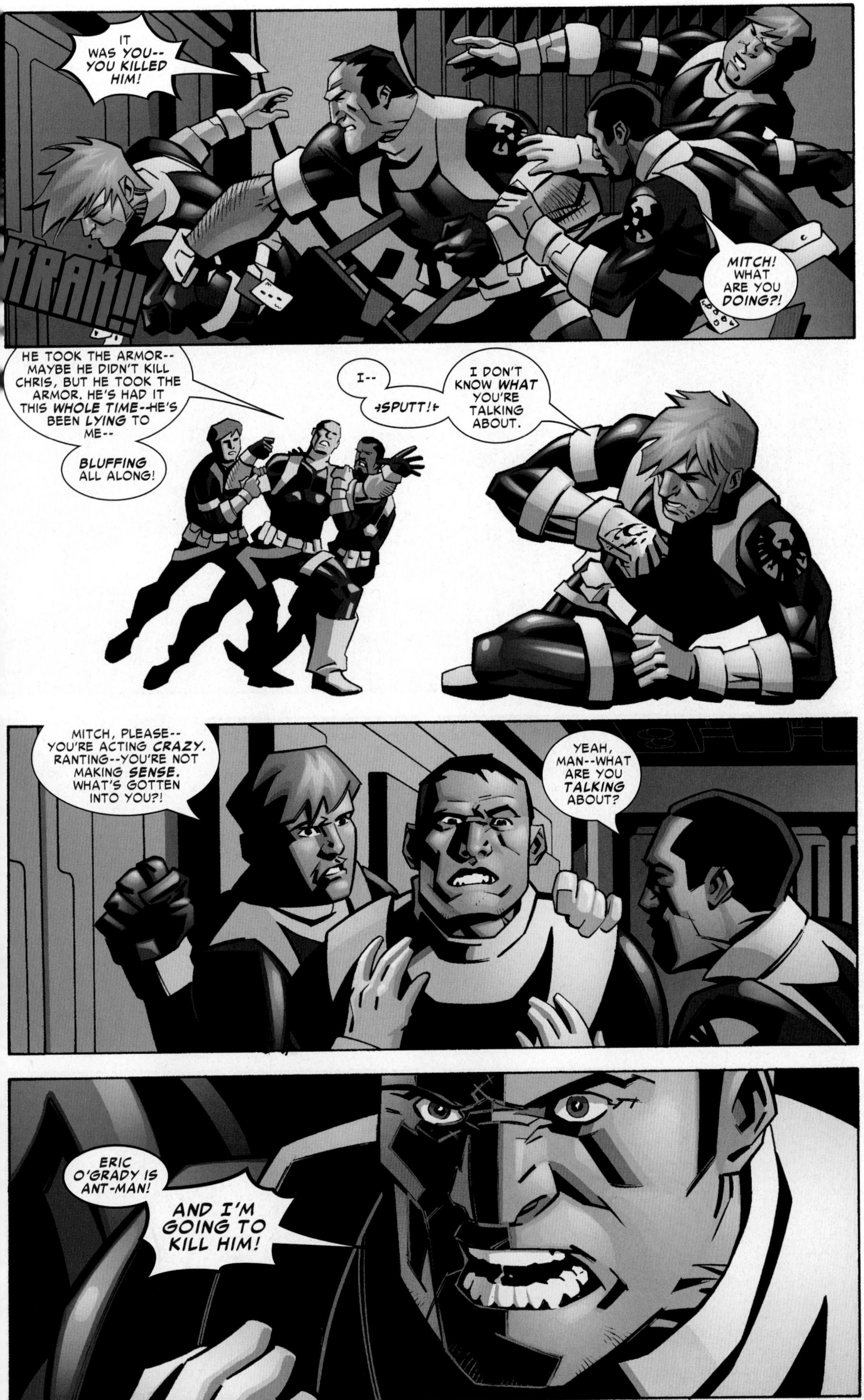
IT WAS YOU--YOU KILLED HIM!
KRAK!!
MITCH! WHAT ARE YOU DOING?!
HE TOOK THE ARMOR--MAYBE HE DIDN'T KILL CHRIS, BUT HE TOOK THE ARMOR. HE'S HAD IT THIS WHOLE TIME--HE'S BEEN LYING TO ME--
BLUFFING ALL ALONG!
I--
SPUTT!
I DON'T KNOW WHAT YOU'RE TALKING ABOUT.
MITCH, PLEASE--YOU'RE ACTING CRAZY. RANTING--YOU'RE NOT MAKING SENSE. WHAT'S GOTTEN INTO YOU?!
YEAH, MAN--WHAT ARE YOU TALKING ABOUT?
ERIC O'GRADY IS ANT-MAN!
AND I'M GOING TO KILL HIM!

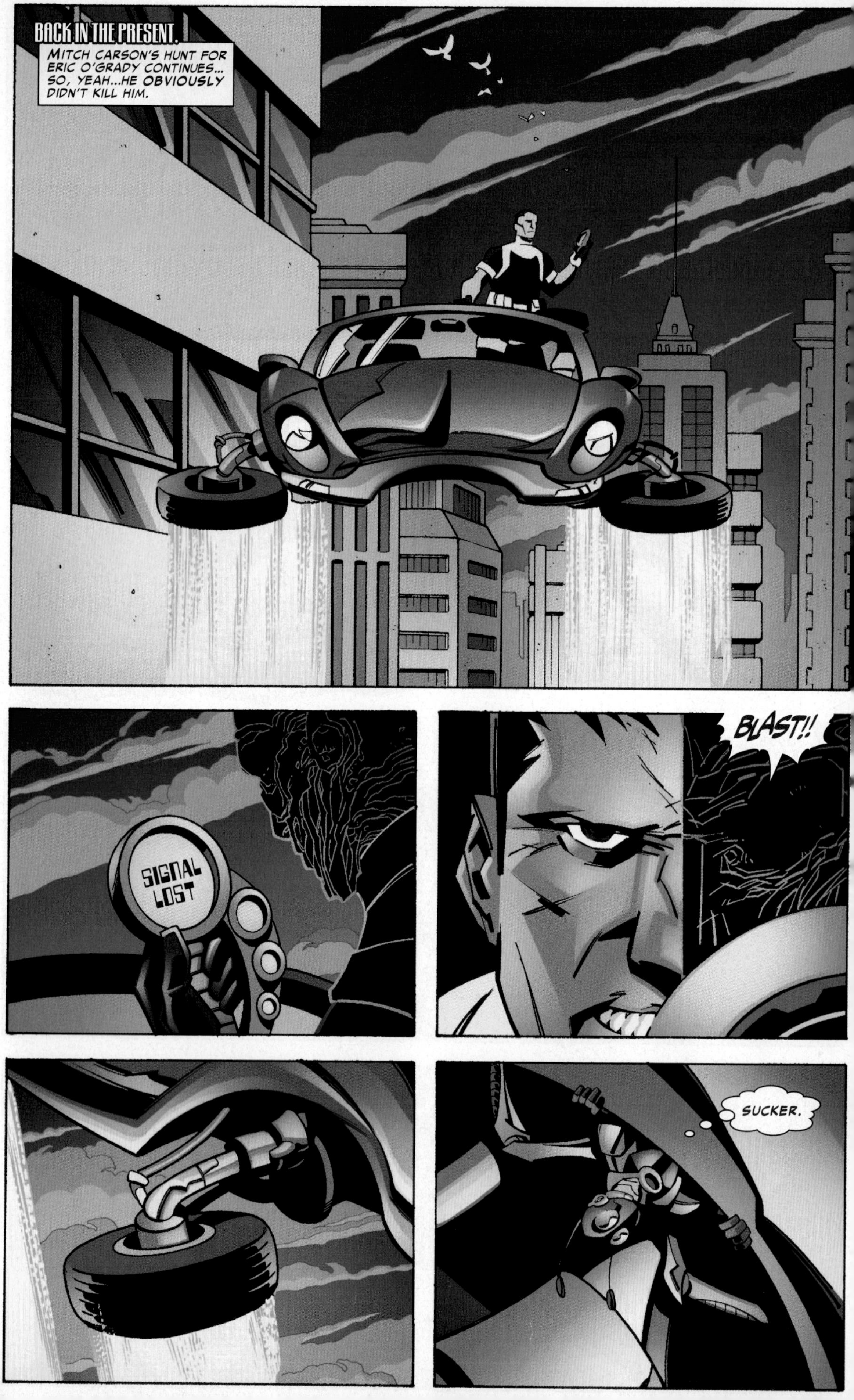
BACK IN THE PRESENT.
MITCH CARSON'S HUNT FOR ERIC O'GRADY CONTINUES... SO, YEAH...HE OBVIOUSLY DIDN'T KILL HIM.
SIGNAL LOST
BLAST!!
SUCKER.

#6

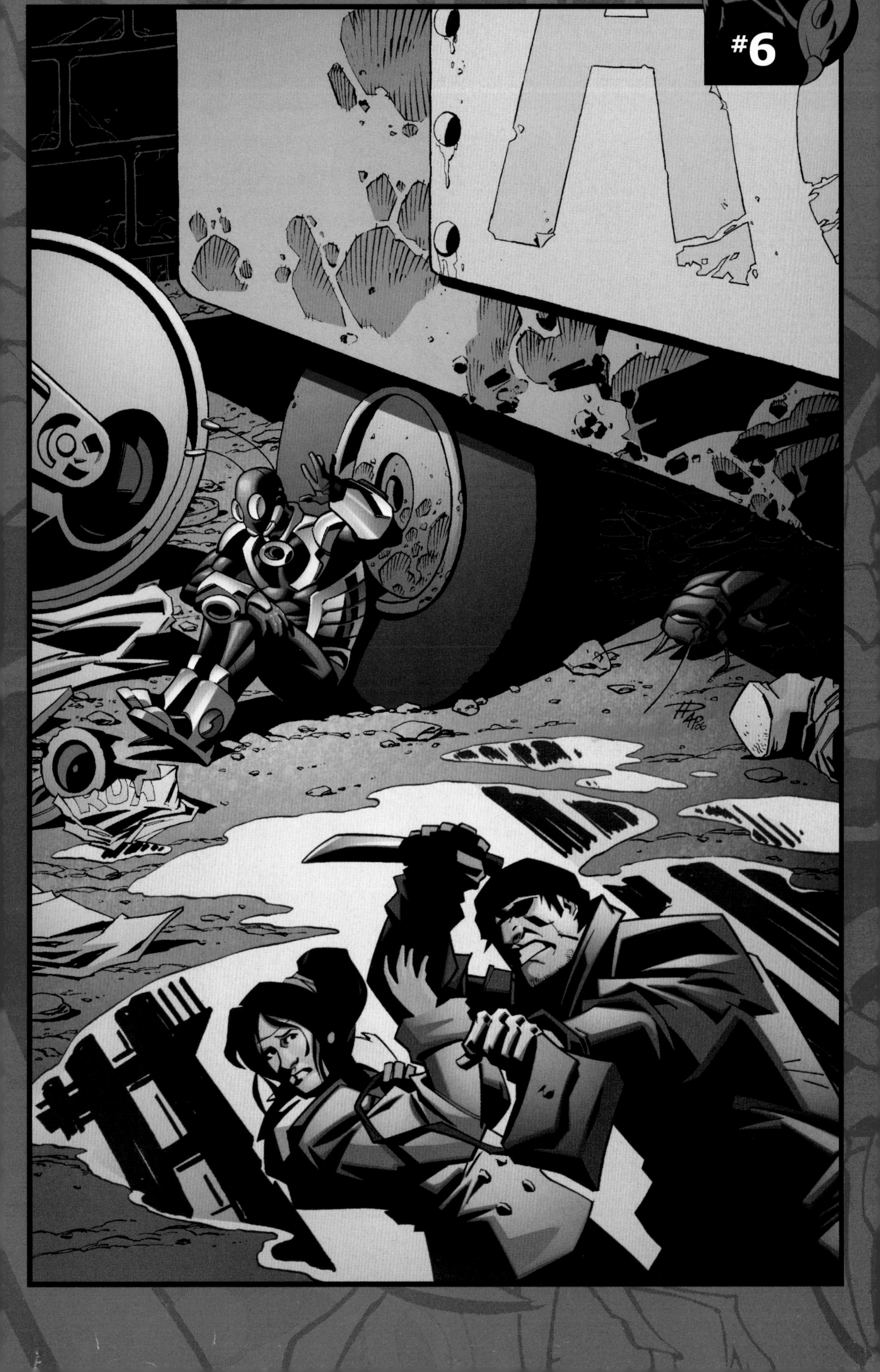

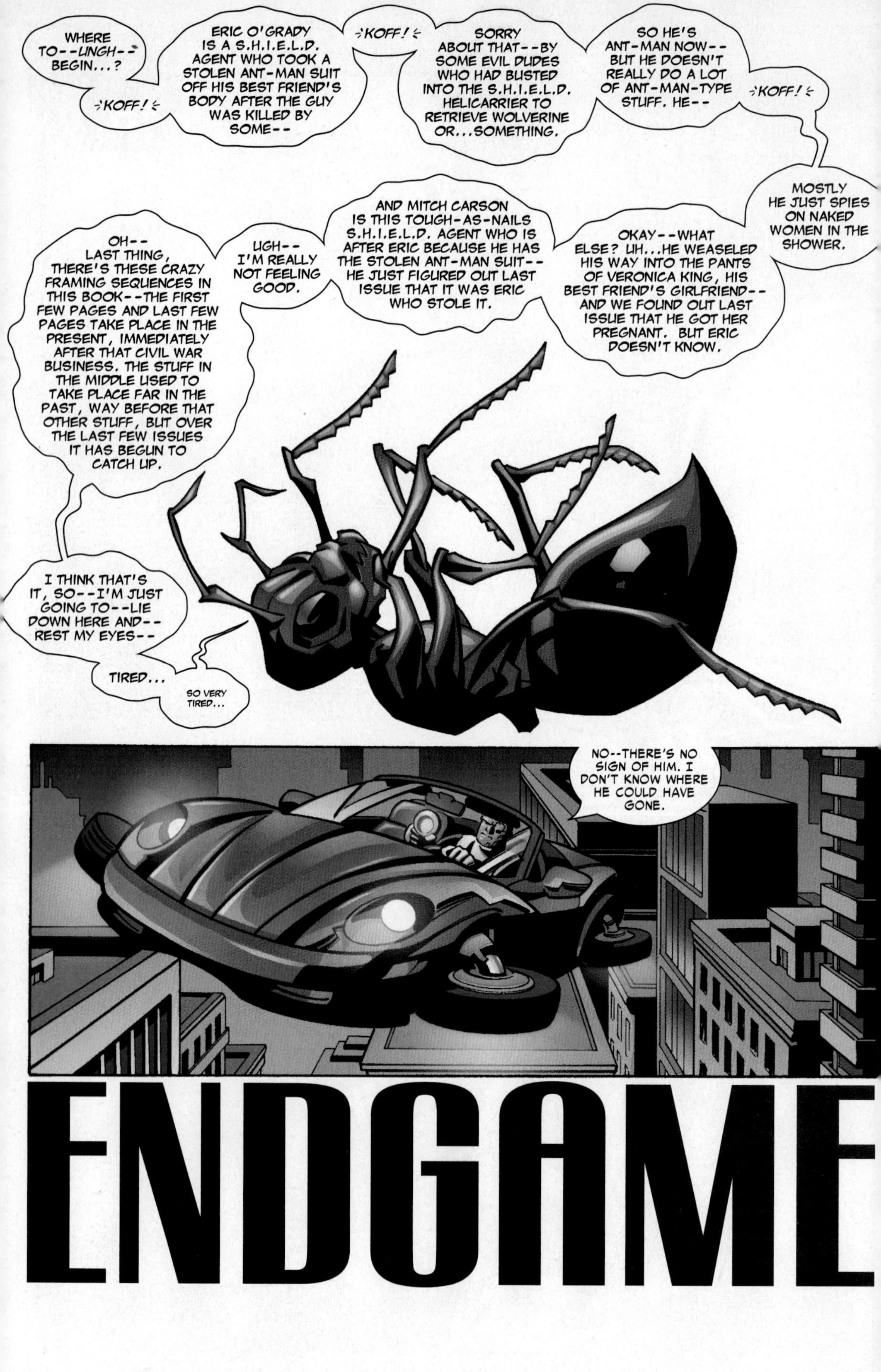

WHERE TO--UNGH--BEGIN...?
KOFF!
ERIC O'GRADY IS A S.H.I.E.L.D. AGENT WHO TOOK A STOLEN ANT-MAN SUIT OFF HIS BEST FRIEND'S BODY AFTER THE GUY WAS KILLED BY SOME--
KOFF!
SORRY ABOUT THAT--BY SOME EVIL DUDES WHO HAD BUSTED INTO THE S.H.I.E.L.D. HELICARRIER TO RETRIEVE WOLVERINE OR...SOMETHING.
SO HE'S ANT-MAN NOW--BUT HE DOESN'T REALLY DO A LOT OF ANT-MAN-TYPE STUFF. HE--
KOFF!
MOSTLY HE JUST SPIES ON NAKED WOMEN IN THE SHOWER.
OKAY--WHAT ELSE? UH...HE WEASELED HIS WAY INTO THE PANTS OF VERONICA KING, HIS BEST FRIEND'S GIRLFRIEND--AND WE FOUND OUT LAST ISSUE THAT HE GOT HER PREGNANT. BUT ERIC DOESN'T KNOW.
AND MITCH CARSON IS THIS TOUGH-AS-NAILS S.H.I.E.L.D. AGENT WHO IS AFTER ERIC BECAUSE HE HAS THE STOLEN ANT-MAN SUIT--HE JUST FIGURED OUT LAST ISSUE THAT IT WAS ERIC WHO STOLE IT.
UGH--I'M REALLY NOT FEELING GOOD.
OH--LAST THING, THERE'S THESE CRAZY FRAMING SEQUENCES IN THIS BOOK--THE FIRST FEW PAGES AND LAST FEW PAGES TAKE PLACE IN THE PRESENT, IMMEDIATELY AFTER THAT CIVIL WAR BUSINESS. THE STUFF IN THE MIDDLE USED TO TAKE PLACE FAR IN THE PAST, WAY BEFORE THAT OTHER STUFF, BUT OVER THE LAST FEW ISSUES IT HAS BEGUN TO CATCH UP.
I THINK THAT'S IT, SO--I'M JUST GOING TO--LIE DOWN HERE AND--REST MY EYES--
TIRED...
SO VERY TIRED...
NO--THERE'S NO SIGN OF HIM. I DON'T KNOW WHERE HE COULD HAVE GONE.
ENDGAME

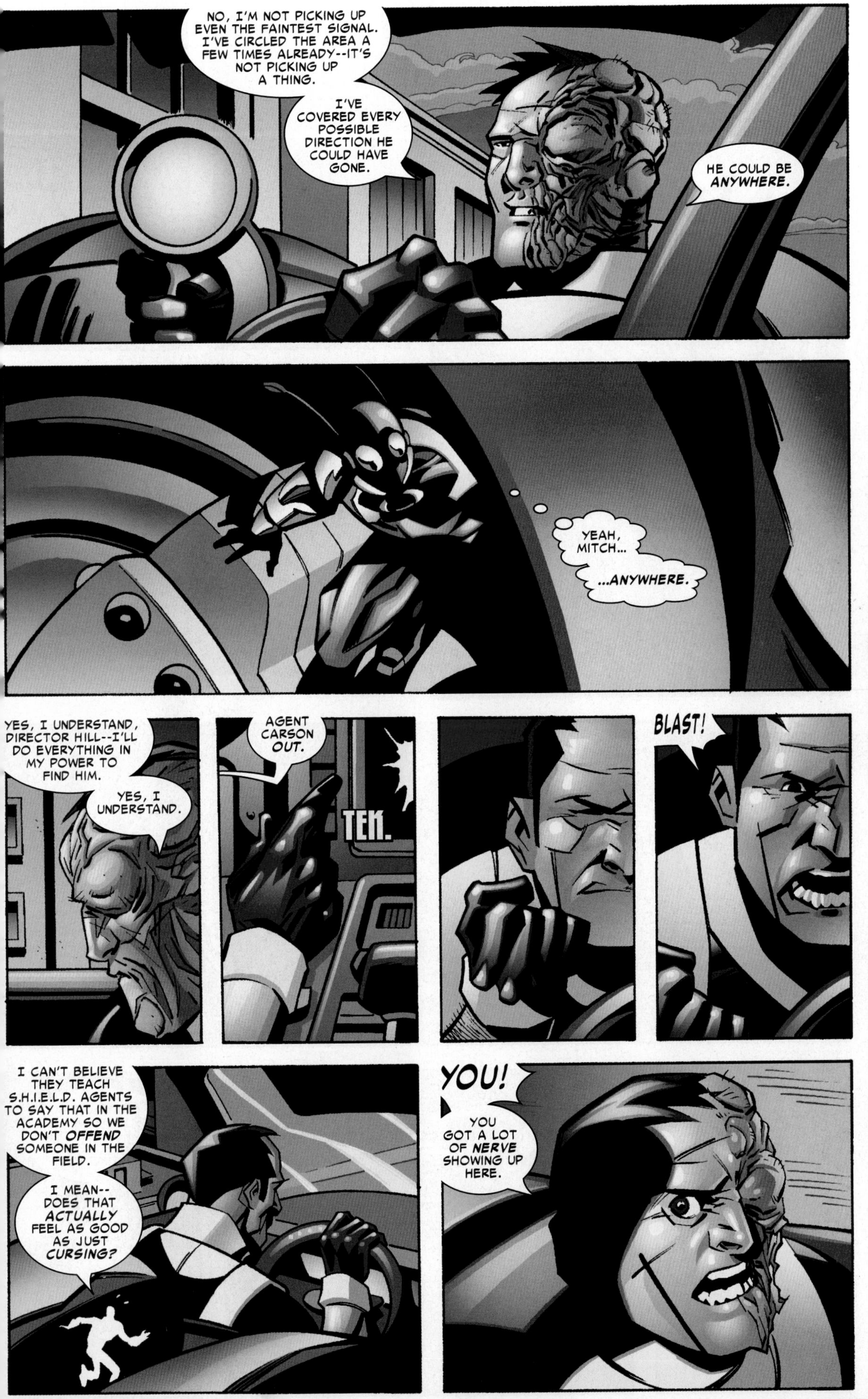
NO, I'M NOT PICKING UP EVEN THE FAINTEST SIGNAL. I'VE CIRCLED THE AREA A FEW TIMES ALREADY--IT'S NOT PICKING UP A THING.
I'VE COVERED EVERY POSSIBLE DIRECTION HE COULD HAVE GONE.
HE COULD BE ANYWHERE.
YEAH, MITCH...
...ANYWHERE.
YES, I UNDERSTAND, DIRECTOR HILL--I'LL DO EVERYTHING IN MY POWER TO FIND HIM.
YES, I UNDERSTAND.
AGENT CARSON OUT.
TEK.
BLAST!
I CAN'T BELIEVE THEY TEACH S.H.I.E.L.D. AGENTS TO SAY THAT IN THE ACADEMY SO WE DON'T OFFEND SOMEONE IN THE FIELD.
I MEAN-- DOES THAT ACTUALLY FEEL AS GOOD AS JUST CURSING?
YOU!
YOU GOT A LOT OF NERVE SHOWING UP HERE.

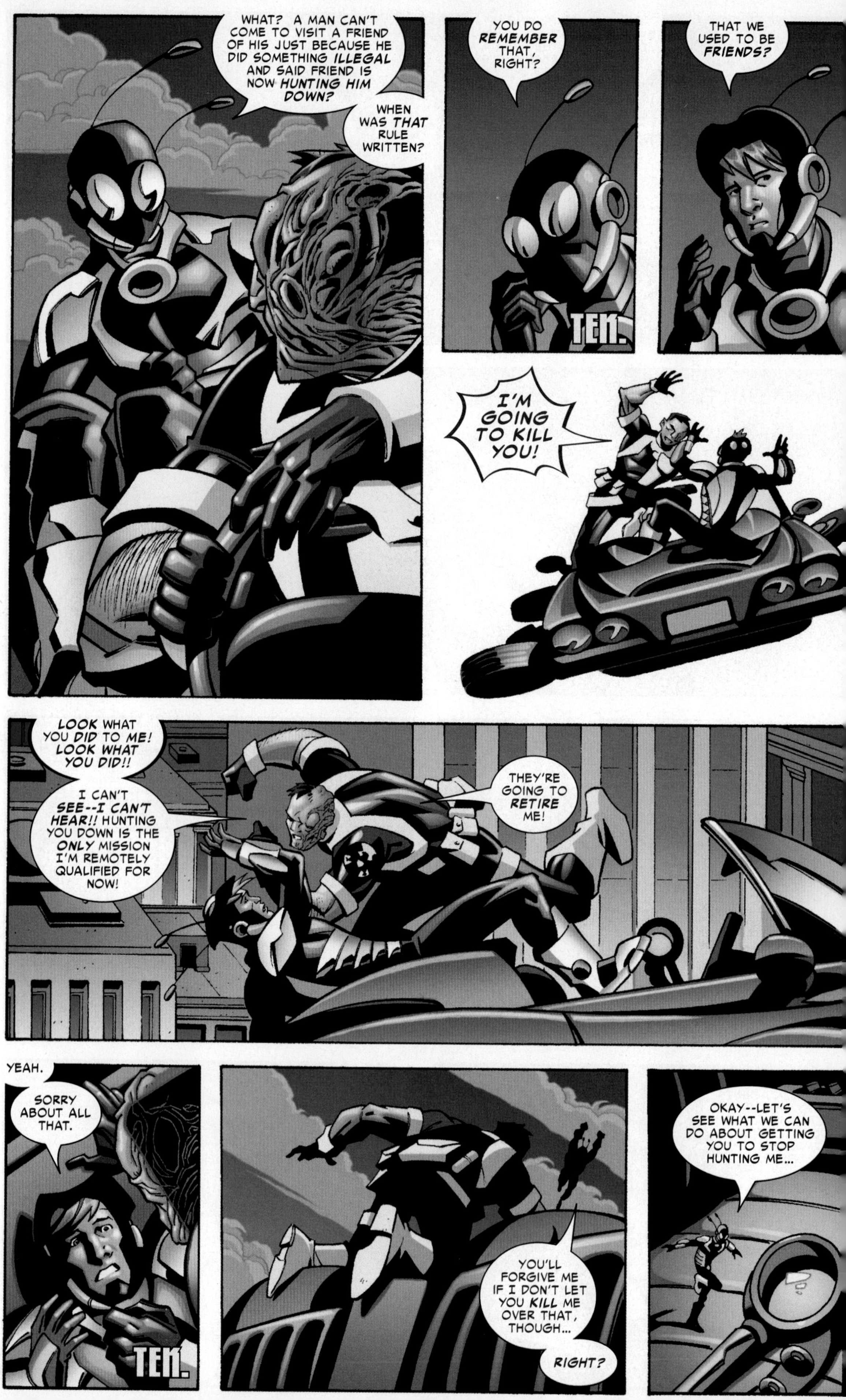
WHAT? A MAN CAN'T COME TO VISIT A FRIEND OF HIS JUST BECAUSE HE DID SOMETHING ILLEGAL AND SAID FRIEND IS NOW HUNTING HIM DOWN?
WHEN WAS THAT RULE WRITTEN?
YOU DO REMEMBER THAT, RIGHT?
TEK.
THAT WE USED TO BE FRIENDS?
I'M GOING TO KILL YOU!
LOOK WHAT YOU DID TO ME! LOOK WHAT YOU DID!!
I CAN'T SEE--I CAN'T HEAR!! HUNTING YOU DOWN IS THE ONLY MISSION I'M REMOTELY QUALIFIED FOR NOW!
THEY'RE GOING TO RETIRE ME!
YEAH.
SORRY ABOUT ALL THAT.
TEK.
YOU'LL FORGIVE ME IF I DON'T LET YOU KILL ME OVER THAT, THOUGH...
RIGHT?
OKAY--LET'S SEE WHAT WE CAN DO ABOUT GETTING YOU TO STOP HUNTING ME...

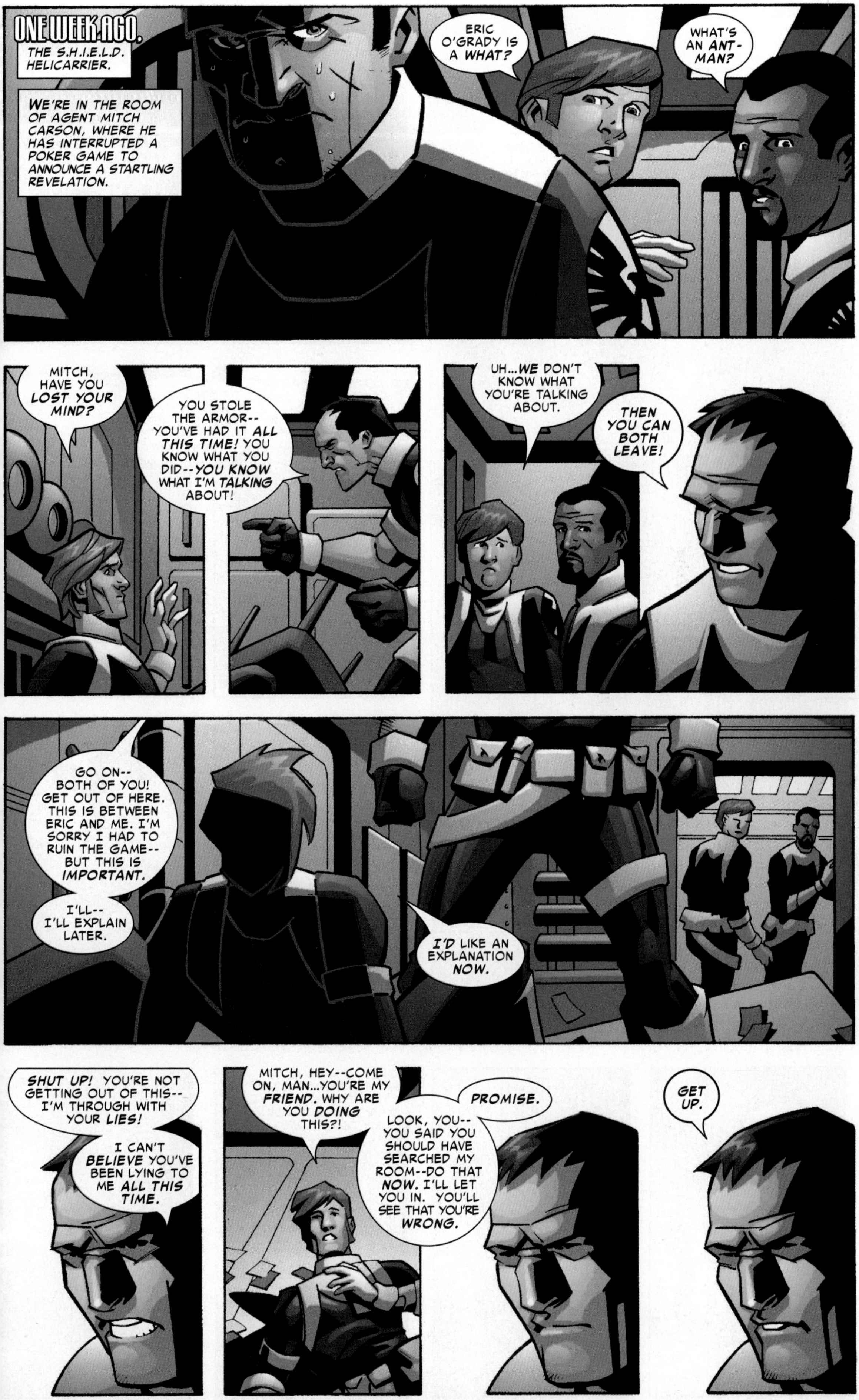
ONE WEEK AGO.
THE S.H.I.E.L.D. HELICARRIER.
WE'RE IN THE ROOM OF AGENT MITCH CARSON, WHERE HE HAS INTERRUPTED A POKER GAME TO ANNOUNCE A STARTLING REVELATION.
ERIC O'GRADY IS A WHAT?
WHAT'S AN ANT-MAN?
MITCH, HAVE YOU LOST YOUR MIND?
YOU STOLE THE ARMOR--YOU'VE HAD IT ALL THIS TIME! YOU KNOW WHAT YOU DID--YOU KNOW WHAT I'M TALKING ABOUT!
UH...WE DON'T KNOW WHAT YOU'RE TALKING ABOUT.
THEN YOU CAN BOTH LEAVE!
GO ON--BOTH OF YOU! GET OUT OF HERE. THIS IS BETWEEN ERIC AND ME. I'M SORRY I HAD TO RUIN THE GAME--BUT THIS IS IMPORTANT.
I'LL--I'LL EXPLAIN LATER.
I'D LIKE AN EXPLANATION NOW.
SHUT UP! YOU'RE NOT GETTING OUT OF THIS--I'M THROUGH WITH YOUR LIES!
I CAN'T BELIEVE YOU'VE BEEN LYING TO ME ALL THIS TIME.
MITCH, HEY--COME ON, MAN...YOU'RE MY FRIEND. WHY ARE YOU DOING THIS?!
LOOK, YOU--YOU SAID YOU SHOULD HAVE SEARCHED MY ROOM--DO THAT NOW. I'LL LET YOU IN. YOU'LL SEE THAT YOU'RE WRONG.
PROMISE.
GET UP.

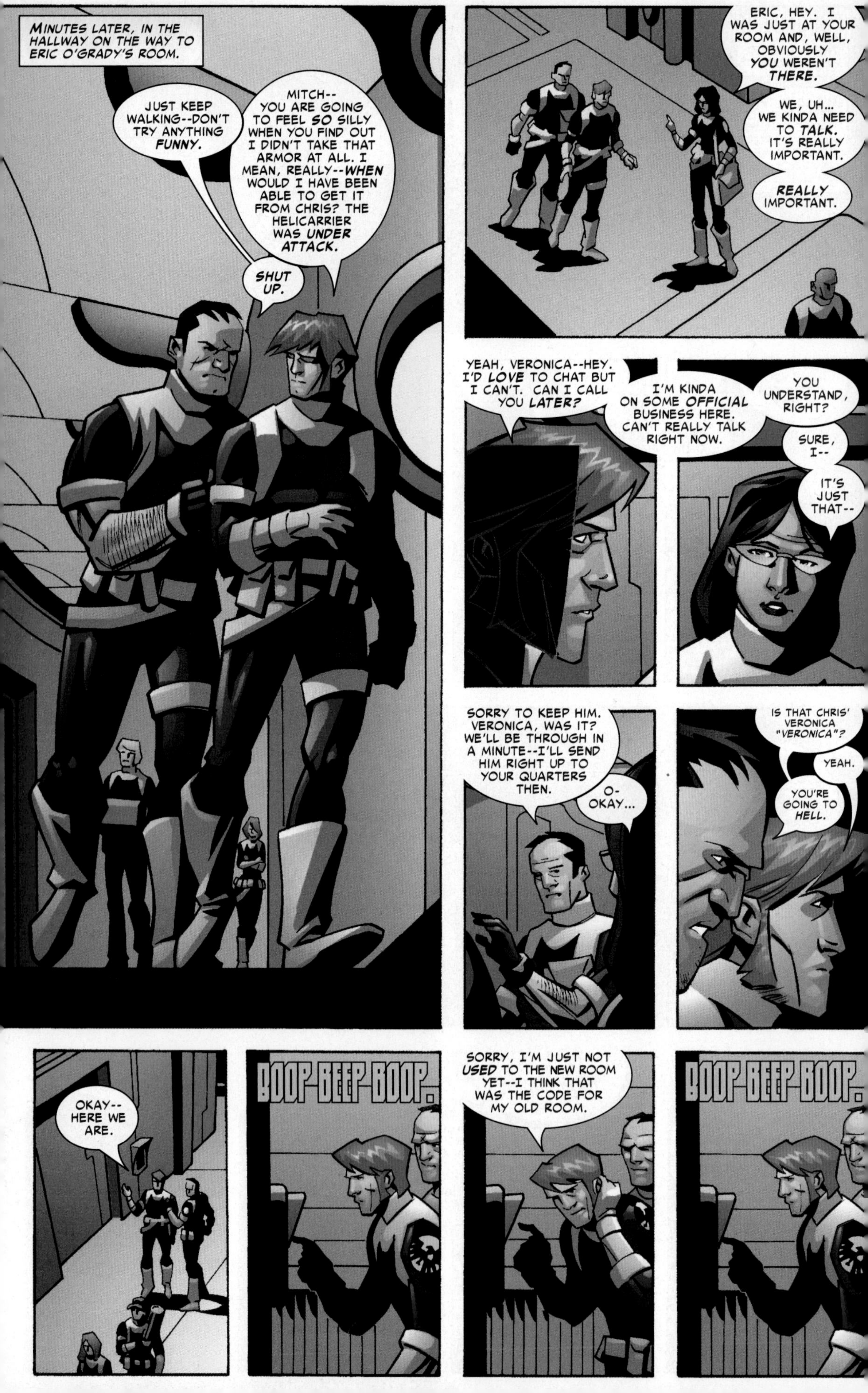
MINUTES LATER, IN THE HALLWAY ON THE WAY TO ERIC O'GRADY'S ROOM.
JUST KEEP WALKING--DON'T TRY ANYTHING FUNNY.
MITCH-- YOU ARE GOING TO FEEL SO SILLY WHEN YOU FIND OUT I DIDN'T TAKE THAT ARMOR AT ALL. I MEAN, REALLY--WHEN WOULD I HAVE BEEN ABLE TO GET IT FROM CHRIS? THE HELICARRIER WAS UNDER ATTACK.
SHUT UP.
ERIC, HEY. I WAS JUST AT YOUR ROOM AND, WELL, OBVIOUSLY YOU WEREN'T THERE.
WE, UH... WE KINDA NEED TO TALK. IT'S REALLY IMPORTANT.
REALLY IMPORTANT.
YEAH, VERONICA--HEY. I'D LOVE TO CHAT BUT I CAN'T. CAN I CALL YOU LATER?
I'M KINDA ON SOME OFFICIAL BUSINESS HERE. CAN'T REALLY TALK RIGHT NOW.
YOU UNDERSTAND, RIGHT?
SURE, I--
IT'S JUST THAT--
SORRY TO KEEP HIM. VERONICA, WAS IT? WE'LL BE THROUGH IN A MINUTE--I'LL SEND HIM RIGHT UP TO YOUR QUARTERS THEN.
O-OKAY...
IS THAT CHRIS' VERONICA "VERONICA"?
YEAH.
YOU'RE GOING TO HELL.
OKAY-- HERE WE ARE.
BOOP-BEEP-BOOP.
SORRY, I'M JUST NOT USED TO THE NEW ROOM YET--I THINK THAT WAS THE CODE FOR MY OLD ROOM.
BOOP-BEEP-BOOP.

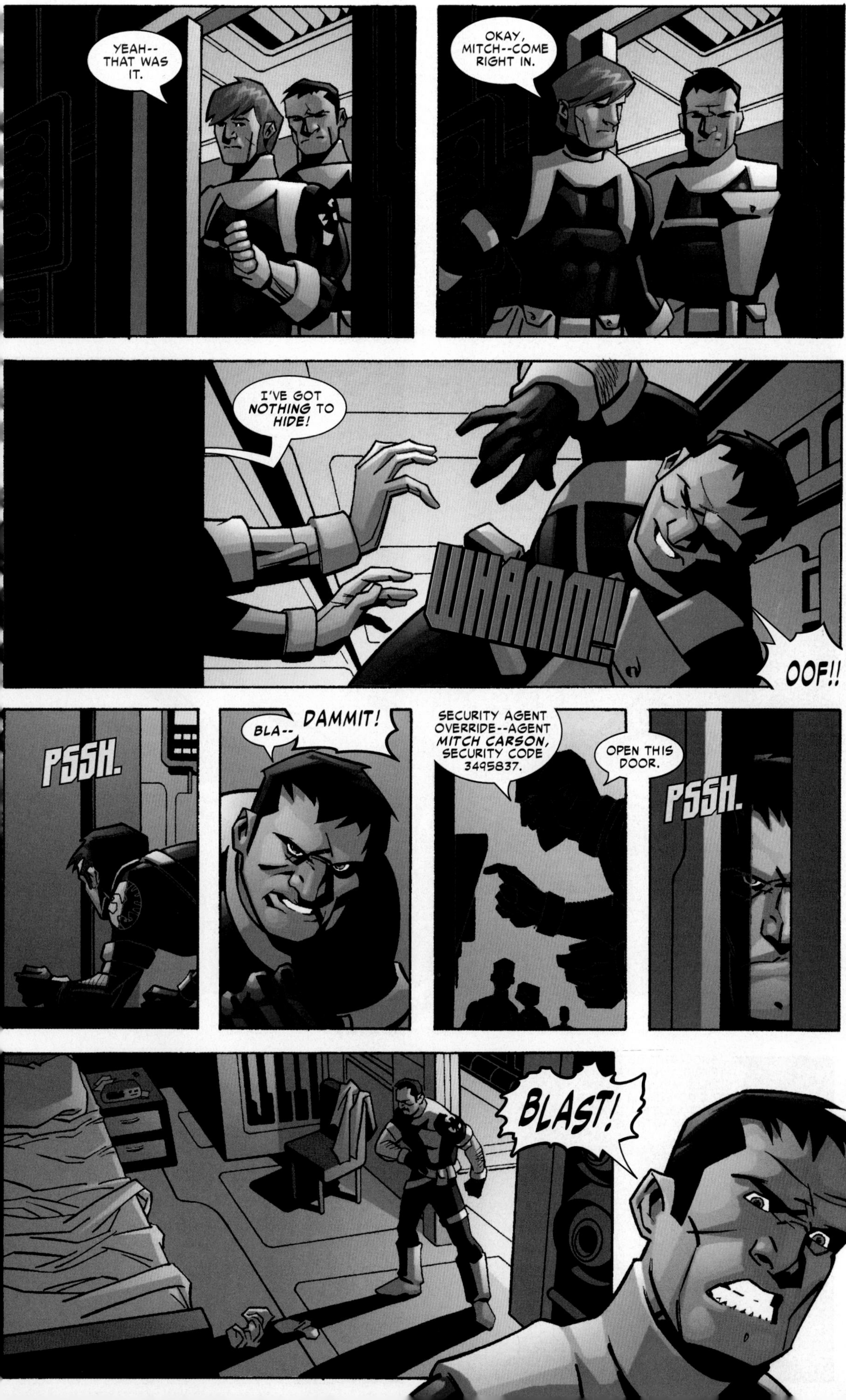
YEAH-- THAT WAS IT.
OKAY, MITCH--COME RIGHT IN.
I'VE GOT NOTHING TO HIDE!
WHAMM!!
OOF!!
PSSH.
BLA--
DAMMIT!
SECURITY AGENT OVERRIDE--AGENT MITCH CARSON, SECURITY CODE 3495837.
OPEN THIS DOOR.
PSSH.
BLAST!

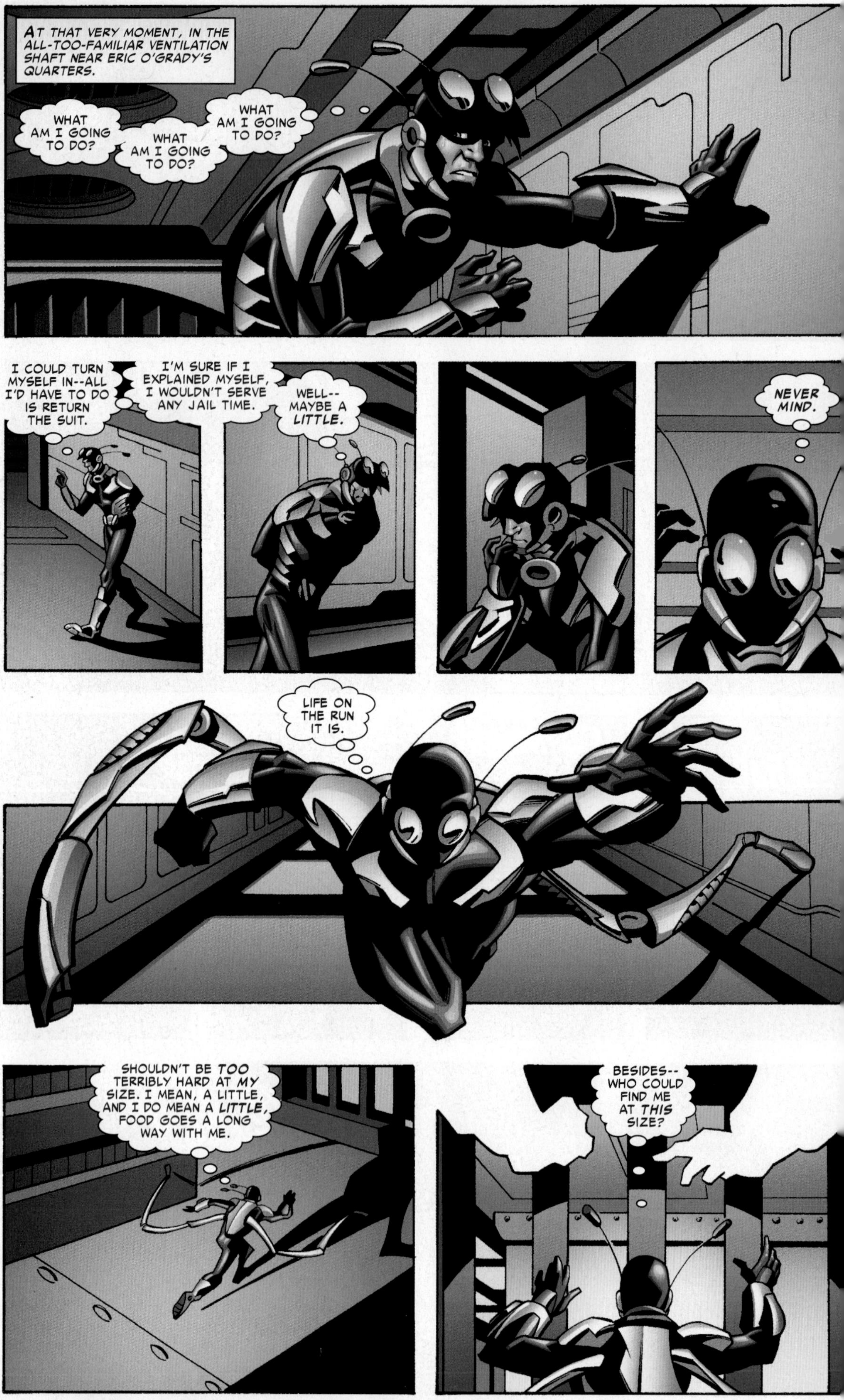
AT THAT VERY MOMENT, IN THE ALL-TOO-FAMILIAR VENTILATION SHAFT NEAR ERIC O'GRADY'S QUARTERS.
WHAT AM I GOING TO DO?
WHAT AM I GOING TO DO?
WHAT AM I GOING TO DO?
I COULD TURN MYSELF IN--ALL I'D HAVE TO DO IS RETURN THE SUIT.
I'M SURE IF I EXPLAINED MYSELF, I WOULDN'T SERVE ANY JAIL TIME.
WELL-- MAYBE A LITTLE.
NEVER MIND.
LIFE ON THE RUN IT IS.
SHOULDN'T BE TOO TERRIBLY HARD AT MY SIZE. I MEAN, A LITTLE, AND I DO MEAN A LITTLE, FOOD GOES A LONG WAY WITH ME.
BESIDES-- WHO COULD FIND ME AT THIS SIZE?

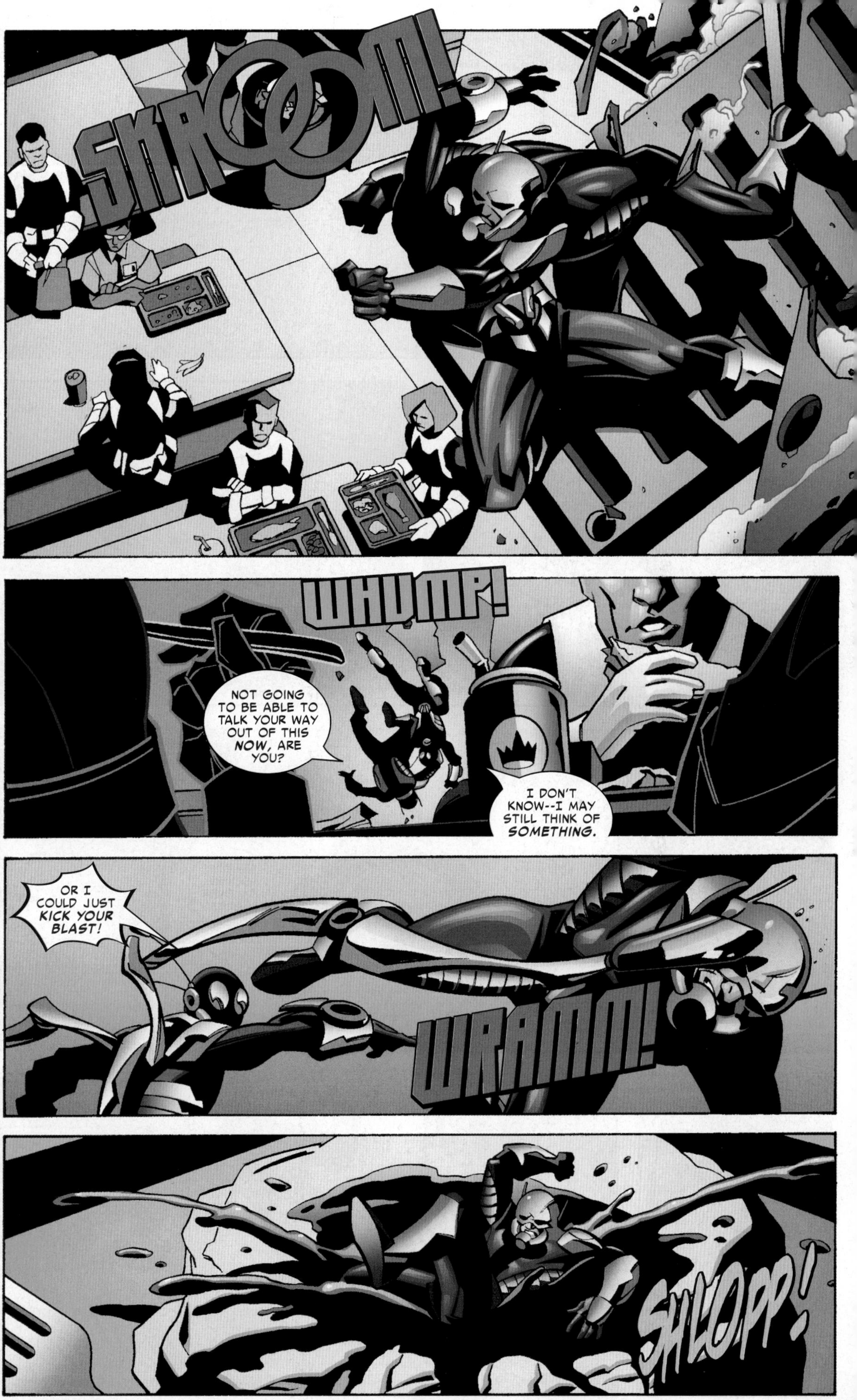
SKROOM!
WHUMP!
NOT GOING TO BE ABLE TO TALK YOUR WAY OUT OF THIS NOW, ARE YOU?
I DON'T KNOW--I MAY STILL THINK OF SOMETHING.
OR I COULD JUST KICK YOUR BLAST!
WRAMM!
SHLOPP!

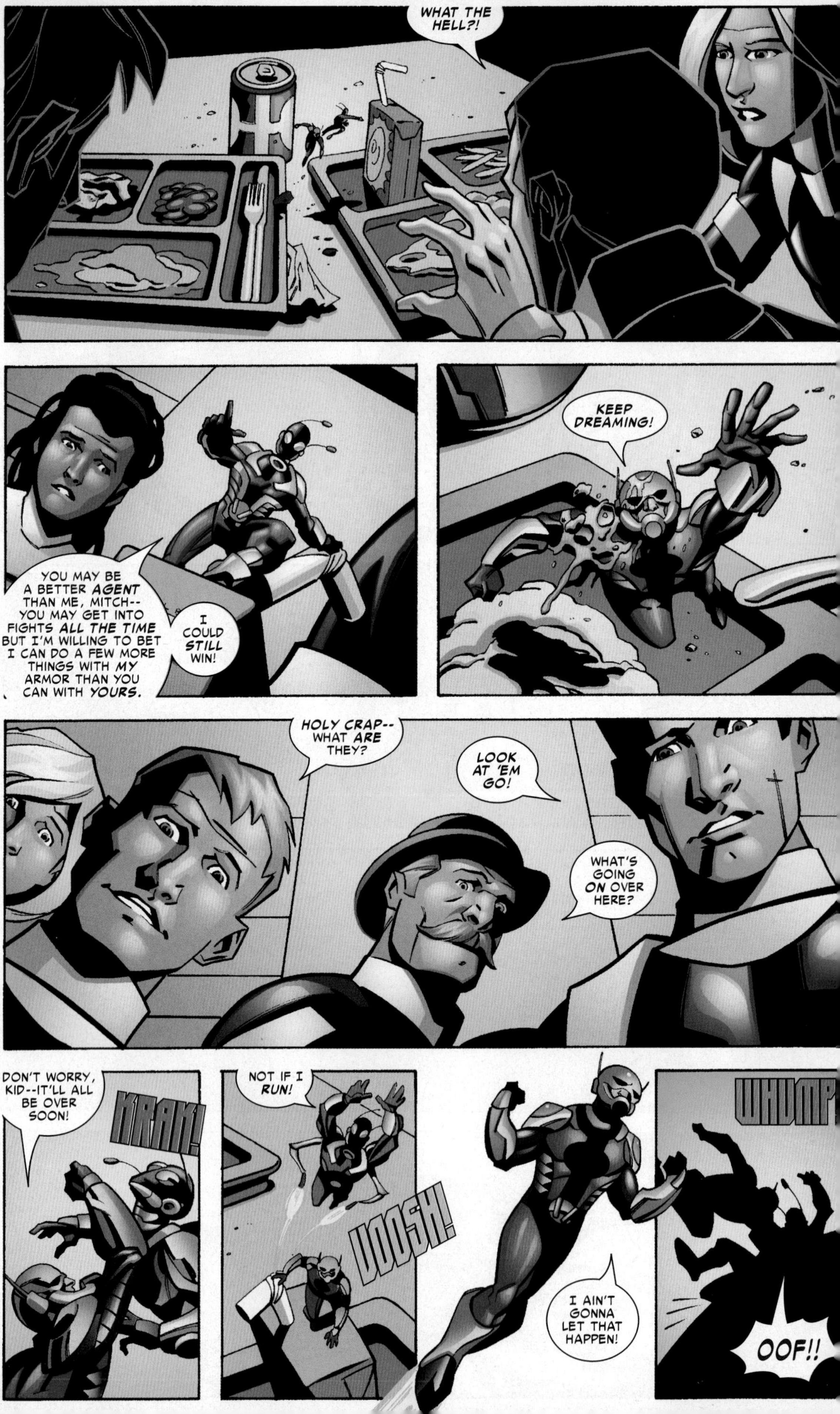

WHAT THE HELL?!
YOU MAY BE A BETTER AGENT THAN ME, MITCH-- YOU MAY GET INTO FIGHTS ALL THE TIME BUT I'M WILLING TO BET I CAN DO A FEW MORE THINGS WITH MY ARMOR THAN YOU CAN WITH YOURS.
I COULD STILL WIN!
KEEP DREAMING!
HOLY CRAP-- WHAT ARE THEY?
LOOK AT 'EM GO!
WHAT'S GOING ON OVER HERE?
DON'T WORRY, KID--IT'LL ALL BE OVER SOON!
KRAK!
NOT IF I RUN!
VOOSH!
I AIN'T GONNA LET THAT HAPPEN!
OOF!!

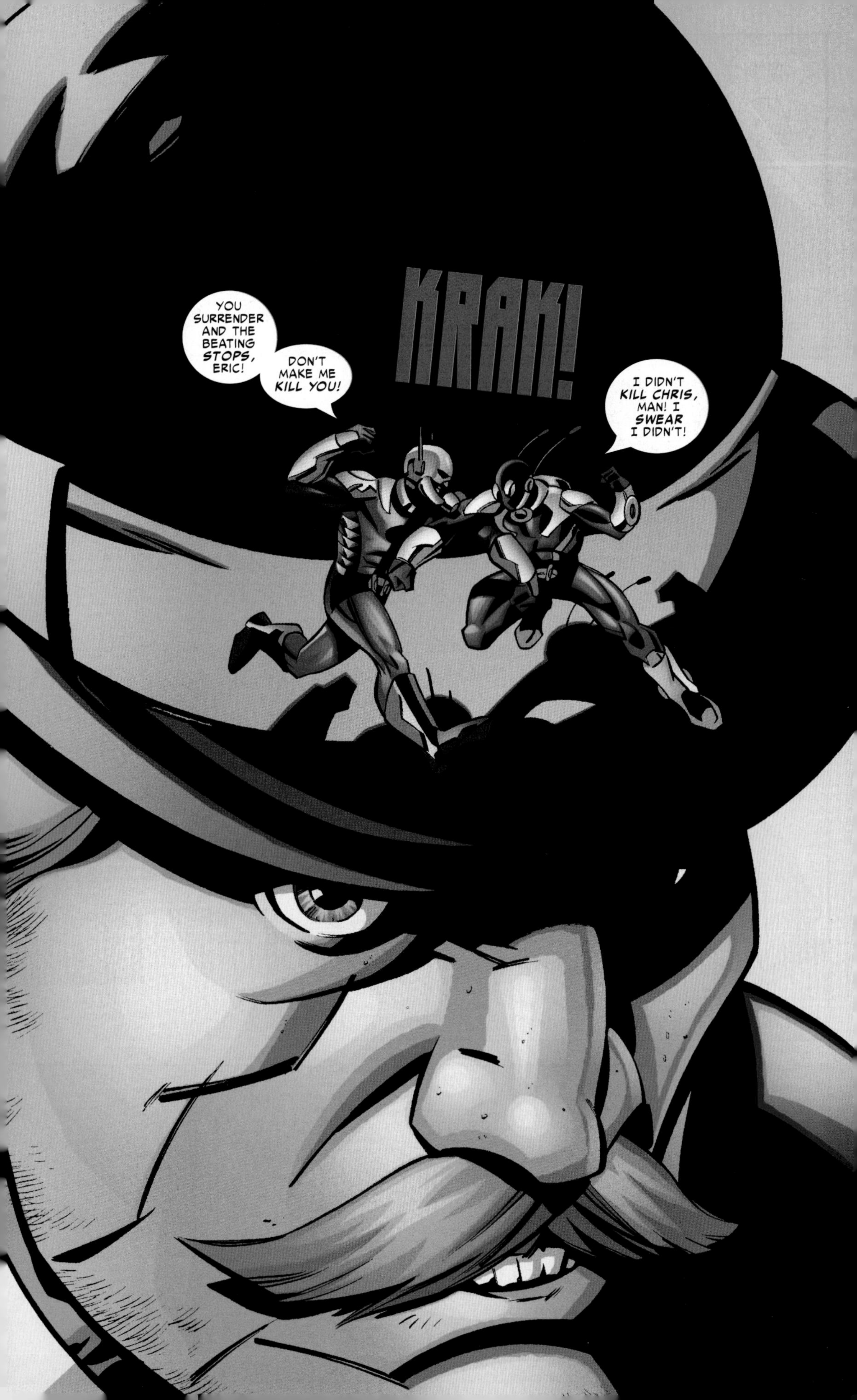
KRAK!
YOU SURRENDER AND THE BEATING STOPS, ERIC!
DON'T MAKE ME KILL YOU!
I DIDN'T KILL CHRIS, MAN! I SWEAR I DIDN'T!

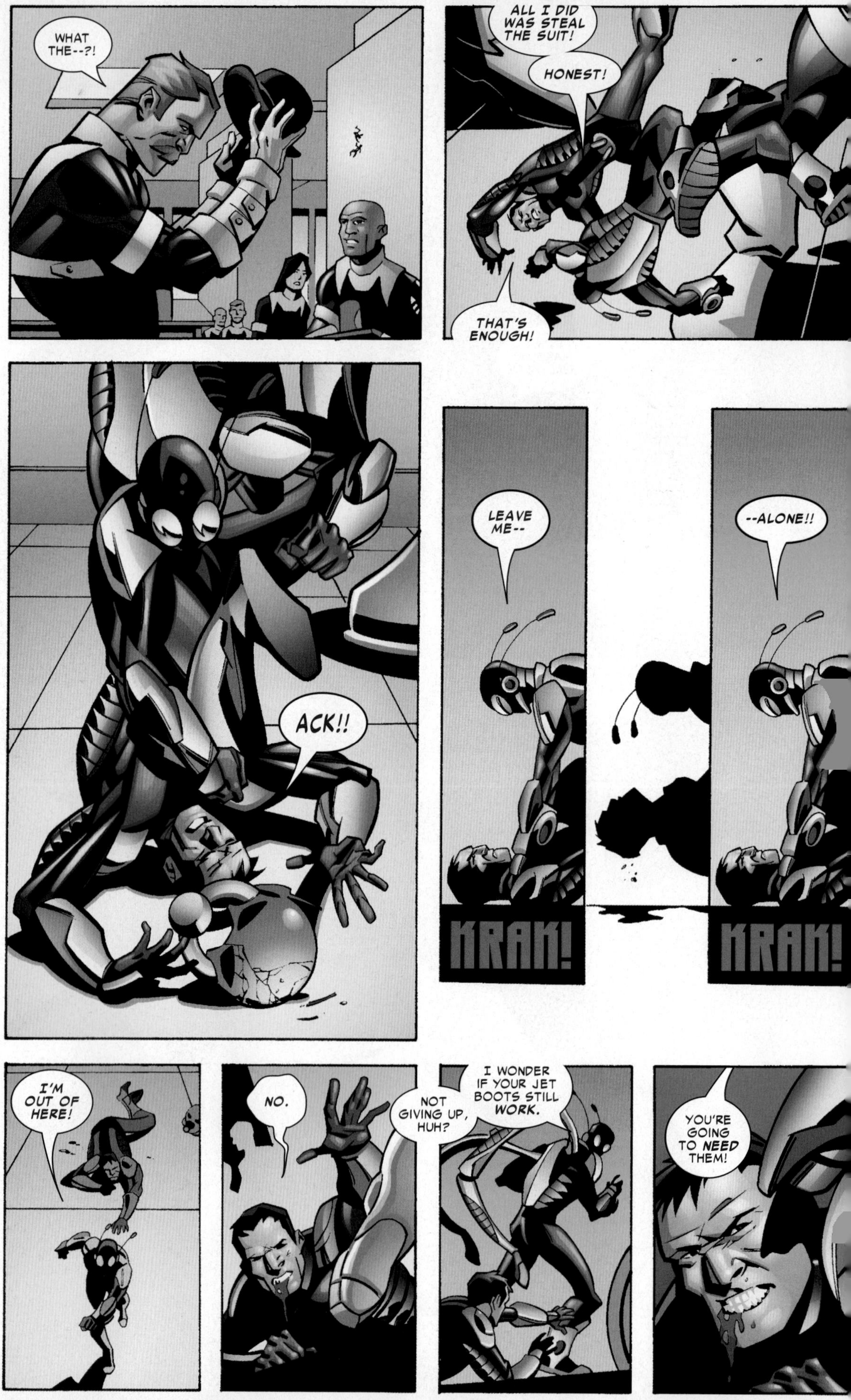
WHAT THE--?!
ALL I DID WAS STEAL THE SUIT!
HONEST!
THAT'S ENOUGH!
ACK!!
LEAVE ME--
KRAK!
--ALONE!!
KRAK!
I'M OUT OF HERE!
NO.
NOT GIVING UP, HUH?
I WONDER IF YOUR JET BOOTS STILL WORK.
YOU'RE GOING TO NEED THEM!

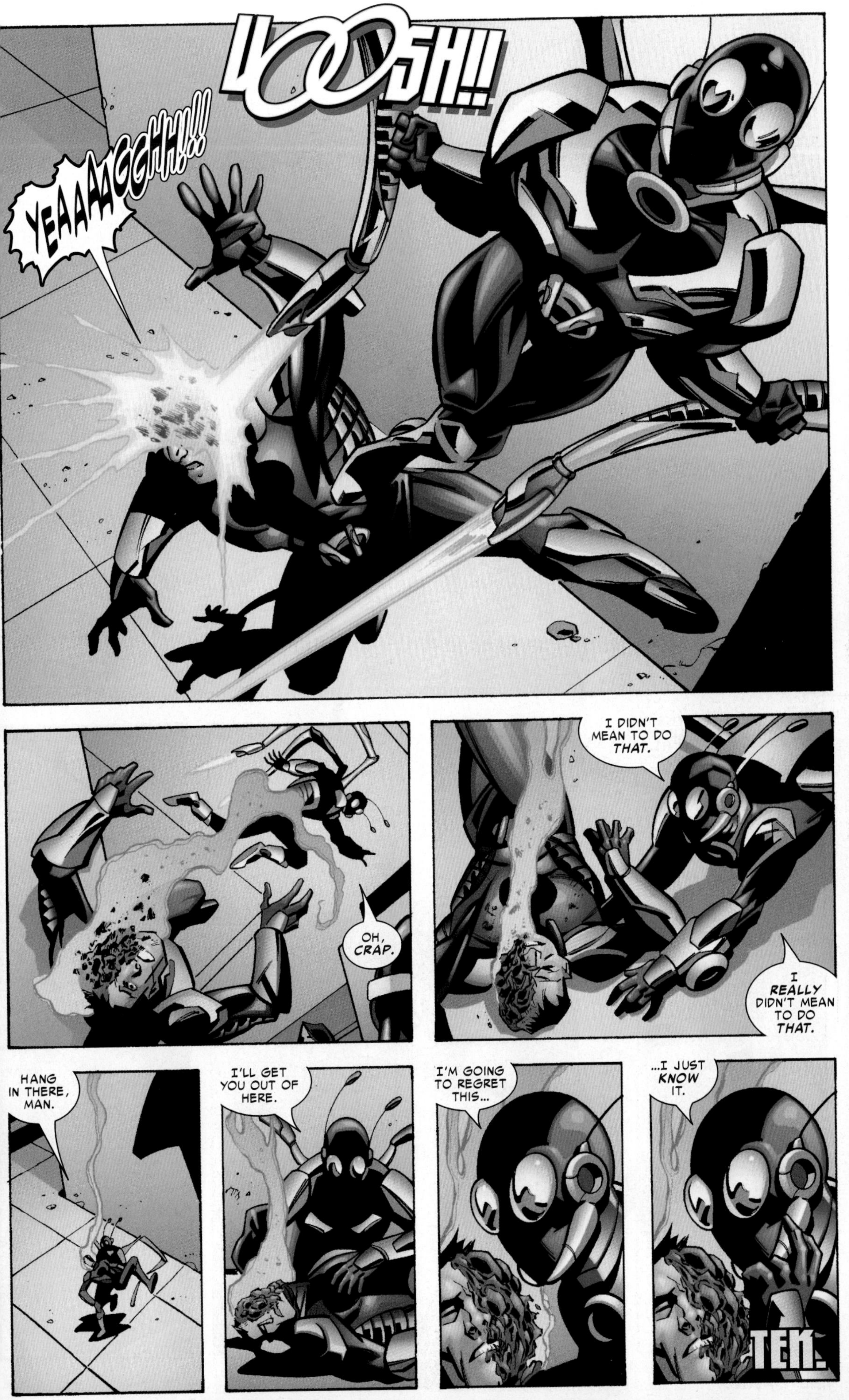
WOOSH!!
YEAAAAGGHH!!!
OH, CRAP.
I DIDN'T MEAN TO DO THAT.
I REALLY DIDN'T MEAN TO DO THAT.
HANG IN THERE, MAN.
I'LL GET YOU OUT OF HERE.
I'M GOING TO REGRET THIS...
...I JUST KNOW IT.
TEK.

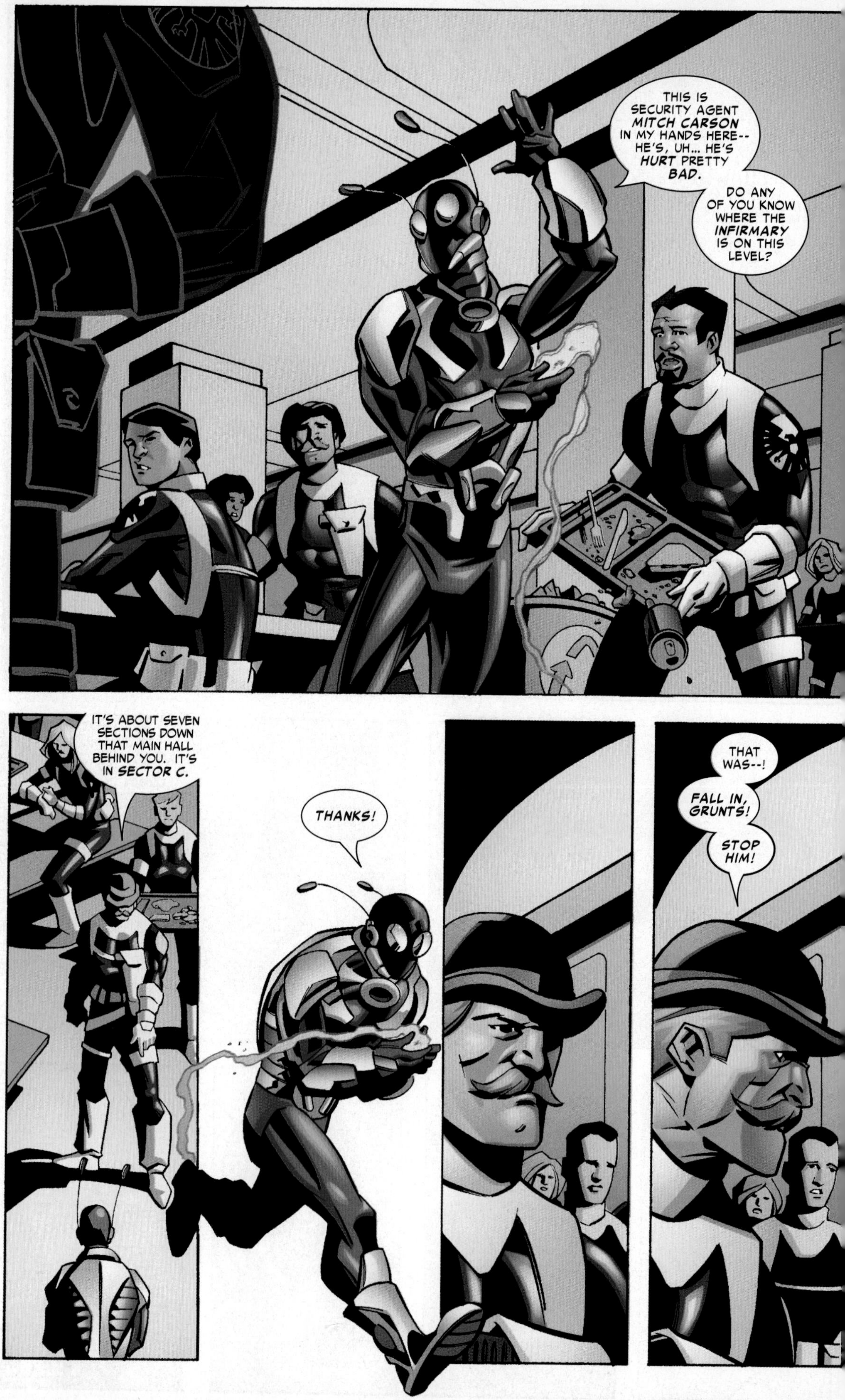
THIS IS SECURITY AGENT MITCH CARSON IN MY HANDS HERE-- HE'S, UH... HE'S HURT PRETTY BAD.
DO ANY OF YOU KNOW WHERE THE INFIRMARY IS ON THIS LEVEL?
IT'S ABOUT SEVEN SECTIONS DOWN THAT MAIN HALL BEHIND YOU. IT'S IN SECTOR C.
THANKS!
THAT WAS--!
FALL IN, GRUNTS!
STOP HIM!

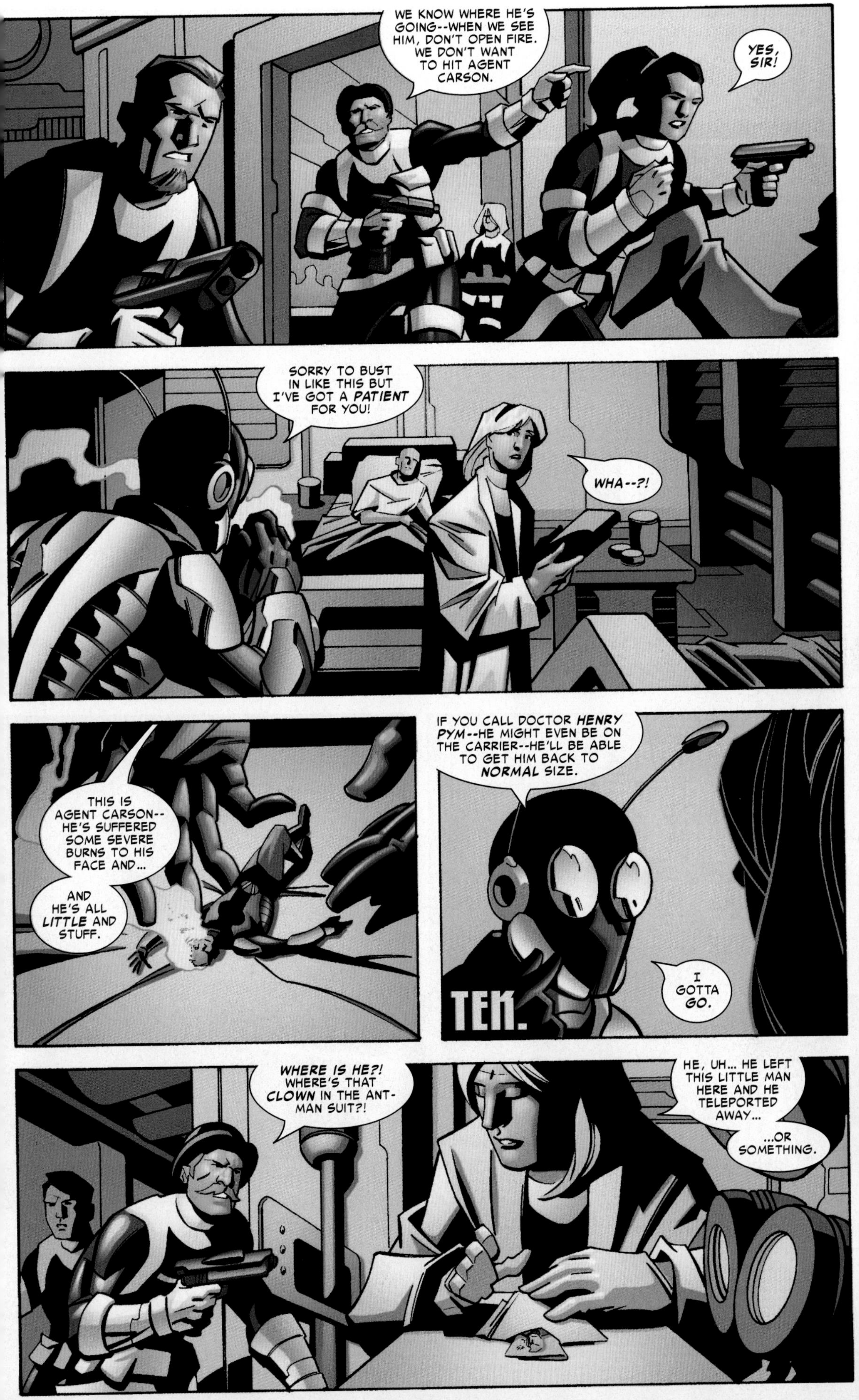
WE KNOW WHERE HE'S GOING--WHEN WE SEE HIM, DON'T OPEN FIRE. WE DON'T WANT TO HIT AGENT CARSON.
YES, SIR!
SORRY TO BUST IN LIKE THIS BUT I'VE GOT A PATIENT FOR YOU!
WHA--?!
THIS IS AGENT CARSON--HE'S SUFFERED SOME SEVERE BURNS TO HIS FACE AND...
AND HE'S ALL LITTLE AND STUFF.
IF YOU CALL DOCTOR HENRY PYM--HE MIGHT EVEN BE ON THE CARRIER--HE'LL BE ABLE TO GET HIM BACK TO NORMAL SIZE.
TEK.
I GOTTA GO.
WHERE IS HE?! WHERE'S THAT CLOWN IN THE ANT-MAN SUIT?!
HE, UH... HE LEFT THIS LITTLE MAN HERE AND HE TELEPORTED AWAY...
...OR SOMETHING.

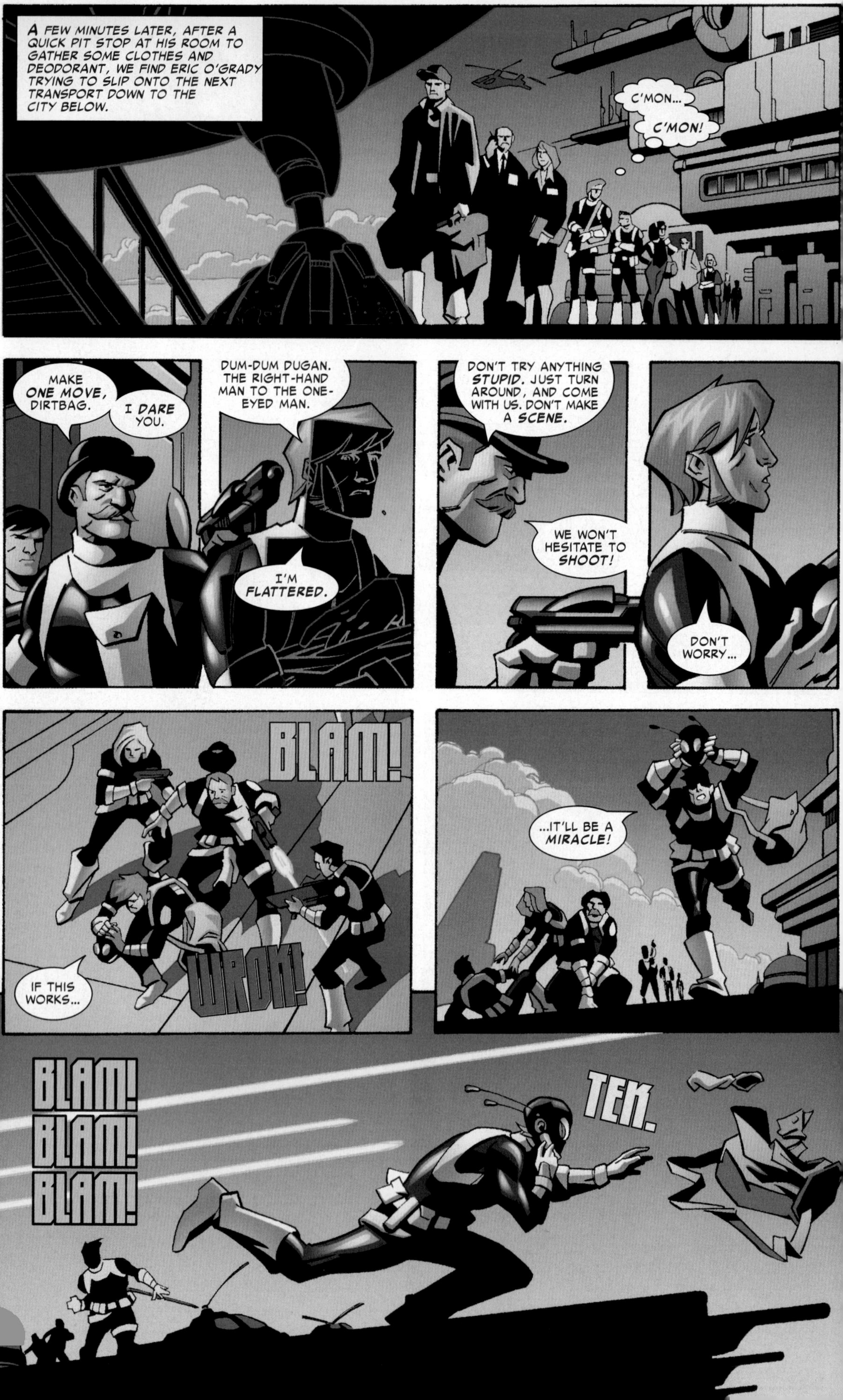
A FEW MINUTES LATER, AFTER A QUICK PIT STOP AT HIS ROOM TO GATHER SOME CLOTHES AND DEODORANT, WE FIND ERIC O'GRADY TRYING TO SLIP ONTO THE NEXT TRANSPORT DOWN TO THE CITY BELOW.
C'MON...
C'MON!
MAKE ONE MOVE, DIRTBAG.
I DARE YOU.
DUM-DUM DUGAN. THE RIGHT-HAND MAN TO THE ONE-EYED MAN.
I'M FLATTERED.
DON'T TRY ANYTHING STUPID. JUST TURN AROUND, AND COME WITH US. DON'T MAKE A SCENE.
WE WON'T HESITATE TO SHOOT!
DON'T WORRY...
BLAM!
IF THIS WORKS...
WROK!
...IT'LL BE A MIRACLE!
BLAM!
BLAM!
BLAM!
TEK.

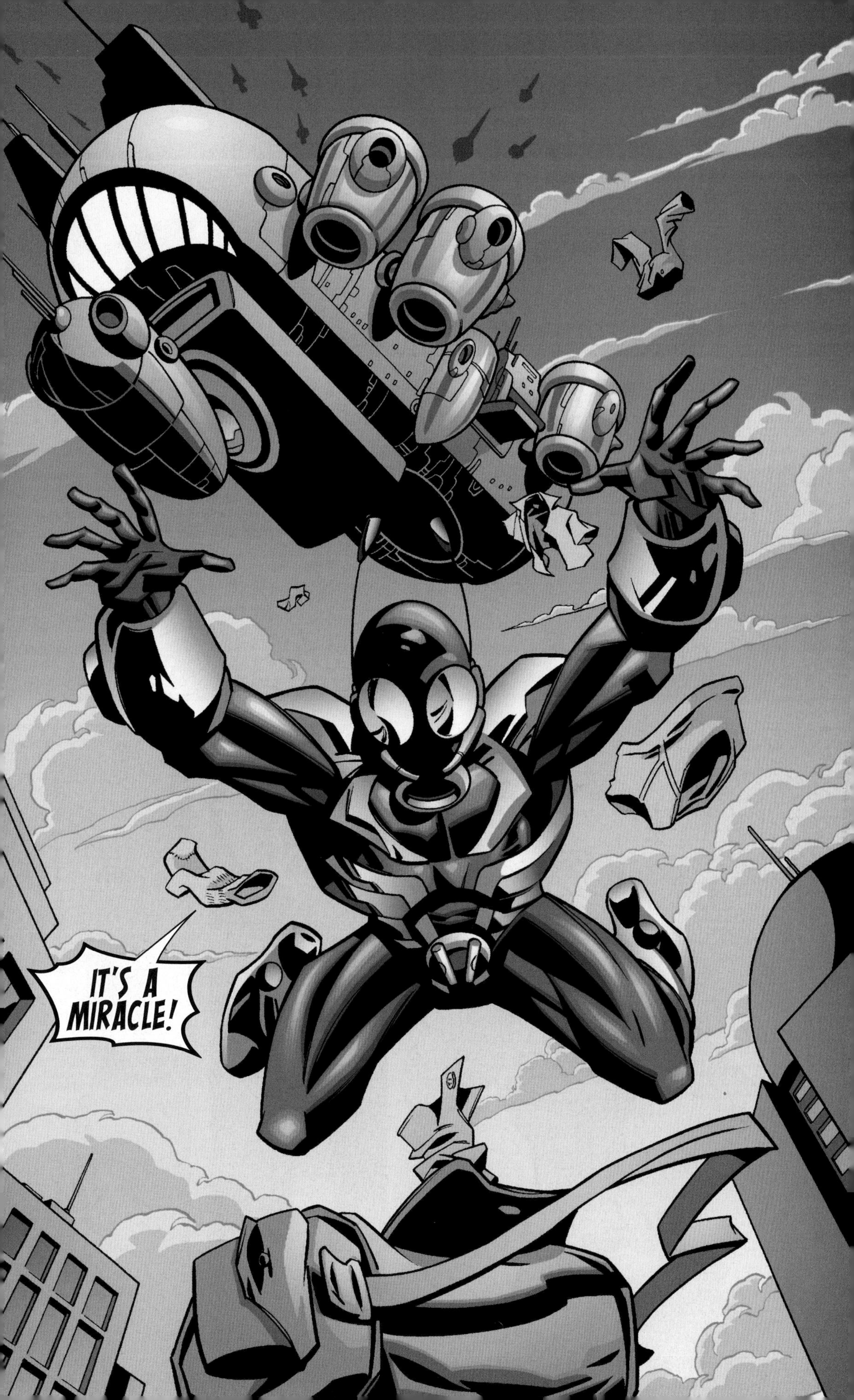
IT'S A MIRACLE!

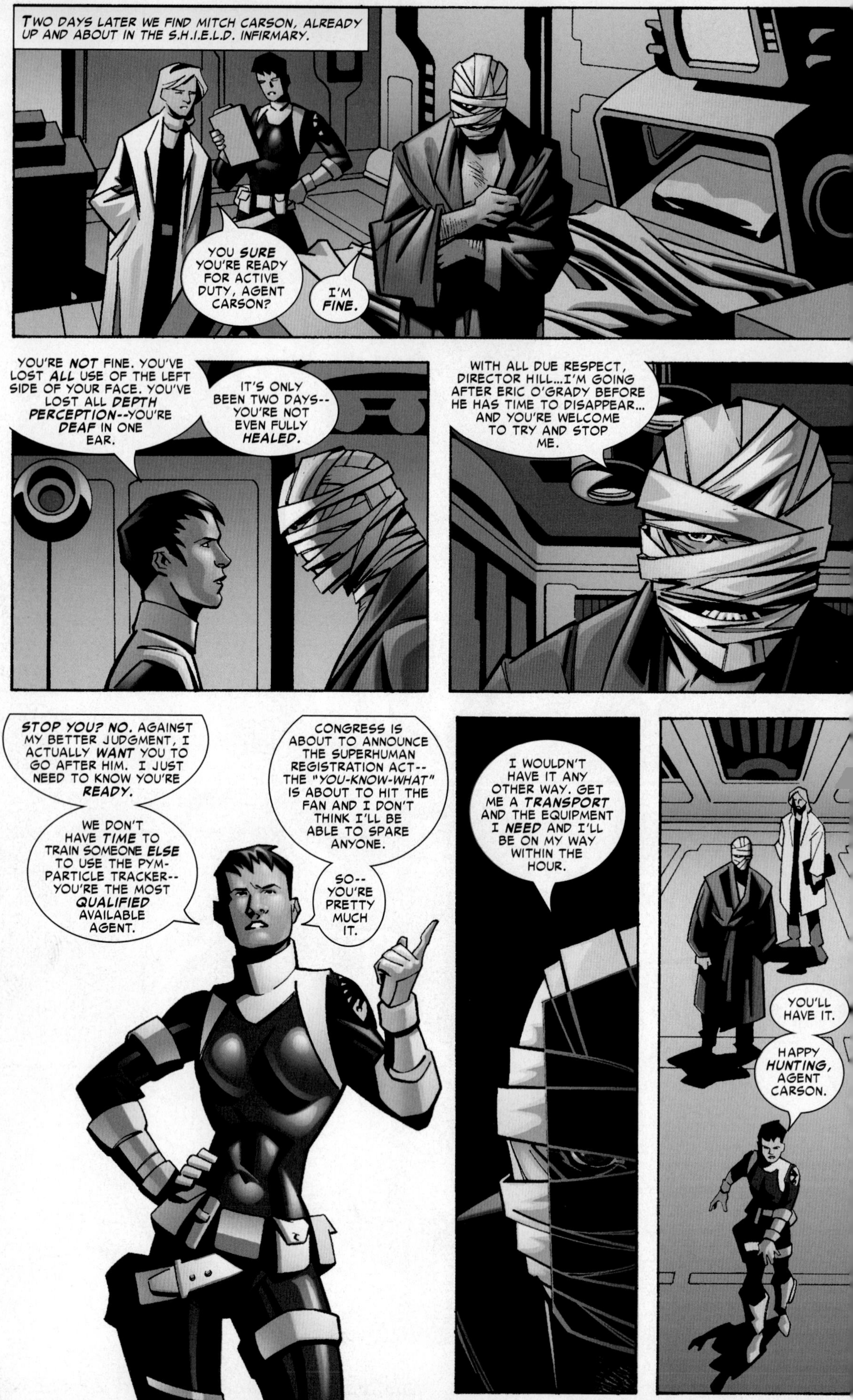
TWO DAYS LATER WE FIND MITCH CARSON, ALREADY UP AND ABOUT IN THE S.H.I.E.L.D. INFIRMARY.
YOU SURE YOU'RE READY FOR ACTIVE DUTY, AGENT CARSON?
I'M FINE.
YOU'RE NOT FINE. YOU'VE LOST ALL USE OF THE LEFT SIDE OF YOUR FACE. YOU'VE LOST ALL DEPTH PERCEPTION--YOU'RE DEAF IN ONE EAR.
IT'S ONLY BEEN TWO DAYS--YOU'RE NOT EVEN FULLY HEALED.
WITH ALL DUE RESPECT, DIRECTOR HILL...I'M GOING AFTER ERIC O'GRADY BEFORE HE HAS TIME TO DISAPPEAR... AND YOU'RE WELCOME TO TRY AND STOP ME.
STOP YOU? NO. AGAINST MY BETTER JUDGMENT, I ACTUALLY WANT YOU TO GO AFTER HIM. I JUST NEED TO KNOW YOU'RE READY.
WE DON'T HAVE TIME TO TRAIN SOMEONE ELSE TO USE THE PYM-PARTICLE TRACKER--YOU'RE THE MOST QUALIFIED AVAILABLE AGENT.
CONGRESS IS ABOUT TO ANNOUNCE THE SUPERHUMAN REGISTRATION ACT--THE "YOU-KNOW-WHAT" IS ABOUT TO HIT THE FAN AND I DON'T THINK I'LL BE ABLE TO SPARE ANYONE.
SO--YOU'RE PRETTY MUCH IT.
I WOULDN'T HAVE IT ANY OTHER WAY. GET ME A TRANSPORT AND THE EQUIPMENT I NEED AND I'LL BE ON MY WAY WITHIN THE HOUR.
YOU'LL HAVE IT.
HAPPY HUNTING, AGENT CARSON.

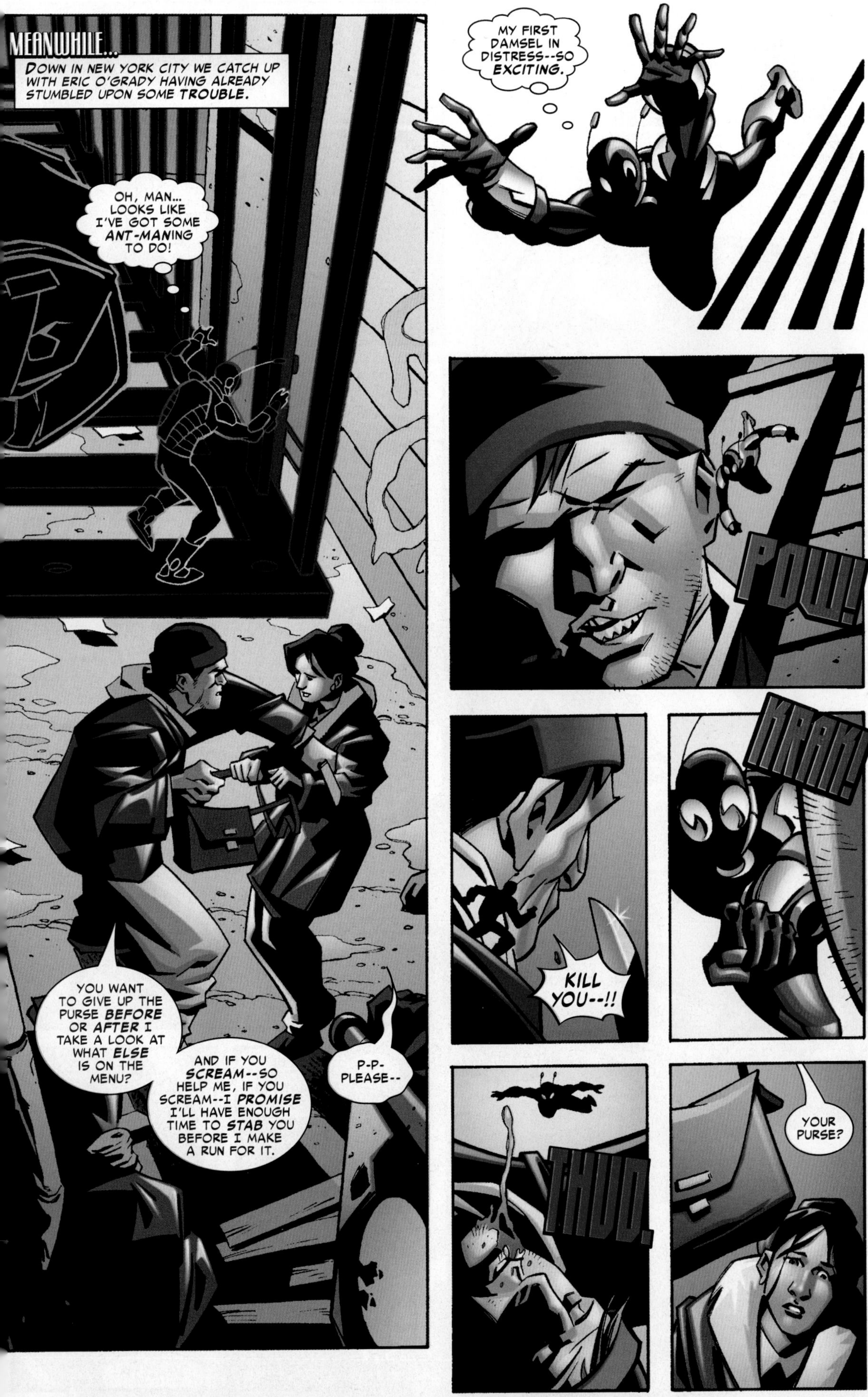

MEANWHILE...
DOWN IN NEW YORK CITY WE CATCH UP WITH ERIC O'GRADY HAVING ALREADY STUMBLED UPON SOME TROUBLE.
OH, MAN... LOOKS LIKE I'VE GOT SOME ANT-MANING TO DO!
YOU WANT TO GIVE UP THE PURSE BEFORE OR AFTER I TAKE A LOOK AT WHAT ELSE IS ON THE MENU?
AND IF YOU SCREAM--SO HELP ME, IF YOU SCREAM--I PROMISE I'LL HAVE ENOUGH TIME TO STAB YOU BEFORE I MAKE A RUN FOR IT.
P-P-PLEASE--
MY FIRST DAMSEL IN DISTRESS--SO EXCITING.
POW!
KILL YOU--!!
KRAK!
THUD.
YOUR PURSE?

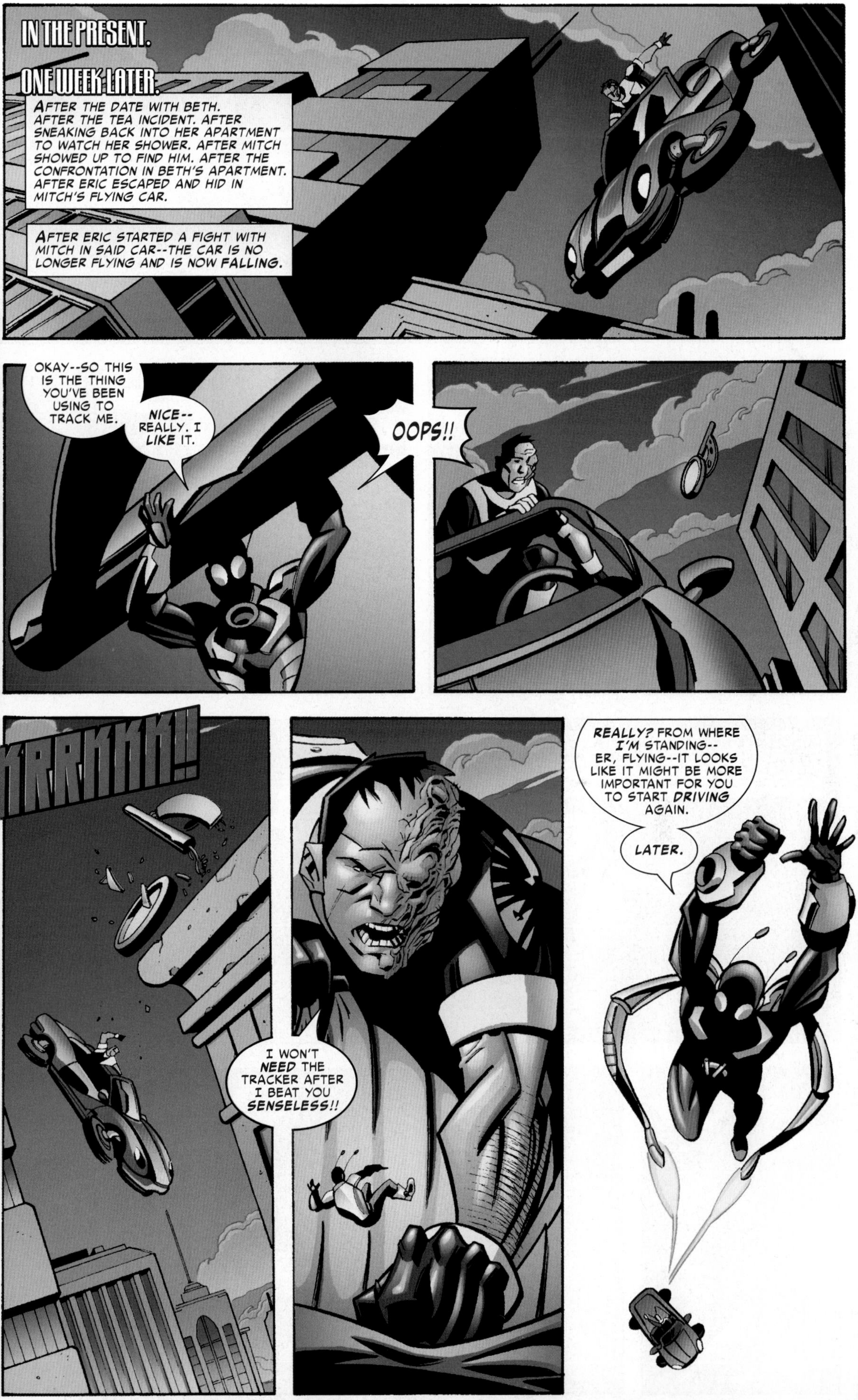
IN THE PRESENT.
ONE WEEK LATER.
AFTER THE DATE WITH BETH. AFTER THE TEA INCIDENT. AFTER SNEAKING BACK INTO HER APARTMENT TO WATCH HER SHOWER. AFTER MITCH SHOWED UP TO FIND HIM. AFTER THE CONFRONTATION IN BETH'S APARTMENT. AFTER ERIC ESCAPED AND HID IN MITCH'S FLYING CAR.
AFTER ERIC STARTED A FIGHT WITH MITCH IN SAID CAR--THE CAR IS NO LONGER FLYING AND IS NOW FALLING.
OKAY--SO THIS IS THE THING YOU'VE BEEN USING TO TRACK ME.
NICE--REALLY. I LIKE IT.
OOPS!!
KRRKKK!!
I WON'T NEED THE TRACKER AFTER I BEAT YOU SENSELESS!!
REALLY? FROM WHERE I'M STANDING--ER, FLYING--IT LOOKS LIKE IT MIGHT BE MORE IMPORTANT FOR YOU TO START DRIVING AGAIN.
LATER.

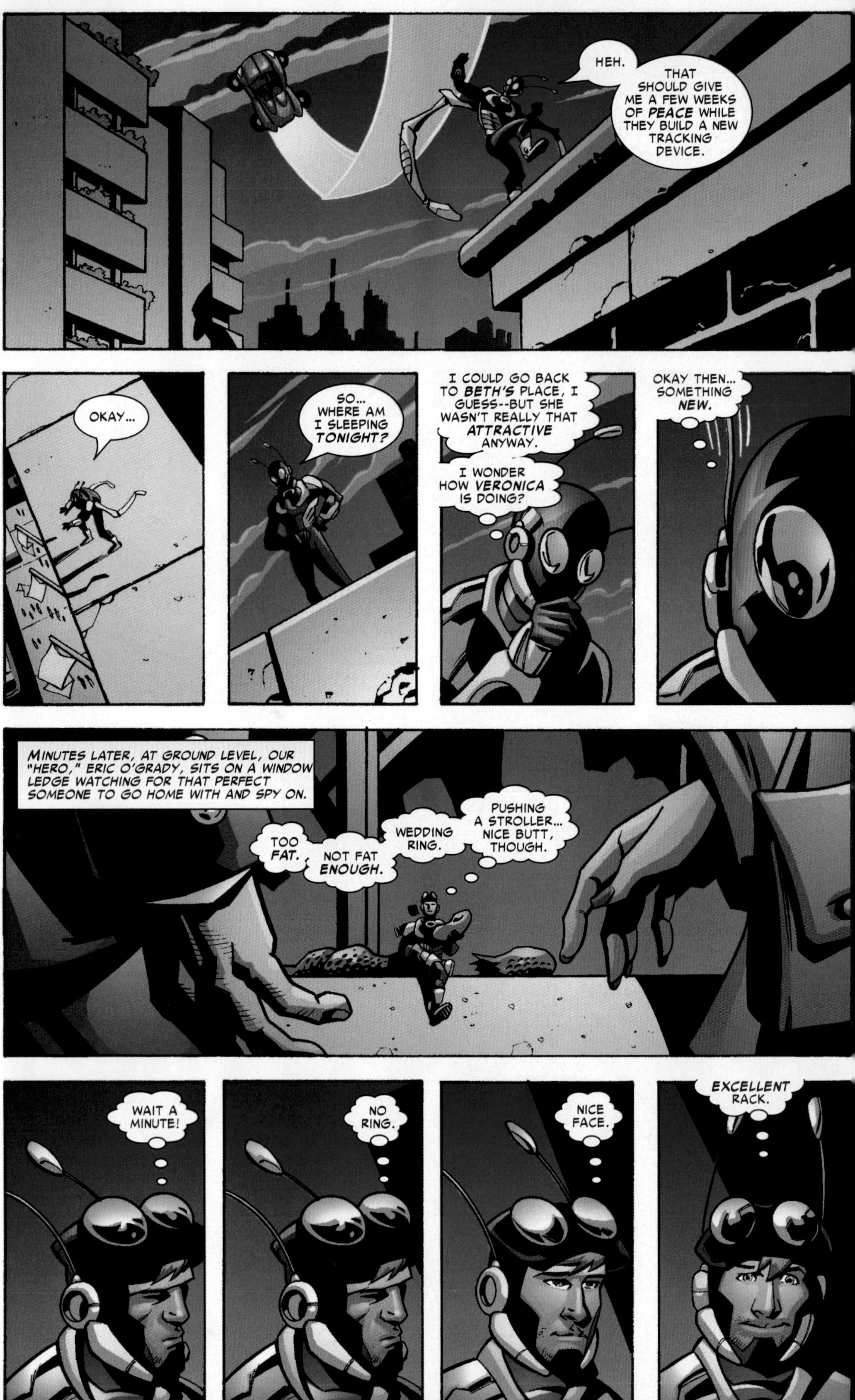
HEH.
THAT SHOULD GIVE ME A FEW WEEKS OF PEACE WHILE THEY BUILD A NEW TRACKING DEVICE.
OKAY...
SO... WHERE AM I SLEEPING TONIGHT?
I COULD GO BACK TO BETH'S PLACE, I GUESS--BUT SHE WASN'T REALLY THAT ATTRACTIVE ANYWAY.
I WONDER HOW VERONICA IS DOING?
OKAY THEN... SOMETHING NEW.
MINUTES LATER, AT GROUND LEVEL, OUR "HERO," ERIC O'GRADY, SITS ON A WINDOW LEDGE WATCHING FOR THAT PERFECT SOMEONE TO GO HOME WITH AND SPY ON.
TOO FAT.
NOT FAT ENOUGH.
WEDDING RING.
PUSHING A STROLLER... NICE BUTT, THOUGH.
WAIT A MINUTE!
NO RING.
NICE FACE.
EXCELLENT RACK.

#7

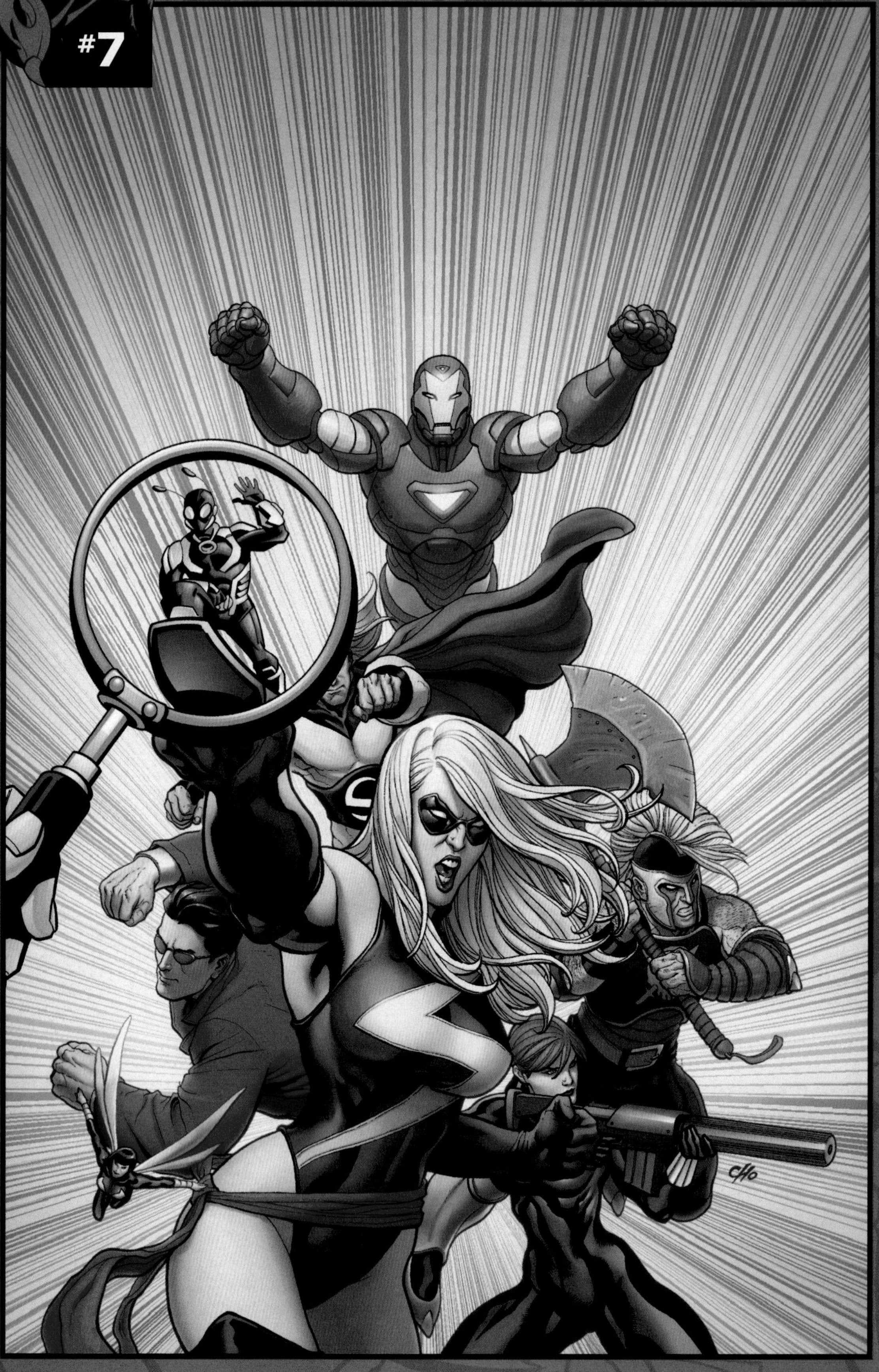
CHO

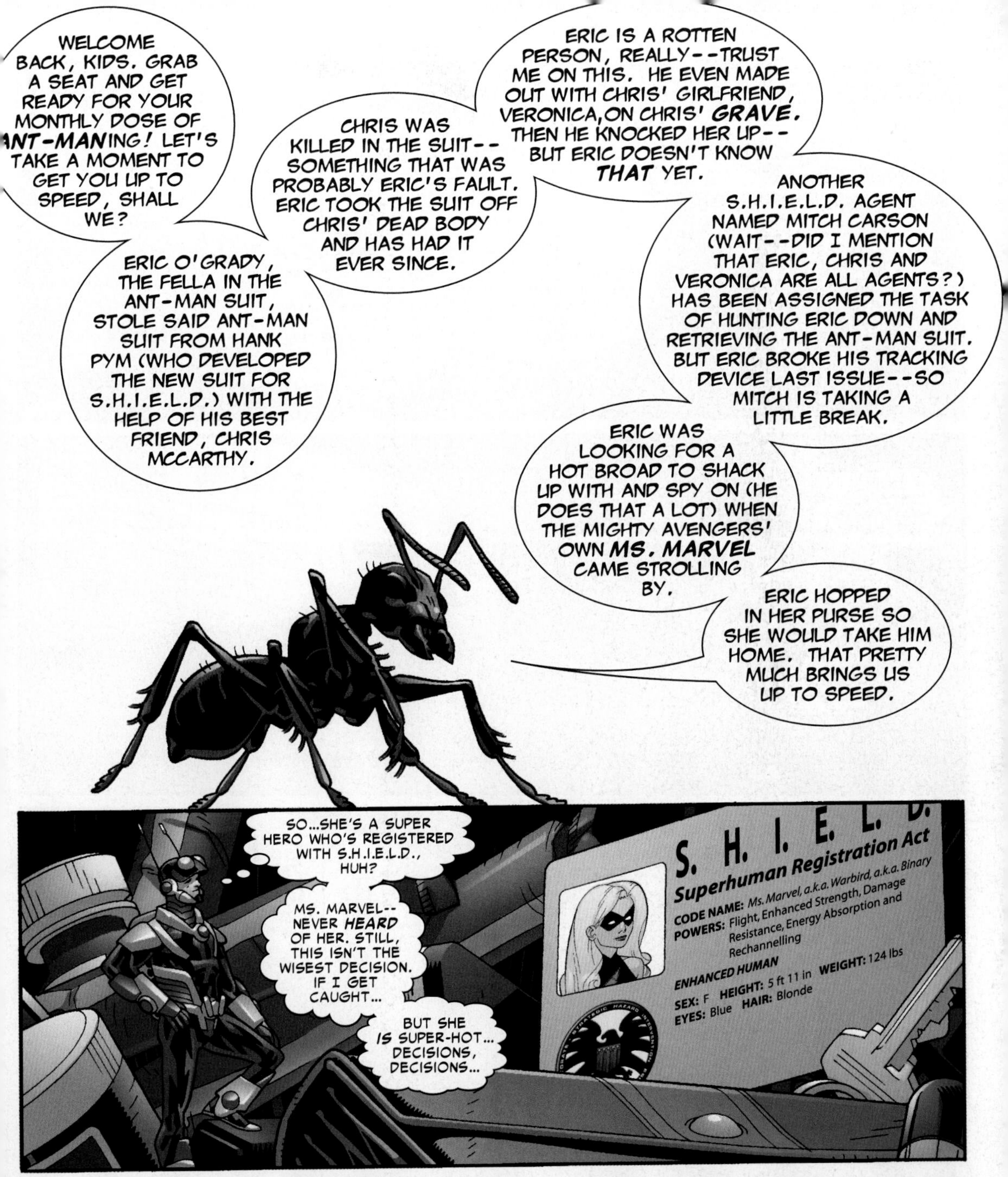
WELCOME BACK, KIDS. GRAB A SEAT AND GET READY FOR YOUR MONTHLY DOSE OF ANT-MANING! LET'S TAKE A MOMENT TO GET YOU UP TO SPEED, SHALL WE?
ERIC O'GRADY, THE FELLA IN THE ANT-MAN SUIT, STOLE SAID ANT-MAN SUIT FROM HANK PYM (WHO DEVELOPED THE NEW SUIT FOR S.H.I.E.L.D.) WITH THE HELP OF HIS BEST FRIEND, CHRIS MCCARTHY.
CHRIS WAS KILLED IN THE SUIT--SOMETHING THAT WAS PROBABLY ERIC'S FAULT. ERIC TOOK THE SUIT OFF CHRIS' DEAD BODY AND HAS HAD IT EVER SINCE.
ERIC IS A ROTTEN PERSON, REALLY--TRUST ME ON THIS. HE EVEN MADE OUT WITH CHRIS' GIRLFRIEND, VERONICA, ON CHRIS' GRAVE. THEN HE KNOCKED HER UP--BUT ERIC DOESN'T KNOW THAT YET.
ANOTHER S.H.I.E.L.D. AGENT NAMED MITCH CARSON (WAIT--DID I MENTION THAT ERIC, CHRIS AND VERONICA ARE ALL AGENTS?) HAS BEEN ASSIGNED THE TASK OF HUNTING ERIC DOWN AND RETRIEVING THE ANT-MAN SUIT. BUT ERIC BROKE HIS TRACKING DEVICE LAST ISSUE--SO MITCH IS TAKING A LITTLE BREAK.
ERIC WAS LOOKING FOR A HOT BROAD TO SHACK UP WITH AND SPY ON (HE DOES THAT A LOT) WHEN THE MIGHTY AVENGERS' OWN MS. MARVEL CAME STROLLING BY.
ERIC HOPPED IN HER PURSE SO SHE WOULD TAKE HIM HOME. THAT PRETTY MUCH BRINGS US UP TO SPEED.
SO...SHE'S A SUPER HERO WHO'S REGISTERED WITH S.H.I.E.L.D., HUH?
MS. MARVEL--NEVER HEARD OF HER. STILL, THIS ISN'T THE WISEST DECISION. IF I GET CAUGHT...
BUT SHE IS SUPER-HOT... DECISIONS, DECISIONS...
S. H. I. E. L. D.
Superhuman Registration Act
CODE NAME: Ms. Marvel, a.k.a. Warbird, a.k.a. Binary
POWERS: Flight, Enhanced Strength, Damage Resistance, Energy Absorption and Rechannelling
ENHANCED HUMAN
SEX: F HEIGHT: 5 ft 11 in WEIGHT: 124 lbs
EYES: Blue HAIR: Blonde

# UNINVITED

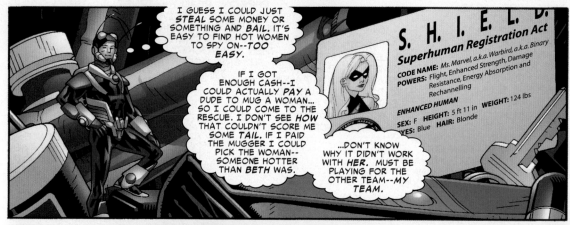

I GUESS I COULD JUST *STEAL* SOME MONEY OR SOMETHING AND *BAIL*. IT'S EASY TO FIND HOT WOMEN TO SPY ON--*TOO EASY*.

IF I GOT ENOUGH *CASH*--I COULD ACTUALLY *PAY* A DUDE TO MUG A WOMAN... SO I COULD COME TO THE RESCUE. I DON'T SEE *HOW* THAT COULDN'T SCORE ME SOME *TAIL*. IF I PAID THE MUGGER I COULD PICK THE WOMAN-- SOMEONE HOTTER THAN *BETH* WAS.

...DON'T KNOW WHY IT DIDN'T WORK WITH *HER*. MUST BE PLAYING FOR THE OTHER TEAM--*MY TEAM*.

**S.H.I.E.L.D.**
*Superhuman Registration Act*
CODE NAME: *Ms. Marvel, a.k.a. Warbird, a.k.a. Binary*
POWERS: Flight, Enhanced Strength, Damage Resistance, Energy Absorption and Rechannelling
*ENHANCED HUMAN*
SEX: F   HEIGHT: 5 ft 11 in   WEIGHT: 124 lbs
EYES: Blue   HAIR: Blonde

OKAY... LET'S SEE WHAT WE'VE GOT HERE.

*CASH*.

*CASH*.

*CASH*.

COME ON, *CASH*.

**S.H.I.E.L.D.**
*Superhuman Registration Act*
CODE NAME: *Ms. Marvel, a.k.a. Warbird, a.k.a. Binary*
POWERS: Flight, Enhanced Strength, Damage Resistance, Energy Absorption and Rechannelling
*ENHANCED HUMAN*
5 ft 11 in   WEIGHT: 124 lbs

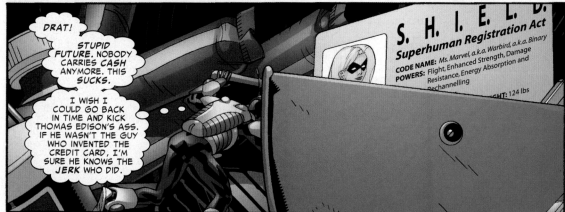

*DRAT!*

STUPID *FUTURE*. NOBODY CARRIES *CASH* ANYMORE. THIS *SUCKS*.

I WISH I COULD GO BACK IN TIME AND KICK THOMAS EDISON'S ASS. IF HE WASN'T THE GUY WHO INVENTED THE CREDIT CARD, I'M SURE HE KNOWS THE *JERK* WHO DID.

**S.H.I.E.L.D.**
*Superhuman Registration Act*
CODE NAME: *Ms. Marvel, a.k.a. Warbird, a.k.a. Binary*
POWERS: Flight, Enhanced Strength, Damage Resistance, Energy Absorption and Rechannelling
124 lbs

WELL, I'M NOT LEAVING HERE *EMPTY-HANDED*. I BET THIS BROAD'S GOT ALL KINDS OF COOL STUFF BACK AT HER LAIR.

I COULD PROBABLY MAKE OFF WITH A DINOSAUR, OR A *GIANT PENNY*.

HEH...*ANT-MAN* WITH A *GIANT* PENNY.

THAT'S... *IRONIC* OR SOMETHING...

*ZZZ.*

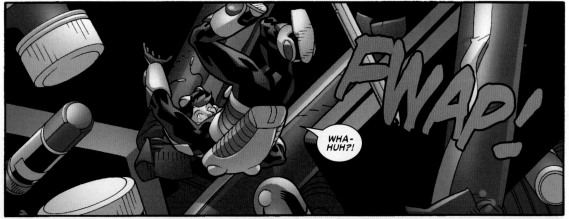

WHA-HUH?!

OKAY-- THAT'S IT. I'M AWAKE-- I'M--

I'M GETTING OUT OF HERE.

HELLO?

SEEMS THE "COAST"--OR WHATEVER IT IS THEY SAY--IS CLEAR.

HUH--WHAT IS THIS? A CRAPPY ONE-BEDROOM APARTMENT? THIS THING DOESN'T EVEN HAVE WINDOWS.

IS THAT A SKYLIGHT IN THERE? ARE WE ON THE TOP FLOOR? LOOKS LIKE WHEREVER WE ARE SHE JUST MOVED IN.

PSSHHHHHHH

HM. MY "ANT-SENSES" ARE TELLING ME THAT SOUNDS UNMISTAKABLY NOT UNLIKE A SHOWER RUNNING.

I MUST GO IMMEDIATELY--TO INVESTIGATE!

VOOOSH!

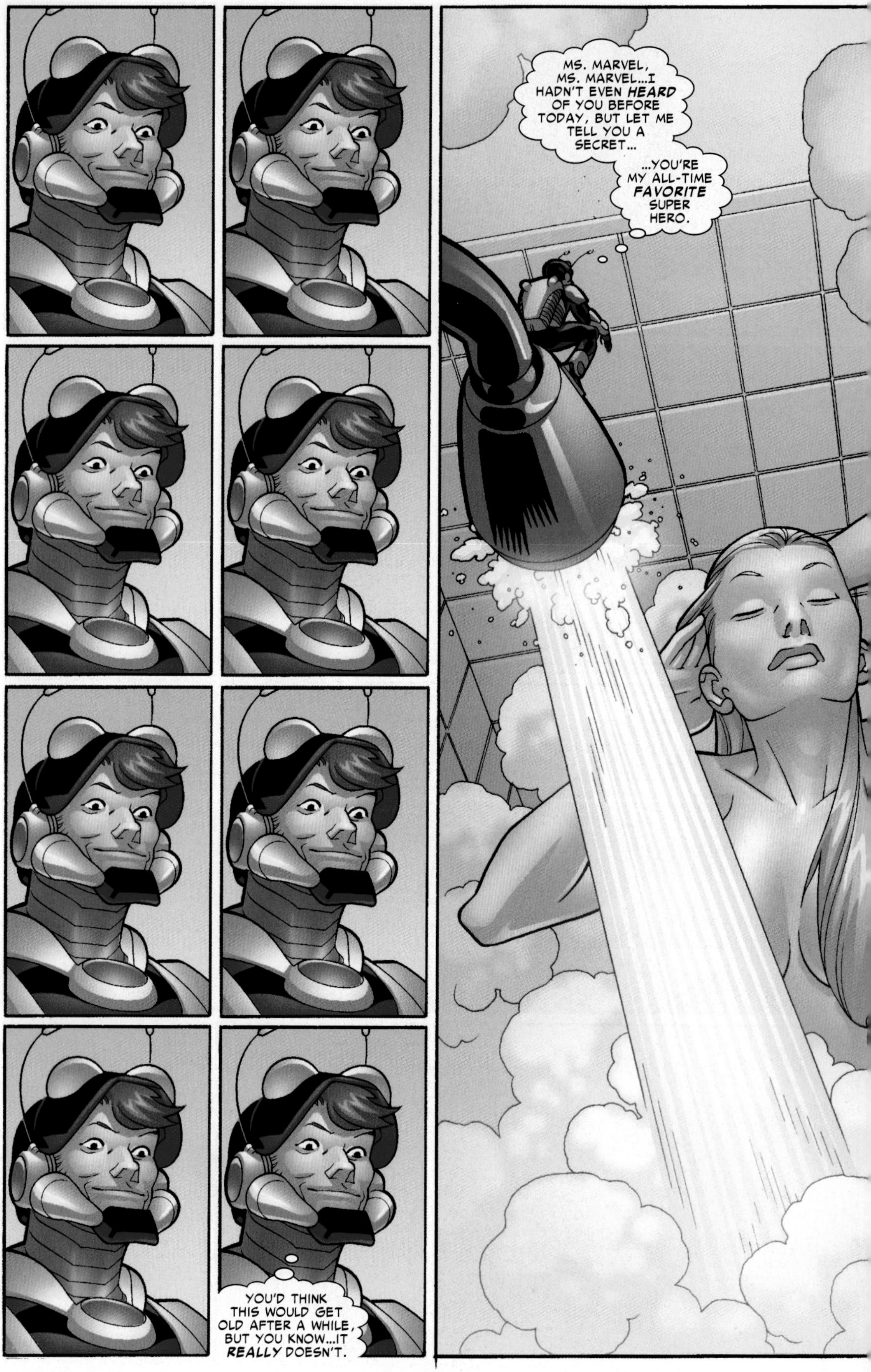
MS. MARVEL, MS. MARVEL...I HADN'T EVEN HEARD OF YOU BEFORE TODAY, BUT LET ME TELL YOU A SECRET...
...YOU'RE MY ALL-TIME FAVORITE SUPER HERO.
YOU'D THINK THIS WOULD GET OLD AFTER A WHILE, BUT YOU KNOW...IT REALLY DOESN'T.

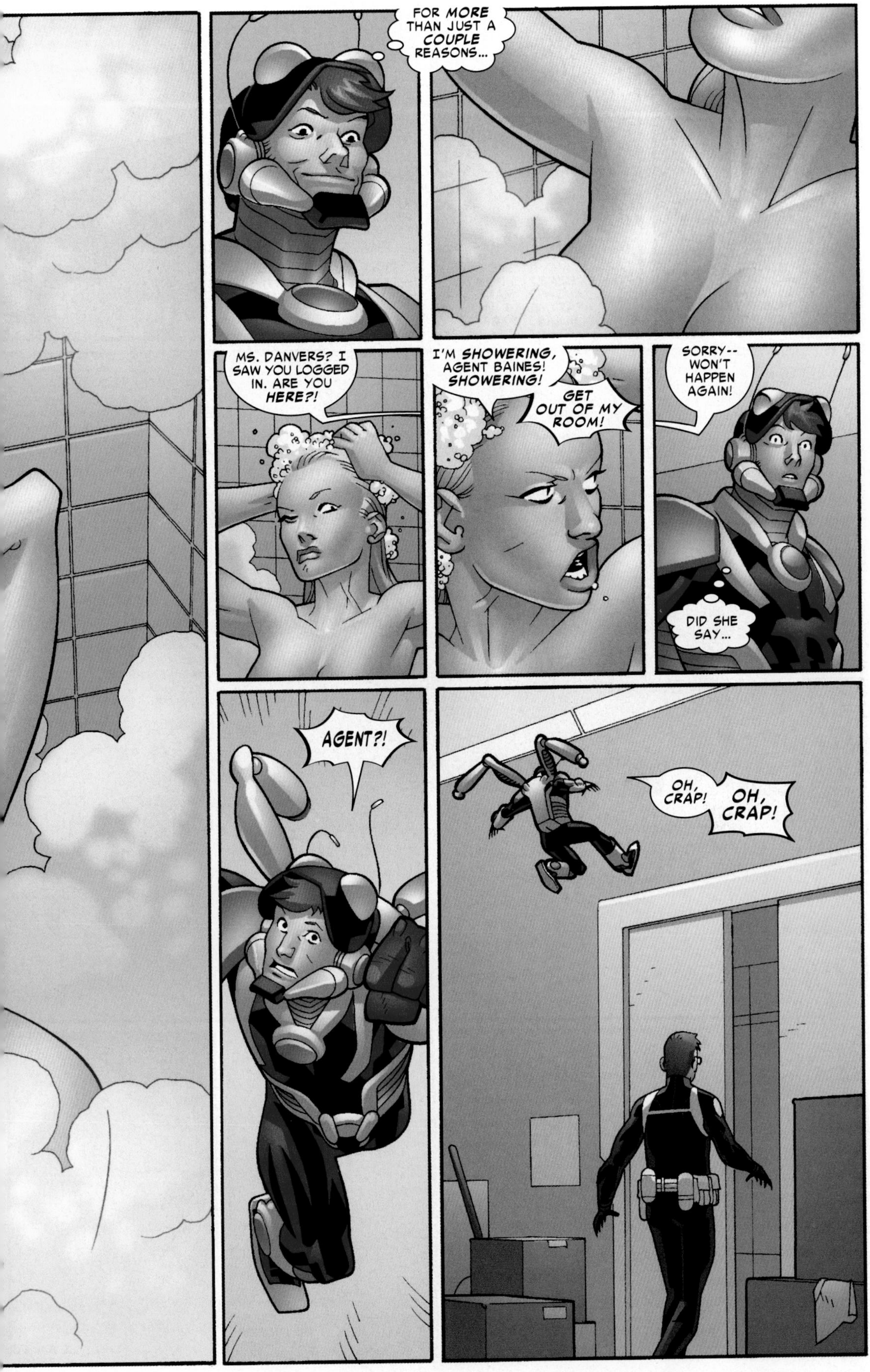
FOR MORE THAN JUST A COUPLE REASONS...
MS. DANVERS? I SAW YOU LOGGED IN. ARE YOU HERE?!
I'M SHOWERING, AGENT BAINES! SHOWERING!
GET OUT OF MY ROOM!
SORRY-- WON'T HAPPEN AGAIN!
DID SHE SAY...
AGENT?!
OH, CRAP!
OH, CRAP!

THAT'S A S.H.I.E.L.D. AGENT--THE SAME KIND THAT ARE HUNTING ME DOWN LIKE A DOG.

WHAT WOULD THEY BE DOING HERE?

AND WHERE IS HERE? I DON'T KNOW OF MANY APARTMENTS WITH SLIDING STAR TREK DOORS.

I AM SCREWED-- I AM SO SCREWED.

HOW MANY GUYS ARE IN THIS PLACE?!

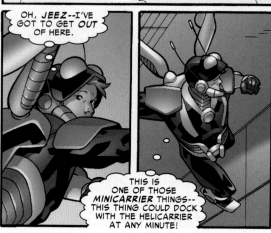

OH, JEEZ--I'VE GOT TO GET OUT OF HERE.

THIS IS ONE OF THOSE MINICARRIER THINGS-- THIS THING COULD DOCK WITH THE HELICARRIER AT ANY MINUTE!

TOK.

WE COULD BE ON OUR WAY THERE, RIGHT NOW!

I AM SO SCREWED.

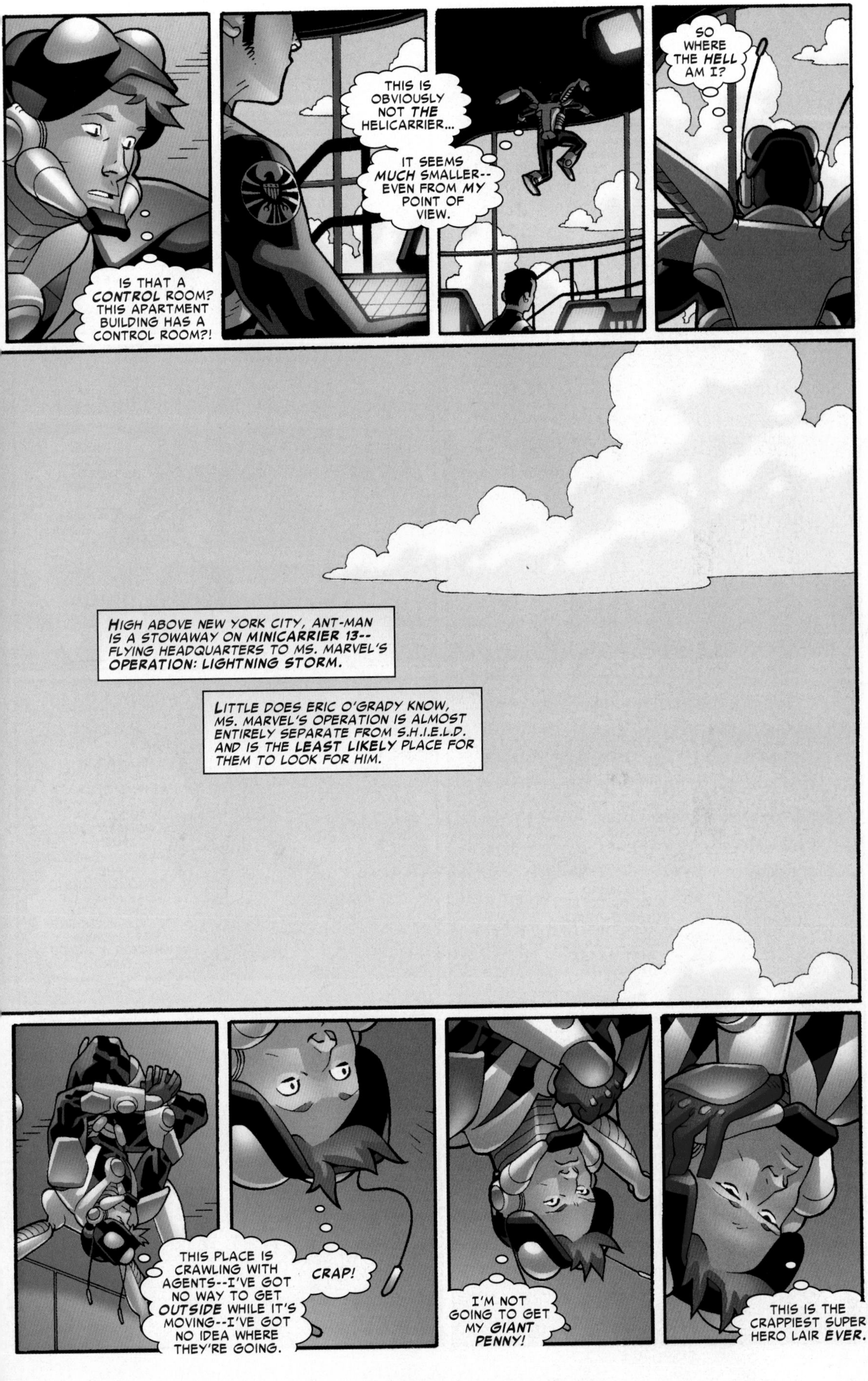
IS THAT A CONTROL ROOM? THIS APARTMENT BUILDING HAS A CONTROL ROOM?!
THIS IS OBVIOUSLY NOT THE HELICARRIER...
IT SEEMS MUCH SMALLER-- EVEN FROM MY POINT OF VIEW.
SO WHERE THE HELL AM I?
HIGH ABOVE NEW YORK CITY, ANT-MAN IS A STOWAWAY ON MINICARRIER 13-- FLYING HEADQUARTERS TO MS. MARVEL'S OPERATION: LIGHTNING STORM.
LITTLE DOES ERIC O'GRADY KNOW, MS. MARVEL'S OPERATION IS ALMOST ENTIRELY SEPARATE FROM S.H.I.E.L.D. AND IS THE LEAST LIKELY PLACE FOR THEM TO LOOK FOR HIM.
THIS PLACE IS CRAWLING WITH AGENTS--I'VE GOT NO WAY TO GET OUTSIDE WHILE IT'S MOVING--I'VE GOT NO IDEA WHERE THEY'RE GOING.
CRAP!
I'M NOT GOING TO GET MY GIANT PENNY!
THIS IS THE CRAPPIEST SUPER HERO LAIR EVER.

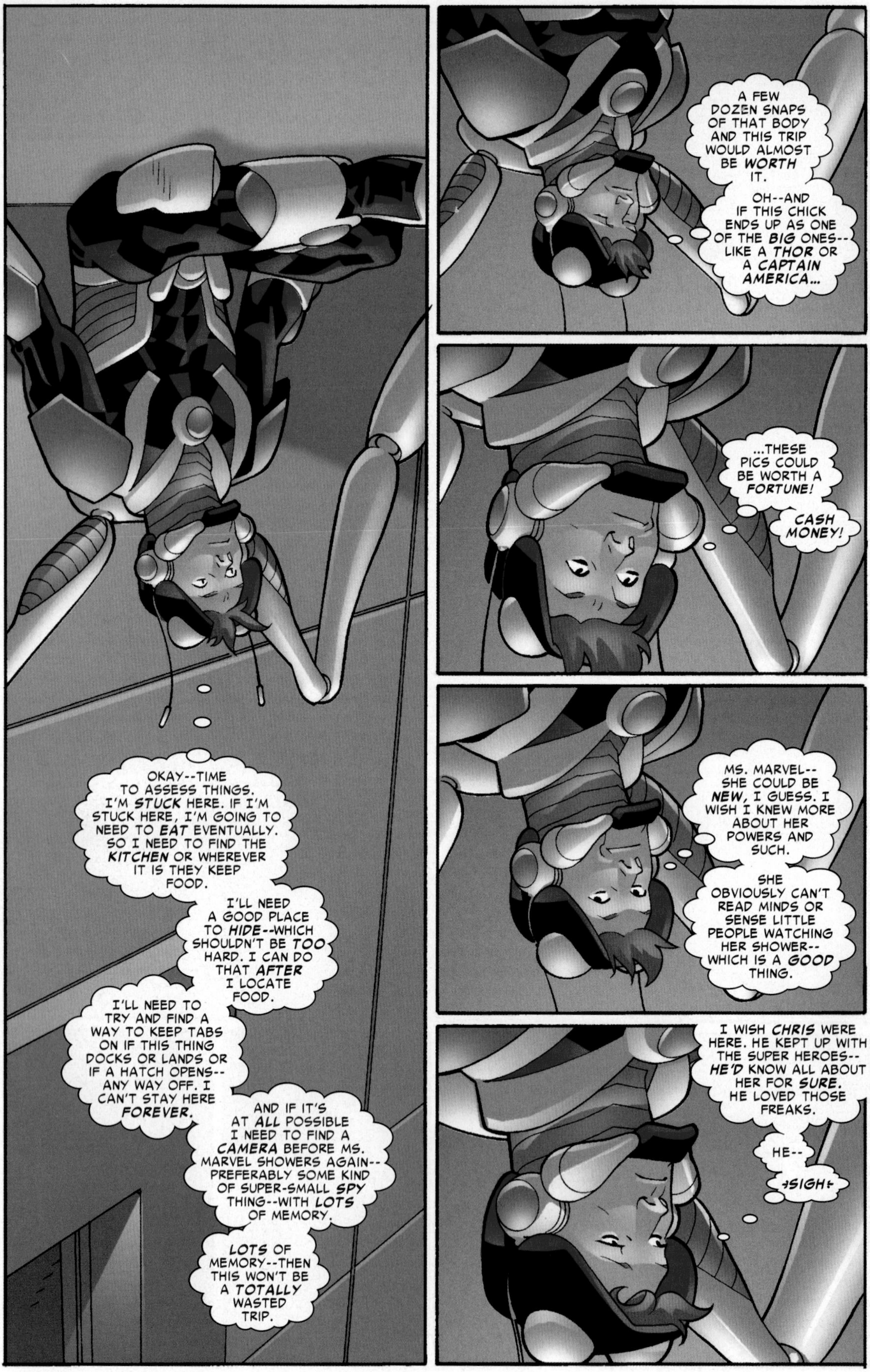
OKAY--TIME TO ASSESS THINGS. I'M STUCK HERE. IF I'M STUCK HERE, I'M GOING TO NEED TO EAT EVENTUALLY. SO I NEED TO FIND THE KITCHEN OR WHEREVER IT IS THEY KEEP FOOD.
I'LL NEED A GOOD PLACE TO HIDE--WHICH SHOULDN'T BE TOO HARD. I CAN DO THAT AFTER I LOCATE FOOD.
I'LL NEED TO TRY AND FIND A WAY TO KEEP TABS ON IF THIS THING DOCKS OR LANDS OR IF A HATCH OPENS--ANY WAY OFF. I CAN'T STAY HERE FOREVER.
AND IF IT'S AT ALL POSSIBLE I NEED TO FIND A CAMERA BEFORE MS. MARVEL SHOWERS AGAIN--PREFERABLY SOME KIND OF SUPER-SMALL SPY THING--WITH LOTS OF MEMORY.
LOTS OF MEMORY--THEN THIS WON'T BE A TOTALLY WASTED TRIP.
A FEW DOZEN SNAPS OF THAT BODY AND THIS TRIP WOULD ALMOST BE WORTH IT.
OH--AND IF THIS CHICK ENDS UP AS ONE OF THE BIG ONES--LIKE A THOR OR A CAPTAIN AMERICA...
...THESE PICS COULD BE WORTH A FORTUNE!
CASH MONEY!
MS. MARVEL--SHE COULD BE NEW, I GUESS. I WISH I KNEW MORE ABOUT HER POWERS AND SUCH.
SHE OBVIOUSLY CAN'T READ MINDS OR SENSE LITTLE PEOPLE WATCHING HER SHOWER--WHICH IS A GOOD THING.
I WISH CHRIS WERE HERE. HE KEPT UP WITH THE SUPER HEROES--HE'D KNOW ALL ABOUT HER FOR SURE. HE LOVED THOSE FREAKS.
HE--
SIGH

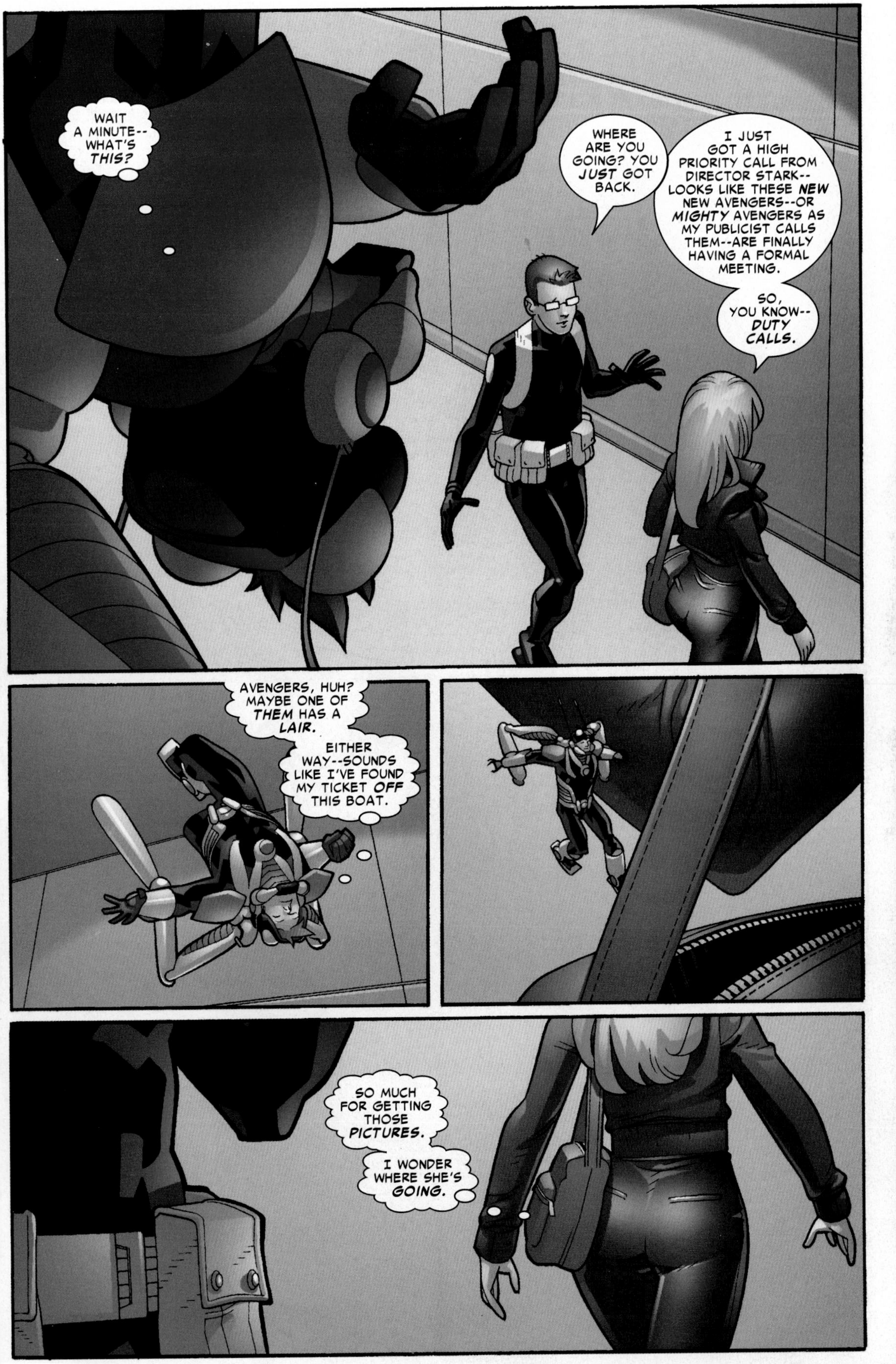
WAIT A MINUTE-- WHAT'S THIS?
WHERE ARE YOU GOING? YOU JUST GOT BACK.
I JUST GOT A HIGH PRIORITY CALL FROM DIRECTOR STARK-- LOOKS LIKE THESE NEW NEW AVENGERS--OR MIGHTY AVENGERS AS MY PUBLICIST CALLS THEM--ARE FINALLY HAVING A FORMAL MEETING.
SO, YOU KNOW-- DUTY CALLS.
AVENGERS, HUH? MAYBE ONE OF THEM HAS A LAIR.
EITHER WAY--SOUNDS LIKE I'VE FOUND MY TICKET OFF THIS BOAT.
SO MUCH FOR GETTING THOSE PICTURES.
I WONDER WHERE SHE'S GOING.

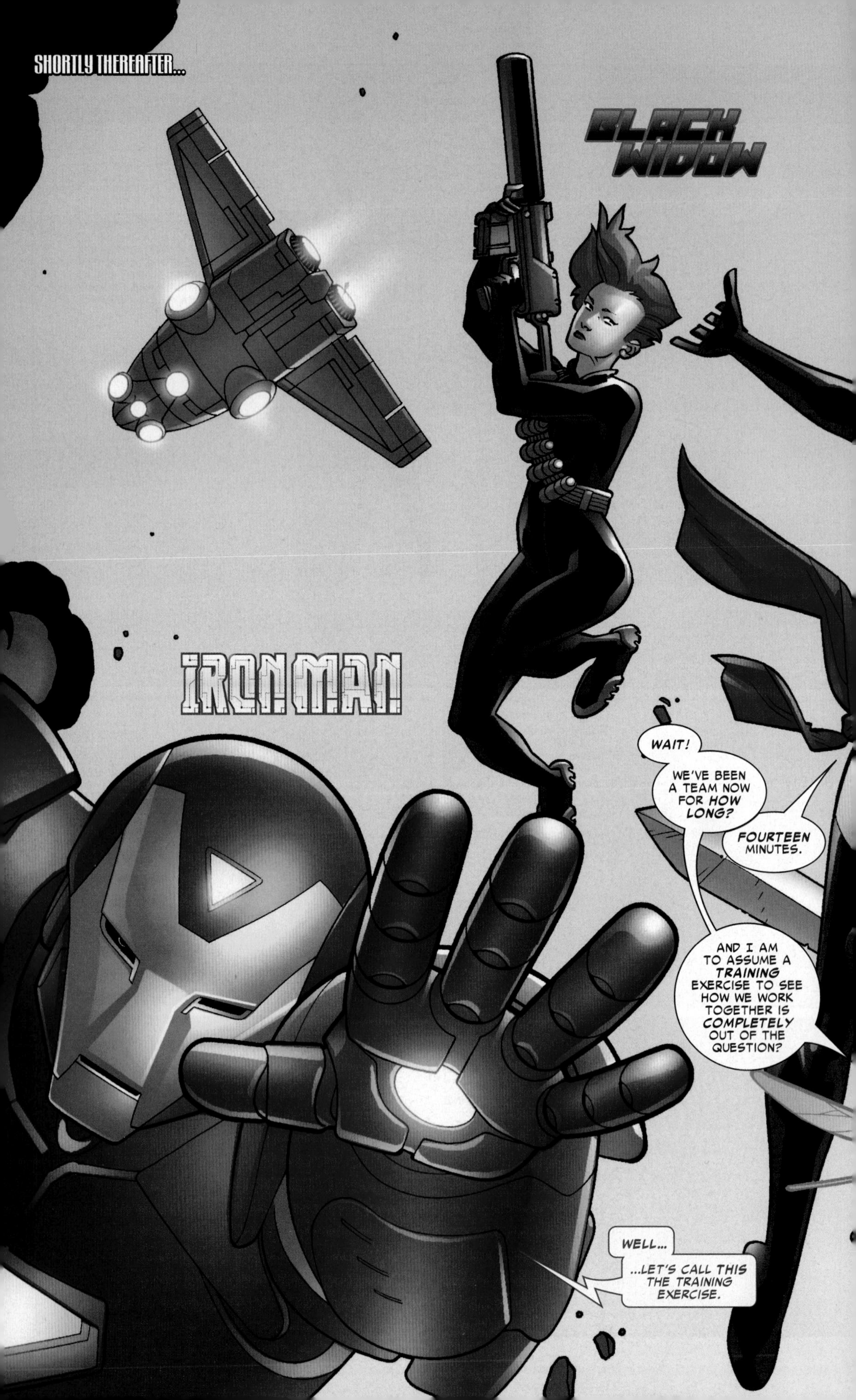
SHORTLY THEREAFTER...
BLACK WIDOW
IRON MAN
WAIT!
WE'VE BEEN A TEAM NOW FOR HOW LONG?
FOURTEEN MINUTES.
AND I AM TO ASSUME A TRAINING EXERCISE TO SEE HOW WE WORK TOGETHER IS COMPLETELY OUT OF THE QUESTION?
WELL...
...LET'S CALL THIS THE TRAINING EXERCISE.

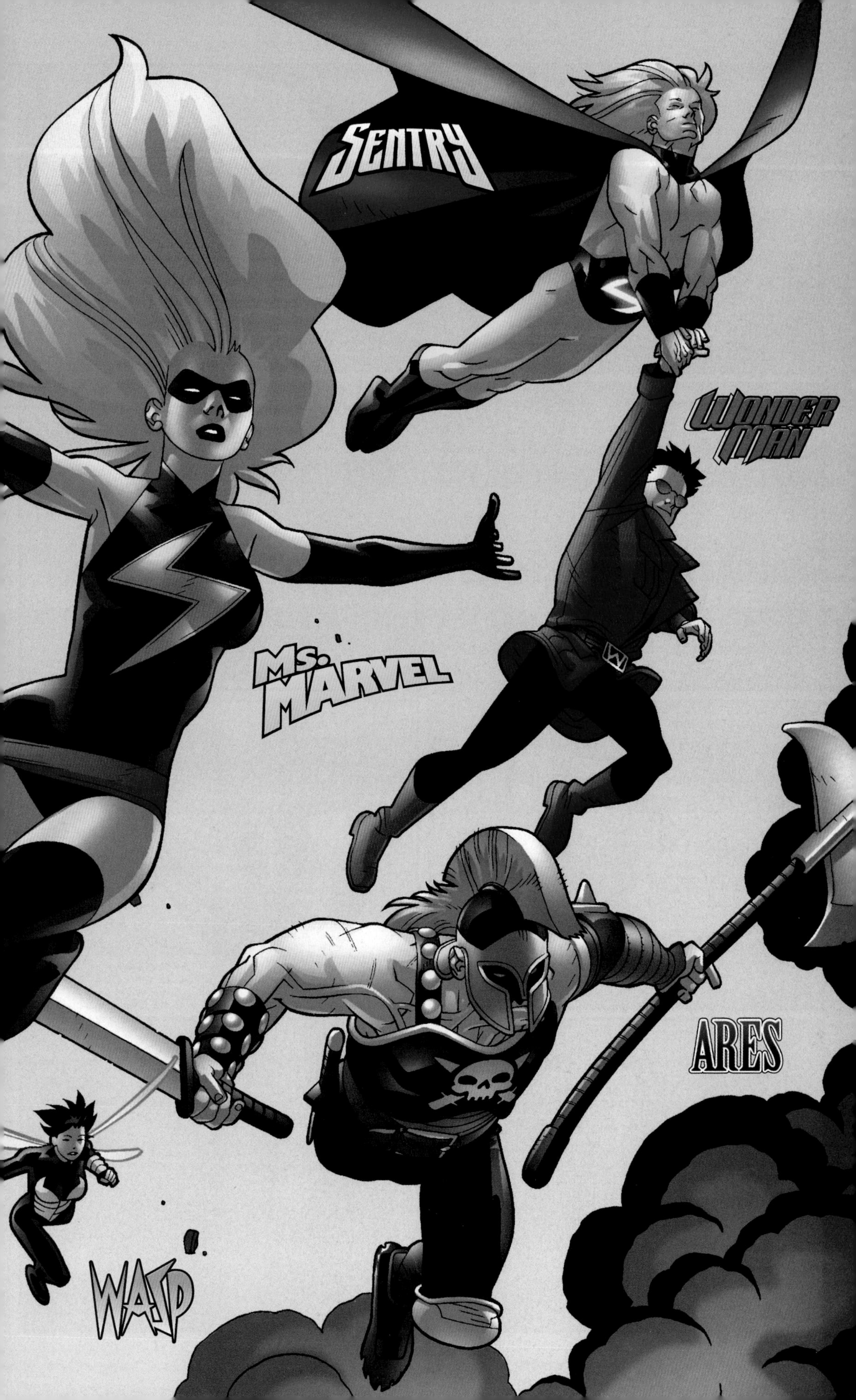
SENTRY
WONDER MAN
Ms. MARVEL
ARES
WASP

I CAN'T DECIDE WHAT I'M GOING TO MISS MOST ABOUT THIS WOMAN...

OKAY-- I'M GETTING *OFF* THIS RIDE--*RIGHT NOW.*

AVENGERS-- YOU'RE ON YOUR *OWN* WITH THIS ONE.

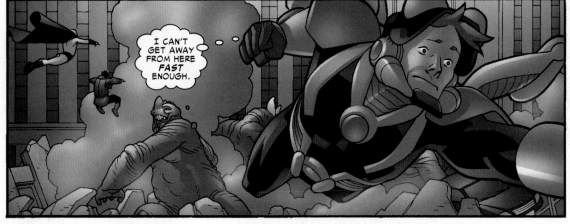

I CAN'T GET AWAY FROM HERE *FAST* ENOUGH.

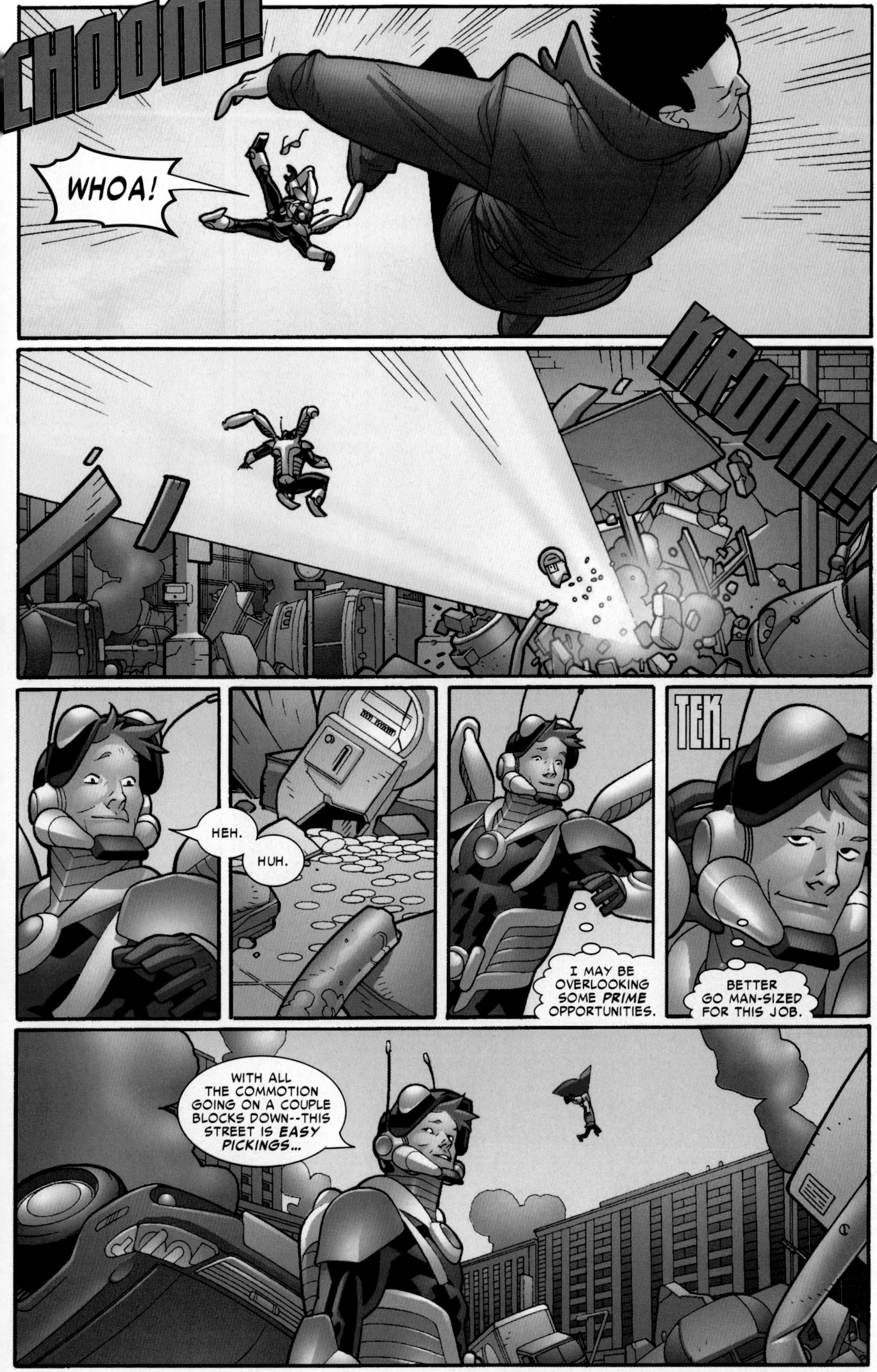
CHOOM!!
WHOA!
KROOM!!
HEH.
HUH.
I MAY BE OVERLOOKING SOME *PRIME* OPPORTUNITIES.
TEK.
BETTER GO MAN-SIZED FOR THIS JOB.
WITH ALL THE COMMOTION GOING ON A COUPLE BLOCKS DOWN--THIS STREET IS *EASY PICKINGS*...

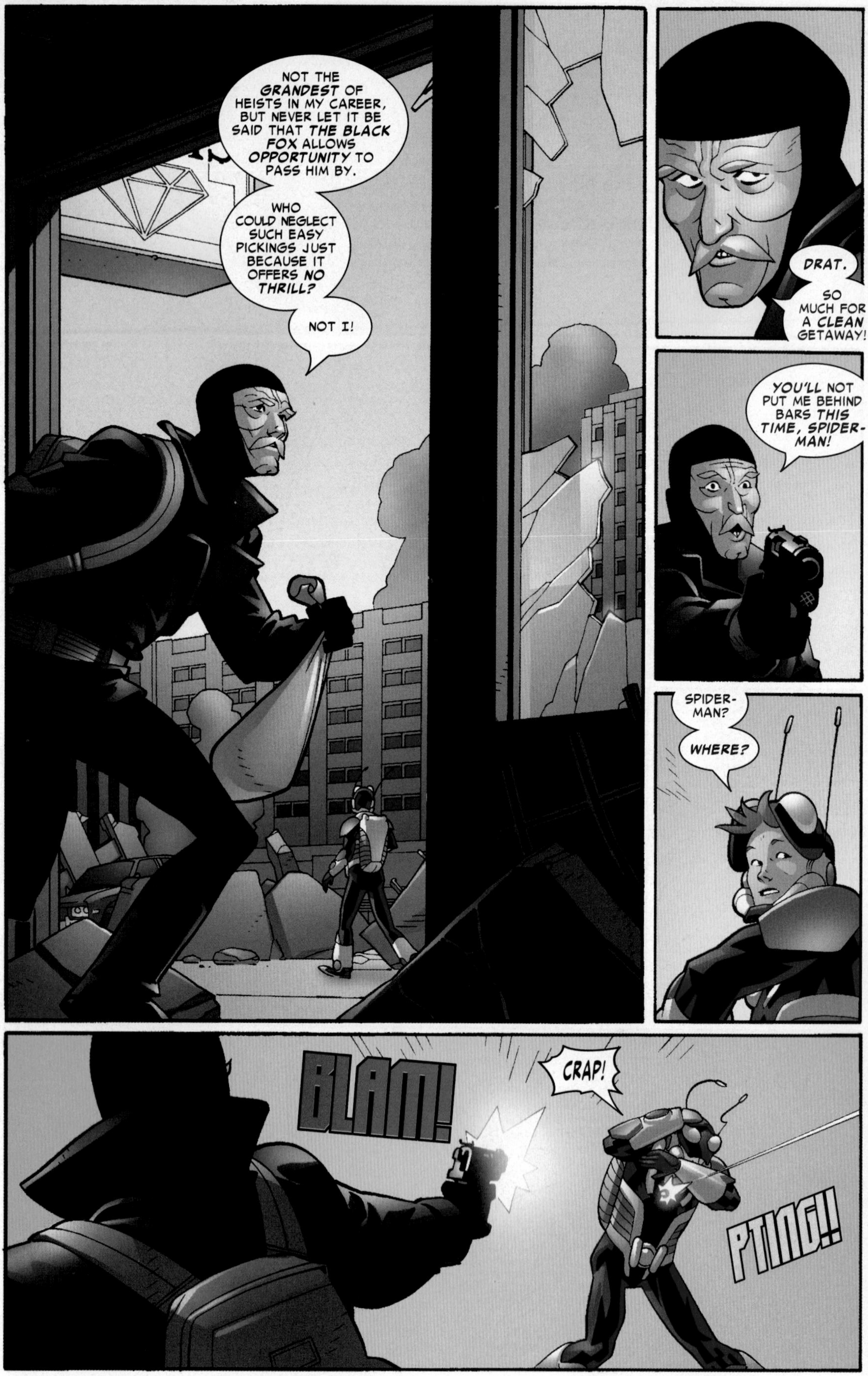
NOT THE GRANDEST OF HEISTS IN MY CAREER, BUT NEVER LET IT BE SAID THAT THE BLACK FOX ALLOWS OPPORTUNITY TO PASS HIM BY.
WHO COULD NEGLECT SUCH EASY PICKINGS JUST BECAUSE IT OFFERS NO THRILL?
NOT I!
DRAT.
SO MUCH FOR A CLEAN GETAWAY!
YOU'LL NOT PUT ME BEHIND BARS THIS TIME, SPIDER-MAN!
SPIDER-MAN?
WHERE?
BLAM!
CRAP!
PTING!!

SPIDER-MAN--YOU THINK I'M SPIDER-MAN?!

WHAT THE HECK?!

HE WAS ALL OVER THE NEWS WEARING THE SAME COSTUME YOU'RE WEARING-- IT'S AN *HONEST* MISTAKE.

REGARDLESS, I DON'T REALLY *CARE* WHO YOU ARE--AS LONG AS YOU'RE DEAD.

OR AT LEAST INCAPACITATED TO THE POINT THAT YOU CAN'T INTERFERE WITH MY *RETREAT.*

SORRY ABOUT YOUR LUCK, GRANDPA-- I'M NOT ABOUT TO LET EITHER OF THOSE HAPPEN.

I SEE NO REASON FOR THIS TO GET *PHYSICAL--*

TEK.

HUH?

OKAY. I'M GOING *HOME* NOW.

OKAY-- HERE COMES THE *ANT-MAN SPECIAL!*

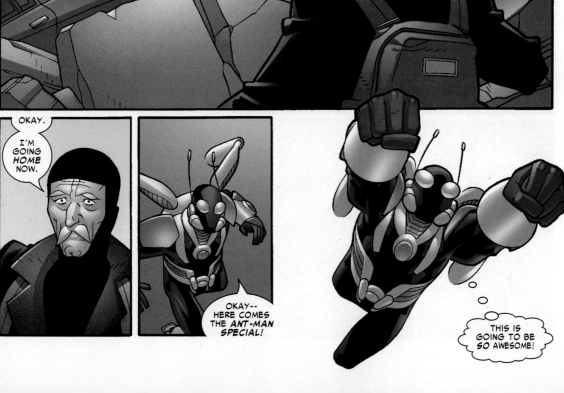

THIS IS GOING TO BE *SO AWESOME!*

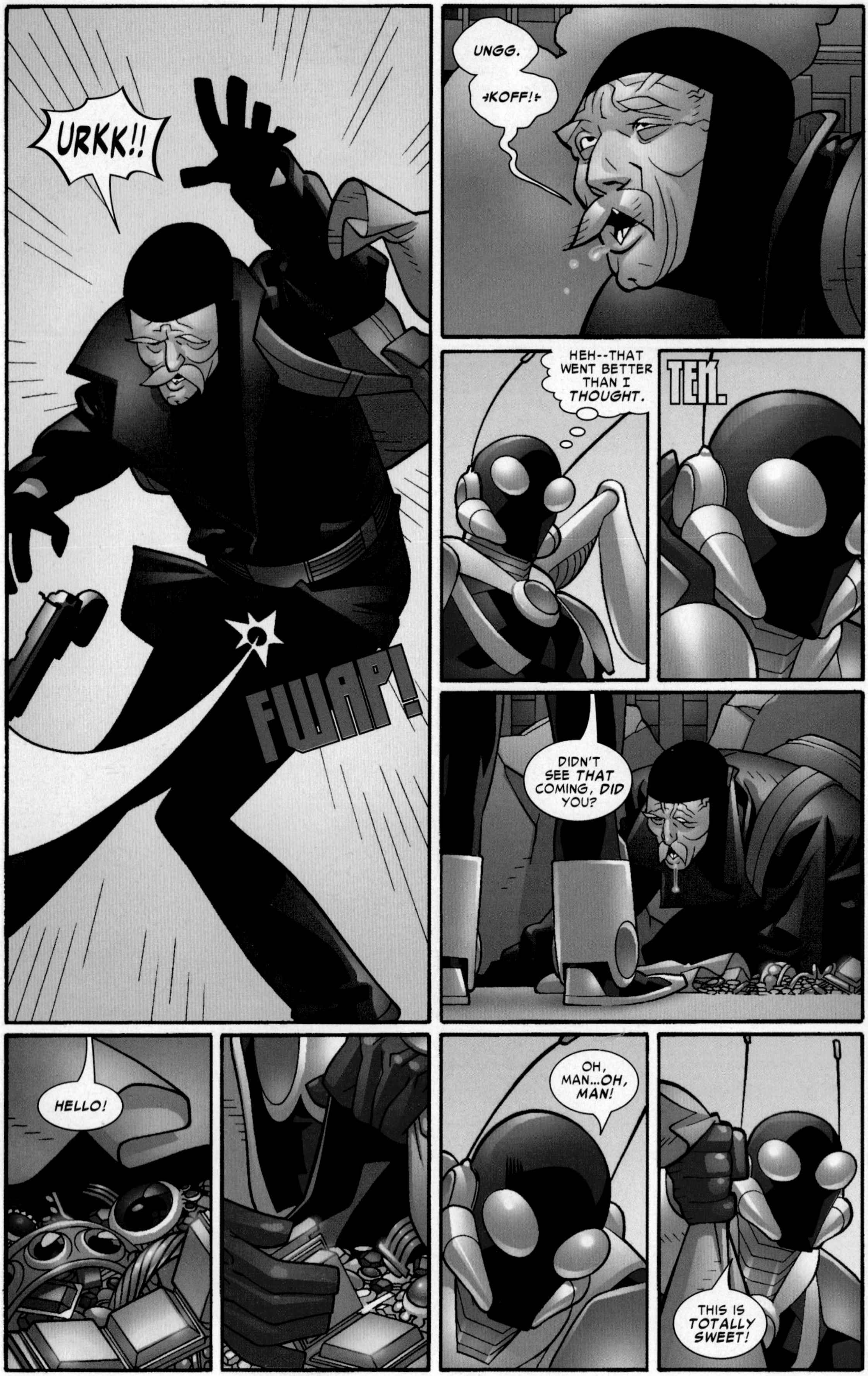
URKK!!
FWAP!
UNGG.
*KOFF!*
HEH--THAT WENT BETTER THAN I THOUGHT.
TEK.
DIDN'T SEE THAT COMING, DID YOU?
HELLO!
OH, MAN...OH, MAN!
THIS IS TOTALLY SWEET!

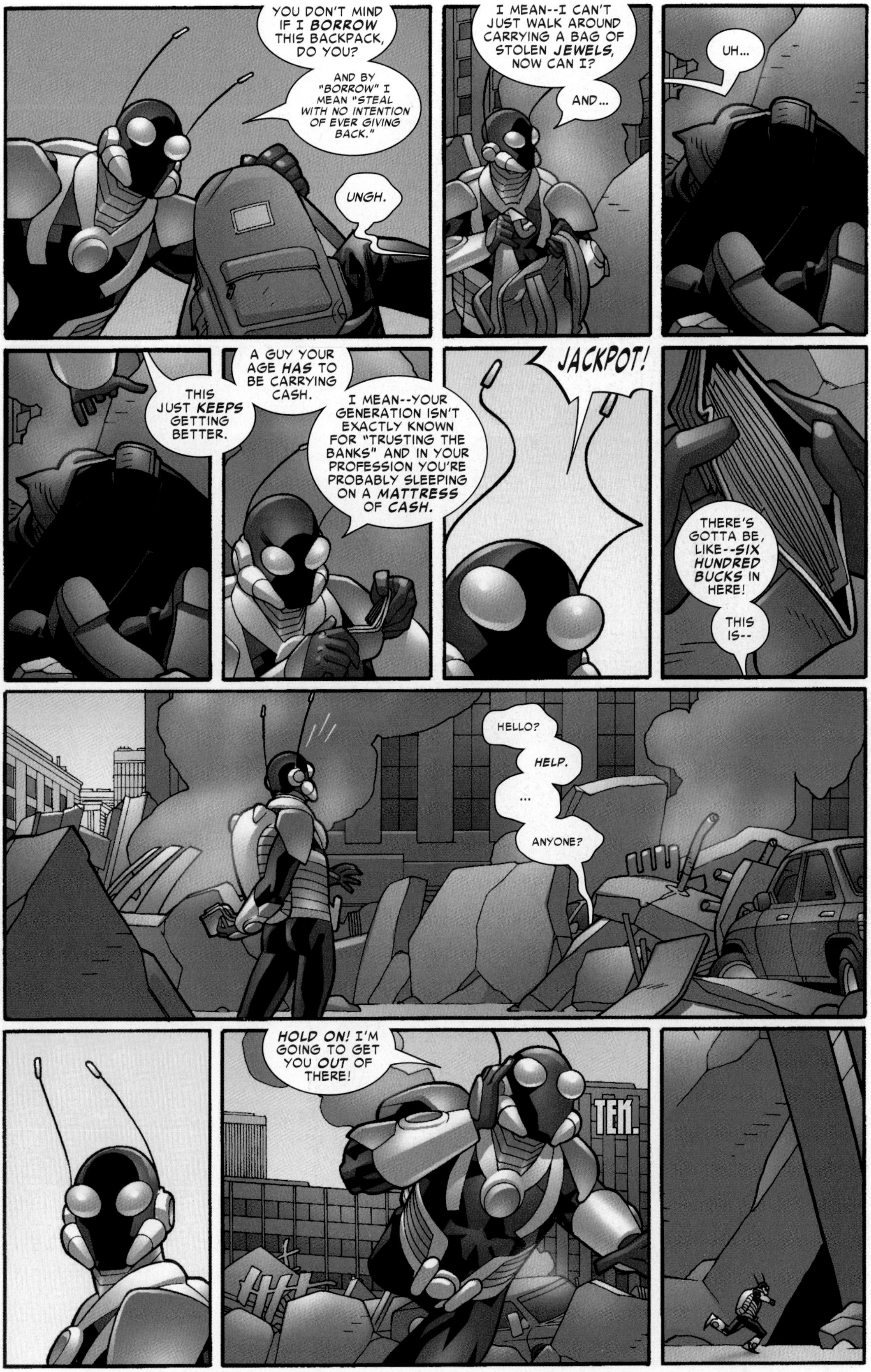
YOU DON'T MIND IF I BORROW THIS BACKPACK, DO YOU?
AND BY "BORROW" I MEAN "STEAL WITH NO INTENTION OF EVER GIVING BACK."
UNGH.
I MEAN--I CAN'T JUST WALK AROUND CARRYING A BAG OF STOLEN JEWELS, NOW CAN I?
AND...
UH...
THIS JUST KEEPS GETTING BETTER.
A GUY YOUR AGE HAS TO BE CARRYING CASH.
I MEAN--YOUR GENERATION ISN'T EXACTLY KNOWN FOR "TRUSTING THE BANKS" AND IN YOUR PROFESSION YOU'RE PROBABLY SLEEPING ON A MATTRESS OF CASH.
JACKPOT!
THERE'S GOTTA BE, LIKE--SIX HUNDRED BUCKS IN HERE!
THIS IS--
HELLO?
HELP.
...
ANYONE?
HOLD ON! I'M GOING TO GET YOU OUT OF THERE!
TEK.

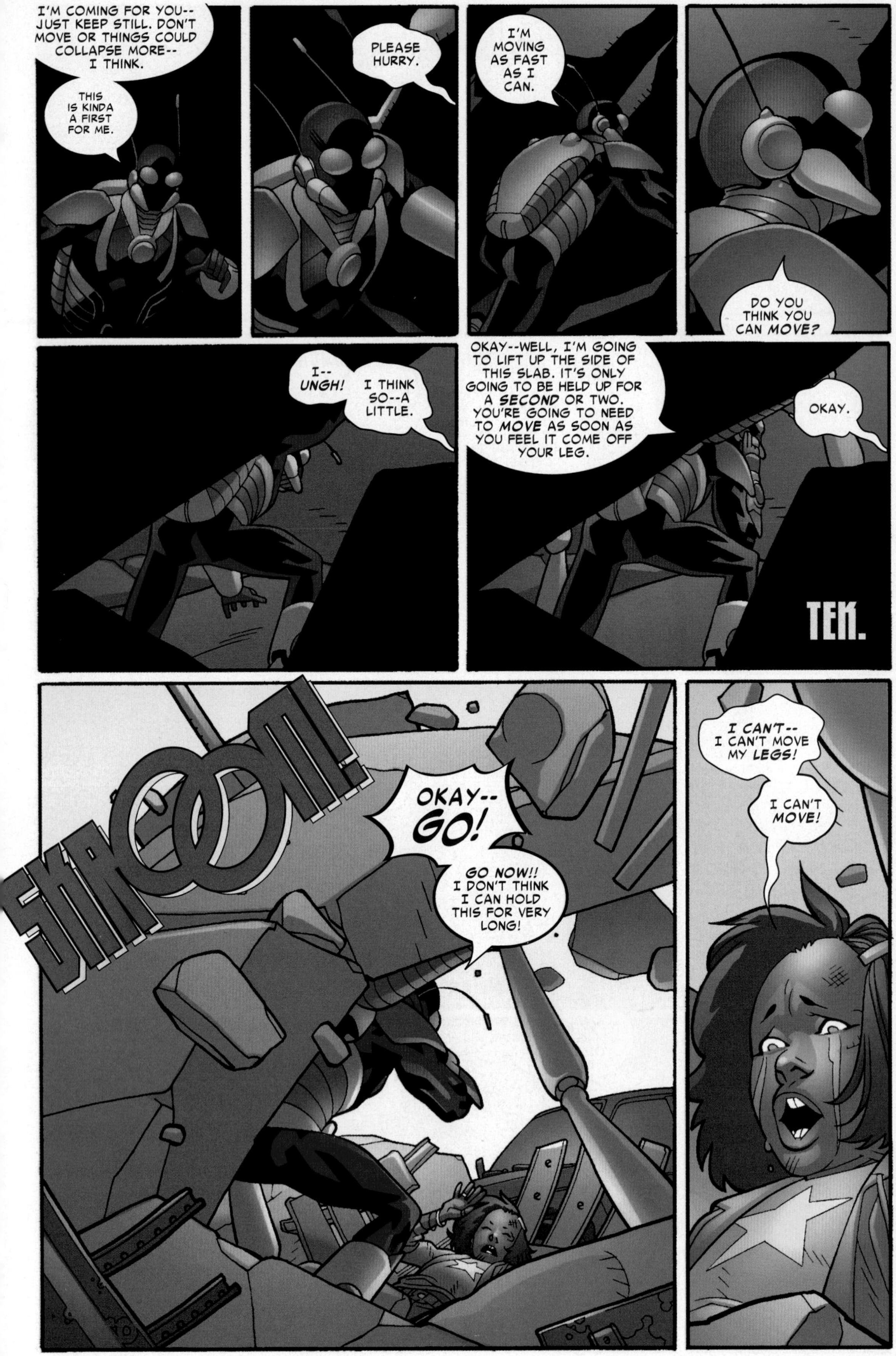
I'M COMING FOR YOU--
JUST KEEP STILL. DON'T MOVE OR THINGS COULD COLLAPSE MORE--
I THINK.
THIS IS KINDA A FIRST FOR ME.
PLEASE HURRY.
I'M MOVING AS FAST AS I CAN.
DO YOU THINK YOU CAN MOVE?
I-- UNGH!
I THINK SO--A LITTLE.
OKAY--WELL, I'M GOING TO LIFT UP THE SIDE OF THIS SLAB. IT'S ONLY GOING TO BE HELD UP FOR A SECOND OR TWO. YOU'RE GOING TO NEED TO MOVE AS SOON AS YOU FEEL IT COME OFF YOUR LEG.
OKAY.
TEK.
SKROOM!
OKAY-- GO!
GO NOW!! I DON'T THINK I CAN HOLD THIS FOR VERY LONG!
I CAN'T-- I CAN'T MOVE MY LEGS!
I CAN'T MOVE!

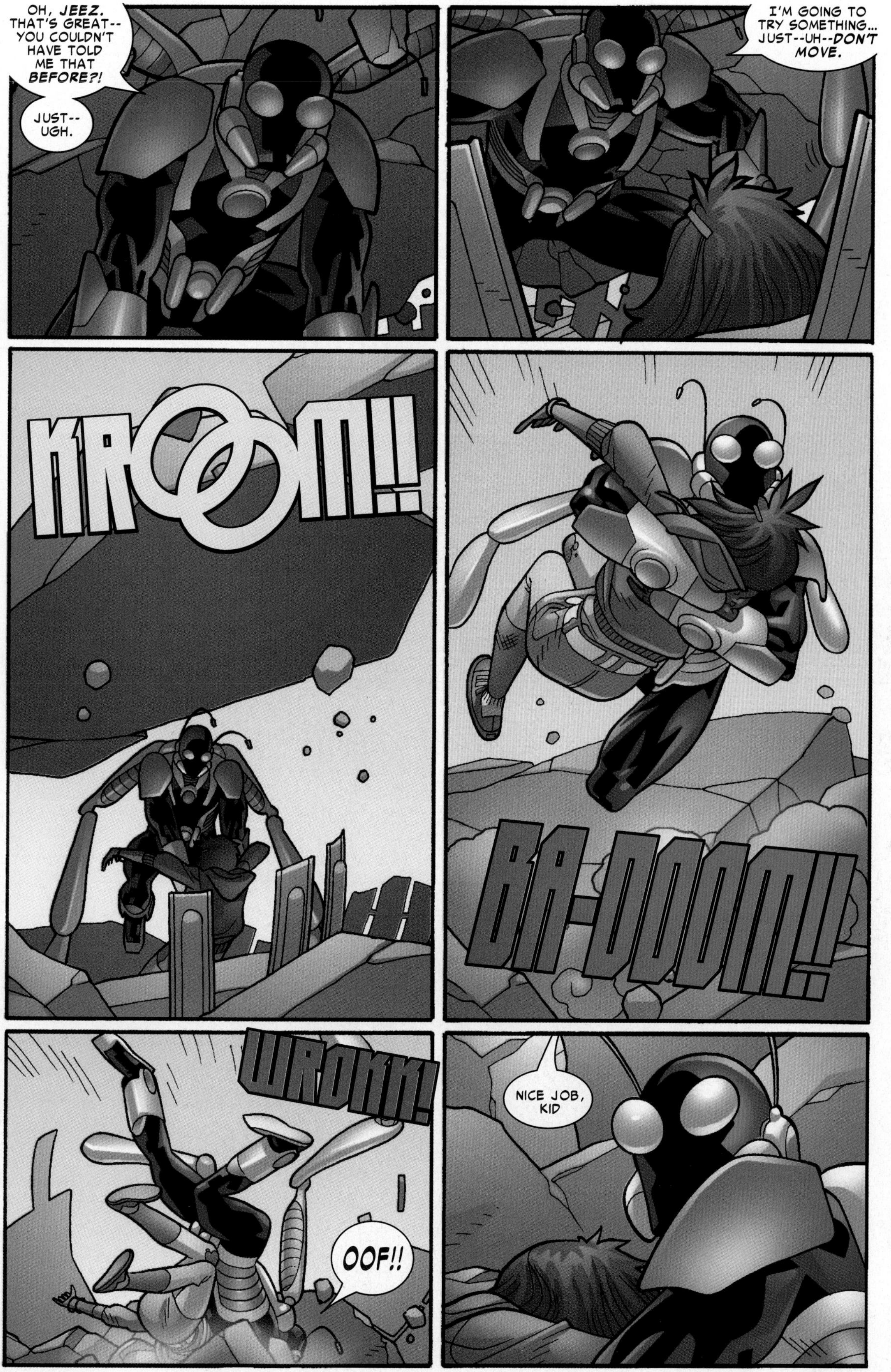
OH, JEEZ. THAT'S GREAT-- YOU COULDN'T HAVE TOLD ME THAT BEFORE?!
JUST-- UGH.
I'M GOING TO TRY SOMETHING... JUST--UH--DON'T MOVE.
KROOM!!
BA-DOOOM!!
WROKK!
OOF!!
NICE JOB, KID

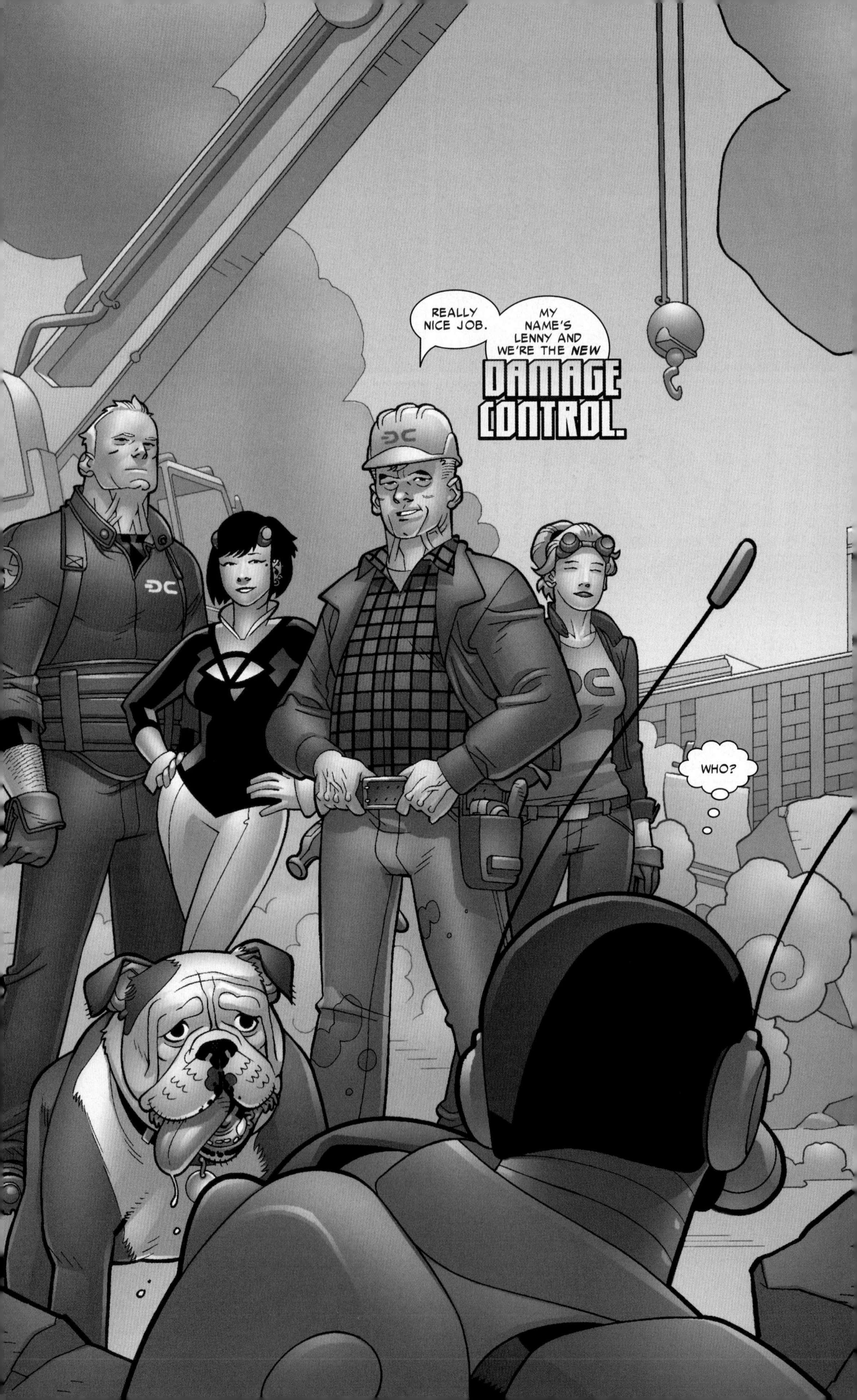
REALLY NICE JOB.
MY NAME'S LENNY AND WE'RE THE NEW
DAMAGE CONTROL.
WHO?

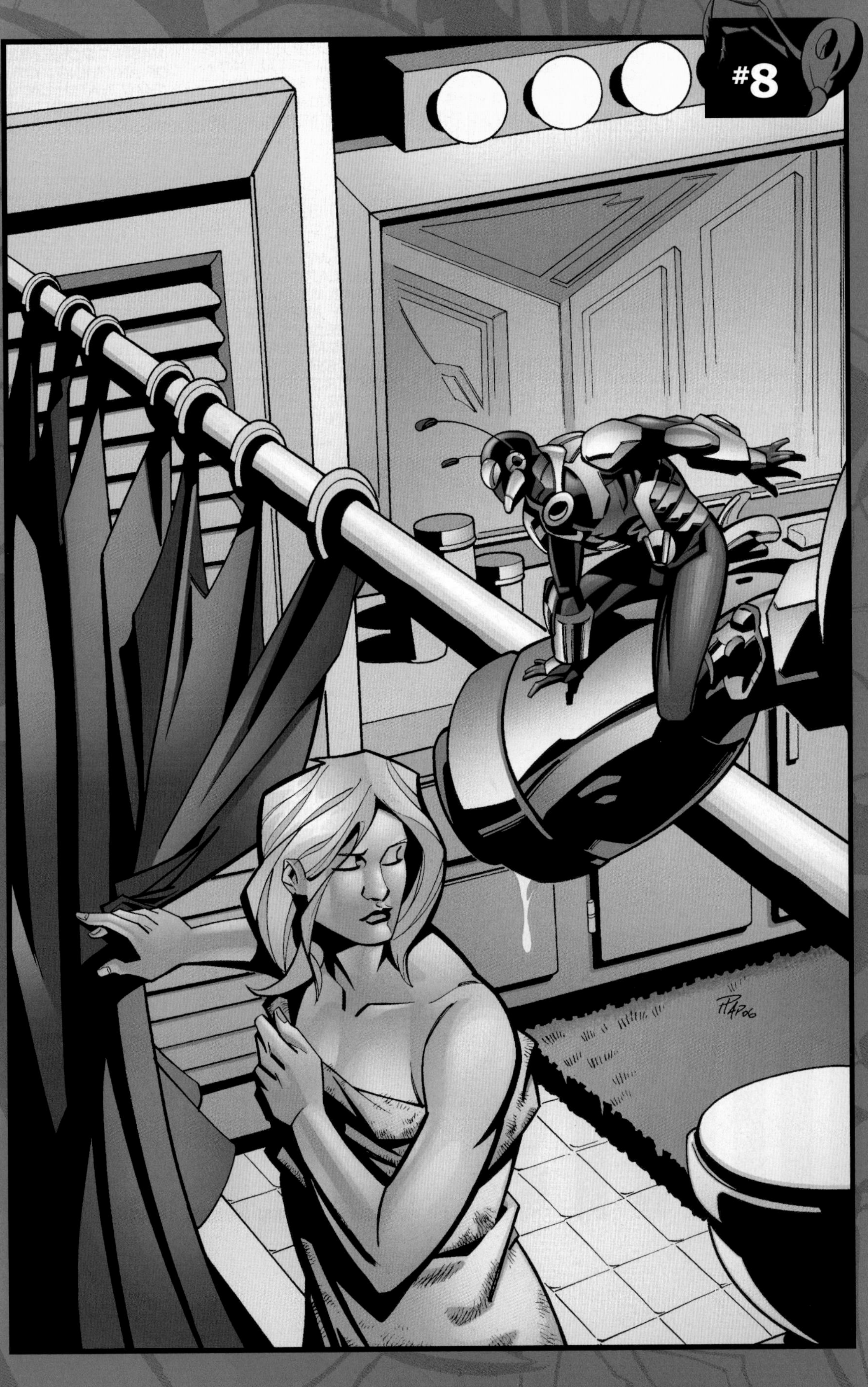
#8

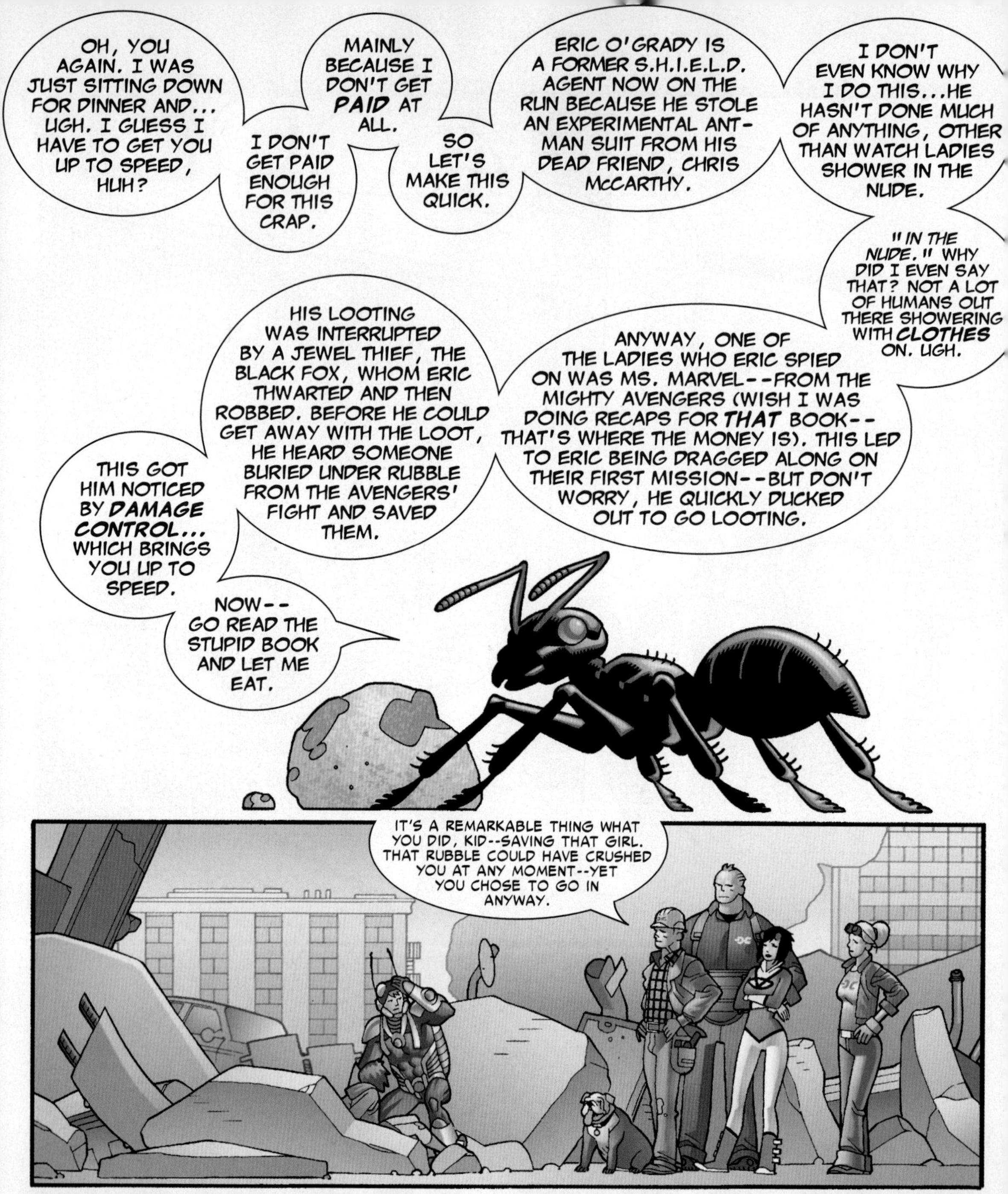
OH, YOU AGAIN. I WAS JUST SITTING DOWN FOR DINNER AND... UGH. I GUESS I HAVE TO GET YOU UP TO SPEED, HUH?
I DON'T GET PAID ENOUGH FOR THIS CRAP.
MAINLY BECAUSE I DON'T GET PAID AT ALL.
SO LET'S MAKE THIS QUICK.
ERIC O'GRADY IS A FORMER S.H.I.E.L.D. AGENT NOW ON THE RUN BECAUSE HE STOLE AN EXPERIMENTAL ANT-MAN SUIT FROM HIS DEAD FRIEND, CHRIS McCARTHY.
I DON'T EVEN KNOW WHY I DO THIS...HE HASN'T DONE MUCH OF ANYTHING, OTHER THAN WATCH LADIES SHOWER IN THE NUDE.
"IN THE NUDE." WHY DID I EVEN SAY THAT? NOT A LOT OF HUMANS OUT THERE SHOWERING WITH CLOTHES ON. UGH.
ANYWAY, ONE OF THE LADIES WHO ERIC SPIED ON WAS MS. MARVEL--FROM THE MIGHTY AVENGERS (WISH I WAS DOING RECAPS FOR THAT BOOK--THAT'S WHERE THE MONEY IS). THIS LED TO ERIC BEING DRAGGED ALONG ON THEIR FIRST MISSION--BUT DON'T WORRY, HE QUICKLY DUCKED OUT TO GO LOOTING.
HIS LOOTING WAS INTERRUPTED BY A JEWEL THIEF, THE BLACK FOX, WHOM ERIC THWARTED AND THEN ROBBED. BEFORE HE COULD GET AWAY WITH THE LOOT, HE HEARD SOMEONE BURIED UNDER RUBBLE FROM THE AVENGERS' FIGHT AND SAVED THEM.
THIS GOT HIM NOTICED BY DAMAGE CONTROL... WHICH BRINGS YOU UP TO SPEED.
NOW--GO READ THE STUPID BOOK AND LET ME EAT.
IT'S A REMARKABLE THING WHAT YOU DID, KID--SAVING THAT GIRL. THAT RUBBLE COULD HAVE CRUSHED YOU AT ANY MOMENT--YET YOU CHOSE TO GO IN ANYWAY.

# DIRTY DEEDS

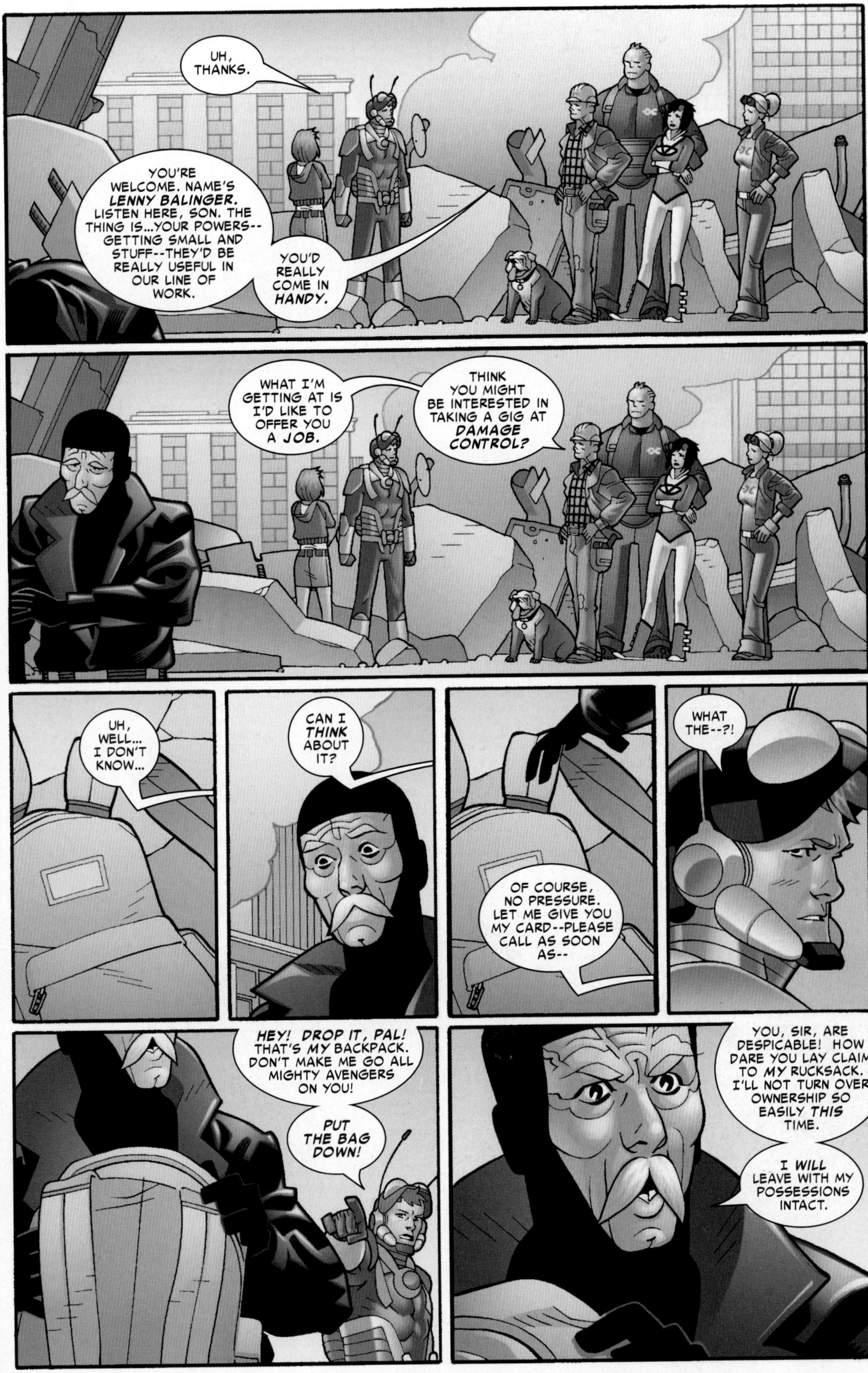
UH, THANKS.
YOU'RE WELCOME. NAME'S LENNY BALINGER. LISTEN HERE, SON. THE THING IS...YOUR POWERS--GETTING SMALL AND STUFF--THEY'D BE REALLY USEFUL IN OUR LINE OF WORK.
YOU'D REALLY COME IN HANDY.
WHAT I'M GETTING AT IS I'D LIKE TO OFFER YOU A JOB.
THINK YOU MIGHT BE INTERESTED IN TAKING A GIG AT DAMAGE CONTROL?
UH, WELL... I DON'T KNOW...
CAN I THINK ABOUT IT?
OF COURSE, NO PRESSURE. LET ME GIVE YOU MY CARD--PLEASE CALL AS SOON AS--
WHAT THE--?!
HEY! DROP IT, PAL! THAT'S MY BACKPACK. DON'T MAKE ME GO ALL MIGHTY AVENGERS ON YOU!
PUT THE BAG DOWN!
YOU, SIR, ARE DESPICABLE! HOW DARE YOU LAY CLAIM TO MY RUCKSACK. I'LL NOT TURN OVER OWNERSHIP SO EASILY THIS TIME.
I WILL LEAVE WITH MY POSSESSIONS INTACT.

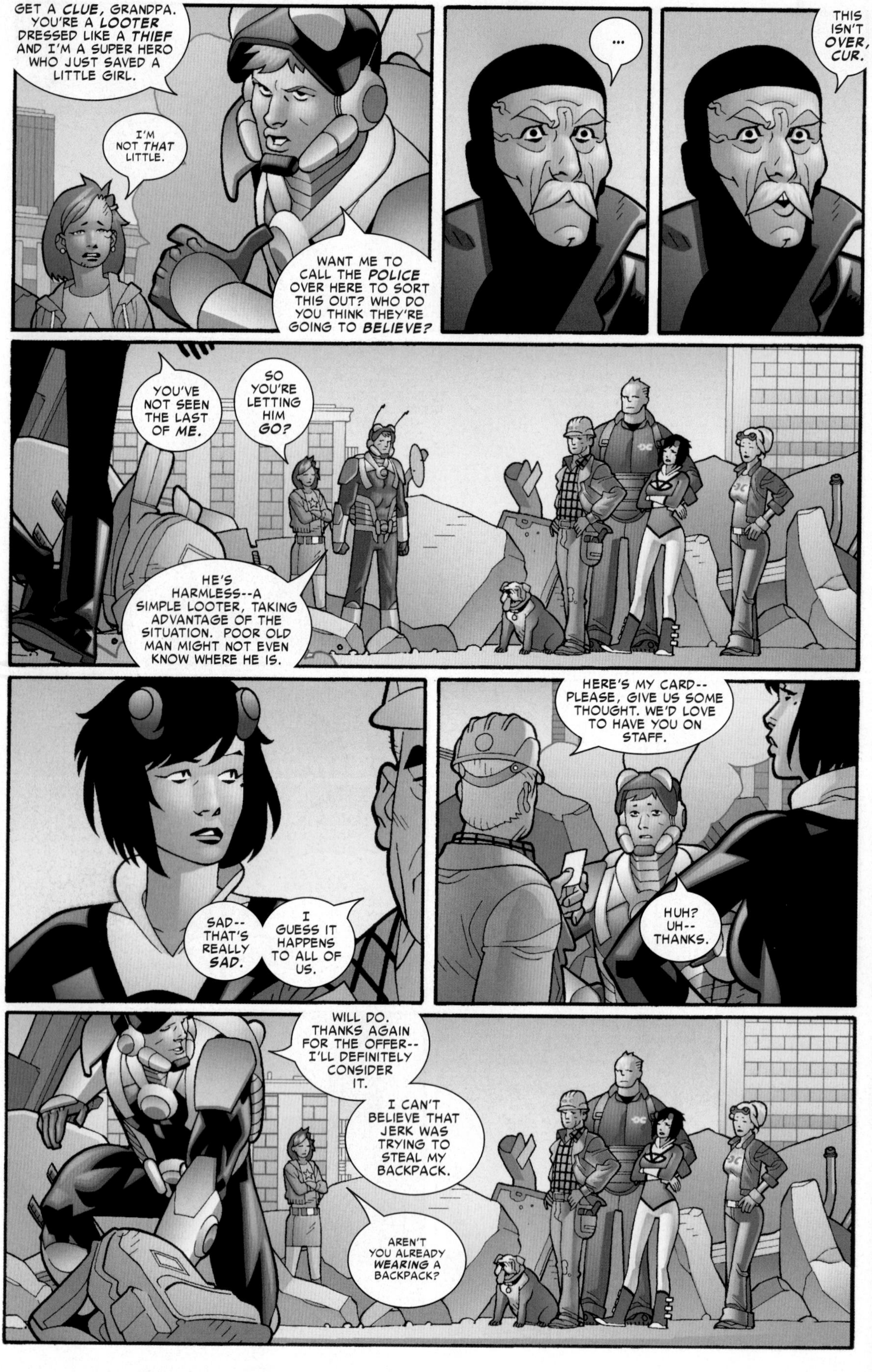

GET A *CLUE*, GRANDPA. YOU'RE A *LOOTER* DRESSED LIKE A *THIEF* AND I'M A SUPER HERO WHO JUST SAVED A LITTLE GIRL.
I'M NOT *THAT* LITTLE.
WANT ME TO CALL THE *POLICE* OVER HERE TO SORT THIS OUT? WHO DO YOU THINK THEY'RE GOING TO *BELIEVE?*
...
THIS ISN'T *OVER, CUR.*
YOU'VE NOT SEEN THE LAST OF *ME.*
SO YOU'RE LETTING HIM *GO?*
HE'S HARMLESS--A SIMPLE LOOTER, TAKING ADVANTAGE OF THE SITUATION. POOR OLD MAN MIGHT NOT EVEN KNOW WHERE HE IS.
SAD--THAT'S REALLY *SAD.*
I GUESS IT HAPPENS TO ALL OF US.
HERE'S MY CARD--PLEASE, GIVE US SOME THOUGHT. WE'D LOVE TO HAVE YOU ON STAFF.
HUH? UH--THANKS.
WILL DO. THANKS AGAIN FOR THE OFFER--I'LL DEFINITELY CONSIDER IT.
I CAN'T BELIEVE THAT JERK WAS TRYING TO STEAL MY BACKPACK.
AREN'T YOU ALREADY *WEARING* A BACKPACK?

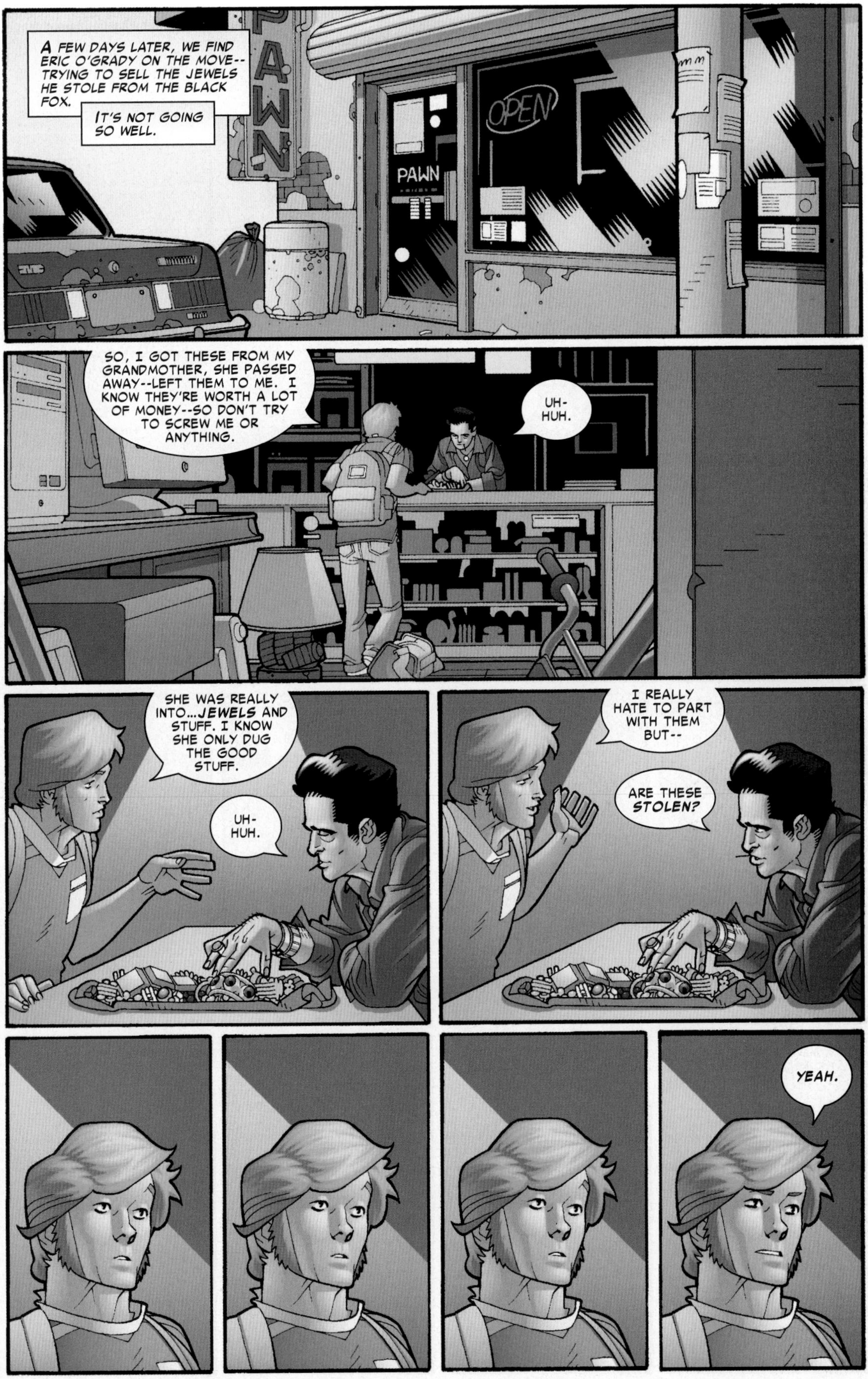
A FEW DAYS LATER, WE FIND ERIC O'GRADY ON THE MOVE--TRYING TO SELL THE JEWELS HE STOLE FROM THE BLACK FOX.
IT'S NOT GOING SO WELL.
PAWN
OPEN
PAWN
SO, I GOT THESE FROM MY GRANDMOTHER, SHE PASSED AWAY--LEFT THEM TO ME. I KNOW THEY'RE WORTH A LOT OF MONEY--SO DON'T TRY TO SCREW ME OR ANYTHING.
UH-HUH.
SHE WAS REALLY INTO...JEWELS AND STUFF. I KNOW SHE ONLY DUG THE GOOD STUFF.
UH-HUH.
I REALLY HATE TO PART WITH THEM BUT--
ARE THESE STOLEN?
YEAH.

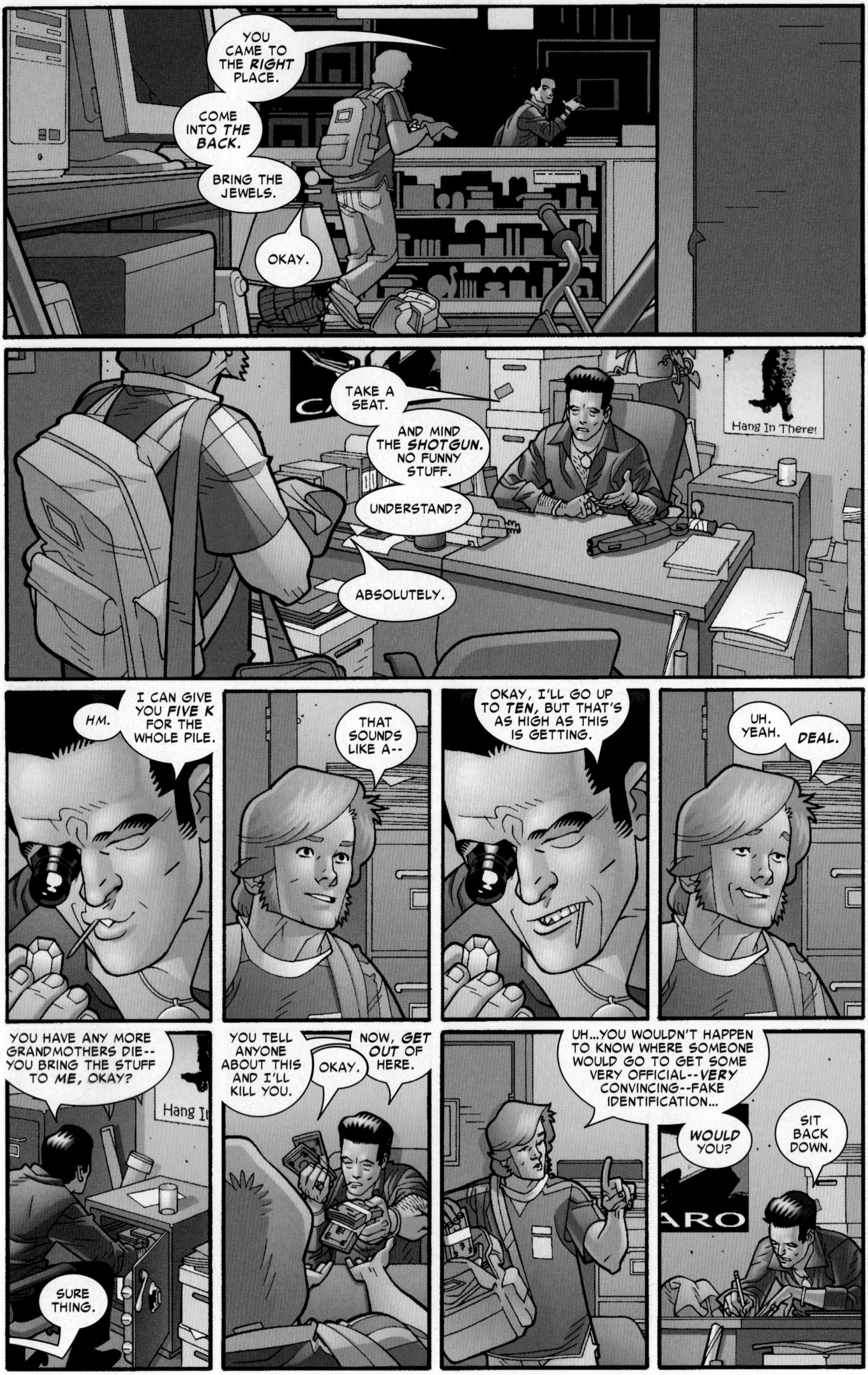
YOU CAME TO THE RIGHT PLACE.
COME INTO THE BACK.
BRING THE JEWELS.
OKAY.
TAKE A SEAT.
AND MIND THE SHOTGUN. NO FUNNY STUFF.
UNDERSTAND?
Hang In There!
ABSOLUTELY.
HM.
I CAN GIVE YOU FIVE K FOR THE WHOLE PILE.
THAT SOUNDS LIKE A--
OKAY, I'LL GO UP TO TEN, BUT THAT'S AS HIGH AS THIS IS GETTING.
UH. YEAH.
DEAL.
YOU HAVE ANY MORE GRANDMOTHERS DIE-- YOU BRING THE STUFF TO ME, OKAY?
SURE THING.
YOU TELL ANYONE ABOUT THIS AND I'LL KILL YOU.
OKAY.
NOW, GET OUT OF HERE.
UH...YOU WOULDN'T HAPPEN TO KNOW WHERE SOMEONE WOULD GO TO GET SOME VERY OFFICIAL--VERY CONVINCING--FAKE IDENTIFICATION...
WOULD YOU?
SIT BACK DOWN.

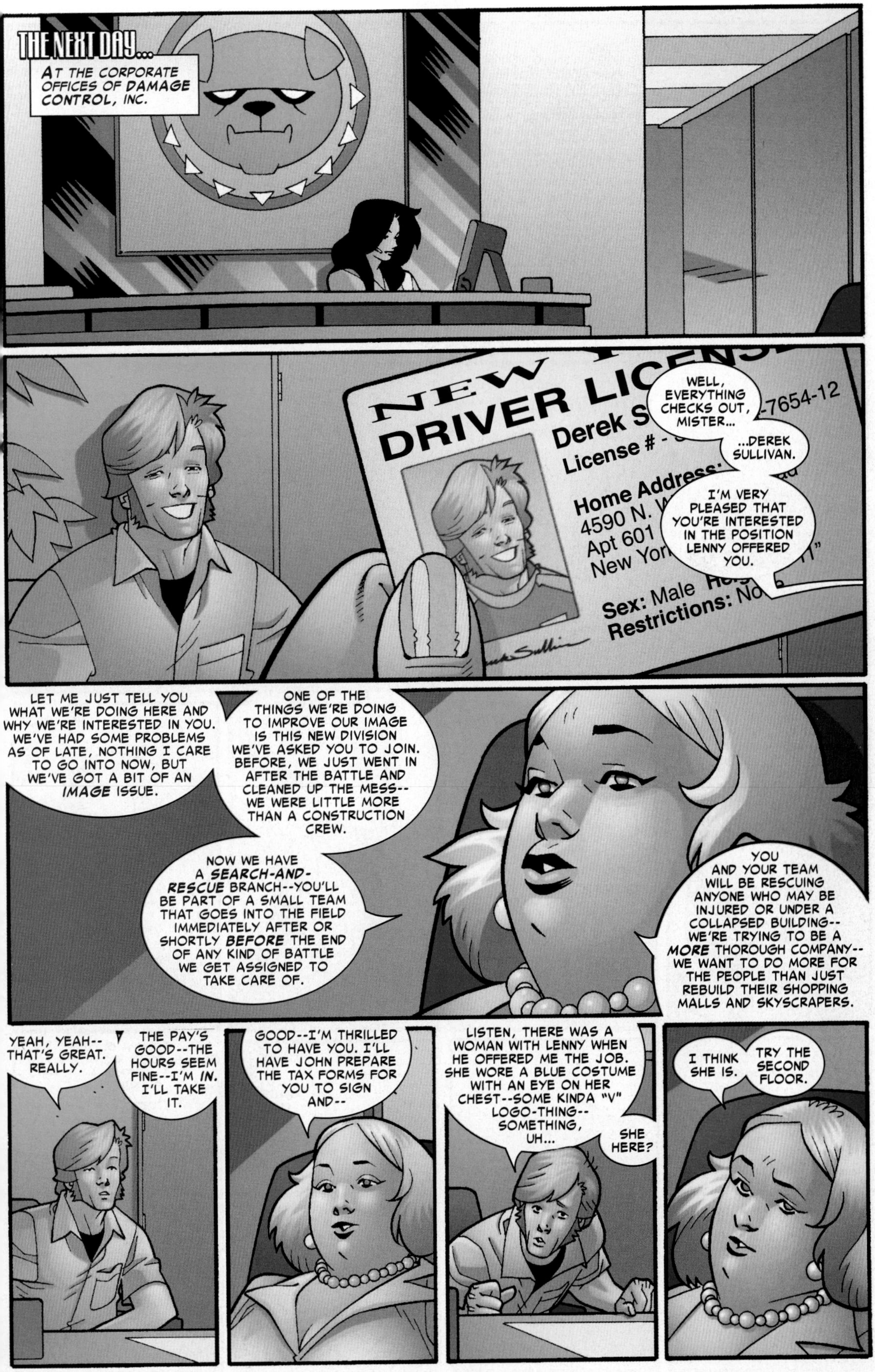
THE NEXT DAY...
AT THE CORPORATE OFFICES OF DAMAGE CONTROL, INC.
NEW Y
DRIVER LICENSE
Derek S
License # -
-7654-12
Home Address:
4590 N. W
Apt 601
New York
Sex: Male
Restrictions: No
WELL, EVERYTHING CHECKS OUT, MISTER...
...DEREK SULLIVAN.
I'M VERY PLEASED THAT YOU'RE INTERESTED IN THE POSITION LENNY OFFERED YOU.
LET ME JUST TELL YOU WHAT WE'RE DOING HERE AND WHY WE'RE INTERESTED IN YOU. WE'VE HAD SOME PROBLEMS AS OF LATE, NOTHING I CARE TO GO INTO NOW, BUT WE'VE GOT A BIT OF AN IMAGE ISSUE.
ONE OF THE THINGS WE'RE DOING TO IMPROVE OUR IMAGE IS THIS NEW DIVISION WE'VE ASKED YOU TO JOIN. BEFORE, WE JUST WENT IN AFTER THE BATTLE AND CLEANED UP THE MESS--WE WERE LITTLE MORE THAN A CONSTRUCTION CREW.
NOW WE HAVE A SEARCH-AND-RESCUE BRANCH--YOU'LL BE PART OF A SMALL TEAM THAT GOES INTO THE FIELD IMMEDIATELY AFTER OR SHORTLY BEFORE THE END OF ANY KIND OF BATTLE WE GET ASSIGNED TO TAKE CARE OF.
YOU AND YOUR TEAM WILL BE RESCUING ANYONE WHO MAY BE INJURED OR UNDER A COLLAPSED BUILDING--WE'RE TRYING TO BE A MORE THOROUGH COMPANY--WE WANT TO DO MORE FOR THE PEOPLE THAN JUST REBUILD THEIR SHOPPING MALLS AND SKYSCRAPERS.
YEAH, YEAH--THAT'S GREAT. REALLY.
THE PAY'S GOOD--THE HOURS SEEM FINE--I'M IN. I'LL TAKE IT.
GOOD--I'M THRILLED TO HAVE YOU. I'LL HAVE JOHN PREPARE THE TAX FORMS FOR YOU TO SIGN AND--
LISTEN, THERE WAS A WOMAN WITH LENNY WHEN HE OFFERED ME THE JOB. SHE WORE A BLUE COSTUME WITH AN EYE ON HER CHEST--SOME KINDA "V" LOGO-THING--SOMETHING, UH...
SHE HERE?
I THINK SHE IS.
TRY THE SECOND FLOOR.

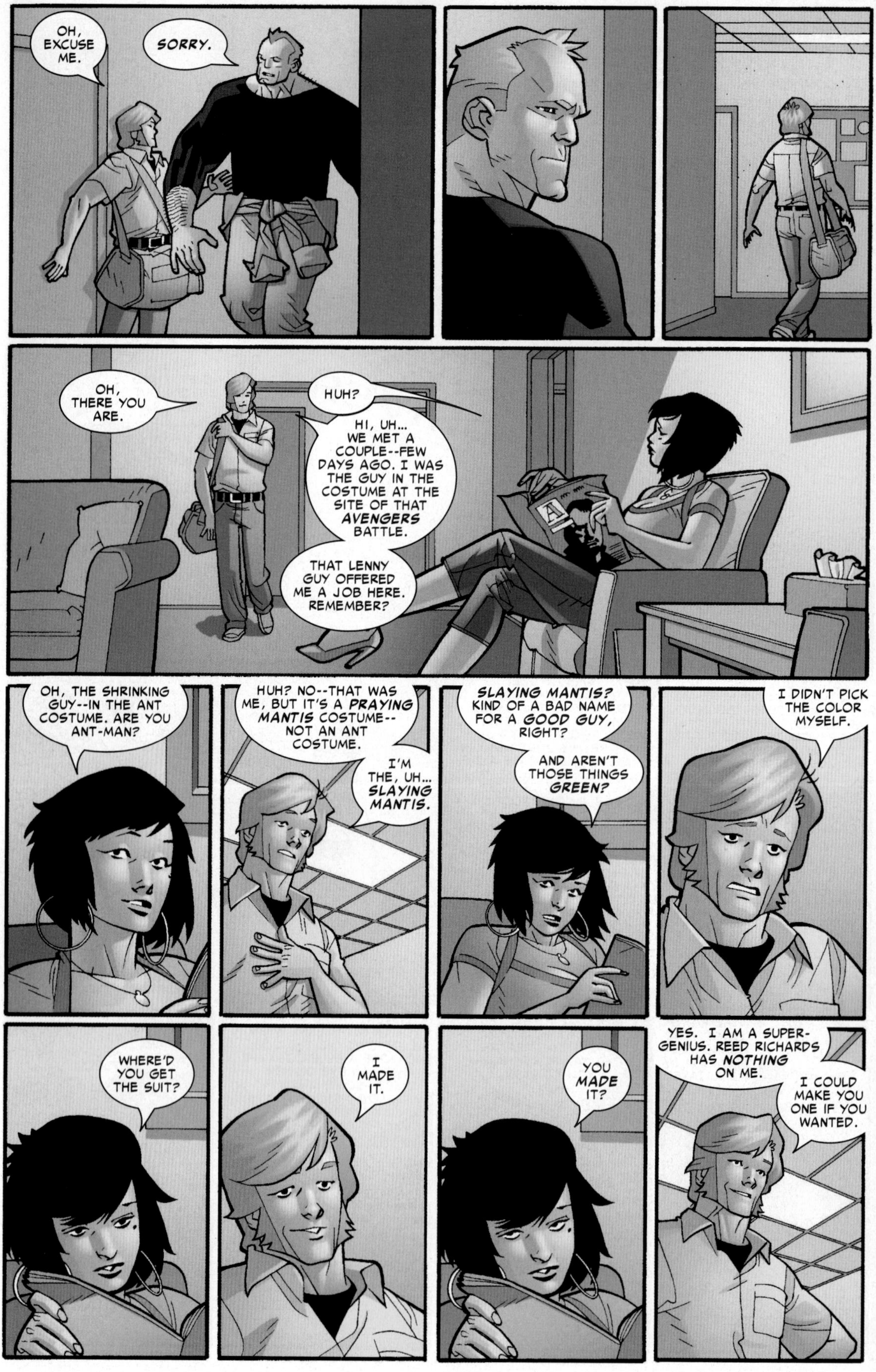
OH, EXCUSE ME.
SORRY.
OH, THERE YOU ARE.
HUH?
HI, UH... WE MET A COUPLE--FEW DAYS AGO. I WAS THE GUY IN THE COSTUME AT THE SITE OF THAT AVENGERS BATTLE.
THAT LENNY GUY OFFERED ME A JOB HERE. REMEMBER?
OH, THE SHRINKING GUY--IN THE ANT COSTUME. ARE YOU ANT-MAN?
HUH? NO--THAT WAS ME, BUT IT'S A PRAYING MANTIS COSTUME--NOT AN ANT COSTUME.
I'M THE, UH... SLAYING MANTIS.
SLAYING MANTIS? KIND OF A BAD NAME FOR A GOOD GUY, RIGHT?
AND AREN'T THOSE THINGS GREEN?
I DIDN'T PICK THE COLOR MYSELF.
WHERE'D YOU GET THE SUIT?
I MADE IT.
YOU MADE IT?
YES. I AM A SUPER-GENIUS. REED RICHARDS HAS NOTHING ON ME.
I COULD MAKE YOU ONE IF YOU WANTED.

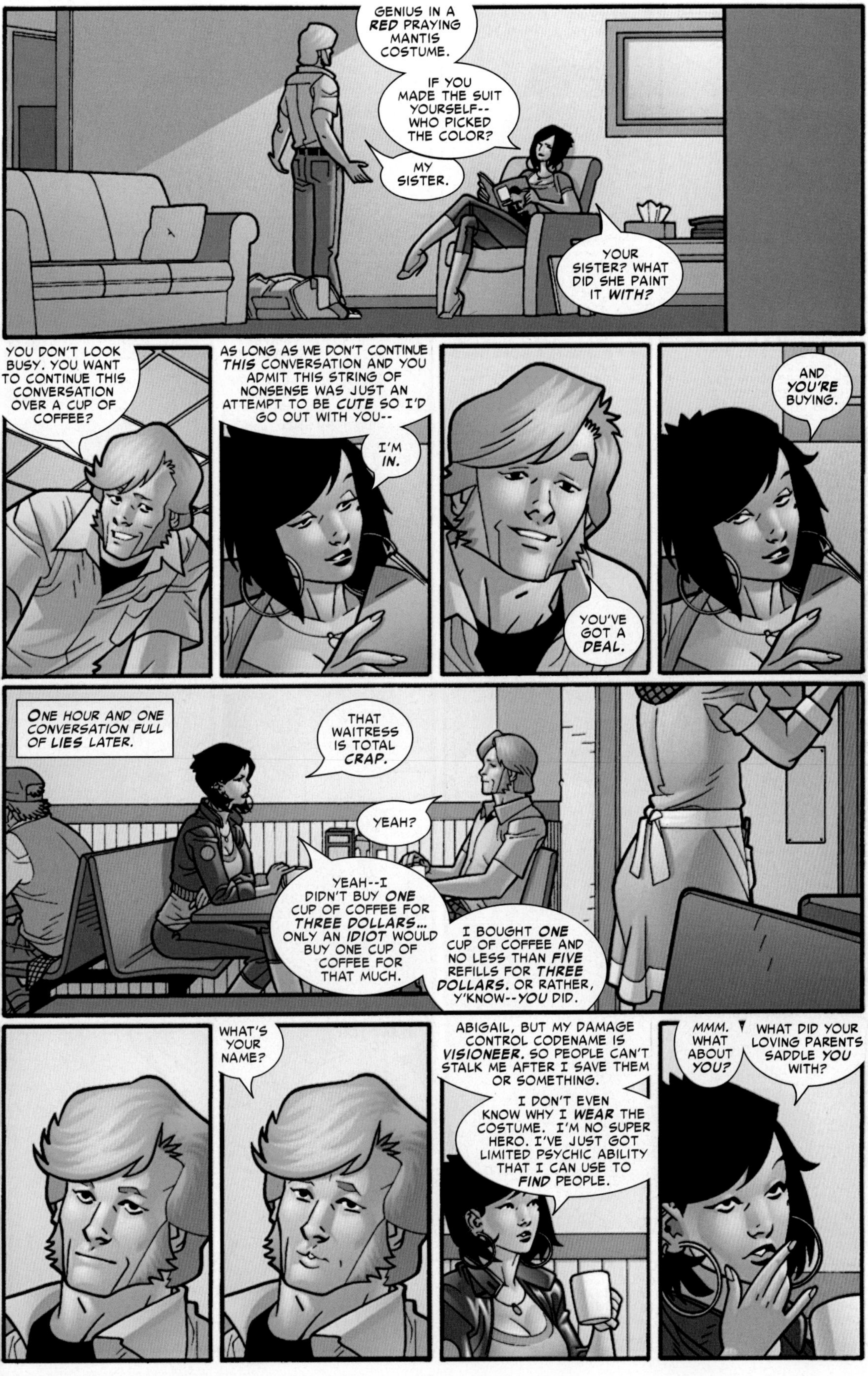
GENIUS IN A RED PRAYING MANTIS COSTUME.
IF YOU MADE THE SUIT YOURSELF-- WHO PICKED THE COLOR?
MY SISTER.
YOUR SISTER? WHAT DID SHE PAINT IT WITH?
YOU DON'T LOOK BUSY. YOU WANT TO CONTINUE THIS CONVERSATION OVER A CUP OF COFFEE?
AS LONG AS WE DON'T CONTINUE THIS CONVERSATION AND YOU ADMIT THIS STRING OF NONSENSE WAS JUST AN ATTEMPT TO BE CUTE SO I'D GO OUT WITH YOU--
I'M IN.
YOU'VE GOT A DEAL.
AND YOU'RE BUYING.
ONE HOUR AND ONE CONVERSATION FULL OF LIES LATER.
THAT WAITRESS IS TOTAL CRAP.
YEAH?
YEAH--I DIDN'T BUY ONE CUP OF COFFEE FOR THREE DOLLARS... ONLY AN IDIOT WOULD BUY ONE CUP OF COFFEE FOR THAT MUCH.
I BOUGHT ONE CUP OF COFFEE AND NO LESS THAN FIVE REFILLS FOR THREE DOLLARS. OR RATHER, Y'KNOW--YOU DID.
WHAT'S YOUR NAME?
ABIGAIL, BUT MY DAMAGE CONTROL CODENAME IS VISIONEER. SO PEOPLE CAN'T STALK ME AFTER I SAVE THEM OR SOMETHING.
I DON'T EVEN KNOW WHY I WEAR THE COSTUME. I'M NO SUPER HERO. I'VE JUST GOT LIMITED PSYCHIC ABILITY THAT I CAN USE TO FIND PEOPLE.
MMM. WHAT ABOUT YOU?
WHAT DID YOUR LOVING PARENTS SADDLE YOU WITH?

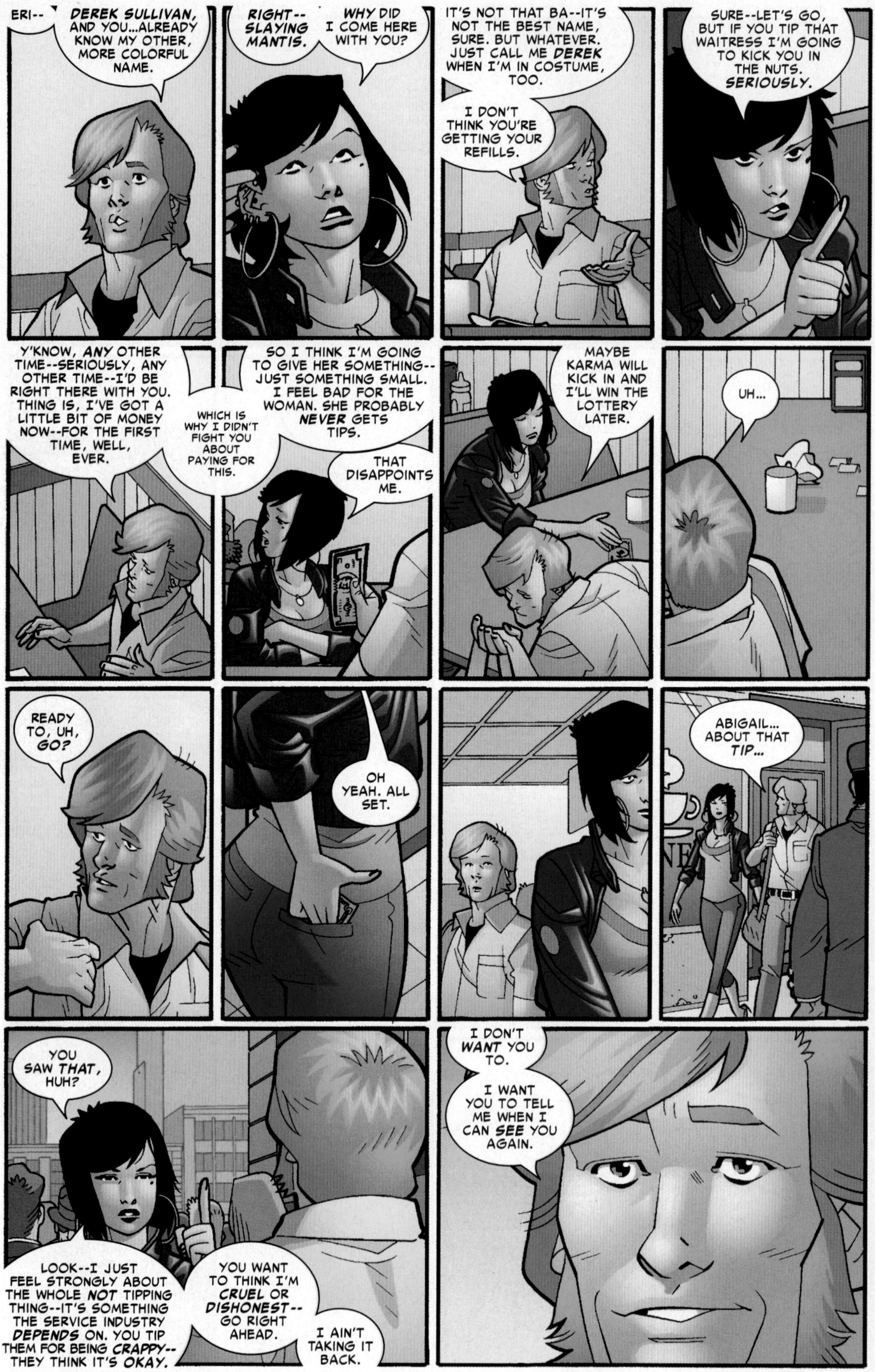
ERI--
DEREK SULLIVAN, AND YOU...ALREADY KNOW MY OTHER, MORE COLORFUL NAME.
RIGHT-- SLAYING MANTIS.
WHY DID I COME HERE WITH YOU?
IT'S NOT THAT BA--IT'S NOT THE BEST NAME, SURE. BUT WHATEVER. JUST CALL ME DEREK WHEN I'M IN COSTUME, TOO.
I DON'T THINK YOU'RE GETTING YOUR REFILLS.
SURE--LET'S GO, BUT IF YOU TIP THAT WAITRESS I'M GOING TO KICK YOU IN THE NUTS. SERIOUSLY.
Y'KNOW, ANY OTHER TIME--SERIOUSLY, ANY OTHER TIME--I'D BE RIGHT THERE WITH YOU. THING IS, I'VE GOT A LITTLE BIT OF MONEY NOW--FOR THE FIRST TIME, WELL, EVER.
WHICH IS WHY I DIDN'T FIGHT YOU ABOUT PAYING FOR THIS.
SO I THINK I'M GOING TO GIVE HER SOMETHING-- JUST SOMETHING SMALL. I FEEL BAD FOR THE WOMAN. SHE PROBABLY NEVER GETS TIPS.
THAT DISAPPOINTS ME.
MAYBE KARMA WILL KICK IN AND I'LL WIN THE LOTTERY LATER.
UH...
READY TO, UH, GO?
OH YEAH. ALL SET.
ABIGAIL... ABOUT THAT TIP...
YOU SAW THAT, HUH?
LOOK--I JUST FEEL STRONGLY ABOUT THE WHOLE NOT TIPPING THING--IT'S SOMETHING THE SERVICE INDUSTRY DEPENDS ON. YOU TIP THEM FOR BEING CRAPPY-- THEY THINK IT'S OKAY.
YOU WANT TO THINK I'M CRUEL OR DISHONEST-- GO RIGHT AHEAD.
I AIN'T TAKING IT BACK.
I DON'T WANT YOU TO.
I WANT YOU TO TELL ME WHEN I CAN SEE YOU AGAIN.

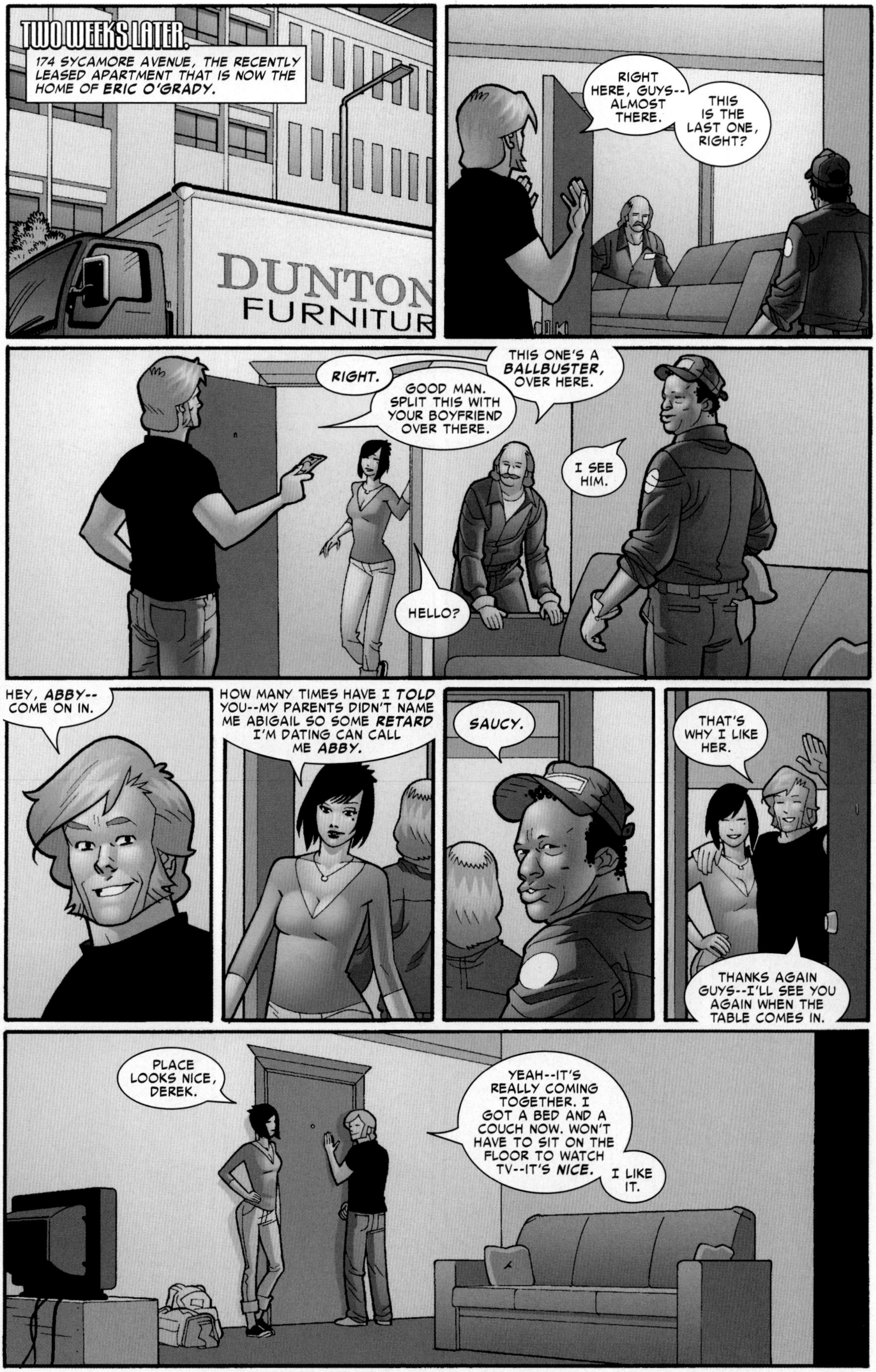

TWO WEEKS LATER.
174 SYCAMORE AVENUE, THE RECENTLY LEASED APARTMENT THAT IS NOW THE HOME OF ERIC O'GRADY.
DUNTON FURNITUR
RIGHT HERE, GUYS-- ALMOST THERE.
THIS IS THE LAST ONE, RIGHT?
RIGHT.
THIS ONE'S A BALLBUSTER, OVER HERE.
GOOD MAN. SPLIT THIS WITH YOUR BOYFRIEND OVER THERE.
I SEE HIM.
HELLO?
HEY, ABBY-- COME ON IN.
HOW MANY TIMES HAVE I TOLD YOU--MY PARENTS DIDN'T NAME ME ABIGAIL SO SOME RETARD I'M DATING CAN CALL ME ABBY.
SAUCY.
THAT'S WHY I LIKE HER.
THANKS AGAIN GUYS--I'LL SEE YOU AGAIN WHEN THE TABLE COMES IN.
PLACE LOOKS NICE, DEREK.
YEAH--IT'S REALLY COMING TOGETHER. I GOT A BED AND A COUCH NOW. WON'T HAVE TO SIT ON THE FLOOR TO WATCH TV--IT'S NICE.
I LIKE IT.

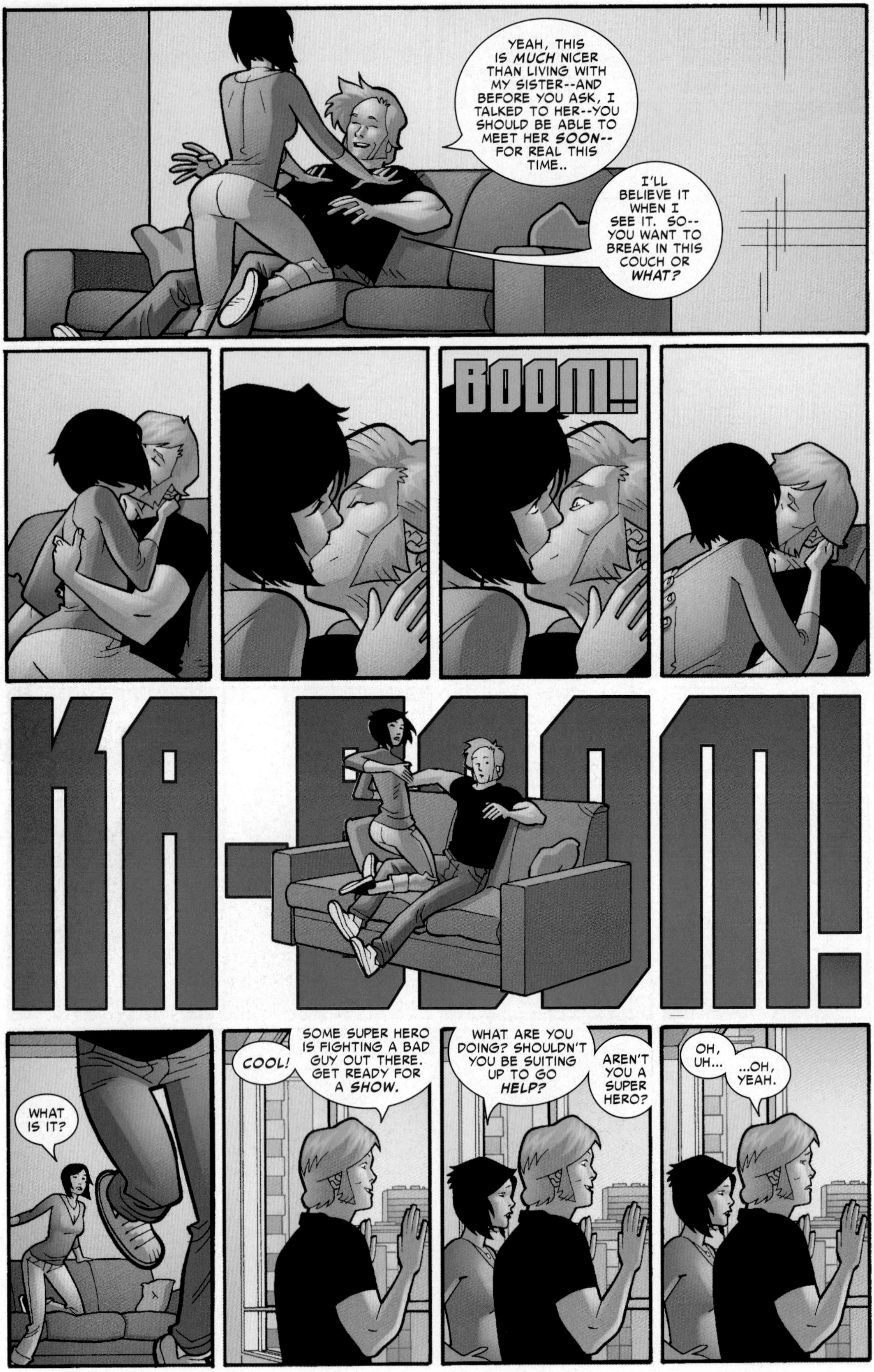
YEAH, THIS IS MUCH NICER THAN LIVING WITH MY SISTER--AND BEFORE YOU ASK, I TALKED TO HER--YOU SHOULD BE ABLE TO MEET HER SOON-- FOR REAL THIS TIME..
I'LL BELIEVE IT WHEN I SEE IT. SO-- YOU WANT TO BREAK IN THIS COUCH OR WHAT?
BOOM!!
KA-BOOM!
WHAT IS IT?
COOL!
SOME SUPER HERO IS FIGHTING A BAD GUY OUT THERE. GET READY FOR A SHOW.
WHAT ARE YOU DOING? SHOULDN'T YOU BE SUITING UP TO GO HELP?
AREN'T YOU A SUPER HERO?
OH, UH...
...OH, YEAH.

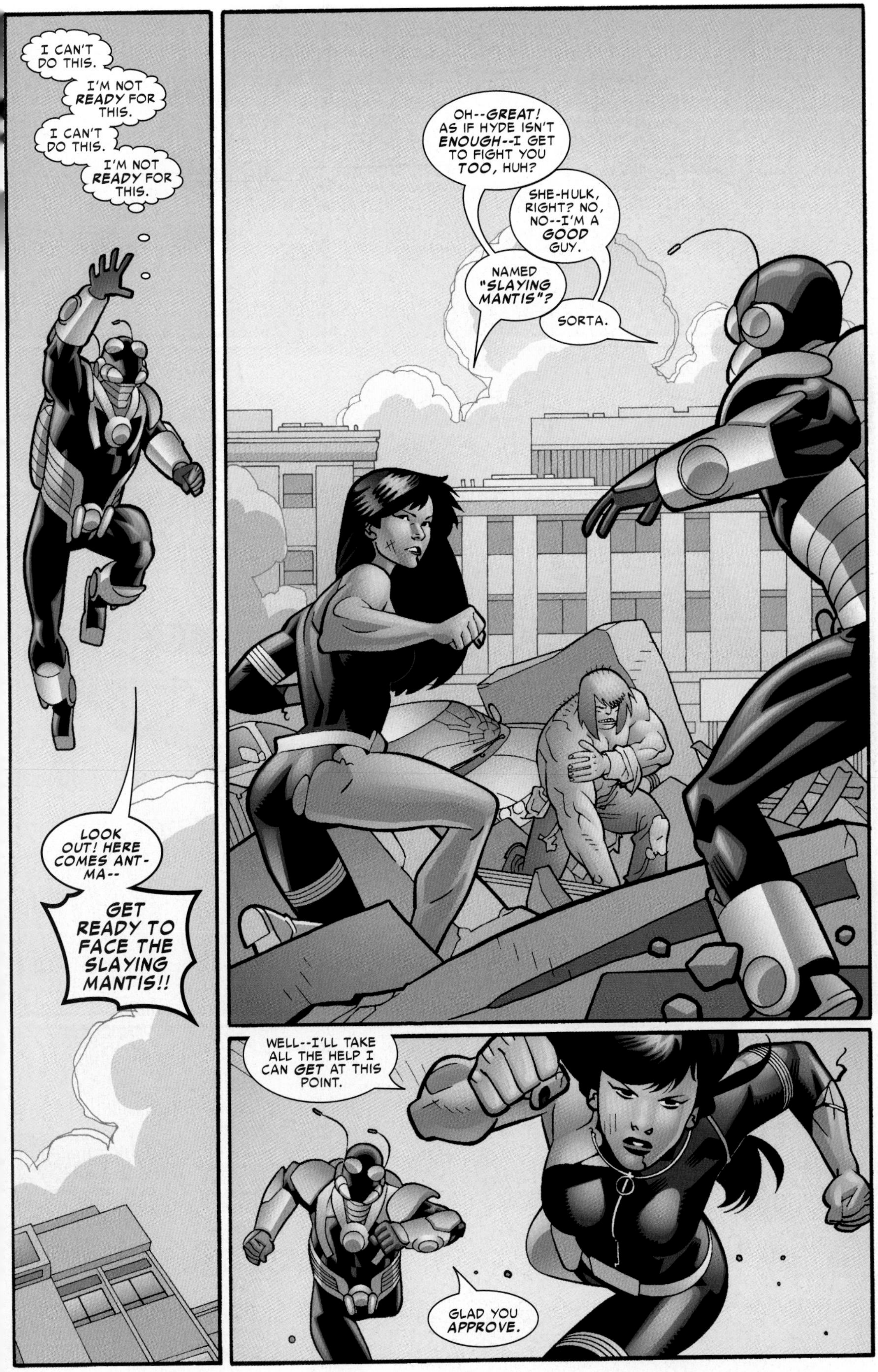

I CAN'T DO THIS.
I'M NOT READY FOR THIS.
I CAN'T DO THIS.
I'M NOT READY FOR THIS.
OH--GREAT! AS IF HYDE ISN'T ENOUGH--I GET TO FIGHT YOU TOO, HUH?
SHE-HULK, RIGHT? NO, NO--I'M A GOOD GUY.
NAMED "SLAYING MANTIS"?
SORTA.
LOOK OUT! HERE COMES ANT-MA--
GET READY TO FACE THE SLAYING MANTIS!!
WELL--I'LL TAKE ALL THE HELP I CAN GET AT THIS POINT.
GLAD YOU APPROVE.

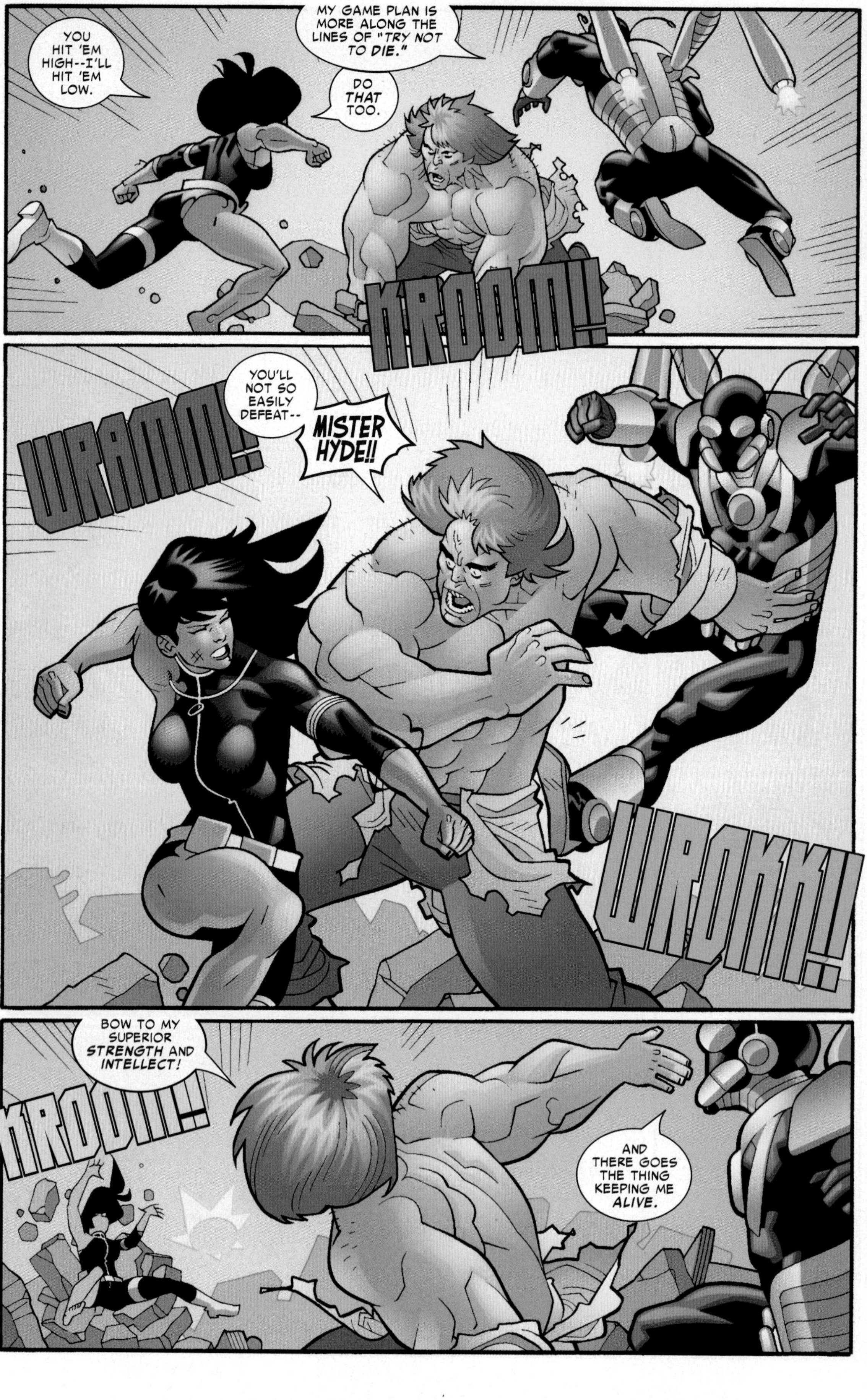
YOU HIT 'EM HIGH--I'LL HIT 'EM LOW.
MY GAME PLAN IS MORE ALONG THE LINES OF "TRY NOT TO DIE."
DO THAT TOO.
KROOM!!
YOU'LL NOT SO EASILY DEFEAT--
MISTER HYDE!!
WRAMM!!
WROKK!!
BOW TO MY SUPERIOR STRENGTH AND INTELLECT!
KROOM!!
AND THERE GOES THE THING KEEPING ME ALIVE.

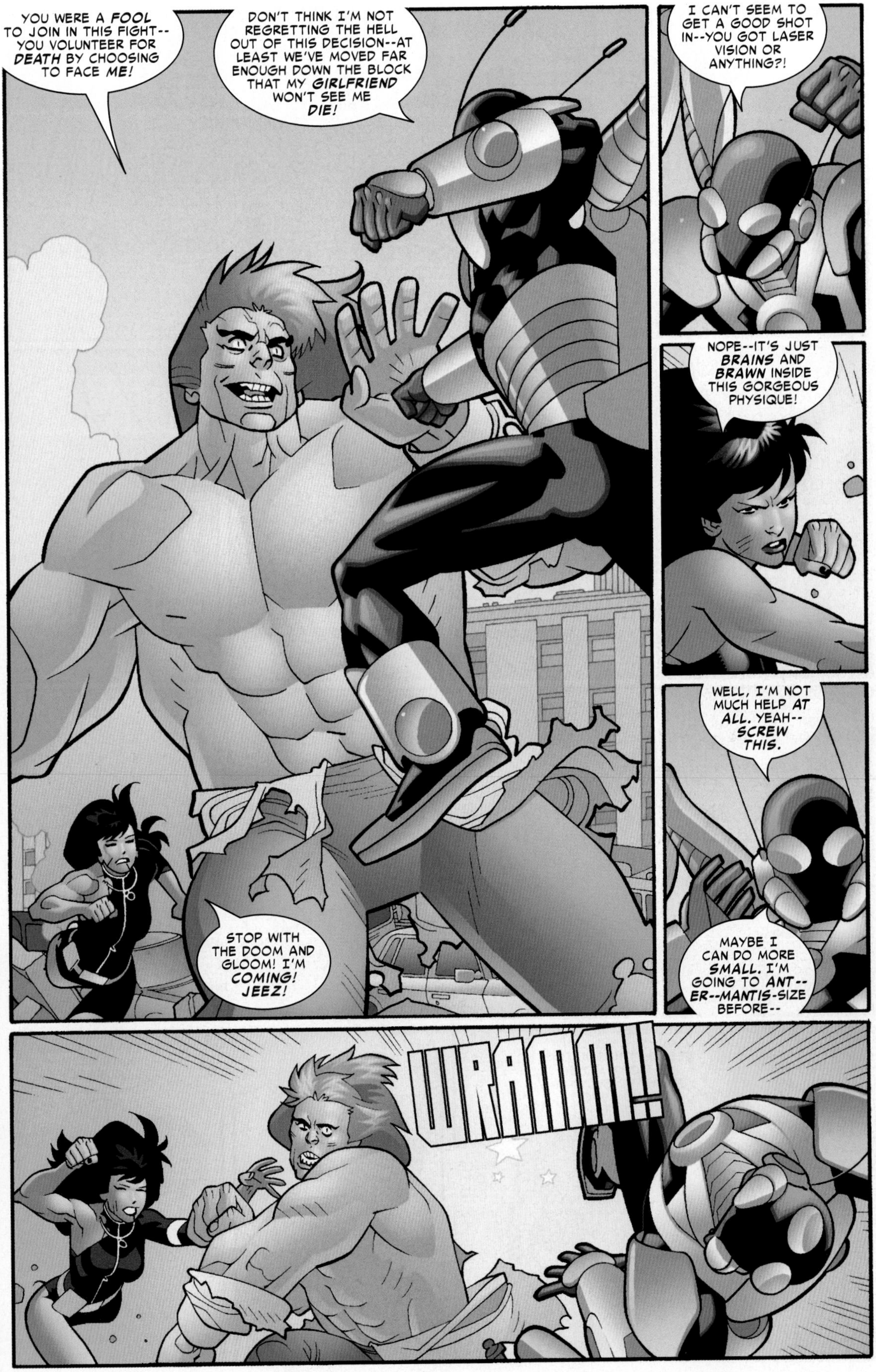
YOU WERE A FOOL TO JOIN IN THIS FIGHT--YOU VOLUNTEER FOR DEATH BY CHOOSING TO FACE ME!
DON'T THINK I'M NOT REGRETTING THE HELL OUT OF THIS DECISION--AT LEAST WE'VE MOVED FAR ENOUGH DOWN THE BLOCK THAT MY GIRLFRIEND WON'T SEE ME DIE!
STOP WITH THE DOOM AND GLOOM! I'M COMING! JEEZ!
I CAN'T SEEM TO GET A GOOD SHOT IN--YOU GOT LASER VISION OR ANYTHING?!
NOPE--IT'S JUST BRAINS AND BRAWN INSIDE THIS GORGEOUS PHYSIQUE!
WELL, I'M NOT MUCH HELP AT ALL. YEAH--SCREW THIS.
MAYBE I CAN DO MORE SMALL. I'M GOING TO ANT-- ER--MANTIS-SIZE BEFORE--
WRAMM!!

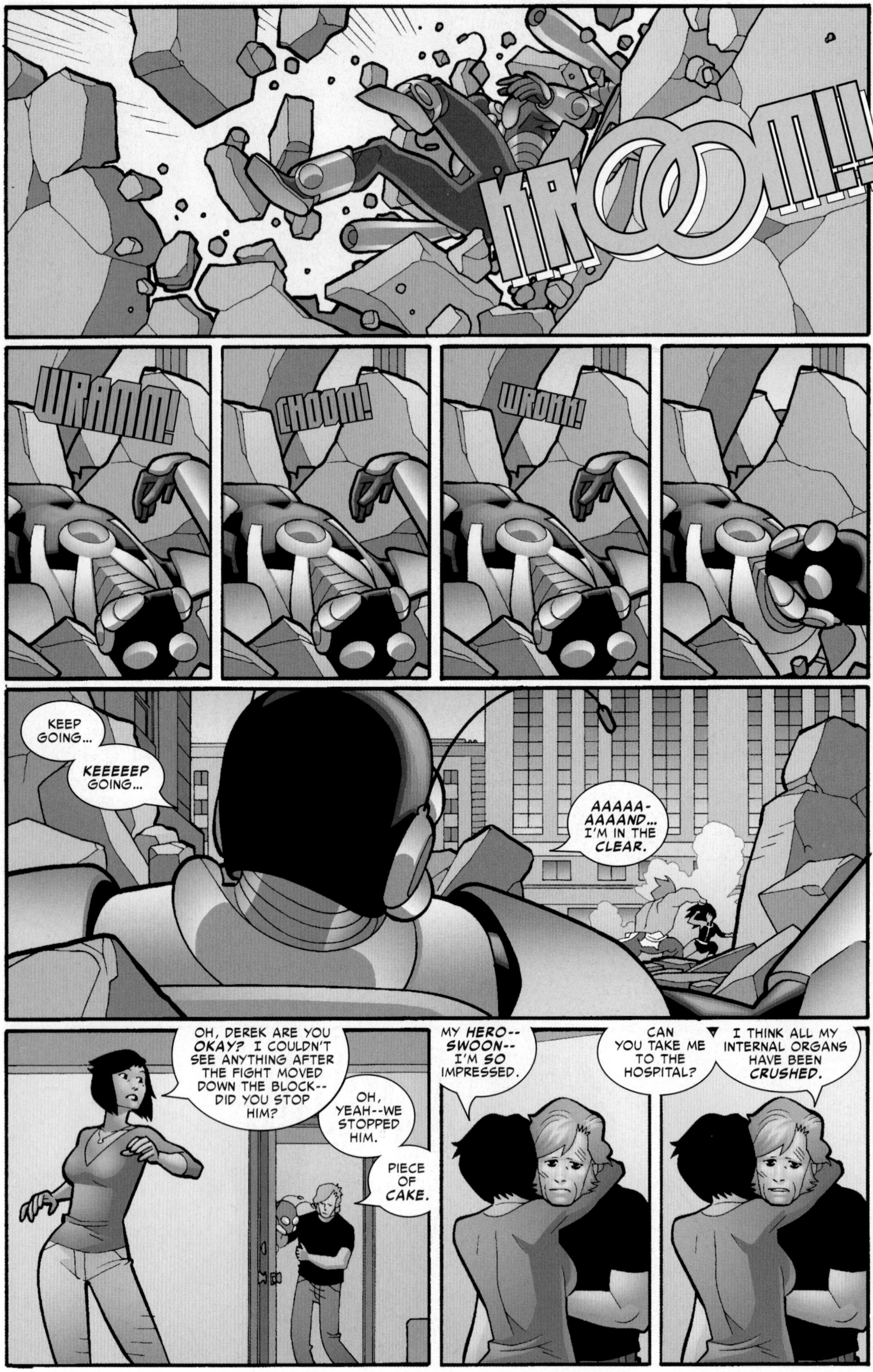
KROOOM!!!
WRAMM!
CHOOM!
WRONK!
KEEP GOING...
KEEEEEP GOING...
AAAAA-AAAAND... I'M IN THE CLEAR.
OH, DEREK ARE YOU OKAY? I COULDN'T SEE ANYTHING AFTER THE FIGHT MOVED DOWN THE BLOCK--DID YOU STOP HIM?
OH, YEAH--WE STOPPED HIM.
PIECE OF CAKE.
MY HERO--SWOON--I'M SO IMPRESSED.
CAN YOU TAKE ME TO THE HOSPITAL?
I THINK ALL MY INTERNAL ORGANS HAVE BEEN CRUSHED.

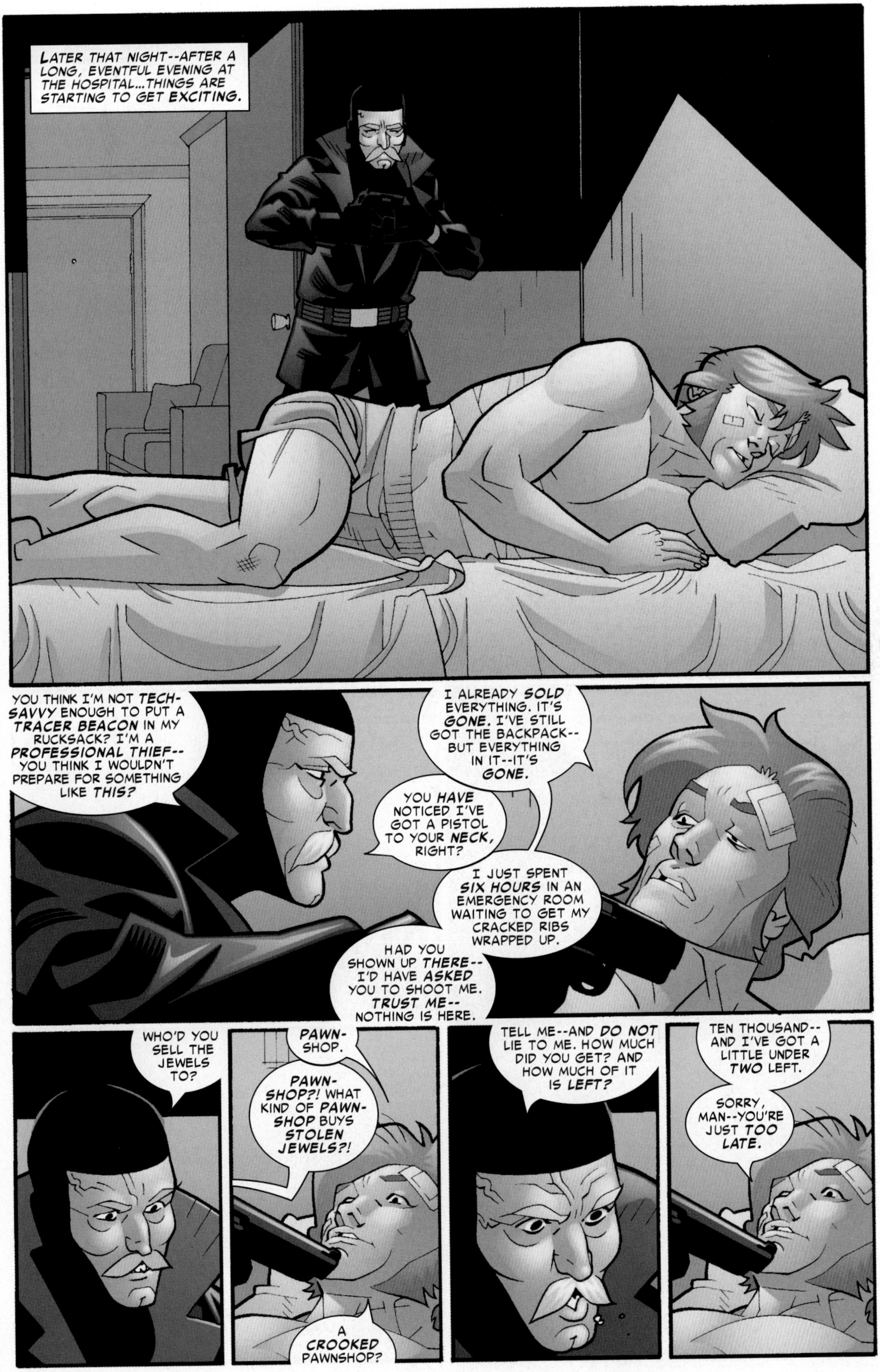
LATER THAT NIGHT--AFTER A LONG, EVENTFUL EVENING AT THE HOSPITAL...THINGS ARE STARTING TO GET EXCITING.
YOU THINK I'M NOT TECH-SAVVY ENOUGH TO PUT A TRACER BEACON IN MY RUCKSACK? I'M A PROFESSIONAL THIEF--YOU THINK I WOULDN'T PREPARE FOR SOMETHING LIKE THIS?
I ALREADY SOLD EVERYTHING. IT'S GONE. I'VE STILL GOT THE BACKPACK--BUT EVERYTHING IN IT--IT'S GONE.
YOU HAVE NOTICED I'VE GOT A PISTOL TO YOUR NECK, RIGHT?
I JUST SPENT SIX HOURS IN AN EMERGENCY ROOM WAITING TO GET MY CRACKED RIBS WRAPPED UP.
HAD YOU SHOWN UP THERE--I'D HAVE ASKED YOU TO SHOOT ME. TRUST ME--NOTHING IS HERE.
WHO'D YOU SELL THE JEWELS TO?
PAWN-SHOP.
PAWN-SHOP?! WHAT KIND OF PAWN-SHOP BUYS STOLEN JEWELS?!
A CROOKED PAWNSHOP?
TELL ME--AND DO NOT LIE TO ME. HOW MUCH DID YOU GET? AND HOW MUCH OF IT IS LEFT?
TEN THOUSAND--AND I'VE GOT A LITTLE UNDER TWO LEFT.
SORRY, MAN--YOU'RE JUST TOO LATE.

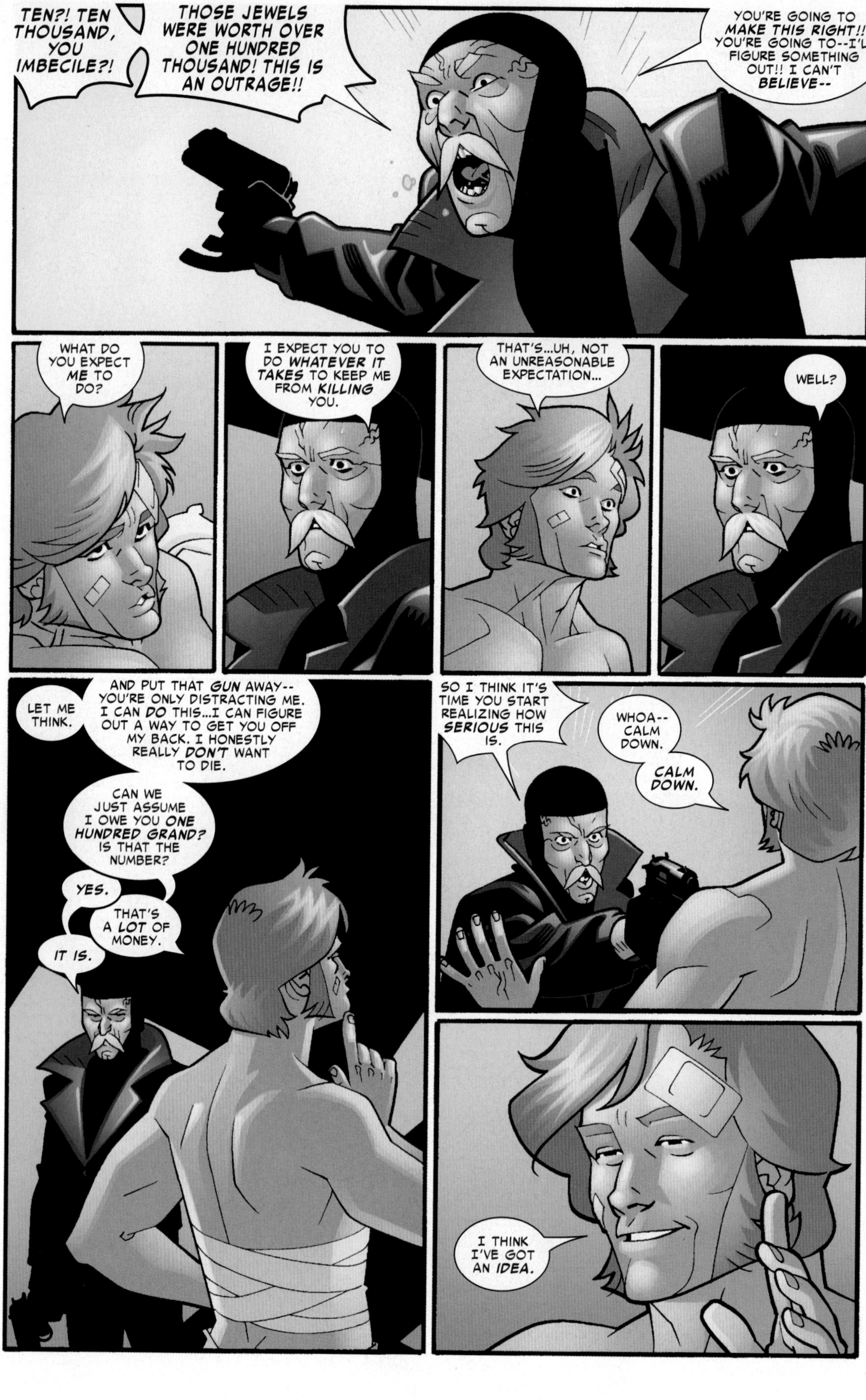
TEN?! TEN THOUSAND, YOU IMBECILE?!
THOSE JEWELS WERE WORTH OVER ONE HUNDRED THOUSAND! THIS IS AN OUTRAGE!!
YOU'RE GOING TO MAKE THIS RIGHT!! YOU'RE GOING TO--I'LL FIGURE SOMETHING OUT!! I CAN'T BELIEVE--
WHAT DO YOU EXPECT ME TO DO?
I EXPECT YOU TO DO WHATEVER IT TAKES TO KEEP ME FROM KILLING YOU.
THAT'S...UH, NOT AN UNREASONABLE EXPECTATION...
WELL?
LET ME THINK.
AND PUT THAT GUN AWAY--YOU'RE ONLY DISTRACTING ME. I CAN DO THIS...I CAN FIGURE OUT A WAY TO GET YOU OFF MY BACK. I HONESTLY REALLY DON'T WANT TO DIE.
CAN WE JUST ASSUME I OWE YOU ONE HUNDRED GRAND? IS THAT THE NUMBER?
YES.
THAT'S A LOT OF MONEY.
IT IS.
SO I THINK IT'S TIME YOU START REALIZING HOW SERIOUS THIS IS.
WHOA--CALM DOWN.
CALM DOWN.
I THINK I'VE GOT AN IDEA.

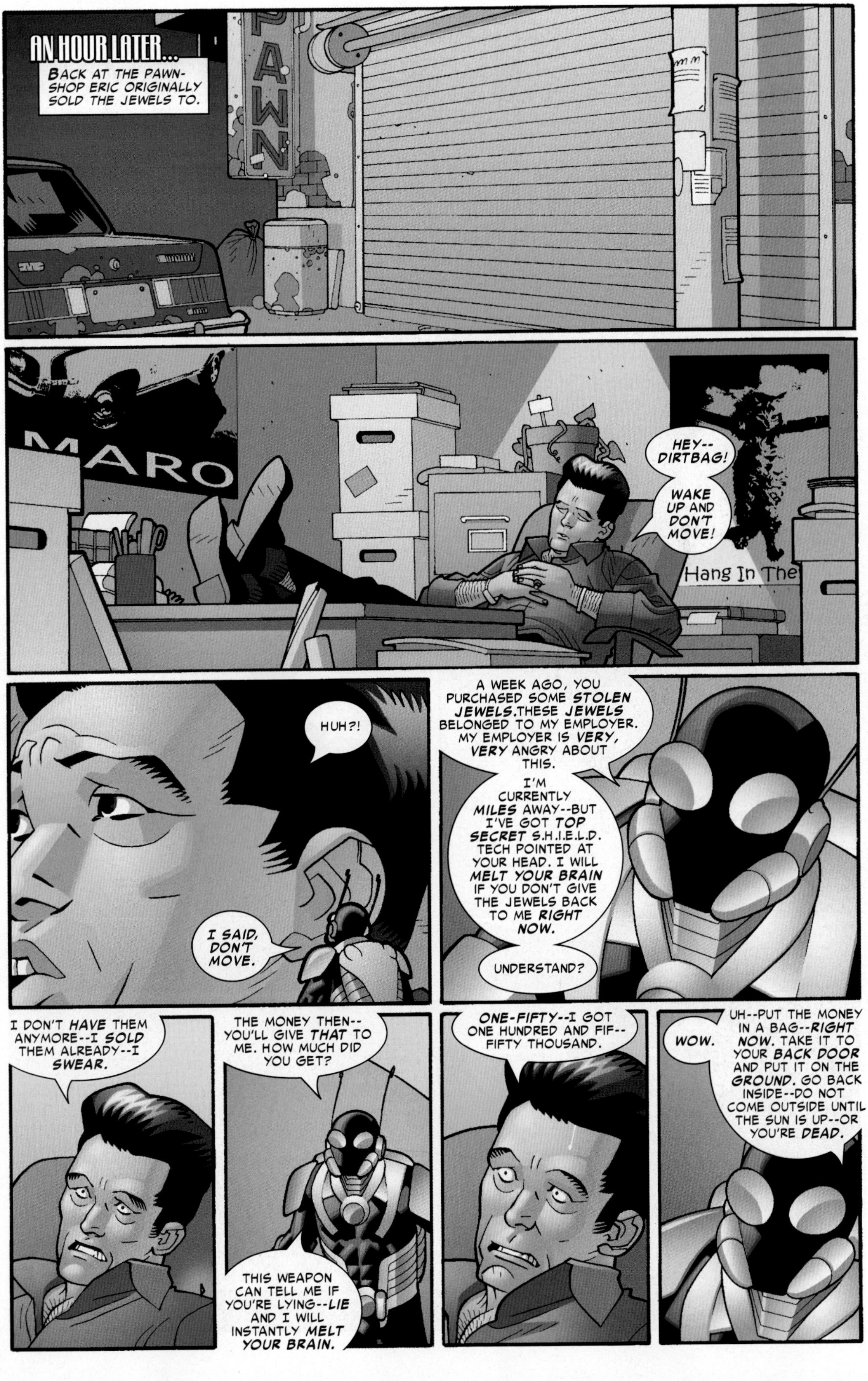
AN HOUR LATER...
BACK AT THE PAWN-SHOP ERIC ORIGINALLY SOLD THE JEWELS TO.
PAWN
MARO
HEY-- DIRTBAG!
WAKE UP AND DON'T MOVE!
Hang In The
HUH?!
I SAID, DON'T MOVE.
A WEEK AGO, YOU PURCHASED SOME STOLEN JEWELS.THESE JEWELS BELONGED TO MY EMPLOYER. MY EMPLOYER IS VERY, VERY ANGRY ABOUT THIS.
I'M CURRENTLY MILES AWAY--BUT I'VE GOT TOP SECRET S.H.I.E.L.D. TECH POINTED AT YOUR HEAD. I WILL MELT YOUR BRAIN IF YOU DON'T GIVE THE JEWELS BACK TO ME RIGHT NOW.
UNDERSTAND?
I DON'T HAVE THEM ANYMORE--I SOLD THEM ALREADY--I SWEAR.
THE MONEY THEN-- YOU'LL GIVE THAT TO ME. HOW MUCH DID YOU GET?
THIS WEAPON CAN TELL ME IF YOU'RE LYING--LIE AND I WILL INSTANTLY MELT YOUR BRAIN.
ONE-FIFTY--I GOT ONE HUNDRED AND FIF-- FIFTY THOUSAND.
WOW.
UH--PUT THE MONEY IN A BAG--RIGHT NOW. TAKE IT TO YOUR BACK DOOR AND PUT IT ON THE GROUND. GO BACK INSIDE--DO NOT COME OUTSIDE UNTIL THE SUN IS UP--OR YOU'RE DEAD.

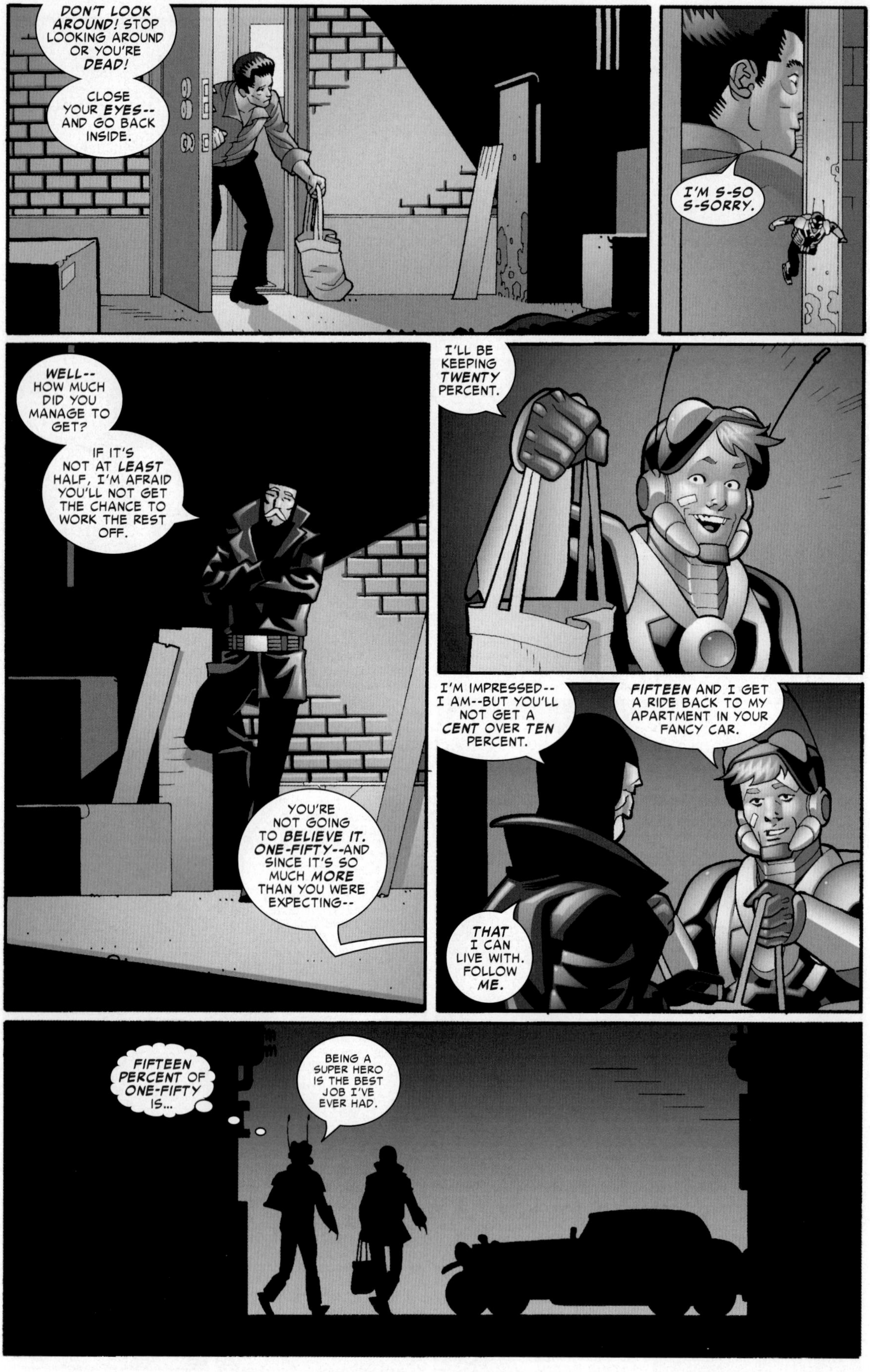
DON'T LOOK AROUND! STOP LOOKING AROUND OR YOU'RE DEAD!
CLOSE YOUR EYES-- AND GO BACK INSIDE.
I'M S-SO S-SORRY.
WELL-- HOW MUCH DID YOU MANAGE TO GET?
IF IT'S NOT AT LEAST HALF, I'M AFRAID YOU'LL NOT GET THE CHANCE TO WORK THE REST OFF.
YOU'RE NOT GOING TO BELIEVE IT. ONE-FIFTY--AND SINCE IT'S SO MUCH MORE THAN YOU WERE EXPECTING--
I'LL BE KEEPING TWENTY PERCENT.
I'M IMPRESSED-- I AM--BUT YOU'LL NOT GET A CENT OVER TEN PERCENT.
FIFTEEN AND I GET A RIDE BACK TO MY APARTMENT IN YOUR FANCY CAR.
THAT I CAN LIVE WITH. FOLLOW ME.
FIFTEEN PERCENT OF ONE-FIFTY IS...
BEING A SUPER HERO IS THE BEST JOB I'VE EVER HAD.

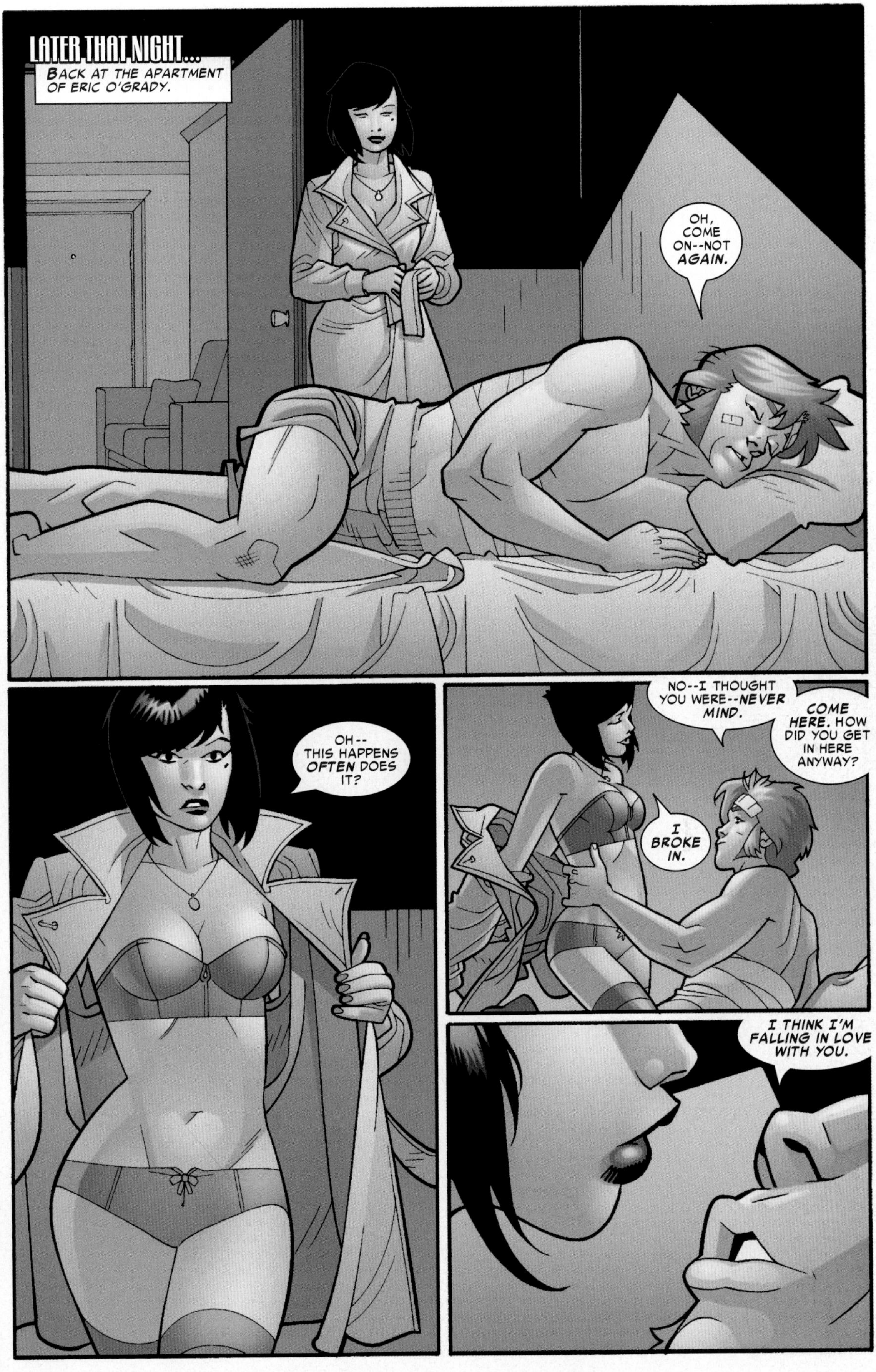
LATER THAT NIGHT...
BACK AT THE APARTMENT OF ERIC O'GRADY.
OH, COME ON--NOT AGAIN.
OH-- THIS HAPPENS OFTEN DOES IT?
NO--I THOUGHT YOU WERE--NEVER MIND.
COME HERE. HOW DID YOU GET IN HERE ANYWAY?
I BROKE IN.
I THINK I'M FALLING IN LOVE WITH YOU.

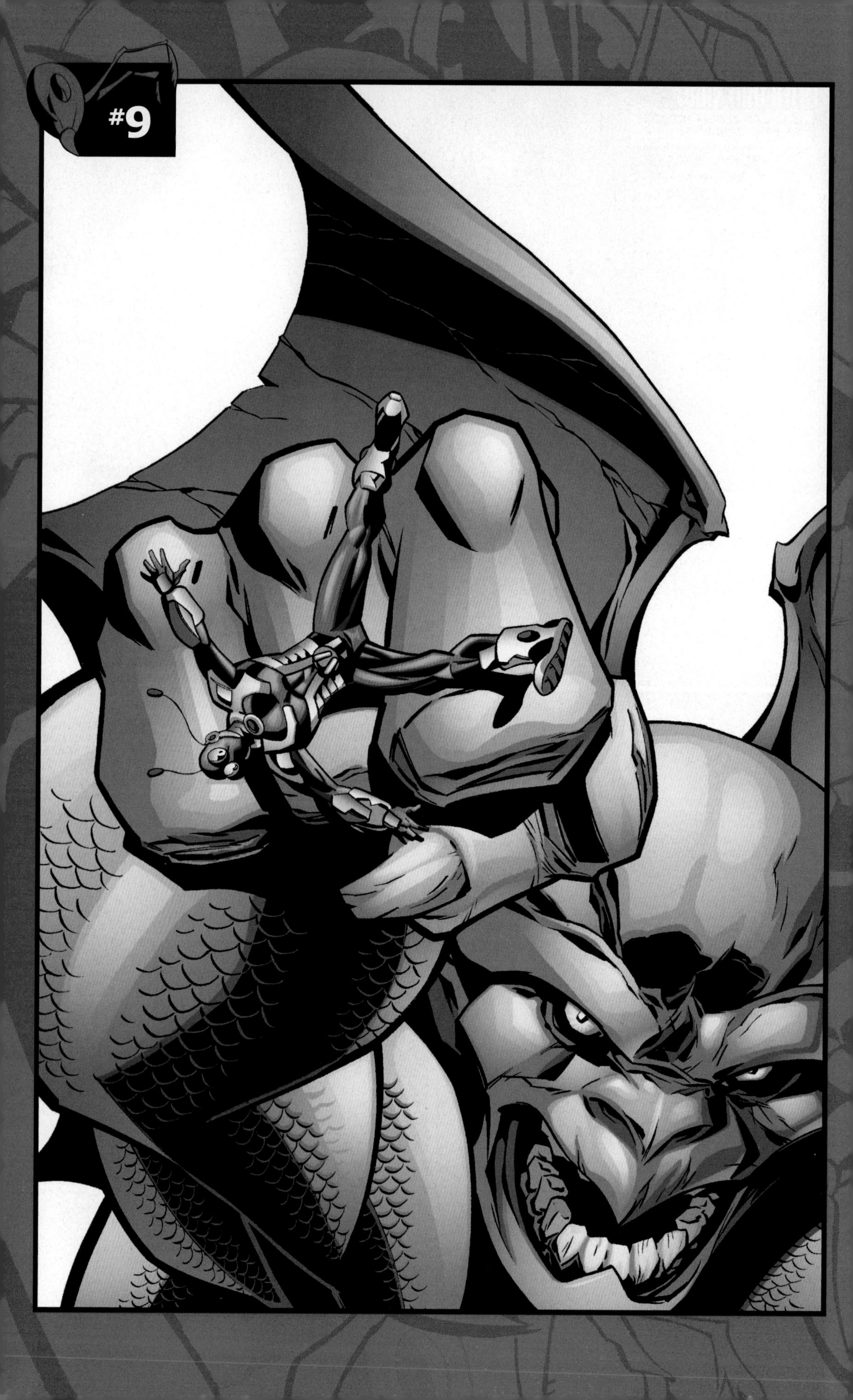
#9

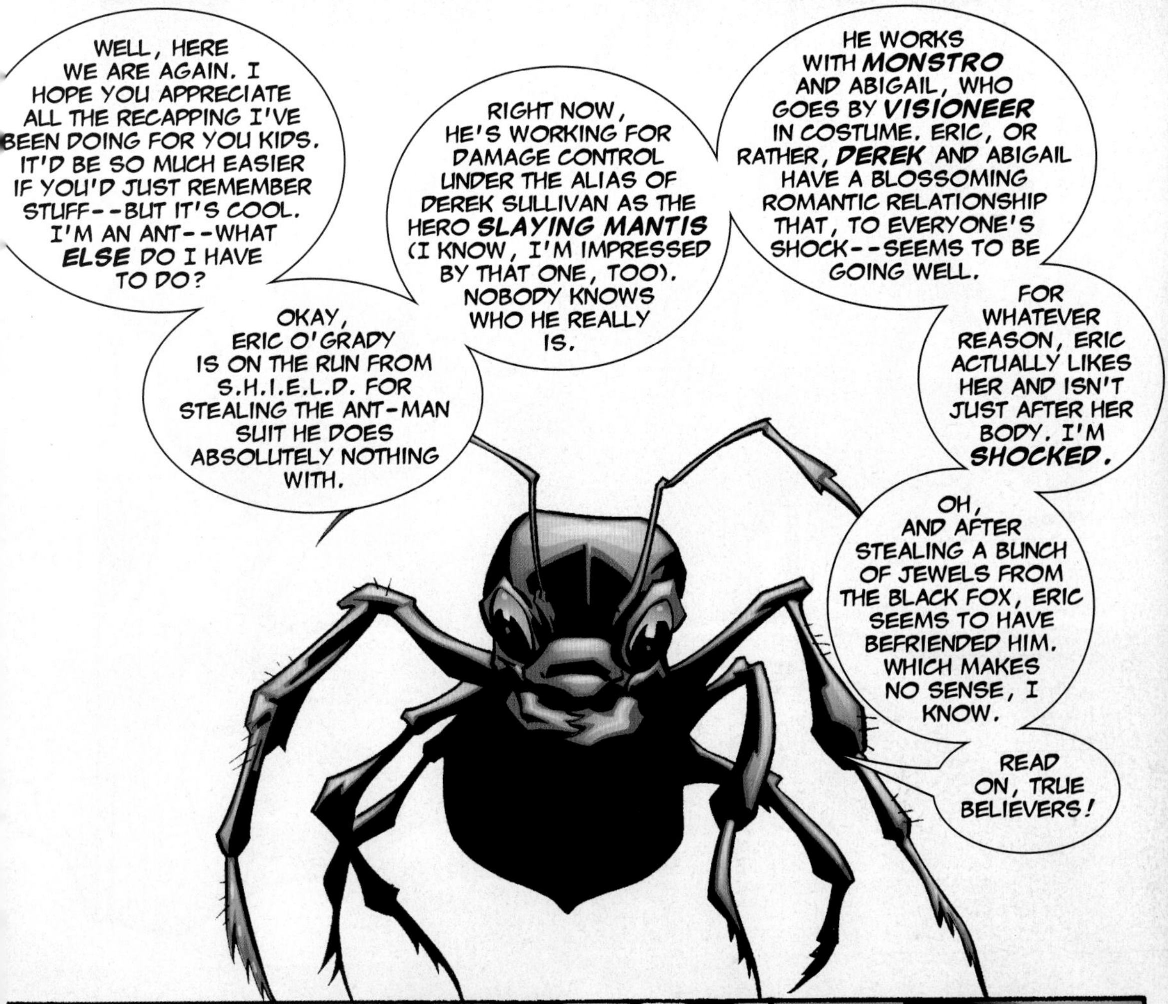
WELL, HERE WE ARE AGAIN. I HOPE YOU APPRECIATE ALL THE RECAPPING I'VE BEEN DOING FOR YOU KIDS. IT'D BE SO MUCH EASIER IF YOU'D JUST REMEMBER STUFF--BUT IT'S COOL. I'M AN ANT--WHAT ELSE DO I HAVE TO DO?
OKAY, ERIC O'GRADY IS ON THE RUN FROM S.H.I.E.L.D. FOR STEALING THE ANT-MAN SUIT HE DOES ABSOLUTELY NOTHING WITH.
RIGHT NOW, HE'S WORKING FOR DAMAGE CONTROL UNDER THE ALIAS OF DEREK SULLIVAN AS THE HERO SLAYING MANTIS (I KNOW, I'M IMPRESSED BY THAT ONE, TOO). NOBODY KNOWS WHO HE REALLY IS.
HE WORKS WITH MONSTRO AND ABIGAIL, WHO GOES BY VISIONEER IN COSTUME. ERIC, OR RATHER, DEREK AND ABIGAIL HAVE A BLOSSOMING ROMANTIC RELATIONSHIP THAT, TO EVERYONE'S SHOCK--SEEMS TO BE GOING WELL.
FOR WHATEVER REASON, ERIC ACTUALLY LIKES HER AND ISN'T JUST AFTER HER BODY. I'M SHOCKED.
OH, AND AFTER STEALING A BUNCH OF JEWELS FROM THE BLACK FOX, ERIC SEEMS TO HAVE BEFRIENDED HIM. WHICH MAKES NO SENSE, I KNOW.
READ ON, TRUE BELIEVERS!

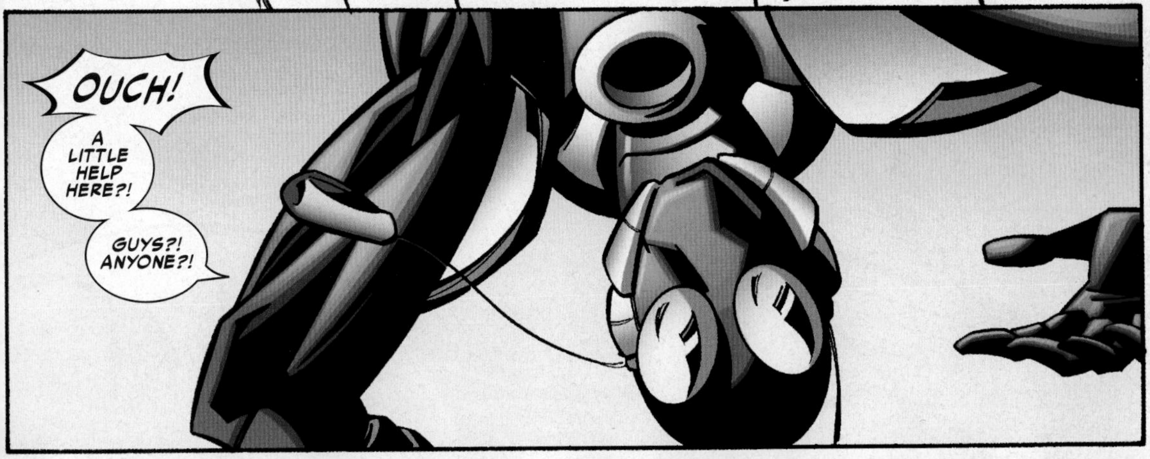
OUCH!
A LITTLE HELP HERE?!
GUYS?! ANYONE?!

# LOVE'S LONELY EMBRACE

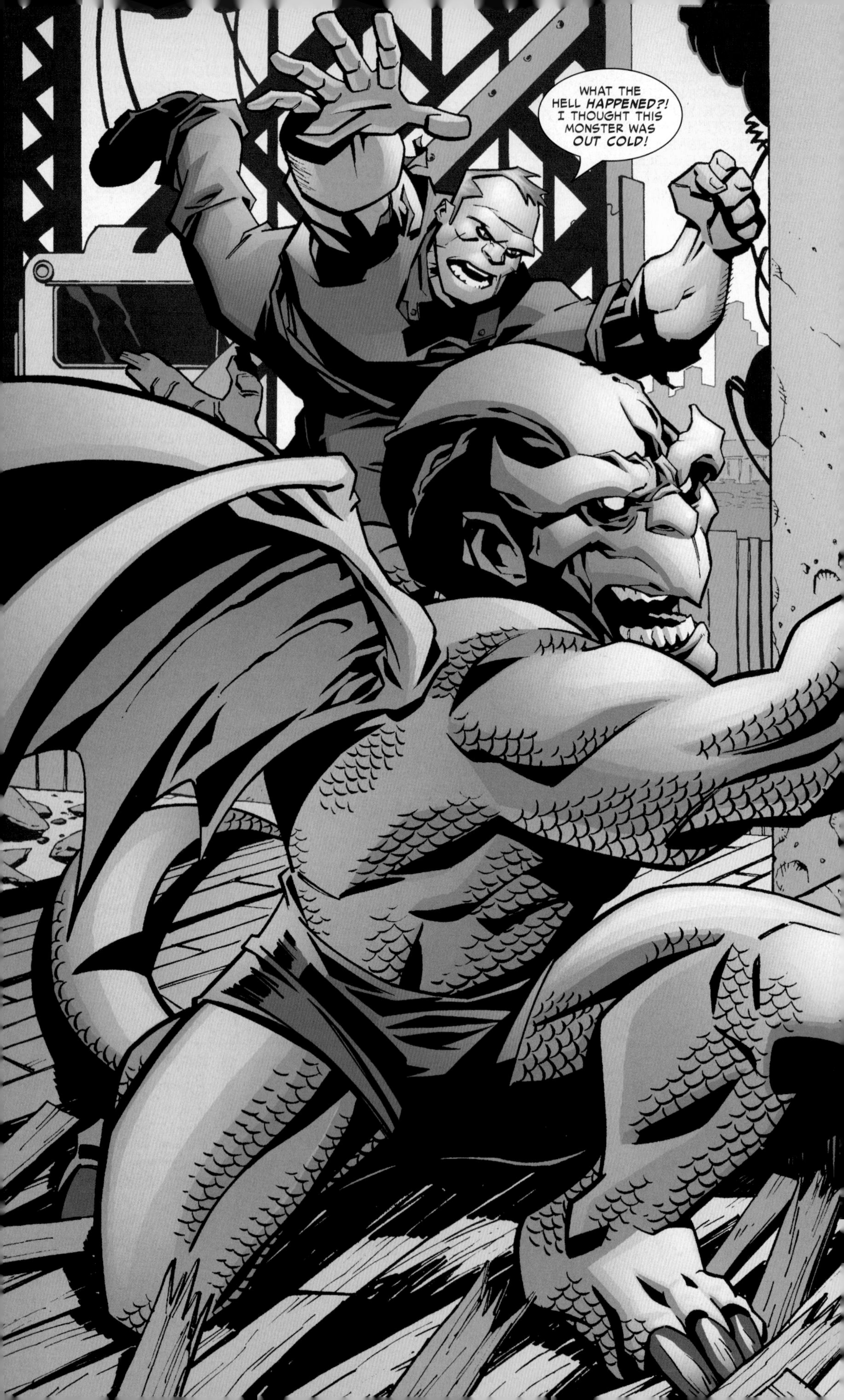
WHAT THE HELL HAPPENED?! I THOUGHT THIS MONSTER WAS OUT COLD!

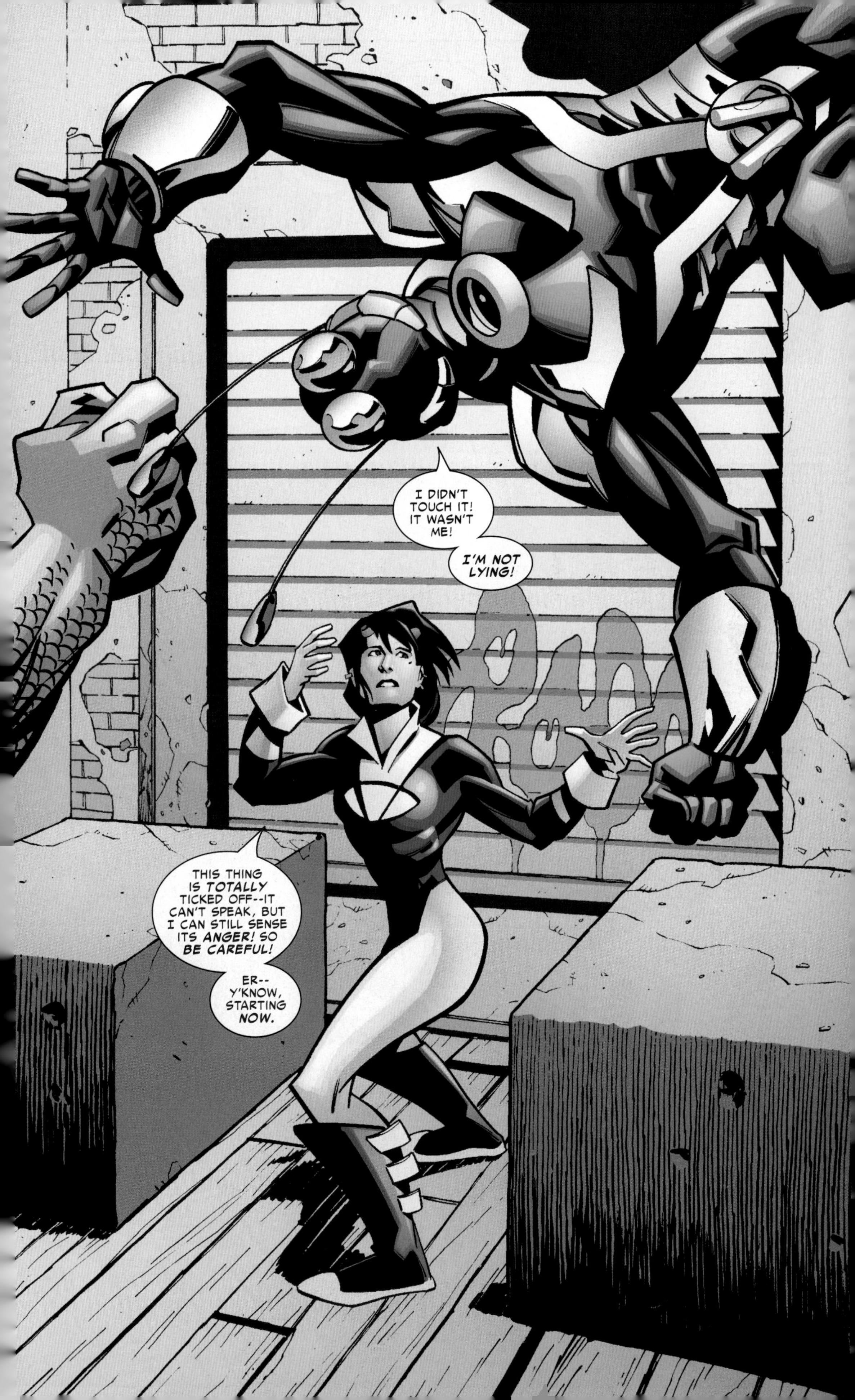
I DIDN'T TOUCH IT! IT WASN'T ME!
I'M NOT LYING!
THIS THING IS TOTALLY TICKED OFF--IT CAN'T SPEAK, BUT I CAN STILL SENSE ITS ANGER! SO BE CAREFUL!
ER-- Y'KNOW, STARTING NOW.

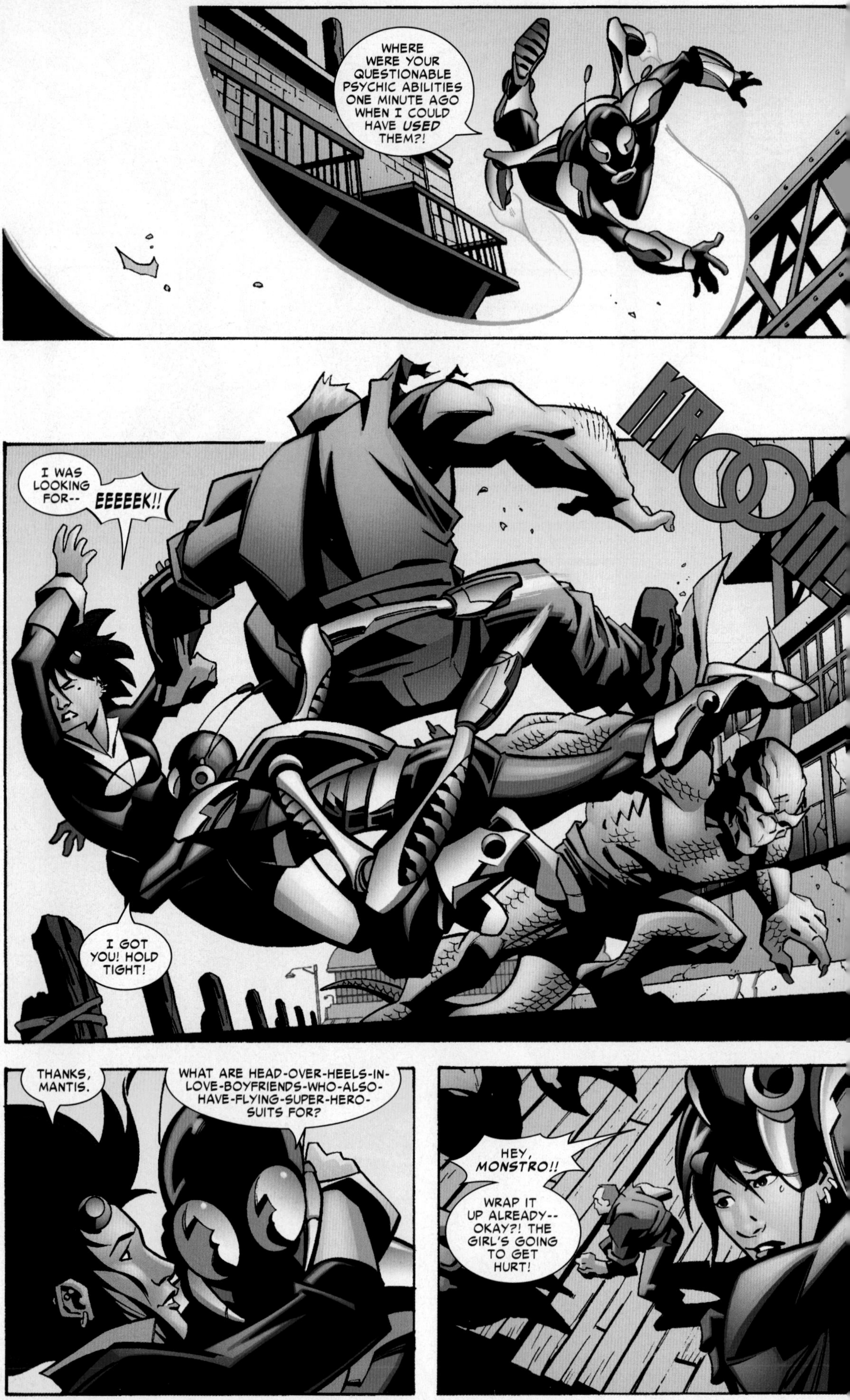
WHERE WERE YOUR QUESTIONABLE PSYCHIC ABILITIES ONE MINUTE AGO WHEN I COULD HAVE USED THEM?!
KROOM
I WAS LOOKING FOR--
EEEEEK!!
I GOT YOU! HOLD TIGHT!
THANKS, MANTIS.
WHAT ARE HEAD-OVER-HEELS-IN-LOVE-BOYFRIENDS-WHO-ALSO-HAVE-FLYING-SUPER-HERO-SUITS FOR?
HEY, MONSTRO!!
WRAP IT UP ALREADY--OKAY?! THE GIRL'S GOING TO GET HURT!

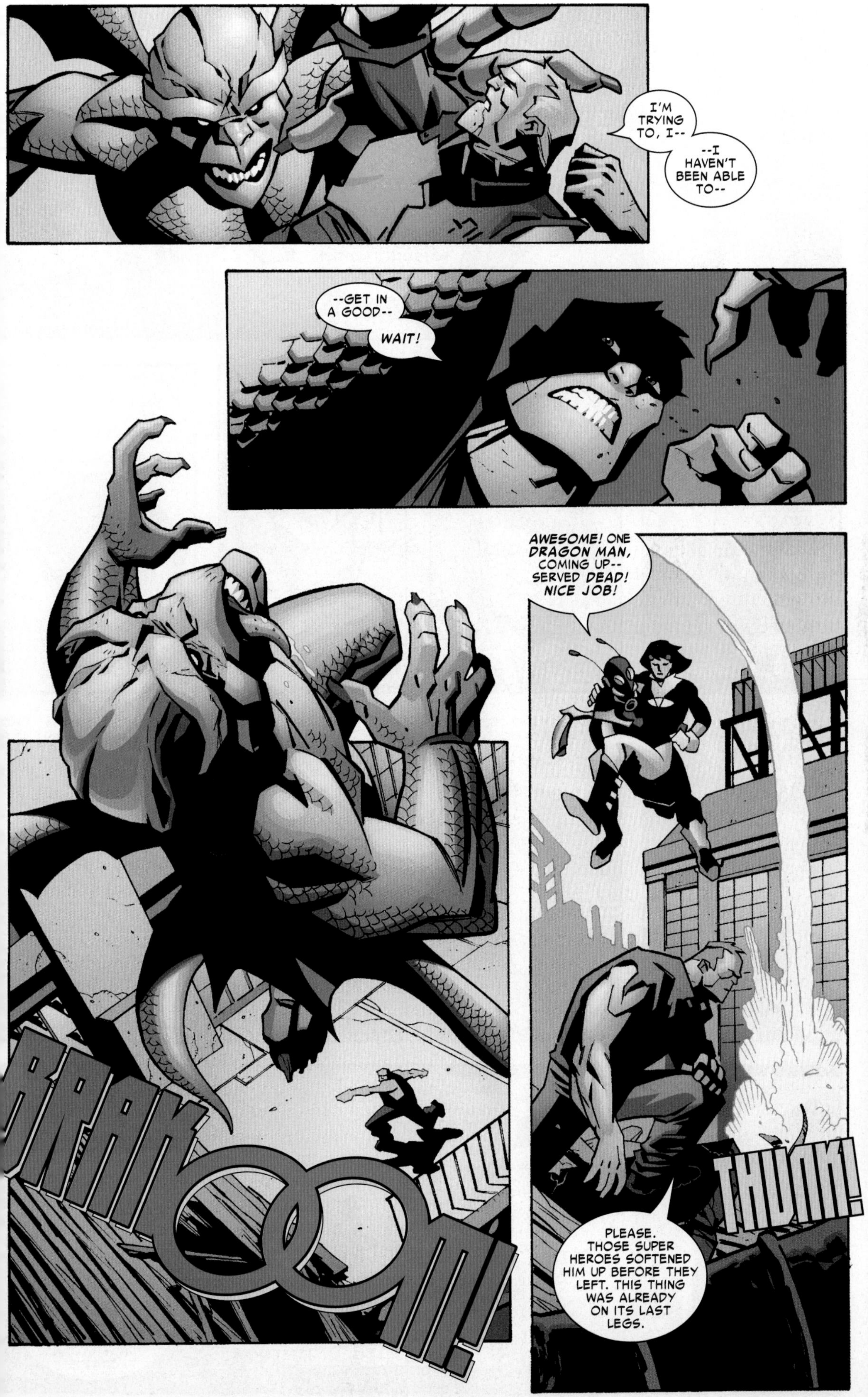
I'M TRYING TO, I--
--I HAVEN'T BEEN ABLE TO--
--GET IN A GOOD--
WAIT!
BRAKOOM!
AWESOME! ONE DRAGON MAN, COMING UP-- SERVED DEAD! NICE JOB!
THUNK!
PLEASE. THOSE SUPER HEROES SOFTENED HIM UP BEFORE THEY LEFT. THIS THING WAS ALREADY ON ITS LAST LEGS.

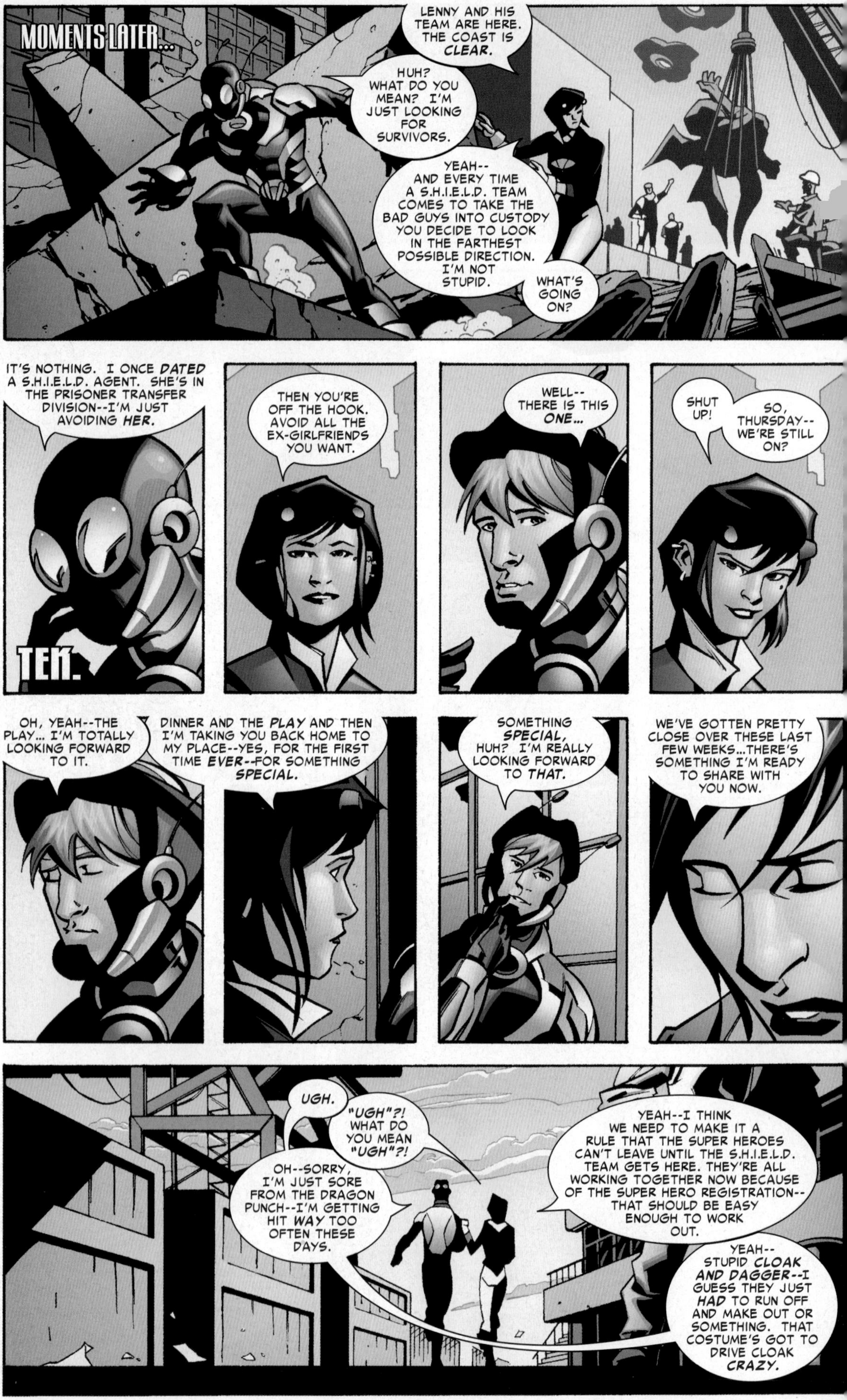
MOMENTS LATER...
LENNY AND HIS TEAM ARE HERE. THE COAST IS CLEAR.
HUH? WHAT DO YOU MEAN? I'M JUST LOOKING FOR SURVIVORS.
YEAH-- AND EVERY TIME A S.H.I.E.L.D. TEAM COMES TO TAKE THE BAD GUYS INTO CUSTODY YOU DECIDE TO LOOK IN THE FARTHEST POSSIBLE DIRECTION. I'M NOT STUPID.
WHAT'S GOING ON?
IT'S NOTHING. I ONCE DATED A S.H.I.E.L.D. AGENT. SHE'S IN THE PRISONER TRANSFER DIVISION--I'M JUST AVOIDING HER.
TEK.
THEN YOU'RE OFF THE HOOK. AVOID ALL THE EX-GIRLFRIENDS YOU WANT.
WELL-- THERE IS THIS ONE...
SHUT UP!
SO, THURSDAY-- WE'RE STILL ON?
OH, YEAH--THE PLAY... I'M TOTALLY LOOKING FORWARD TO IT.
DINNER AND THE PLAY AND THEN I'M TAKING YOU BACK HOME TO MY PLACE--YES, FOR THE FIRST TIME EVER--FOR SOMETHING SPECIAL.
SOMETHING SPECIAL, HUH? I'M REALLY LOOKING FORWARD TO THAT.
WE'VE GOTTEN PRETTY CLOSE OVER THESE LAST FEW WEEKS...THERE'S SOMETHING I'M READY TO SHARE WITH YOU NOW.
UGH.
"UGH"?! WHAT DO YOU MEAN "UGH"?!
OH--SORRY, I'M JUST SORE FROM THE DRAGON PUNCH--I'M GETTING HIT WAY TOO OFTEN THESE DAYS.
YEAH--I THINK WE NEED TO MAKE IT A RULE THAT THE SUPER HEROES CAN'T LEAVE UNTIL THE S.H.I.E.L.D. TEAM GETS HERE. THEY'RE ALL WORKING TOGETHER NOW BECAUSE OF THE SUPER HERO REGISTRATION--THAT SHOULD BE EASY ENOUGH TO WORK OUT.
YEAH-- STUPID CLOAK AND DAGGER--I GUESS THEY JUST HAD TO RUN OFF AND MAKE OUT OR SOMETHING. THAT COSTUME'S GOT TO DRIVE CLOAK CRAZY.

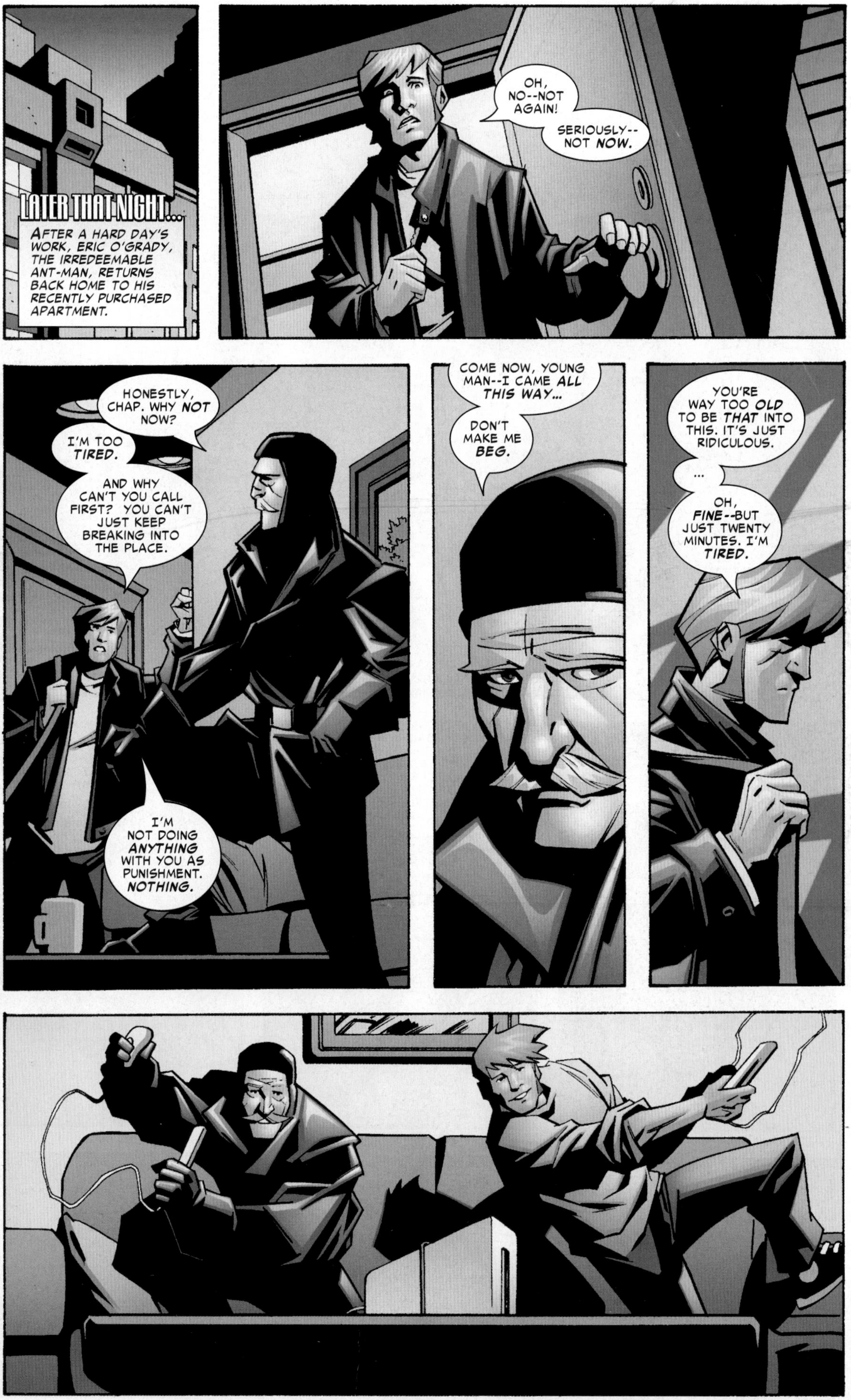
LATER THAT NIGHT...
AFTER A HARD DAY'S WORK, ERIC O'GRADY, THE IRREDEEMABLE ANT-MAN, RETURNS BACK HOME TO HIS RECENTLY PURCHASED APARTMENT.
OH, NO--NOT AGAIN!
SERIOUSLY--NOT NOW.
HONESTLY, CHAP. WHY NOT NOW?
I'M TOO TIRED.
AND WHY CAN'T YOU CALL FIRST? YOU CAN'T JUST KEEP BREAKING INTO THE PLACE.
I'M NOT DOING ANYTHING WITH YOU AS PUNISHMENT. NOTHING.
COME NOW, YOUNG MAN--I CAME ALL THIS WAY...
DON'T MAKE ME BEG.
YOU'RE WAY TOO OLD TO BE THAT INTO THIS. IT'S JUST RIDICULOUS.
...
OH, FINE--BUT JUST TWENTY MINUTES. I'M TIRED.

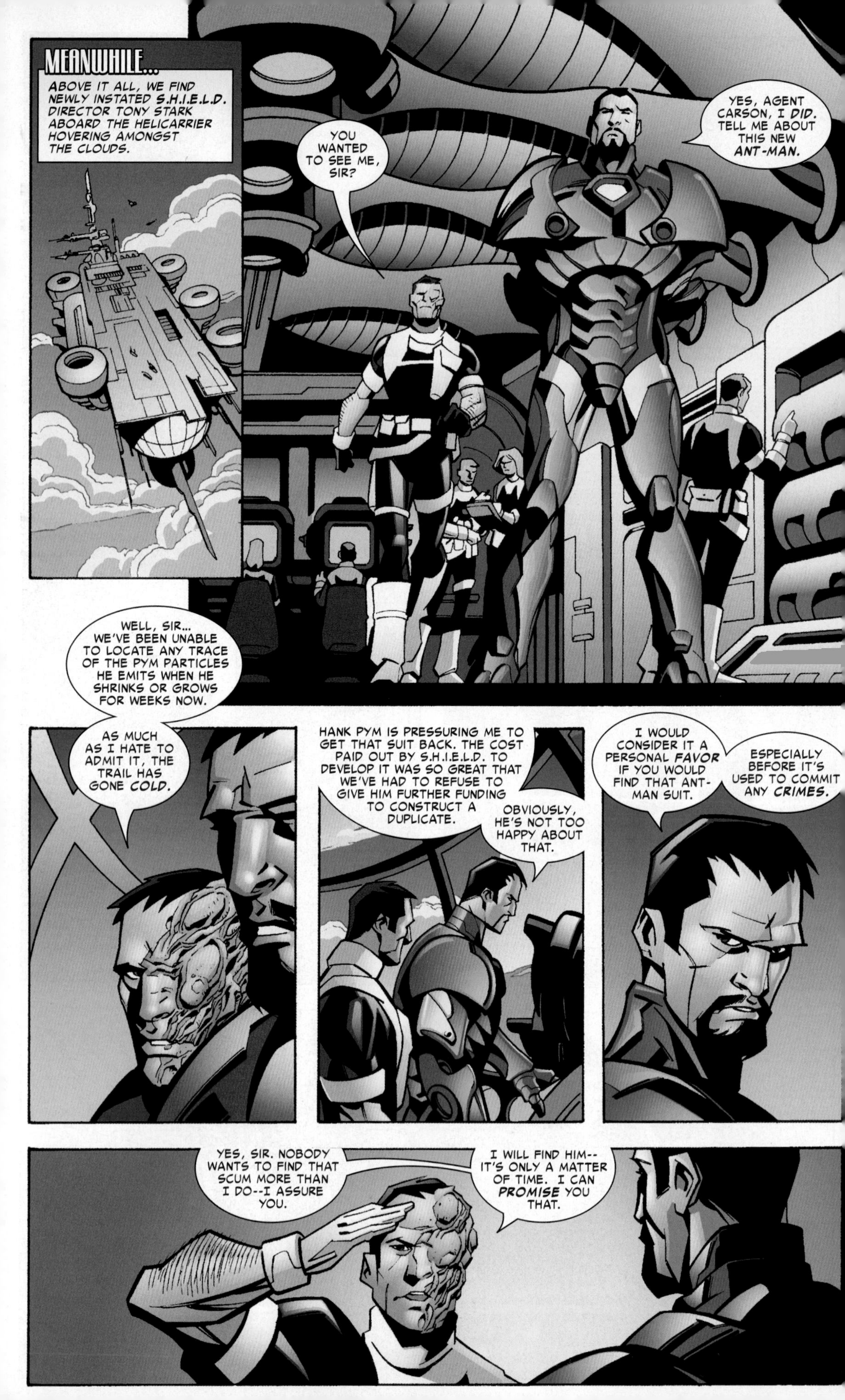
MEANWHILE...
ABOVE IT ALL, WE FIND NEWLY INSTATED S.H.I.E.L.D. DIRECTOR TONY STARK ABOARD THE HELICARRIER HOVERING AMONGST THE CLOUDS.
YOU WANTED TO SEE ME, SIR?
YES, AGENT CARSON, I DID. TELL ME ABOUT THIS NEW ANT-MAN.
WELL, SIR... WE'VE BEEN UNABLE TO LOCATE ANY TRACE OF THE PYM PARTICLES HE EMITS WHEN HE SHRINKS OR GROWS FOR WEEKS NOW.
AS MUCH AS I HATE TO ADMIT IT, THE TRAIL HAS GONE COLD.
HANK PYM IS PRESSURING ME TO GET THAT SUIT BACK. THE COST PAID OUT BY S.H.I.E.L.D. TO DEVELOP IT WAS SO GREAT THAT WE'VE HAD TO REFUSE TO GIVE HIM FURTHER FUNDING TO CONSTRUCT A DUPLICATE.
OBVIOUSLY, HE'S NOT TOO HAPPY ABOUT THAT.
I WOULD CONSIDER IT A PERSONAL FAVOR IF YOU WOULD FIND THAT ANT-MAN SUIT.
ESPECIALLY BEFORE IT'S USED TO COMMIT ANY CRIMES.
YES, SIR. NOBODY WANTS TO FIND THAT SCUM MORE THAN I DO--I ASSURE YOU.
I WILL FIND HIM--IT'S ONLY A MATTER OF TIME. I CAN PROMISE YOU THAT.

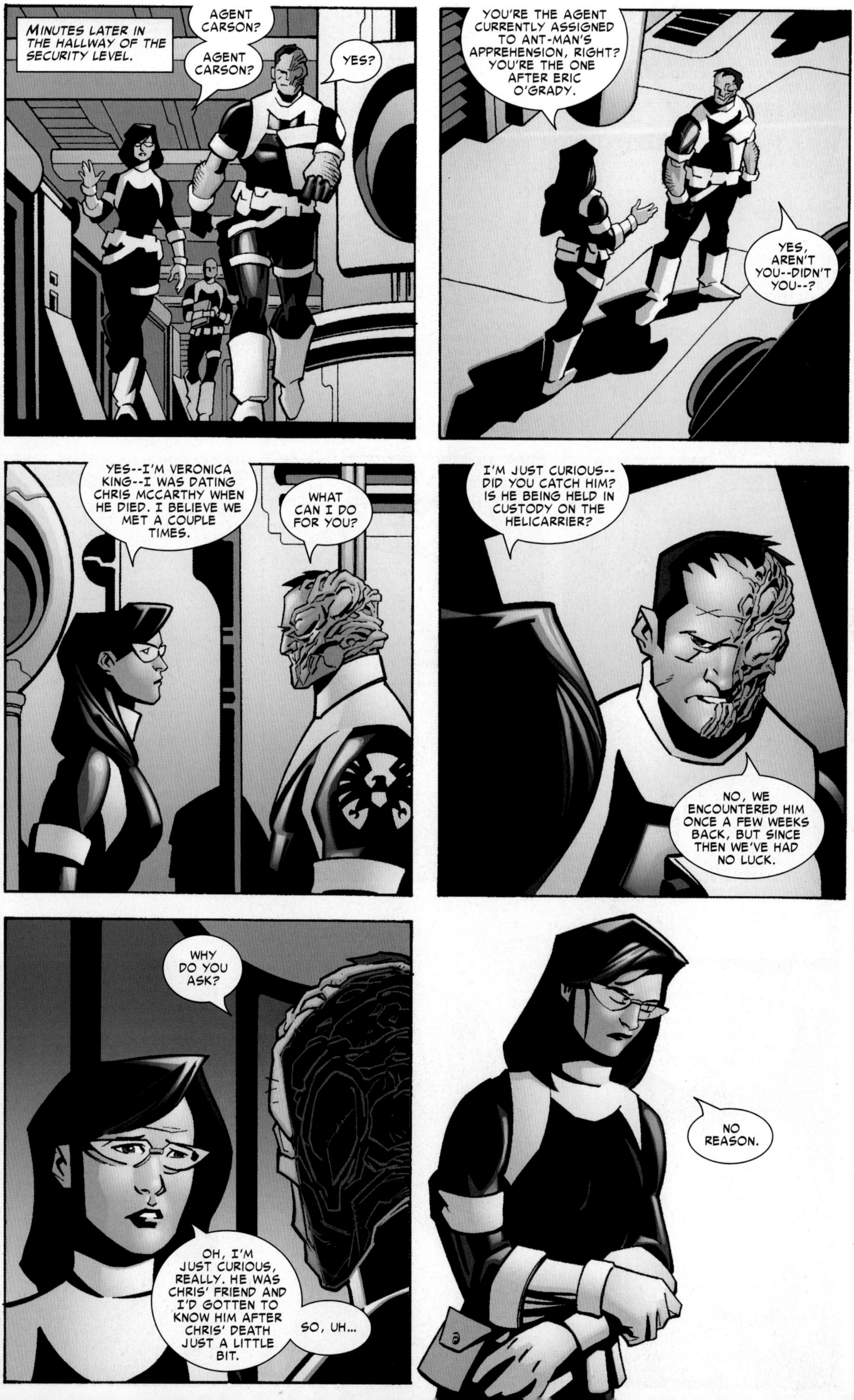
MINUTES LATER IN THE HALLWAY OF THE SECURITY LEVEL.
AGENT CARSON?
AGENT CARSON?
YES?
YOU'RE THE AGENT CURRENTLY ASSIGNED TO ANT-MAN'S APPREHENSION, RIGHT? YOU'RE THE ONE AFTER ERIC O'GRADY.
YES, AREN'T YOU--DIDN'T YOU--?
YES--I'M VERONICA KING--I WAS DATING CHRIS McCARTHY WHEN HE DIED. I BELIEVE WE MET A COUPLE TIMES.
WHAT CAN I DO FOR YOU?
I'M JUST CURIOUS--DID YOU CATCH HIM? IS HE BEING HELD IN CUSTODY ON THE HELICARRIER?
NO, WE ENCOUNTERED HIM ONCE A FEW WEEKS BACK, BUT SINCE THEN WE'VE HAD NO LUCK.
WHY DO YOU ASK?
OH, I'M JUST CURIOUS, REALLY. HE WAS CHRIS' FRIEND AND I'D GOTTEN TO KNOW HIM AFTER CHRIS' DEATH JUST A LITTLE BIT.
SO, UH...
NO REASON.

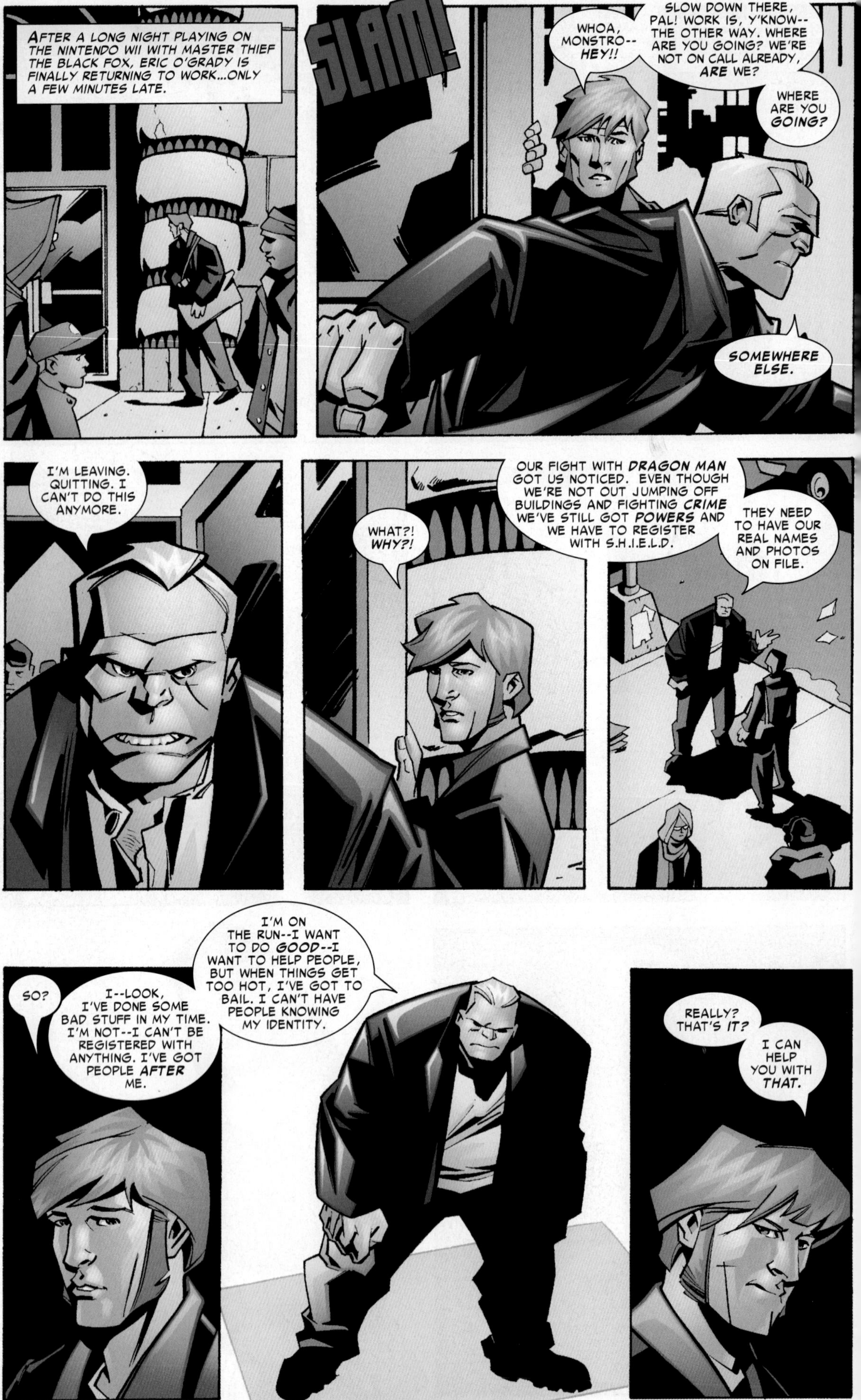
AFTER A LONG NIGHT PLAYING ON THE NINTENDO WII WITH MASTER THIEF THE BLACK FOX, ERIC O'GRADY IS FINALLY RETURNING TO WORK...ONLY A FEW MINUTES LATE.
SLAM!
WHOA, MONSTRO-- HEY!!
SLOW DOWN THERE, PAL! WORK IS, Y'KNOW-- THE OTHER WAY. WHERE ARE YOU GOING? WE'RE NOT ON CALL ALREADY, ARE WE?
WHERE ARE YOU GOING?
SOMEWHERE ELSE.
I'M LEAVING. QUITTING. I CAN'T DO THIS ANYMORE.
WHAT?! WHY?!
OUR FIGHT WITH DRAGON MAN GOT US NOTICED. EVEN THOUGH WE'RE NOT OUT JUMPING OFF BUILDINGS AND FIGHTING CRIME WE'VE STILL GOT POWERS AND WE HAVE TO REGISTER WITH S.H.I.E.L.D.
THEY NEED TO HAVE OUR REAL NAMES AND PHOTOS ON FILE.
SO?
I--LOOK, I'VE DONE SOME BAD STUFF IN MY TIME. I'M NOT--I CAN'T BE REGISTERED WITH ANYTHING. I'VE GOT PEOPLE AFTER ME.
I'M ON THE RUN--I WANT TO DO GOOD--I WANT TO HELP PEOPLE, BUT WHEN THINGS GET TOO HOT, I'VE GOT TO BAIL. I CAN'T HAVE PEOPLE KNOWING MY IDENTITY.
REALLY? THAT'S IT?
I CAN HELP YOU WITH THAT.

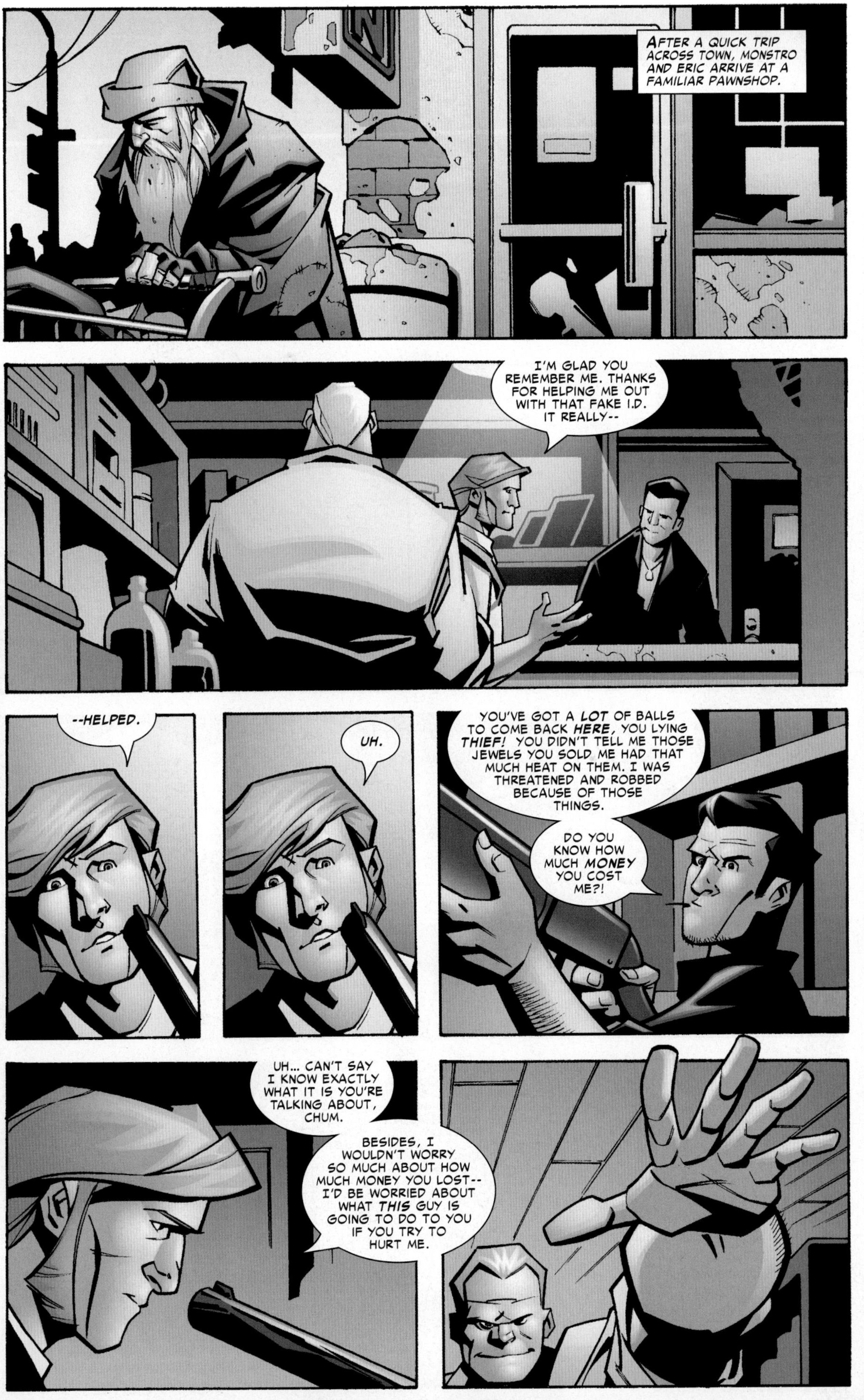
AFTER A QUICK TRIP ACROSS TOWN, MONSTRO AND ERIC ARRIVE AT A FAMILIAR PAWNSHOP.
I'M GLAD YOU REMEMBER ME. THANKS FOR HELPING ME OUT WITH THAT FAKE I.D. IT REALLY--
--HELPED.
UH.
YOU'VE GOT A LOT OF BALLS TO COME BACK HERE, YOU LYING THIEF! YOU DIDN'T TELL ME THOSE JEWELS YOU SOLD ME HAD THAT MUCH HEAT ON THEM. I WAS THREATENED AND ROBBED BECAUSE OF THOSE THINGS.
DO YOU KNOW HOW MUCH MONEY YOU COST ME?!
UH... CAN'T SAY I KNOW EXACTLY WHAT IT IS YOU'RE TALKING ABOUT, CHUM.
BESIDES, I WOULDN'T WORRY SO MUCH ABOUT HOW MUCH MONEY YOU LOST-- I'D BE WORRIED ABOUT WHAT THIS GUY IS GOING TO DO TO YOU IF YOU TRY TO HURT ME.

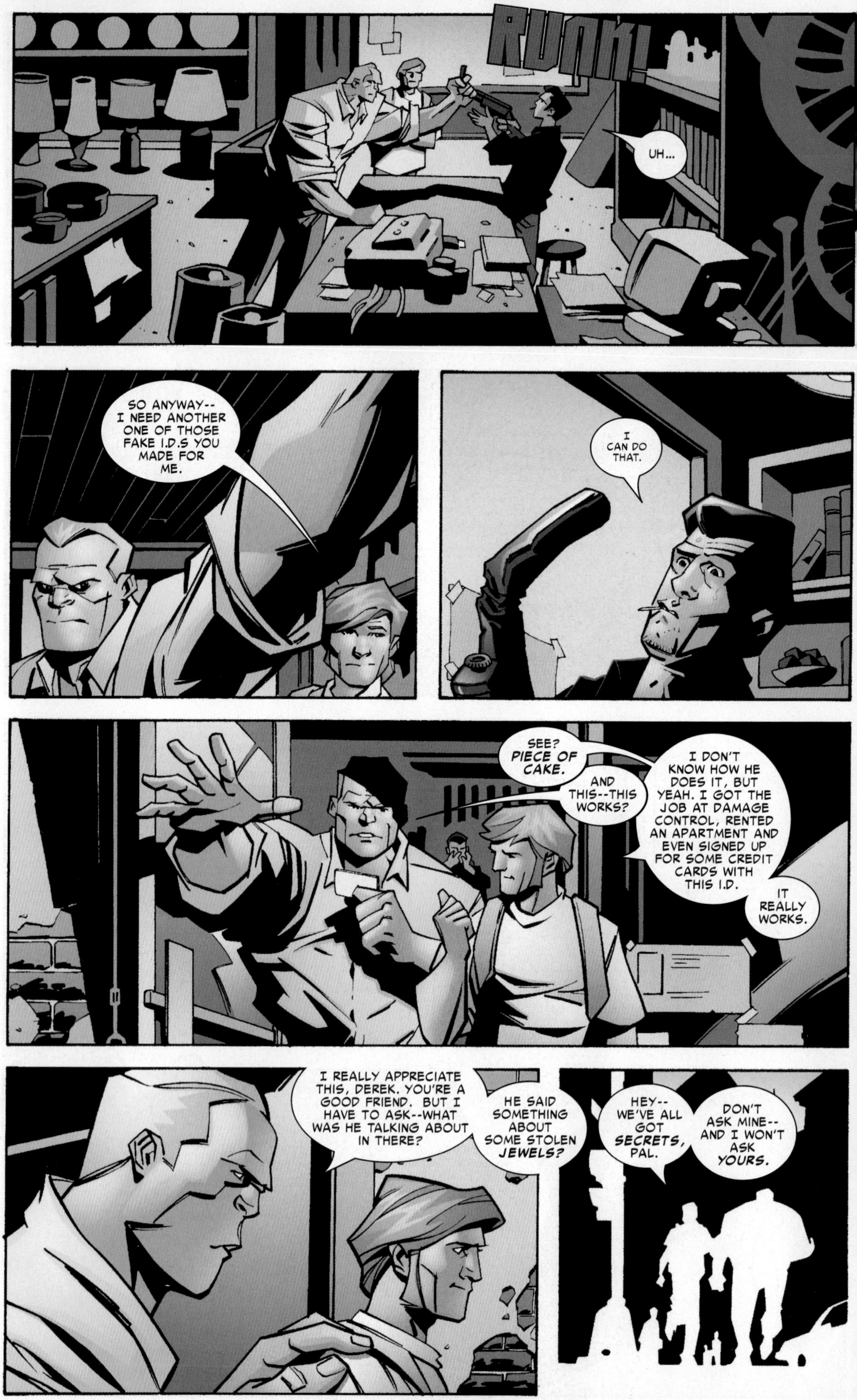
RUNK!
UH...
SO ANYWAY-- I NEED ANOTHER ONE OF THOSE FAKE I.D.S YOU MADE FOR ME.
I CAN DO THAT.
SEE? PIECE OF CAKE.
AND THIS--THIS WORKS?
I DON'T KNOW HOW HE DOES IT, BUT YEAH. I GOT THE JOB AT DAMAGE CONTROL, RENTED AN APARTMENT AND EVEN SIGNED UP FOR SOME CREDIT CARDS WITH THIS I.D.
IT REALLY WORKS.
I REALLY APPRECIATE THIS, DEREK. YOU'RE A GOOD FRIEND. BUT I HAVE TO ASK--WHAT WAS HE TALKING ABOUT IN THERE?
HE SAID SOMETHING ABOUT SOME STOLEN JEWELS?
HEY-- WE'VE ALL GOT SECRETS, PAL.
DON'T ASK MINE-- AND I WON'T ASK YOURS.

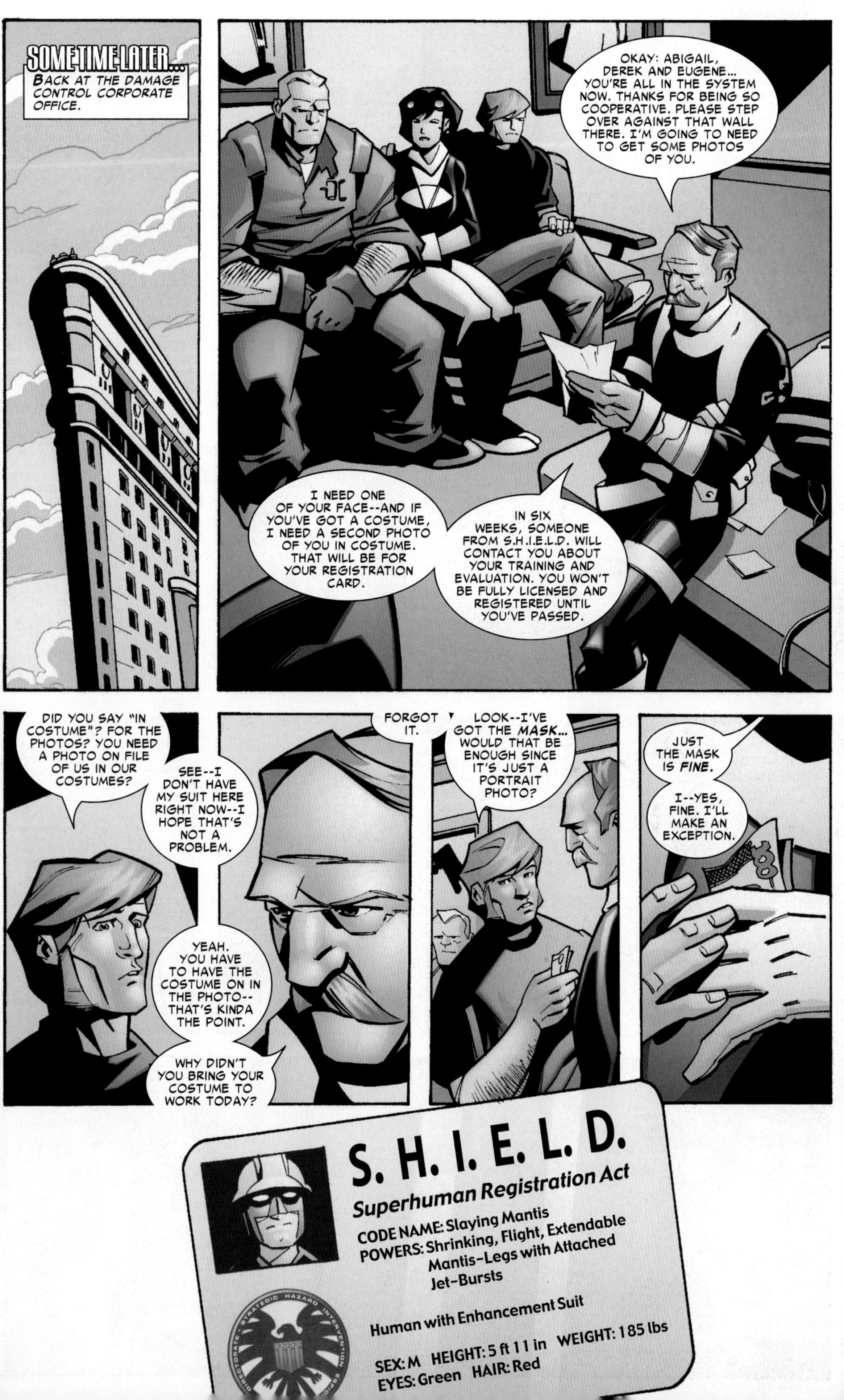
SOME TIME LATER...
BACK AT THE DAMAGE CONTROL CORPORATE OFFICE.
OKAY: ABIGAIL, DEREK AND EUGENE... YOU'RE ALL IN THE SYSTEM NOW. THANKS FOR BEING SO COOPERATIVE. PLEASE STEP OVER AGAINST THAT WALL THERE. I'M GOING TO NEED TO GET SOME PHOTOS OF YOU.
I NEED ONE OF YOUR FACE--AND IF YOU'VE GOT A COSTUME, I NEED A SECOND PHOTO OF YOU IN COSTUME. THAT WILL BE FOR YOUR REGISTRATION CARD.
IN SIX WEEKS, SOMEONE FROM S.H.I.E.L.D. WILL CONTACT YOU ABOUT YOUR TRAINING AND EVALUATION. YOU WON'T BE FULLY LICENSED AND REGISTERED UNTIL YOU'VE PASSED.
DID YOU SAY "IN COSTUME"? FOR THE PHOTOS? YOU NEED A PHOTO ON FILE OF US IN OUR COSTUMES?
SEE--I DON'T HAVE MY SUIT HERE RIGHT NOW--I HOPE THAT'S NOT A PROBLEM.
YEAH. YOU HAVE TO HAVE THE COSTUME ON IN THE PHOTO--THAT'S KINDA THE POINT.
WHY DIDN'T YOU BRING YOUR COSTUME TO WORK TODAY?
FORGOT IT.
LOOK--I'VE GOT THE MASK... WOULD THAT BE ENOUGH SINCE IT'S JUST A PORTRAIT PHOTO?
JUST THE MASK IS FINE.
I--YES, FINE. I'LL MAKE AN EXCEPTION.
S. H. I. E. L. D.
Superhuman Registration Act
CODE NAME: Slaying Mantis
POWERS: Shrinking, Flight, Extendable Mantis-Legs with Attached Jet-Bursts
Human with Enhancement Suit
SEX: M HEIGHT: 5 ft 11 in WEIGHT: 185 lbs
EYES: Green HAIR: Red

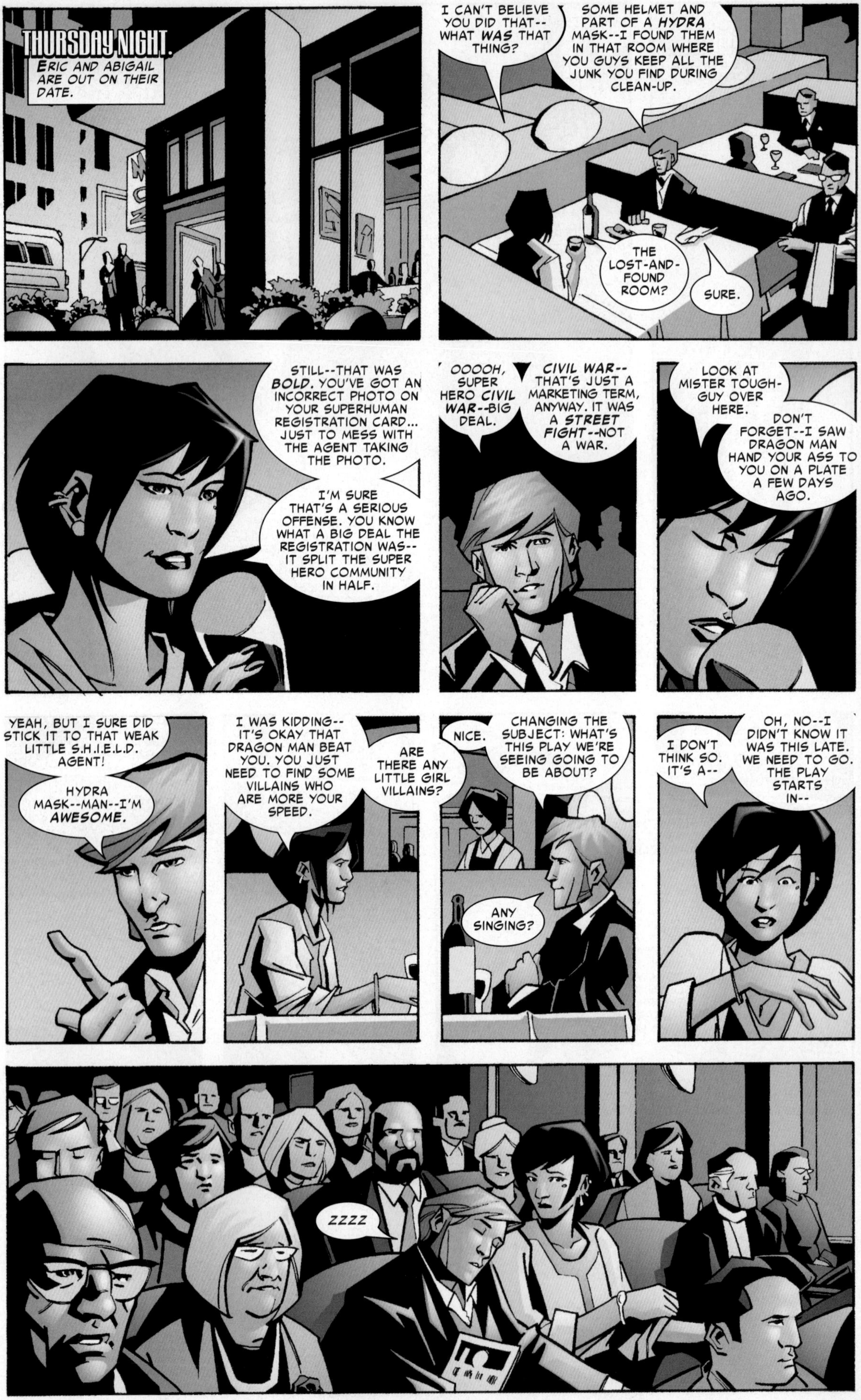
THURSDAY NIGHT.
ERIC AND ABIGAIL ARE OUT ON THEIR DATE.
I CAN'T BELIEVE YOU DID THAT-- WHAT WAS THAT THING?
SOME HELMET AND PART OF A HYDRA MASK--I FOUND THEM IN THAT ROOM WHERE YOU GUYS KEEP ALL THE JUNK YOU FIND DURING CLEAN-UP.
THE LOST-AND-FOUND ROOM?
SURE.
STILL--THAT WAS BOLD. YOU'VE GOT AN INCORRECT PHOTO ON YOUR SUPERHUMAN REGISTRATION CARD... JUST TO MESS WITH THE AGENT TAKING THE PHOTO.
I'M SURE THAT'S A SERIOUS OFFENSE. YOU KNOW WHAT A BIG DEAL THE REGISTRATION WAS-- IT SPLIT THE SUPER HERO COMMUNITY IN HALF.
OOOOH, SUPER HERO CIVIL WAR--BIG DEAL.
CIVIL WAR-- THAT'S JUST A MARKETING TERM, ANYWAY. IT WAS A STREET FIGHT--NOT A WAR.
LOOK AT MISTER TOUGH-GUY OVER HERE.
DON'T FORGET--I SAW DRAGON MAN HAND YOUR ASS TO YOU ON A PLATE A FEW DAYS AGO.
YEAH, BUT I SURE DID STICK IT TO THAT WEAK LITTLE S.H.I.E.L.D. AGENT!
HYDRA MASK--MAN--I'M AWESOME.
I WAS KIDDING-- IT'S OKAY THAT DRAGON MAN BEAT YOU. YOU JUST NEED TO FIND SOME VILLAINS WHO ARE MORE YOUR SPEED.
ARE THERE ANY LITTLE GIRL VILLAINS?
NICE.
CHANGING THE SUBJECT: WHAT'S THIS PLAY WE'RE SEEING GOING TO BE ABOUT?
ANY SINGING?
I DON'T THINK SO. IT'S A--
OH, NO--I DIDN'T KNOW IT WAS THIS LATE. WE NEED TO GO. THE PLAY STARTS IN--
ZZZZ

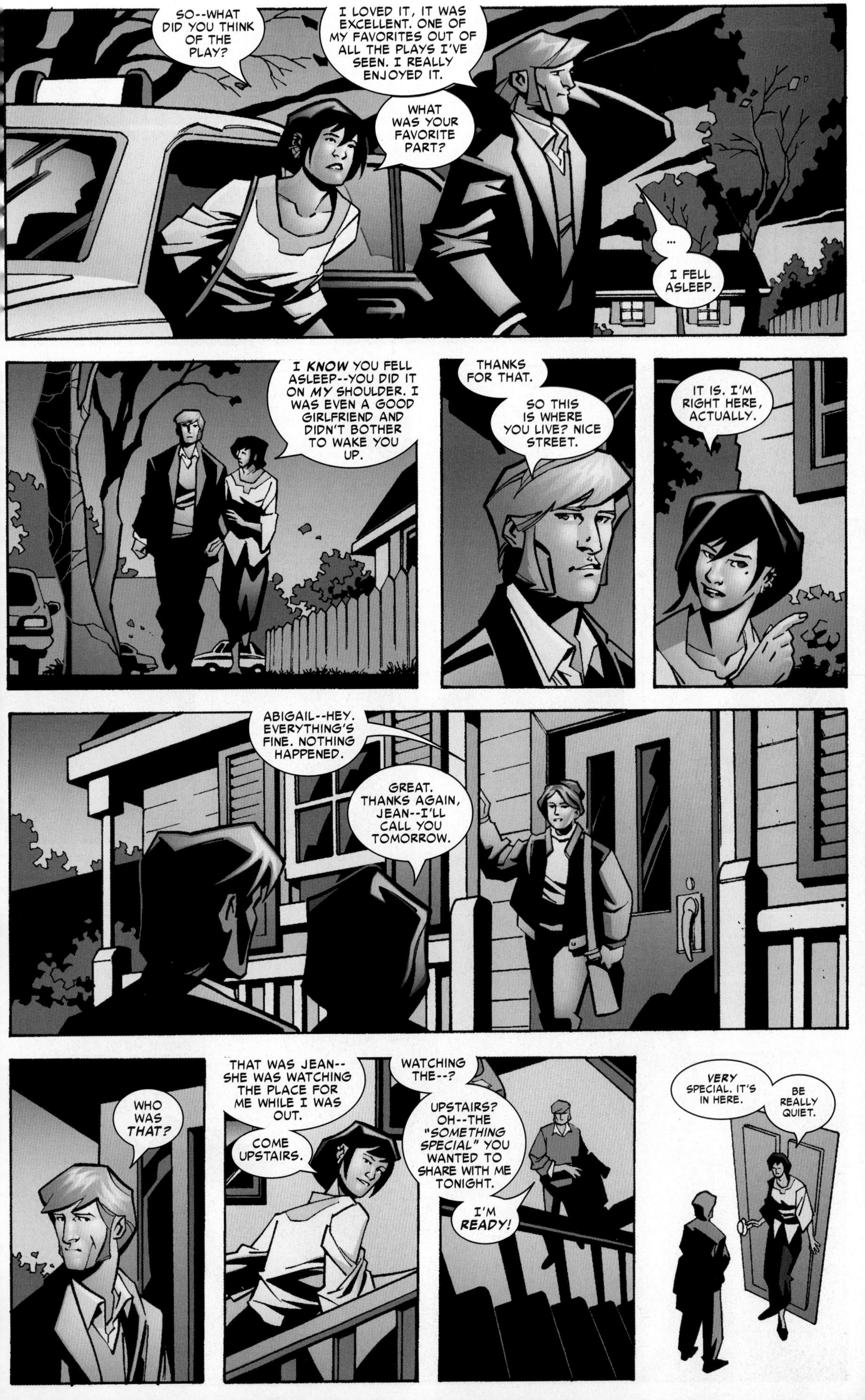
SO--WHAT DID YOU THINK OF THE PLAY?
I LOVED IT, IT WAS EXCELLENT. ONE OF MY FAVORITES OUT OF ALL THE PLAYS I'VE SEEN. I REALLY ENJOYED IT.
WHAT WAS YOUR FAVORITE PART?
...
I FELL ASLEEP.
I KNOW YOU FELL ASLEEP--YOU DID IT ON MY SHOULDER. I WAS EVEN A GOOD GIRLFRIEND AND DIDN'T BOTHER TO WAKE YOU UP.
THANKS FOR THAT.
SO THIS IS WHERE YOU LIVE? NICE STREET.
IT IS. I'M RIGHT HERE, ACTUALLY.
ABIGAIL--HEY. EVERYTHING'S FINE. NOTHING HAPPENED.
GREAT. THANKS AGAIN, JEAN--I'LL CALL YOU TOMORROW.
WHO WAS THAT?
THAT WAS JEAN--SHE WAS WATCHING THE PLACE FOR ME WHILE I WAS OUT.
COME UPSTAIRS.
WATCHING THE--?
UPSTAIRS? OH--THE "SOMETHING SPECIAL" YOU WANTED TO SHARE WITH ME TONIGHT.
I'M READY!
VERY SPECIAL. IT'S IN HERE.
BE REALLY QUIET.

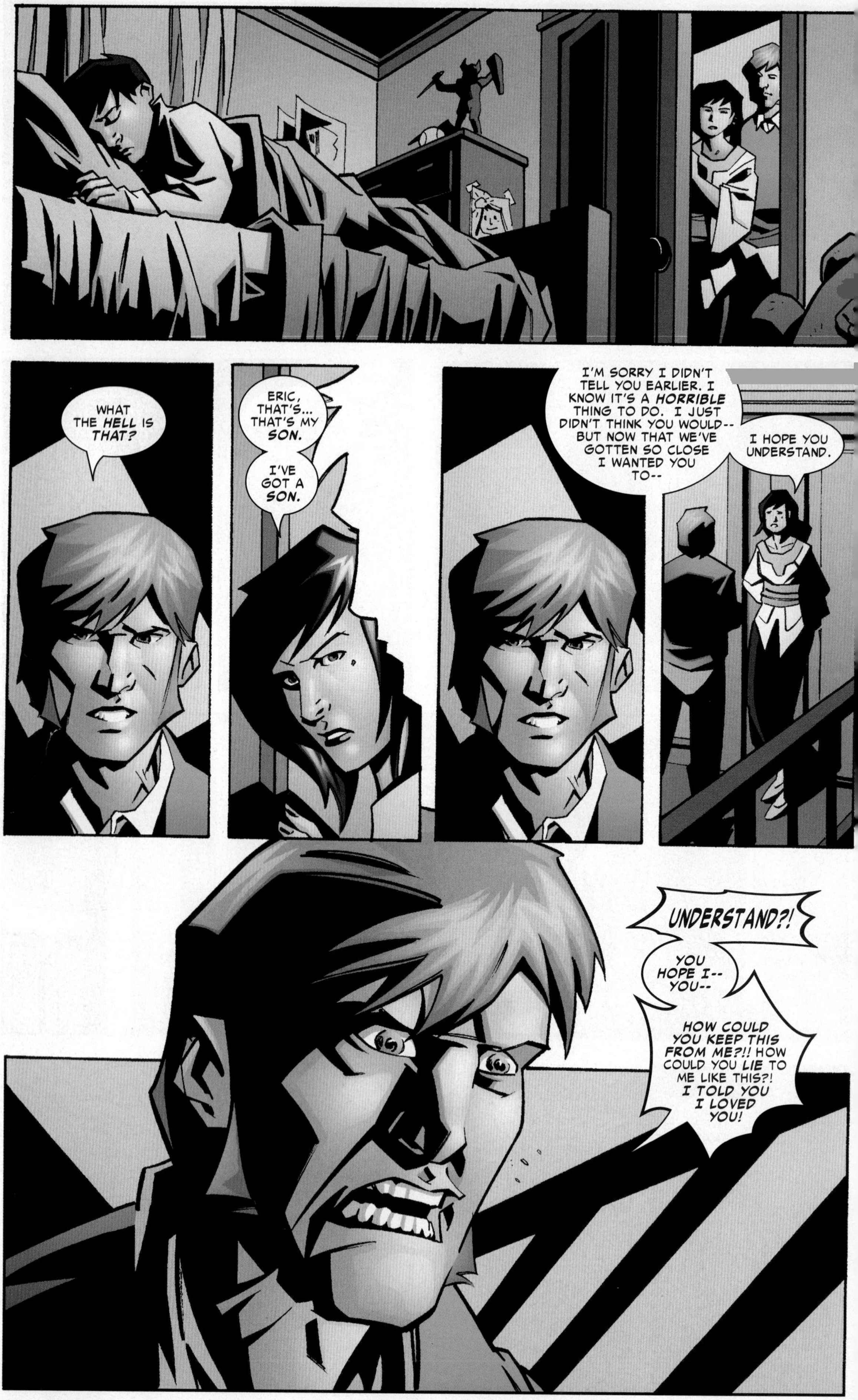
WHAT THE HELL IS THAT?
ERIC, THAT'S... THAT'S MY SON.
I'VE GOT A SON.
I'M SORRY I DIDN'T TELL YOU EARLIER. I KNOW IT'S A HORRIBLE THING TO DO. I JUST DIDN'T THINK YOU WOULD-- BUT NOW THAT WE'VE GOTTEN SO CLOSE I WANTED YOU TO--
I HOPE YOU UNDERSTAND.
UNDERSTAND?!
YOU HOPE I-- YOU--
HOW COULD YOU KEEP THIS FROM ME?!! HOW COULD YOU LIE TO ME LIKE THIS?! I TOLD YOU I LOVED YOU!

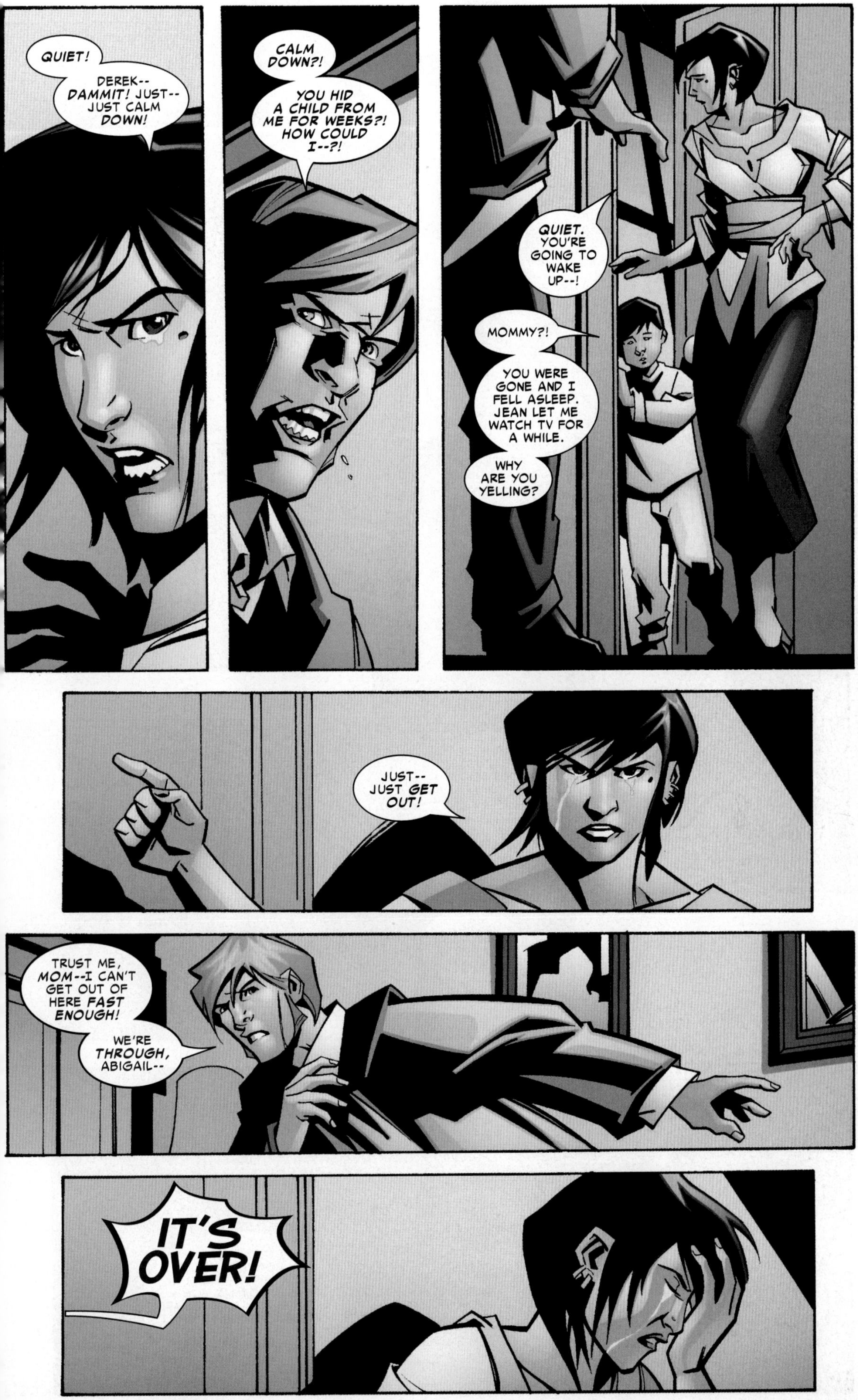
QUIET!
DEREK-- DAMMIT! JUST-- JUST CALM DOWN!
CALM DOWN?!
YOU HID A CHILD FROM ME FOR WEEKS?! HOW COULD I--?!
QUIET. YOU'RE GOING TO WAKE UP--!
MOMMY?!
YOU WERE GONE AND I FELL ASLEEP. JEAN LET ME WATCH TV FOR A WHILE.
WHY ARE YOU YELLING?
JUST-- JUST GET OUT!
TRUST ME, MOM--I CAN'T GET OUT OF HERE FAST ENOUGH!
WE'RE THROUGH, ABIGAIL--
IT'S OVER!

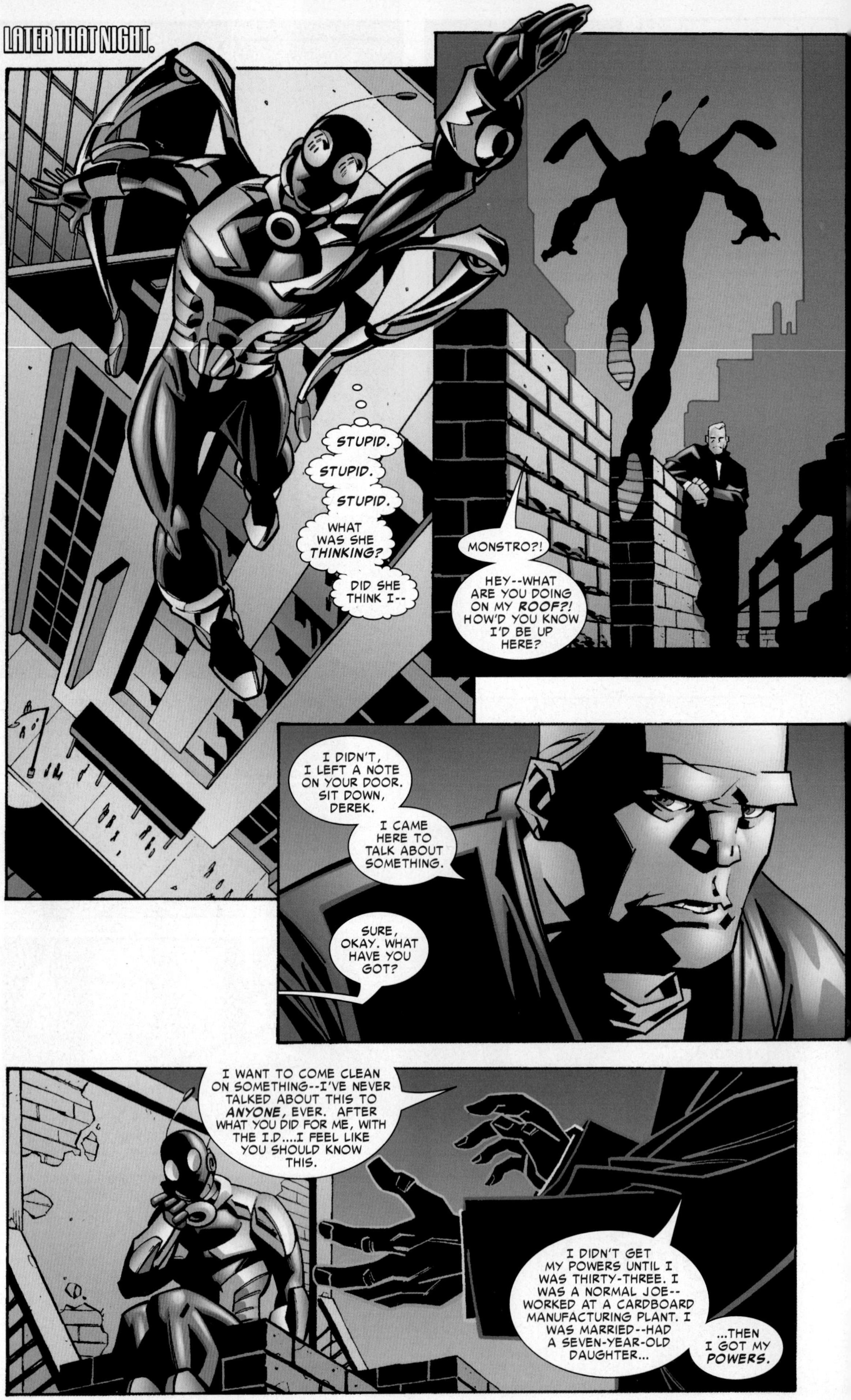
LATER THAT NIGHT.
STUPID.
STUPID.
STUPID.
WHAT WAS SHE THINKING?
DID SHE THINK I--
MONSTRO?!
HEY--WHAT ARE YOU DOING ON MY ROOF?! HOW'D YOU KNOW I'D BE UP HERE?
I DIDN'T, I LEFT A NOTE ON YOUR DOOR. SIT DOWN, DEREK.
I CAME HERE TO TALK ABOUT SOMETHING.
SURE, OKAY. WHAT HAVE YOU GOT?
I WANT TO COME CLEAN ON SOMETHING--I'VE NEVER TALKED ABOUT THIS TO ANYONE, EVER. AFTER WHAT YOU DID FOR ME, WITH THE I.D....I FEEL LIKE YOU SHOULD KNOW THIS.
I DIDN'T GET MY POWERS UNTIL I WAS THIRTY-THREE. I WAS A NORMAL JOE--WORKED AT A CARDBOARD MANUFACTURING PLANT. I WAS MARRIED--HAD A SEVEN-YEAR-OLD DAUGHTER...
...THEN I GOT MY POWERS.

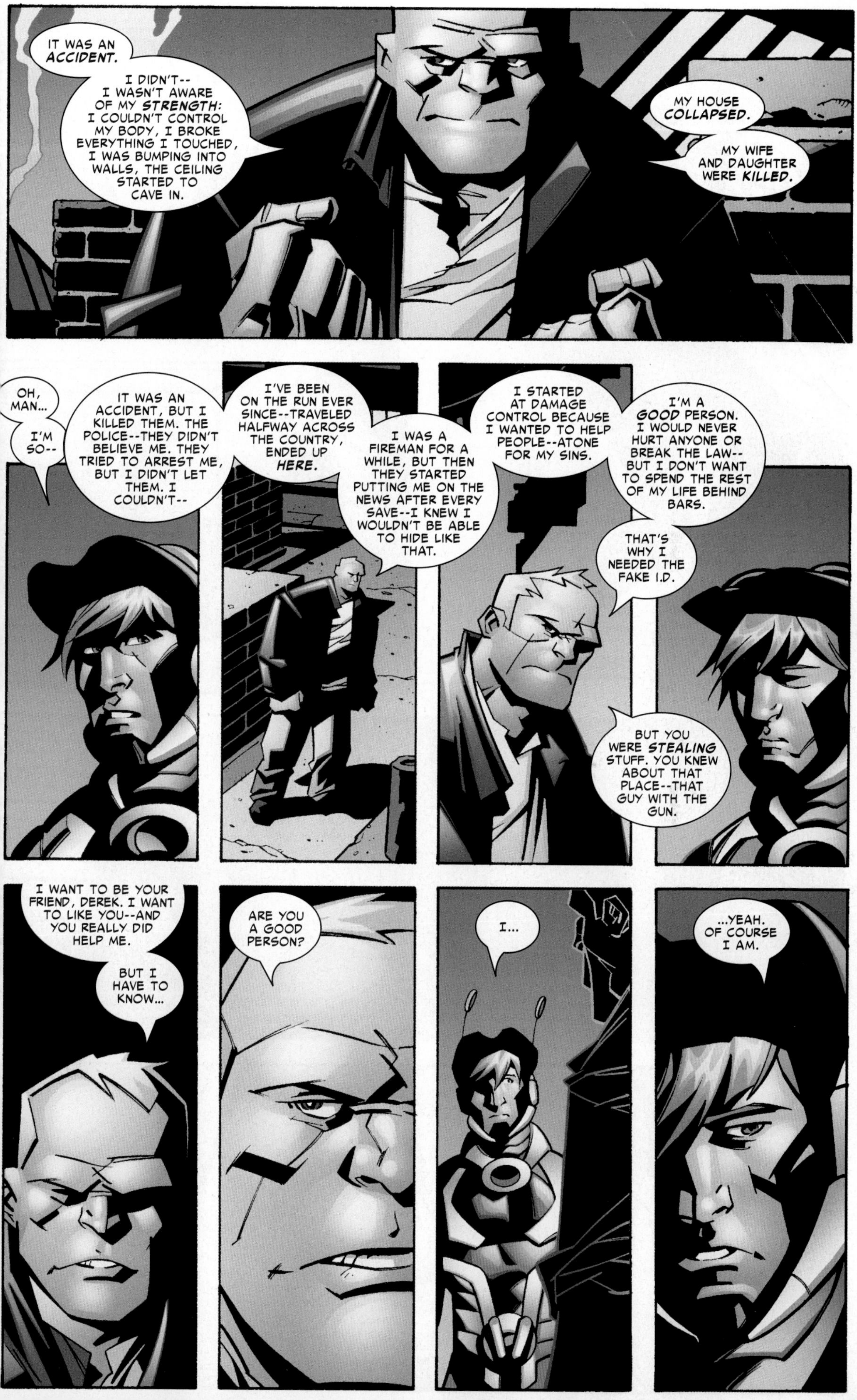

IT WAS AN ACCIDENT.
I DIDN'T-- I WASN'T AWARE OF MY STRENGTH: I COULDN'T CONTROL MY BODY, I BROKE EVERYTHING I TOUCHED, I WAS BUMPING INTO WALLS, THE CEILING STARTED TO CAVE IN.
MY HOUSE COLLAPSED.
MY WIFE AND DAUGHTER WERE KILLED.
OH, MAN...
I'M SO--
IT WAS AN ACCIDENT, BUT I KILLED THEM. THE POLICE--THEY DIDN'T BELIEVE ME. THEY TRIED TO ARREST ME, BUT I DIDN'T LET THEM. I COULDN'T--
I'VE BEEN ON THE RUN EVER SINCE--TRAVELED HALFWAY ACROSS THE COUNTRY, ENDED UP HERE.
I WAS A FIREMAN FOR A WHILE, BUT THEN THEY STARTED PUTTING ME ON THE NEWS AFTER EVERY SAVE--I KNEW I WOULDN'T BE ABLE TO HIDE LIKE THAT.
I STARTED AT DAMAGE CONTROL BECAUSE I WANTED TO HELP PEOPLE--ATONE FOR MY SINS.
I'M A GOOD PERSON. I WOULD NEVER HURT ANYONE OR BREAK THE LAW--BUT I DON'T WANT TO SPEND THE REST OF MY LIFE BEHIND BARS.
THAT'S WHY I NEEDED THE FAKE I.D.
BUT YOU WERE STEALING STUFF. YOU KNEW ABOUT THAT PLACE--THAT GUY WITH THE GUN.
I WANT TO BE YOUR FRIEND, DEREK. I WANT TO LIKE YOU--AND YOU REALLY DID HELP ME.
BUT I HAVE TO KNOW...
ARE YOU A GOOD PERSON?
I...
...YEAH. OF COURSE I AM.

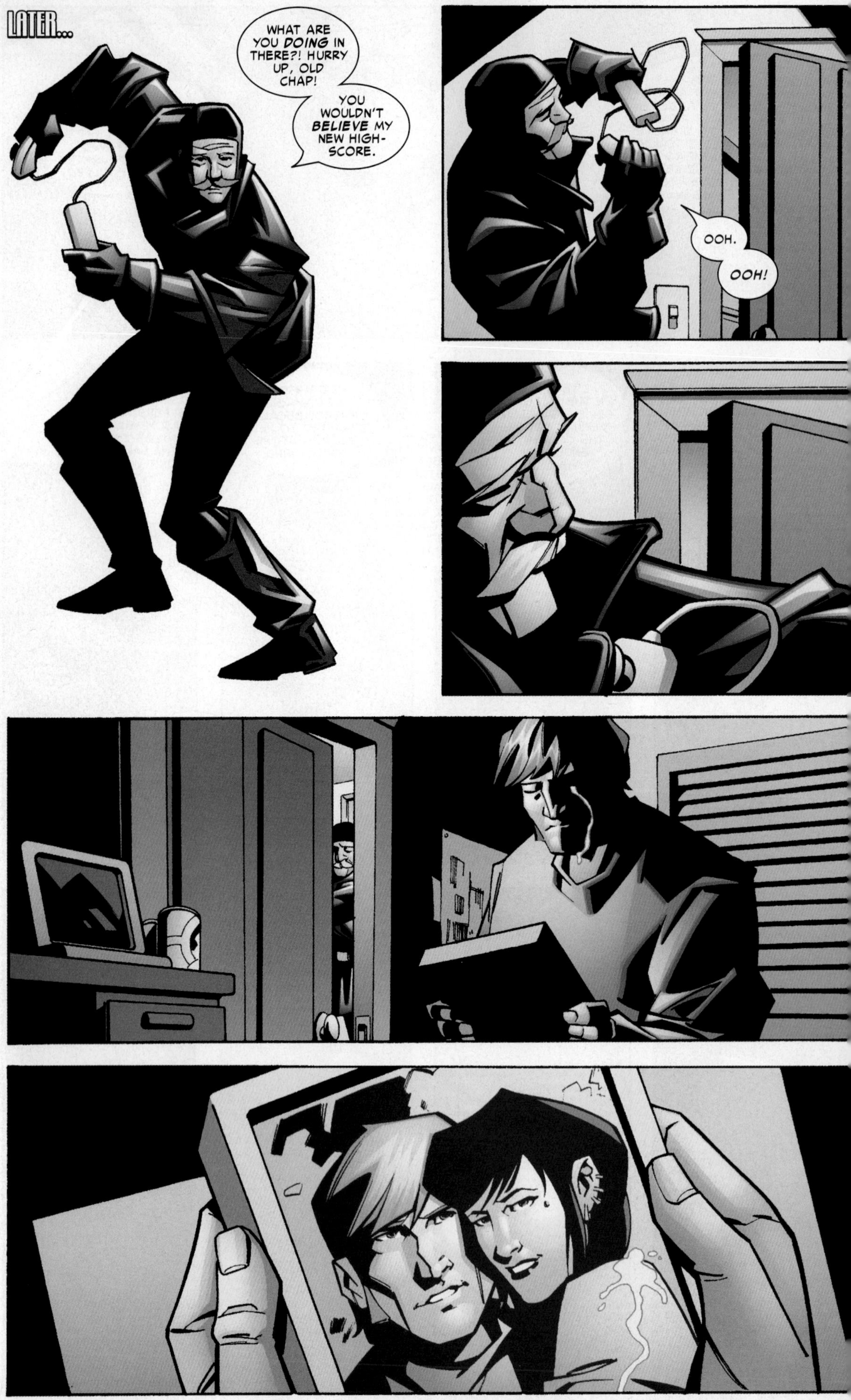
LATER...
WHAT ARE YOU DOING IN THERE?! HURRY UP, OLD CHAP!
YOU WOULDN'T BELIEVE MY NEW HIGH-SCORE.
OOH.
OOH!

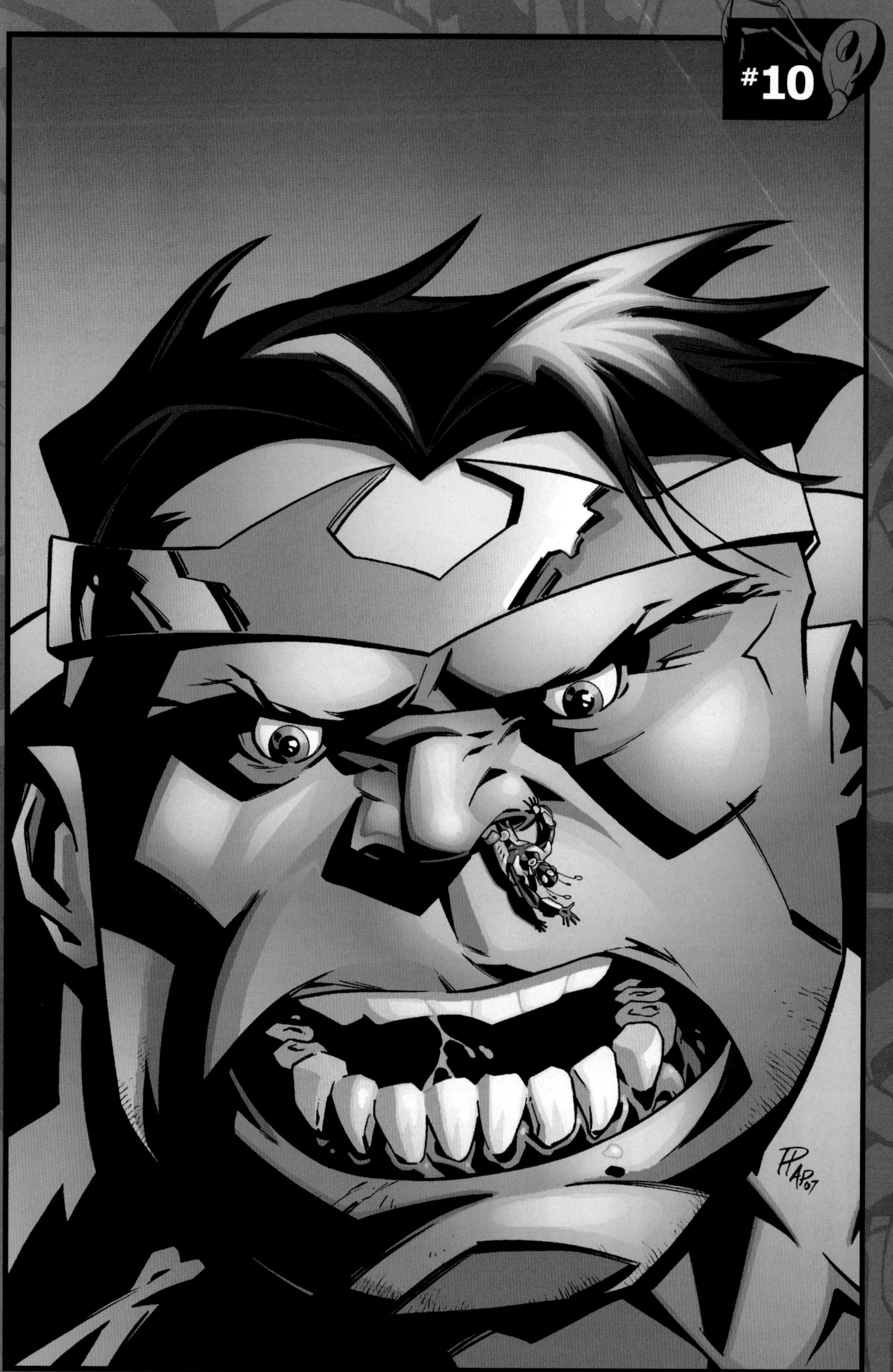
#10

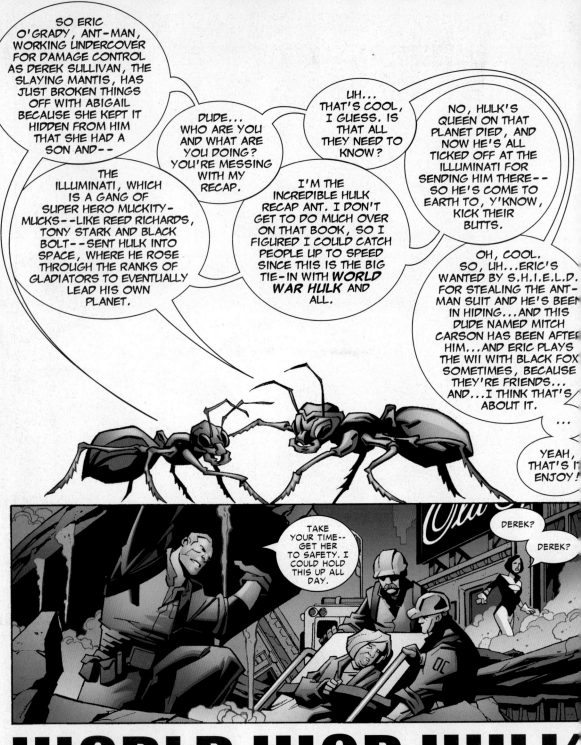

SO ERIC O'GRADY, ANT-MAN, WORKING UNDERCOVER FOR DAMAGE CONTROL AS DEREK SULLIVAN, THE SLAYING MANTIS, HAS JUST BROKEN THINGS OFF WITH ABIGAIL BECAUSE SHE KEPT IT HIDDEN FROM HIM THAT SHE HAD A SON AND--

THE ILLUMINATI, WHICH IS A GANG OF SUPER HERO MUCKITY-MUCKS--LIKE REED RICHARDS, TONY STARK AND BLACK BOLT--SENT HULK INTO SPACE, WHERE HE ROSE THROUGH THE RANKS OF GLADIATORS TO EVENTUALLY LEAD HIS OWN PLANET.

DUDE... WHO ARE YOU AND WHAT ARE YOU DOING? YOU'RE MESSING WITH MY RECAP.

I'M THE INCREDIBLE HULK RECAP ANT. I DON'T GET TO DO MUCH OVER ON THAT BOOK, SO I FIGURED I COULD CATCH PEOPLE UP TO SPEED SINCE THIS IS THE BIG TIE-IN WITH *WORLD WAR HULK* AND ALL.

UH... THAT'S COOL, I GUESS. IS THAT ALL THEY NEED TO KNOW?

NO, HULK'S QUEEN ON THAT PLANET DIED, AND NOW HE'S ALL TICKED OFF AT THE ILLUMINATI FOR SENDING HIM THERE-- SO HE'S COME TO EARTH TO, Y'KNOW, KICK THEIR BUTTS.

OH, COOL. SO, UH...ERIC'S WANTED BY S.H.I.E.L.D. FOR STEALING THE ANT-MAN SUIT AND HE'S BEEN IN HIDING...AND THIS DUDE NAMED MITCH CARSON HAS BEEN AFTER HIM...AND ERIC PLAYS THE WII WITH BLACK FOX SOMETIMES, BECAUSE THEY'RE FRIENDS... AND...I THINK THAT'S ABOUT IT.

...

YEAH, THAT'S IT ENJOY!

TAKE YOUR TIME-- GET HER TO SAFETY. I COULD HOLD THIS UP ALL DAY.

DEREK?

DEREK?

# WORLD WAR HULK

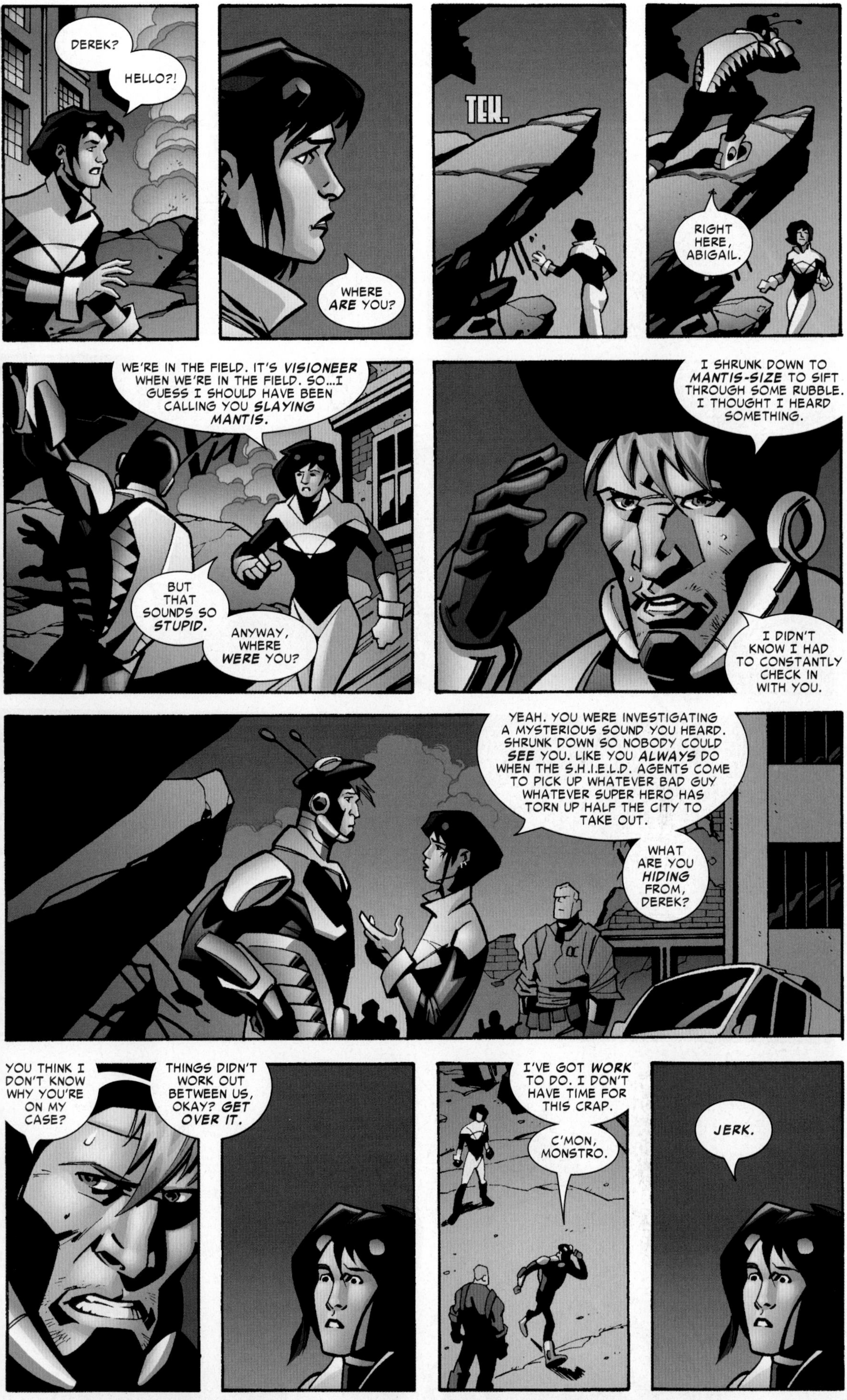
DEREK?
HELLO?!
WHERE ARE YOU?
TEK.
RIGHT HERE, ABIGAIL.
WE'RE IN THE FIELD. IT'S VISIONEER WHEN WE'RE IN THE FIELD. SO...I GUESS I SHOULD HAVE BEEN CALLING YOU SLAYING MANTIS.
BUT THAT SOUNDS SO STUPID.
ANYWAY, WHERE WERE YOU?
I SHRUNK DOWN TO MANTIS-SIZE TO SIFT THROUGH SOME RUBBLE. I THOUGHT I HEARD SOMETHING.
I DIDN'T KNOW I HAD TO CONSTANTLY CHECK IN WITH YOU.
YEAH. YOU WERE INVESTIGATING A MYSTERIOUS SOUND YOU HEARD. SHRUNK DOWN SO NOBODY COULD SEE YOU. LIKE YOU ALWAYS DO WHEN THE S.H.I.E.L.D. AGENTS COME TO PICK UP WHATEVER BAD GUY WHATEVER SUPER HERO HAS TORN UP HALF THE CITY TO TAKE OUT.
WHAT ARE YOU HIDING FROM, DEREK?
YOU THINK I DON'T KNOW WHY YOU'RE ON MY CASE?
THINGS DIDN'T WORK OUT BETWEEN US, OKAY? GET OVER IT.
I'VE GOT WORK TO DO. I DON'T HAVE TIME FOR THIS CRAP.
C'MON, MONSTRO.
JERK.

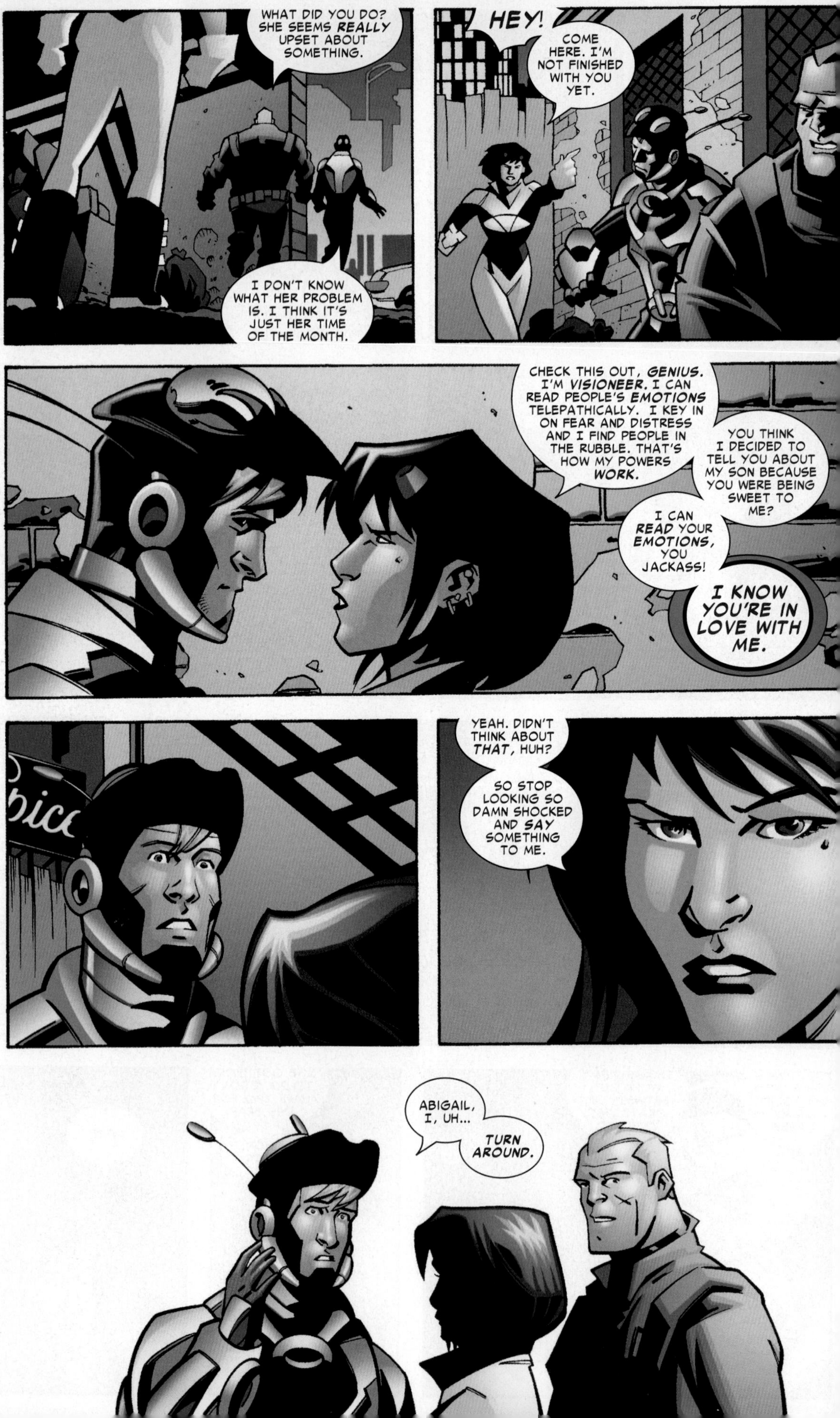
WHAT DID YOU DO? SHE SEEMS REALLY UPSET ABOUT SOMETHING.
I DON'T KNOW WHAT HER PROBLEM IS. I THINK IT'S JUST HER TIME OF THE MONTH.
HEY!
COME HERE. I'M NOT FINISHED WITH YOU YET.
CHECK THIS OUT, GENIUS. I'M VISIONEER. I CAN READ PEOPLE'S EMOTIONS TELEPATHICALLY. I KEY IN ON FEAR AND DISTRESS AND I FIND PEOPLE IN THE RUBBLE. THAT'S HOW MY POWERS WORK.
YOU THINK I DECIDED TO TELL YOU ABOUT MY SON BECAUSE YOU WERE BEING SWEET TO ME?
I CAN READ YOUR EMOTIONS, YOU JACKASS!
I KNOW YOU'RE IN LOVE WITH ME.
YEAH. DIDN'T THINK ABOUT THAT, HUH?
SO STOP LOOKING SO DAMN SHOCKED AND SAY SOMETHING TO ME.
ABIGAIL, I, UH...
TURN AROUND.

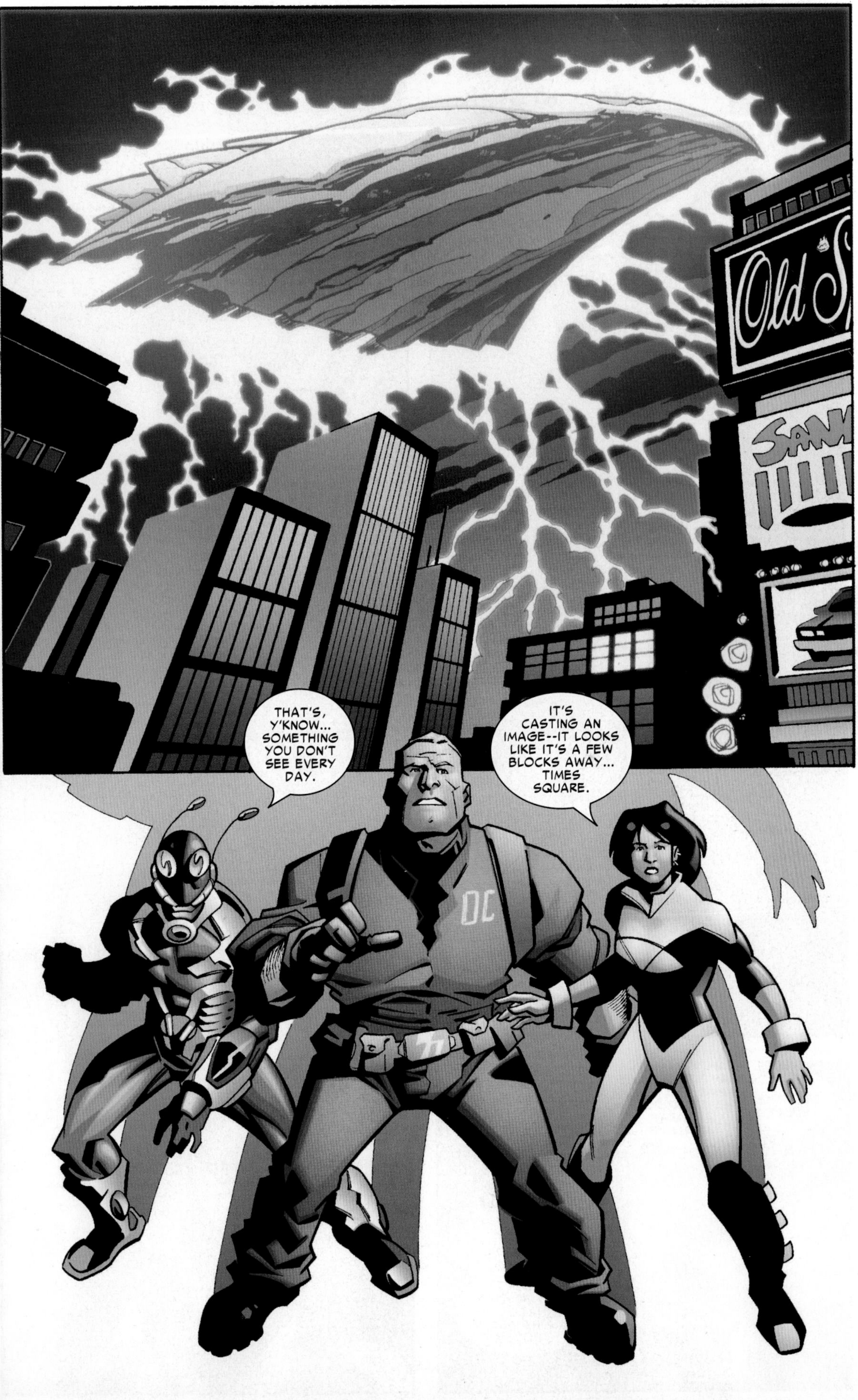
Old S
THAT'S, Y'KNOW... SOMETHING YOU DON'T SEE EVERY DAY.
IT'S CASTING AN IMAGE--IT LOOKS LIKE IT'S A FEW BLOCKS AWAY... TIMES SQUARE.
DC

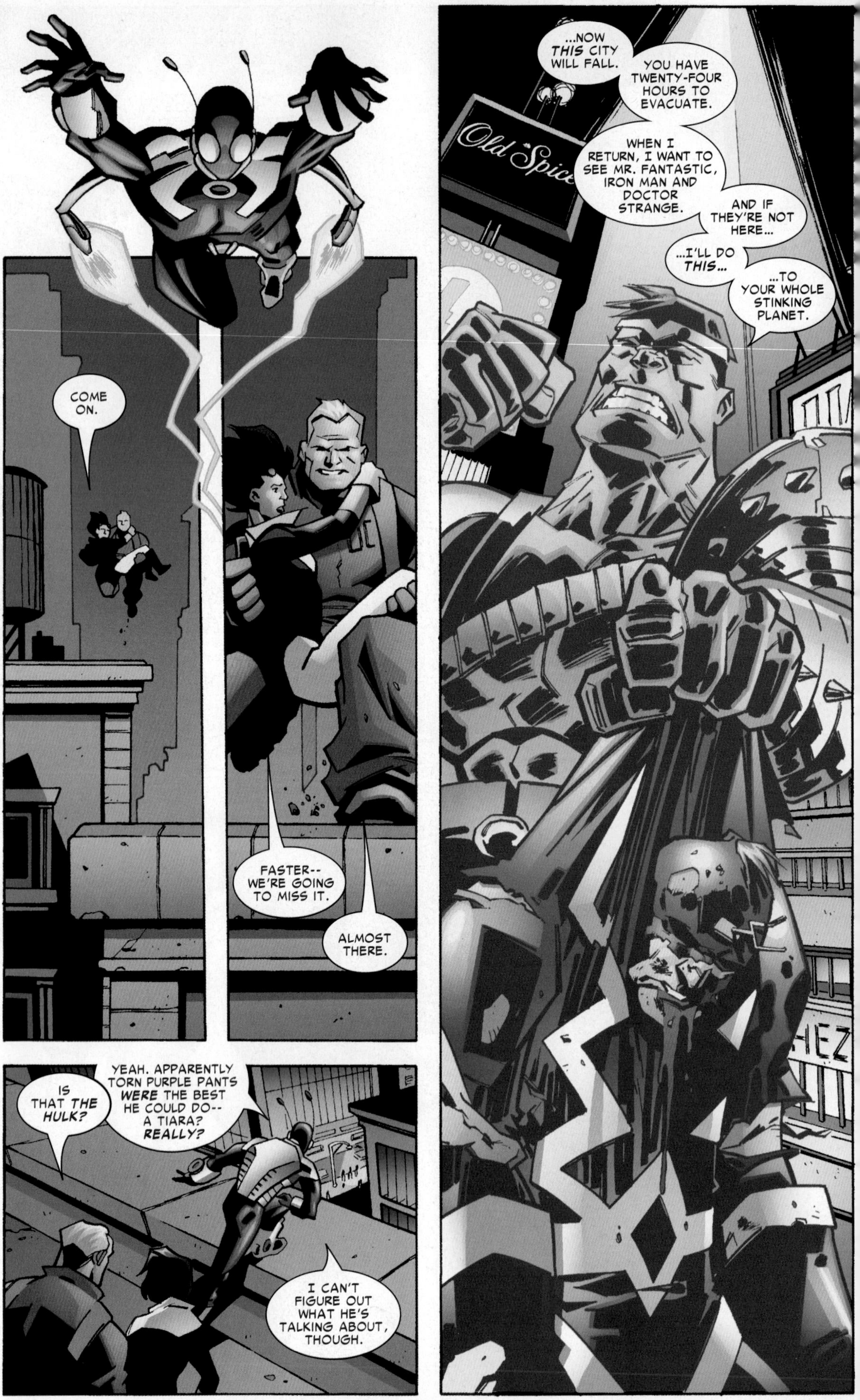
COME ON.
FASTER-- WE'RE GOING TO MISS IT.
ALMOST THERE.
IS THAT THE HULK?
YEAH. APPARENTLY TORN PURPLE PANTS WERE THE BEST HE COULD DO-- A TIARA? REALLY?
I CAN'T FIGURE OUT WHAT HE'S TALKING ABOUT, THOUGH.
Old Spice
...NOW THIS CITY WILL FALL.
YOU HAVE TWENTY-FOUR HOURS TO EVACUATE.
WHEN I RETURN, I WANT TO SEE MR. FANTASTIC, IRON MAN AND DOCTOR STRANGE.
AND IF THEY'RE NOT HERE...
...I'LL DO THIS...
...TO YOUR WHOLE STINKING PLANET.

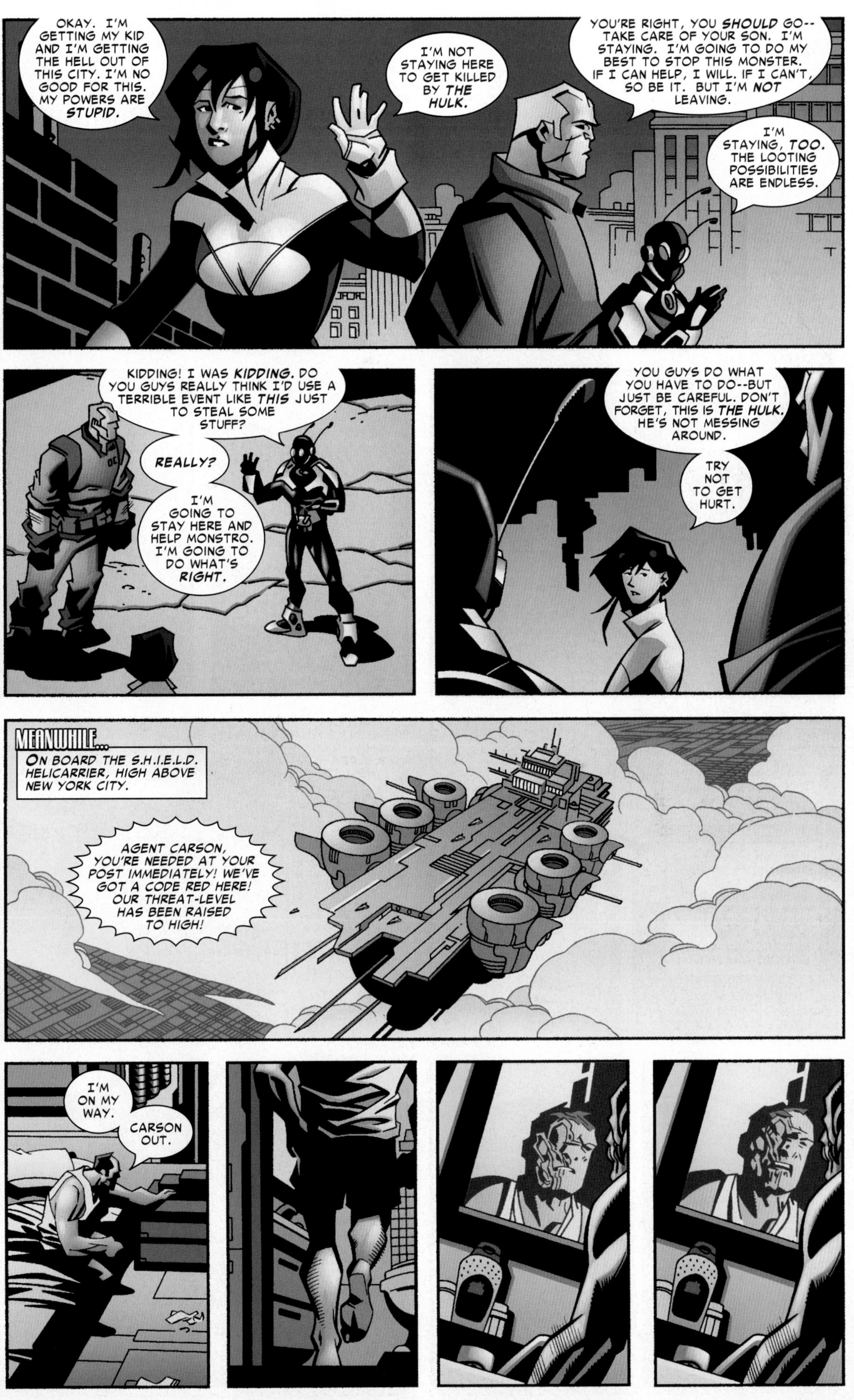
OKAY. I'M GETTING MY KID AND I'M GETTING THE HELL OUT OF THIS CITY. I'M NO GOOD FOR THIS. MY POWERS ARE STUPID.
I'M NOT STAYING HERE TO GET KILLED BY THE HULK.
YOU'RE RIGHT, YOU SHOULD GO-- TAKE CARE OF YOUR SON. I'M STAYING. I'M GOING TO DO MY BEST TO STOP THIS MONSTER. IF I CAN HELP, I WILL. IF I CAN'T, SO BE IT. BUT I'M NOT LEAVING.
I'M STAYING, TOO. THE LOOTING POSSIBILITIES ARE ENDLESS.
KIDDING! I WAS KIDDING. DO YOU GUYS REALLY THINK I'D USE A TERRIBLE EVENT LIKE THIS JUST TO STEAL SOME STUFF?
REALLY?
I'M GOING TO STAY HERE AND HELP MONSTRO. I'M GOING TO DO WHAT'S RIGHT.
YOU GUYS DO WHAT YOU HAVE TO DO--BUT JUST BE CAREFUL. DON'T FORGET, THIS IS THE HULK. HE'S NOT MESSING AROUND.
TRY NOT TO GET HURT.
MEANWHILE...
ON BOARD THE S.H.I.E.L.D. HELICARRIER, HIGH ABOVE NEW YORK CITY.
AGENT CARSON, YOU'RE NEEDED AT YOUR POST IMMEDIATELY! WE'VE GOT A CODE RED HERE! OUR THREAT-LEVEL HAS BEEN RAISED TO HIGH!
I'M ON MY WAY.
CARSON OUT.

SMREESSH!!

RARRGGH!!

O'GRADY--

--ERIC O'GRADY...

I'M GOING TO KILL YOU FOR WHAT YOU'VE DONE TO ME.

I'M GOING TO KILL YOU.

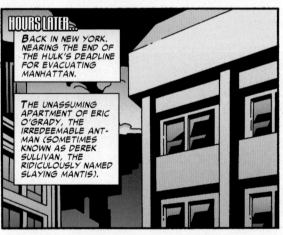

HOURS LATER...

BACK IN NEW YORK. NEARING THE END OF THE HULK'S DEADLINE FOR EVACUATING MANHATTAN.

THE UNASSUMING APARTMENT OF ERIC O'GRADY, THE IRREDEEMABLE ANT-MAN (SOMETIMES KNOWN AS DEREK SULLIVAN, THE RIDICULOUSLY NAMED SLAYING MANTIS).

ERIC, OLD FRIEND? IT'S YOUR COMPATRIOT, THE BLACK FOX. HELLO?

I ASSURE YOU, I DIDN'T WANT TO BREAK IN. I WAS JUST COMING TO MAKE SURE YOU'VE EVACUATED. ARE YOU STILL HERE?

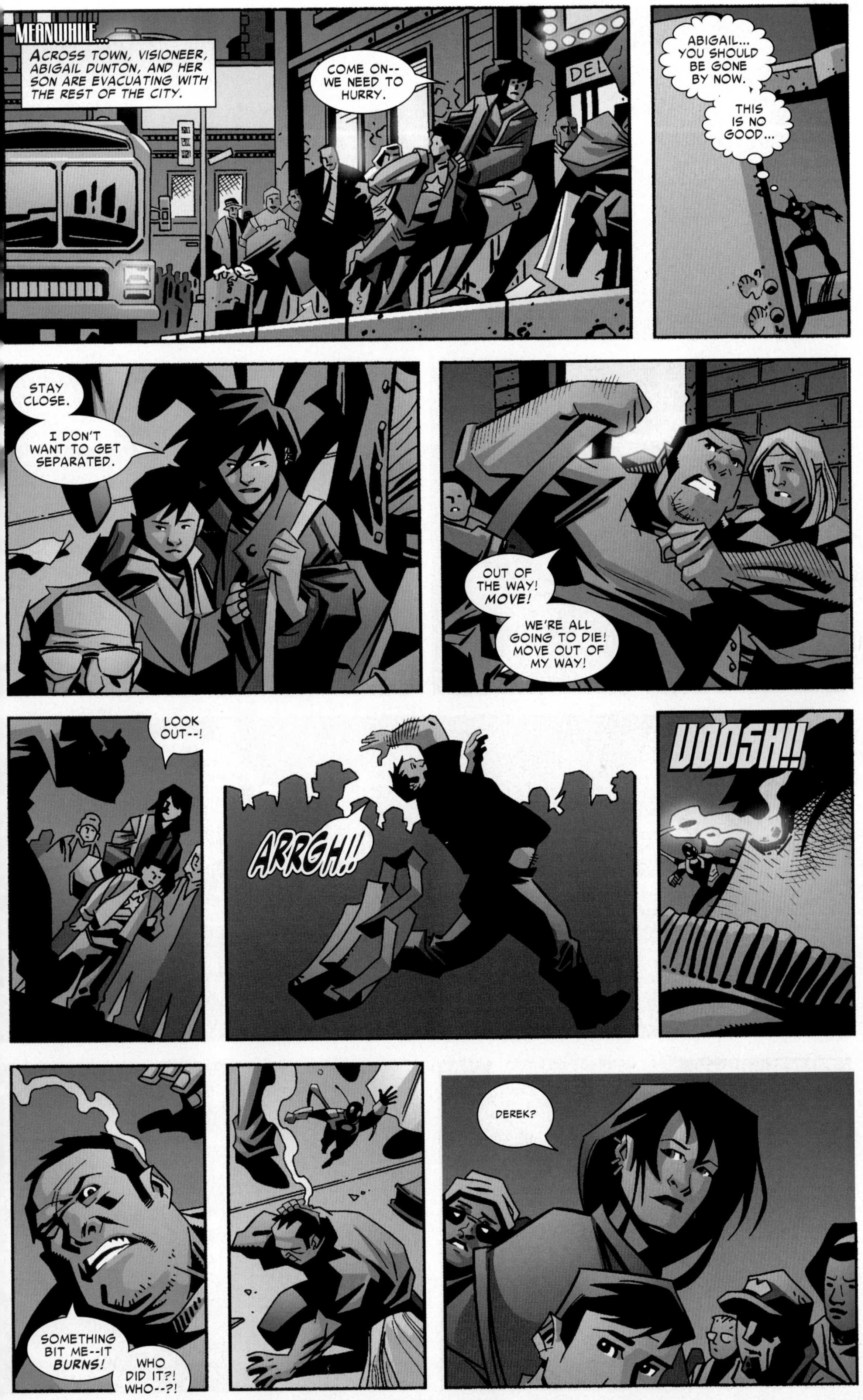
MEANWHILE...
ACROSS TOWN, VISIONEER, ABIGAIL DUNTON, AND HER SON ARE EVACUATING WITH THE REST OF THE CITY.
COME ON-- WE NEED TO HURRY.
DEL
ABIGAIL... YOU SHOULD BE GONE BY NOW.
THIS IS NO GOOD...
STAY CLOSE.
I DON'T WANT TO GET SEPARATED.
OUT OF THE WAY! MOVE!
WE'RE ALL GOING TO DIE! MOVE OUT OF MY WAY!
LOOK OUT--!
ARRGH!!
VOOSH!!
SOMETHING BIT ME--IT BURNS!
WHO DID IT?! WHO--?!
DEREK?

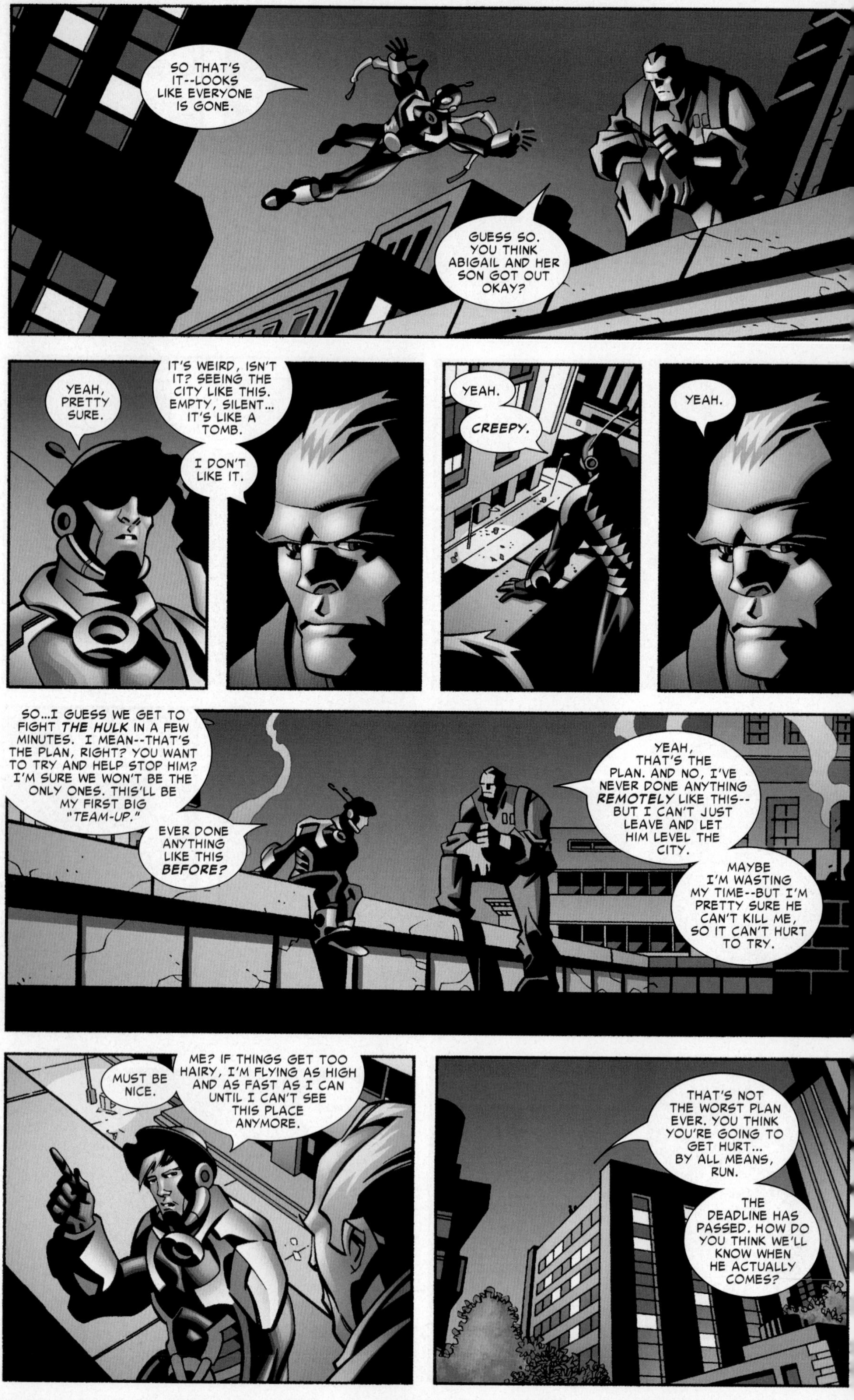
SO THAT'S IT--LOOKS LIKE EVERYONE IS GONE.
GUESS SO. YOU THINK ABIGAIL AND HER SON GOT OUT OKAY?
YEAH, PRETTY SURE.
IT'S WEIRD, ISN'T IT? SEEING THE CITY LIKE THIS. EMPTY, SILENT... IT'S LIKE A TOMB.
I DON'T LIKE IT.
YEAH.
CREEPY.
YEAH.
SO...I GUESS WE GET TO FIGHT THE HULK IN A FEW MINUTES. I MEAN--THAT'S THE PLAN, RIGHT? YOU WANT TO TRY AND HELP STOP HIM? I'M SURE WE WON'T BE THE ONLY ONES. THIS'LL BE MY FIRST BIG "TEAM-UP."
EVER DONE ANYTHING LIKE THIS BEFORE?
YEAH, THAT'S THE PLAN. AND NO, I'VE NEVER DONE ANYTHING REMOTELY LIKE THIS--BUT I CAN'T JUST LEAVE AND LET HIM LEVEL THE CITY.
MAYBE I'M WASTING MY TIME--BUT I'M PRETTY SURE HE CAN'T KILL ME, SO IT CAN'T HURT TO TRY.
MUST BE NICE.
ME? IF THINGS GET TOO HAIRY, I'M FLYING AS HIGH AND AS FAST AS I CAN UNTIL I CAN'T SEE THIS PLACE ANYMORE.
THAT'S NOT THE WORST PLAN EVER. YOU THINK YOU'RE GOING TO GET HURT... BY ALL MEANS, RUN.
THE DEADLINE HAS PASSED. HOW DO YOU THINK WE'LL KNOW WHEN HE ACTUALLY COMES?

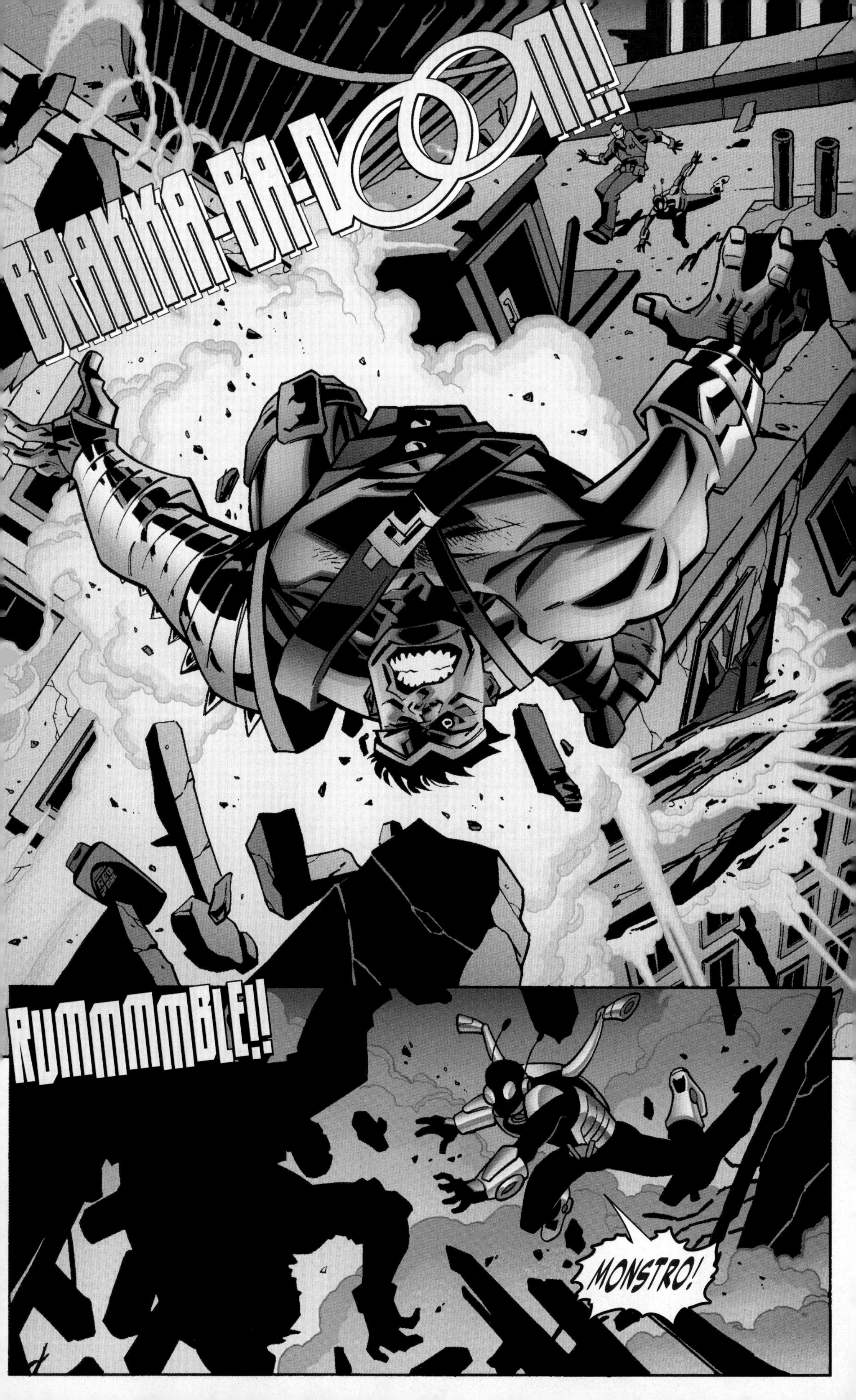
BRAKKA-BA-BOOM!!
RUMMMMBLE!!
MONSTRO!

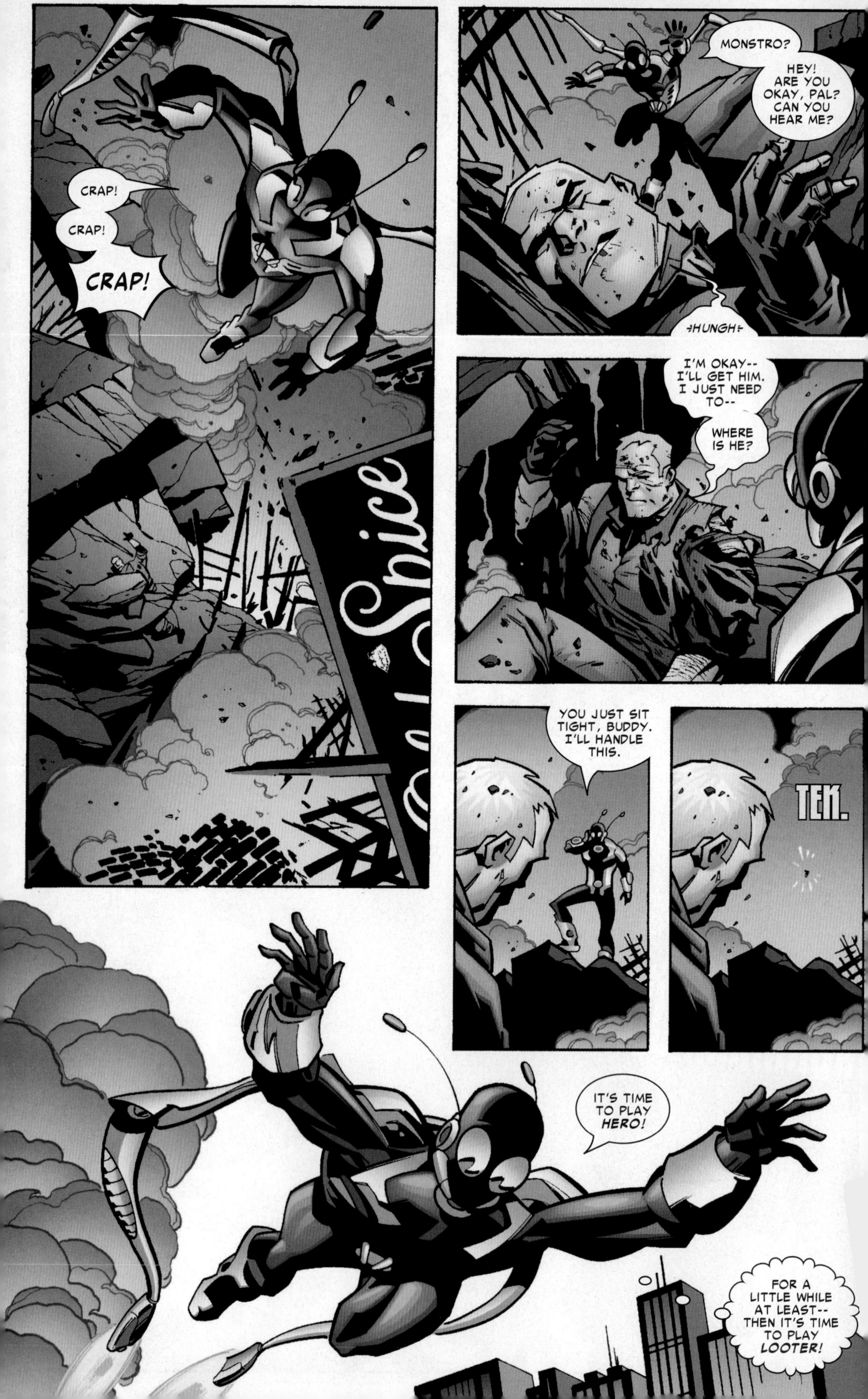
CRAP!
CRAP!
CRAP!
Spice
MONSTRO?
HEY! ARE YOU OKAY, PAL? CAN YOU HEAR ME?
HUNGH
I'M OKAY-- I'LL GET HIM. I JUST NEED TO--
WHERE IS HE?
YOU JUST SIT TIGHT, BUDDY. I'LL HANDLE THIS.
TEK.
IT'S TIME TO PLAY HERO!
FOR A LITTLE WHILE AT LEAST-- THEN IT'S TIME TO PLAY LOOTER!

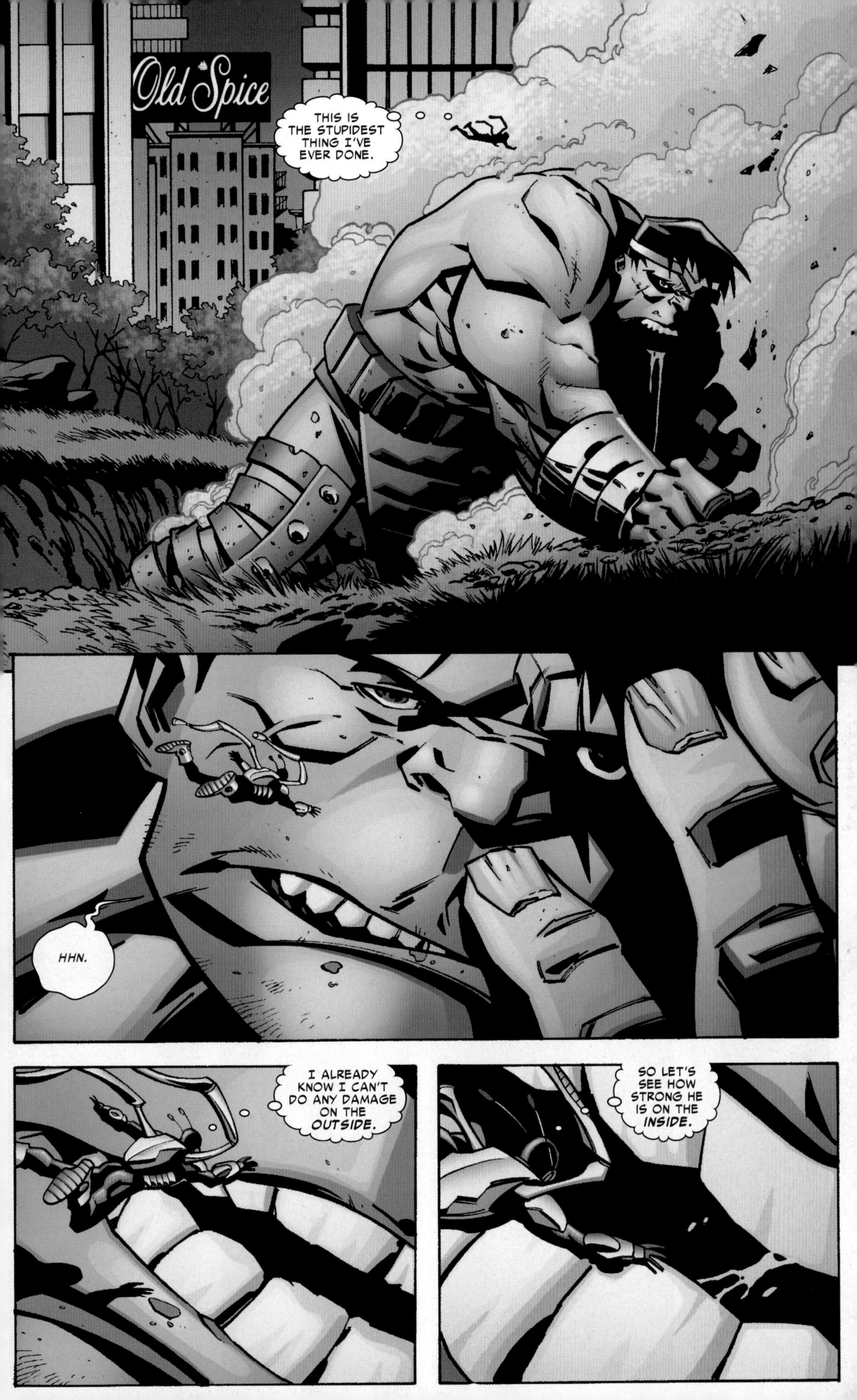
Old Spice
THIS IS THE STUPIDEST THING I'VE EVER DONE.
HHN.
I ALREADY KNOW I CAN'T DO ANY DAMAGE ON THE *OUTSIDE*.
SO LET'S SEE HOW STRONG HE IS ON THE *INSIDE*.

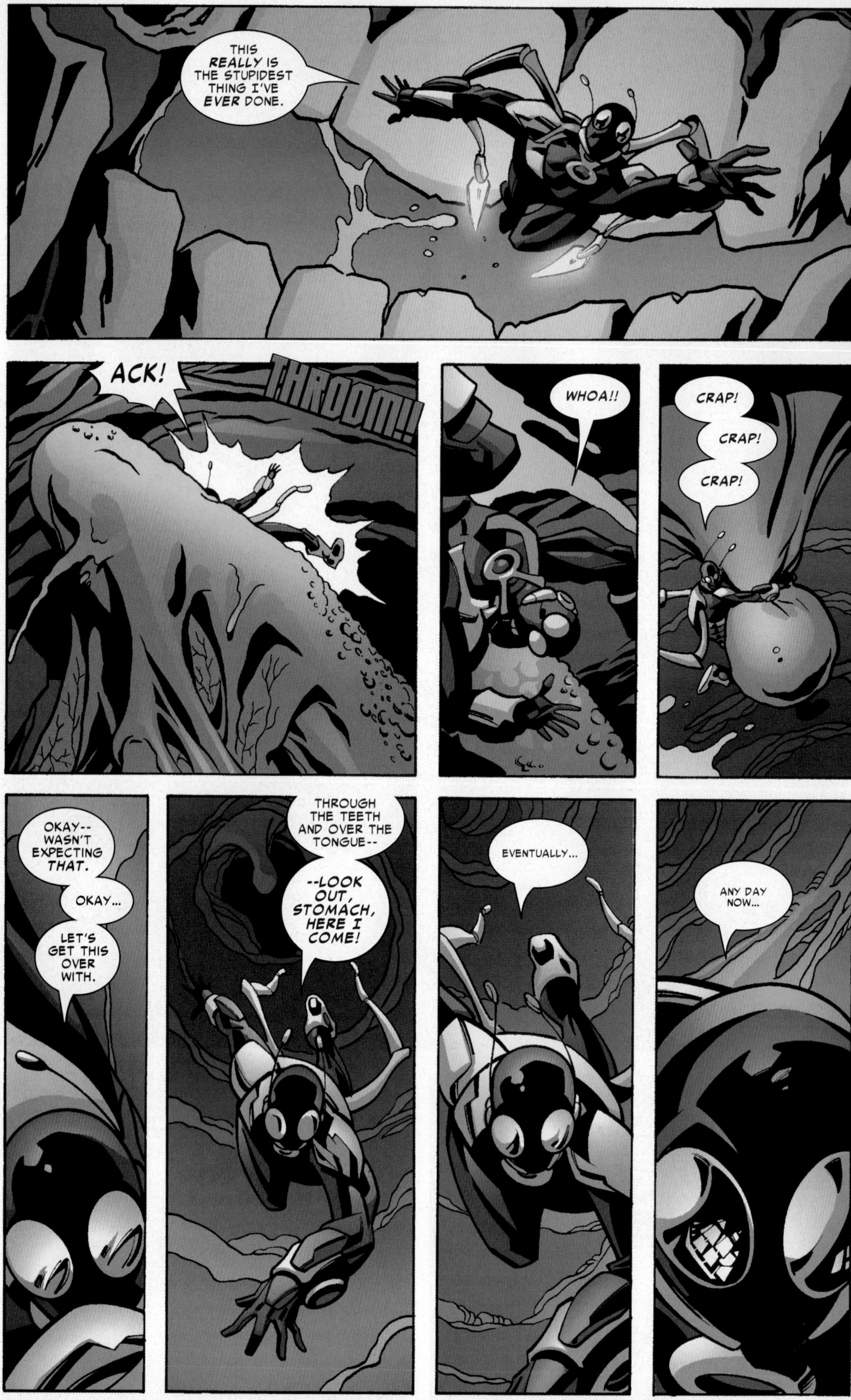
THIS REALLY IS THE STUPIDEST THING I'VE EVER DONE.
ACK!
THROOM!!
WHOA!!
CRAP!
CRAP!
CRAP!
OKAY-- WASN'T EXPECTING THAT.
OKAY...
LET'S GET THIS OVER WITH.
THROUGH THE TEETH AND OVER THE TONGUE--
--LOOK OUT, STOMACH, HERE I COME!
EVENTUALLY...
ANY DAY NOW...

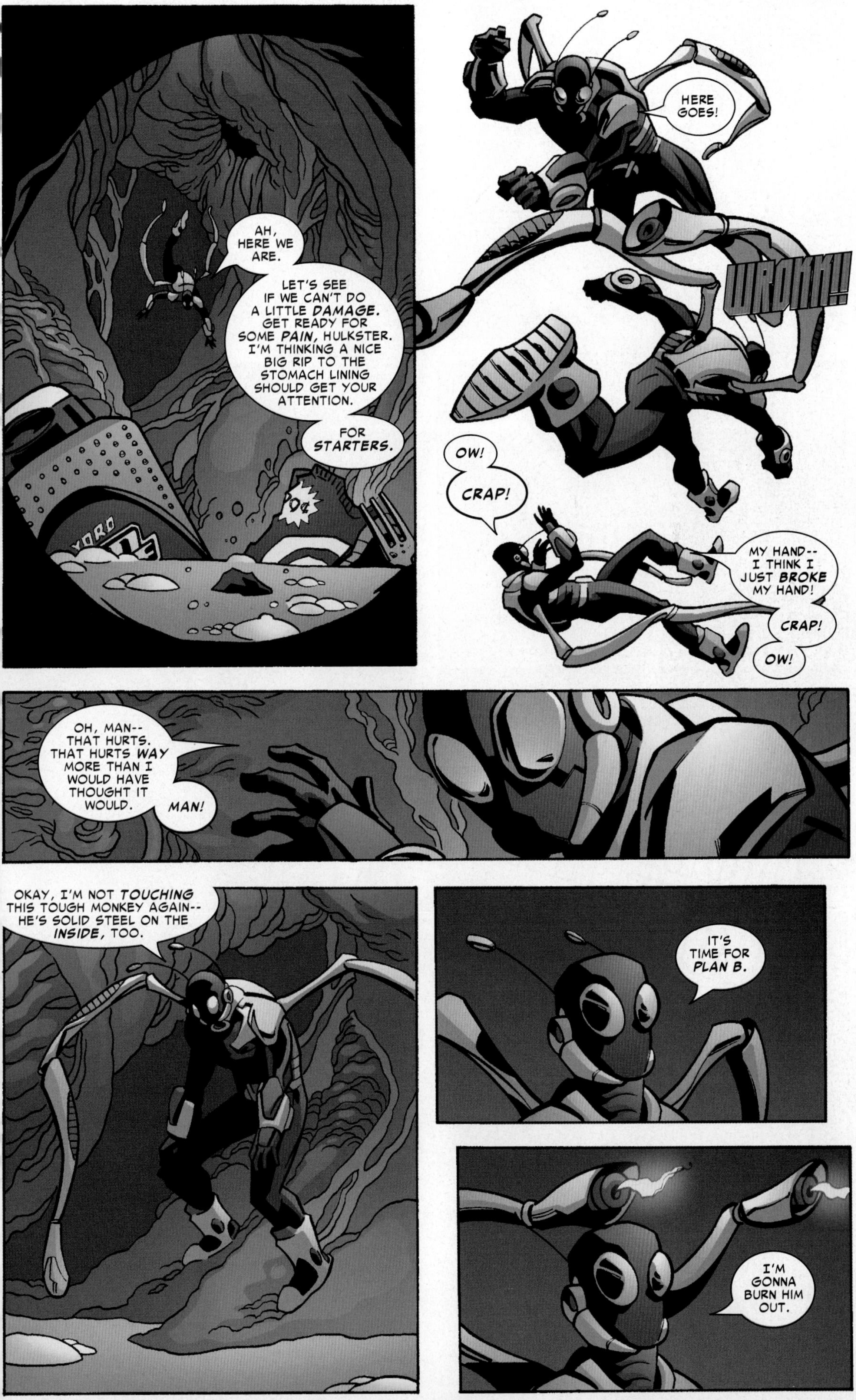
AH, HERE WE ARE.
LET'S SEE IF WE CAN'T DO A LITTLE *DAMAGE.* GET READY FOR SOME *PAIN,* HULKSTER. I'M THINKING A NICE BIG RIP TO THE STOMACH LINING SHOULD GET YOUR ATTENTION.
FOR *STARTERS.*
HERE GOES!
WROKK!!
OW!
CRAP!
MY HAND-- I THINK I JUST *BROKE* MY HAND!
CRAP!
OW!
OH, MAN-- THAT HURTS. THAT HURTS *WAY* MORE THAN I WOULD HAVE THOUGHT IT WOULD.
*MAN!*
OKAY, I'M NOT *TOUCHING* THIS TOUGH MONKEY AGAIN-- HE'S SOLID STEEL ON THE *INSIDE,* TOO.
IT'S TIME FOR *PLAN B.*
I'M GONNA BURN HIM OUT.

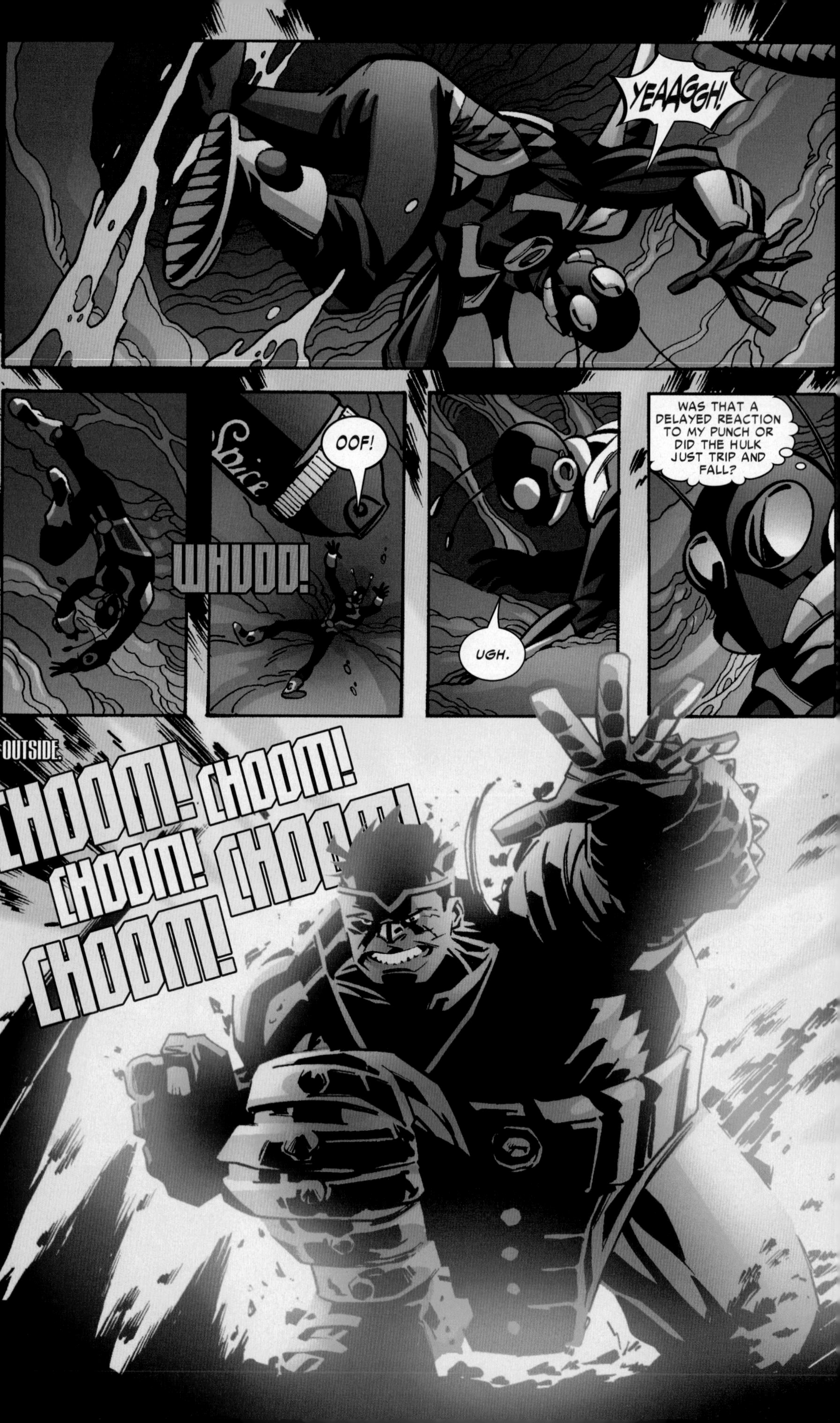
YEAAGGH!
OOF!
WHUDD!
UGH.
WAS THAT A DELAYED REACTION TO MY PUNCH OR DID THE HULK JUST TRIP AND FALL?
OUTSIDE.
CHOOM! CHOOM! CHOOM! CHOOM! CHOOM!

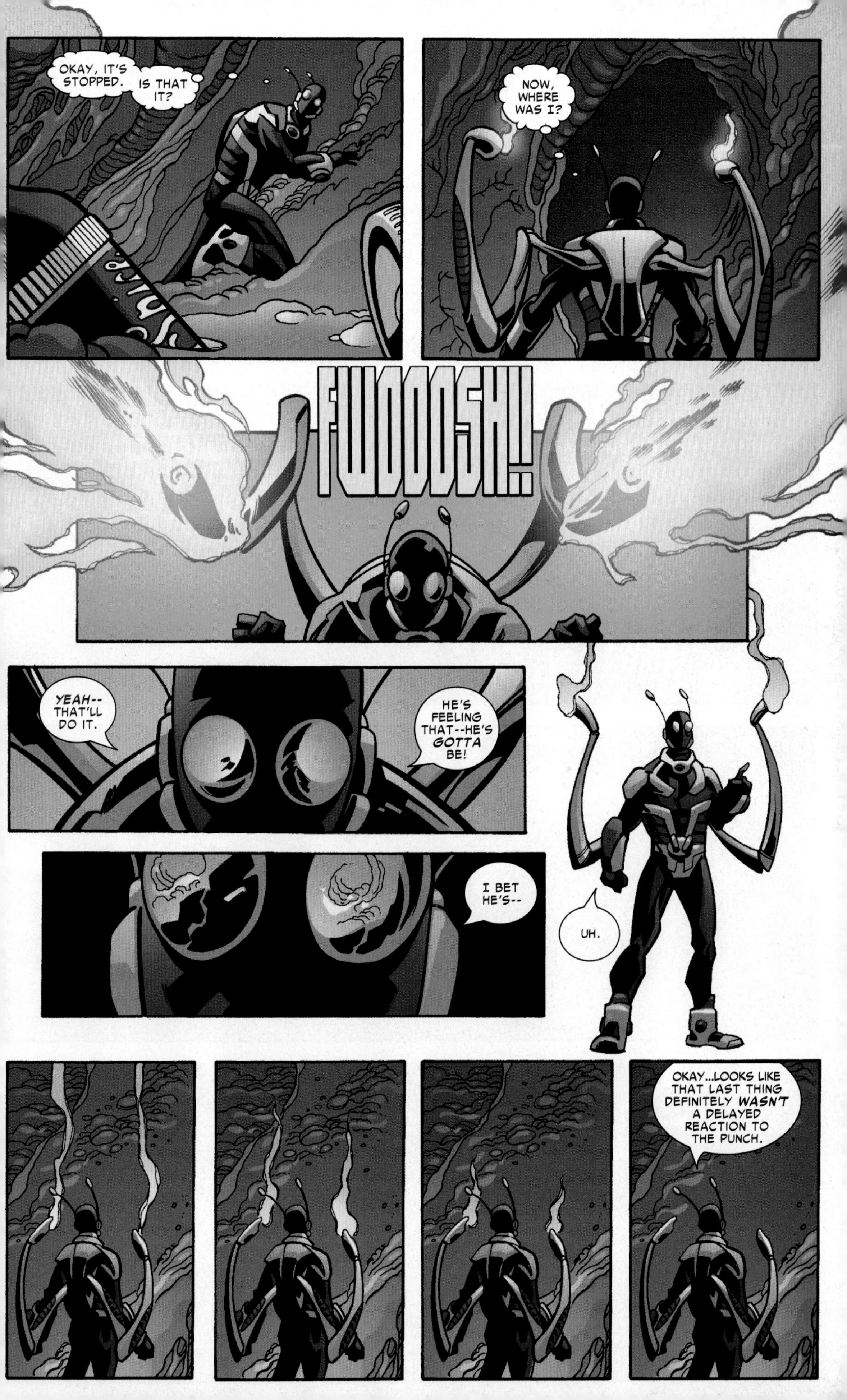
OKAY, IT'S STOPPED.
IS THAT IT?
NOW, WHERE WAS I?
FWOOOSH!!
YEAH--THAT'LL DO IT.
HE'S FEELING THAT--HE'S GOTTA BE!
I BET HE'S--
UH.
OKAY...LOOKS LIKE THAT LAST THING DEFINITELY WASN'T A DELAYED REACTION TO THE PUNCH.

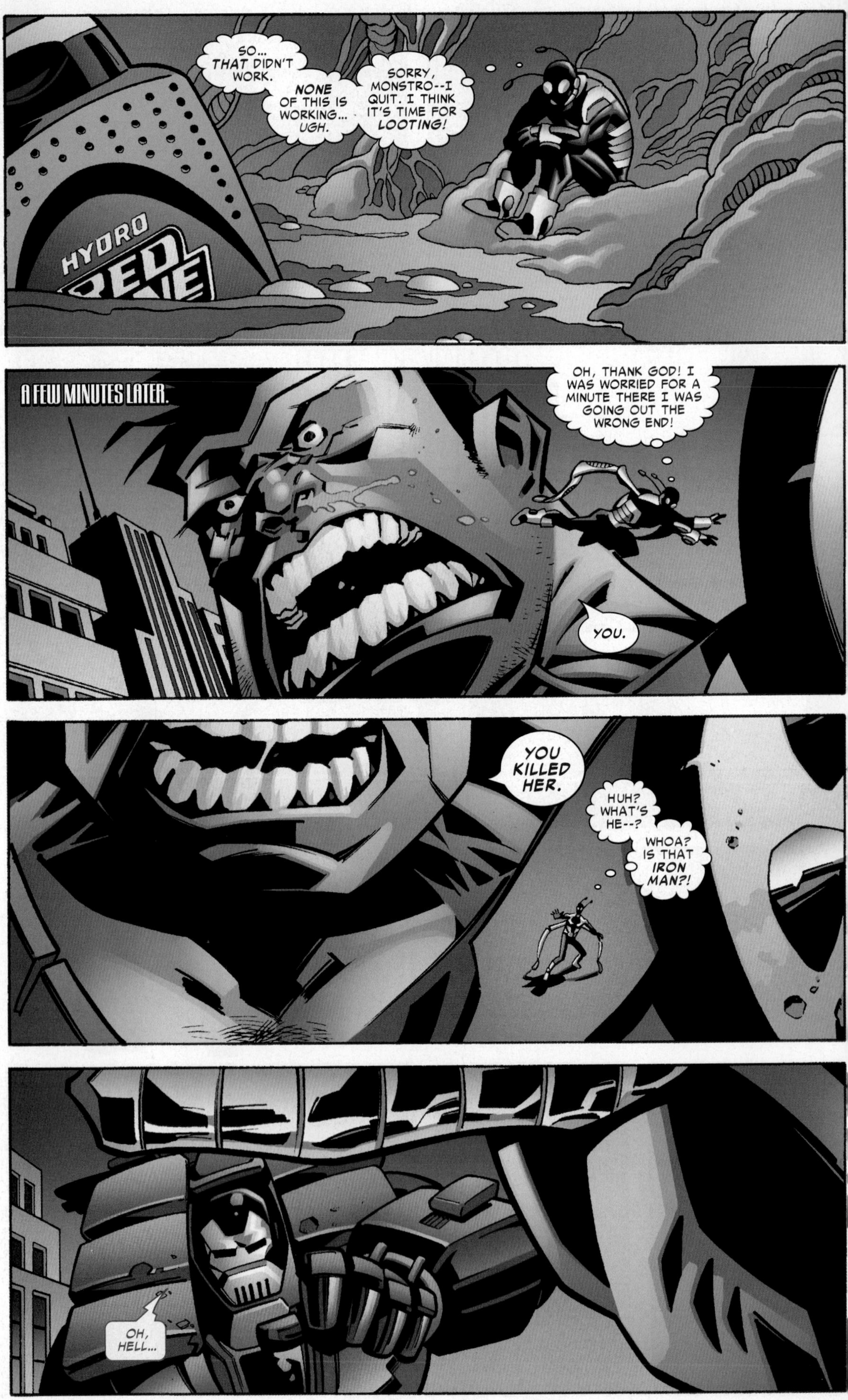
SO... THAT DIDN'T WORK.
NONE OF THIS IS WORKING... UGH.
SORRY, MONSTRO--I QUIT. I THINK IT'S TIME FOR LOOTING!
HYDRO RED
A FEW MINUTES LATER.
OH, THANK GOD! I WAS WORRIED FOR A MINUTE THERE I WAS GOING OUT THE WRONG END!
YOU.
YOU KILLED HER.
HUH? WHAT'S HE--?
WHOA? IS THAT IRON MAN?!
OH, HELL...

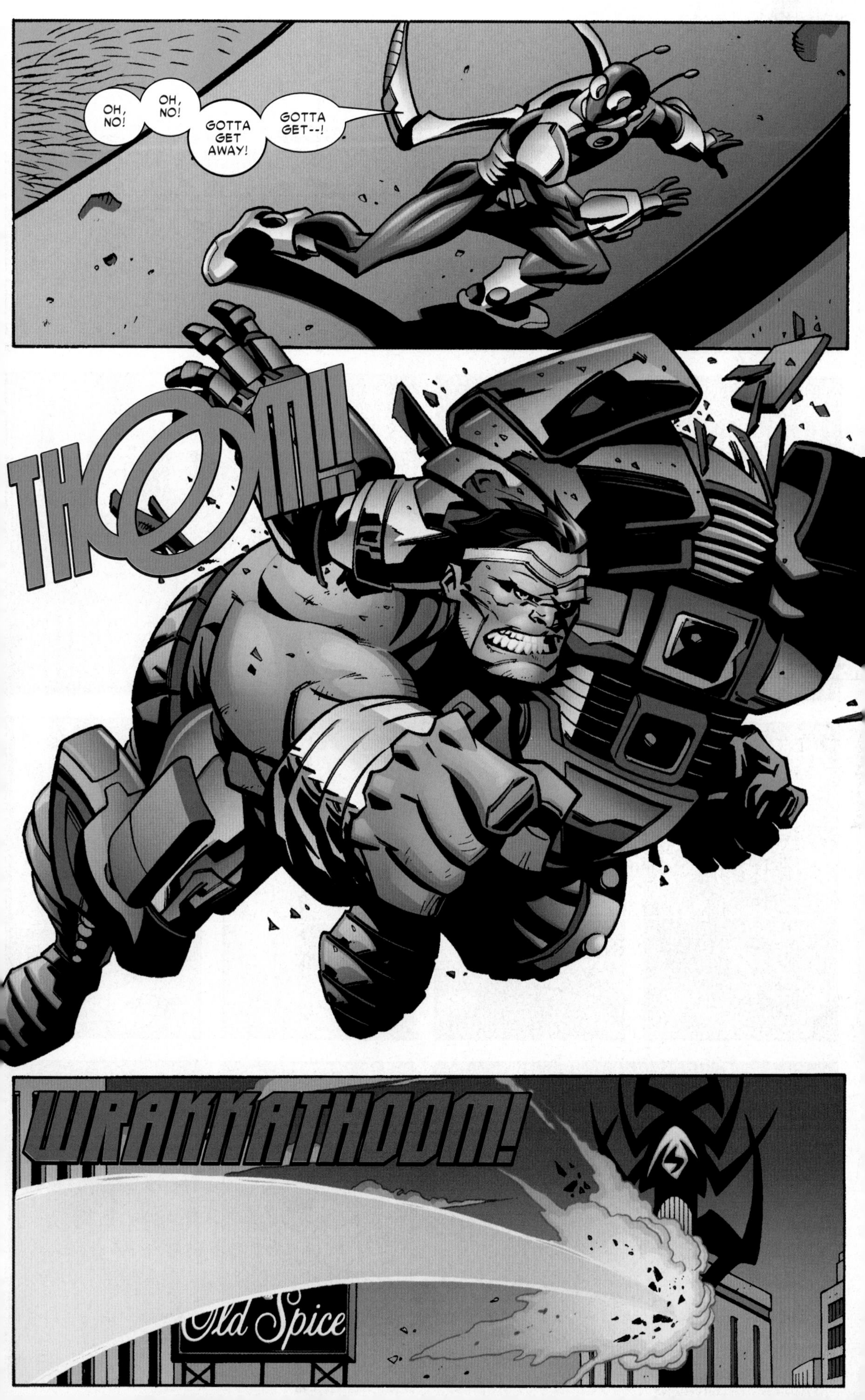
OH, NO!
OH, NO!
GOTTA GET AWAY!
GOTTA GET--!
THOOM!!
WRAKKATHOOM!
Old Spice

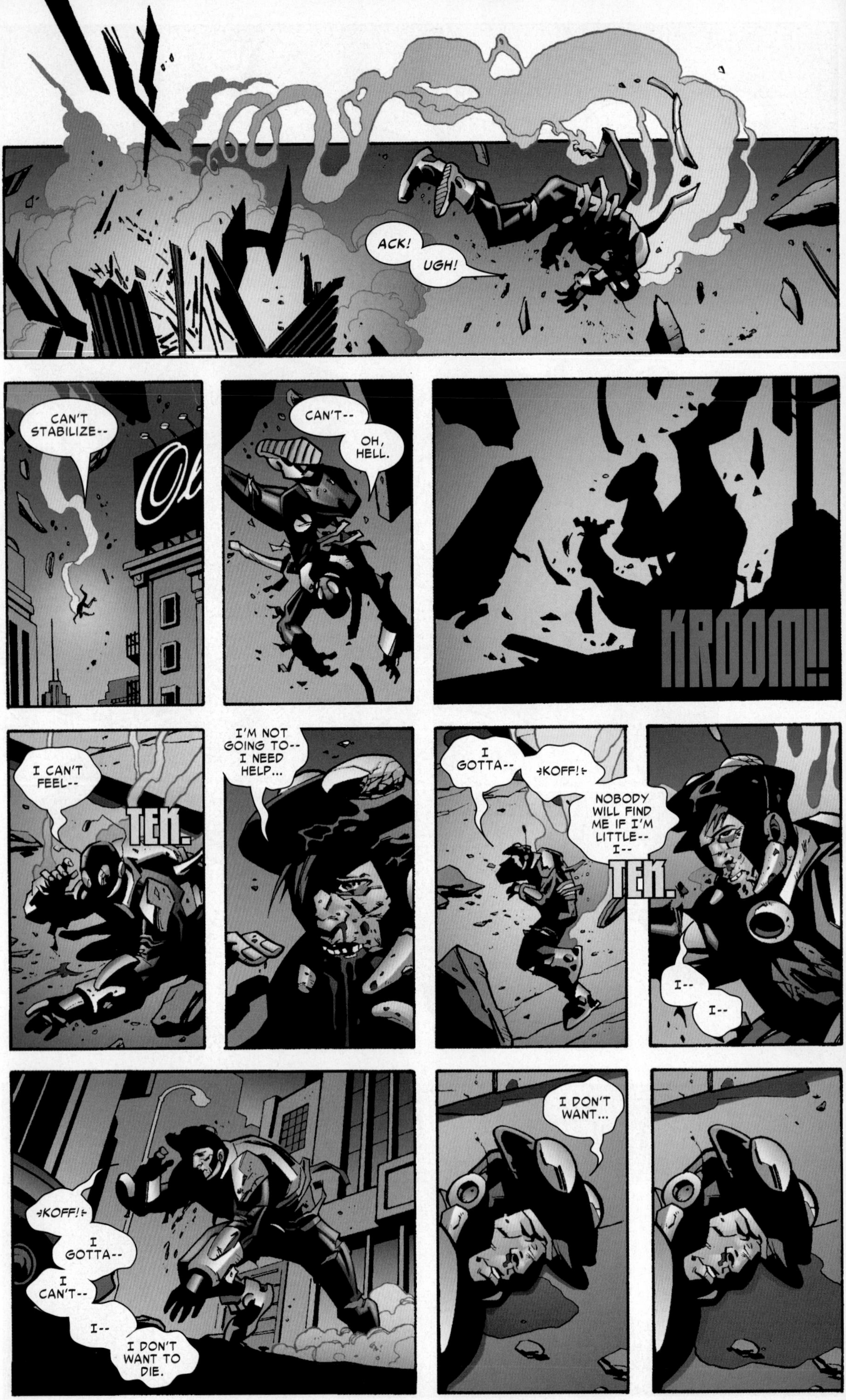
ACK!
UGH!
CAN'T STABILIZE--
CAN'T--
OH, HELL.
KROOM!!
I CAN'T FEEL--
TEK.
I'M NOT GOING TO-- I NEED HELP...
I GOTTA--
KOFF!
NOBODY WILL FIND ME IF I'M LITTLE-- I--
TEK.
I--
I--
KOFF!
I GOTTA--
I CAN'T--
I--
I DON'T WANT TO DIE.
I DON'T WANT...

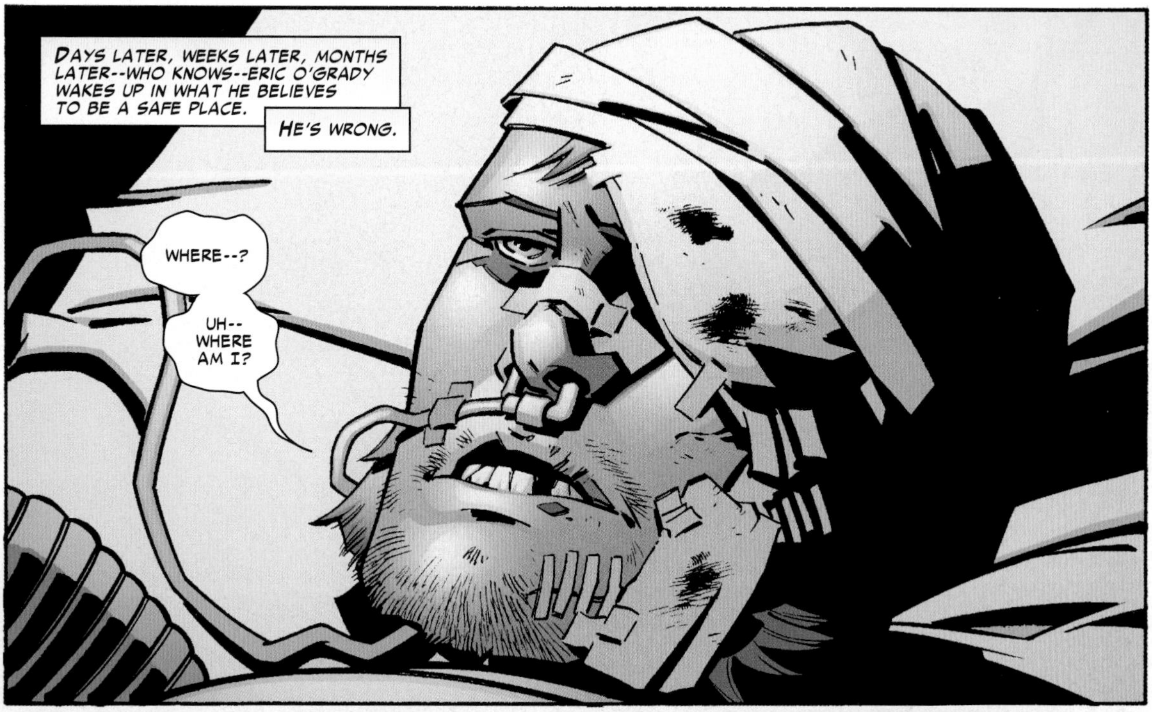
DAYS LATER, WEEKS LATER, MONTHS LATER--WHO KNOWS--ERIC O'GRADY WAKES UP IN WHAT HE BELIEVES TO BE A SAFE PLACE.
HE'S WRONG.
WHERE--?
UH-- WHERE AM I?

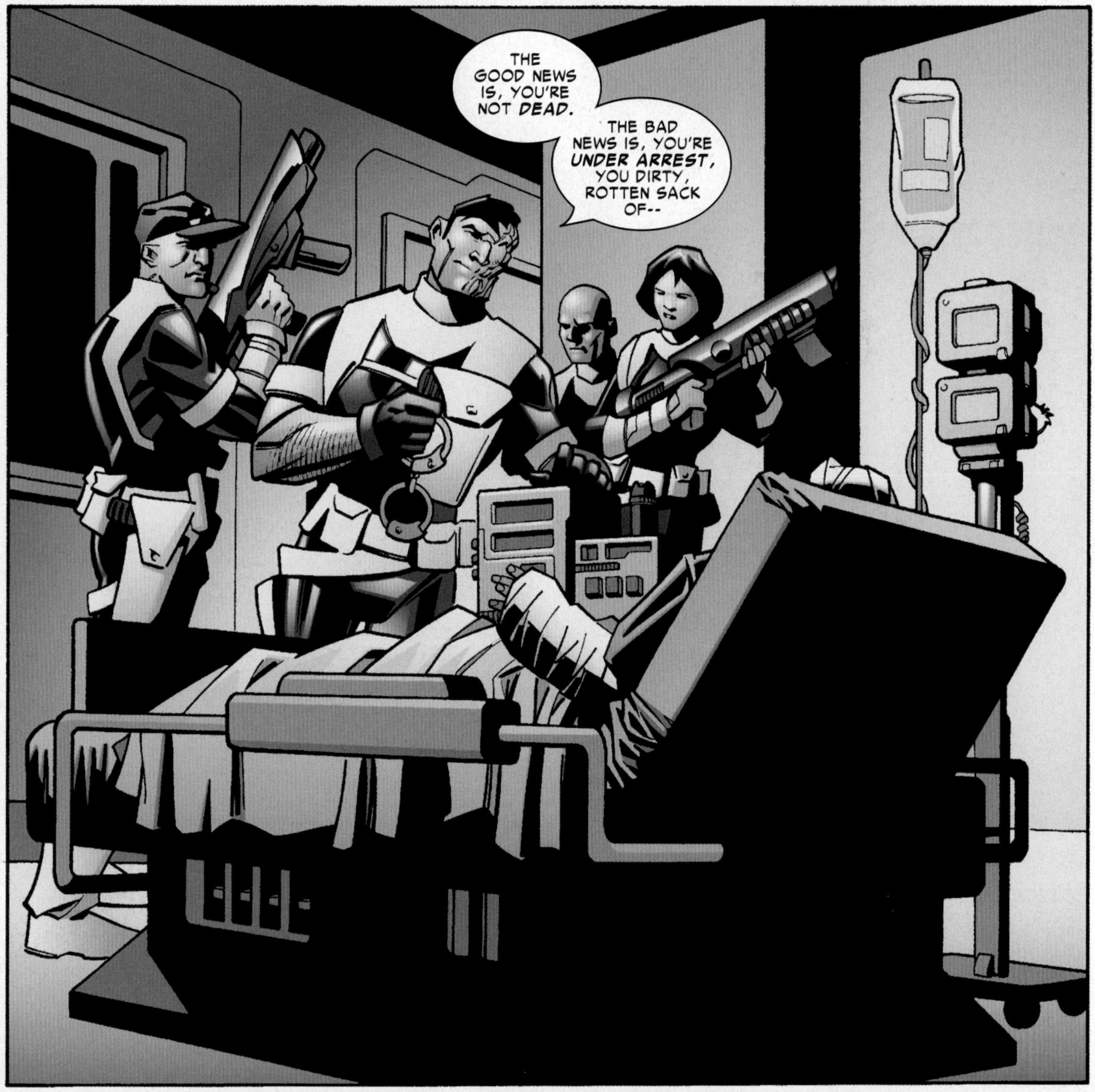
THE GOOD NEWS IS, YOU'RE NOT DEAD.
THE BAD NEWS IS, YOU'RE UNDER ARREST, YOU DIRTY, ROTTEN SACK OF--

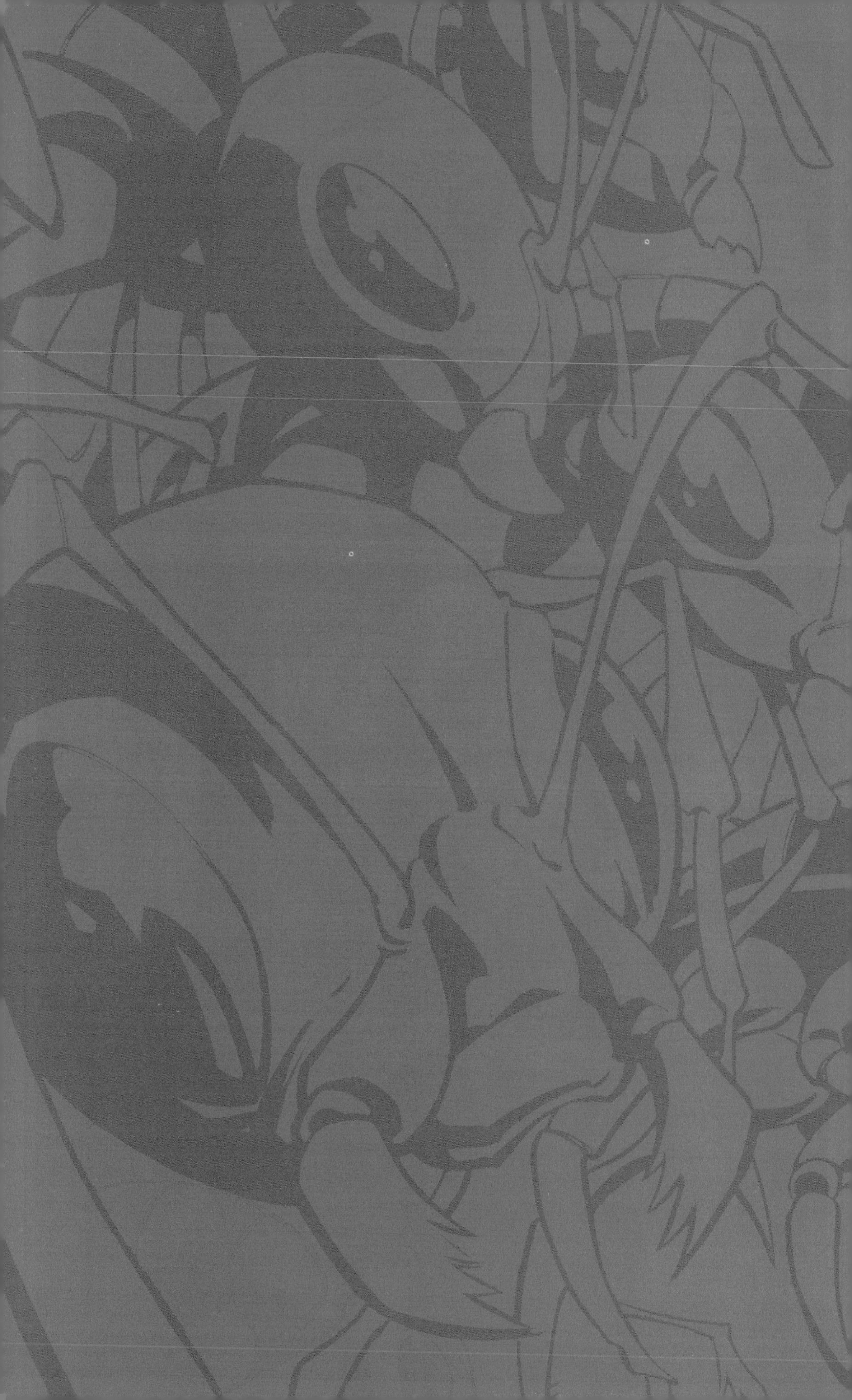

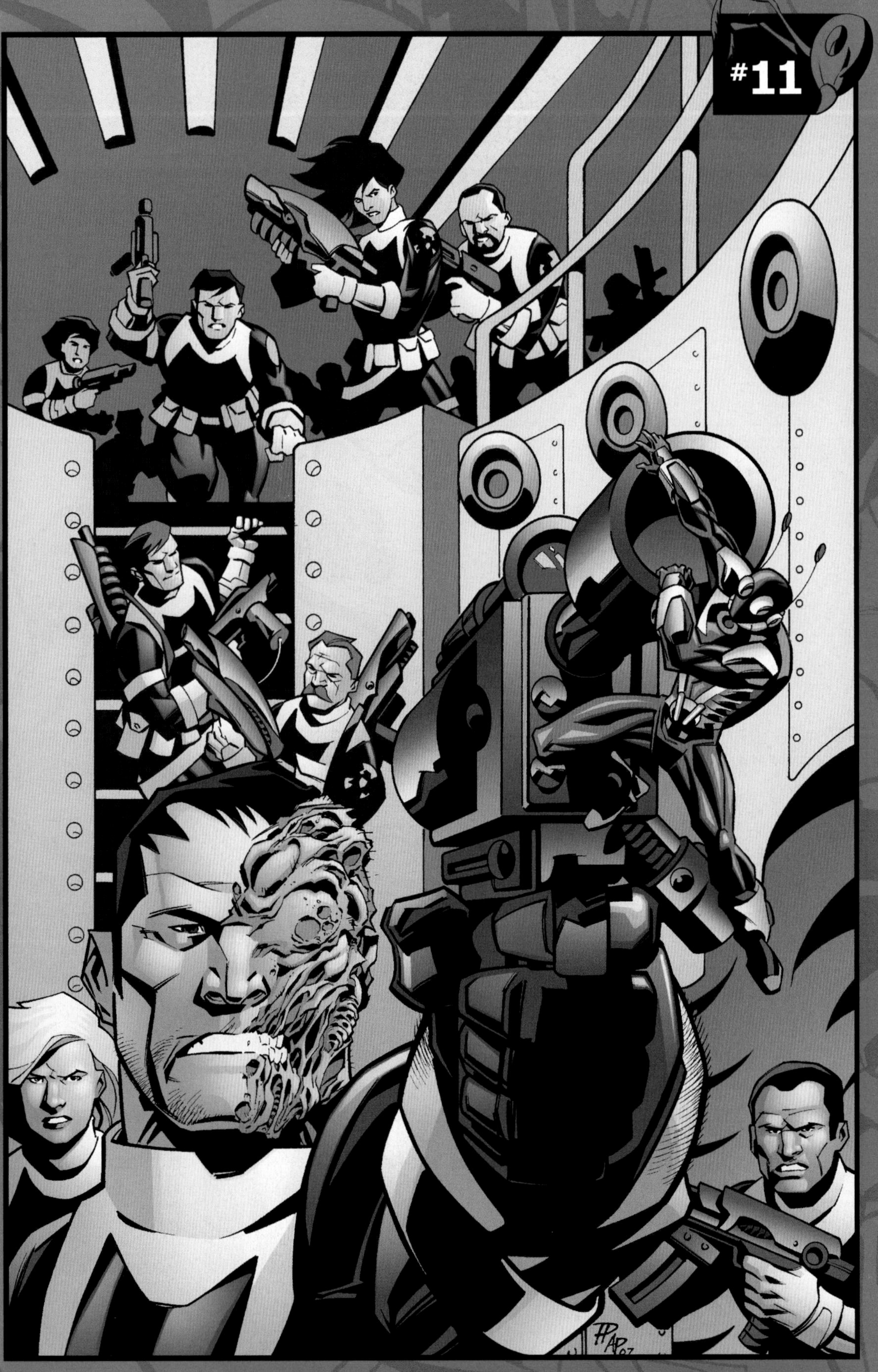
#11

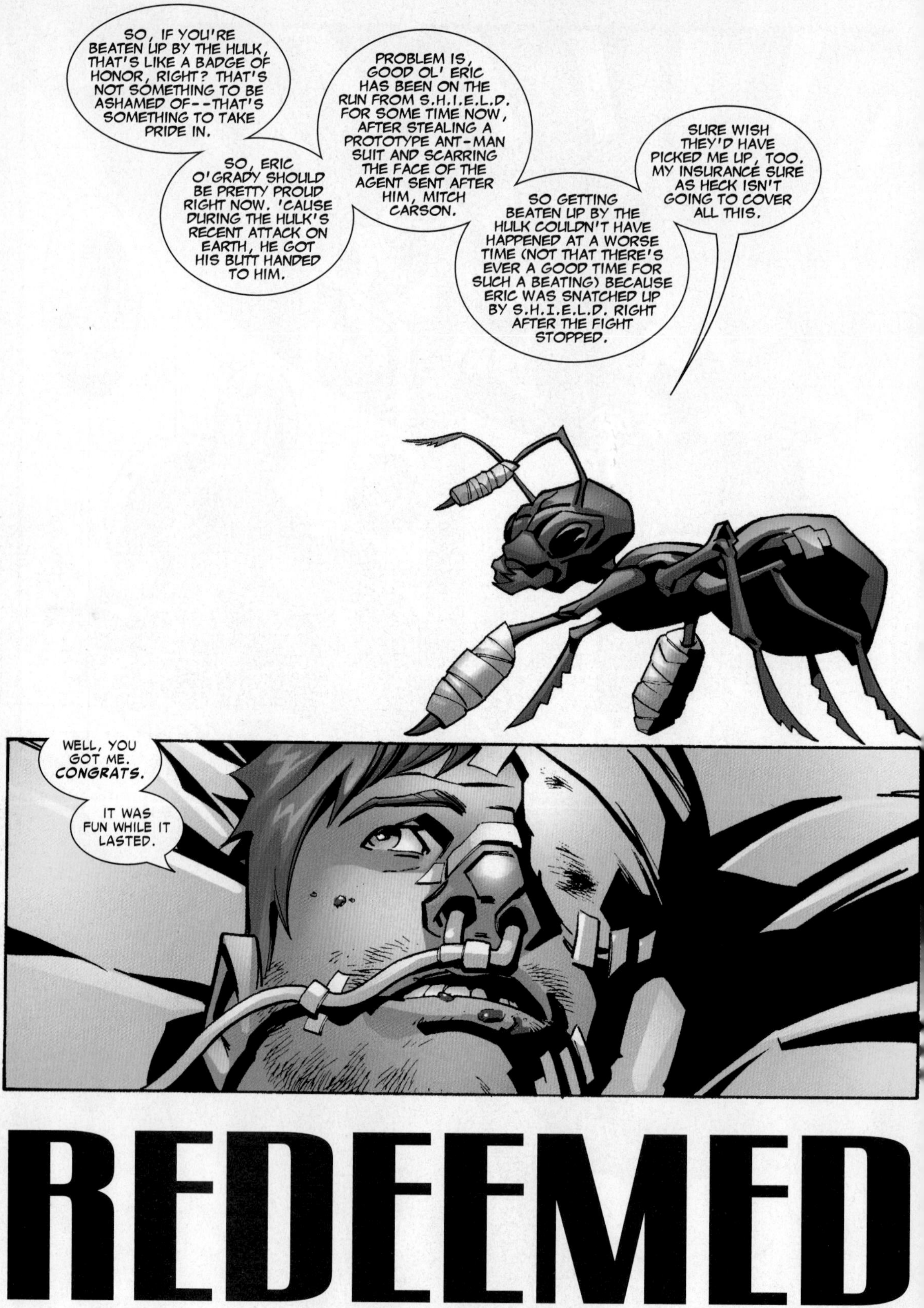
SO, IF YOU'RE BEATEN UP BY THE HULK, THAT'S LIKE A BADGE OF HONOR, RIGHT? THAT'S NOT SOMETHING TO BE ASHAMED OF--THAT'S SOMETHING TO TAKE PRIDE IN.
SO, ERIC O'GRADY SHOULD BE PRETTY PROUD RIGHT NOW. 'CAUSE DURING THE HULK'S RECENT ATTACK ON EARTH, HE GOT HIS BUTT HANDED TO HIM.
PROBLEM IS, GOOD OL' ERIC HAS BEEN ON THE RUN FROM S.H.I.E.L.D. FOR SOME TIME NOW, AFTER STEALING A PROTOTYPE ANT-MAN SUIT AND SCARRING THE FACE OF THE AGENT SENT AFTER HIM, MITCH CARSON.
SO GETTING BEATEN UP BY THE HULK COULDN'T HAVE HAPPENED AT A WORSE TIME (NOT THAT THERE'S EVER A GOOD TIME FOR SUCH A BEATING) BECAUSE ERIC WAS SNATCHED UP BY S.H.I.E.L.D. RIGHT AFTER THE FIGHT STOPPED.
SURE WISH THEY'D HAVE PICKED ME UP, TOO. MY INSURANCE SURE AS HECK ISN'T GOING TO COVER ALL THIS.
WELL, YOU GOT ME. CONGRATS.
IT WAS FUN WHILE IT LASTED.

# REDEEMED

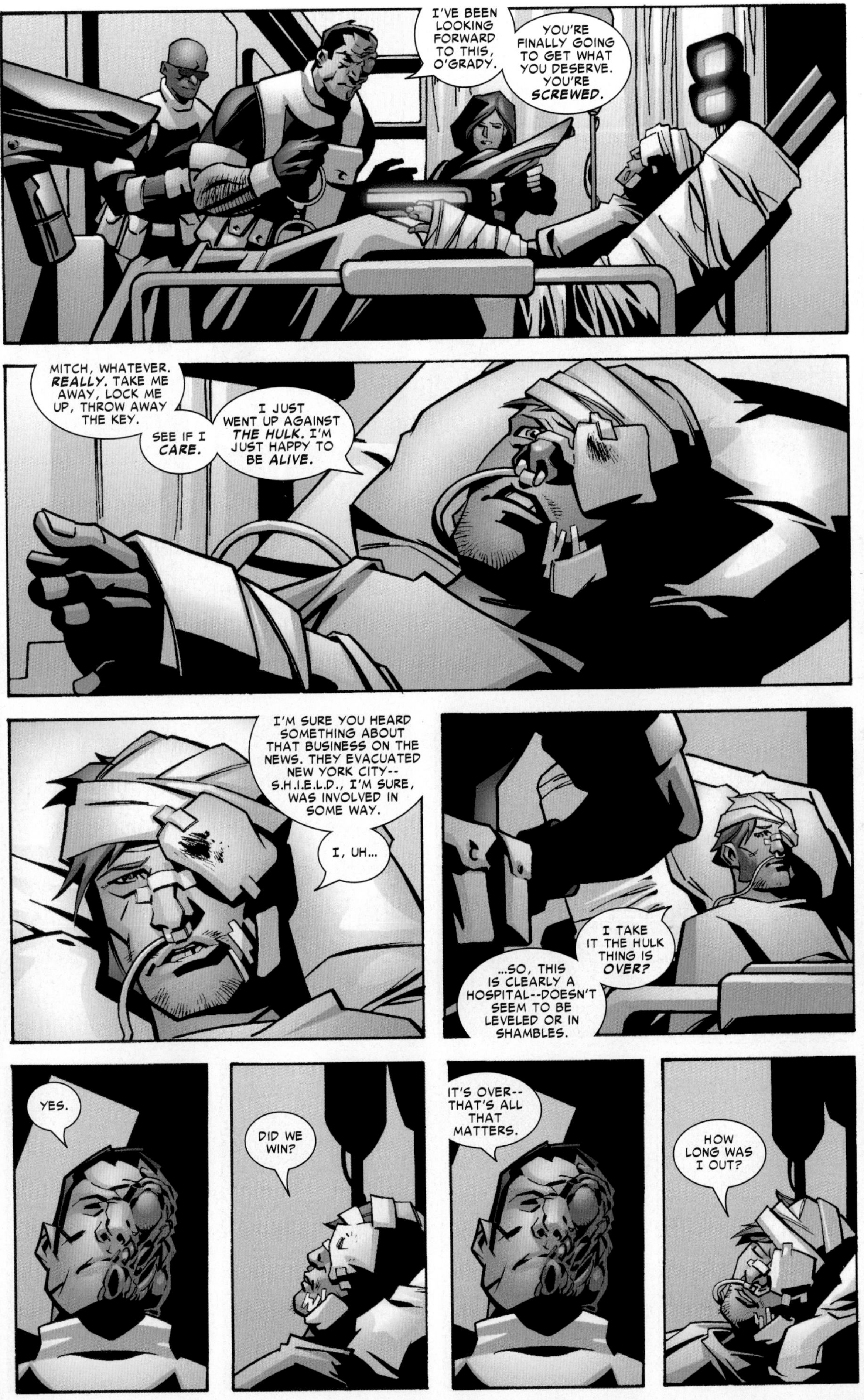
I'VE BEEN LOOKING FORWARD TO THIS, O'GRADY.
YOU'RE FINALLY GOING TO GET WHAT YOU DESERVE. YOU'RE SCREWED.
MITCH, WHATEVER. REALLY. TAKE ME AWAY, LOCK ME UP, THROW AWAY THE KEY.
SEE IF I CARE.
I JUST WENT UP AGAINST THE HULK. I'M JUST HAPPY TO BE ALIVE.
I'M SURE YOU HEARD SOMETHING ABOUT THAT BUSINESS ON THE NEWS. THEY EVACUATED NEW YORK CITY-- S.H.I.E.L.D., I'M SURE, WAS INVOLVED IN SOME WAY.
I, UH...
...SO, THIS IS CLEARLY A HOSPITAL--DOESN'T SEEM TO BE LEVELED OR IN SHAMBLES.
I TAKE IT THE HULK THING IS OVER?
YES.
DID WE WIN?
IT'S OVER-- THAT'S ALL THAT MATTERS.
HOW LONG WAS I OUT?

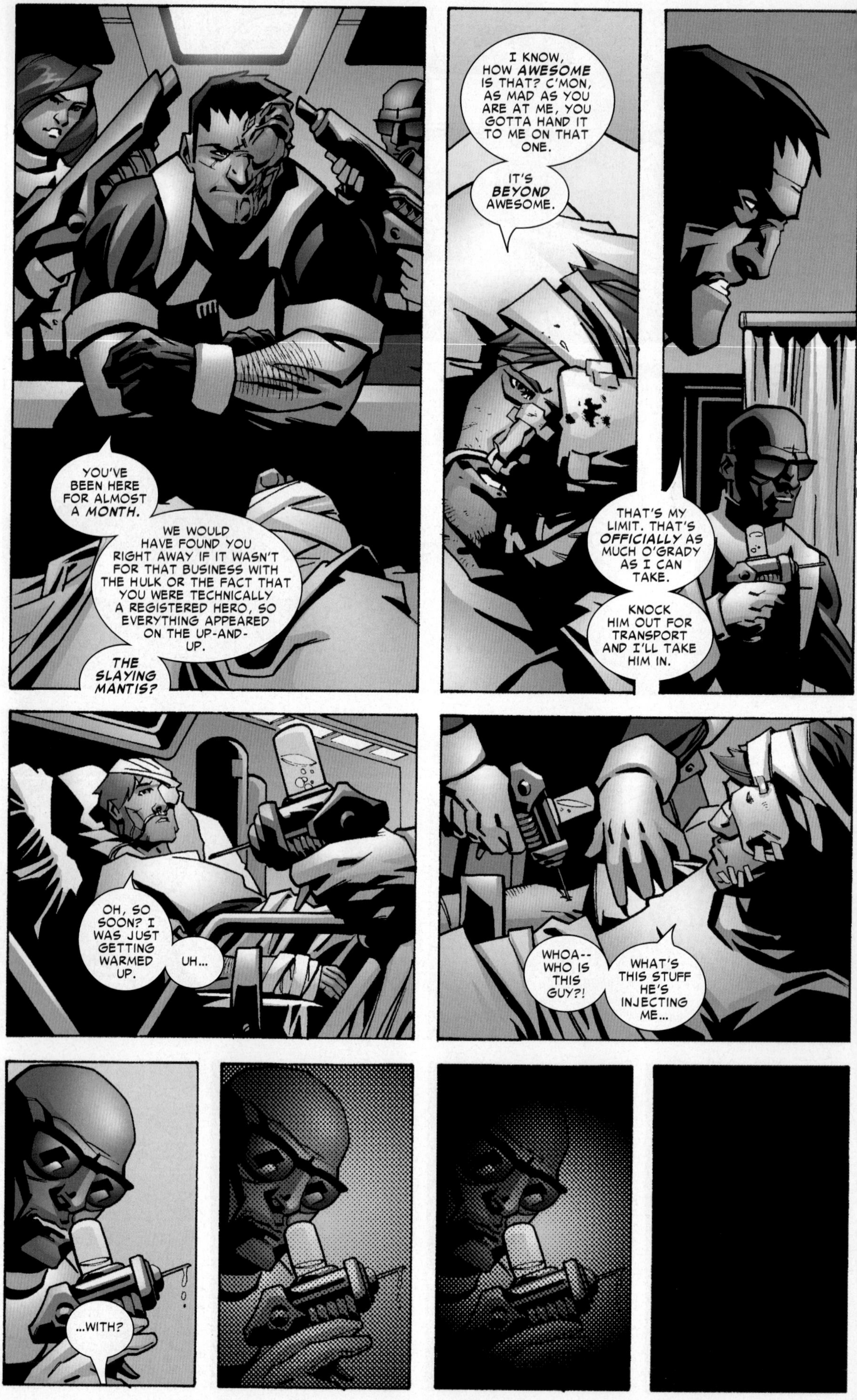
YOU'VE BEEN HERE FOR ALMOST A MONTH.
WE WOULD HAVE FOUND YOU RIGHT AWAY IF IT WASN'T FOR THAT BUSINESS WITH THE HULK OR THE FACT THAT YOU WERE TECHNICALLY A REGISTERED HERO, SO EVERYTHING APPEARED ON THE UP-AND-UP.
THE SLAYING MANTIS?
I KNOW, HOW AWESOME IS THAT? C'MON, AS MAD AS YOU ARE AT ME, YOU GOTTA HAND IT TO ME ON THAT ONE.
IT'S BEYOND AWESOME.
THAT'S MY LIMIT. THAT'S OFFICIALLY AS MUCH O'GRADY AS I CAN TAKE.
KNOCK HIM OUT FOR TRANSPORT AND I'LL TAKE HIM IN.
OH, SO SOON? I WAS JUST GETTING WARMED UP.
UH...
WHOA-- WHO IS THIS GUY?!
WHAT'S THIS STUFF HE'S INJECTING ME...
...WITH?

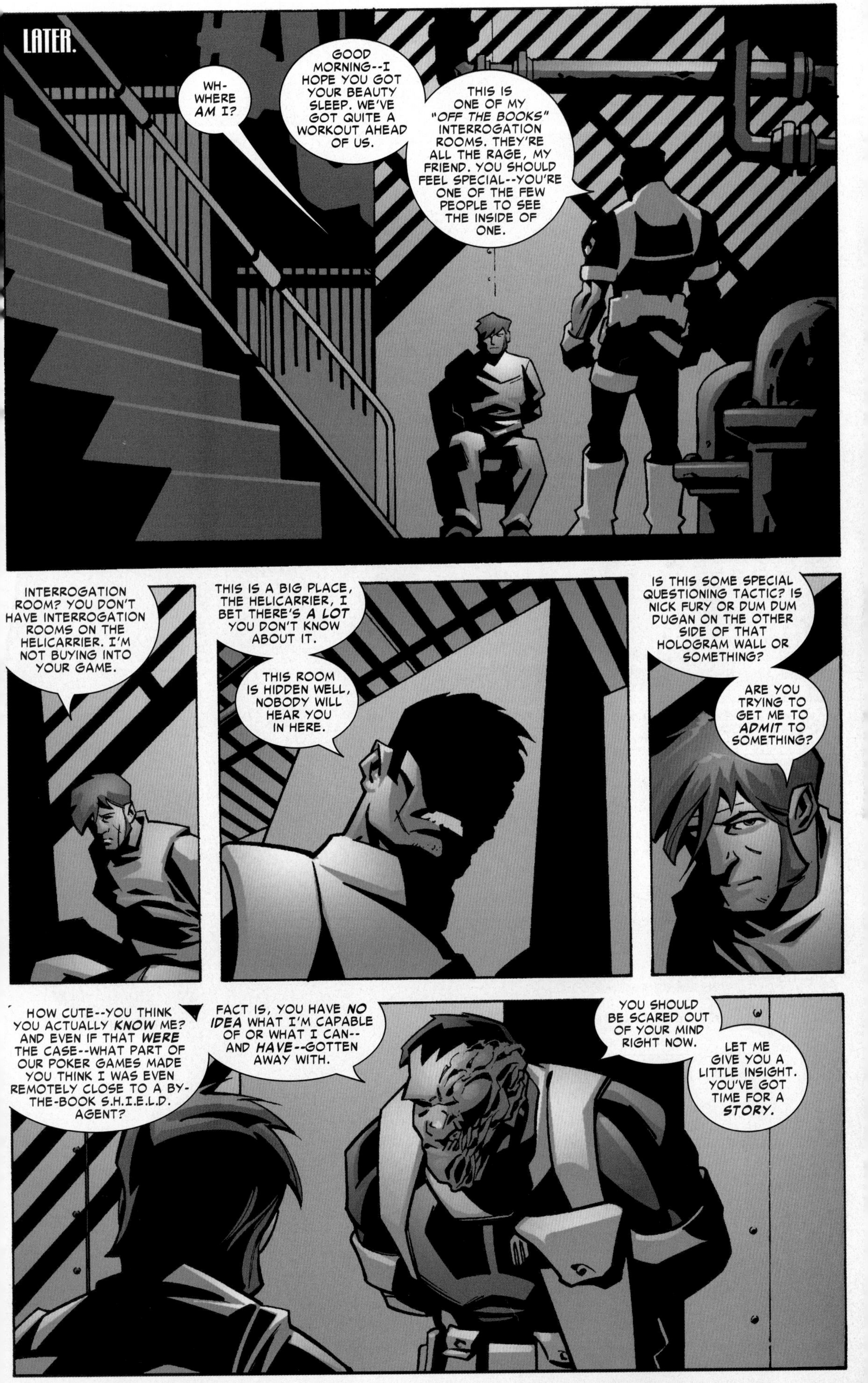

LATER.
WH-WHERE AM I?
GOOD MORNING--I HOPE YOU GOT YOUR BEAUTY SLEEP. WE'VE GOT QUITE A WORKOUT AHEAD OF US.
THIS IS ONE OF MY "OFF THE BOOKS" INTERROGATION ROOMS. THEY'RE ALL THE RAGE, MY FRIEND. YOU SHOULD FEEL SPECIAL--YOU'RE ONE OF THE FEW PEOPLE TO SEE THE INSIDE OF ONE.
INTERROGATION ROOM? YOU DON'T HAVE INTERROGATION ROOMS ON THE HELICARRIER. I'M NOT BUYING INTO YOUR GAME.
THIS IS A BIG PLACE, THE HELICARRIER, I BET THERE'S A LOT YOU DON'T KNOW ABOUT IT.
THIS ROOM IS HIDDEN WELL, NOBODY WILL HEAR YOU IN HERE.
IS THIS SOME SPECIAL QUESTIONING TACTIC? IS NICK FURY OR DUM DUM DUGAN ON THE OTHER SIDE OF THAT HOLOGRAM WALL OR SOMETHING?
ARE YOU TRYING TO GET ME TO ADMIT TO SOMETHING?
HOW CUTE--YOU THINK YOU ACTUALLY KNOW ME? AND EVEN IF THAT WERE THE CASE--WHAT PART OF OUR POKER GAMES MADE YOU THINK I WAS EVEN REMOTELY CLOSE TO A BY-THE-BOOK S.H.I.E.L.D. AGENT?
FACT IS, YOU HAVE NO IDEA WHAT I'M CAPABLE OF OR WHAT I CAN--AND HAVE--GOTTEN AWAY WITH.
YOU SHOULD BE SCARED OUT OF YOUR MIND RIGHT NOW.
LET ME GIVE YOU A LITTLE INSIGHT. YOU'VE GOT TIME FOR A STORY.

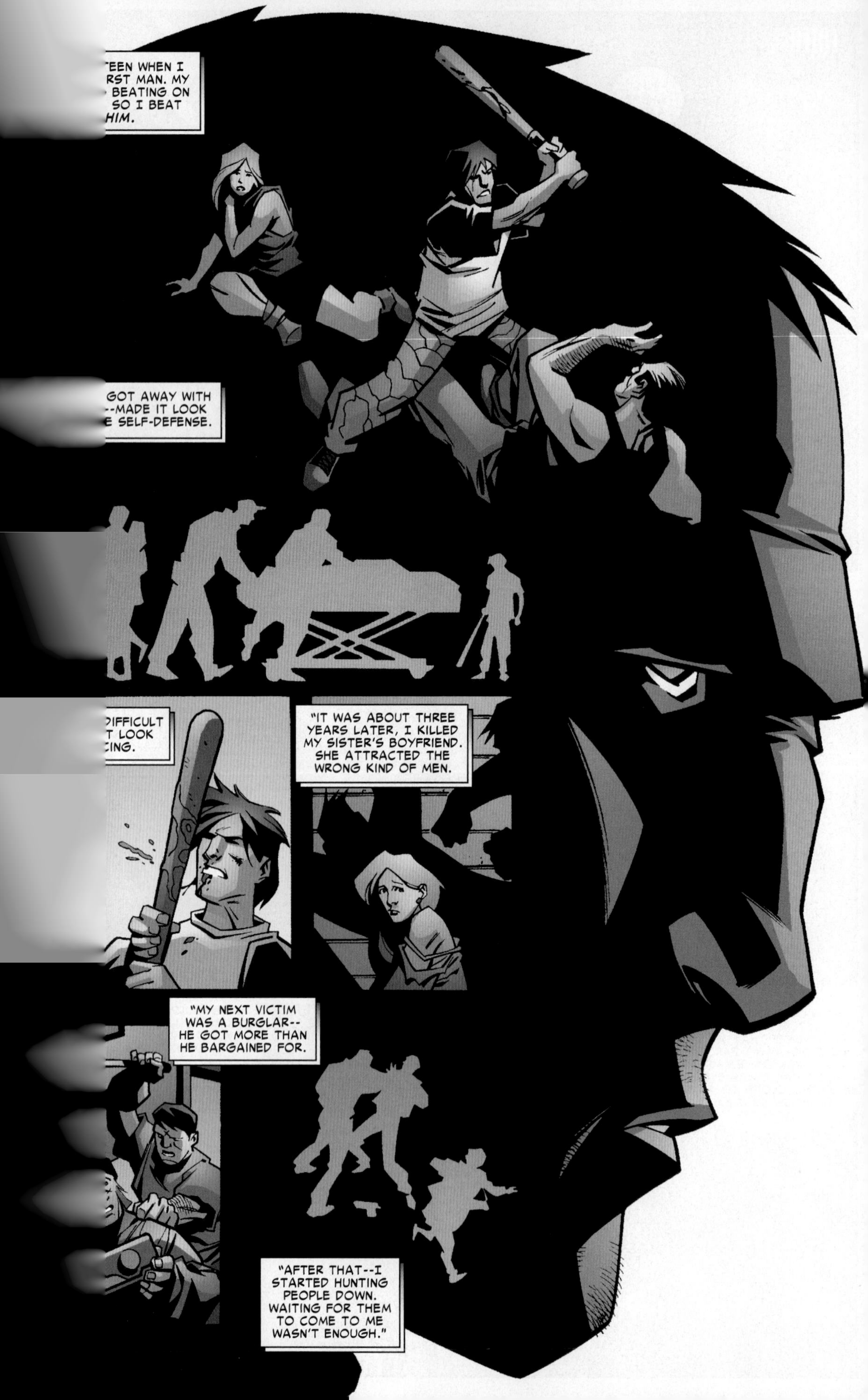
TEEN WHEN I RST MAN. MY BEATING ON SO I BEAT HIM.
GOT AWAY WITH --MADE IT LOOK SELF-DEFENSE.
DIFFICULT T LOOK CING.
"IT WAS ABOUT THREE YEARS LATER, I KILLED MY SISTER'S BOYFRIEND. SHE ATTRACTED THE WRONG KIND OF MEN.
"MY NEXT VICTIM WAS A BURGLAR-- HE GOT MORE THAN HE BARGAINED FOR.
"AFTER THAT--I STARTED HUNTING PEOPLE DOWN. WAITING FOR THEM TO COME TO ME WASN'T ENOUGH."

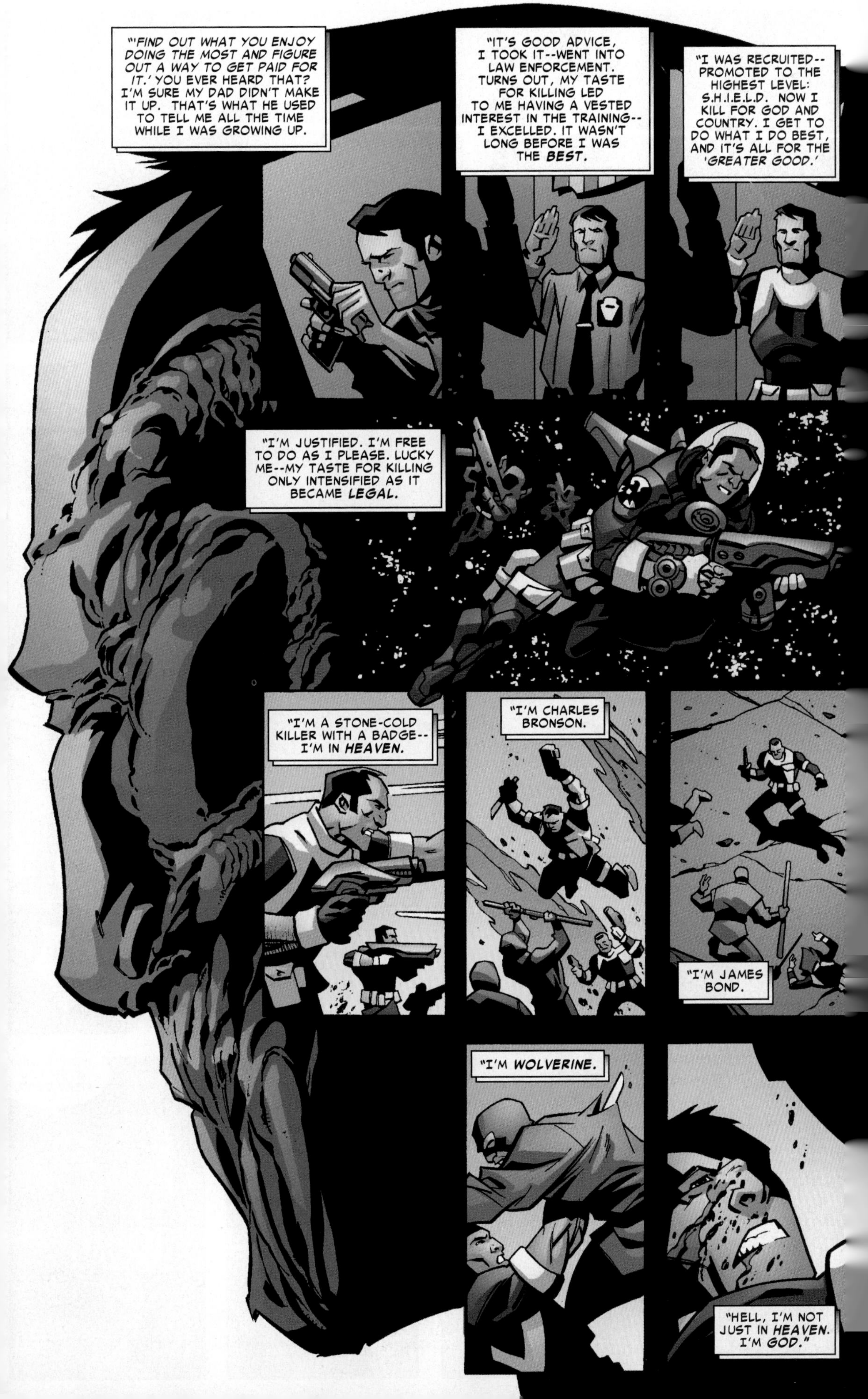
"'FIND OUT WHAT YOU ENJOY DOING THE MOST AND FIGURE OUT A WAY TO GET PAID FOR IT.' YOU EVER HEARD THAT? I'M SURE MY DAD DIDN'T MAKE IT UP. THAT'S WHAT HE USED TO TELL ME ALL THE TIME WHILE I WAS GROWING UP.
"IT'S GOOD ADVICE, I TOOK IT--WENT INTO LAW ENFORCEMENT. TURNS OUT, MY TASTE FOR KILLING LED TO ME HAVING A VESTED INTEREST IN THE TRAINING--I EXCELLED. IT WASN'T LONG BEFORE I WAS THE BEST.
"I WAS RECRUITED--PROMOTED TO THE HIGHEST LEVEL: S.H.I.E.L.D. NOW I KILL FOR GOD AND COUNTRY. I GET TO DO WHAT I DO BEST, AND IT'S ALL FOR THE 'GREATER GOOD.'
"I'M JUSTIFIED. I'M FREE TO DO AS I PLEASE. LUCKY ME--MY TASTE FOR KILLING ONLY INTENSIFIED AS IT BECAME LEGAL.
"I'M A STONE-COLD KILLER WITH A BADGE--I'M IN HEAVEN.
"I'M CHARLES BRONSON.
"I'M JAMES BOND.
"I'M WOLVERINE.
"HELL, I'M NOT JUST IN HEAVEN. I'M GOD."

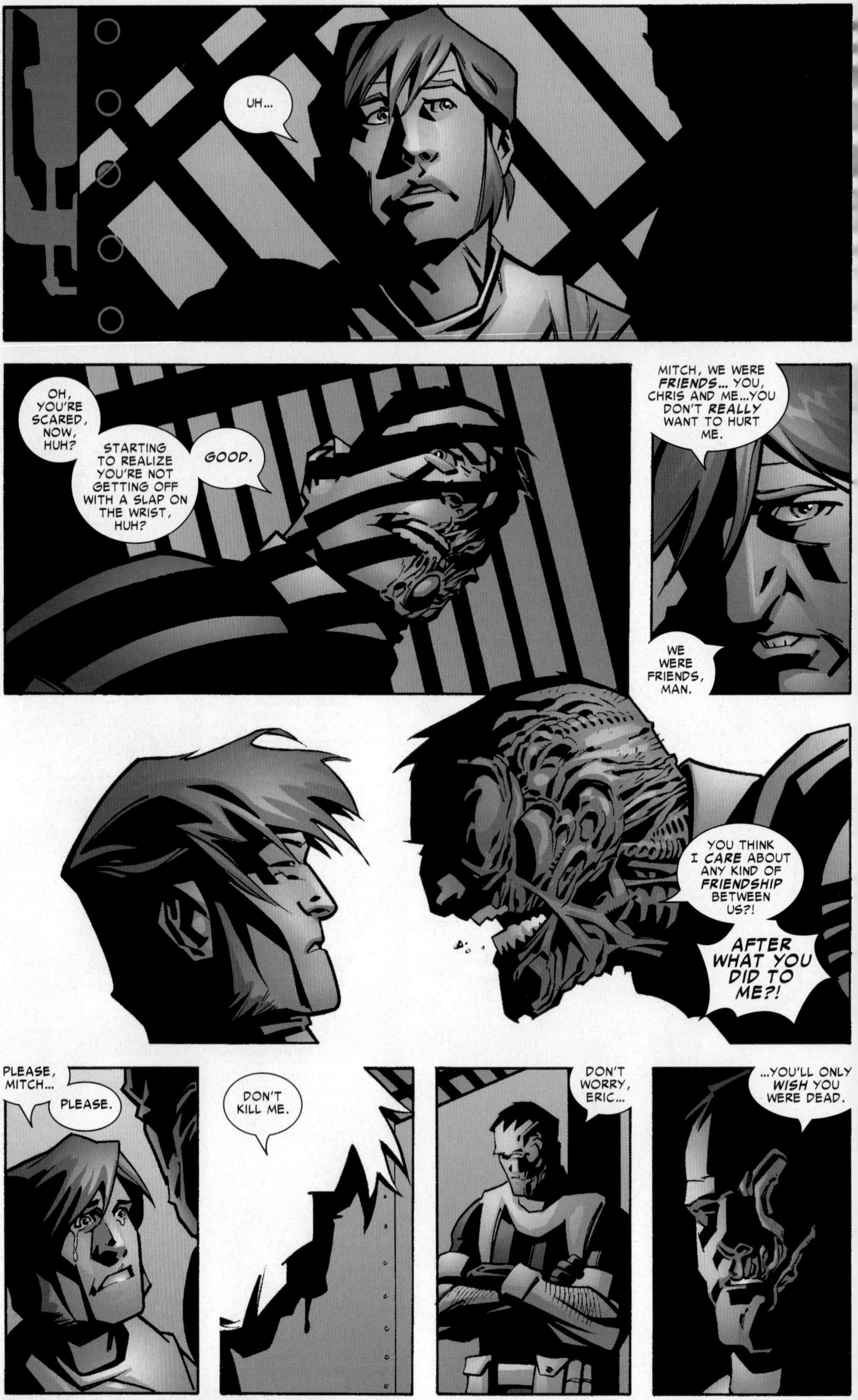
UH...
OH, YOU'RE SCARED, NOW, HUH?
STARTING TO REALIZE YOU'RE NOT GETTING OFF WITH A SLAP ON THE WRIST, HUH?
GOOD.
MITCH, WE WERE FRIENDS... YOU, CHRIS AND ME...YOU DON'T REALLY WANT TO HURT ME.
WE WERE FRIENDS, MAN.
YOU THINK I CARE ABOUT ANY KIND OF FRIENDSHIP BETWEEN US?!
AFTER WHAT YOU DID TO ME?!
PLEASE, MITCH...
PLEASE.
DON'T KILL ME.
DON'T WORRY, ERIC...
...YOU'LL ONLY WISH YOU WERE DEAD.

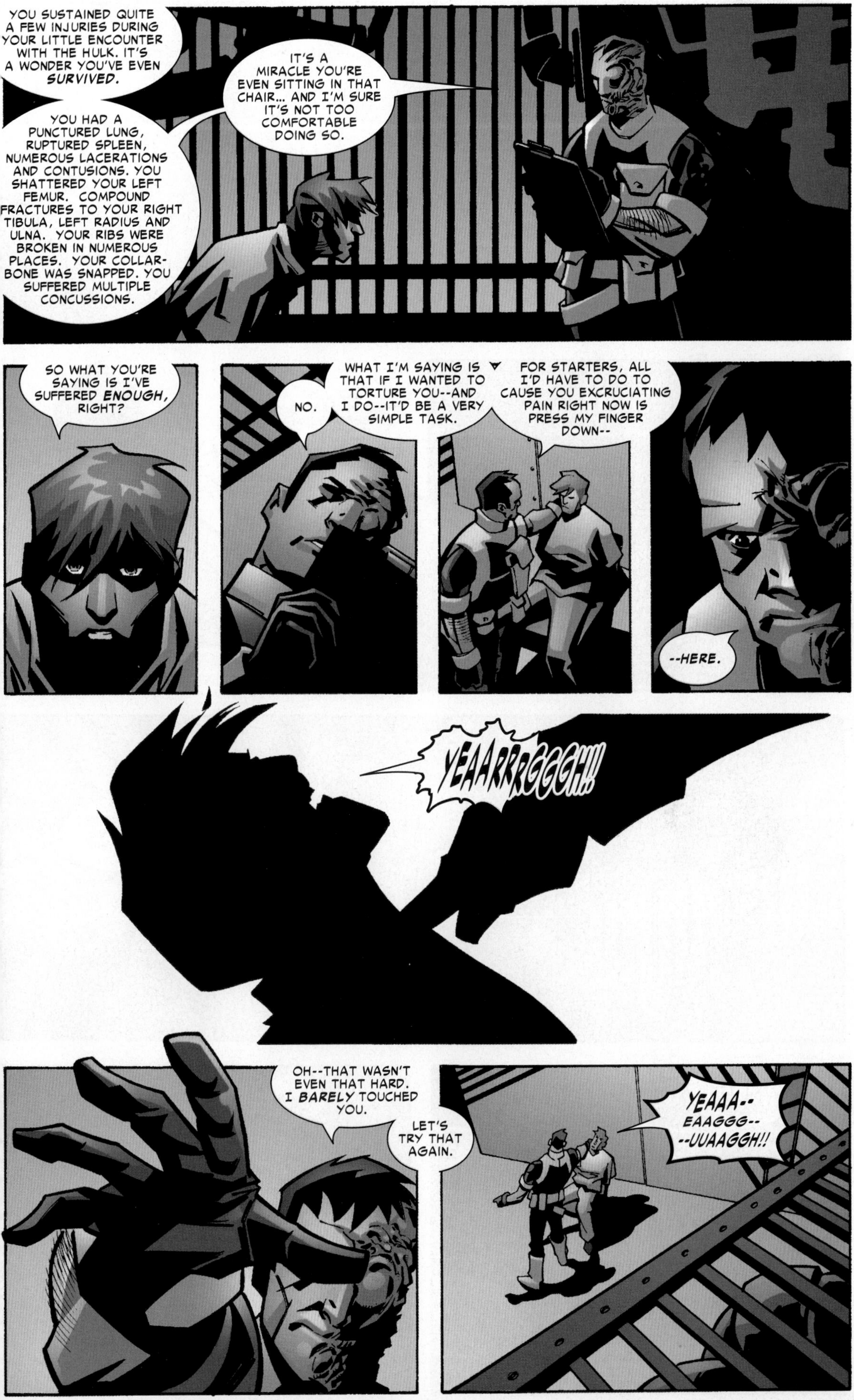
YOU SUSTAINED QUITE A FEW INJURIES DURING YOUR LITTLE ENCOUNTER WITH THE HULK. IT'S A WONDER YOU'VE EVEN SURVIVED.
YOU HAD A PUNCTURED LUNG, RUPTURED SPLEEN, NUMEROUS LACERATIONS AND CONTUSIONS. YOU SHATTERED YOUR LEFT FEMUR. COMPOUND FRACTURES TO YOUR RIGHT TIBULA, LEFT RADIUS AND ULNA. YOUR RIBS WERE BROKEN IN NUMEROUS PLACES. YOUR COLLAR-BONE WAS SNAPPED. YOU SUFFERED MULTIPLE CONCUSSIONS.
IT'S A MIRACLE YOU'RE EVEN SITTING IN THAT CHAIR... AND I'M SURE IT'S NOT TOO COMFORTABLE DOING SO.
SO WHAT YOU'RE SAYING IS I'VE SUFFERED ENOUGH, RIGHT?
NO.
WHAT I'M SAYING IS THAT IF I WANTED TO TORTURE YOU--AND I DO--IT'D BE A VERY SIMPLE TASK.
FOR STARTERS, ALL I'D HAVE TO DO TO CAUSE YOU EXCRUCIATING PAIN RIGHT NOW IS PRESS MY FINGER DOWN--
--HERE.
YEAARRRGGGH!!
OH--THAT WASN'T EVEN THAT HARD. I BARELY TOUCHED YOU.
LET'S TRY THAT AGAIN.
YEAAA--
EAAGGG--
--UUAAGGH!!

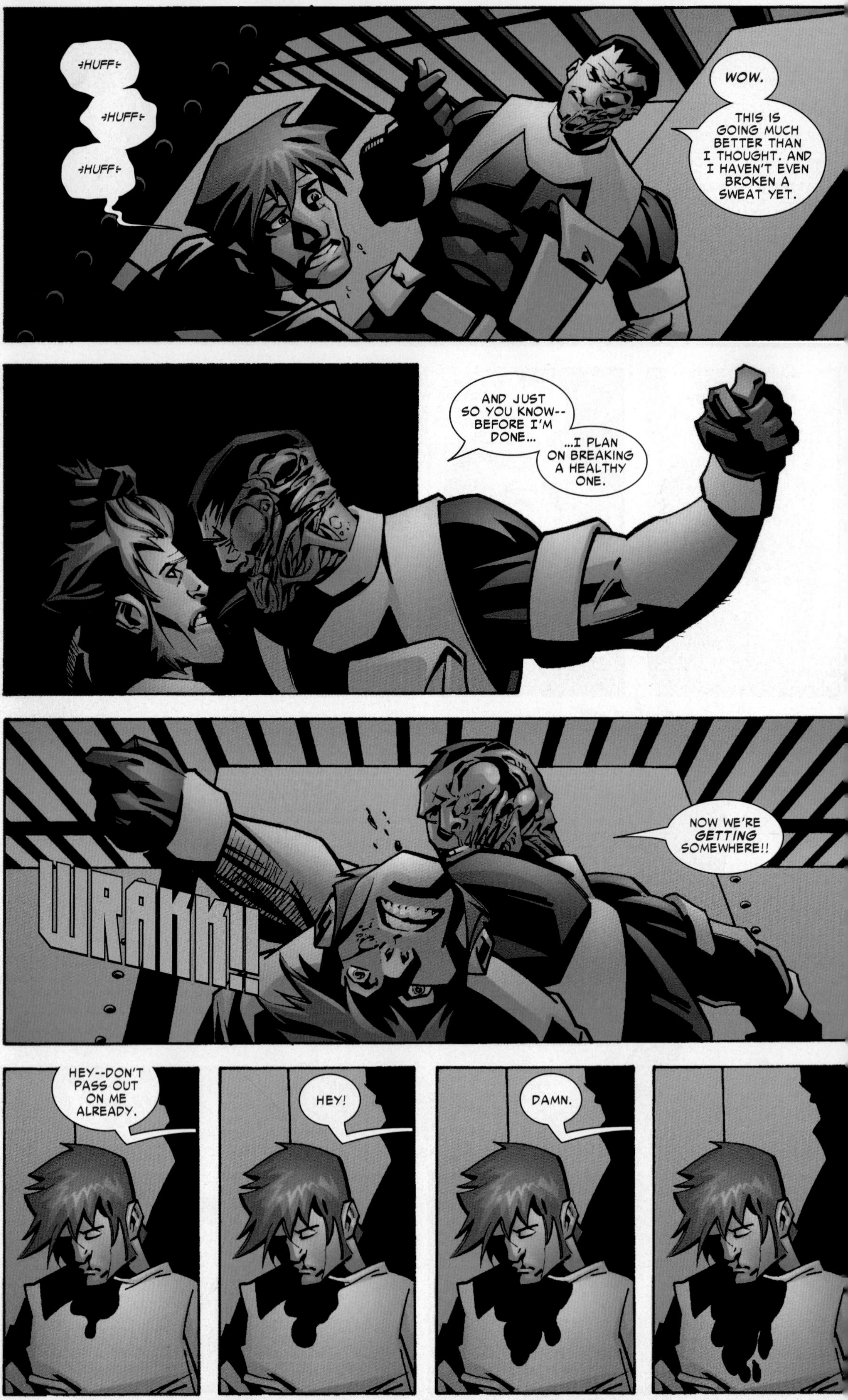

-HUFF-
-HUFF-
-HUFF-
WOW.
THIS IS GOING MUCH BETTER THAN I THOUGHT. AND I HAVEN'T EVEN BROKEN A SWEAT YET.
AND JUST SO YOU KNOW-- BEFORE I'M DONE...
...I PLAN ON BREAKING A HEALTHY ONE.
WRAKK!!
NOW WE'RE GETTING SOMEWHERE!!
HEY--DON'T PASS OUT ON ME ALREADY.
HEY!
DAMN.

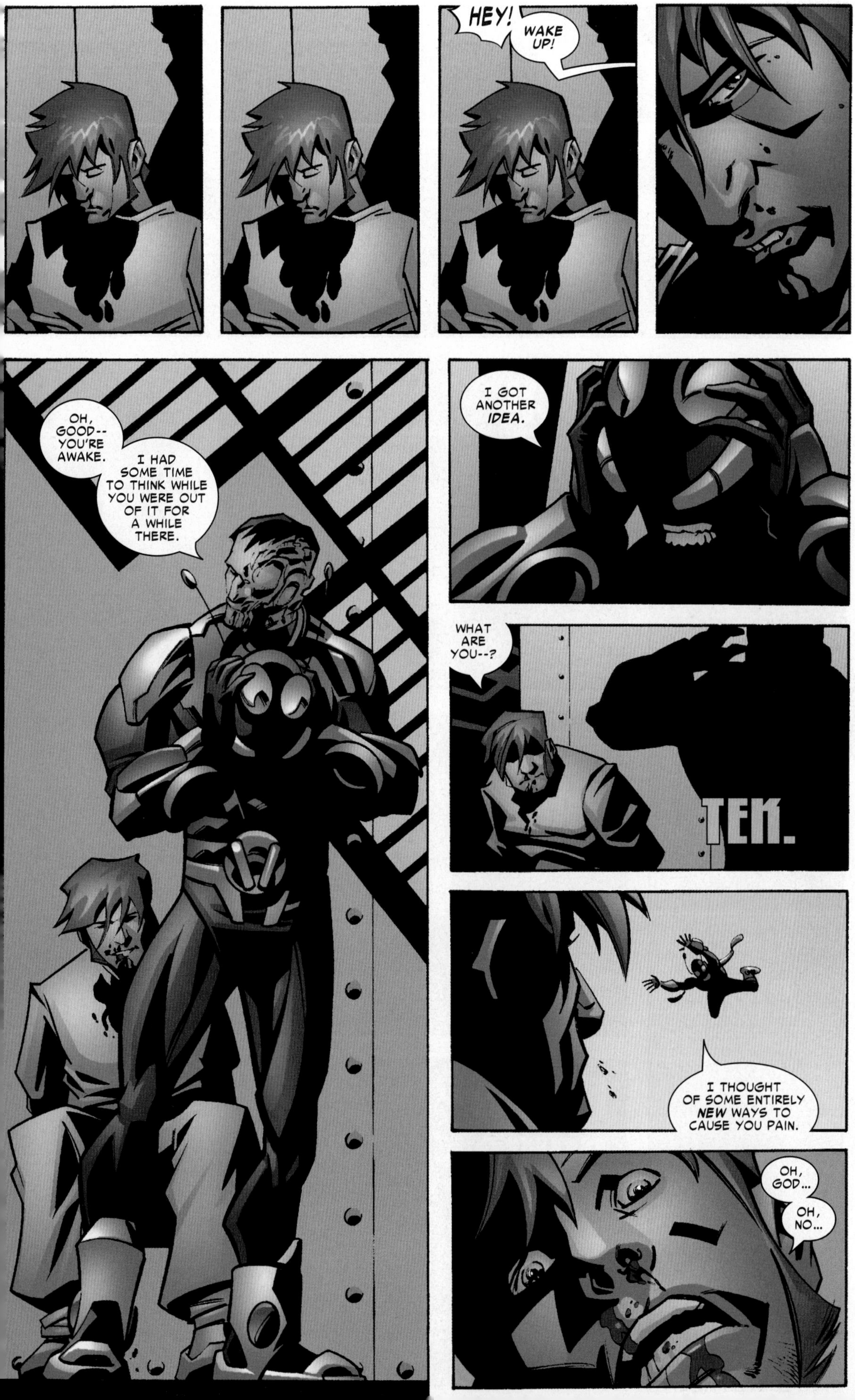
HEY!
WAKE UP!
OH, GOOD-- YOU'RE AWAKE.
I HAD SOME TIME TO THINK WHILE YOU WERE OUT OF IT FOR A WHILE THERE.
I GOT ANOTHER IDEA.
WHAT ARE YOU--?
TEK.
I THOUGHT OF SOME ENTIRELY NEW WAYS TO CAUSE YOU PAIN.
OH, GOD...
OH, NO...

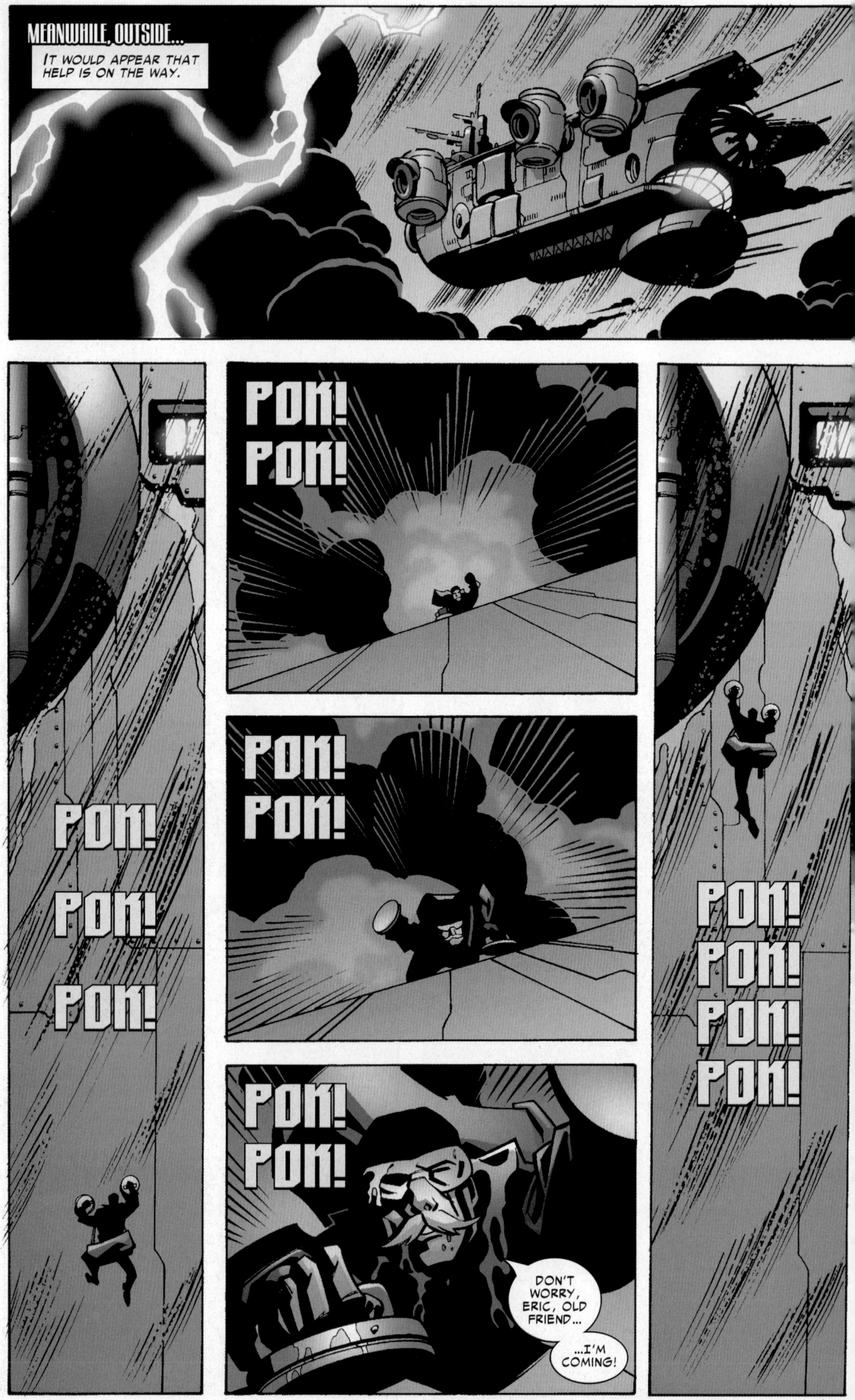
MEANWHILE, OUTSIDE...
IT WOULD APPEAR THAT HELP IS ON THE WAY.
POK! POK! POK!
POK! POK!
POK! POK!
POK! POK!
DON'T WORRY, ERIC, OLD FRIEND...
...I'M COMING!
POK! POK! POK! POK!

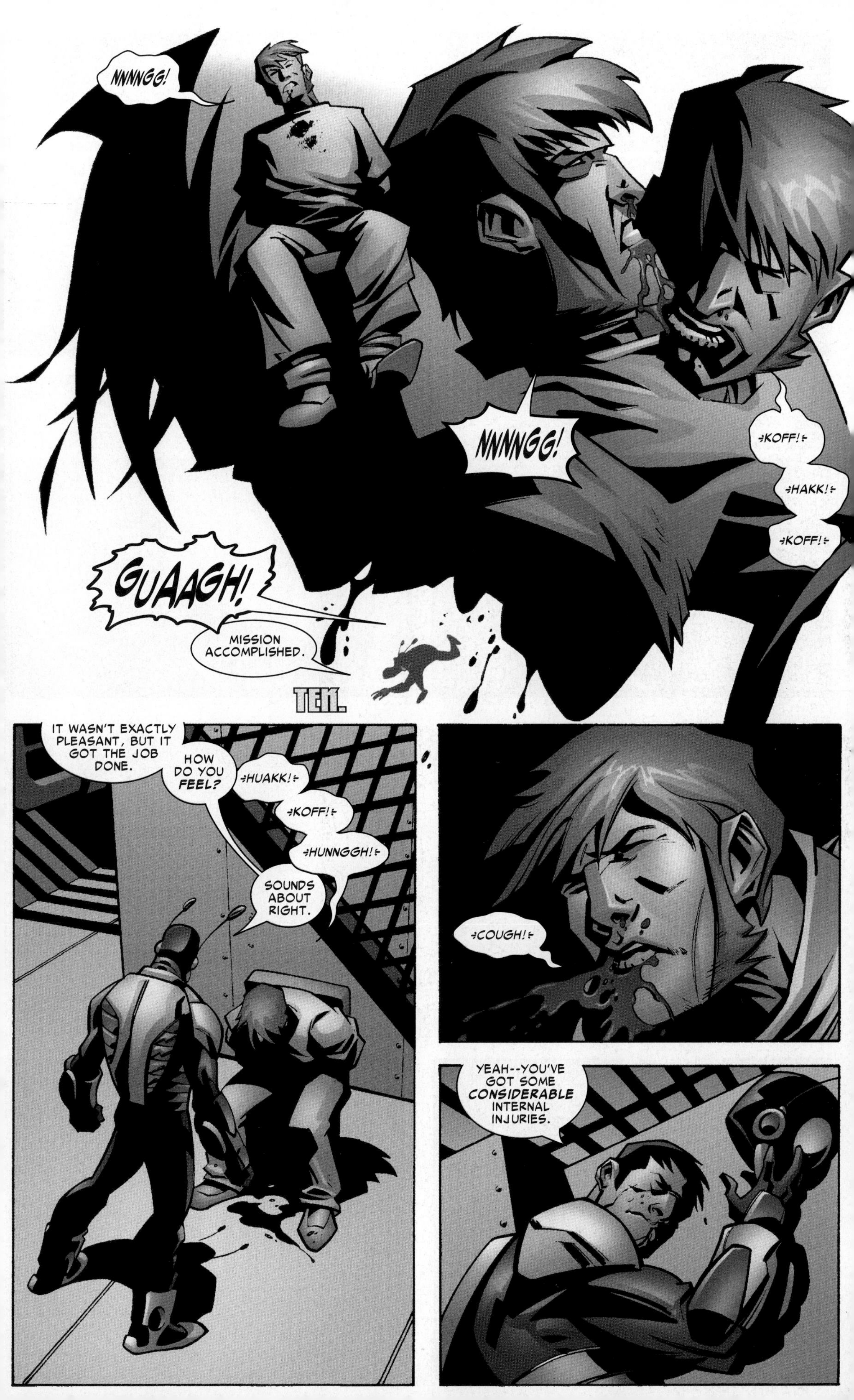
NNNNGG!
NNNNGG!
KOFF!
HAKK!
KOFF!
GUAAGH!
MISSION ACCOMPLISHED.
TEN.
IT WASN'T EXACTLY PLEASANT, BUT IT GOT THE JOB DONE.
HOW DO YOU FEEL?
HUAKK!
KOFF!
HUNNGGH!
SOUNDS ABOUT RIGHT.
COUGH!
YEAH--YOU'VE GOT SOME CONSIDERABLE INTERNAL INJURIES.

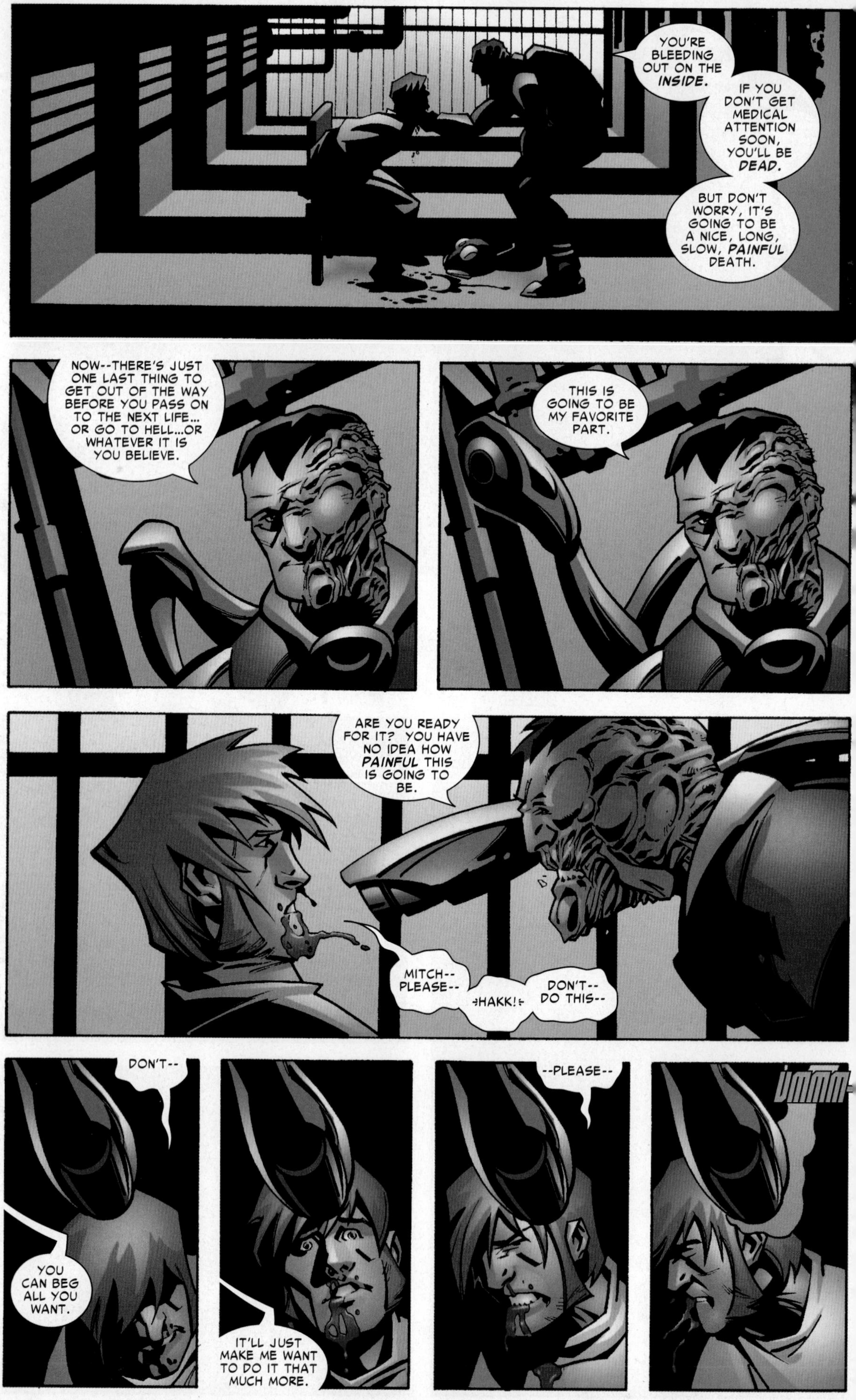
YOU'RE BLEEDING OUT ON THE *INSIDE.*
IF YOU DON'T GET MEDICAL ATTENTION SOON, YOU'LL BE *DEAD.*
BUT DON'T WORRY, IT'S GOING TO BE A NICE, LONG, SLOW, *PAINFUL* DEATH.
NOW--THERE'S JUST ONE LAST THING TO GET OUT OF THE WAY BEFORE YOU PASS ON TO THE NEXT LIFE... OR GO TO HELL...OR WHATEVER IT IS YOU BELIEVE.
THIS IS GOING TO BE MY FAVORITE PART.
ARE YOU READY FOR IT? YOU HAVE NO IDEA HOW *PAINFUL* THIS IS GOING TO BE.
MITCH-- PLEASE--
HAKK!
DON'T-- DO THIS--
DON'T--
YOU CAN BEG ALL YOU WANT.
IT'LL JUST MAKE ME WANT TO DO IT THAT MUCH MORE.
--PLEASE--
VMMM

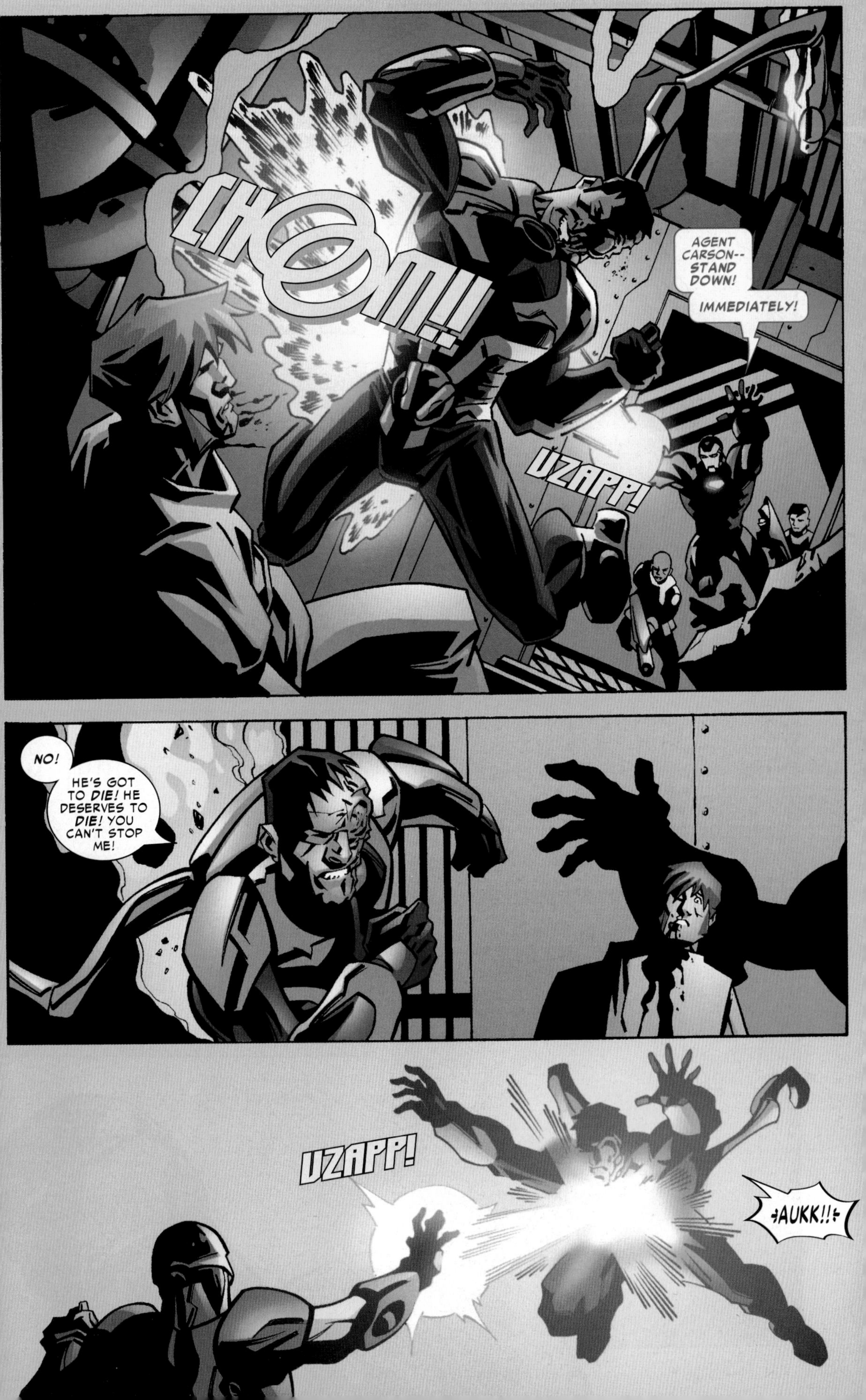
CHOOM!!
AGENT CARSON-- STAND DOWN!
IMMEDIATELY!
UZAPP!
NO!
HE'S GOT TO DIE! HE DESERVES TO DIE! YOU CAN'T STOP ME!
UZAPP!
AUKK!!

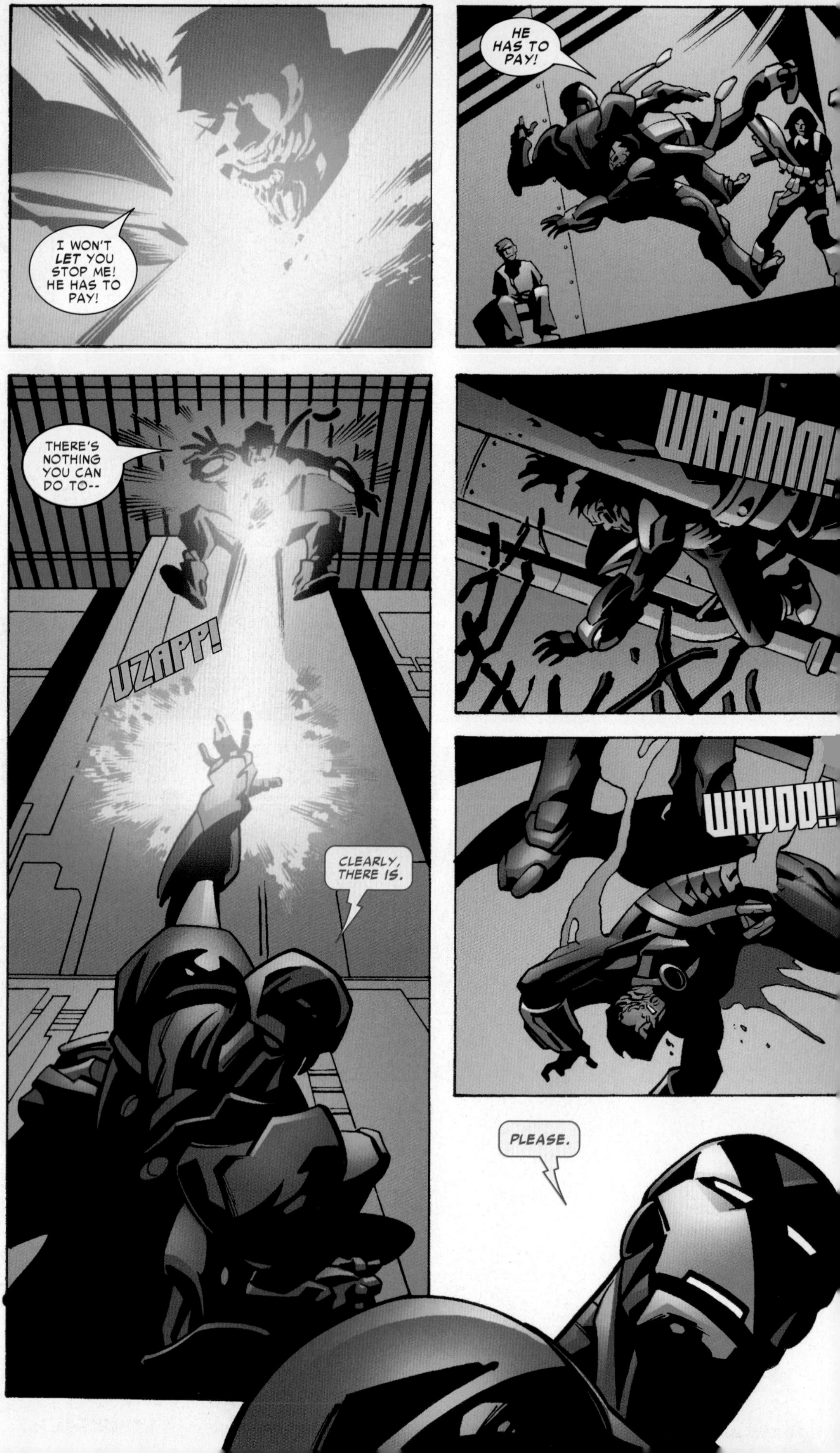
I WON'T LET YOU STOP ME! HE HAS TO PAY!
HE HAS TO PAY!
THERE'S NOTHING YOU CAN DO TO--
UZAPP!
CLEARLY, THERE IS.
WRAMM!
WHUDD!!
PLEASE.

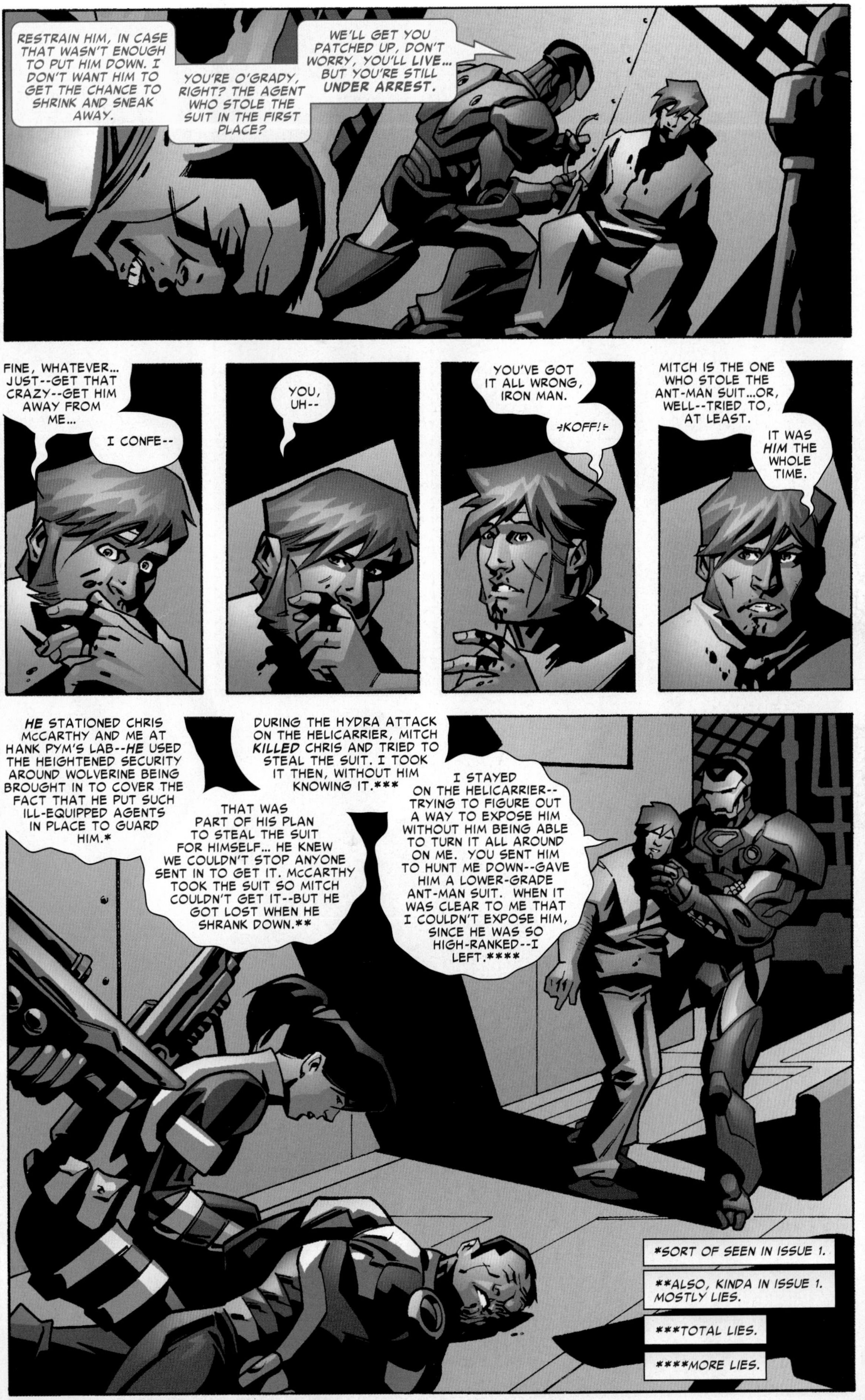

RESTRAIN HIM, IN CASE THAT WASN'T ENOUGH TO PUT HIM DOWN. I DON'T WANT HIM TO GET THE CHANCE TO SHRINK AND SNEAK AWAY.
YOU'RE O'GRADY, RIGHT? THE AGENT WHO STOLE THE SUIT IN THE FIRST PLACE?
WE'LL GET YOU PATCHED UP, DON'T WORRY, YOU'LL LIVE... BUT YOU'RE STILL UNDER ARREST.
FINE, WHATEVER... JUST--GET THAT CRAZY--GET HIM AWAY FROM ME...
I CONFE--
YOU, UH--
YOU'VE GOT IT ALL WRONG, IRON MAN.
KOFF!
MITCH IS THE ONE WHO STOLE THE ANT-MAN SUIT...OR, WELL--TRIED TO, AT LEAST.
IT WAS HIM THE WHOLE TIME.
HE STATIONED CHRIS McCARTHY AND ME AT HANK PYM'S LAB--HE USED THE HEIGHTENED SECURITY AROUND WOLVERINE BEING BROUGHT IN TO COVER THE FACT THAT HE PUT SUCH ILL-EQUIPPED AGENTS IN PLACE TO GUARD HIM.*
THAT WAS PART OF HIS PLAN TO STEAL THE SUIT FOR HIMSELF... HE KNEW WE COULDN'T STOP ANYONE SENT IN TO GET IT. McCARTHY TOOK THE SUIT SO MITCH COULDN'T GET IT--BUT HE GOT LOST WHEN HE SHRANK DOWN.**
DURING THE HYDRA ATTACK ON THE HELICARRIER, MITCH KILLED CHRIS AND TRIED TO STEAL THE SUIT. I TOOK IT THEN, WITHOUT HIM KNOWING IT.***
I STAYED ON THE HELICARRIER--TRYING TO FIGURE OUT A WAY TO EXPOSE HIM WITHOUT HIM BEING ABLE TO TURN IT ALL AROUND ON ME. YOU SENT HIM TO HUNT ME DOWN--GAVE HIM A LOWER-GRADE ANT-MAN SUIT. WHEN IT WAS CLEAR TO ME THAT I COULDN'T EXPOSE HIM, SINCE HE WAS SO HIGH-RANKED--I LEFT.****
*SORT OF SEEN IN ISSUE 1.
**ALSO, KINDA IN ISSUE 1. MOSTLY LIES.
***TOTAL LIES.
****MORE LIES.

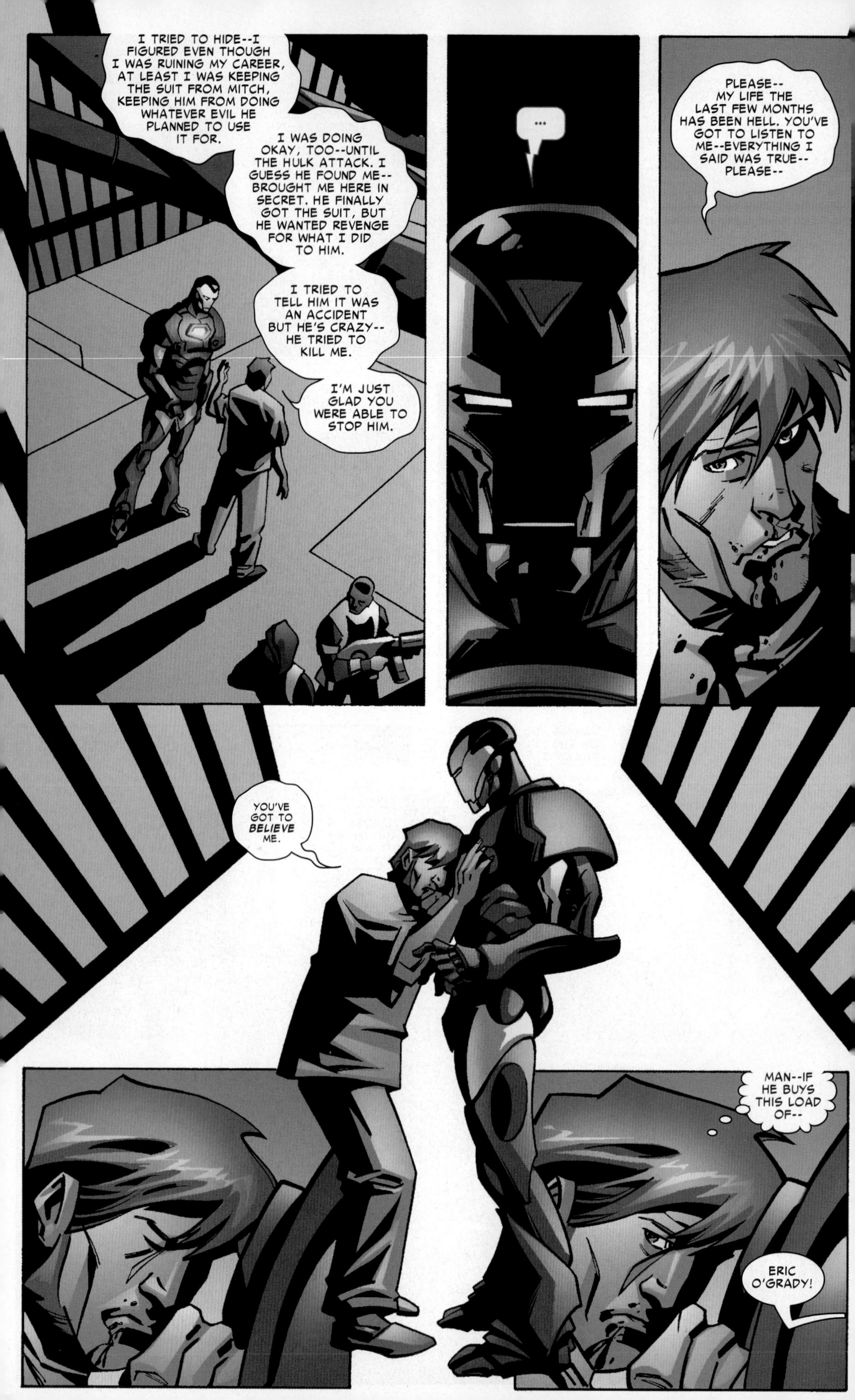
I TRIED TO HIDE--I FIGURED EVEN THOUGH I WAS RUINING MY CAREER, AT LEAST I WAS KEEPING THE SUIT FROM MITCH, KEEPING HIM FROM DOING WHATEVER EVIL HE PLANNED TO USE IT FOR.
I WAS DOING OKAY, TOO--UNTIL THE HULK ATTACK. I GUESS HE FOUND ME--BROUGHT ME HERE IN SECRET. HE FINALLY GOT THE SUIT, BUT HE WANTED REVENGE FOR WHAT I DID TO HIM.
I TRIED TO TELL HIM IT WAS AN ACCIDENT BUT HE'S CRAZY--HE TRIED TO KILL ME.
I'M JUST GLAD YOU WERE ABLE TO STOP HIM.
...
PLEASE--MY LIFE THE LAST FEW MONTHS HAS BEEN HELL. YOU'VE GOT TO LISTEN TO ME--EVERYTHING I SAID WAS TRUE--PLEASE--
YOU'VE GOT TO *BELIEVE* ME.
MAN--IF HE BUYS THIS LOAD OF--
ERIC O'GRADY!

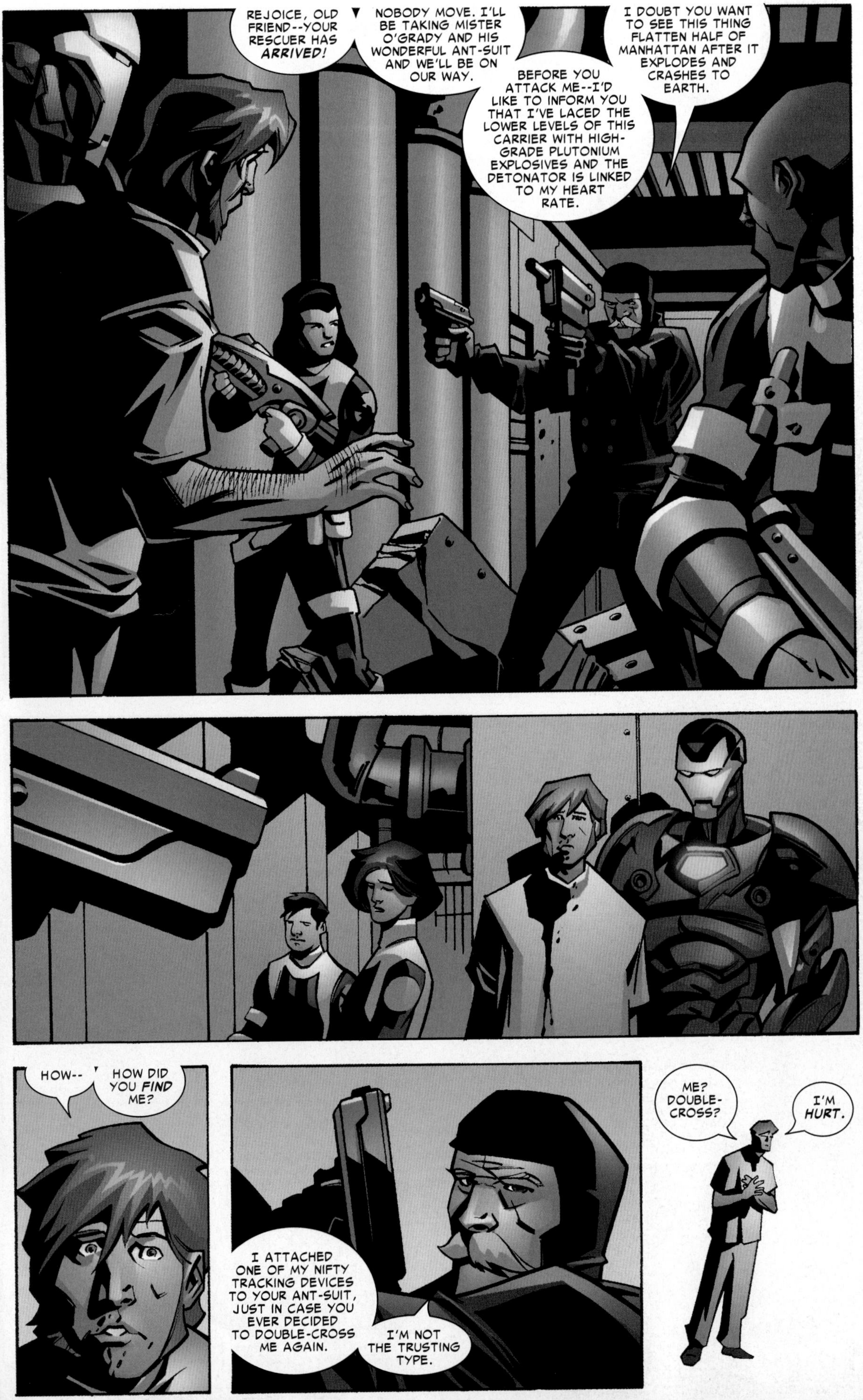
REJOICE, OLD FRIEND--YOUR RESCUER HAS *ARRIVED!*
NOBODY MOVE. I'LL BE TAKING MISTER O'GRADY AND HIS WONDERFUL ANT-SUIT AND WE'LL BE ON OUR WAY.
BEFORE YOU ATTACK ME--I'D LIKE TO INFORM YOU THAT I'VE LACED THE LOWER LEVELS OF THIS CARRIER WITH HIGH-GRADE PLUTONIUM EXPLOSIVES AND THE DETONATOR IS LINKED TO MY HEART RATE.
I DOUBT YOU WANT TO SEE THIS THING FLATTEN HALF OF MANHATTAN AFTER IT EXPLODES AND CRASHES TO EARTH.
HOW--
HOW DID YOU *FIND* ME?
I ATTACHED ONE OF MY NIFTY TRACKING DEVICES TO YOUR ANT-SUIT, JUST IN CASE YOU EVER DECIDED TO DOUBLE-CROSS ME AGAIN.
I'M NOT THE TRUSTING TYPE.
ME? DOUBLE-CROSS?
I'M *HURT.*

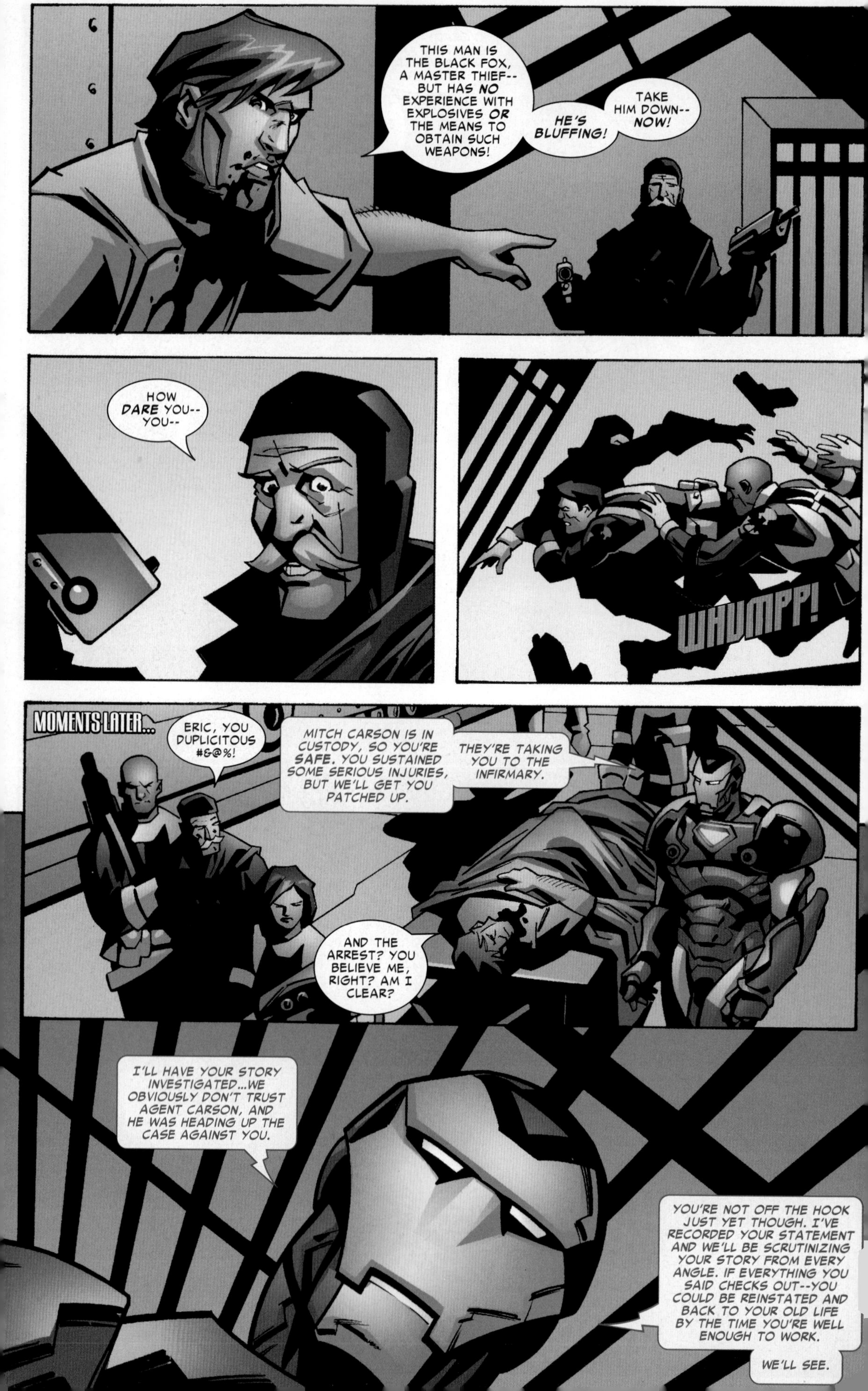
THIS MAN IS THE BLACK FOX, A MASTER THIEF-- BUT HAS NO EXPERIENCE WITH EXPLOSIVES OR THE MEANS TO OBTAIN SUCH WEAPONS!
HE'S BLUFFING!
TAKE HIM DOWN-- NOW!
HOW DARE YOU-- YOU--
WHUMPP!
MOMENTS LATER...
ERIC, YOU DUPLICITOUS #&@%!
MITCH CARSON IS IN CUSTODY, SO YOU'RE SAFE. YOU SUSTAINED SOME SERIOUS INJURIES, BUT WE'LL GET YOU PATCHED UP.
THEY'RE TAKING YOU TO THE INFIRMARY.
AND THE ARREST? YOU BELIEVE ME, RIGHT? AM I CLEAR?
I'LL HAVE YOUR STORY INVESTIGATED...WE OBVIOUSLY DON'T TRUST AGENT CARSON, AND HE WAS HEADING UP THE CASE AGAINST YOU.
YOU'RE NOT OFF THE HOOK JUST YET THOUGH. I'VE RECORDED YOUR STATEMENT AND WE'LL BE SCRUTINIZING YOUR STORY FROM EVERY ANGLE. IF EVERYTHING YOU SAID CHECKS OUT--YOU COULD BE REINSTATED AND BACK TO YOUR OLD LIFE BY THE TIME YOU'RE WELL ENOUGH TO WORK.
WE'LL SEE.

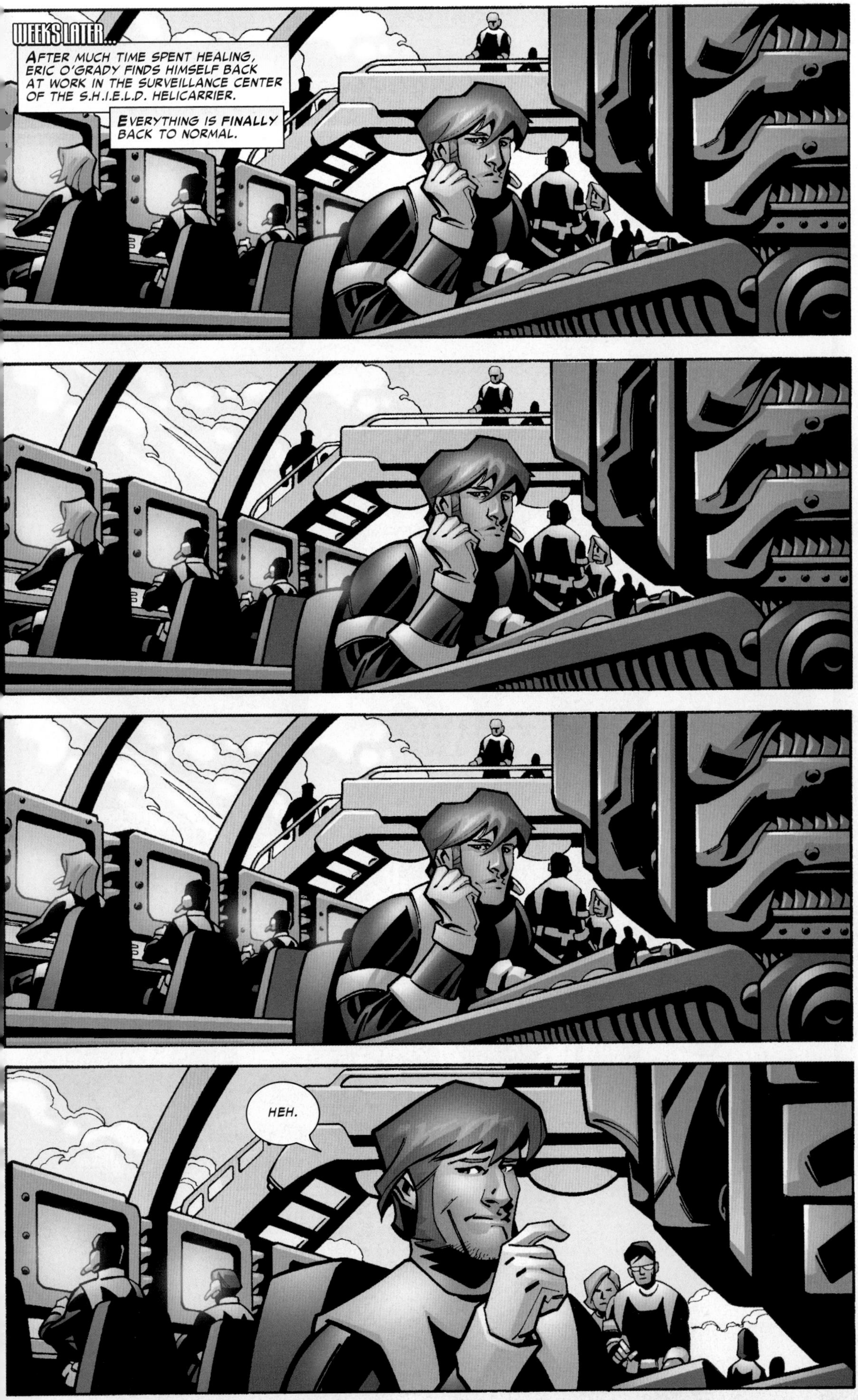
WEEKS LATER...
AFTER MUCH TIME SPENT HEALING, ERIC O'GRADY FINDS HIMSELF BACK AT WORK IN THE SURVEILLANCE CENTER OF THE S.H.I.E.L.D. HELICARRIER.
EVERYTHING IS FINALLY BACK TO NORMAL.
HEH.

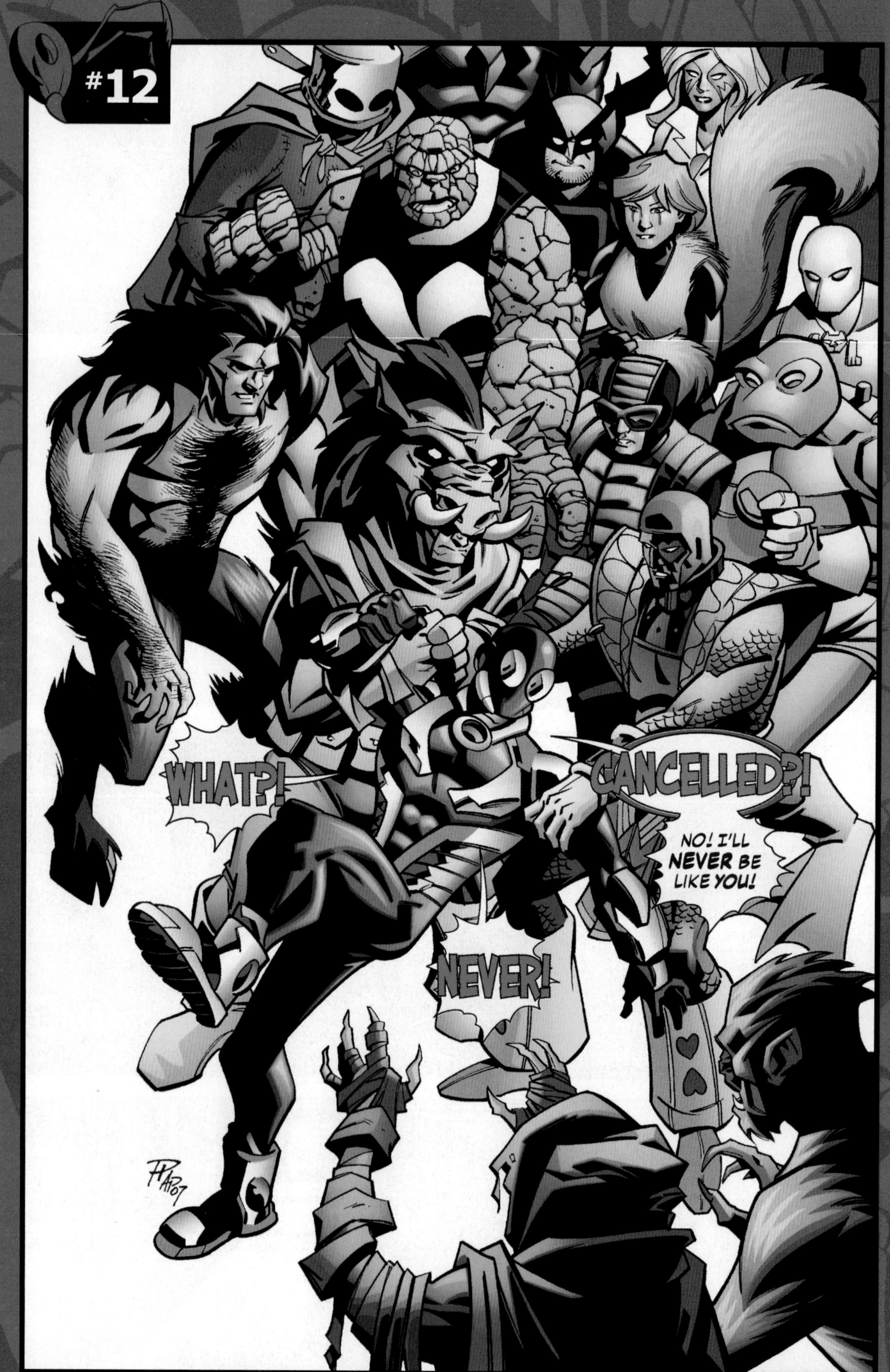
#12
WHAT?!
CANCELLED?!
NO! I'LL NEVER BE LIKE YOU!
NEVER!

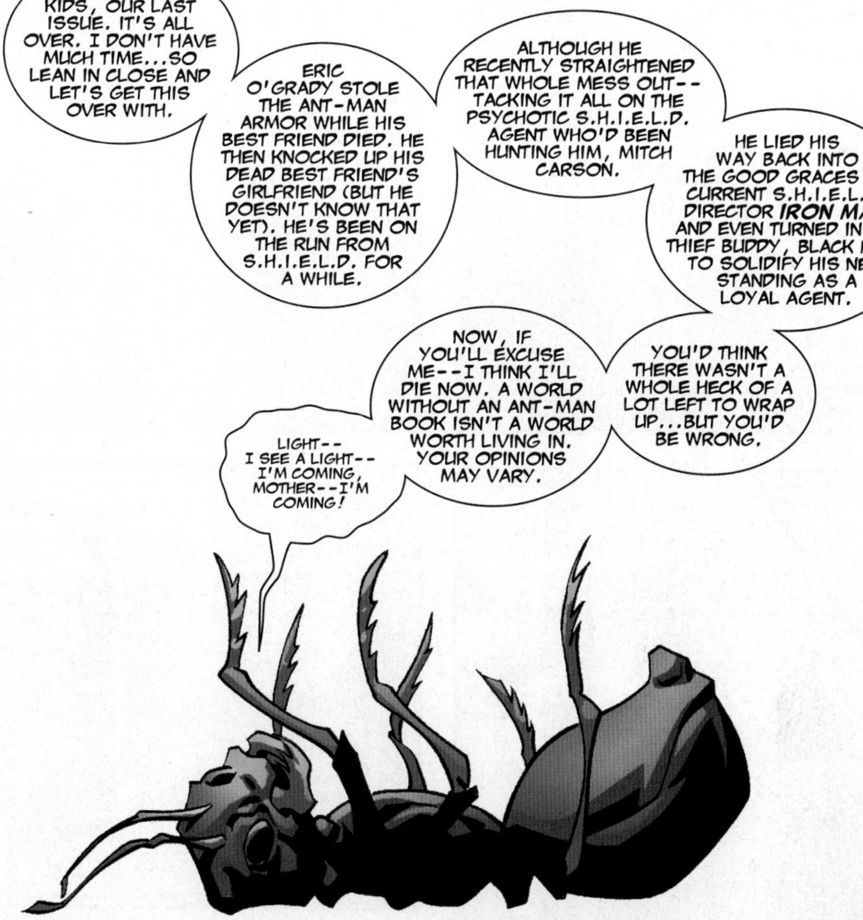
THIS IS IT, KIDS, OUR LAST ISSUE. IT'S ALL OVER. I DON'T HAVE MUCH TIME...SO LEAN IN CLOSE AND LET'S GET THIS OVER WITH.
ERIC O'GRADY STOLE THE ANT-MAN ARMOR WHILE HIS BEST FRIEND DIED. HE THEN KNOCKED UP HIS DEAD BEST FRIEND'S GIRLFRIEND (BUT HE DOESN'T KNOW THAT YET). HE'S BEEN ON THE RUN FROM S.H.I.E.L.D. FOR A WHILE.
ALTHOUGH HE RECENTLY STRAIGHTENED THAT WHOLE MESS OUT--TACKING IT ALL ON THE PSYCHOTIC S.H.I.E.L.D. AGENT WHO'D BEEN HUNTING HIM, MITCH CARSON.
HE LIED HIS WAY BACK INTO THE GOOD GRACES OF CURRENT S.H.I.E.L.D. DIRECTOR IRON MAN AND EVEN TURNED IN HIS THIEF BUDDY, BLACK FOX, TO SOLIDIFY HIS NEW STANDING AS A LOYAL AGENT.
YOU'D THINK THERE WASN'T A WHOLE HECK OF A LOT LEFT TO WRAP UP...BUT YOU'D BE WRONG.
NOW, IF YOU'LL EXCUSE ME--I THINK I'LL DIE NOW. A WORLD WITHOUT AN ANT-MAN BOOK ISN'T A WORLD WORTH LIVING IN. YOUR OPINIONS MAY VARY.
LIGHT--I SEE A LIGHT--I'M COMING, MOTHER--I'M COMING!

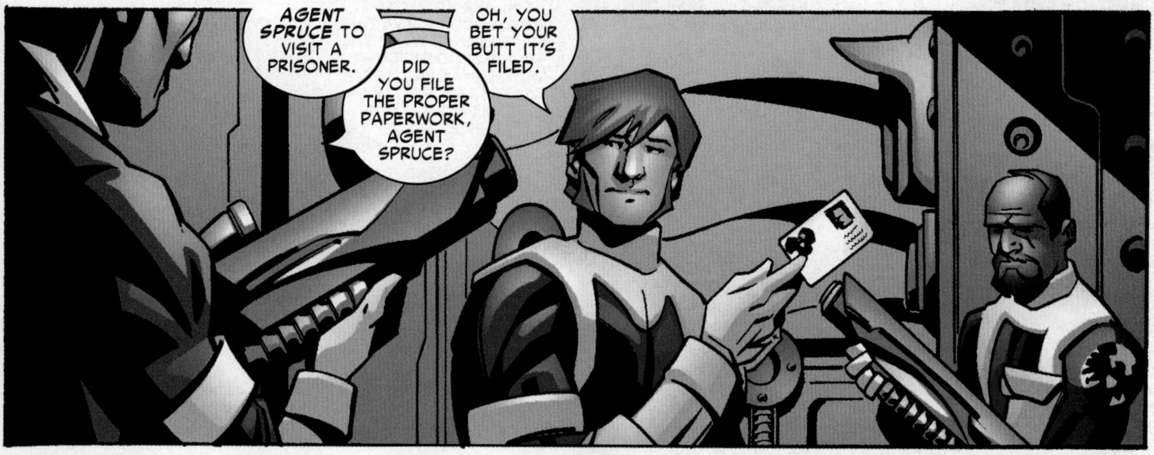
AGENT SPRUCE TO VISIT A PRISONER.
DID YOU FILE THE PROPER PAPERWORK, AGENT SPRUCE?
OH, YOU BET YOUR BUTT IT'S FILED.

# THE END IS THE BEGINNING

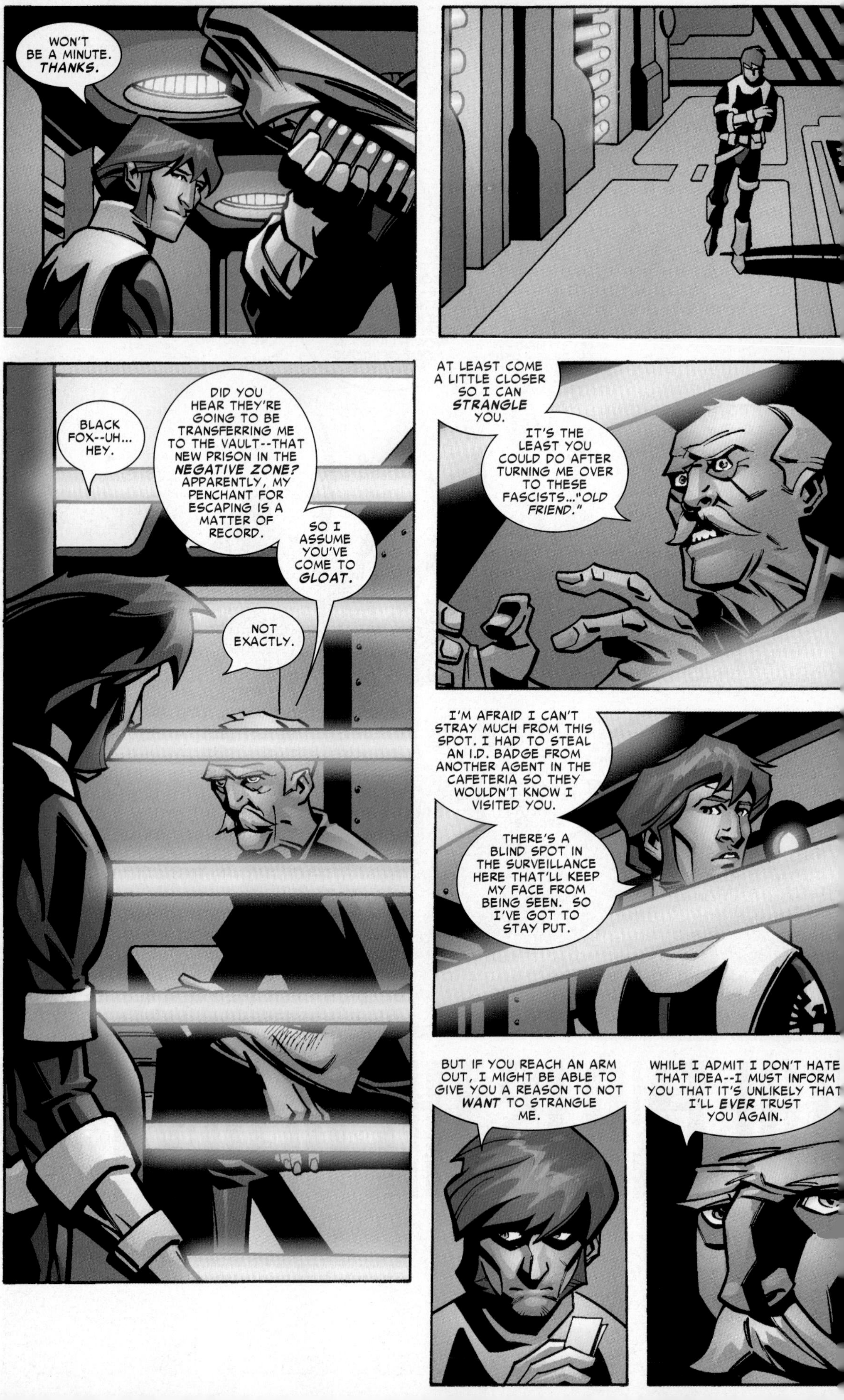

WON'T BE A MINUTE. THANKS.
BLACK FOX--UH... HEY.
DID YOU HEAR THEY'RE GOING TO BE TRANSFERRING ME TO THE VAULT--THAT NEW PRISON IN THE NEGATIVE ZONE? APPARENTLY, MY PENCHANT FOR ESCAPING IS A MATTER OF RECORD.
SO I ASSUME YOU'VE COME TO GLOAT.
NOT EXACTLY.
AT LEAST COME A LITTLE CLOSER SO I CAN STRANGLE YOU.
IT'S THE LEAST YOU COULD DO AFTER TURNING ME OVER TO THESE FASCISTS..."OLD FRIEND."
I'M AFRAID I CAN'T STRAY MUCH FROM THIS SPOT. I HAD TO STEAL AN I.D. BADGE FROM ANOTHER AGENT IN THE CAFETERIA SO THEY WOULDN'T KNOW I VISITED YOU.
THERE'S A BLIND SPOT IN THE SURVEILLANCE HERE THAT'LL KEEP MY FACE FROM BEING SEEN. SO I'VE GOT TO STAY PUT.
BUT IF YOU REACH AN ARM OUT, I MIGHT BE ABLE TO GIVE YOU A REASON TO NOT WANT TO STRANGLE ME.
WHILE I ADMIT I DON'T HATE THAT IDEA--I MUST INFORM YOU THAT IT'S UNLIKELY THAT I'LL EVER TRUST YOU AGAIN.

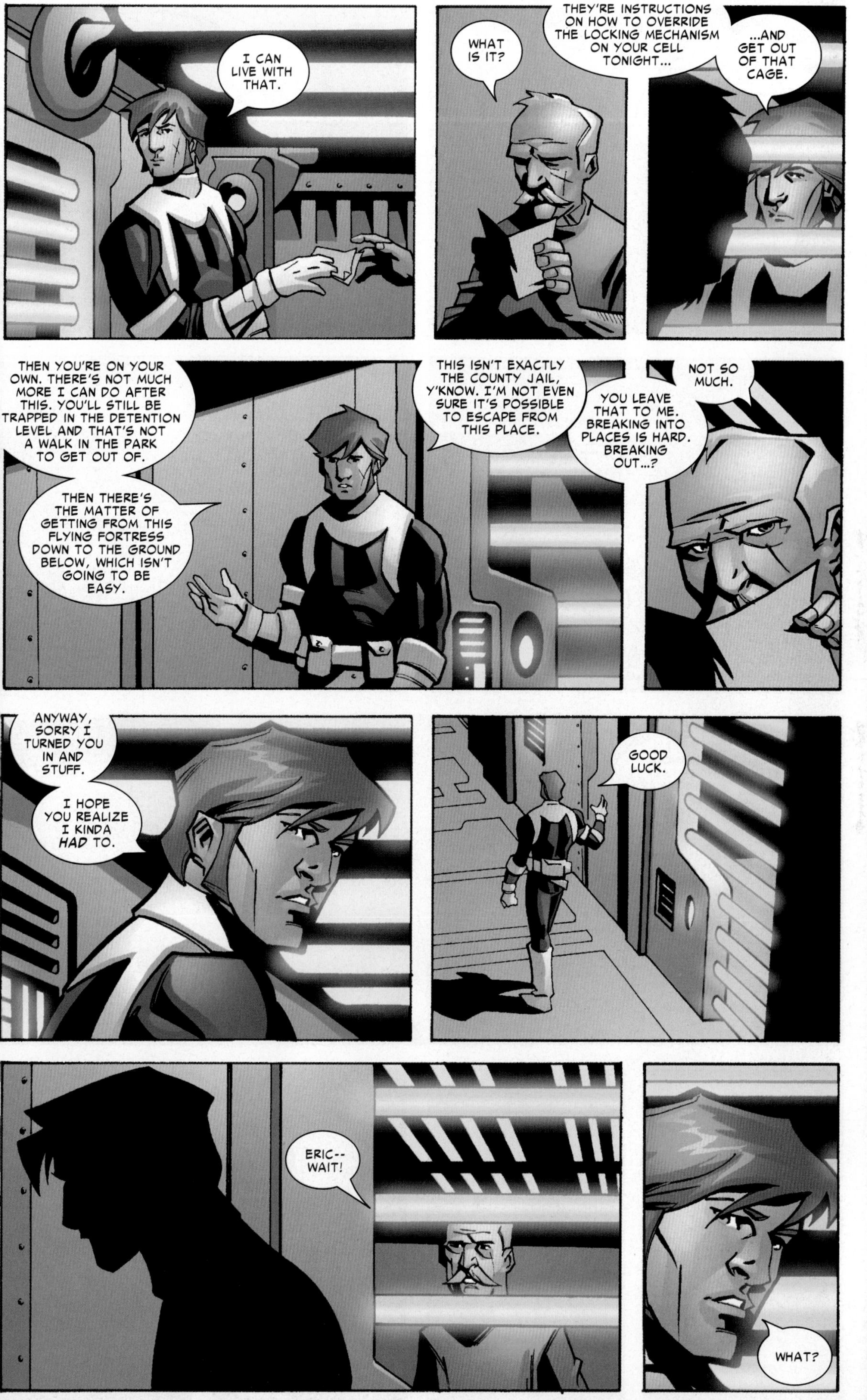
I CAN LIVE WITH THAT.
WHAT IS IT?
THEY'RE INSTRUCTIONS ON HOW TO OVERRIDE THE LOCKING MECHANISM ON YOUR CELL TONIGHT...
...AND GET OUT OF THAT CAGE.
THEN YOU'RE ON YOUR OWN. THERE'S NOT MUCH MORE I CAN DO AFTER THIS. YOU'LL STILL BE TRAPPED IN THE DETENTION LEVEL AND THAT'S NOT A WALK IN THE PARK TO GET OUT OF.
THEN THERE'S THE MATTER OF GETTING FROM THIS FLYING FORTRESS DOWN TO THE GROUND BELOW, WHICH ISN'T GOING TO BE EASY.
THIS ISN'T EXACTLY THE COUNTY JAIL, Y'KNOW. I'M NOT EVEN SURE IT'S POSSIBLE TO ESCAPE FROM THIS PLACE.
YOU LEAVE THAT TO ME. BREAKING INTO PLACES IS HARD. BREAKING OUT...?
NOT SO MUCH.
ANYWAY, SORRY I TURNED YOU IN AND STUFF.
I HOPE YOU REALIZE I KINDA *HAD* TO.
GOOD LUCK.
ERIC--WAIT!
WHAT?

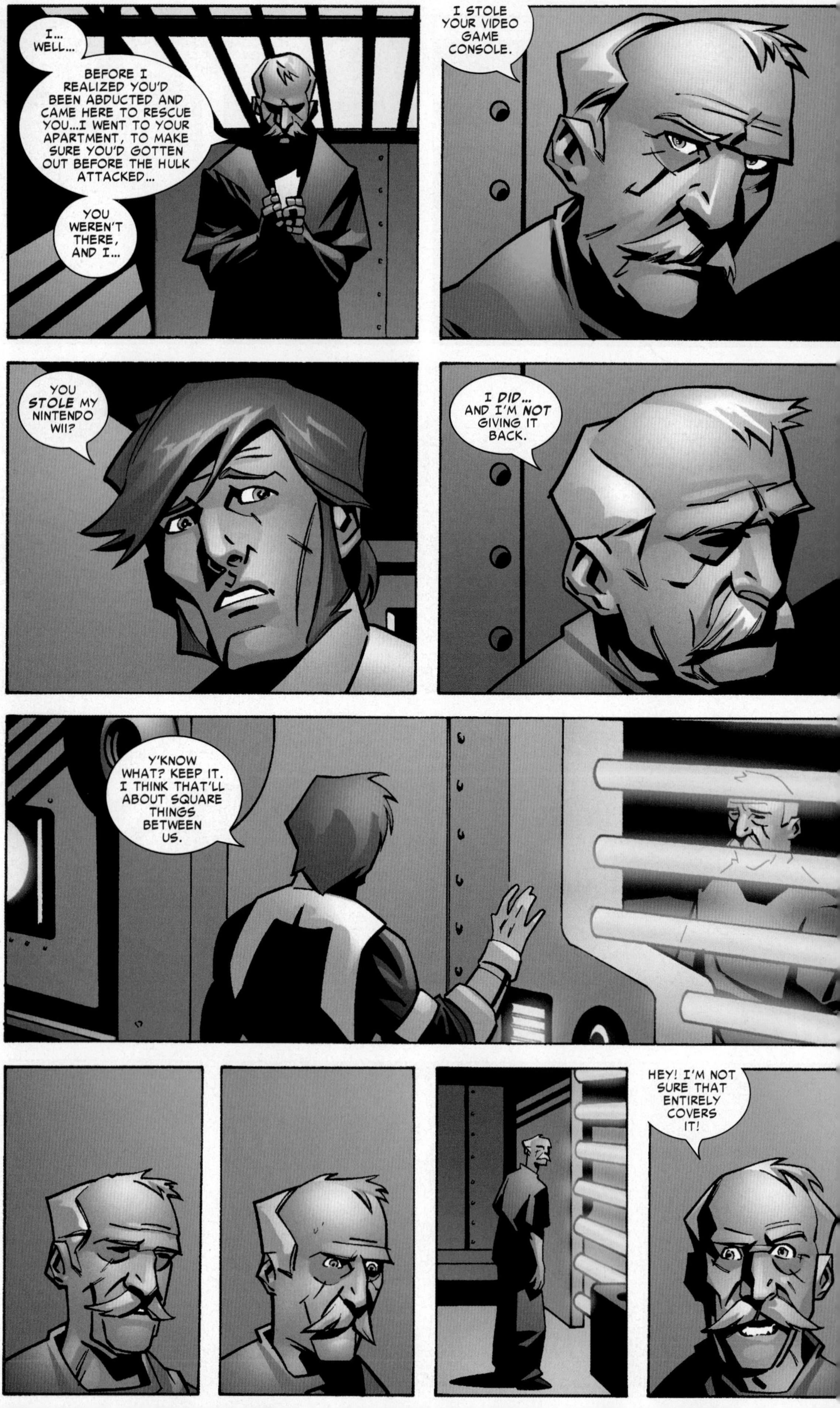
I... WELL...
BEFORE I REALIZED YOU'D BEEN ABDUCTED AND CAME HERE TO RESCUE YOU...I WENT TO YOUR APARTMENT, TO MAKE SURE YOU'D GOTTEN OUT BEFORE THE HULK ATTACKED...
YOU WEREN'T THERE, AND I...
I STOLE YOUR VIDEO GAME CONSOLE.
YOU STOLE MY NINTENDO WII?
I DID... AND I'M NOT GIVING IT BACK.
Y'KNOW WHAT? KEEP IT. I THINK THAT'LL ABOUT SQUARE THINGS BETWEEN US.
HEY! I'M NOT SURE THAT ENTIRELY COVERS IT!

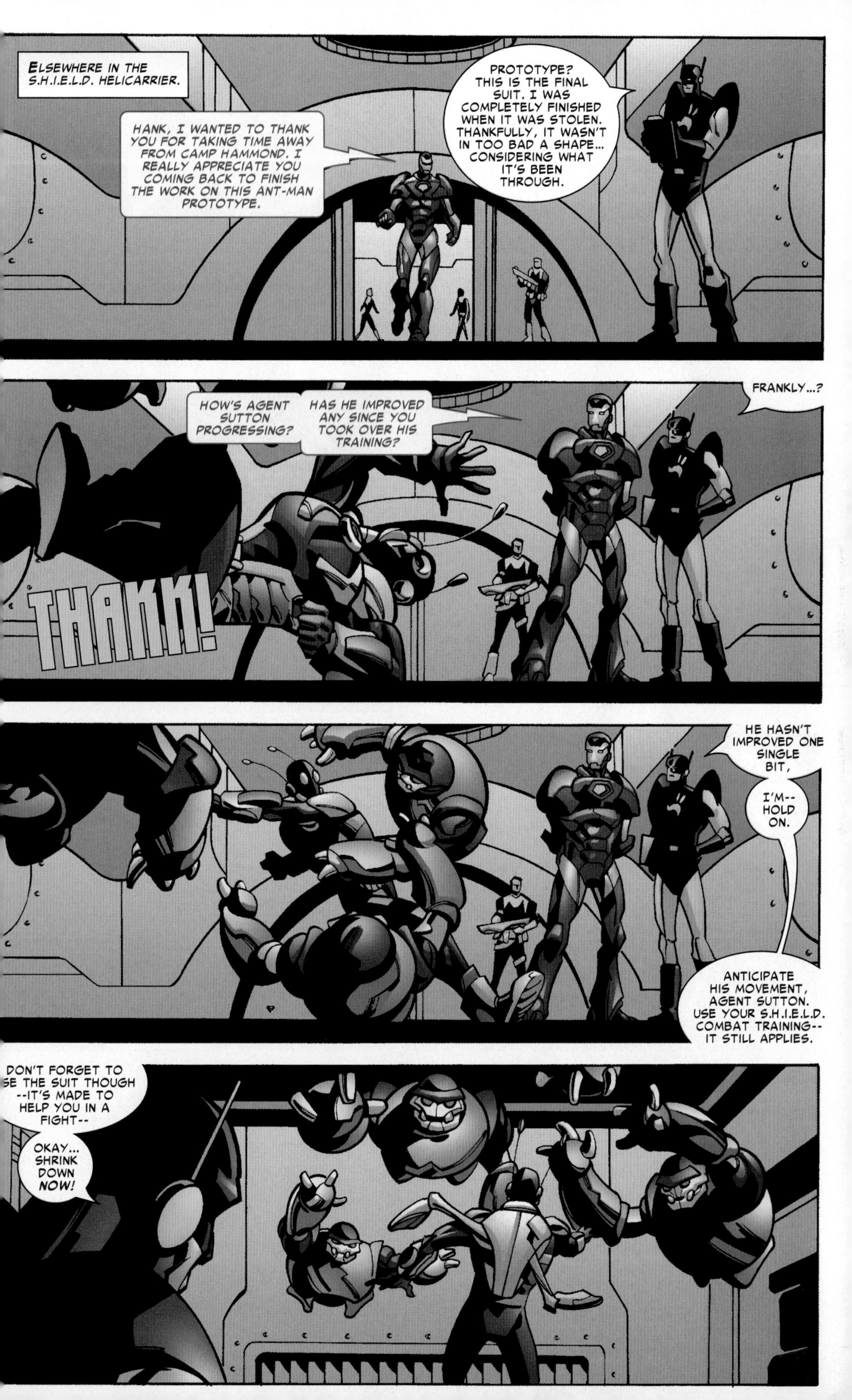

ELSEWHERE IN THE S.H.I.E.L.D. HELICARRIER.
HANK, I WANTED TO THANK YOU FOR TAKING TIME AWAY FROM CAMP HAMMOND. I REALLY APPRECIATE YOU COMING BACK TO FINISH THE WORK ON THIS ANT-MAN PROTOTYPE.
PROTOTYPE? THIS IS THE FINAL SUIT. I WAS COMPLETELY FINISHED WHEN IT WAS STOLEN. THANKFULLY, IT WASN'T IN TOO BAD A SHAPE... CONSIDERING WHAT IT'S BEEN THROUGH.
HOW'S AGENT SUTTON PROGRESSING?
HAS HE IMPROVED ANY SINCE YOU TOOK OVER HIS TRAINING?
FRANKLY...?
THAKK!
HE HASN'T IMPROVED ONE SINGLE BIT,
I'M-- HOLD ON.
ANTICIPATE HIS MOVEMENT, AGENT SUTTON. USE YOUR S.H.I.E.L.D. COMBAT TRAINING-- IT STILL APPLIES.
DON'T FORGET TO SE THE SUIT THOUGH --IT'S MADE TO HELP YOU IN A FIGHT--
OKAY... SHRINK DOWN NOW!

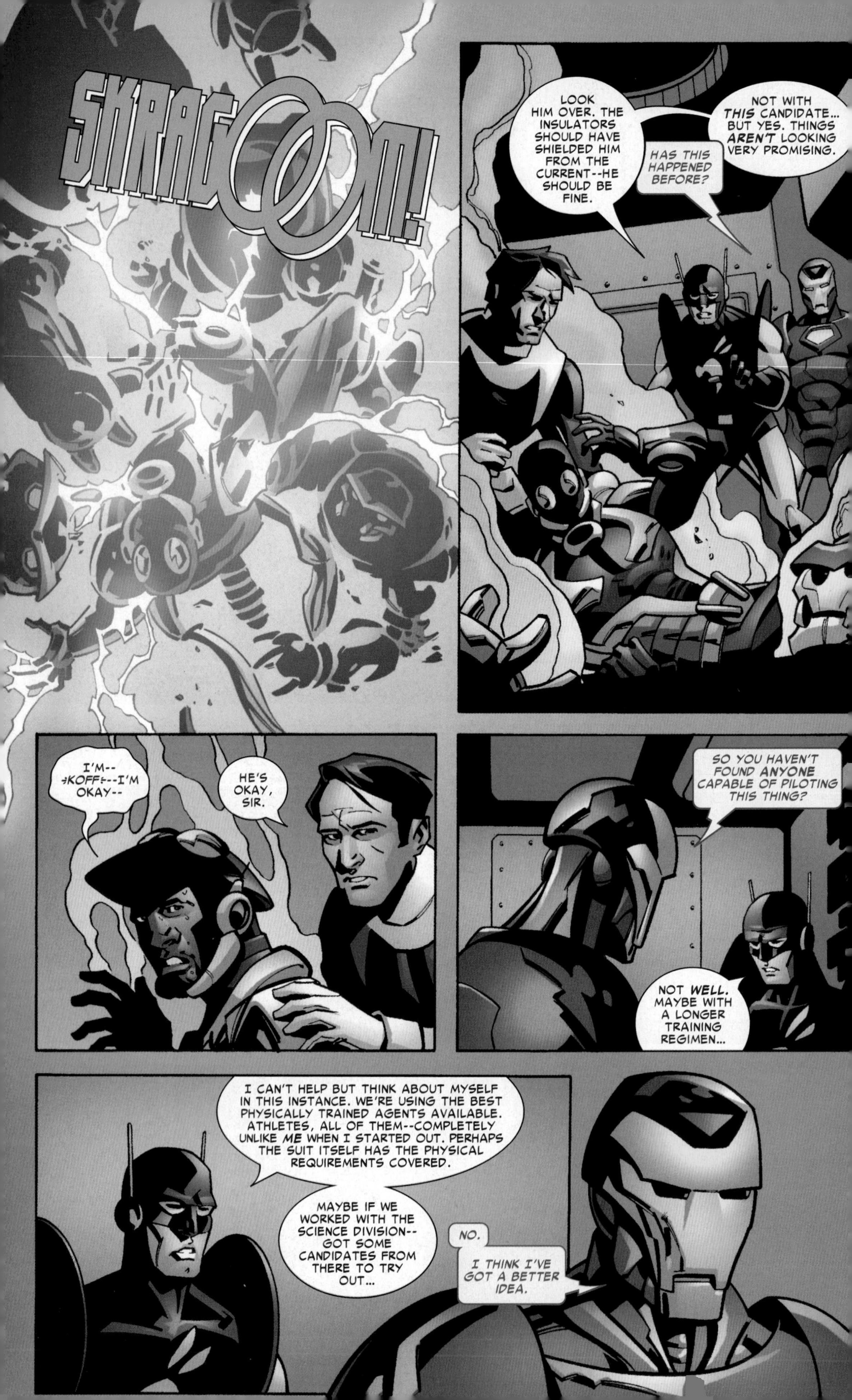
SKRAGOOM!
LOOK HIM OVER. THE INSULATORS SHOULD HAVE SHIELDED HIM FROM THE CURRENT--HE SHOULD BE FINE.
HAS THIS HAPPENED BEFORE?
NOT WITH THIS CANDIDATE... BUT YES. THINGS AREN'T LOOKING VERY PROMISING.
I'M-- *KOFF*--I'M OKAY--
HE'S OKAY, SIR.
SO YOU HAVEN'T FOUND ANYONE CAPABLE OF PILOTING THIS THING?
NOT WELL. MAYBE WITH A LONGER TRAINING REGIMEN...
I CAN'T HELP BUT THINK ABOUT MYSELF IN THIS INSTANCE. WE'RE USING THE BEST PHYSICALLY TRAINED AGENTS AVAILABLE. ATHLETES, ALL OF THEM--COMPLETELY UNLIKE ME WHEN I STARTED OUT. PERHAPS THE SUIT ITSELF HAS THE PHYSICAL REQUIREMENTS COVERED.
MAYBE IF WE WORKED WITH THE SCIENCE DIVISION--GOT SOME CANDIDATES FROM THERE TO TRY OUT...
NO.
I THINK I'VE GOT A BETTER IDEA.

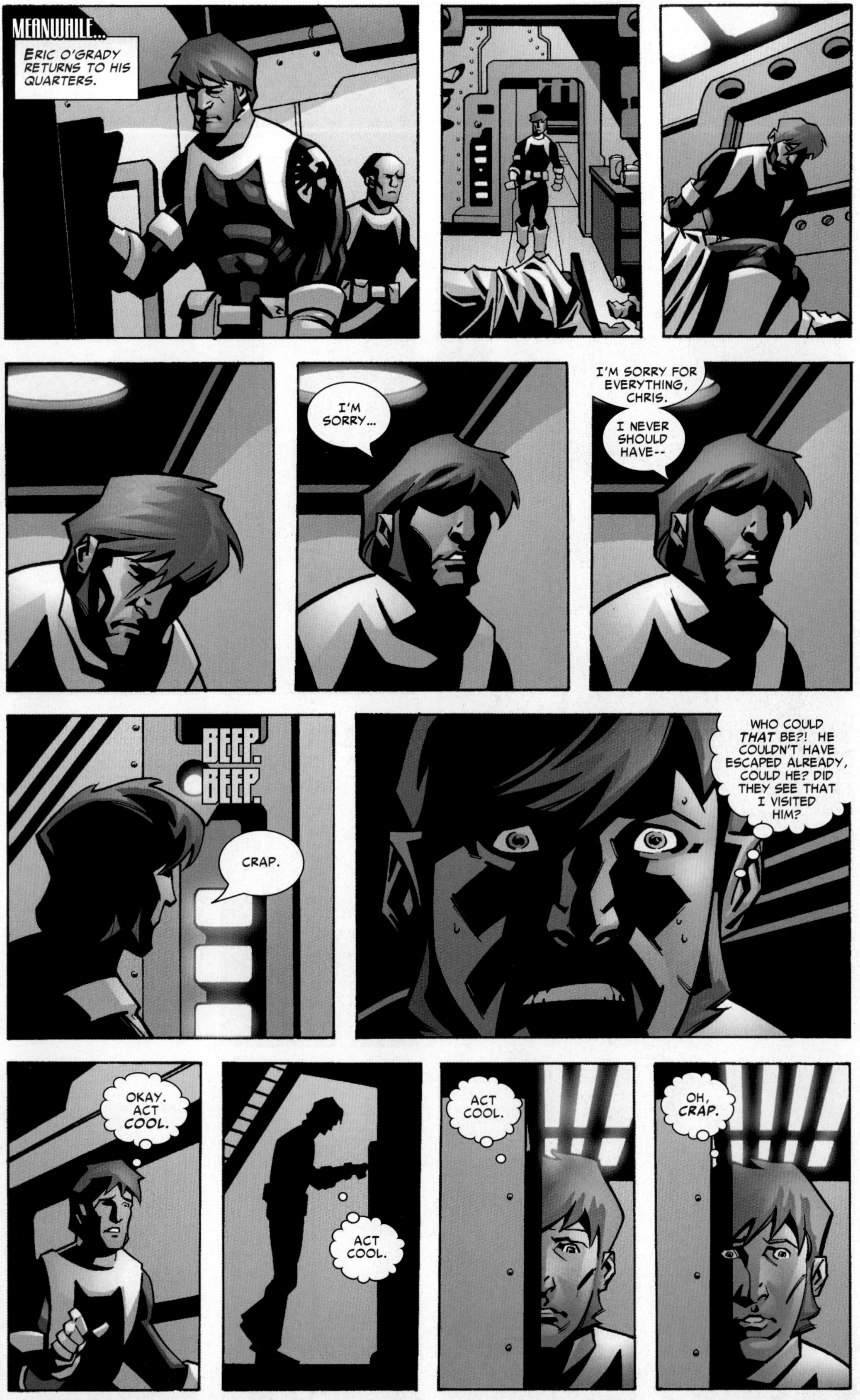
MEANWHILE...
ERIC O'GRADY RETURNS TO HIS QUARTERS.
I'M SORRY...
I'M SORRY FOR EVERYTHING, CHRIS.
I NEVER SHOULD HAVE--
BEEP. BEEP.
CRAP.
WHO COULD THAT BE?! HE COULDN'T HAVE ESCAPED ALREADY, COULD HE? DID THEY SEE THAT I VISITED HIM?
OKAY. ACT COOL.
ACT COOL.
ACT COOL.
OH, CRAP.

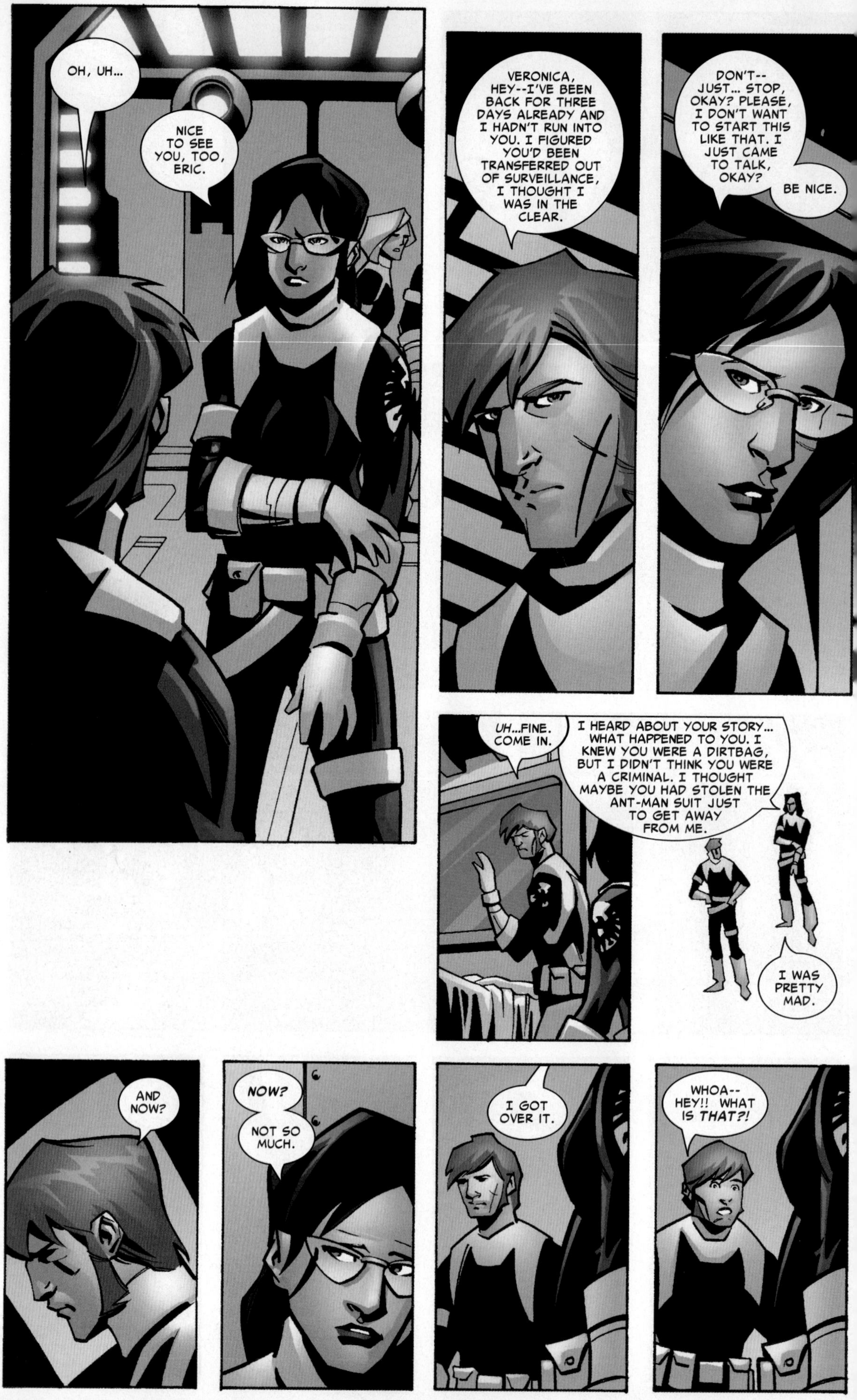
OH, UH...
NICE TO SEE YOU, TOO, ERIC.
VERONICA, HEY--I'VE BEEN BACK FOR THREE DAYS ALREADY AND I HADN'T RUN INTO YOU. I FIGURED YOU'D BEEN TRANSFERRED OUT OF SURVEILLANCE, I THOUGHT I WAS IN THE CLEAR.
DON'T-- JUST... STOP, OKAY? PLEASE, I DON'T WANT TO START THIS LIKE THAT. I JUST CAME TO TALK, OKAY?
BE NICE.
UH...FINE. COME IN.
I HEARD ABOUT YOUR STORY... WHAT HAPPENED TO YOU. I KNEW YOU WERE A DIRTBAG, BUT I DIDN'T THINK YOU WERE A CRIMINAL. I THOUGHT MAYBE YOU HAD STOLEN THE ANT-MAN SUIT JUST TO GET AWAY FROM ME.
I WAS PRETTY MAD.
AND NOW?
NOW?
NOT SO MUCH.
I GOT OVER IT.
WHOA-- HEY!! WHAT IS THAT?!

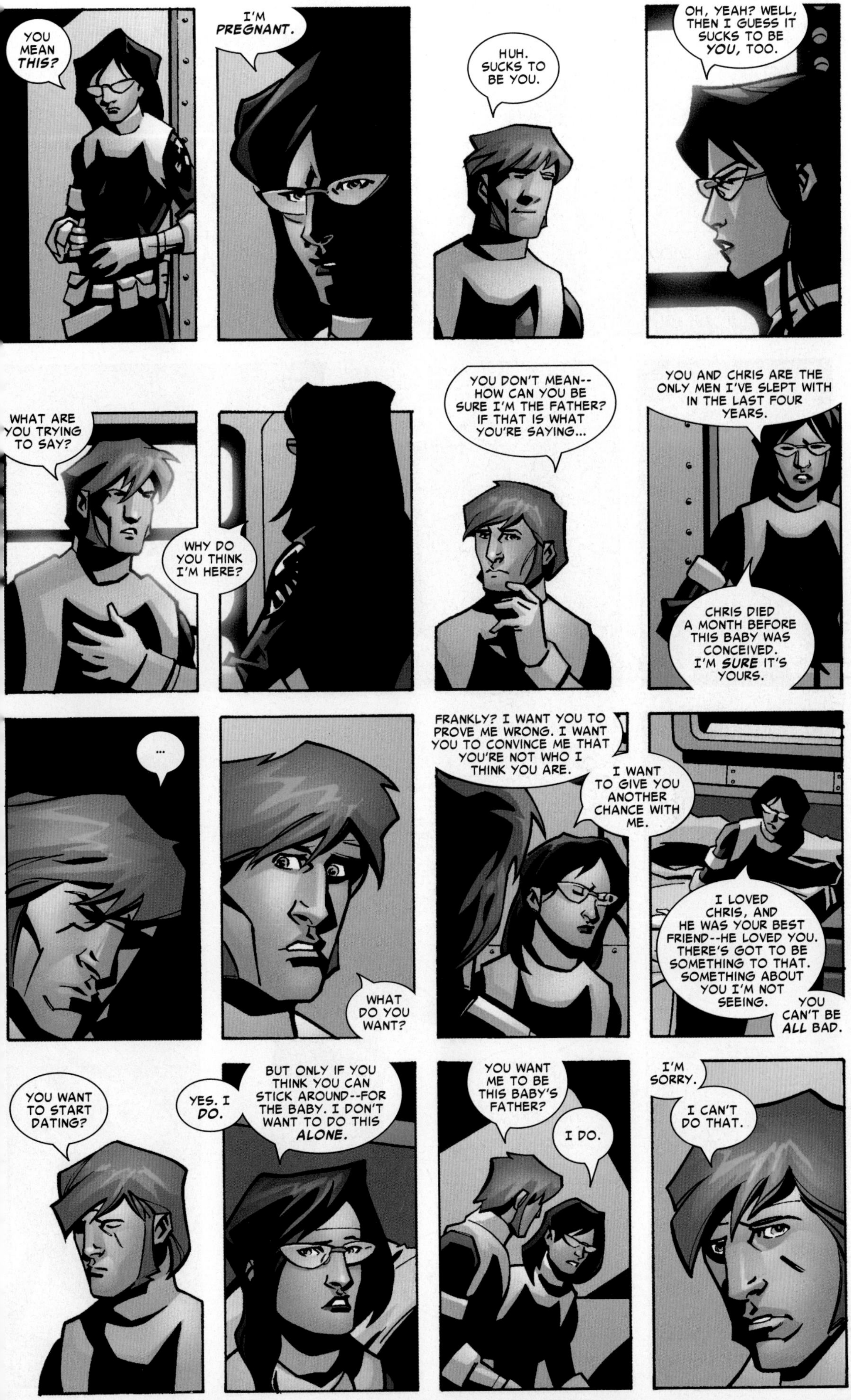
YOU MEAN THIS?
I'M PREGNANT.
HUH. SUCKS TO BE YOU.
OH, YEAH? WELL, THEN I GUESS IT SUCKS TO BE YOU, TOO.
WHAT ARE YOU TRYING TO SAY?
WHY DO YOU THINK I'M HERE?
YOU DON'T MEAN-- HOW CAN YOU BE SURE I'M THE FATHER? IF THAT IS WHAT YOU'RE SAYING...
YOU AND CHRIS ARE THE ONLY MEN I'VE SLEPT WITH IN THE LAST FOUR YEARS.
CHRIS DIED A MONTH BEFORE THIS BABY WAS CONCEIVED. I'M SURE IT'S YOURS.
...
WHAT DO YOU WANT?
FRANKLY? I WANT YOU TO PROVE ME WRONG. I WANT YOU TO CONVINCE ME THAT YOU'RE NOT WHO I THINK YOU ARE.
I WANT TO GIVE YOU ANOTHER CHANCE WITH ME.
I LOVED CHRIS, AND HE WAS YOUR BEST FRIEND--HE LOVED YOU. THERE'S GOT TO BE SOMETHING TO THAT. SOMETHING ABOUT YOU I'M NOT SEEING.
YOU CAN'T BE ALL BAD.
YOU WANT TO START DATING?
YES. I DO.
BUT ONLY IF YOU THINK YOU CAN STICK AROUND--FOR THE BABY. I DON'T WANT TO DO THIS ALONE.
YOU WANT ME TO BE THIS BABY'S FATHER?
I DO.
I'M SORRY.
I CAN'T DO THAT.

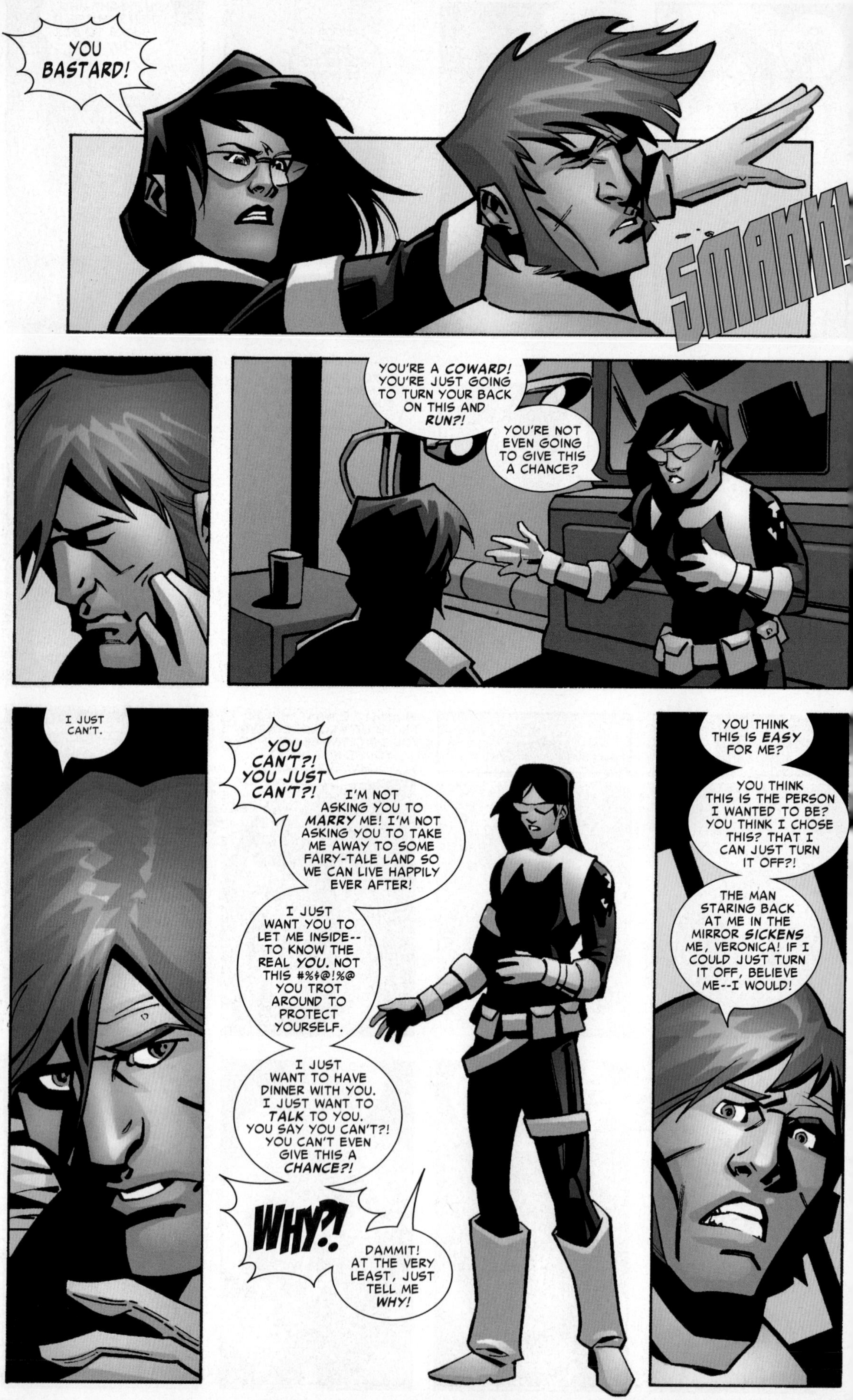
YOU BASTARD!
SMAKK!
YOU'RE A COWARD! YOU'RE JUST GOING TO TURN YOUR BACK ON THIS AND RUN?!
YOU'RE NOT EVEN GOING TO GIVE THIS A CHANCE?
I JUST CAN'T.
YOU CAN'T?! YOU JUST CAN'T?!
I'M NOT ASKING YOU TO MARRY ME! I'M NOT ASKING YOU TO TAKE ME AWAY TO SOME FAIRY-TALE LAND SO WE CAN LIVE HAPPILY EVER AFTER!
I JUST WANT YOU TO LET ME INSIDE-- TO KNOW THE REAL YOU. NOT THIS #%$@!%@ YOU TROT AROUND TO PROTECT YOURSELF.
I JUST WANT TO HAVE DINNER WITH YOU. I JUST WANT TO TALK TO YOU. YOU SAY YOU CAN'T?! YOU CAN'T EVEN GIVE THIS A CHANCE?!
WHY?!
DAMMIT! AT THE VERY LEAST, JUST TELL ME WHY!
YOU THINK THIS IS EASY FOR ME?
YOU THINK THIS IS THE PERSON I WANTED TO BE? YOU THINK I CHOSE THIS? THAT I CAN JUST TURN IT OFF?!
THE MAN STARING BACK AT ME IN THE MIRROR SICKENS ME, VERONICA! IF I COULD JUST TURN IT OFF, BELIEVE ME--I WOULD!

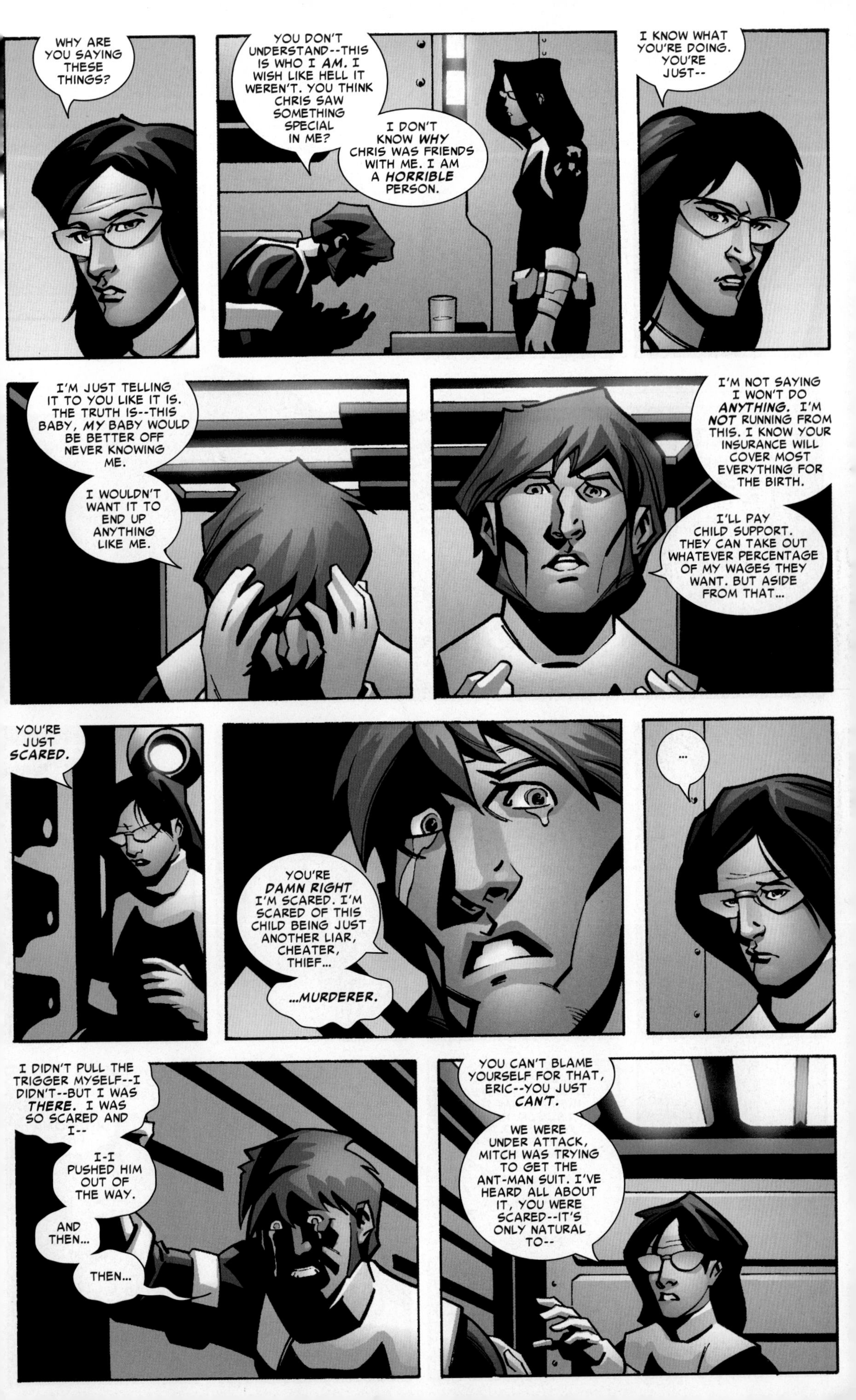
WHY ARE YOU SAYING THESE THINGS?
YOU DON'T UNDERSTAND--THIS IS WHO I AM. I WISH LIKE HELL IT WEREN'T. YOU THINK CHRIS SAW SOMETHING SPECIAL IN ME?
I DON'T KNOW WHY CHRIS WAS FRIENDS WITH ME. I AM A HORRIBLE PERSON.
I KNOW WHAT YOU'RE DOING. YOU'RE JUST--
I'M JUST TELLING IT TO YOU LIKE IT IS. THE TRUTH IS--THIS BABY, MY BABY WOULD BE BETTER OFF NEVER KNOWING ME.
I WOULDN'T WANT IT TO END UP ANYTHING LIKE ME.
I'M NOT SAYING I WON'T DO ANYTHING. I'M NOT RUNNING FROM THIS. I KNOW YOUR INSURANCE WILL COVER MOST EVERYTHING FOR THE BIRTH.
I'LL PAY CHILD SUPPORT. THEY CAN TAKE OUT WHATEVER PERCENTAGE OF MY WAGES THEY WANT. BUT ASIDE FROM THAT...
YOU'RE JUST SCARED.
YOU'RE DAMN RIGHT I'M SCARED. I'M SCARED OF THIS CHILD BEING JUST ANOTHER LIAR, CHEATER, THIEF...
...MURDERER.
...
I DIDN'T PULL THE TRIGGER MYSELF--I DIDN'T--BUT I WAS THERE. I WAS SO SCARED AND I--
I-I PUSHED HIM OUT OF THE WAY.
AND THEN...
THEN...
YOU CAN'T BLAME YOURSELF FOR THAT, ERIC--YOU JUST CAN'T.
WE WERE UNDER ATTACK, MITCH WAS TRYING TO GET THE ANT-MAN SUIT. I'VE HEARD ALL ABOUT IT, YOU WERE SCARED--IT'S ONLY NATURAL TO--

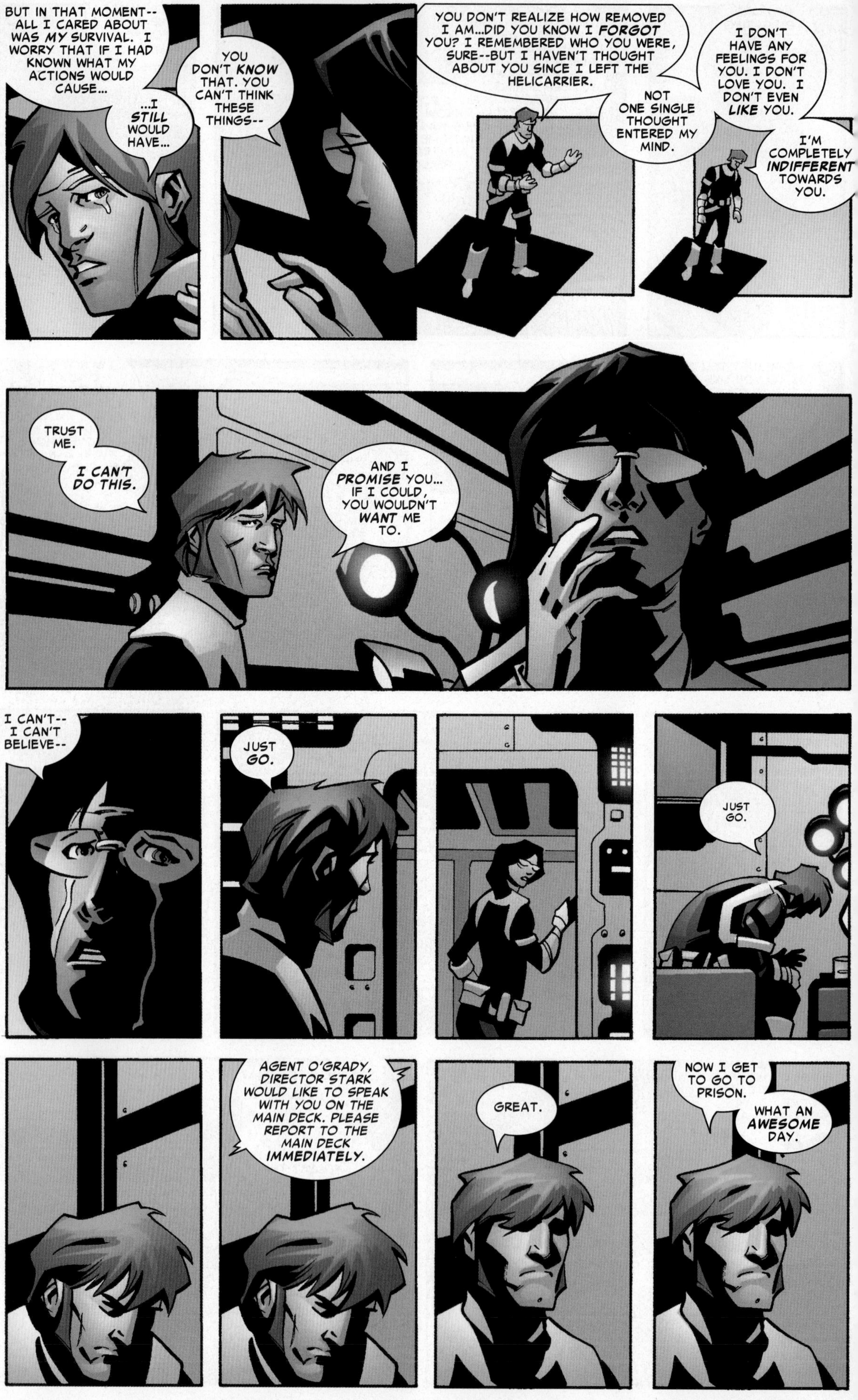
BUT IN THAT MOMENT-- ALL I CARED ABOUT WAS MY SURVIVAL. I WORRY THAT IF I HAD KNOWN WHAT MY ACTIONS WOULD CAUSE...
...I STILL WOULD HAVE...
YOU DON'T KNOW THAT. YOU CAN'T THINK THESE THINGS--
YOU DON'T REALIZE HOW REMOVED I AM...DID YOU KNOW I FORGOT YOU? I REMEMBERED WHO YOU WERE, SURE--BUT I HAVEN'T THOUGHT ABOUT YOU SINCE I LEFT THE HELICARRIER.
NOT ONE SINGLE THOUGHT ENTERED MY MIND.
I DON'T HAVE ANY FEELINGS FOR YOU. I DON'T LOVE YOU. I DON'T EVEN LIKE YOU.
I'M COMPLETELY INDIFFERENT TOWARDS YOU.
TRUST ME.
I CAN'T DO THIS.
AND I PROMISE YOU... IF I COULD, YOU WOULDN'T WANT ME TO.
I CAN'T-- I CAN'T BELIEVE--
JUST GO.
JUST GO.
AGENT O'GRADY, DIRECTOR STARK WOULD LIKE TO SPEAK WITH YOU ON THE MAIN DECK. PLEASE REPORT TO THE MAIN DECK IMMEDIATELY.
GREAT.
NOW I GET TO GO TO PRISON.
WHAT AN AWESOME DAY.

MOMENTS LATER, ERIC O'GRADY ARRIVES ON THE COMMAND DECK OF THE S.H.I.E.L.D. HELICARRIER.

UH...AGENT ERIC O'GRADY REPORTING FOR DUTY, SIR.

AT EASE, AGENT.

FIRST OFF, I'D LIKE TO APOLOGIZE AGAIN FOR THE HELL AGENT MITCH CARSON PUT YOU THROUGH. THIS ORGANIZATION IS NOT PERFECT, BUT WE SHOULD BE ABLE TO AVOID PEOPLE LIKE THAT SLIPPING THROUGH THE CRACKS.

I TRUST YOU'RE HEALING WELL?

Y-YEAH, PRETTY MUCH GOOD AS NEW, FOR THE MOST PART AT LEAST. JUST KINDA SORE, REALLY.

THAT'S GOOD TO HEAR. BUT THAT'S NOT REALLY THE REASON I CALLED YOU HERE.

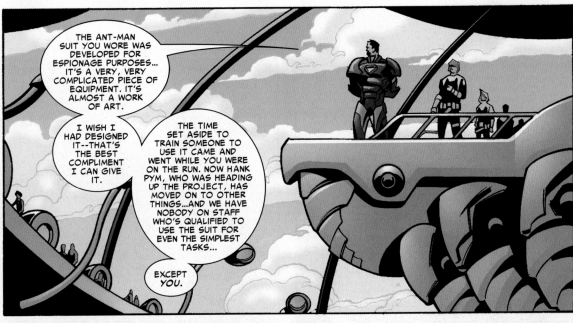

THE ANT-MAN SUIT YOU WORE WAS DEVELOPED FOR ESPIONAGE PURPOSES... IT'S A VERY, VERY COMPLICATED PIECE OF EQUIPMENT. IT'S ALMOST A WORK OF ART.

I WISH I HAD DESIGNED IT--THAT'S THE BEST COMPLIMENT I CAN GIVE IT.

THE TIME SET ASIDE TO TRAIN SOMEONE TO USE IT CAME AND WENT WHILE YOU WERE ON THE RUN. NOW HANK PYM, WHO WAS HEADING UP THE PROJECT, HAS MOVED ON TO OTHER THINGS...AND WE HAVE NOBODY ON STAFF WHO'S QUALIFIED TO USE THE SUIT FOR EVEN THE SIMPLEST TASKS...

EXCEPT YOU.

ARE YOU ASKING ME TO HELP TRAIN SOMEONE TO USE THE ANT-MAN SUIT?

NOT EXACTLY.

PLEASE, COME WITH ME.

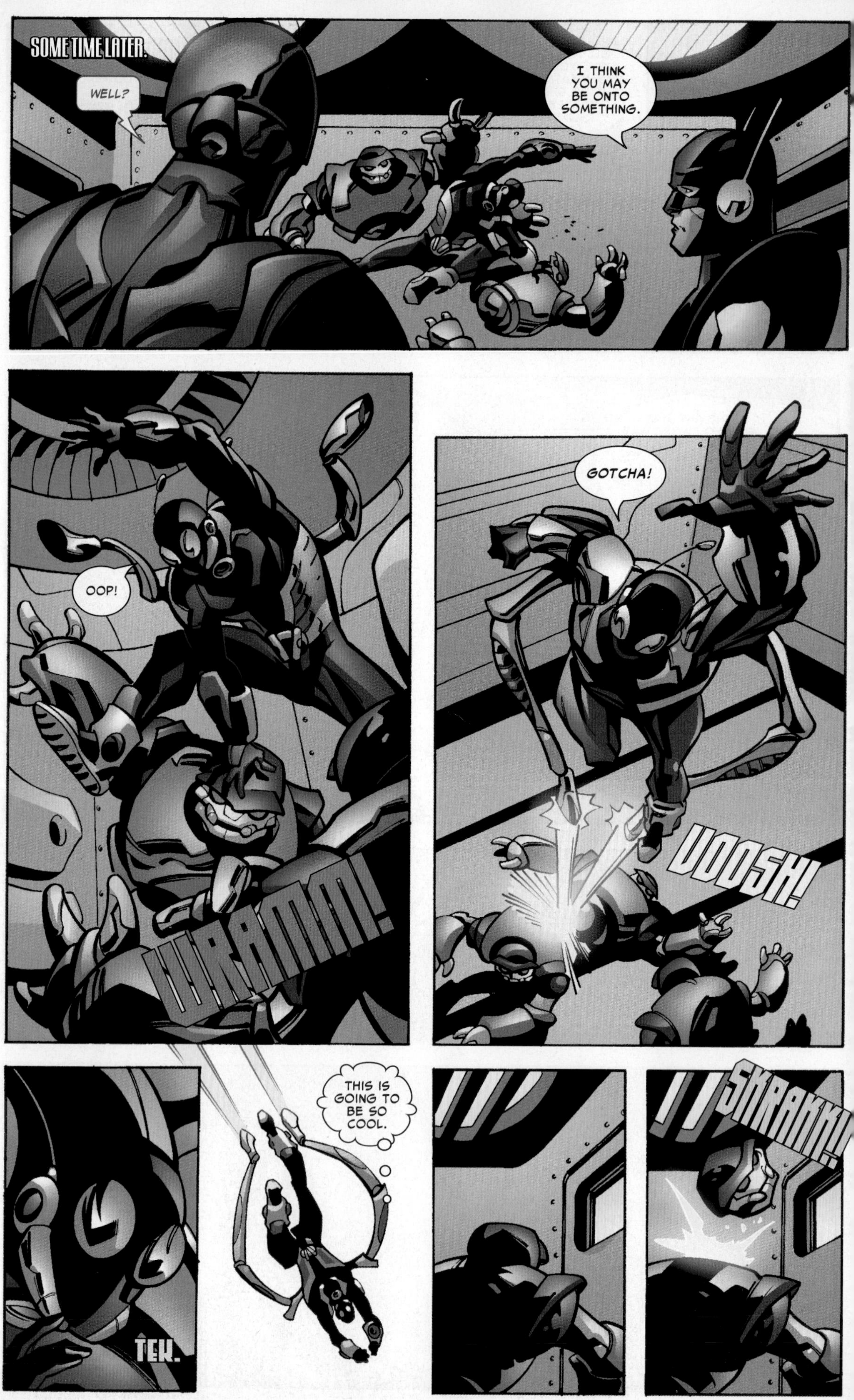

SOME TIME LATER.
WELL?
I THINK YOU MAY BE ONTO SOMETHING.
OOP!
WRAMMM!
GOTCHA!
VOOSH!
TEK.
THIS IS GOING TO BE SO COOL.
SKRAKK!

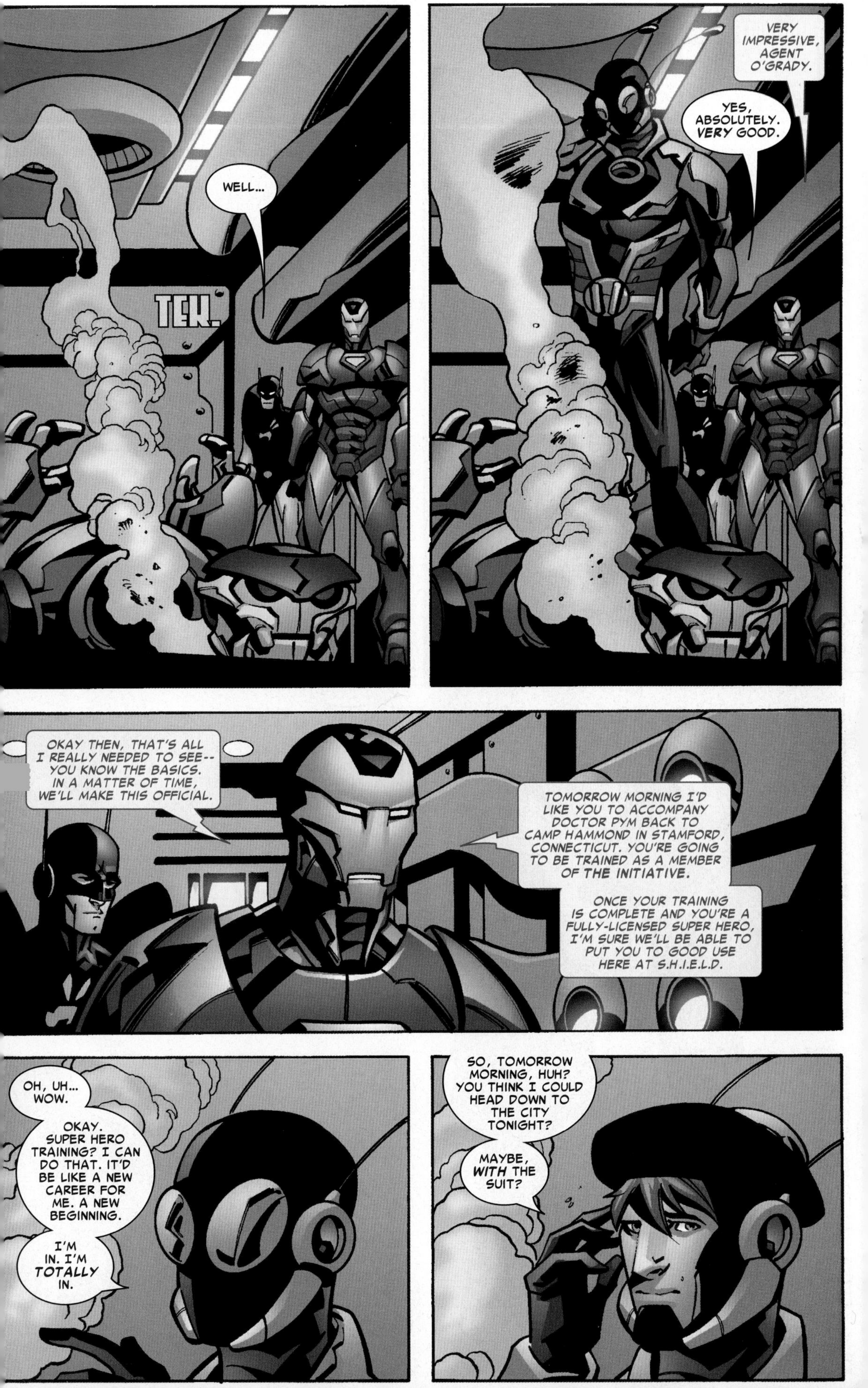
WELL...
TEK.
VERY IMPRESSIVE, AGENT O'GRADY.
YES, ABSOLUTELY. VERY GOOD.
OKAY THEN, THAT'S ALL I REALLY NEEDED TO SEE-- YOU KNOW THE BASICS. IN A MATTER OF TIME, WE'LL MAKE THIS OFFICIAL.
TOMORROW MORNING I'D LIKE YOU TO ACCOMPANY DOCTOR PYM BACK TO CAMP HAMMOND IN STAMFORD, CONNECTICUT. YOU'RE GOING TO BE TRAINED AS A MEMBER OF THE INITIATIVE.
ONCE YOUR TRAINING IS COMPLETE AND YOU'RE A FULLY-LICENSED SUPER HERO, I'M SURE WE'LL BE ABLE TO PUT YOU TO GOOD USE HERE AT S.H.I.E.L.D.
OH, UH... WOW.
OKAY. SUPER HERO TRAINING? I CAN DO THAT. IT'D BE LIKE A NEW CAREER FOR ME. A NEW BEGINNING.
I'M IN. I'M TOTALLY IN.
SO, TOMORROW MORNING, HUH? YOU THINK I COULD HEAD DOWN TO THE CITY TONIGHT?
MAYBE, WITH THE SUIT?

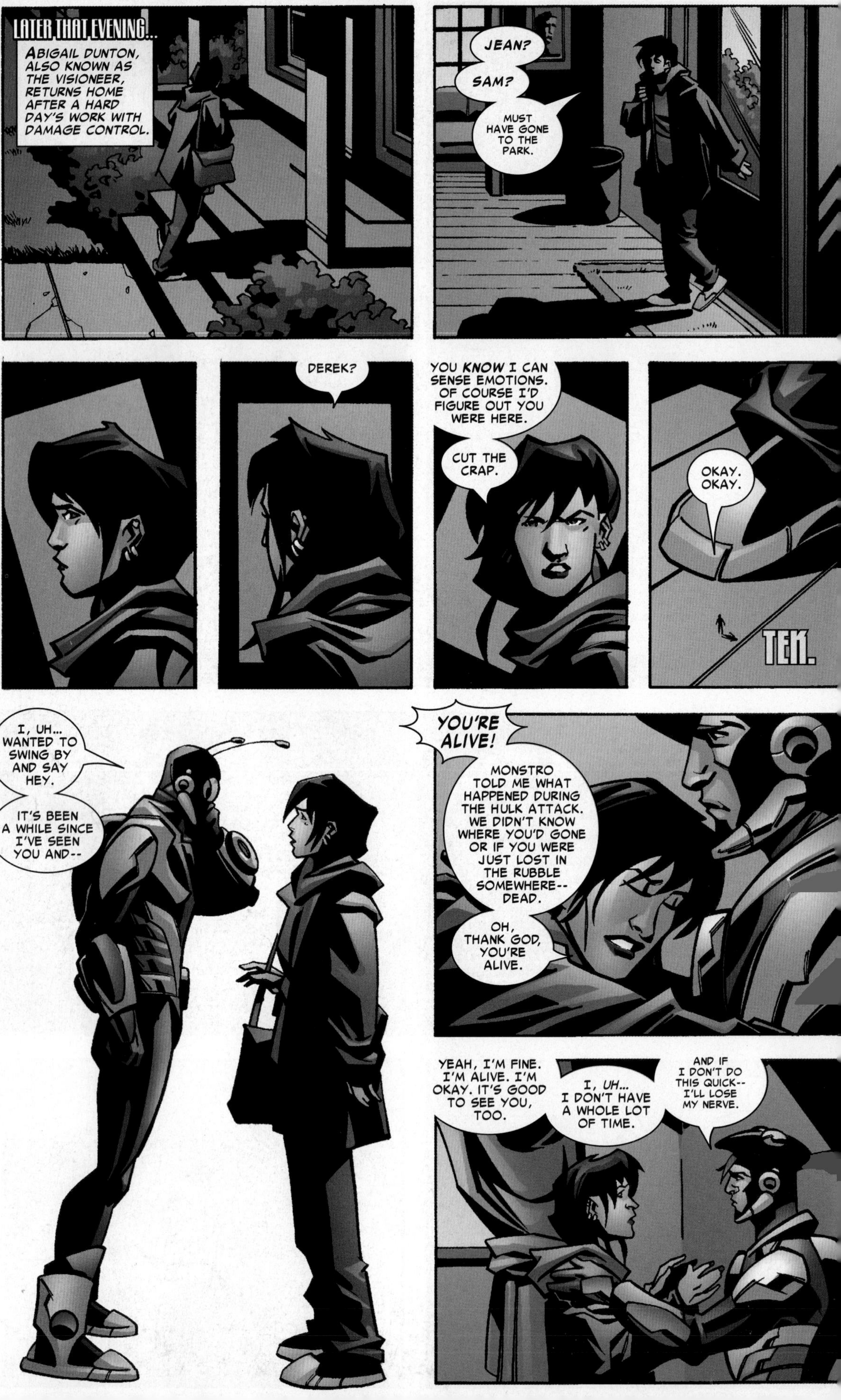
LATER THAT EVENING...
ABIGAIL DUNTON, ALSO KNOWN AS THE VISIONEER, RETURNS HOME AFTER A HARD DAY'S WORK WITH DAMAGE CONTROL.
JEAN?
SAM?
MUST HAVE GONE TO THE PARK.
DEREK?
YOU KNOW I CAN SENSE EMOTIONS. OF COURSE I'D FIGURE OUT YOU WERE HERE.
CUT THE CRAP.
OKAY. OKAY.
TEK.
I, UH... WANTED TO SWING BY AND SAY HEY.
IT'S BEEN A WHILE SINCE I'VE SEEN YOU AND--
YOU'RE ALIVE!
MONSTRO TOLD ME WHAT HAPPENED DURING THE HULK ATTACK. WE DIDN'T KNOW WHERE YOU'D GONE OR IF YOU WERE JUST LOST IN THE RUBBLE SOMEWHERE--DEAD.
OH, THANK GOD, YOU'RE ALIVE.
YEAH, I'M FINE. I'M ALIVE. I'M OKAY. IT'S GOOD TO SEE YOU, TOO.
I, UH... I DON'T HAVE A WHOLE LOT OF TIME.
AND IF I DON'T DO THIS QUICK--I'LL LOSE MY NERVE.

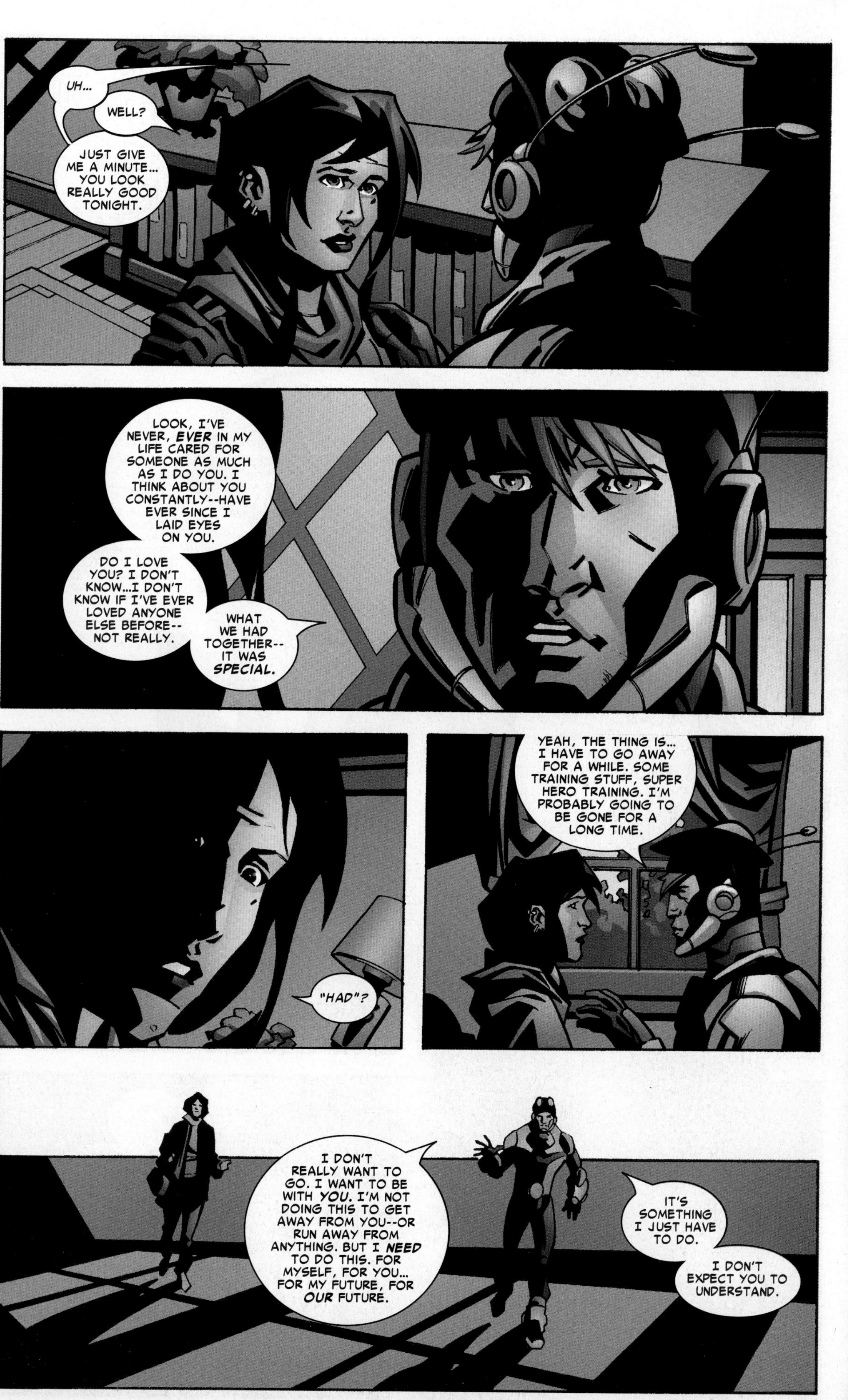
UH...
WELL?
JUST GIVE ME A MINUTE... YOU LOOK REALLY GOOD TONIGHT.
LOOK, I'VE NEVER, EVER IN MY LIFE CARED FOR SOMEONE AS MUCH AS I DO YOU. I THINK ABOUT YOU CONSTANTLY--HAVE EVER SINCE I LAID EYES ON YOU.
DO I LOVE YOU? I DON'T KNOW...I DON'T KNOW IF I'VE EVER LOVED ANYONE ELSE BEFORE--NOT REALLY.
WHAT WE HAD TOGETHER--IT WAS SPECIAL.
"HAD"?
YEAH, THE THING IS... I HAVE TO GO AWAY FOR A WHILE. SOME TRAINING STUFF, SUPER HERO TRAINING. I'M PROBABLY GOING TO BE GONE FOR A LONG TIME.
I DON'T REALLY WANT TO GO. I WANT TO BE WITH YOU. I'M NOT DOING THIS TO GET AWAY FROM YOU--OR RUN AWAY FROM ANYTHING. BUT I NEED TO DO THIS. FOR MYSELF, FOR YOU... FOR MY FUTURE, FOR OUR FUTURE.
IT'S SOMETHING I JUST HAVE TO DO.
I DON'T EXPECT YOU TO UNDERSTAND.

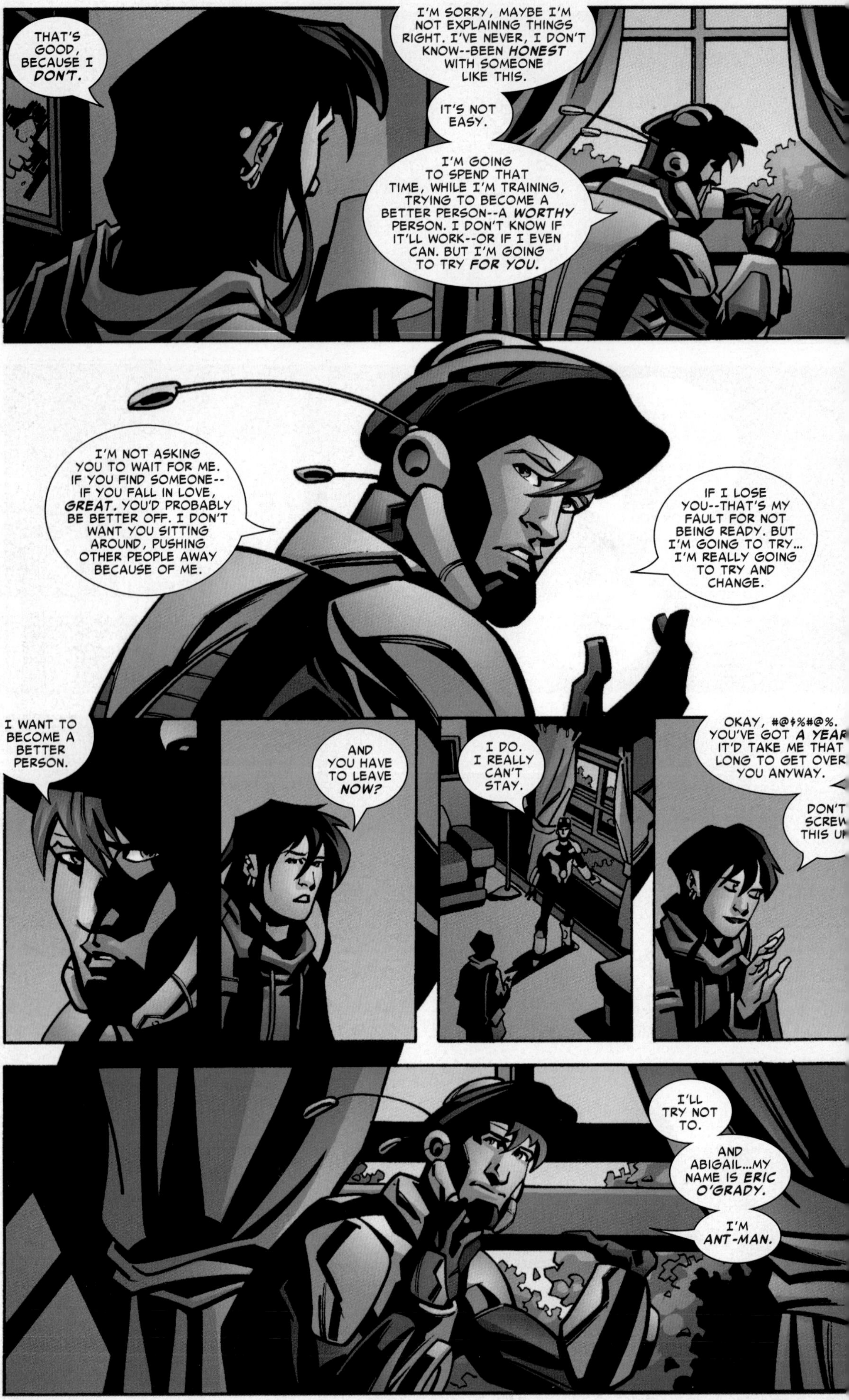
THAT'S GOOD, BECAUSE I DON'T.
I'M SORRY, MAYBE I'M NOT EXPLAINING THINGS RIGHT. I'VE NEVER, I DON'T KNOW--BEEN HONEST WITH SOMEONE LIKE THIS.
IT'S NOT EASY.
I'M GOING TO SPEND THAT TIME, WHILE I'M TRAINING, TRYING TO BECOME A BETTER PERSON--A WORTHY PERSON. I DON'T KNOW IF IT'LL WORK--OR IF I EVEN CAN. BUT I'M GOING TO TRY FOR YOU.
I'M NOT ASKING YOU TO WAIT FOR ME. IF YOU FIND SOMEONE-- IF YOU FALL IN LOVE, GREAT. YOU'D PROBABLY BE BETTER OFF. I DON'T WANT YOU SITTING AROUND, PUSHING OTHER PEOPLE AWAY BECAUSE OF ME.
IF I LOSE YOU--THAT'S MY FAULT FOR NOT BEING READY. BUT I'M GOING TO TRY... I'M REALLY GOING TO TRY AND CHANGE.
I WANT TO BECOME A BETTER PERSON.
AND YOU HAVE TO LEAVE NOW?
I DO. I REALLY CAN'T STAY.
OKAY, #@$%#@%. YOU'VE GOT A YEAR IT'D TAKE ME THAT LONG TO GET OVER YOU ANYWAY.
DON'T SCREW THIS U
I'LL TRY NOT TO.
AND ABIGAIL...MY NAME IS ERIC O'GRADY.
I'M ANT-MAN.

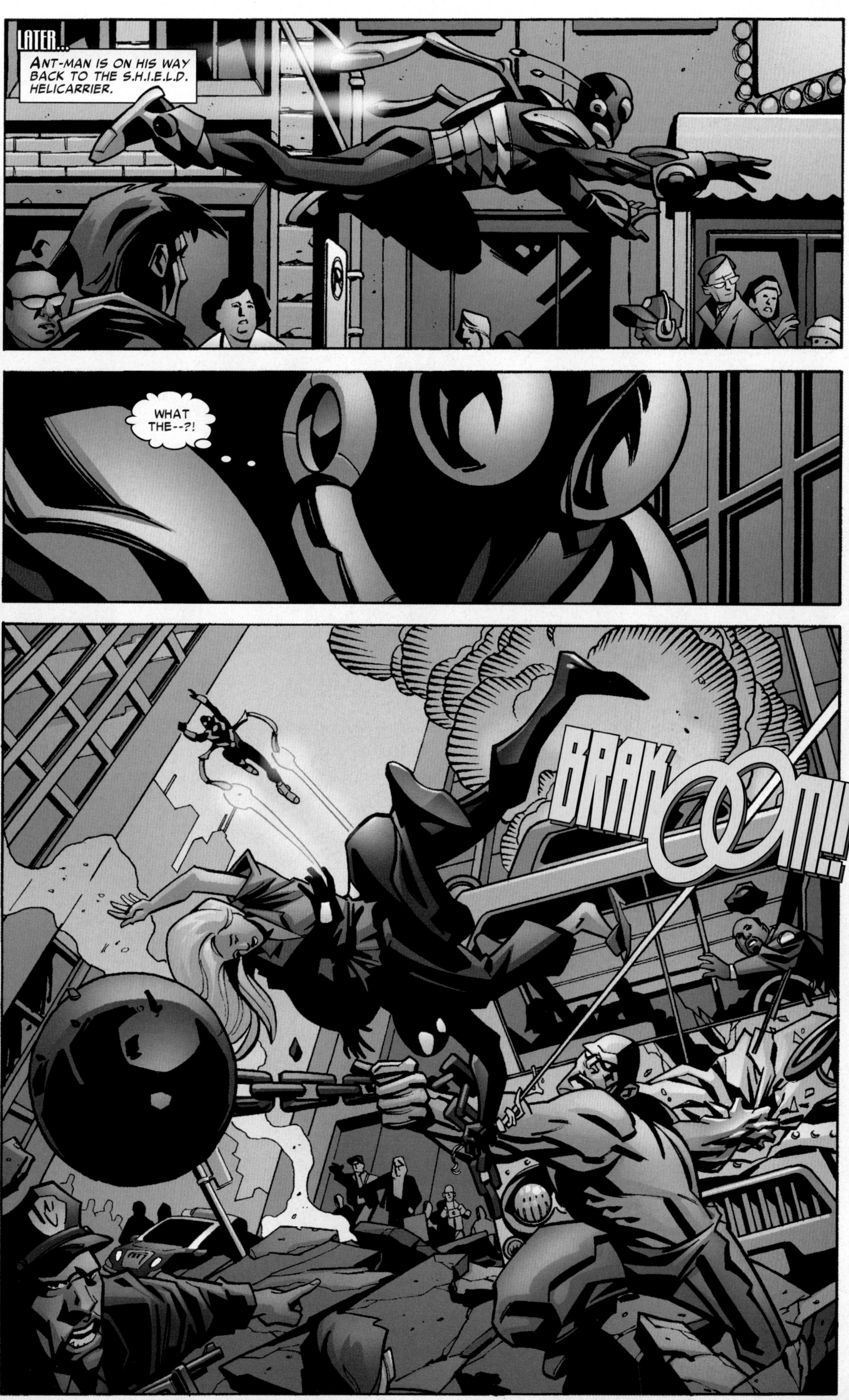
LATER...
ANT-MAN IS ON HIS WAY BACK TO THE S.H.I.E.L.D. HELICARRIER.
WHAT THE--?!
BRAKOOM!!

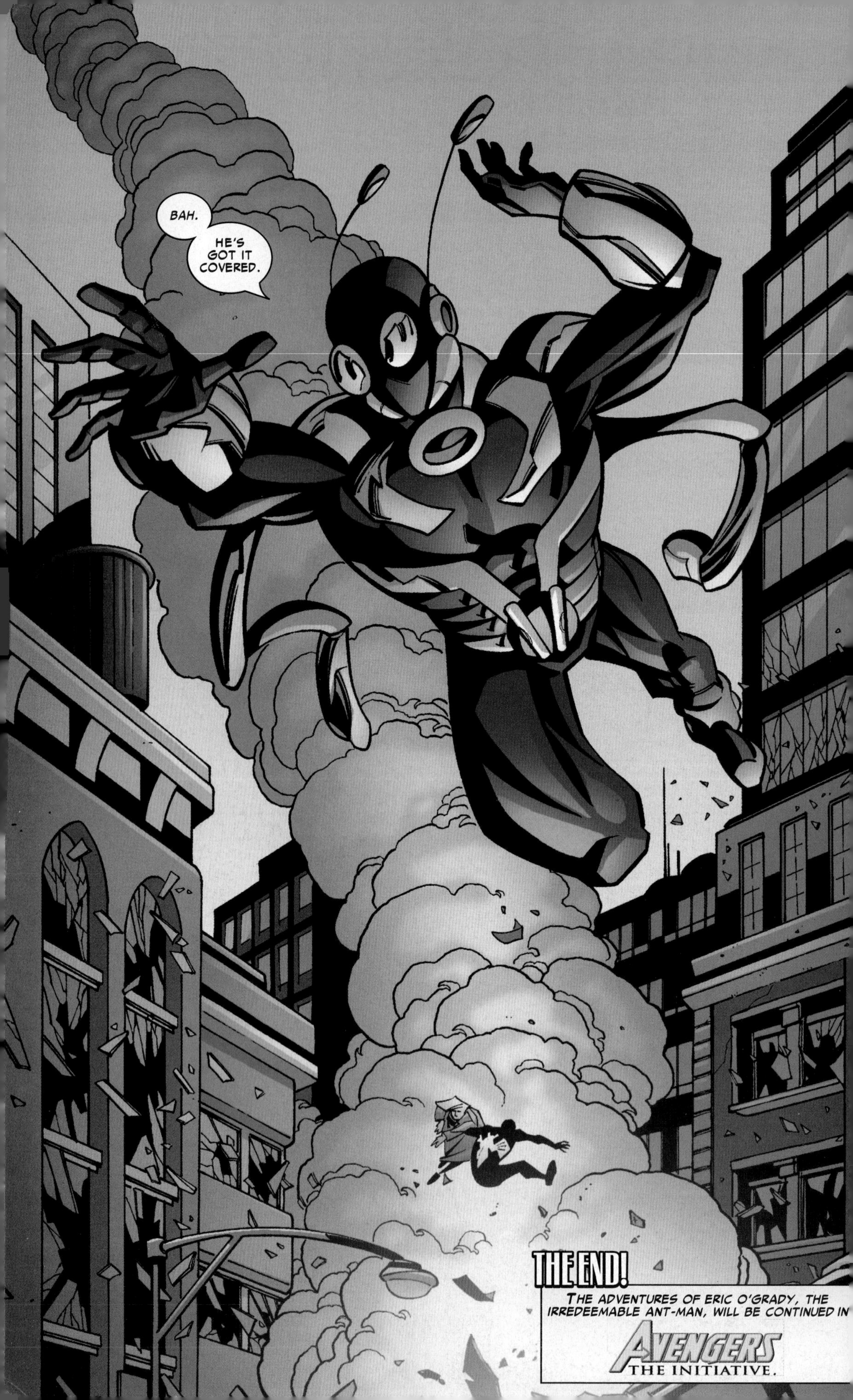
BAH.
HE'S GOT IT COVERED.
THE END!
THE ADVENTURES OF ERIC O'GRADY, THE IRREDEEMABLE ANT-MAN, WILL BE CONTINUED IN
AVENGERS THE INITIATIVE.

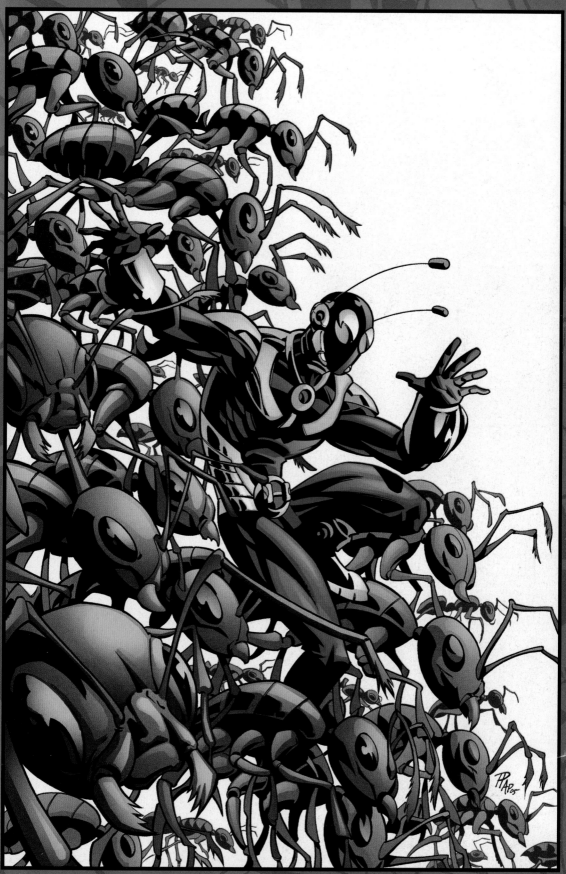

PROMOTIONAL ART BY PHIL HESTER, ANDE PARKS & BILL CRABTREE